PRINCIPLES OF BANKING LAW

PRINCIPLES OF BANKING LAW

Second Edition

ROSS CRANSTON

OXFORD

UNIVERSITY PRESS

OXFORD

UNIVERSITY PRESS

Great Clarendon Street, Oxford OX2 6DP

Oxford University Press is a department of the University of Oxford.
It furthers the University's objective of excellence in research,
scholarship, and education by publishing worldwide in

Oxford New York

Auckland Cape Town Dar es Salaam Hong Kong Karachi Kuala Lumpur
Madrid Melbourne Mexico City Nairobi New Delhi Shanghai Taipei Toronto

With offices in

Argentina Austria Brazil Chile Czech Republic France Greece
Guatemala Hungary Italy Japan South Korea Poland Portugal
Singapore Switzerland Thailand Turkey Ukraine Vietnam

Oxford is a registered trade mark of Oxford University Press
in the UK and in certain other countries

Published in the United States
by Oxford University Press Inc., New York

© Ross Cranston 2002

British Library Cataloguing in Publication Data
Data available

Library of Congress Cataloging in Publication Data
Data available

ISBN-13: 978–0–19–925331–9
ISBN-10: 0–19–925331–5

5

Typeset in Adobe Minion
by RefineCatch Limited, Bungay, Suffolk
Printed in Great Britain
on acid-free paper by
Biddles Ltd, King's Lynn, Norfolk

For Molly, my daughter

PREFACE

In his *Capitalism, Socialism and Democracy*, Joseph Shumpeter wrote that capitalism 'is by nature a form or method of economic change and not only never is but never can be stationary'. The many changes in the world of banking since the first edition of this book illustrate this truth. Institutionally, the tendency for banks to become multifunctional bodies has become more pronounced, although this has not provided a path to success for all. The regulatory system has been transformed to reflect multifunctional banking—notably in the UK, the Financial Services and Markets Act 2000 (FSMA 2000) confirmed the Financial Services Authority (FSA) as the combined regulator for banking, securities, and insurance. The internationalisation of banking has also continued apace, leading to new responses in both regulatory and soft law, as well as to the way courts handle issues such as jurisdiction. The story has been not only one of a continuation of existing trends. There are new institutions, such as the European Central Bank and e money. Moreover, new laws address new concerns—governments have responded to both money laundering and terrorist financing by placing additional duties on banks to know both their customers and their correspondents. The threat to systemic stability through the failure of a large value payment system has led, amongst other things, to the Settlement Finality directive of the Europen Community.

The aims and compass of this edition have not changed from those of the first. It is not an exhaustive treatment of the subject but, as the title indicates, an account of its contours. A certain authorial satisfaction derives from having in the first edition correctly identified several aspects of how the law was developing. For example, the House of Lords decision in *Etridge* confirms my long held view—first made public in an address to the Chancery Bar Association in 1994—that manifest disadvantage is not a separate requirement for undue influence.[1] My argument for a rethink of the law of confidentiality in respect of banks receives some support from a Court of Appeal decision to the effect that there is no justification for bankers' opinions, without the express consent of customers to forfeit the secrecy of their account.[2] These successes, if that is what they are, are tinged with a jealousy that legal writers elsewhere have a more publicly acknowledged involvement in moulding the law's development. They should also be coupled with confessions of failure—for example, the argument that dishonesty should be a test for knowing receipt has taken such a pounding that one is almost embarrassed to expose it to further public gaze.[3] My defence of the *Liggett* doctrine in the first edition was clearly misconceived, although the problem the case addressed still awaits solution.[4]

The special debts I incurred in writing the first edition—to Bill Blair, Roy Goode, Joe Norton, and Philip Wood—are compounded by their renewed assistance for this

---

[1] 214–15 below. [2] 181 below. [3] 194–5 below. [4] 250–1 below.

edition. To their names should be added those of Christos Hadjiemmanuil and Richard Hooley, not least for their own very fine writing on the subject. As with the first edition, many others have contributed—from my chambers, the wider legal community, government, regulatory agencies, and the academic world.

OUTLINE CONTENTS

CONTENTS

PART III PAYMENT AND PAYMENT SYSTEMS

TABLE OF CASES

TABLE OF LEGISLATION

TABLE OF CONVENTIONS

LIST OF WEB SITES CONTAINING INFORMATION ON BANKING LAW*

web site address	Organization	Comments
www.aba.com	American Bankers Association	
www.aciforex.com	ACI—The Financial Markets Association	Contains the model code for foreign exchange dealing
www.apacs.org.uk	Association for Payment Clearing Services	
www.aplma.com	Asia-Pacific Loan Market Association	
www.bailii.org	British and Irish Legal Information Institute	Contains free, mainly appellant cases from the UK, Ireland, Australia, New Zealand, Hong Kong, and others
www.bankingcode.org.uk	Banking Code Standards Board	Copies of Banking Codes available
www.bankofengland.co.uk	Bank of England	
www.bba.org.uk	British Bankers' Association	
www.bis.org	Bank for International Settlements	Excellent and essential site
www.bondmarkets.com	Bond Market Association	Contains master agreements
www.chips.org	The Clearing House Inter-Bank Payments System	Contains Chips Rules
www.ebrd.com	European Bank for Reconstruction and Development	
www.ecb.int	European Central Bank	A valuable site, with links to European Central Banks
www.emta.org	Trade Association for the Emerging Markets	
www.euroclear.com	Euroclear (the international clearing and settlement system for securities)	
europa.eu.int	European Union On-line	Difficult site to negotiate
www.fbe.be	European Banking Federation	
www.federalreserve.gov	US Federal Reserve	
www.financial-ombudsman.org.uk	The Financial Ombudsman Service	
www.fsa.gov.uk	Financial Services Authority	An essential site; contains the handbook
www.german-banks.com	Association of German Banks	
www.gpo.gov	Official US Federal Government website	
www.hcch.net	Hague Conference on Private International Law	
www.hm-treasury.gov.uk	Her Majesty's Treasury	
www.house.gov/financialservices	US House of Representatives Financial Services Committee	
www.iccwbo.org	International Chamber of Commerce	

web site address	Organisation	Comments
www.iib.org	Institute for International Bankers	
www.imf.org	The International Monetary Fund	
www.ipma.org.uk	International Primary Market Association	
www.irti.org	Islamic Research and Training Institute	Contains material on Islamic banking
www.isma.org	International Securities Market Association	
www.isda.org	International Swaps and Derivatives Association	Contains master agreements
www.lawcom.gov.uk	Law Commission for England and Wales	
www.loan-market-assoc.com	Loan Market Association	
www.lsta.org	Loan Syndications and Trading Association	
www.ny.frb.org	New York Federal Reserve Bank	
www.occ.treas.gov	US Office of the Comptroller of Currency	
www1.oecd.org/fatf	Financial Action Task Force on Money Laundering	
www.oft.gov.uk	Office of Fair Trading	
www.open.gov.uk	UK Government Information Services	Contains list of government department and agency websites
www.parliament.uk	House of Lords	Recent judgments
www.privy-council.org.uk	Privy Council	Contains Privy Council opinions
www.sec.gov	**US Securities and Exchange Commission**	
www.senate.gov/~banking	Senate Banking Committee	
www.swift.com	Swift (the payment messaging system)	
www.thetakeoverpanel.org.uk	The Takeover Panel	Contains copy of the Takeovers Code
www.uncitral.org	United Nations Commission on International Trade Law	Contains conventions and model law on payment and trade
www.worldbank.org	The World Bank	

* Many trade associations do not make rules, agreements, etc. available to non-members.

PART I

BANKS, BANKING, AND BANK REGULATION

1

BANKING AND BANK ORGANIZATIONS

An appreciation of the nature of banks and of banking activities, and how these are changing, is essential background to a study of banking law. It is possible only to skate the surface in a book of this nature, but this Chapter addresses two aspects of what banking involves and how it is organized. One aspect is how banks are structured internally. Thus banks have traditionally relied on a branch network for what are described in this book as their core activities—taking deposits and lending. These days there is a tension between maintaining a branch network, which has been thought important to customer satisfaction and selling other services, and the cost considerations. What is happening is a rationalization of branches, a change in the nature of some branches, greater automation, and internet banking.[1] Moreover, the one corporate entity has become the banking group, as many banks have established separate subsidiaries for separate activities. While branches are not typically incorporated, it is common now for banks to hive off activities into subsidiaries. Thus point-of-sale finance and corporate finance may be effected from members of the banking group other than the core bank.

Coupled with this has been the move towards the German model of universal banking. In other words, large banks are typically multifunctional institutions, engaged not only in core banking but in a range of other activities. At the retail level this is partly because individual customers have become wealthier and more sophisticated. Money has been drawn away from deposit accounts to unit trusts, life assurance, and pension plans. Banks have thus become involved in the distribution and provision of these services as their captive deposit base has been eroded. The mirror of this has been the banks themselves choosing higher risk, higher return activities. As is well known, banks have become players in foreign exchange, securities, and derivatives markets, on their own account, as well as on behalf of customers. Trading profile, as well as fee-income, is the goal.

In Britain the typical multifunctional bank has been formed by the merger of what used to be separate activity institutions—the clearing bank (called the commercial

---

[1] J. Chetham, *Issues in European Banking* (London, Financial Times Management Reports, 1994); E. Gardner and J. Falzon (eds.), *Strategic Challenges in European Banking* (Basingstoke, Macmillan, 1999); J.-P. Danthine, *et al.*, *The Future of European Banking* (London, CEPR, 1999).

bank elsewhere), the merchant bank (the investment bank in US terms), and the stockbroker and securities dealer (in US terms, the broker-dealer). Commercial banking involves at its core taking deposits, effecting customers' payment instructions, and providing finance in a variety of ways. Investment banking comprises a range of activities, including capital market activities, investment management, corporate financing and advice, and derivatives products. Securities and derivatives dealing for customers has been mentioned. As we shall see, insurance is typically tacked on to all of this as well.[2]

I. THE NATURE OF BANKING

Before turning to these aspects of how banks are organized, however, it is as well to start with the nature of banking. It will be evident from what has already been said that the term 'banking' can no longer be identified with the business of a banking group, since the multifunctional bank engages in a whole range of activities not associated with traditional banking—securities dealing, investment management, and insurance to name but three. How, then, can banking be defined?

A. COMMON LAW DEFINITIONS

A number of definitions of banking emerged at common law. Perhaps the most authoritative is that adopted in *United Dominions Trust Ltd.* v. *Kirkwood*,[3] when the court drew on the usual characteristics of banking set out in *Paget's Law of Banking*,[4] a standard textbook. As Lord Denning MR put it:

There are, therefore, two characteristics usually found in bankers today: (i) They accept money from, and collect cheques for, their customers and place them to their credit; (ii) They honour cheques or orders drawn on them by their customers when presented for payment and debit their customers accordingly. These two characteristics carry with them also a third, namely: (iii) They keep current accounts, or something of that nature, in their books in which the credits and debits are entered.[5]

Such an analysis cannot be regarded as sufficient. First, it ties itself to payment through the cheque system, thus excluding traditional savings and co-operative banks, quite apart from merchant (investment) banking. More importantly, cheques are only one way in which payments are effected: indeed, before too long, cheques will have had their day.[6] For this reason the more generalized analysis of Isaacs J in the Australian High Court, specifically rejected by Lord Denning MR, is to be preferred. It

---

[2] e.g. J. Canals, *Competitive Strategies in European Banking* (Oxford, Clarendon, 1993), 232.
[3] [1966] 2 QB 431 (CA).
[4] See now 11th edn., M. Hapgood (ed.), London, Butterworths, 1996, 104.
[5] At 447. See also 465, *per* Diplock LJ.   [6] 256 below.

is worth quoting at some length, because it encapsulates a great deal of what this book is about:

The essential characteristics of the business of banking are . . . the collection of money by receiving deposits upon loan, repayable when and as expressly or impliedly agreed upon, and the utilization of the money so collected by lending it again in such sums as are required. These are the essential functions of a bank as an instrument of society. It is, in effect, a financial reservoir receiving streams of currency in every direction, and from which there issue outflowing streams where and as required to sustain and fructify or assist commercial, industrial or other enterprises or adventures . . . The methods by which the functions of a bank are effected—as by current account, deposit account at call, fixed deposit account, orders, cheques, secured loans, discounting bills, note issue, letters of credit, telegraphic transfers, and any other modes that may be developed by the necessities of business—are merely accidental and auxiliary circumstances, any of which may or may not exist in any particular case.[7]

Moreover, to universalize the *Kirkwood*, or any, definition ignores the point that definitions are developed in a particular context. The notions of 'bank' and 'banking' will bear different shades of meaning turning on the issue. Broadly speaking the jurisprudence about the meaning of banking has arisen in three contexts. The first revolves around regulation: for example, is a particular body in breach of the law since it is carrying on banking business in the jurisdiction without a banking licence?[8] Secondly, some legislation confers a privilege or protection on 'banks' without defining them, and the issue becomes whether a particular body can take advantage of it. For example under section 4(1) of the Cheques Act 1957, *bankers* (undefined) who convert cheques by collecting them for customers have a defence if they can establish that they acted in good faith and without negligence.[9] Thirdly, those seeking to avoid a payment obligation have occasionally argued that it arose on an illegal contract, which is void or unenforceable because it is owed by or to an unlicensed bank.

The judicial approach in each of these three contexts has been influenced by the circumstances. In the case of the third type of case, for example, such claims can smack of the unmeritorious. Consequently, the courts may strain to find that the creditor is, in fact, a bank and its rights and obligations enforceable by action. Indeed this is what happened in *Kirkwood*. These days, however, the issue is unlikely to arise in the same way as in that decision, since it will be quite clear whether or not a body is an unlicensed bank. (In *Kirkwood* the issue was whether UDT was an unlicensed moneylender: under the legislation it did not have to be licensed if it was a bank—undefined in the particular legislation.) The contending policy considerations in this type of case include, on the one hand, that to deny recovery of a loan to the unlicensed bank may be a deterrent to unlawful banking. The corollary is, however, that the unlicensed bank, unable to recover the moneys which it has lent, will be disabled as a

---

[7] See *Comrs. of the State Savings Bank of Victoria* v. *Permewan, Wright & Co. Ltd.* (1915) 19 CLR 457, 470–1.
[8] e.g. *Koh Kim Chai* v. *Asia Commercial Banking Corporation Ltd.* [1984] 1 WLR 850 (PC).
[9] See also, s. 1; Bills of Exchange Act 1882, ss. 60, 80, 81A.

practical matter from voluntarily repaying its own depositors. (Under section 29 of the UK Financial Services and Markets Act 2000 (FSMA 2000), those depositing moneys with the 'bank' may be able to recover them as a matter of law.)

No more will be said in this book about the common law definitions of banks. The crucial issue these days is how banks are defined in statutory law.

B. STATUTORY DEFINITIONS

Internationally, statutory definitions of banks and banking take different forms. At one end of the spectrum is the approach which defines as a bank any body recognized as such by a governmental authority. In the absence of any indication of the criteria required for such recognition, this approach confers too great a discretion on the state. Falling somewhere along the spectrum is a second approach, which lists the activities which banking encompasses. The German Banking Act adopts the list approach.[10] There are difficulties. First it must be made clear which activities on the list, if not all, a body must perform to be treated as a bank. Moreover, the law must specify whether banks are confined only to these, and incidental, activities—it will not always be an easy issue which activities are incidental—or whether they have a free rein. More fundamentally, the list approach will soon become dated as the business of banking changes, so that there must be a mechanism for its constant updating.

At the other end of the spectrum is the formulary approach: banking is defined in terms of a few, generalized characteristics. Again there are problems. As with the list approach, can banks go beyond the activities specified in the formula? What are the essential features of the formula—deposit taking from the public coupled with granting credits for its own account (the EC approach); or some other approach, such as deposit-taking, granting credits, and the ability to make payments to third parties on behalf of customers? Moreover, since the formulary approach is by nature all-encompassing, how is it to be confined? Specific exemptions will be needed to exclude what will otherwise be caught.

Whether the list or formulary approach is adopted, it is clear that bodies may act like banks yet not be categorized in law as banks. If taking deposits *from the public* is defined as the essential ingredient of banking then the finance house able to fund itself from the wholesale markets, or the co-operative taking deposits from within its membership, would probably not be caught. If banking means deposit taking coupled with *making loans,* an investment fund will be able to avoid classification as a bank by using its moneys to purchase short-term government paper or other money market instruments. Economists sometimes refer to such bodies as 'non-bank banks' or 'non-bank financial intermediaries'. That they may escape the banking net is not necessarily a bad thing—it depends on whether this thwarts the legislative aims.[11]

---

[10] §1(1) respectively.   [11] 66ff. below.

C. THE UK APPROACH

No longer does the UK use the term banking as an authorizable activity, although it slips back into the details of the regulatory regime. In broad terms section 19 of the Financial Services and Markets Act 2000 (FSMA 2000) provides that no person may carry on (or purport to carry on) a regulated activity in the UK unless authorized or exempt. This is known as the general prohibition. Regulated activities are set out in Schedule 2, and what this book describes as core banking is there in terms of accepting deposits and home mortgage lending. Home mortgage lending is nothing more than lending (dealt with in Chapter 11) on security (dealt with in Chapter 15), although there are special controls over its marketing because of its importance to ordinary people and their potential vulnerability in undertaking what for most will be the largest financial commitment of their lives.[12] Also listed as regulated activity are a range of investment banking activities, which are mentioned throughout the book but notably in Chapter 12. Breach of the prohibition attracts criminal penalties, although it should be noted that this does not affect the liability of the deposit-taker to repay any deposit.[13] Finally, it is well to note here that an authorized person cannot be in breach of the general prohibition, even if its permission does not include the particular regulated activity. Such behaviour is dealt with as a regulatory, rather than a criminal, breach. In using the concept of accepting deposits, the legislation conflates two aims. One is the aim of preventing ordinary consumers from being fleeced by fly by night operators, taking money deposits for 'investment'. Even though they may call themselves bankers, such persons have nothing to do with banking. The other aim is to define those bodies which will be subject to the regulatory regime for banks set out in FSMA 2000, which is a much wider remit.

The first aim—consumer protection—took form in the Protection of Depositors Act 1963. In the present legislation, FSMA 2000, it involves the general prohibition on unauthorized deposit taking, breaching the detailed provisions on financial promotion, and false claims to be authorized or exempt. Injunctions can be obtained under section 380 of the FSMA 2000 against persons contravening these provisions, and restitution orders made under section 382. There is little overlap between unauthorized deposit-taking and banking; indeed, banks were exempted from the full impact of the 1963 Act. Yet when the first overall statutory regime for bank regulation in the United Kingdom was introduced by the Banking Act 1979, the concept of deposit-taking in the 1963 Act was simply incorporated as its crux. This was despite the fact that an EC definition of credit institutions (banks) for bank regulatory purposes—deposit-taking from the public coupled with granting credits for its own

---

[12] In December 2001 the government announced that the Financial Services Authority would have responsibility for regulating the selling of home mortgages: see HM Treasury, *Regulating Mortgages. Consultation Document*, February 2002. See also European Commission Recommendation on Pre-Contractual Information to be given to consumers by lenders offering home loans, COM (2001) 477, [2001] OJ L69/25.

[13] FSMA 2000, ss. 23, 26(4). See also s. 29 (court may order immediate repayment even if time deposit).

account—had already been adopted in the First EC Banking Directive of 1977.[14] Both approaches now coexist, side by side, in the UK provisions implementing the EC Credit Institutions Directive.[15]

As it stands, deposit-taking, to be caught by FSMA 2000, must be by way of business. Deposit is defined as a sum of money paid on terms under which it will be repaid, with or without interest or a premium, and either on demand or at a time or in circumstances agreed. However, it does not include money paid which is referable to the provision of property or services or the giving of security. Examples of these exceptions include advance payments for goods and services, deposits payable in relation to the purchase of land, and moneys payable by way of security for the performance of a contract.[16] Because of its width, the meaning of 'deposit' is further confined by excluding matters such as loans by banks and others in the lending business, inter-company loans, and loans between relatives.[17] Among the deposits exempted by regulations from the scope of the Act are payments for short-term debt instruments issued by corporate borrowers.[18] Moreover, the money received by way of deposit must be lent to others, or any other of the body's activities must be financed out of money so received.[19]

The statutory definition has an extraterritorial application, in that, although acceptance of the deposit must be in the United Kingdom, the deposit taking business can be based abroad.[20] Thus the representative offices of non-EU banks would be in breach of the Act if they took deposits in the United Kingdom. A foreign bank which lends money commercially in the jurisdiction but does not take deposits is not caught.[21]

D. THE EC APPROACH

Taking deposits (or other repayable funds) from the public and granting credits on its own account—this, in essence, is the definition of credit institution used in Article 1 of the Credit Institutions Directive of the European Community. It accords with what banks have traditionally done. It also encompasses the activity of specialized banks such as savings banks, although some of these institutions are specifically excluded from the ambit of the Directive. The term public is undefined but this could turn on how the undertaking received the deposit—had it made a private approach or solicited the public at large? However, the concept of public seems to depend more on the character of those depositing—are they from a private group, restricted class, or the public generally?

Under the Directive undertakings other than credit institutions are categorized as 'financial institutions' if they do not accept deposits or other repayable funds from

---

[14] Dir. 77/780/EEC [1977] OJ L322/30.   [15] 64, 433 below.

[16] Financial Services and Markets Act 2000 (Regulated Activities) Order 2001, SI 2001 No 544, art. 5(2).

[17] art. 6(1)(b).   [18] 329 below.

[19] art. 5(1).   [20] S. 19(1).

[21] See *Hafton Properties Ltd.* v. *McHugh (Inspector of Taxes)* [1987] STC 16.

the public, but do, as their principal activity, lend or carry on any of the activities mentioned in the Annex.[22] The term also includes those undertakings other than credit institutions which are the holding companies of a financial group—at least one credit institution and other financial institutions—called financial holding companies.

For the purposes of this book the EC definition is adopted—public deposit-taking and granting credits on its own account—when it is necessary to refer to banking in a general way. Intimately connected with these activities is providing customers with payment services. For convenience these activities together are termed 'core banking', as distinct from the many other activities and services in which banks are now involved.

II. BANKING STRUCTURES

These days almost all banks have a head office and other offices. If engaged in core banking—taking deposits, granting credits, and providing payment services—these other offices will generally be branches. Branches do not have a legal personality separate from that of the head office but will be carrying out some at least of what is associated with core banking.[23] When established abroad, however, branches may be separately subsidiarized for legal and other reasons. If a bank is a multifunctional bank it may separately subsidiarize some of its activities. In other words the multi-functional bank may consist of a group of companies: hence use of the term banking group or banking conglomerate. If it is also international in character members of the banking group may be incorporated abroad. In simplified form the structure of such a bank may be something like the following:

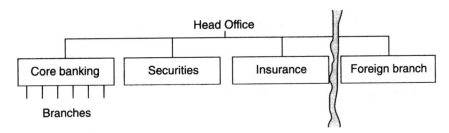

A. BRANCHES

Traditionally the branches of banks had considerable autonomy; their managers wielded important decision-making power on matters like lending, and they person-ally had a high status in their local communities. It is against this background that the common law relating to branches has developed. In recent times, however, banks have pruned their branch networks, especially following bank mergers. The majority of banks have also downgraded their branches, removing discretion from management

---

[22] 100 below.   [23] Cf. definition in the EC Credit Institutions Dir., Art. 1.

and concentrating important services in regional centres. Branches are linked to each other electronically. The common law has not caught up with these changes.

(i) The Principle of Branch Separateness

From the nineteenth century the common law treated the branches of a bank for some purposes as distinct entities from their head office, even though not separately incorporated. Thus a basic rule became that a customer must make demand for payment of money deposited at the branch of the bank where the account is kept.[24] In as much as courts have been explicit about localization of this obligation to pay, they have put it on the basis of an implied term in the deposit contract rather than as a matter of law.[25] A corollary of the basic rule is that probably countermand of a payment instruction must be made at the branch where the original order was given.[26] However, while a customer has had to make demand at the branch where the account is kept, somewhat inconsistently the courts have given banks the privilege of combining the accounts of a customer held at different branches when one of them is in deficit.[27] The origin of this basic rule about where payment must be demanded was that it was the customer's branch which had the most ready access to the true state of his or her account. Built onto the basic rule is that English law regards the law of the place where the account is kept as the proper law of a bank account for conflict of laws purposes.[28]

This principle of the separateness of branches was accepted throughout the common law world, including the United States.[29] As regards branches in different countries, it has been adopted in the Uniform Customs and Practices for Documentary Credits (UCP 500) and in the UNCITRAL Model Law on International Credit Transfers.[30] Given the organizational and technological developments in banking, however, there must be a question mark over its future. Branches are linked electronically and there seems no reason why payment instructions should not be effected at any branch, at least within a single jurisdiction. Ordinary customers can now withdraw moneys (make demand) wherever an automatic teller machine is located, and with telephone and internet banking need not have a branch at all. Other aspects of separateness, such as the notion that notice given to the head office may not constitute notice to the branches, sit ill in the modern day.

Even if the law is brought up to date as regards payment instructions the proper law of a bank account—in the absence of express provisions—can remain that of the jurisdiction where the customer has the account. But that is because that is the one with which the banking contract has its closest connection, rather than as a consequence of any notion of the separateness of bank branches.

---

[24] *N. Joachimson* v. *Swiss Bank Corp.* [1921] 3 KB 110 (CA).   [25] *Ibid.* 129–30.
[26] J. Vroegop, 'The Statutes of Bank Branches' [1990] 11 *JIBL* 445, 447.
[27] *Garnett* v. *McKewan* (1872) LR 8 Exch. 10.
[28] *Libyan Arab Foreign Bank* v. *Bankers Trust* [1989] 1 QB 728.
[29] e.g. *United States* v. *National City Bank*, 321 F 2d 14 (2nd Cir. 1963), revd. on other grounds, 379 US 378 (1965).
[30] Art. 2; art. 1(3) respectively.

(ii) Head Office Liability for Branches

Branch failure is one area where the common law courts have sometimes rejected the principle of branch separateness. Instead they have applied the ordinary rule that the bank as a whole is liable for the debts of any of its offices not separately incorporated.[31] (In principle the head office would also be liable for separately incorporated branches or affiliates if it had guaranteed their liabilities.) The problem has mainly arisen where a bank's branches abroad have been closed because of civil war or have been expropriated, or a moratorium has been imposed by the host government on their repayment of deposits. Depositors have then claimed against the bank elsewhere. Such claims are, of course, subject to contract: for example, a contract of deposit could expressly limit claims to the particular branch which entered it and subject the deposit contract to the local law and the exclusive jurisdiction of the local courts.[32]

As a result of a series of court decisions making the head offices of American banks liable in these circumstances federal legislation was enacted in 1994—followed by New York legislation—to give them statutory protection against such claims, where they have not expressly agreed in writing to repay deposits made with their foreign branches.[33] Customers henceforth have to bear certain sovereign and other risks if they bank with American banks abroad. The statutory protection does not extend to non-payment because of illiquidity or insolvency.

In favour of this approach it may be said that if customers situated outside a jurisdiction make deposits at branches of banks in the jurisdiction for the higher interest rates payable, they should bear the risk of the government in that jurisdiction imposing, say, a moratorium. Customers should take the rough with the smooth. The approach seems to neglect the inter-office business of some international banks, which take advantage of the ability of particular branches to raise funds more cheaply, and which book loans and other transactions at branches where there are favourable tax, regulatory, or management considerations. If banks can arbitrage, why not customers?

Moreover, what of, say, those who choose a foreign bank because of its international standing, not knowing of any legal restriction on claims? And is the risk of expropriation on the same plane in fact as the risk of a moratorium? In the case of expropriation without compensation, the depositor may lose everything if he or she cannot recover from the bank's head office. By the same token the bank will have already lost its business as a result of the expropriation of its branch, without having then to compensate depositors. On the other hand, the bank is probably in a better position

[31] e.g. *Leader, Plunkett and Leader* v. *Direction der Disconto Gesellschaft* (1914) 31 TLR 83; *United Commercial Bank Ltd.* v. *Okara Grain Buyers Syndicate Ltd.*, AIR 1968 SC 1115; *Citibank, NA* v. *Wells Fargo Asia Ltd.*, 936 F 2d 723 (2nd Cir. 1991).

[32] W. Blair, 'Liability for foreign branch deposits in English law', in R. Cranston (ed.), *The Making of Commercial Law* (Oxford, Clarendon, 1997); R. Herring and F. Kübler, 'The Allocation of Risk in Cross-border Deposit Transactions' (1995) 89 *NWU LR* 942; E. Kwaw, *Grey Areas in Eurocurrency Deposits and Placements* (Aldershot, Dartmouth, 1994), 141–52.

[33] 12 USC 633, 1828(q); New York Banking Law, 1994 McKinney's Session Laws, c.265, §138(2)(a).

to have its government put pressure on the expropriating state for compensation by comparison with the individual depositors. With moratoria or exchange control, however, the depositor suffers only from delay or by being paid in local currency. It may be said that this is a type of sovereign risk, like currency fluctuations, which any depositor must bear, especially since they may be getting a higher rate of interest by depositing abroad. Of course, a moratorium may be indefinite, and exchange control so onerous, as to approach expropriation.

(iii) Restrictions on Branching

Traditionally there have been no restrictions on UK banks wanting to establish branches. A not inconsiderable number of other jurisdictions have limited the capacity of their banks to set up branch networks, even within the jurisdiction, although in recent times this type of restriction has been loosened.

The United States is the classic case, where the states have divided between those prohibiting branching completely, those restricting branches to one county within the state, and those permitting branching state-wide. At the federal level the McFadden Act of 1927 was supposed to impose barriers to interstate branching mirroring those at state level.[34] The legislation reflected a belief in locally controlled banks, fear of big business and federalism. Yet the pressure of competition and the drive for efficiencies through economies of scale have placed the law under great strain. Interstate branching has been loosened up, but by no means left uncontrolled.[35]

B. REPRESENTATIVE OFFICES

For the sake of completeness, it is as well to note that a bank may conduct its business in another jurisdiction through a representative office, as well as a branch, subsidiary, or incorporated affiliate. Representative offices perform a limited range of functions, such as developing relationships with correspondent banks to support head office activities, increasing the bank's profile within the market place, acting as a point of contact with the bank, and providing information to head office about developments in the economy, financial markets, and regulation. The legal position of each is different. Both the representative office and branch are part of the legal entity which is the bank. The subsidiary and incorporated affiliate are not. Moreover, the regulatory implications differ. Branches which engage in deposit taking or other regulated activity must, if they are not part of an EU bank, obtain authorization and comply with the more detailed regulatory requirements established under FSMA 2000. The same applies to subsidiaries and incorporated affiliates, even of EU banks.[36] So long as representative offices do not stray into regulated activity or financial promotion or falsely claim to be authorized, they are not subject to a formal regime of regulation.

---

[34] 44 Stat. 1228 (1927).   [35] 12 USC §§215, 215a, 215a–1.   [36] 432 below.

C. BANKING GROUPS

The corporate group is a feature of modern economic activity—banking is no exception. Consequently, some of the problems thrown up for the law by banking groups are similar to those much discussed in relation to corporate groups generally. One problem is the technical one of defining the boundaries of a corporate group when a legislative scheme is to have group-wide coverage. We shall see in Chapter 3 how this matter has arisen in relation to the consolidated supervision of banking groups.[37] The definition of a corporate group may vary depending on the purpose, e.g. regulation or accounting. Also discussed there in the context of multifunctional banking groups is the more general policy problem of regulatory gaps and overlaps.[38] These are accentuated when a banking group extends across borders. It is not only a problem of its prudential regulation but of controlling how banks are used by others. It is now twenty years since Templeman LJ issued a salutary warning in the English Court of Appeal that it was high time that banks looked very carefully at their subsidiaries in certain offshore jurisdictions 'to ensure that there was no longer any scope for those companies being used as a cloak for fraud'.[39]

A classic problem with corporate groups is the responsibility of a parent when a subsidiary or affiliate is in difficulty. This problem may be more acute when a subsidiary or affiliate of a bank is engaged not in core banking but in some other, possibly riskier, activity. Generally speaking there can be no objection as a matter of company law if the parent bank intervenes successfully, and at no long-term cost, to set a subsidiary or affiliate bank on its feet.[40] In English terms the parent's directors would be acting *bona fide* in the parent's interests in doing so. But what if the parent decides to cut the subsidiary or affiliate loose?

Unlike German law, the common law developed no theory of enterprise liability. It applied the notion of the limited liability of individual investor-shareholders in the different context of parent companies of wholly and partially owned subsidiaries. Especially in the United States, 'piercing the veil' jurisprudence has had some impact on the notion that members of a corporate group are invariably to be treated as separate entities. English law adopts a stricter approach, but liability on this and other grounds (e.g. a parent bank may be treated as a shadow director of a subsidiary which is wrongfully trading under section 214 of the Insolvency Act 1986) cannot be ruled out.

The administrative application of corporate separateness in the banking context involves, however, a paradox. On the one hand, bank regulators may seek letters of comfort from substantial shareholders. This approach has been used for banks established in the United Kingdom. Thus bank regulators seek to overcome the legal

---

[37] 108 below.   [38] 104 below.

[39] *Idmac Industrial Designers and Management Consultants BV* v. *Midland Bank, The Times*, 8 October 1981.

[40] A. Hirsch, 'Changing Role of Multinational Banks', in K. L. Koh *et al.* (eds.), *Current Developments in International Securities, Commodities and Financial Futures Markets* (Singapore, Butterworths, 1987), 95.

separateness which the law sanctions by imposing a moral, albeit not a legally water-tight, commitment of support.[41] On the other hand bank regulators sometimes require subsidiarization for certain activities, with a view to reducing the risk of contagion, ensuring capital adequacy and facilitating supervision. There are limited examples in the United Kingdom, such as insurance, but this policy takes its most pronounced form in the American concept of firewalls.[42]

D. BANK MERGERS AND ACQUISITIONS

Mergers and acquisitions have in recent times transformed the face of banking. As a result there are now banks with an awesome economic power, a truly global reach, and providing the whole range of financial services. Even banks with less comprehensive ambitions have used mergers and acquisitions to expand in their home base or region.

As well as being driven by the factors which operate in other economic sectors—motives of grandeur, a desire for economies of scale, cost savings and efficiency gains, and shareholder pressure for performance—mergers and acquisitions in banking have been prompted by specific features.[43] Improvements in information technology is one, given its centrality to banking operations. Another has been the requirement to meet capital adequacy standards, and more generally to secure against the much greater risks associated these days with banking. The removal of legal barriers to what banks can do (and in the European Community and United States where they can do it) has also led to mergers and acquisitions and to the modern multifunctional financial institution. Moreover, bank rescues have sometimes been effected through a failed institution being taken over by a healthy one. Especially, but not only, in this context the legal structure of the acquisition will be shaped by the desire to avoid certain liabilities, and perhaps also to take over only parts of the business.

The increased concentration in banking has left public policy—and the law as an expression of it—well behind. Largely unaddressed are the social and economic consequences of these mergers and acquisitions—concerns expressed for an earlier era by Louis D. (later Justice) Brandeis in his *Other People's Money And How the Bankers Use It* (1914).[44] Moreover, the complexity of the new breed of large, multifunctional bank means that, if seriously distressed, any wind-up is fraught with difficulties and likely to be disorderly.[45] Banks which are too big or too important to fail compound the problem of moral hazard and are a contingent liability on the public purse. Yet another dimension is that regulators find it increasingly difficult to monitor the multifarious activities of the multinational, multifunctional bank. To these aspects,

[41] A. Page, 'The State and Corporate Groups in the United Kingdom', in D. Sugarman and G. Teubner (eds.), *Regulating Corporate Groups in Europe*, (Nomos, Baden-Baden, 1990), 262–3.
[42] 100 below.
[43] S. Davis, *Bank Mergers. Lessons for the Future* (Basingstoke, Macmillan, 2001).
[44] New York, Harper Torchbook edn., 1967.
[45] Group of Ten, *Consolidation in the Financial Sector* (Basle, BIS, 2001), 15, 19.

including bank rescues, we return in Chapter 3, but our concern here is with the private law aspects of bank mergers.

(i) The Mechanics of Merger

At a basic level the law must provide for the mechanics of bank mergers and acquisitions. In some jurisdictions these are separate from the ordinary law.[46] Presumably the justification is the convenience of having a self-contained code. As a matter of legal technique, however, there need be no difference between a merger or acquisition involving a bank and any other enterprise. That is the approach in Britain. Possibly the one exception is the conversion of a mutual, co-operative, or trust institution into an ordinary bank, which can raise the special difficulty of protecting the interests of its members. In these situations English courts have sometimes not given sufficient weight to the mutual character of such bodies.[47]

That as a matter of technique bank mergers and acquisitions fall under the ordinary law does not mean, of course, that there will not be attendant difficulties. What is the legal nature of the 'merger' or 'acquisition': is it a takover where the separate legal personality of the two banks continues, have the two actually been amalgamated into a new legal entity, or has one purchased the assets and liabilities of the other? The purchase of assets and liabilities is used when part only of a bank is being acquired, for example, when a bank is selling off its unincorporated branch in a foreign jurisdiction. The purchase of assets means complying with the different sale rules for each type of asset. The special problems involved in purchasing loan assets are dealt with elsewhere in this book.[48]

Where a bank is threatened with insolvency, its acquisition by, or merger with, another bank is less likely to be effected by contract. Once the insolvency laws apply, however, there are difficulties if, for example, the acquiring bank wishes to cap the liabilities of the acquired bank, although this may be necessary to make the acquisition financially viable. Any move away from the ordinary *pari passu* principle of insolvency law needs justification.[49]

(ii) Prerequisites to Merger

A second level is whether the law imposes any standards on mergers and acquisitions involving banks. It is not unusual (but by no means universal) for banking legislation to require approval of the Ministry of Finance, central bank, or bank regulator for a merger or acquisition. Typically the legislation indicates in very broad terms how the discretion is to be exercised (e.g. national interest; to ensure financial soundness). Article 31 of the Japanese Banking Law sets out the criteria which the Ministry of Finance must consider in a little more detail than laws elsewhere:

---

[46] Bank Act (Canada), SC 1991, c.46, ss. 283–92.

[47] *Ross* v. *Lord Advocate* [1986] 1 WLR 1077, [1986] 3 All ER 79 (HL). Cf. *Cheltenham and Gloucester Building Society* v. *Building Societies Commission* [1995] Ch. 185.

[48] 360 below.

[49] See e.g., *Barings plc* v. *Internationale Nederlanden Group NV*, unreported, 31 August 1995 (CA).

(1) The merger, transfer or acquisition . . . is justifiable in light of the harmony of demand and supply for funds and users' benefit in the community . . .

(2) Merger, etc., will not disturb financial order, such as undermining fair competition among financial institutions; and

(3) [The bank is highly likely] to carry on banking business appropriately, fairly and efficiently after the merger, etc.

Sometimes the need for approval is used to block or filter mergers and acquisitions of local banks by foreign interests.[50] In fact there may be specific controls on the foreign ownership of banks.[51]

Whatever the position in the past, bank regulators in the United Kingdom do not seek now to control the acquisition, for protectionist reasons, of one bank by another, even if the other is a foreign bank. As a result of the FSMA 2000, the UK now has specific powers for bank mergers. A court must approve any transfer of a banking business, and to do so must have before it a certificate of the bank's regulator that the transferee has adequate financial resources.[52] A merger or acquisition would only be blocked on prudential grounds—under the statutory provisions for the vetting of controllers of banks—when the merger or acquisition was for a quick investment gain or for the purpose of sale or of breaking up the target bank in ways which are detrimental to depositors.[53]

There are also standards applied to bank mergers and acquisitions derived from competition (antitrust) policy. These standards might be general, as in the European Community, where Articles 81 and 82 and the Merger Control Regulation apply to banking.[54] Where they are specific to banking, as with the Bank Merger Act and Bank Holding Company Act of the United States, they are patterned in the main on general law standards.[55]

What is at first glance surprising is that so few mergers and acquisitions of banks have fallen into the antitrust net. In the past there were some isolated examples in Britain, but there because the bidder was a foreign bank and the target a major national bank.[56] The Cruickshank Report called for UK merger law to be tightened to ensure effective competition is promoted, to allow the entry of new providers and to improve services. Until then it recommended that all proposed mergers of banks, with material shares in a particular market or related markets, should be referred to

---

[50] P. Portier and R. Narelet-Novalhier, 'French Bank Mergers' [2000] *JIBL* 97, 99.

[51] Banks (Shareholdings) Act 1972 (Australia). Cf. Banking Act 1959, s. 63.

[52] Ss. 106, 111, Sched. 12, pt. 2.

[53] C. Hadjiemmanuil, *Banking Regulation and the Bank of England* (London, LLP Ltd., 1996), 253.

[54] Case 172/80 *Züchner* v. *Bayerische Vereinsbank AG* [1981] ECR 2021; Merger Control Regulation, Council Reg. 4064/89 [1990] OJ L257/13. Art. 3(5)(a) provides a very limited exemption for banks (those dealing in securities which hold securities on a temporary basis only).

[55] S. Huber, *Bank Officer's Handbook of Government Regulation* (2nd edn., Boston, Mass., WGL, 1989), ch. 14.

[56] See Monopolies and Mergers Commission, *Hong Kong and Shanghai Banking Corporation/Royal Bank of Scotland*, Cmnd. 8472, 1982.

the Competition Commission for investigation.[57] It may be that a decision of the Competition Commission in 2001 heralds an invigorated approach: a merger between one of the big four banks and a former building society was judged anticompetitive by eliminating an important force for change in the market for personal deposit accounts and the highly concentrated market for banking services for small and medium sized enterprises.[58] The European Commission competition authorities have proved relatively benign. In 1992 the European Commission declared that the acquisition of a major UK bank, resulting in the fifth largest bank in Europe by shareholders' funds, was consistent with the Merger Control Regulation: there was no appreciable overlap in the activity of the two banks in any Member State in some fifteen separate sectors, and even in the United Kingdom the reduction in competition would have no appreciable adverse effect on competition.[59] Despite the legion of bank mergers in the United States, challenges on antitrust grounds seem rare.[60]

(iii) Private-Law Consequences

At yet another level bank mergers and acquisitions have consequences in private law. Later this Chapter examines one such consequence—the conflicts of interest arising in the multifunctional bank, the latter often being the product of a conglomerate merger or acquisition. Another private law consequence covers bank confidentiality, dealt with in Chapter 6: technically there is a breach of the duty of confidentiality if a bank reveals its customers' affairs to the entity which acquires it, or with which it is amalgamated. There are a variety of other private law consequences: A bequeaths shares in Bank X, but on her death she holds shares in Bank Y which she exchanged for the former when Bank Y successfully took over Bank X; B claims that his guarantee to Bank P is discharged on the bank being acquired by Bank Q; Banks R and S having merged, C claims that the security originally given to Bank R does not extend to the further advances made by the merged bank.

In each case the solution demands further legal and factual inquiry. Did A in the example above have any other bank shares at the time of her death? Is B's contention confined to advances after the acquisition, the acquisition resulting in the total absorption of Bank P by Bank Q? Is the security in standard form, being for the benefit of successors, assigns, and companies with which Bank R amalgamates? And so on. Since such situations raise tricky issues, it has been the practice in the United Kingdom in the case of major transactions to solve them by legislation in cases where the separate entities are not to continue as before. A private Act of Parliament is passed for each 'merger'—an unnecessarily expensive and complicated procedure.[61]

---

[57] D. Cruickshank, *Competition in UK Banking* (London, HMSO, 2000).

[58] Competition Commission, *Lloyds TSB Group plc and Abbey National plc*, Cm. 5208, 2001.

[59] Case No IV/M213—Hong Kong and Shanghai Bank/Midland, 21 June 1992, para. 14. See also case IV/M611—Dresdner Bank/Kleinwort Benson, 28 July 1995.

[60] See S. Rhoades, 'Consolidation of the Banking Industry and the Merger Guidelines' (1992) 37 *Antitrust Bull.* 689.

[61] e.g. Citibank International Act 1993; Hill Samuel Bank and United Dominions Trust Act 1994.

FSMA 2000 now provides framework legislation under which these private law consequences can also flow from a court order approving a bank merger.[62] There is the separate issue of whether a merger is recognized under the laws of other jurisdictions. Basically, all the assets and liabilities of the merging banks must be transferred to the surviving bank for universal succession.

E. BANK INSOLVENCY

As with bank mergers and acquisitions, some jurisdictions have a special regime for bank insolvencies. Thus from the ninteenth century the United States developed special rules for the liquidation of banks. Under them, shareholders might be required to inject extra funds in the event of a bank failure, liquidations were to be handled speedily, and government was given a monopoly power to close banks. The justification was the special character of banks, in particular the problem of systemic risk. By reassuring depositors, the special rules were supposed to reduce systemic risk.[63] In more recent times the rationale for special laws for bank insolvency has been to minimize calls on the deposit insurance fund. Since the American experience is that banks are particularly prone to insider abuse, this is the basis for some of the especially strict rules imposed on insiders in a bank insolvency.

Elsewhere, as in the United Kingdom, banks are dealt with under the ordinary insolvency laws.[64] These are beyond the scope of this book, although aspects make an appearance at various points. The policy of not having a separate regime is, no doubt, that matters can be handled speedily under the general insolvency laws, as can the problem of insider abuse and the effect on counterparties.[65] Systemic risk is addressed by lender-of-last-resort facilities and measures of prudential regulation, including those concerning bank rescue.[66] Deposit insurance is now mandatory in the European Community; it satisfies claims independently of the insolvency laws, although the scheme itself is in effect subrogated to those paid out.[67]

There has been much discussion about the problems associated with cross-border insolvency. The liquidation of the Bank of Credit and Commerce International (BCCI) highlighted these. This was an international bank, with its ultimate holding company in Luxembourg. London and the Cayman Islands were the places where its two main divisions were incorporated. Insolvency proceedings were instituted in all three of these jurisdictions. The courts there approved a pooling agreement, whereby the assets would be distributed rateably.[68] In other jurisdictions, however, bank

---

[62] Ss. 106, 111–12.

[63] P. Swire, 'Bank Insolvency Law Now that it Matters Again' (1992) 42 *Duke LJ* 469.

[64] E. Hüpkes, *The Legal Aspects of Bank Insolvency* (Hague, Kluwer, 2000), 19–22, 67–80.

[65] e.g. *Re Chancery plc* [1991] BCC 171, [1991] BCLC 712.

[66] 93, 110 below.

[67] Directive on deposit-guarantee schemes, 94/19/EC [1994] OJ L135/5, Art. 12; 78 below.

[68] e.g. *Re Bank of Credit and Commerce International (No 2)* [1992] BCC 715, [1992] BCLC 579 (CA). See C. Grierson, 'Issues in Concurrent Insolvency Jurisdiction' in J. Ziegel, *Current Developments in International and Comparative Corporate Insolvency Law* (Oxford, Clarendon, 1994).

regulators and local liquidators ring-fenced BCCI assets so that local creditors had first claim. In effect this occurred in the United States, where creditors were fully paid off. Doubly objectionable was that the United States treated as BCCI's assets in the United States, moneys in clearing accounts in New York.[69] These were there because payment obligations in US dollars, but having nothing to do with anyone in the United States, are often routed through New York.[70]

As indicated, some jurisdictions adopt a co-operative approach with an international insolvency, so as to achieve a fairer distribution of the assets. Thus the English courts have long said that they will lend assistance to foreign liquidators in a winding-up, recognizing their title to assets and permitting ancillary proceedings in England to secure local assets for them. Some of the relevant jurisprudence evolved in the winding up of banks.[71] Moreover, section 426 of the Insolvency Act 1986 obliges courts in the United Kingdom to provide assistance to other courts, notably those of the county of incorporation. Assistance can include staying an action by local creditors.[72]

The failure of some jurisdictions to extend comity to others has given added impetus to initiatives for international measures to govern cross-border insolvency. The aim of these is to prevent creditors from one jurisdiction stealing a march on those in others, for example by the ring-fencing of assets in that jurisdiction for local creditors. Of immediate relevance in the banking context is the European Community Directive on the reorganization and winding-up of credit institutions. Under the Directive, insolvency proceedings against banks in their home state (where they have their registered office) will be recognized throughout the Community.[73] Separate insolvency proceedings against branches in other Member States are precluded, although to further confidence in cross-border banking, the Directive expressly provides that creditors must be treated equally with creditors in the home state. This approach of mutual recognition also applies to formal reorganization proceedings, short of insolvency, where a bank is being restored to financial health and there may be measures such as a suspension of payments or enforcement, or a reduction of claims. The Directive contains a number of fairly standard conflict of laws rules to be applied in a winding-up or reorganization: thus netting and repurchase requirements are governed by the law of the contract, and so too are transactions carried out on regulated markets.

---

[69] H. Scott, 'Multinational Bank Insolvencies: The United States and BCCI', *ibid.*
[70] 234 below.
[71] e.g. *Re English, Scottish and Australian Chartered Bank* [1893] Ch. 385.
[72] e.g. *Re Bank of Credit and Commerce International, SA* [1993] BCC 787.
[73] Dir. 2001/24/EC on the reorganization and winding-up of credit institutions [2001] OJ L125/15, Arts. 9–10.

III. THE MULTIFUNCTIONAL BANK

A. GROWTH OF MULTIFUNCTIONAL BANKING

Historically in England core (commercial) and merchant (investment) banking were carried on separately. Core banking was carried on by private bankers, later joined by the joint-stock banks. Investment banking was the province of the merchant banks, providing trade finance and arranging securities issues for foreign governments and companies operating around the world. The institutional history, rather than any policy decision that it was risky to associate core banking with securities activities, seems to explain the distinctive spheres of activities. The separateness of functions was reinforced by conservatism and cartelization: there was no desire on the part of insiders to change matters, and outsiders could not break the mould. Certainly there was no major legal impediment to multifunctional banking, in which commercial and investment banking are combined.

Multifunctional banking came with full force in the 1980s, a product of international economic pressures, financial scandals, and the government's ideological commitment to market forces. The internationalization of finance through the growth of the London Euromarkets, the significant force of foreign, especially US and Japanese, banks and securities houses in the City of London, the innovations in banking and financial techniques, and the introduction of new technology—all pushed in the direction of financial liberalization. As in other areas, so too in banking and finance, it has often been specific crises which have given rise to change. The so-called 'Big Bang' of the mid-1980s was consistent with the deregulatory policy expounded by the government.[74]

Not uncharacteristically for Britain, no legislation heralded the 'Big Bang', except the very short Restrictive Trade Practices (Stock Exchange) Act 1984. Rather the Stock Exchange changed its rules to permit outside bodies to acquire up to 100 per cent of a member firm, and to end the separation of brokers and jobbers (to put the latter another way, to replace single with dual capacity). The restructuring which subsequently occurred meant that within a very short time almost every large Stock Exchange firm was sold out to a bank, UK or foreign.

In Germany, by contrast, universal banking can be traced back several centuries. Private bankers engaged in deposit taking, lending, and securities underwriting from the eighteenth century, and the joint-stock banks of the nineteenth century operated as universal banks from the outset. Institutionally, however, the banks divided between commercial banks, savings banks, and a very healthy co-operative banking sector. By contrast the American history is not straightforward. The National Bank Act of 1864 prohibited national banks from dealing in non-governmental securities, but this restriction was removed in 1913. It was only because the financial collapse of

---

[74] See L. C. B. Gower, ' "Big Bang" and City Regulation' (1988) 51 *MLR* 1, 2–5.

the late 1920s was blamed in large part on the securities activities of banks, that the United States adopted the strict segregation of the Glass–Steagall Act in 1933.[75]

B. LEGAL PROBLEMS WITH MULTIFUNCTIONAL BANKS

The emergence of the multifunctional bank has raised a variety of legal issues. Prominent among them is that of risk, as core banking is combined with other financial activities. It is this concern which prompted the separation of core banking from securities activities in the US Glass–Steagall Act. Discussion of this aspect of multifunctional banking is postponed until Chapter 3, on banking regulation. Then there is the concentration of economic power in the multifunctional bank and the competition and antitrust concerns associated with this. This was touched on in the discussion of bank mergers, although we saw that the law has been a particular weak reed in this regard.

The remainder of this section confines itself to a third issue, the conflicts of interest thrown up in the operation of the multifunctional bank. Consider when an issue of securities is being underwritten by a bank or when a bank is a market-maker in securities, i.e. holds itself out as willing to buy and sell particular securities. The bank may be tempted to recommend these securities to customers, or place them in accounts or funds it is managing, if they are unsold in the case of an underwriting, or the bank has taken a position as a market-maker. A variation of this example is if the securities-retailing or fund-management arms of a bank are placing a company's securities at the same time as its corporate-finance arm is about to undercut their value, e.g. call default on a loan by the company. A third example occurs if a bank is tempted to trade upon or divulge to favoured customers information it obtains about a corporate customer or a customer to whom it is giving financial advice. A fourth example of a conflict of interest is when a bank finances a company which is bidding to take over another of its customers.[76]

Relevant to these and a variety of other conflicts of interest are provisions in the general and the regulatory law. In the general law the most obvious proscription against conflicts of interest is if there is a fiduciary relationship. As for regulatory law, the securities laws contain a variety of provisions.

(i) Applying the General Law to Multifunctional Banks

The difficulties in applying fiduciary law to multifunctional banks are both conceptual and institutional. Conceptually there must be a fiduciary relationship before equity intervenes to prevent, or to remedy, a conflict of interest. While the trustee–beneficiary and agent–principal relationships give rise to fiduciary obligations, it is none too clear

---

[75] 99 below.
[76] N. Poser, 'Chinese Wall or Emperor's New Clothes? Regulatory Conflicts of Interest of Securities Firms in the US and the UK' (1988) 9 *Mich. YB Int'l Legal Stud.* 91, 96–7.

on what basis a court will say that fiduciary obligations otherwise arise in commercial relationships.[77]

Institutionally, the problem is that fiduciary law developed at a time when organizations were relatively simple. Its application to the multifunctional bank is not an easy matter. One problem is knowledge: can the knowledge of different parts of a multifunctional bank be attributed to the business as a whole, even if one part does not know in fact what another part knows, and especially if there are barriers such as Chinese walls which prevent the free flow of information? In this respect the position with senior officials is fairly straightforward. Where they straddle more than one department of a bank, knowledge may in practice pass between the departments. Moreover, as the 'brains and nerve centre' of a bank, their state of mind or knowledge can as a matter of English law be attributed to the bank, whether or not in fact knowledge has passed between departments.

Whether the knowledge of lesser officials, within the scope of their employment, is attributable to the business as a whole is another matter. Generally the court must ask whose knowledge, for the purpose of the rule, was intended to count as the company's.[78] There is English authority that since a corporation is one entity in law, however many departments it may be divided into, if one department acts (as agent) for a customer, and another, unbeknown to the first, acts contrary to the interests of the customer, the company as a whole will be in breach of fiduciary duty.[79] Strictly speaking, this was not a case about the attribution of knowledge, although it shows how an institution can be treated as one entity in law. One possible solution in the context of a multifunctional bank is to presume that knowledge exists throughout the bank unless the contrary is proved. Another is to argue that the knowledge acquired by a department is attributable to the bank as a whole only if the circumstances are such that it is the former's duty to communicate it to the latter. But in both cases it is difficult to see in principle how a bank by its own actions can confine the duty to communicate irrespective of what the customer would normally expect given the scope of any fiduciary duty.

The subsidiarization of separate parts of a multifunctional bank defeats any reasoning based on the bank being one entity in law (whatever the business realities). In that case for knowledge to be attributable to members of the group as a whole there would have to be a relationship of principal and agent between the separate corporate entities or, even more difficult, the corporate veil between them must be pierced. Just because members of the group have common directors does not mean that their knowledge from one company will be attributable to other members of the group of which they are directors. However if, say, a director of the parent company has a responsibility to oversee subsidiaries, then the parent should in principle be presumed to possess his or her knowledge in relation to them.

---

[77]   189–91 below.

[78]   *Meridian Global Funds Management Asia Ltd.* v. *Securities Commission* [1995] 2 AC 500 (PC).

[79]   *Harrods Ltd.* v. *Lemon* [1931] 2 KB 157 (CA). See *Lloyds Bank Ltd.* v. *E. B. Savory & Co.* [1933] AC 201 (HL).

The difficulties of the general law do not cease even if it can be established that fiduciary duties arise in a particular context of a multifunctional bank. For there is uncertainty about what the common law rules prescribe. In some cases it has been said of fiduciaries that they ought never to have acted at all, certainly not without making a full disclosure to the customers of the conflicting interests to obtain their fully informed consent. Full disclosure, however, may be in breach of a duty of confidentiality to another customer. Does the duty of confidentiality trump other duties?[80] The strict view is that the only solution is that the fiduciary should desist completely from acting. In this situation the fiduciary bank would therefore have to inform the customer that it is unable to advise or assist.[81]

However, the difficulty again is that one department of a multifunctional bank may not know of important information known in another department, or of a conflict of interest as a result of what another department is doing. A Chinese wall may be in operation designed to achieve ignorance on the part of particular departments of a bank about what other departments know or are doing.[82] A strict application of fiduciary rules would mean that the Chinese wall would offer no defence in the case of a breach of the duty of loyalty to a customer or of the duty not to put the bank's interests before those of a customer. Rather, the bank would have to take positive steps to ensure that there is disclosure, where this is possible, or that the bank desists from acting. Such positive steps to desist would include a restricted-list procedure, whereby the bank would make no recommendations about, and would not deal in, the securities of a company as soon as it entered into a close business relationship with that company.[83]

While the duty of confidentiality is an absolute duty (and not simply one to take reasonable care), there is no rule of law that Chinese walls cannot be adequate in eliminating the risk of confidential information leaking from one part of a multifunctional bank to another. But where a bank has confidential information from one customer, and proposes to act for a second customer with interests adverse to those of the first, the onus is on the bank to show that there are effective measures in place and that there is no risk of information leaking.[84] The risk of leakage must be real, not fanciful or theoretical: the crucial issue is whether the Chinese wall will work to prevent the confidential information being inadvertently disclosed.[85] It may be especially difficult to show that a transaction-specific Chinese wall will be effective, as opposed to one already established as part of the organizational structure of the bank.

[80] Cf. *Winterton Constructions Pty. Ltd.* v. *Hambros Australia Ltd.* (1992) 111 ALR 649.

[81] See e.g. *Standard Investments Ltd.* v. *Canadian Imperial Bank of Commerce* (1986) 22 DLR (4th) 410, 436 (Ont.CA). Cf. *Washington Steel Corp.* v. *TW Corp.*, 602 F 2d 594 (1979).

[82] See C. Hollander and S. Salzedo, *Conflicts of Interest and Chinese Walls* (London, Sweet & Maxwell, 2000), ch. 7; C. Nakajima and E. Sheffield, *Conflicts of Interest and Chinese Walls* (London, Butterworths, 2002).

[83] M. Lipton and R. Mazur, 'The Chinese Wall Solution to the Conflict Problems of Securities Firms' (1975) 50 *NYU LR* 459, 466–8. See also V. Brudeney, 'Insiders, Outsiders, and Informational Advantages under the Federal Securities Laws' (1979) 93 *Harv. LR* 322.

[84] *Bolkiah (Prince Jefri)* v. *KPMG (a firm)* [1999] 2 AC 222.

[85] *Young* v. *Robson Rhodes (a firm)* [1999] 3 All ER 524.

(ii) Law Reform?

It may be thought that its uncertain application and the strictness of the 'disclose or desist' rule mean that common law is outdated. Conflicts of interest must simply be accepted as an inevitable feature of multifunctional banks. It would be undesirable if the general law and regulatory law—which in some respects is more lenient—demanded contradictory behaviour of the one bank. There should be a legislative safe harbour, following this line of thought, if a bank has in place effective Chinese walls, established in accordance with regulatory requirements and if (i) it withholds information from a customer or the information is not available for the customer's use; or (ii) there is a conflict of duty and interest, or a conflict of duties, of which its different arms are unaware because of the wall.[86]

However, it can be argued that in its pristine form the common law is a valuable deterrent to unacceptable behaviour. Precisely because a fiduciary relationship may be held to exist, and because severe consequences flow from that, a multifunctional bank will be well advised to take a cautious line. Chinese walls are not an answer to many conflicts of interest; additional steps are necessary, such as the no-recommendation policy. In any event, the common law continues. The FSMA 2000 does not expressly abrogate it as it does much of the old law on gaming contracts.[87] Compliance with rules made under the Act does not necessarily provide an excuse for deviation from common law strictness. But the common law is, as ever, a flexible instrument. There is no doubt that a judge applying the common law would look to current good practice. If the latter is embodied in the rules made under FSMA 2000,[88] the courts could easily mould the common law to current expectations.

C. THE SECURITIES LAWS AND CONFLICTS OF INTEREST

(i) Insider Dealing

The basic thrust of the insider dealing legislation is to impose criminal penalties—there are no civil penalties and contracts are not unenforceable or void—on insiders who deal in securities, who encourage another to deal, or who communicate inside information to another.[89] It has been traditional to divide insiders between insiders in the strict sense and tippees. Insiders in the strict sense are those connected with a company. For present purposes bank officials would be in this category if there were a business relationship between their bank and the company.[90]

---

[86] Law Commission, *Fiduciary Duties and Regulatory Rules*, Law Com. No 236, Cm. 3049, 1995, 99–100.

[87] FSMA 2000, ss. 147, 412.   [88] FSA Handbook, Conduct of Business, r. 2.4.

[89] Criminal Justice Act 1993, s. 52. This replaces previous legislation: it gives effect to the EC Insider Dealing Dir., 89/592/EEC, [1989] OJ L334/30. See K. Hopt, 'Inside Information and Conflicts of Interest of Banks and Other Financial Intermediaries in European Law', in K. Hopt and E. Wymeersch (eds.), *European Insider Dealing* (London, Butterworths, 1991), 221–31; B. Rider and M. Ashe (eds.), *The Fiduciary, the Insider and the Conflict* (Dublin, Brehon Sweet & Maxwell, 1995).

[90] Criminal Justice Act 1993, s. 57(2)(a)(ii).

Thus those in the bank's corporate finance arm would be caught. In a multi-functional bank they would fall foul by dealing themselves or by informing, say, the bank's securities arm, expecting it to deal. A less obvious example is where banks take charges over listed securities: they may be precluded from enforcing their security by the possession of price-sensitive information, notwithstanding that the information may have been acquired inadvertently or without any suggestion of impropriety.[91] Tippees are those who obtain what they know is inside information from someone known to be an inside source. The insider or tippee must have non-public information which is specific or precise and which, if it were generally known, would be likely to have a significant effect on the price of the securities.[92] Just how specific the information has to be is a matter of debate, although knowledge of a company's impending plans or results would most likely be covered.

From this brief outline, it is obvious that there is a heavy burden in prosecuting insider-dealing offences—quite apart from the problems of uncovering evidence of wrongdoing. Establishing insider dealing by a bank official in a company's securities requires proof of a considerable number of acts and states of knowledge. Not surprisingly, relatively few prosecutions have been instituted since insider dealing has been on the statute book. Secondly, and more importantly, insider dealing is narrowly defined. The legislation does not cover institutions (as opposed to individuals) which benefit from insider dealing. Nor does it cover non-public information which, while confidential, is not price-sensitive. The state of a company's bank account may fall into this category. The prohibition is confined to dealing on a regulated market or through a professional intermediary. Thus the official of a bank dealing over the counter would not be caught if the bank did not hold itself out as a securities dealer.

Underpinning the legislative controls on insider dealing are various provisions in the rules made under the FSMA 2000 and in the Takeovers Code. For example, market abuse rules of the Financial Services Authority go one step further and in effect prohibit a bank from effecting a transaction if an individual employed or associated with it would be prohibited from dealing by the insider dealing legislation. Breach of the rules gives rise to the possible imposition of penalties. The rules do not apply if a Chinese wall prevents the individual effecting or arranging the transaction for the bank from knowing the circumstances giving rise to the prohibition.[93] The Takeovers Code prohibits generally dealings in the securities of a target company by someone like a bank, privy to confidential price sensitive information concerning an offer.

---

[91] Financial Law Panel, *Insider Dealing and Charges over Securities* (London, Financial Law Panel, 1996).
[92] Criminal Justice Act 1993, s. 56(1).
[93] FSA Handbook, The Code of Market Conduct, E1.4.4, C1.4.24.

(ii) FSMA 2000 Provisions

Under the Investment Services Directive (ISD), host countries must draw up conduct-of-business rules incorporating the principle of avoiding conflicts of interest and, when they exist, ensuring clients fair treatment.[94] Chinese walls are not mentioned, and Member States have a wide discretion concerning what to do. Consequently there is considerable divergence on how conflicts of interest are mitigated.[95]

In the United Kingdom, various provisions under the FSMA 2000 address the issue of conflicts of interest. Breach of them may lead to disciplinary action, an injunction, a restitution order, or proceedings by private investors under the Act for the loss resulting from the breach. This is not the place to explain at length the complex pattern of FSMA regulation. At a general level are the principles of the Financial Services Authority (FSA), which are the general statement of the fundamental obligations of all regulated firms, derived from the FSA's rule-making powers set out in FSMA 2000. Compliance with the Principles feeds into the fit and proper standard in the threshold conditions for authorization (discussed in Chapter 3). Breach of a Principle makes a firm liable for disciplinary action and the FSA may apply to court for an injunction or restitution order. No action for damages is possible. For present purposes Principle 8 is relevant. It does not apply to clients which are market counterparties. Principle 8 provides: 'A firm must manage conflicts of interest fairly, both between itself and its customers and between a customer and another client'.

Then there are the Conduct of Business rules of the FSA, made under section 147 of the FSMA 2000. Most important for present purposes is Rule 7.1 which sets out the prohibition on conflict of interest and material interests: a firm must not knowingly advise, or deal in the exercise of discretion, if it has or may have a material interest in a transaction to be entered into, with, or for a customer; a relationship which gives or may give rise to a conflict of interest in relation to such a transaction; an interest in a transaction which is, or may be, in conflict with the interest of any of the firm's customers; or customers with conflicting interests in relation to a transaction. However, the rule exculpates a firm if it takes reasonable steps to ensure fair treatment for customers, and the FSA Handbook enunciates various steps a firm may take: disclosure, relying on a policy of independence, Chinese walls, or declining to act. In disclosing an interest to a customer, a firm must be able to demonstrate 'that it has taken reasonable steps to ensure that the customer does not object to that material interest or conflict of interest'—which falls slightly short of the common law, since a beneficiary of a fiduciary duty must give his or her fully informed consent to a breach.[96]

---

[94] Dir. 93/22/EEC [1993] OJ L141/27, Art. 11(1).

[95] M. Tison, 'Conduct of Business Rules and their Implementation in the EU Member States', in G. Ferrarini, K. Hopt, and E. Wymeersh (eds.), *Capital Markets in the Age of the Euro* (Hague, Kluwer, 2002), 69–73. N. O'Neil, 'The Investment Services Directive', in R. Cranston (ed.), *The Single Market and the Law of Banking* (2nd edn., London, LLP, 1995), 202.

[96] FSA Handbook, Conduct of Business E7.1.6(2).

When it is impractical for a firm to disclose to the customer in this way, it may demonstrate fair treatment by adopting a policy of independence, under which the relevant employee is required to disregard the firm's material interest, although private customers must be notified that there may be a potential interest or conflict. As for Chinese walls, Rule 2.4.1. makes clear that the arrangements must be 'maintained', i.e. reasonable steps must be taken to ensure that the arrangements remain effective and are adequately monitored so that information is withheld and not used in circumstances where the firm would otherwise be obliged to disclose it to, or use it for the benefit of, a client. Compliance provides a defence to criminal proceedings under section 397 of the Act for misleading statements or practices, FSA enforcement action, and an action in damages by private persons.[97] Rule 2.4.6 goes on to provide that a firm is not taken to act with knowledge if none of the relevant individuals involved on its behalf acts with knowledge. Again this falls short of the common law in as much as the common law attributes to the bank as a whole the knowledge of one of its parts, whatever Chinese walls are in place. Indeed declining to act—the fourth method of achieving fair treatment for customers mentioned—is the only one on all fours with the common law.

Other aspects of the FSA's rules address conflicts of interest. For example, the controversial polarization rules are designed to ensure that private customers contemplating so-called 'packet products' (unit trusts, life assurance policies, etc.) are not confused about the capacity in which the bank is acting. A bank must choose: it must market only its own packet products, or if it markets packet products on an independent basis it must be truly independent and seek out the best advice for a customer. Banks have largely followed the first route, and have thus acquired or linked with life assurance and unit trust companies.

As would be expected, there are some difficulties with the regulatory rules relating to conflicts of interest. First, there is their interpretation. For example, the rule about conflicts of interest and material interests applies only if a bank knowingly advises or deals. Does a bank knowingly act whenever its officers know? The problem of attributing knowledge, especially in the multifunctional, and indeed multinational, bank has been alluded to. The difficulties of interpretation are compounded by the mosaic of rules. Secondly, the rules do not seem to deal with certain conflicts adequately. A good example is the firm 'front running' its research, in other words dealing knowing that a research report may affect the price. The FSA provides in one of its rules that a firm may deal ahead of its research, *inter alia*, if it discloses in the research that it has done or may do so.[98] Publication of the fact of front-running hardly protects customers—except in the general sense that they may be deterred from dealing with banks which do so.

---

[97] S. 397(4), (5)(c).
[98] FSA Handbook, Conduct of Business, r.7.3.4(5).

D. SELF-REGULATION AND CONFLICTS OF INTEREST

A hallmark of the traditional English approach to regulation has been the use of informal mechanisms of control by bodies such as the Bank of England and an emphasis on self-regulation by financial institutions. Over the years both the Panel on Takeovers and Mergers and the Stock Exchange have laid down prescriptions about conflicts of interest. In part these have led banks to take various internal steps to deal with the problem. The provisions in the Takeovers Code are illustrative.

(i) The Takeovers Code

The current Takeovers Code, which the Panel administers, contains a number of provisions relevant to conflicts of interest. Under the Code, the Panel does not regard as an appropriate person to give independent advice someone (a) who is in the same group as the financial adviser to a bidder; or (b) who has a significant interest in or financial connection with either a bidder or the target company of such a kind as to create a conflict of interest.[99] The Code recognizes that in other cases not covered by this rule segregation may not be enough to overcome a conflict of interest. In an example it says that a financial adviser to an offeror may have material confidential information relating to a target because it was a previous client or because of involvement in an earlier transaction. In certain circumstances, for instance, the conflict of interest arising may be incapable of resolution simply by isolating information within the bank or by assigning different personnel to a transaction. Instead it may necessitate the financial adviser declining to act. The Code does not go further in identifying the circumstances in which segregation is not sufficient and in which a bank must refuse to act.

The Code also contains a number of rules which recognize that a multifunctional bank may also be engaged in fund management or market-making as well as, for example, advising a bidder or target company in a takeover situation.[100] Under the Code, a fund manager managing investment accounts on a discretionary basis which is connected with the offeror is presumed to be acting in concert with the offeror in respect of those investment accounts, once the identity of the offeror or potential offeror is publicly known. Under the Code various consequences flow from a party being regarded as a concert party: for example, the aggregated shareholding of the concert parties may mean that a full bid has to be made to a company, once the trigger of 30 per cent of its shares set out in the Code has been acquired. The Code provides, however, that what it calls an 'exempt fund manager' is not presumed to be acting in concert.[101] To be an exempt fund manager, a financial institution must satisfy the Panel that fund management is being conducted on a day-to-day basis quite separately within the organization. Not only must there be total segregation of those operations,

---

[99] *The City Code on Takeovers and Mergers* (London, Panel on Takeovers and Mergers), r.3.3.

[100] *The Takeover Panel, Report on the year ended 31 March 1996* (London, Panel on Takeovers and Mergers, 1996), 11–12.

[101] R. 7.2(b).

but also they must be conducted without regard for the interests of other parts of the bank or of its customers.

(ii) Institutional Measures

The common law, the criminalization of insider trading, the implementation of the Financial Services Act 1986 and FSMA 2000, and the code and rulings of the Take-overs Panel have all played a part in the banks themselves taking structural measures to deal with conflicts of interests.

One measure has been segmentation through subsidiarization. We have already touched on this. The different arms of many, but certainly not all, banks have been located in separate subsidiaries. This is one step towards implementing policies requiring segregation and avoiding common law liability. Of course practical factors such as capitalization and corporate acquisition have also been at work in whether or not subsidiaries exist. Subsidiarization does not overcome the conflicts which can arise through contacts, official and unofficial, between the personnel in different parts of a bank. It cannot overcome certain conflicts within the one arm, such as self-dealing and dual agency.

A second step has been the creation of Chinese walls which, as we have seen, are designed to stem the flow of information between different parts of the bank. Insti-tutionally a Chinese wall can involve physical separation (in some cases separate entrances or the occupation of different buildings); separate files for the functions separated by the Chinese wall with no access for someone on one side of the wall to a file on the other side; consequent restrictions on physical access and controls on computer access and fail-safe systems; and controlled procedures for the movement of personnel between different parts of a bank.[102] In some financial institutions, Chinese walls are underpinned by stop lists and no-recommendation policies. The reason is that, whereas under the FSMA 2000 an effective Chinese wall by itself is regarded as a defence to the breach of important regulatory rules, as we have seen the common law sometimes requires more—disclosure or the cessation of the activity.

Thirdly, banks have appointed compliance officers, some being directors at board level. Compliance procedures are required by the rules made under the FSMA 2000. Compliance officers have varying authority to lay down procedures, to call for infor-mation from different parts of the bank, and to instruct the operating parts on the steps to be taken to deal with the problems.[103] Coupled with the appointment of compliance officers are training sessions for personnel and the preparation of compli-ance manuals. The latter may contain a summary of legal and non-legal prescriptions, standard operating procedures, instructions on record keeping, and customer agreements.

---

[102] H. McVea, *Financial Conglomerations and the Chinese Wall* (Oxford, Clarendon, 1993).

[103] R. Bosworth-Davies, 'The Compliance Officer's Role', in B. Rider and M. Ashe (eds.), The *Fiduciary, the Insider and the Conflict* (Dublin, Brehon Sweet & Maxwell, 1995).

IV. BANKS AND INDUSTRY

So far we have been looking at the role of banks in the financial sector. As we have seen most banks perform a range of financial functions from core banking through financial advice to securities activities. We turn now to the relationship of banks to commerce and industry more generally. A great deal of this book is about the relationship between the two—how banks provide industry with payment services, depository services, financial advice, financing, and so on. The focus here is narrower, given that the Chapter is about what banks do and their organizational features. Three aspects are addressed: the extent to which banks can carry on non-financial activities; the degree of ownership of banks by industrial corporations; and, conversely, the ownership of industrial corporations by banks. To the extent that a structural overlap occurs it raises a number of issues for public policy. In general terms they are those relevant in the context of the multifunctional financial group: bank safety, conflicts of interest, and economic concentration.

A. BANKS AND NON-FINANCIAL ACTIVITIES

In England banking and industry have long been structurally separated. This had its origins in the limits imposed on the Bank of England when it was founded. As a result of pressure from merchants, who feared unfair competition, a prohibition on commercial activities was written into the relevant legislation.[104] In 1844 it became possible to incorporate joint-stock banks under the Joint Stock Banks Act. The Act did not expressly mention non-banking activities. However, the jurisprudence seemed to expect that joint-stock banks should not engage in non-financial activities. Conversely, it was regarded as unlawful for commercial enterprises to engage in banking because they had not been incorporated under the Act.[105] For the early merchant banks there was no such boundary. As their name suggests many merchant banks began as merchants. But by the mid-nineteenth century they followed the dictates of the division of labour. They shed their non-banking activities and concentrated on financing through discounting bills of exchange and distributing the securities which governments and subsequently companies issued.[106]

There is no explicit restriction in FSMA 2000 on banks engaging in commercial activities, comparable to the legislation in other jurisdictions which, for example, bans banks from engaging 'in wholesale or retail trade, including import and export trade'.[107] However, banks must conduct their business under the Act in a prudent manner and

---

[104] Bank of England Act 1694, s. 26 (5 & 6 Will. & Mary, c. 20).

[105] e.g. *O'Connor* v. *Bradshaw* (1850) 5 Ex. 882, 155 ER 386; *Re District Savings Bank Ltd.* (1861) 3 De G F & 1335, 45 ER 907.

[106] S. Chapman, *The Rise of Merchant Banking* (London, George Allen & Unwin, 1984), 126.

[107] Banking and Financial Institutions Act 1989 (Malaysia), s. 32.

must safeguard the interests of depositors. Arguably these factors could be jeopard-
ized by a significant expansion beyond banking and financial activities. Moreover, the
Act contains a practical barrier to such expansion since prudence also turns on the
nature and scale of an institution's operations, and to the risks to depositors inherent
in its operations and in the operations of any other member of the corporate
group. Thus prudential requirements may limit in practice the non-banking activities
of banks.

The separation of banking and non-banking activities was adopted elsewhere. The
National Bank Act 1864 of the United States confined chartered banks to accepting
deposits, extending loans, and incidental activities. State and private banks ranged
more widely, beginning first with securities distribution and then with insurance. The
reaction after the 1929 crash was to separate banking and securities activity (the
Glass–Steagall Act). Once licensed a bank was limited to a single line of business (core
banking) and certain closely related activities. The Bank Holding Company Act of
1956, as amended in 1970, forced bank holding companies to divest themselves of
any subsidiaries the activities of which were not closely related to banking. Apparently
this was not so much because Congress feared that these non-banking activities
threatened bank stability but more because it feared economic concentration. Despite
changes to Glass–Steagall in 1999, the institutional separation of banking and
commerce remains.[108]

Yet the separation of banking and commerce has not been universal. The French
approach has been inspired by the concept of commercial and industrial freedom
proclaimed in 1791. If the French banks founded in the nineteenth century confined
themselves to banking, that was by strategic choice, not legal obligation. In modern
France there are numerous financial institutions which have been created or bought
by large industrial or commercial groups.[109] Similarly in Germany: by the turn of the
century the major German banks with their large capital funds occupied significant
numbers of seats on the boards of industry, and in many cases also provided the
board chairmen. Nowadays a German bank, once licensed, may engage in a wide
range of activities, even if not enumerated in the Banking Act. As well as providing a
wide range of financial services their substantial role in German industry continues.[110]
As for Japan, the story is well-known. From the Meiji restoration in 1868, and the
adoption of a national policy of industrialization, banks were part of the zaibatsu,
the conglomerates owned by wealthy families. The major change after 1945 has been
that the banks moved from a secondary, to a leadership, role in modern Japanese
conglomerates (the keiretsu).[111]

Even in countries which favour a strict separation of banking and non-banking

[108] 99 below.

[109] B. Sousi, 'French Banking Regulations' (1993) 19 *Brooklyn J Int'l. L* 85, 90.

[110] M. Gruson, 'Banking Regulation in Germany', in M. Gruson and R. Reisner (eds.), *Regulation of
Foreign Banks* (3rd edn., New York, Matthew Bender, 2000).

[111] R. Gilson and M. Roe, 'Understanding the Japanese Keiretsu' (1993) 102 *Yale Law journal* 871, 879–82;
L. Miles, 'Corporate Governance in Japan' [1998] *Bus. LR* 61.

activities, such separation is breaking down under market pressures. Most jurisdictions now adopt the universal banking model, even if in practice some of their banks resist the temptation and continue to specialize. As a result of the Second Banking Directive of the European Community (now the Credit Institutions Directive), Member States have an incentive to remove barriers to what their banks can do.[112] In practice not only does universal banking permit the combination of commercial and investment banks, but in many places it also enables banks to provide a number of other services such as insurance, real-estate brokerage, and travel agency. Moreover, many commercial enterprises are providing the functional equivalent of banking services. Thus some department stores and manufacturers not only provide point of sale credit but they now market a variety of other banking and financial services.

B. INDUSTRIAL OWNERSHIP OF BANKS

One dimension to the relationship between banking and industry is whether a predominantly industrial or commercial enterprise should have a bank as part of its empire. The first concern must be with contagion risk. The bank might be separately subsidiarized, and there might be firewalls in place. For example, bank regulators might prohibit the parent or other members of the conglomerate from depositing with the bank, and limit severely the extent to which the latter can assist other members of the group in times of crisis. But there is a large question mark over the efficacy of firewalls, and the experience is that members of a corporate group find it difficult to disavow each other when individual solvency is threatened.[113]

Secondly, the potential conflicts of interest are patent. The parent and other members of the group must be prevented from milking the public's deposits with the bank by means of excessive dividends and management fees. Favourable loans are another threat, as are debts owed by the bank to others in the group which, if paid early, could prejudice depositors who would continue to bear any risk of the bank's default.[114] Thirdly, there is the issue of economic concentration. Perhaps it is this which is the strongest argument of all in seeking to preserve something of a separation of banks from commercial and industrial conglomerates.

With this as background it should not be surprising that many jurisdictions object to predominantly commercial and industrial enterprises owning banks. In some this is written into the law. A general limit such as 20 per cent is put on the permissible shareholding in a bank of any one person or group of persons acting in concert.[115] The shareholding limit might not apply to ownership by another financial institution, thus permitting a financial conglomerate to subsidiarize. Another consequence of this exception is that foreign banks can establish subsidiaries in these jurisdictions,

---

[112] 100 below.

[113] A. Hirsch, 'The Regulation of Financial Conglomerates and "Contagion Risk"', in Z. Mikdashi (ed.), *Financial Strategies and Public Policies* (London, Macmillan, 1993), 86–8.

[114] Cf. R. Clark, 'The Regulation of Financial Holding Companies' (1979) 92 *Harv. LR* 787, 803.

[115] e.g. Banks (Shareholdings) Act 1972 (Australia), s. 10.

provided other conditions are satisfied. As well as divestment another possible sanction for breach of this type of shareholding limit is to deprive a person exceeding it of any rights attached to the shares.

Elsewhere the prohibition against the industrial or commercial enterprise owning a bank may operate as a matter of policy, in accordance with a broad legislative discretion, while not being mentioned explicitly on the face of the statute. This has been the approach in Britain. There has never been an express limit on commercial enterprises owning shares in banks. However, the Financial Services Authority has a power, in the FSMA 2000, to object to shareholders acquiring control or controlling shareholders of a bank who are not fit and proper, or who would threaten the interests of consumers.[116] At one time the Bank of England had the policy that it might object to an industrial or commercial company acquiring control of a bank where this created a possible conflict of interest in the conduct of a bank's business, or exposed the bank (and thus the wider financial system) to the risk of contagion.[117] As a matter of law the FSA could not apply this approach if those behind the industrial or commercial enterprise satisfied the FSMA 2000 requirements.

At the other end of the spectrum are those jurisdictions which have no law or policy against banks being part of a commercial or industrial group. Until 1993 German law said nothing about the shareholders of banks. Now it has had to bring its law into line with the Credit Institutions Directive of the European Community. Article 16 of the Directive obliges Member States to require persons to notify the home regulator if they are proposing to acquire a qualifying holding in a bank. 'Qualifying holding' is defined in terms of a direct or indirect holding of 10 per cent or more of the capital or voting rights, or a holding which makes it possible to exercise significant influence. Under Article 16(1) persons must also notify the bank regulators if they propose to increase their capital or voting rights so that their holding would cross the specified thresholds of 20 per cent, 33 per cent or 50 per cent, or the bank would become a subsidiary. The regulators can then veto the acquisition if, in view of the need to ensure a sound and prudent management of the bank, they are not satisfied of the suitability of the person. Under the Directive, Member States must have a range of sanctions against breach of these provisions. Despite the introduction of Article 16 into German law, however, German policy—that commercial and industrial enterprises can own banks—is unaffected.

C. BANKS AS OWNERS OF INDUSTRY

Banks maintain equity holdings in companies, first, as part of their own portfolios to meet customer demand and to take advantage of market opportunities. Banks also hold shares in different companies, but as custodians of customers. A third capacity in which they hold the shares of companies is as investment managers. Finally, in some

---

[116] Notably ss. 186(2), 187(3).
[117] Bank of England, *Statement of Principles* (London, Bank of England, 1993), §2.53.

countries, of which Germany and Japan are examples *par excellence*, banks have their own long-term shareholdings in companies and appoint their own officers to the boards. This last capacity has given rise to a lively debate about whether banks in Anglo-Saxon countries ought to become stakeholders in companies on a similar basis. One criticism of their current arm's-length philosophy is that it leads them to favour the short over the long term—corporate closure over corporate rescue—when a fundamentally sound company which they are financing gets into temporary difficulties. The counter-argument is that under the German and Japanese systems the banks and corporate management can gang up to the detriment of other shareholders and other companies.[118] Pressure to enhance shareholder value is leading German banks to reduce their stake in non-financial companies.[119]

That banks hold shares in these various capacities has a number of legal ramifications. In Germany banks vote the shares they hold as custodians. The law requires that the bank must regularly obtain the customer's proxy to do this and seek instructions on how to vote. In practice customers are passive.[120] To limit conflicts of interest, the Control and Transparency in the Corporate Field Act 1998 limits German banks holding more than 5 per cent of a company's shares from exercising voting rights on behalf of clients whose shares it holds as custodian. As investment managers British banks, along with other institutional shareholders, have been urged to take an active interest in the companies in which they have shareholdings. Perhaps this is a faint hope: investment managers wish to be able to sell when the market changes, and their diversified holdings over many companies preclude a close monitoring of all, or even a majority, of them. However, there is still the point that the way the banks vote these shares is a matter of legitimate concern to those on behalf of whom they invest. Therefore it is not surprising that the Cadbury Committee recommended that institutional shareholders such as banks acting as investment managers should disclose their policies on the use of voting rights.[121]

The potential control which banks would and do have as a result of large shareholdings in industrial companies gives rise to several concerns. The first is the fear of monopoly. Thus in the period immediately after World War II, the Allies wished to strip the German and Japanese banks of their dominating influence in the economy. The 1952 deconcentration law for German banks did not last. Similarly in Japan the zaibatsu banks had to sever their links with industry, but these were re-established after the American occupation.[122] In Germany the Monopolkommission has repeatedly recommended that the equity holdings of banks be limited. It has suggested a 5 per

---

[118] See C. Goodhart, *The Central Bank and the Financial System* (London, Macmillan, 1995), 142–55; J. Macey and G. Miller, 'Corporate Governance and Commercial Banking' (1995) 48 *Stan. LR* 73.

[119] R. Essen, 'The Transition of German Universal Banks' [2001] *Eur. BLR* 105, 107.

[120] J. Köndgen, 'Duties of Banks in Voting their Clients' Stock', in T. Baums, R. Buxbaum, and K. Hopt (eds.), *Institutional Investors and Corporate Governance* (Berlin, Gruyter, 1994).

[121] *Report of the Committee on the Financial Aspects of Corporate Governance* (London, Gee & Co., 1992), para. 6.12.

[122] K. Born, *International Banks in the 19th and 20th Centuries* (Stuttgart, Alfred Kröner Verlag, 1983), 311.

cent ceiling in terms of a company's capital. The Monopolkommission has given as reasons the barriers to a takeover of industrial companies because of bank control, the competitive advantages for companies with a close bank relationship, and the negative effect on competition for banking services if companies are tied into their shareholder bank.[123]

If the antitrust concern about large bank shareholdings in companies has failed to have a lasting impact on public policy, this is not the case with controlling such shareholdings in the interest of bank liquidity and limiting a bank's exposure to risk. Bank regulators have successfully argued that the failure of a major shareholding can not only expose a bank to direct losses, but also result in its reputation suffering long-term, as well as leading to systemic risk. Consequently, Article 51 of the Credit Institutions Directive of the European Community limits a bank's 'qualifying holding' (1) to 15 per cent of its own capital in terms of what it can invest in the equity of any one company in the non-banking sector; and (2) to 60 per cent of its own capital in terms of what it can invest in total in the non-banking sector.[124] The Directive does not prevent a bank from holding shares in a company temporarily during a reconstruction or rescue, for purposes of underwriting, or on behalf of others. The Directive does not address the conflict-of-interest problems associated with banks holding shares in industry.

D. 'BANCASSURANCE'

We saw at the very outset of the Chapter that banks have moved into life and other insurance business. The combination of banking and insurance flies under various flags: 'bancassurance', 'Allfinanz', and so on.[125] Apart from banks distributing insurance (insurance broking), the insurance activities of a bank are located in different members of a corporate group. That is because each activity must be separately capitalized. The regulatory regimes also differ. For example, the calculation of solvency varies fundamentally: with banks it is a function of the assets i.e. loans etc., whereas with insurers it is a function of the risk that they may be called on to meet the liabilities of policyholders.[126]

Historically many countries segregated the two activities, often not by design but because they subjected each to different regulatory regimes. This was the position in Britain. Outside Lloyds insurance could only be underwritten by licensed insurers,

---

[123] T. Baums, 'Banks and Corporate Control in Germany', in J. McCahery, S. Picciotto, and C. Scott (eds.), *Corporate Control and Accountability* (Oxford, Clarendon, 1993), 276.

[124] Qualifying holding is a direct or indirect holding which represents 10% of the capital or voting rights or which gives significant influence. See generally C. Lichtenstein, 'Thinking the Unthinkable: What Should Commercial Banks or Their Holding Companies be Allowed to Own?' (1992) 67 *Indiana LJ* 251.

[125] A. Leach, *New Initiatives in European Bancassurance* (London, Pearson, 1996); T. Hoschka, *Bancassurance in Europe* (London, Macmillan, 1994); N. Genetay and P. Molyneux, *Bancassurance* (Basingstoke, Macmillan, 1998).

[126] 90 below; see also P. Woolfson, '"Bancassurance" and community law' [1994] 11 *International Insurance LR* 404.

although there were no legal restrictions on banks having an insurance subsidiary or on bankers distributing the insurance products of others.[127] In other countries such as the United States, the lobbying power of the insurance industry led to more definite restrictions on banks engaging in insurance. The legal separation was the result of the exercise of this power in the various American legislatures. In the courts the issue has often turned on whether particular insurance activities can be treated as incidental to banking business and thus not subject to the separation.[128]

In Europe banks can now generally be owned by, or own, insurance companies. European Community law is permissive; Member States have in the main removed any obstacles. Indeed, the Credit Institutions Directive of the European Communities expressly exempts Member States from having to apply the limits discussed in the previous subsection to banks' ownership of insurance companies.[129] 'Downstream linkages' of this nature are now common in Britain, but, while permissible, upstream linkages are less so.

[127] J. Birds and N. Hird, *Bird's Modern Insurance Law* (5th edn., London, Sweet & Maxwell, 2001), 25.
[128] e.g. *Nationsbank of North Carolina* v. *Variable Annuity Life Insurance Co.*, 115 S Ct. 810 (1995).
[129] Art.12(3).

2

INTERBANK NETWORKS

The previous Chapter dealt with the structural features of banks—how banks are organized, in particular multifunctional banks. The particular concern was how the law moulds the structure of individual banks and the legal consequences of bank structures. This Chapter moves from individual banks to relations between different banks. The issue to be addressed is the various ways in which banks relate to each other. Again the discussion revolves around legal impact and legal consequences, in this case of various types of interbank relations. These relations are contractual in nature; the concept of the network usefully encapsulates the scope of the discussion.

I. NETWORKS

The network of contracts between banks takes various forms. First, contracts might be part of a chain, as where A in London employs her bank (X) to pay dollar funds to B's account with his bank (Y) in Singapore: Bank X might contact its correspondent bank in New York, which in turn contacts Bank Y's correspondent bank there.[1] Secondly, the concept of network covers bilateral transactions between Bank X and Bank Y (a transfer of funds, a deposit on the interbank market, a swap, a sale of loan assets or securities) which are made against the backdrop of a longstanding arrangement or master agreement between them, on the basis of a standard-form contract prepared by an association of financial institutions, or in accordance with the rules of an exchange or a clearing system through which the relevant transactions are routed. Thirdly, the concept of network can be applied to contracts which are bundled, as in a bank syndicate where a number of banks join in financing a particular enterprise or project.

There are of course combinations of these arrangements, where the primary contract falls into one category but the secondary or tertiary contracts fall into another. Thus in the payment example above, the payment will most likely pass through the dollar-clearing system in New York (CHIPS); banks which are members are contractually bound by the CHIPS rules. Likewise, a bilateral deal between banks, say a swap on the standard terms produced by the International Swaps and Derivatives

---

[1] 237 below.

Association (ISDA), may be bolted onto another transaction (e.g. a loan or a bond issue) or will be part of a chain of dealings. Or if a bank syndicate is involved in the issue and distribution of bonds, quite apart from any contracts involving the bond-holders, the issuer might appoint an independent bank as trustee for the bondholders, the banks may enter subscription and selling agreements with the issuer, and the lead bank might enter into arrangements with an international securities clearing system, on behalf of the syndicate.

The concept of network has been invoked in a variety of ways. Some have argued that it can overcome certain conceptual difficulties in the law such as privity of contract. Their argument is, in a way, for a type of 'organizational' liability, with A in the payment transfer example being able to sue any bank in the chain for a mistake, or being able to hold her bank (X) liable for the mistake of another bank, no matter how far down the chain. Others have analysed networks from the angle of economic efficiency: in particular circumstances a network of contracts will minimize transaction costs and maximize flexibility, thus offering real advantages to banks and their customers. Yet others have used the concept of network to theorize about systems. Do networks stand between contract and organization; are they higher order autopoeietic systems distinct from the individual relationships?[2]

Although it is tempting to pursue these various issues, it is beyond the scope of the present book. Nonetheless, this Chapter throws some light on them in the course of its more mundane task of explicating some key banking networks. Beginning with correspondent banking, which has a long history, it then examines interbank markets. These are over-the-counter (OTC) markets rather than exchange markets. Important among them is the interbank deposit market (one part of the money markets), the foreign exchange market, and OTC derivatives markets. Next the Chapter briefly turns to exchange markets (e.g. financial futures exchanges, securities exchanges) and clearing systems. It is not concerned with examining these in depth. Exchange markets really fall outside the scope of banking law. As for clearing systems, there is a full discussion in Part 3 of the book. At this point the concern is to flag the pattern of contracting involved for banks in exchange markets and clearing systems. Finally, the Chapter explores different types of banking syndicates.

The focus of the Chapter is on the relationship between banks themselves. The relationship between banks and customers is taken up in Part 2 of the book. However, an issue which often arises is the relationship between customers and a banking network. That issue is appropriately addressed here. Thus in the payment example, did A impliedly consent to her bank (X) using a correspondent? More importantly, is A impliedly bound by the contract between X and the correspondent? Can she sue X or the correspondent should the latter make a mistake? Take another example: A

---

[2] e.g. J. Adams and R. Brownsword, 'Privity and the Concept of a Network Contract' (1990) 10 *Leg. Stud.* 12; G. Teubner, 'Piercing the Contractual Veil? The Social Responsibility of Contractual Networks', in T. Wilhelmsson (ed.), *Perspectives of Critical Contract Law* (Aldershot, Dartmouth, 1993); H. Collins, *The Law of Contract* (3rd edn., London, Butterworths, 1997).

employs her bank to manage her investments. Is she bound by the rules of the various exchanges on which her bank deals to carry out the task? As we shall see the legal position of the customer *vis-à-vis* banking networks is not always straightforward.

II. CORRESPONDENT BANKING

A. THE NATURE OF CORRESPONDENT BANKING

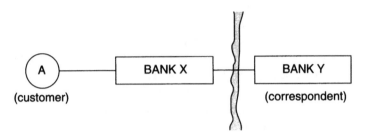

When banks were mainly local they needed banks in other places to perform services on behalf of them and their customers, such as collecting bills of exchange (and occasionally cheques) and advising letters of credit. This is the origin of correspondent banking. In an English context correspondent banking involves international relationships, but in other countries, notably the United States, the fragmentation of banking has meant that correspondent banking had a large domestic element. Even today the international, multifunctional bank will have a very large number of correspondents, so that it can offer customers a full range of services around the world. Even if Bank X has a branch in New York, it may be economically more efficient to appoint a New York bank, Bank Y, to be its correspondent to settle mundane transactions if Bank X's New York branch is geared to investment banking. The relationship between any two correspondents may be extensive and mutual, or it may be entirely one way in which the correspondent acts for the originator in specific transactions only.

The services provided by correspondents these days are numerous and sometimes complex. Trade-related services involve not only letters of credit but handing trade documentation, on demand guarantees and countertrade. Correspondents may provide custodian, money market, and travel facilities.[3] Account services now go beyond collecting bills of exchange to cover cash management (e.g. accounts in a variety of currencies), cheque clearing, foreign exchange services, and payment in general. Banks need access to clearing services in all major currencies—the enormous growth in dealings on money and capital markets has been a driving force—and so use

---

[3] N. Wilkins, *The Correspondent Banking Handbook* (London, Euromoney, 1993).

correspondents which are members of the local system. Banks regarded as sound credit risks will be offered credit related products such as business accounts for credit-card transactions. For the sake of completeness it is as well to note the banker's jargon that the account which Bank X maintains with its correspondent Bank Y is called a nostro account; that which Bank Y maintains with Bank X is called a vostro account.

The relationship between a bank and its correspondents is often one of agency. But not always, and the correspondent may be only an independent contractor providing services for reward, such as conveying messages. In so far as it brings the issuing bank and beneficiary into contractual relations, a correspondent acting as an advising bank in a documentary credit transaction seems to be an agent.[4] If the correspondent confirms the letter of credit then its position changes, because it is now liable as principal to pay if the documents presented by the beneficiary conform. In practice the relationship with a correspondent will probably be governed by a written contract. This could define the branches and services covered, set out the fees payable, and detail the mechanical aspects, such as authentication of messages and accounts to which transfers are to be directed. Specific services may be the subject of separate agreements. Since correspondent banks are the cornerstone if a bank is to service its customers world-wide, errors, losses, and disputes are resolved promptly and without resort to law. Thus the legal aspects of correspondent banking which surface publicly generally involve third parties, other than a bank and its correspondent.

One such aspect is whether, for either regulatory or procedural purposes, Bank X in our example can be regarded as being in New York (e.g. carrying on business for regulatory purposes; carrying on business or having a resident agent so that civil process can be issued against it) by the mere fact that it has appointed Bank Y as its correspondent there. It would seem not. Correspondents typically do not maintain any office on behalf of the foreign principal, exhibit its name, or designate particular employees to carry out its transactions and none other. As a matter of characteriza-tion the correspondent is carrying on its own business, not that of the foreign bank. In advising letters of credit, making payment, and so on Bank Y is performing services in relation to contracts initiated and arranged elsewhere.

B. THE CORRESPONDENT'S ERROR

An important legal issue is whether, in the event of a correspondent bank's error, the customer can sue either the bank or the correspondent it engaged. For example if a customer's payment instructions are carried out incorrectly by the correspondent can the customer recover lost interest or, which will be relevant in some cases, the sum itself (paid away, say, to a fraudster)? More significantly, can the customer recover consequential losses, such as an adverse movement in exchange rates? In some cases consequential losses could be very significant—for example a correspondent does not pay a relatively small sum in time or at all and the owner terminates a charterparty, as

---

[4] Cf. J. Dolan, 'The Correspondent Bank in the Letter-of-credit Transaction' (1992) 109 *Bank. LJ* 396, 422.

it is entitled to do for late payment of hire, and the customer must charter another vessel at much higher rates; or as a result a bidder does not clinch a corporate takeover, and thus misses the considerable profits which were reasonably to be expected.[5]

(i) Customer *v.* Customer's Bank

As far as the customer's bank is concerned, it is fairly clear that it will be authorized to employ a correspondent. The customer impliedly authorizes it to use the usual procedures in carrying out its instructions, or employing correspondents is trade usage. But that is only the beginning of the inquiry. In performing a service, the customer's bank has certain obligations. First, it is obliged strictly to observe its mandate. No breach of this occurs where the error can be laid at the correspondent's door. Nor, generally speaking, will the customer's bank be in breach of its duty of performance. In the main it will not be giving an absolute undertaking that a particular result will be achieved. Rather, it will be bound at most to exercise reasonable care and skill. That it must do in choosing and possibly also supervising the correspondent, but if it selects a reputable bank it is difficult to conceive of a claim succeeding on this basis. In particular circumstances the nature of its contract with the customer will mean that the correspondent's lapses can be sheeted home to it.[6] Given the undeveloped state of the English law of subagency, however, it goes too far to suggest that as a general rule a bank is vicariously liable for the acts of its correspondents or that it undertakes that its correspondents will perform their tasks adequately (e.g. with reasonable care and skill). Even the limited liability of the customer's bank as outlined is subject to contract, and banks invariably protect themselves with exemption clauses.[7] Where the customer is a commercial party these clauses will readily surmount the legislative barriers to unfair contract terms.

Legislation is making some inroads on these common law principles. The European Community Directive on cross-border credit transfers[8] within the European Economic Area imposes liability on a customer's bank for credit transfers in European currencies which are not completed. Liability is strict and banks are released only in the event of *force majeure*. The customer's bank can in turn claim from its correspondent. Claims are limited to the return of the sum with interest and charges; hence this aspect of the Directive is popularly known as the 'money-back guarantee'. Under the Directive Member States can limit claims to payments of €12,500 or less. Thus it is best

---

[5] e.g. *Evra Corporation* v. *Swiss Bank Corporation*, 673 F 2d 951 (7th Cir. 1982); *Lloyds Bank plc* v. *Lynch*, 702 F Supp. 157 (ND Ohio 1988).

[6] The true explanation of *Equitable Trust Company of New York* v. *Dawson Partners Ltd.* (1927) 27 Ll. LR 49 (HL).

[7] For example, under the ICC Uniform Customs and Practices for Documentary Credits (UCP500), banks utilizing the services of another bank for the purposes of giving effect to the instructions of an applicant (customer) 'do so for the account and at the risk of such applicant' (Art. 18a). See also ICC Uniform Rules for Collections (No 522), Art. 11a.

[8] Dir. 97/5/EC, [1997] OJ L43/25; Cross-border Credit Transfer Regulations 1999, SI 1999 No 1876.

seen as a consumer-protection measure. The Directive is derived from Article 14 of the UNCITRAL Model Law on international credit transfers and §4A-402 of the Uniform Commercial Code of the United States.

(ii) Customer *v.* Correspondent Bank

What of a claim by the customer directly against the correspondent? Some civil law systems permit claims by customers on various bases, for example that the correspondent bank is an employee/assistant of the customer's bank.[9] In English law, one possible argument is that customers are third party beneficiaries of the contract between their bank and the correspondent. However, the Contracts (Rights of Third Parties) Act 1999 requires that the contract must expressly provide that third parties (customers) can sue, or must confer a benefit on them. Bank-correspondent contracts typically do not do this. Another way around the strict doctrine of privity of contract is if the customer's bank as agent creates privity between the customer and correspondent. It is unlikely in the ordinary case that the customer's bank as agent creates privity between the customer and the correspondent. To put it in terms of subagency, the subagent would thus be liable both to the agent (the customer's bank) and the principal (the customer) in performing its responsibilities. But in a banking context English courts tend to demand precise proof of privity with the correspondent.[10] This accords with the general understanding that the correspondent bank is *not* an agent additional to, or in substitution for, the customer's bank.

As for tort liability, where the correspondent bank is handling negotiable instruments or securities, the customer as owner may readily establish conversion—a strict-liability tort. But negligence is a different matter. Although US courts have recognized it, and there is a faint suggestion in the English jurisprudence that it is possible in the case of a correspondent bank's error,[11] the weight of English authority is against it. The circumstances would have to be very special for the correspondent bank specifically to have assumed a responsibility to the customer in the relevant sense. Finally, the customer may be able to claim against the correspondent on restitutionary principles—dealt with elsewhere[12]—but this would require very special circumstances.

Were an action against the correspondent possible—as suggested an unlikely event—English law has no definite answer to whether the correspondent could take advantage of an exemption clause in the contract between the customer and its bank or in the contract between the banks themselves (as between the banks themselves, the correspondent bank would be entitled to an indemnity in the absence of an express clause). If an owner consents, expressly or impliedly, to a sub-bailment, the owner's

---

[9] B. Geva, *Bank Collections and Payment Transactions* (Oxford, OUP, 2001), 214, 216, 222.

[10] *Calico Printers Association* v. *Barclays Bank Ltd.* (1930) 36 Com.Cas. 71, 197 (CA); *Royal Products Ltd.* v. *Midland Bank Ltd.* [1981] 2 Lloyd's Rep. 194. Cf. *Bastone & Firminger Ltd.* v. *Nasima Enterprises (Nigeria) Ltd.* [1996] CLC 1902 (an interlocutory decision).

[11] e.g. *United Trading Corpn. SA* v. *Allied Arab Bank Ltd.* (Note) [1985] 2 Lloyd's Rep. 554, 560 (CA).

[12] 245 below.

rights against the sub-bailee will be subject to the terms of the sub-bailment—but this rule has its origins outside the law of contract, and in the case of banks would have only limited application (e.g. where securities are being transferred).[13]

(iii) Consequential Losses

If in the event of a correspondent bank's lapse the customer's bank or the correspondent itself is to be made liable, either at common law or by statute, the issue of consequential damages must be faced up to. As a matter of both policy and principle it seems inappropriate in the ordinary case to make either bank liable for what may be massive economic loss suffered by a customer as a result of a lapse in performing a service for what will typically be a relatively small charge.

As a matter of policy, a sophisticated commercial customer is generally in the best position to take precautions against loss—by timely institution of an instruction, by independently checking that the service has been performed, and by taking immediate remedial action if something goes wrong.[14] As a matter of principle, and assuming the tort measure of damages, it cannot be said that economic loss is reasonably foreseeable where the correspondent has no established banking relationship with the parties to the underlying transaction, where it has no specific knowledge about the nature of the transaction, where it is not put on specific notice of the large losses which could ensue as a result of a lapse on its part, or where it is not made a direct party to the transaction (e.g. appointment as escrow agent).

There are no consequential losses provided under the European Directive on cross-border credit transfers. It is unlikely non-commercial customers will often suffer them and a money-back guarantee will suffice. The UNCITRAL Model Law on international credit transfers provides for consequential losses, but only if a bank has acted with the specific intent to cause loss, or recklessly and with actual knowledge that loss would be likely to result.[15] Consequential losses are severely limited under Article 4A of the Uniform Commercial Code to circumstances where the receiving bank agrees in writing to assume the liability.[16]

Even if consequential losses are available, courts will give effect to plainly expressed exclusion and limitation clauses when commercial parties are involved.[17] Commercial parties cannot expect banks to be ready to accept an exposure to large potential losses in return for relatively low bank charges. A strained construction, seeking to impose

---

[13] *The Pioneer Container* [1994] 2 AC 324 (PC).

[14] Cf. Judge (formerly Professor) Posner's opinion: *Evra Corporation* v. *Swiss Bank Corporation*, 673 F 2d 951 (7th Cir. 1982), cert. denied 459 US 1017. See also *Bradford Trust Co. of Boston* v. *Texas American Bank*, 790 F 2d. 407 (5th Cir. 1986); E. Ellinger, E. Lomnicka, and R. Hooley, *Modern Banking Law* (3rd edn., Oxford, Clarendon, 2002), 505 ff; R. Dole, 'Receiving Bank Liability for Errors in Wholesale Wire Transfers' (1995) 69 *Tulane LR* 877.

[15] Art. 18.

[16] UCC §4A-305. See B. Crawford, 'International Credit Transfers' (1991) 19 *Can.Bus. LJ* 166, 182–5; L. Thévenoz, 'Error and Fraud in Wholesale Funds Transfers' (1991) 42 *Alabama LR* 881, 921; B. Geva, *Bank Collections and Payment Transactions* (Oxford, OUP, 2001), 308–9.

[17] 145 below.

liability on a bank, will be avoided. This will be consistent with the allocation of risk agreed.[18]

C. CORRESPONDENT BANKING, MONEY-LAUNDERING, AND TERRORISM

In recent times the cover which correspondent banking can provide to money-launderers and terrorists has been high on the regulatory agenda. The problem occurs because a bank does not necessarily have first hand knowledge of the controllers or customers of its correspondents. It will simply effect the instructions which the correspondent bank transmits to it on behalf of itself or its customers. There is no real financial incentive to find out with fee-based correspondent services (e.g. making payment or cheque clearing), although greater care is in order when credit is being extended. Nor may a bank be in a strong position to assess the controls which its correspondent has in place to check for money-laundering or terrorist financing. In part this turns on the regulatory regime of the jurisdiction of the correspondent, about which the bank may know even less. Then difficulties of assessment are compounded if the correspondent is acting in turn as correspondent of another bank (a sub-correspondent).

A bank may become suspicious of transactions effected for its correspondent. There may be no obvious reason for a transaction, it may form part of a series which raises doubts, or it may be contrary to what would be expected in terms of any underlying transaction. Both the Basle Committee on Banking Supervision[19] and the Financial Action Task Force on Money Laundering[20] have recommended best practice guidelines. One element parallels the know-your-customer rules for a bank itself to curb laundering. A bank must know its correspondents—their management, their banking activities, and the rigour and quality of their regulatory regimes. Although its knowledge of a correspondent's customers is likely to be less than of its own, it must be assured that the correspondent has strong know-your-customer procedures. When a correspondent's customers have direct access to a correspondent account—a 'payable through' account—the bank should know their identity.

The United States PATRIOT Act imposes an obligation on banks with foreign correspondents to establish due diligence procedures reasonably designed to detect and report instances of money-laundering through those accounts.[21] Enhanced due diligence is demanded for correspondents with offshore banking licences or licences in jurisdictions regarded as non-co-operative by the Financial Action Task Force: the identity of the correspondent's owners must be known, sub-correspondents must be

---

[18] Cf. *DHL International (NZ) Ltd.* v. *Richmond Ltd.* [1993] 3 NZLR 10, 22 (CA); *BDC Ltd.* v. *Hofstrand Farms Ltd.* (1986) 33 BLR 293 (SCC).

[19] *Customer Due Diligence for Banks* (Basle, BIS, 2001).

[20] See examples in Financial Action Task Force on Money Laundering, *Report on Money Laundering Typologies 2001–2002* (FATF-XIII, Paris, 2002), 10–11.

[21] 31 USC §5318(i).

checked, and transactions on the account must be scrupulously monitored. Moreover, no correspondent relationship should be entered into with a shell bank or a bank which permits shell banks to have accounts with it. A shell bank is one with no physical presence in any country. The prohibition does not apply if the shell bank is affiliated to an established banking group.

III. THE INTERBANK MARKETS

Banks constantly contract with one another in wholesale, over-the-counter (OTC) markets. The term OTC is used here by contrast with exchange markets, to indicate that dealings are not on a formal or organized market. However, a particular product may be dealt with on both OTC and exchange markets. Derivatives are a good example. In this section we give attention to three OTC markets: the interbank deposit, foreign exchange, and derivatives markets.

OTC money markets involve the issue and trading of short-term debt claims (less than a year's maturity). The interbank market in wholesale, short-term deposits is one part of the money markets. Indeed the interbank market where banks can borrow and lend short-term (often overnight) is vital if they are to provide payment and liquidity services to individuals and companies without the need to hold large non-interest-bearing reserves. It also enables some banks to provide longer-term funds to customers without first the need to procure the equivalent in retail deposits.[22] The OTC foreign-exchange markets are where currencies are bought and sold by individuals, companies, banks, central banks, and so on. Transactions are both spot and forward. The bulk of foreign-exchange trading occurs between the banks themselves as they continually adjust and readjust their positions: certainly their participation is vital to the liquidity of the market.[23] The most recently developed are the OTC derivatives markets. Swaps are one aspect—the contractual undertaking between parties to deliver a sum of money against another sum of money at specified times. Initially the banks were mainly intermediaries in the derivatives market, but now there are interbank swaps for position taking and laying off risk.

Although there are other OTC interbank markets such as the market in 'distressed debt'[24] the interbank markets mentioned—the interbank deposit market, the foreign exchange market, and the OTC derivatives market—give rise to the majority of interbank transactions. Indeed the transactions on these markets are myriad and the sums involved enormous. In many senses the markets are interlinked. For example,

---

[22] N. Schnadt, *The Domestic Money Markets of the UK, France, Germany and the US* (London, Corporation of London, 1994); C. Furfine, *The Interbank Market During a Crisis* (Basle, BIS Working Paper No 99, 2001).

[23] I. Giddy, *Global Financial Markets* (Lexington, Mass., D. C. Heath & Co., 1994), 6. See also J. Grabbe, *International Financial Markets* (3rd edn., New York, Prentice Hall, 1996); S. Valdez, *An Introduction to Global Financial Markets* (London, Macmillan, 2000).

[24] 360 below.

banks may use the interbank market in short-term deposits to protect against the risks associated with forward foreign-exchange transactions. Moreover, in large financial centres such as London it is difficult to distinguish which aspects are national and which international. As indicated, dealing on all these markets is not only to meet the immediate needs of a bank but also to make arbitrage profits and for speculative gains.

A. CONTRACTING ON INTERBANK MARKETS

Perhaps most importantly for present purposes is the way transactions on these interbank markets are effected. Typically dealers agree a transaction orally and electronically. Brokers are often used to initiate transactions: their advantages are efficiency, that they provide anonymity until a rate is struck, and that they know which banks are able and willing to deal with a principal bank. The accepted practice is that all deals are recorded.[25] Once oral agreement is reached the 'back office' of a bank ensures that a prompt confirmation is dispatched to the other bank. Best practice is that confirmations are sent electronically; written confirmation could arrive after settlement and cause confusion.[26] Confirmations may be provided for in the standard-form documentation which may deem them to be correct if not objected to within a specific period.

Interbank agreements are reached against a background of market practices. In the context of interbank deposits these are reasonably stable; the practices in other markets such as derivatives have evolved rapidly. Under English law market practices which are 'trade usages' give rise to implied terms in a contact, and can thus modify legal duties. In exceptional cases the courts will take judicial notice of a trade usage between banks.[27] The tests to establish a trade usage are well known. As a matter of fact it must be established that a practice is certain, notorious, and considered to be of a legally binding nature. This is not easy, but universal acceptance does not seem necessary, and even a recent practice can acquire these qualities. Although as a matter of law the practice must be reasonable, if a practice on an interbank market were to be factually established and followed it would be unlikely to be said to be unreasonable.[28] Even if a practice meets these tests there are further hurdles. Most significantly an express provision in a contract can negate a trade usage, as can a market rule.[29] The globalization of markets may mean that it is more difficult to establish the high degree of uniformity necessary for a practice to be regarded as a usage in English law.

---

[25] Bank of England, *The Code of Conduct for Non-Investment Products*, 2000, §§30–5.

[26] §§114–15.

[27] *National Bank of Greece SA v. Pinios Shipping Co.* [1990] 1 AC 637, 675.

[28] E. Peden, 'Policy Concerns Behind Implication of Terms in Law' (2001) 117 *LQR* 459, 464, 469.

[29] *Kum v. Wah Tat Bank Ltd.* [1971] 1 Lloyd's Rep. 439 (PC). See also *Lloyds Bank Ltd. v. Swiss Bankverein* (1913) 108 LT 143 (CA) (custom, even if established, repugnant to nature of negotiable securities).

B. STANDARD FORM DOCUMENTATION

These days many interbank transactions are done against a backdrop, not only of market practice, but also of standard-form contracts and regulatory rules. For the wholesale markets in London the Bank of England in its Code of Conduct for Non-Investment Products has recommended the use, wherever possible, of standard documentation and its speedy completion and exchange.[30] The Promisel Report of the Bank for International Settlements (1992) sees good contracting as an important contribution to risk-management.[31]

Typically standard documentation is drawn up by an industry association and executed as a master agreement between banks. Two examples suffice here. In 1997 the British Bankers Association, in association with the Foreign Exchange Committee of New York, the Tokyo Market Practices Committee, and the Canada Foreign Exchange Committee, published its International Foreign Exchange Master Agreement Terms (the IFEMA terms) for bilateral spot and forward transactions. The terms provide for prompt confirmation of transactions, settlement and netting, the rights and obligations of counterparties on default, and the governing law and jurisdiction (parties must chose). Surprisingly, the Guide to the IFEMA terms suggests that, while in New York it is standard practice for banks to execute the terms as a master agreement, in London the terms 'will be presumed' to apply if one of the parties is acting through an office in the United Kingdom unless there is an agreement with broadly similar netting provisions. Because a number of counterparties in the London market have master agreements using other than IFEMA terms, it is difficult to see how the latter can be binding as trade usage. Course of conduct is no surer foundation when the IFEMA terms include matters which by definition have not occurred, notably the default of one of the counterparties.

When swaps were developing in the early 1980s a contract for each was prepared and considerable time could be spent on negotiation. Individual banks developed their own preferred contracts, which led to a 'battle of the forms'. Clearly this became unsatisfactory. The volume of swaps was increasing as banks became market-makers and entered into hedging arrangements simultaneously with the establishment of the terms of a swap. That there should be an enforceable contract as soon as possible after the oral deal, and the desire to reduce the amount of documentation and transaction costs, led first to master agreements, which were incorporated by reference in the shorter agreements establishing what tended to be the variable financial terms in each separate swap.[32] These master agreements differed between the different banks.

The next step was standard documentation, formulated with a view to facilitating a secondary market and to overcoming the 'battle of the forms' which had been occurring. The International Swaps and Derivatives Association (ISDA) was formed

---

[30] §§93–6.

[31] Bank for International Settlements, *Recent Developments in International Interbank Relations* (Basle, Bank for International Settlements, 1992), 101.

[32] D. Cunningham, 'Swaps: Codes, Problems and Regulation', 5 *IFLR*, No 8 (Aug. 1986), 26.

in 1985, and soon after it issued its *Code of Standard Wording, Assumptions and Provisions for Swaps*, 1985 edition. ISDA then moved beyond standard terms for incorporation in individual master agreements to encompass as well standard master agreements. Now there are many ISDA agreements, various sets of definitions, and a number of long- and short-form confirmations. The documentation extends beyond swaps to a range of other derivatives. Attached to the standard-form master agreements are schedules, the content of which vary with individual transactions. To facilitate netting has been a major impetus to ISDA's work.

C. THE TERMS AND THEIR INTERPRETATION

Interbank contracting in financial markets these days is thus far removed from the contract books with their leisurely negotiation, postal rule, and 'battle of the forms'. Deals done on the telephone or electronically are often over in a matter of seconds. As indicated, the London Code of Conduct for Non-Investment Products requires that confirmations should be sent electronically. Often a master agreement between banks avoids the 'battle of the forms', although individual terms will be negotiated. With derivatives it is the schedule which contains the matters which must be negotiated. Instead of a battle of the forms, there may be a battle of the schedules.

If the contract books do not assist directly with legal analysis of interbank contracting then neither does the jurisprudence, for although disputes arise these are hardly ever litigated. Thus we are left with basic principles to address issues such as when contracts on the interbank market are made, the terms of such contracts, and the meaning of the terms. Let us briefly examine these issues.

(i) Timing of a Contract

On principle if parties agree to the essential terms orally or electronically then they can be said to have contracted there and then. This will be the position with the bulk of interbank transactions: the oral conversation or electronic communication will be more than a preliminary exchange or part of the negotiations. Any confirmation is then evidence of the terms agreed, neither a confirmation of negotiations nor the contract itself.

(ii) Contractual Terms

Again as a matter of principle, even in the absence of an express provision the terms of the master agreement will be incorporated in the contract on the basis of reasonable notice, a consistent course of dealing, or a common understanding. With interbank dealings there will almost always be a master agreement in place, even if this is not necessarily the case when banks deal with customers. If the master agreement has not been executed by the parties it may still be binding because the confirmation (say) provides that it will apply as if it had been executed. In the absence of such a provision, it is difficult to see how its terms can apply: course of conduct and trade usage are unlikely to point to one particular master agreement.[33] Inconsistencies between a schedule and the master agreement, and a confirmation and the master agreement, can arise. The master agreement may contain a supremacy clause whereby, say, the confirmation takes priority over the master agreement.

But what if the oral deal and the confirmation are inconsistent? One argument is that the parties intend to reduce their oral contract to written form, and that consequently the parol evidence rule excludes evidence to show the inconsistency.[34] This cannot be right. The whole purpose of sending confirmations is to identify as soon as possible any misunderstandings about the terms actually agreed by the dealers. The recordings of any telephone conversations of dealers are admissible evidence, so if they contain a clear agreement they can be used to overcome a mistake in a confirmation.[35] In any event, English law acknowledges that if an error is made in reducing a contract to writing it can be rectified if otherwise it would be unconscionable for one party to rely on the terms as written. There is also a separate notion of misnomer, for which the doctrine of rectification is unnecessary, when it is obvious to all that a clerical error has been made in transcribing something such as the name of a party.

(iii) Meaning of the Terms

A characteristic of the financial world is the use of jargon. Efficiency, product differentiation, a tendency to mystification, the need to communicate across borders—all contribute to the often impenetrable language of finance. It is a rule of the common law that, where words do not have a plain meaning, the parties may call evidence to establish the interpretation to be placed on them. In effect the parties may provide their own dictionary of the meaning to be attributed to a particular word or phrase. Pre-contractual dealings may be admitted if they constitute the matrix or surrounding circumstances of the genesis and aim of a transaction.[36] Generally speaking extrinsic evidence will not be received in order to contradict a plain meaning, but sometimes a word used in financial dealings will have another meaning. In that situation external evidence is permissible as a matter of interpreting the writing for its trade meaning. An overriding principle which the courts adopt in construing commercial contracts is to avoid a conclusion which flouts commercial sense.[37] However, where there is no obvious absurdity, but simply assertions by each side that its own interpretation is more sensible, a court will give effect to the plain meaning.[38]

---

[33] Cf. A. Hudson, *The Law on Financial Derivatives* (2nd edn., London, Sweet & Maxwell, 1998), 107.

[34] *Intershoe Inc.* v. *Bankers Trust Company*, 77 NY 2d 517; 569 NY 2d 333 (1991), a decision of the New York Court of Appeals applying Art. 2 of the Uniform Commercial Code to foreign currency futures.

[35] *Ventouris* v. *Mountain (No 2)* [1992] 1 WLR 887, [1992] 3 All ER 414 (CA).

[36] *Investors Compensation Scheme Ltd.* v. *West Bromwich Building Society* [1998] 1 WLR 896, [1998] 1 All ER 98 (HL).

[37] *Amoco (UK) Exploration Co.* v. *Teeside Gas Transportation Ltd.* [2001] 1 Lloyd's Rep. 490, [2001] 1 All ER (Comm) 865.

[38] e.g. *Utica City National Bank* v. *Gunn*, 222 NY 204, 208 (1918), Cardozo J; *Prenn* v. *Simmonds* [1971] 1 WLR 1381, 1385, [1971] 3 All ER 237, 241; *Torvald Klaveness A/S* v. *Arni Maritime Corp.* [1994] 1 WLR 1465, 1473, [1994] 4 All ER 998, 1007–8, *per* Lord Mustill.

D. 'SOFT' REGULATORY LAW

Finally, there is the general point that the wholesale OTC markets are taken to be a place where law has an ancillary role—it is assumed that the professional players can protect themselves. Nonetheless, both trade associations and regulatory bodies appreciate that something needs to be done to enhance confidence and to minimize disputes between the professionals. Hence soft law comes into its own. Examples are in London the Code of Conduct for Non-Investment Products, issued by the Bank of England, and the Guidelines for Foreign Exchange Trading Activities (2001), prepared under the auspices of the Federal Reserve Bank of New York. Banks and other institutions active in these markets have also promulgated guidelines of one sort or the other. A detailed discussion of regulatory rules is deferred until later chapters. These codes and guidelines have both a direct and indirect impact on interbank contracting. Directly they oblige transactions to be conducted in a particular way. Indirectly they may constitute trade usage or they may rule out, in practical terms, the possibility of an implied term imposing an obligation to act contrary to their requirements. Of course the chain from the code provision must not be too tenuous if it is to have legal consequences in any particular contract.

IV. EXCHANGE MARKETS AND CLEARING SYSTEMS

The interbank markets just examined are informal in character, and the legal links in particular transactions bilateral. Banks also deal on formal exchange markets—for example, securities markets such as the stock exchanges, or derivative exchanges such as LIFFE (the London International Financial Futures and Options Exchange), the Chicago Board of Trade, the Chicago Mercantile Exchange, or SIMEX (the Singapore International Monetary Exchange)—either on behalf of customers or on their own account. Some of these exchanges have trading floors; others are screen-based. Banks (or at least their subsidiaries) are often members of these exchanges rather than simply effecting transactions through broker members. These days, as with the interbank markets just examined, it is difficult to differentiate between national and international transactions on exchange markets, at least in international financial centres such as London, Chicago, or Singapore.

Banks are also members of clearing systems. Historically these evolved from the clearing houses for bankers' payments of the eighteenth century. At first these were voluntary and informal meetings of clerks sent out by their banks to collect cheques drawn on each others' banks. Gradually they became more formalized. Illustrative is how the town clearing operated in Lombard Street, London early last century:

Each clearing bank sends round to the Clearing House at the times fixed for the clearing, bundles of 'articles' called 'charges', each 'charge' consisting of cheques drawn upon another member of the House. . . . These are exchanged, entered, and added. . . . The 'charges' received by each bank are then taken round to the bank and examined and paid . . . As soon as all the charges are entered and agreed the work of settlement commences. First of all the clearing clerk of each bank strikes a balance between the amounts of his in-clearing and his out-clearing with each other bank; the result is the amount which on the day's working he owes to that other bank, or, as the case may be, the amount which that other bank owes to him . . .

Each bank takes its 'summary sheet', which has a column of the names of all the clearing bankers with a column on each side for the amounts owing to or from these banks. These two columns are added up, and the difference between the two represents the total sum owing to or by the bank in question, 'on general balance'. Each bank keeps an account at the Bank of England, and there is also an account called the Clearing Bankers' Account, and the differences are settled by transfers between these accounts.[39]

As well as the clearing houses for bankers there developed clearing houses for commodities. For example, the London Produce Clearing House (now the London Clearing House) was founded in 1888 to clear coffee and sugar trades. Today it clears derivatives as well as commodity futures.

Despite the technological sophistication of modern clearing systems, the principles at work are basically those which operated in Lombard Street in the early 1900s—clearing through netting (in that case multilateral netting) and then settlement of net amounts (in that case through the central bank). Clearing houses now extend well beyond paper-based payment systems. CHIPS is the well-known electronic clearing system for dollar payments run by the New York Clearing House Association.[40] CHAPS is the London equivalent for sterling payments operated for the banks by the Association for Payment Clearing Services.[41] Clearing systems also exist for securities and derivatives transactions and foreign exchange. Exchange markets are linked to clearing houses; and the clearing houses are in turn linked to banks, so that payment obligations arising in relation to the exchanges can be settled. Clearing systems are dealt with in greater detail in Chapter 10.

A. THE RULES OF THE MARKET/SYSTEM

Once banks become members of an exchange or clearing system they enter into a multilateral contract, notably the contract represented by the exchange or clearing rules. The multilateral contract may arise indirectly, in the sense that a contract between each member and an exchange or clearing system results in a contract among the members as a whole. Alternatively, members of a system may agree together to comply with the rules. The rules are the multilateral contract. In either event, new members of an existing exchange or clearing system will be admitted on the basis of adherence to the existing provisions. Thus bilateral contracts between banks as members of exchanges or clearing systems 'are stitched together and subsumed within

---

[39] E. Sykes, *Banking and Currency* (London, Butterworth, 1905), 107–9.   [40] 279 below.

[41] See B. Geva, 'International Funds Transfers', in C. Reed, I. Walden, and L. Edgar (eds.), *Cross-Border Electronic Banking* (2nd edn., London, LLP, 2000).

a framework of multilateral rights and duties'.[42] Indeed the rules may prescribe a standard form for bilateral contracting to ensure fungibility on an exchange or to facilitate handling by a clearing system.

Some systems of law regard the rules of associations as not being justiciable. The view is that associations are established on a consensual basis, and in the absence of a clear indication that members contemplate the creation of legal relations, their governance is not to be treated as amounting to an enforceable contract. It seems clear, however, that the rules of exchanges and clearing systems are legally binding—in English law either because in accordance with traditional theory, property rights or the right to trade are involved, or because in terms of basic contract theory there is an intention to create legal relations. In the case of some exchanges and clearing systems, it is explicit in the rules that legal relations are intended, doubly so if there is a provision for a governing law. Apart from the rules, however, administrative procedures and technical specifications may not be intended to be legally binding but for guidance only. Regulatory law may demand that the rules be legally enforceable and that members be disciplined for their breach.[43] Not inconsistently, however, the rules of exchanges and clearing systems often provide a dispute-resolution procedure between members to avoid resort to the courts. There may be an internal conciliation, and even arbitration, procedure.

The rules of exchanges and clearing systems are thus enforceable, one member against another, or one member against the exchange or clearing house itself. Typically, there will be a provision in the rules allowing for their variation from time to time. This is because, although in English law a contract cannot be varied without mutual agreement, parties can bind themselves in advance to accept variation without specific agreement. At one end of the spectrum, members must accept the variations made by the operator of an exchange or clearing system. Near the other end of the spectrum, the substance of the rules is democratically decided by the members.

B. THE POSITION OF NON-MEMBER CUSTOMERS

The rules of an exchange or clearing house may impose a particular character on the relationship between members and their customers who are not members. For example, they may treat members not as agents of their (undisclosed) customer principals (leading to a contract: customer A–customer B), but as principals entering back to back or mirrored contracts (customer A–member X; member X–member Y; member Y–customer B). Moreover, the rules may provide for a novation of contracts. The benefits of novation include reduced risk, increased market liquidity, and decreased transaction costs. Novation in netting is addressed later (Chapter 10).

In relation to clearing houses associated with exchange markets it is common for

---

[42] R. Goode, 'The Concept and Implications of a Market in Commercial Law' [1991] *LMCLQ* 177, 180.

[43] e.g. Financial Services and Markets Act 2000 (Recognition Requirements for Investment Exchanges and Clearing Houses) Regulations 2001, SI 2001 No 995, Schedule, paras. 8, 22.

the clearing house itself to be automatically interposed as principal in a transaction. In other words, the rules cause the rights and duties of members in relation to each other to be replaced by rights and duties in relation to the clearing house. The purpose is to have mutuality between each member and the clearing house for set-off purposes: otherwise two separate banks contracting with a defaulting counterparty could not set off their individual losses and gains.[44]

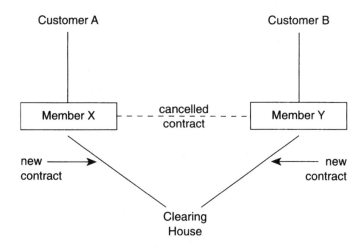

Since the clearing house now bears the risk of default by a member, it must constantly assess the standing of its members; monitor prices, positions, and transactions; and adjust the level of security (collateral) through which members provide it with cover. Novation may also be used in relation to contacts entered on an exchange by non-clearing members. The rules will provide that, for the original contract of a non-clearing member, there will be substituted a parallel contract between the clearing member with which it has an arrangement and the customer, and a related contract between the clearing member and the other party.

    An important question is the extent to which parties which are not members of an exchange or clearing system are bound by its rules. The simplest example is where a customer requests its bank to transfer money to a third party or to effect a transaction on an exchange—is the customer bound by the rules of the clearing system or exchange? The answer depends on the circumstances.[45] Certainly it cannot be said that just because customers are not direct parties to the rules, they are not bound by them because of notions of privity. In English law there is clear authority that one can be bound by the usages of a market, irrespective of one's knowledge of them. Indeed a 'man who employs a banker is bound by the usage of bankers'.[46] The usage becomes

---

[44] P. Wood, *English and International Set-Off* (London, Sweet & Maxwell, 1989), 527–8. See also M. Hains, 'Reflections on the Sydney Futures Exchange Clearing House' (1994) 5 *JBFLP* 257.

[45] See R. Goode, *Commercial Law* (2nd edn., London, Penguin, 1995), 161.

[46] *Hare v. Henty* (1861) 10 CBNS 65, 142 ER 374, 379. See e.g., *Emerald Meats (London) Ltd.* v. *AIB Group (UK) plc* [2002] EWCA Civ. 460. Cf. *Barclays Bank plc* v. *Bank of England* [1985] 1 All ER 385.

binding as an implied term of the customer–bank contract, although where a customer is unaware of it the usage can be implied only if it is reasonable. There is good authority for treating a rule of an exchange or clearing house as usage for the purposes of this principle. In particular circumstances the rules of an exchange or clearing house may be expressly incorporated into customers' contracts with members. In neither case—usage or incorporation—does the exchange or clearing house have a direct action against the customer in contract.

The other side of the coin is the extent to which non-member customers can proceed against the exchange or clearing house itself because of its unfair or improper behaviour. Even with novation, the effect of members acting as principals is that non-member customers are not parties to any contract with the system itself. In these circumstances a customer's best chance is to seek an administrative law remedy or to complain to the regulators.

C. REGULATION OF MARKETS AND CLEARING SYSTEMS

One dimension to the regulation of markets and clearing systems is investor protection. The common law has long frowned on collusive practices on exchange markets; its sanction is to render contracts illegal and unenforceable. Thus manipulation so as to give a false impression of price, including the market practice of stabilization, is caught, although perhaps not if honestly done, on a limited scale and fully disclosed.[47] Investment exchanges are exempted from the general regime of the Financial Services and Markets Act 2000 if their rules are such as to ensure that business is conducted in an orderly fashion, investors protected, and adequate default arrangements are in place.[48] Contracts entered into on investment exchanges are thus moulded by the rules which regulatory law demands on matters such as how business is to be done with clients or where the market member has a direct interest in the transaction. Another dimension to the regulation of markets and clearing systems relates to competition law; its application in the context of payment systems is referred to in Chapter 10.

V. BANK SYNDICATES

A. 'TRUE' SYNDICATES AND PARTICIPATION SYNDICATES

A bank syndicate (or bank consortium) comprises a number of banks associated to carry out some enterprise. Typically the banks will be jointly involved in financing a company, project, or government, whether through a syndicated loan or similar

---

[47] *Scott* v. *Brown, Doering, McNab & Co.* [1892] 2 QB 724 (CA); *Sanderson and Levi* v. *British Mercantile Marine & Share Co. Ltd.*, *The Times*, 19 July 1899. See also FSMA 2000 s. 397(3).

[48] Financial Services and Markets Act 2000 (Recognition Requirements for Investment Exchanges and Clearing Houses) Regulations 2001, SI 2001 No 995, Pt. XVIII.

facility or by arranging, managing, and underwriting an issue of securities. The size of, or risks involved in, the financing may be so large that no one bank can do it alone. The borrower or issuer may wish to involve a number of banks (perhaps from different jurisdictions) or a syndicated financing may have the advantage for it of synchronizing matters such as repayment periods. The syndicate will be put together by a lead (sometimes called an arranger or lead manager) bank or a number of such banks. The syndicate may be a 'true' syndicate, where each bank enters into a direct relationship with the borrower/issuer; or it may be what is sometimes called a 'participation' syndicate, where the lead/arranger bank enters into a bilateral loan or purchases the whole of the issue and then sells 'participations' in the loan or the securities to other banks.[49] There may be dozens of banks in a syndicate but the essence of the arrangements is as follows:

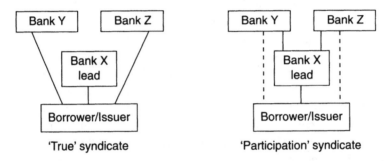

'True' syndicate   'Participation' syndicate

The relationship between the banks on the one hand and the borrower/issuer on the other is examined later.[50] The issue addressed here is the nature of the interbank relationship in a true syndicate. Before considering this issue directly a little needs to be said about the mechanics of syndication and of the relevant terms between the banks themselves. For the sake of simplicity let us assume that the borrower/issuer awards a mandate to one lead bank to arrange the financing and that banks in the syndicate rank equally. (In practice there may be more than one lead and there may be a hierarchy of banks with a management group at the apex.) How this is done (e.g. whether after bidding by potential leads), the nature of decision-making under the mandate when awarded (e.g. as to structuring the syndicate, marketing) and the obligations of the lead to the borrower need not concern us here.[51] The lead bank will then seek to involve other banks—depending on the extent to which they are to retain an interest in the financing—by circulating information about the proposed financing, including an information memorandum from the borrower, and by inviting them to participate. If successful the banks in the syndicate will ultimately

---

[49] A. Armstrong, 'The Evolving Law of Participations', in R. Nassberg (ed.), *Banking and Commercial Lending Law* (Philadelphia, ALI–ABA, 1992), xiii; R. Rendell, 'Current Issues in Participation and Other Co-lending Arrangements', in J. Norton, C.-J. Cheng, and I. Fletcher (eds.), *International Banking Operations and Practices* (Dordrecht, Martinus Nijhoff, 1994).

[50] 304 below.

[51] R. McDonald, *International Syndicated Loans* (London, Euromoney, 1982), chs. 5–6.

sign an agreement in which they undertake to provide or subscribe for so much of the financing. The banks will also agree terms as to the relationship between themselves.

B. THE SEVERALTY CLAUSE IN CONTEXT: SYNDICATED LOANS

The typical syndicated loan (a true syndication) is frequently described as a series of loans which, for convenience, are bundled in one agreement. The severalty clause will provide that the rights and obligations of the members of the syndicate are several; failure by any one bank to perform its obligations does not absolve the other banks of theirs. (Usually no bank is made responsible for the obligations of another bank, although a borrower with bargaining power may be able to have a clause included obliging the agent bank to use reasonable efforts to find another bank to assume the responsibilities of any defaulting bank.[52]) Each bank will be empowered separately to enforce its rights, in as much as these are not relinquished, in other parts of the agreement. In this regard the banks may agree to be bound by a decision of the agent bank and the 'majority banks' (variously defined) on whether certain events of default have occurred (e.g. whether there has been a material adverse change in circumstances affecting the ability of the borrower to perform); whether to call default (i.e. whether to accelerate and cancel the loan); and whether to amend the agreement with respect to, or to waive, certain non-fundamental breaches by the borrower. Rescheduling will be reserved to the banks as a whole; in other words, it will require a unanimous, not just a majority, decision.[53]

There will also be a sharing clause, in which each bank agrees to share with the other banks any recovery from the borrower—a discriminatory repayment but also a recovery by way of set-off—which is in excess of what the other banks have recovered (if anything), taking into account the proportion each has contributed.[54] Sharing may be by way of payment to the other banks or the purchase of participations from them. The sharing clause may subrogate the recovering bank to the portion of the claims it shares with the other banks, which in the case of set-off can allow it to double dip. If the sharing clause extends to recoveries by way of legal proceedings as well, there is an obvious disincentive to a bank to enforce its individual rights pursuant to the severalty clause.

Finally, each bank will appoint the agent bank (often the lead bank) as its agent under the agreement with ministerial functions such as holding any security, receiving and forwarding documents required as a condition precedent to the agreement, setting the interest rate pursuant to the agreement, and acting as the channel for payment and repayment. The agent bank will have no obligation to monitor whether default has occurred—the so-called ostrich clause—but it will be under a duty to

---

[52] P. Wood, *International Loans, Bonds and Securities Regulation* (London, Sweet & Maxwell, 1995), 94.

[53] P. Karamanolis, *The Legal Implications of Sovereign Syndicated Lending* (New York, Oceana, 1992) 137–8, 173.

[54] P. Gabriel, *Legal Aspects of Syndicated Loans* (London, Butterworths, 1986), 185–7.

notify the syndicate if it receives notice of default and it will have a discretion to call default in that event.

C. SUBSCRIPTION AGREEMENTS FOR SECURITIES ISSUES

The subscription agreement in a securities issue differs from the syndicated loan agreement in functional terms. The securities syndicate breaks up after the relatively short time taken for the issue to be placed compared with the years a syndicated loan agreement will last. Generally speaking the banks will not continue to hold the securities unless the issue fails to sell and they are underwriters. In practice the distinction between securities issues and syndicated lending is breaking down in some respect as banks more regularly sell off loan assets.[55] Under the subscription agreement the banks may be in effect individual dealers with no joint rights or obligations. On the other hand they may be jointly and severally responsible for subscribing for the securities.[56] To the extent that a bank defaults the remaining banks therefore undertake to subscribe or purchase themselves in proportion to their commitments. A lead manager is appointed by each bank as its agent to do whatever that bank might do, including entering into agreements with the securities clearing systems and waiving any conditions referred to in the subscription agreement. Most importantly the lead on behalf of the syndicate may terminate the subscription agreement before closing if in its or their opinion there are changed conditions which will prejudice the issue (a *force majeure* clause).[57]

D. LEGAL CHARACTERIZATION OF A SYNDICATE

With this as background we can now approach more sensibly the legal characterization of the relationship in a true bank syndicate. There seem to be at least four possibilities. First, these syndicates constitute a partnership between the banks. Secondly, there is a joint venture in jurisdictions whose laws recognize this creature. Thirdly, a syndicate gives rise to fiduciary relationships, notably between the lead/agent bank and the members of the syndicate. Fourthly, a syndicate is simply an arm's length contractual relationship governed by the terms agreed between the banks.

(i) Partnership

Partnership is an unlikely candidate, not least for the impractical consequences which could follow, such as joint liability of the banks for the individual actions of each and an authority of each bank to bind other members. In any event a bank syndicate does not meet the standard definition of a relationship for carrying on business in

---

[55] 360 below.
[56] H. Scott and P. Wellons, *International Finance* (7th edn., NY, Foundation Press, 2000), 693ff.
[57] T. Prime, *International Bonds and Certificates of Deposit* (London, Butterworths, 1990), 63–6.

common with a view to profit.[58] Assume that the provision of one syndicated loan or that a subscription for one issue has the element of continuity or repetition necessary for the members of the syndicate to be said to be carrying on business. Assume too that there is sufficient mutuality to satisfy the prerequisite that the syndicate carry on the business of lending/subscribing 'in common'. However, there is no sharing of profits as demanded of a partnership, even if the cost of money to the borrower varies with the profitability of the venture. 'The sharing of gross returns does not of itself create a partnership'.[59] Each bank bears its own expense of being in the syndicate, so that whether the interest payable under the syndicated loan or what is obtained in placing the securities constitutes a profit, and if so how much, varies for each bank. The sharing clause in a syndicated loan agreement cannot affect this conclusion.

(ii) Joint Venture

Nor is it any more likely that a bank syndicate is a joint venture—the second possibility—despite a misguided decision of the New York Supreme Court to this effect.[60] In English law 'joint venture' is not a term of art, although it is sometimes applied where firms join together for the limited purpose of a particular commercial venture, perhaps with a sharing of the product of the joint venture rather than the profits.[61] In the United States, however, the joint venture is regarded as a *sui generis* legal relationship: although there is a divergence of views on how it should be characterized, the crucial distinction from partnership is said to be that, despite mutual benefit and profit, it is for a single undertaking.[62] The consequence of finding that the bank syndicate in the *Crédit Français* case was a joint venture was that the plaintiff bank could not sue the borrower separately unless the syndicate as a whole approved. In factual terms the decision is distinguishable since, unlike almost all syndicated loans, this one did not have a severalty clause. Recall that that enables any particular bank to sue the borrower although, as we saw, that right may be illusory if the sharing clause obliges it to share any proceeds recovered. No doubt prompted by this decision syndicate agreements sometimes contain a clear disclaimer that a joint venture or partnership is created.[63]

---

[58] e.g. Partnership Act 1890, s. 1 (UK). Cf. *Re Canada Deposit Insurance Corp. and Canadian Commercial Bank* (1993) 97 DLR (4th) 385 (SCC).

[59] *Ibid.* s. 2(2).

[60] *Crédit Français International SA v. Sociedad Financiera de Comercio CA*, 490 NYS 2d 670 (1985).

[61] e.g. *Smith v. Anderson* (1880) 15 Ch.D. 247, 282 (CA).

[62] *Williston on Contracts* (3rd edn., Mount Kisco, NY, Baker Voorhis & Co. Inc., 1959), ii, para. 318A. Cf. *United Dominions Corpn. Ltd. v. Brian Pty. Ltd.* (1985) 157 CLR 1.

[63] e.g. IPMA Standard Form Agreements Among Managers, cl. 8. IPMA—the International Primary Market Association—comprises the major banks involved in international syndication.

(iii) A Fiduciary Relationship?

That bank syndicates may give rise to fiduciary duties on the part of the lead to the other banks receives support from the *obiter* remarks of the English Court of Appeal (Ackner and Oliver LJJ) in *UBAF Ltd.* v. *European American Banking Corp.*:[64]

The transaction into which the plaintiffs were invited to enter, and did enter, was that of contributing to a syndicate loan where, as it seems to us, quite clearly the defendants were acting in a fiduciary capacity for all the other participants. It was the defendants who received the plaintiff's money and it was the defendants who arranged for and held, on behalf of all the participants, the collateral security for the loan. If, therefore, it was within the defendant's knowledge at any time whilst they were carrying out their fiduciary duties that the security was, as the plaintiffs allege, inadequate, it must, we think, clearly have been their duty to inform the participants of that fact and their continued failure to do so would constitute a continuing breach of their fiduciary duty.

These remarks must be treated with caution as a general statement of the law. The case involved the sale of an existing loan—a participation syndicate in our terms—when the lead/arranger bank was also the trustee of the security for the benefit of participants. In these circumstances the fiduciary obligations of the lead are more obvious than in a true syndicate where there is no security. As is evident in this passage, the consequence of there being a fiduciary duty, if this is correct, is that it compounds the situations in which syndicate members will be able to sue the lead bank where a venture turns sour. Fiduciaries have a duty to act with care and skill, and as well must disclose any conflict of interest in relation to, or benefit from, the borrower or issuer. A variant of the *UBAF* approach is suggested by some commentators: the lead bank is initially the agent of the borrower, but at some point in putting the syndicate together it becomes agent of the syndicate banks and thus owes them fiduciary duties.[65] The 'shifting obligation' theory is elusive about the point at which this metamorphosis occurs.

In fact the US courts are correct when they conclude that the common law requires particular circumstances before a lead bank will owe any fiduciary duties to the syndicate, and that even then it may be a fiduciary in some respects but not others.[66] For example, appointment as the agent bank after a syndicated loan is signed may trigger agent/principal fiduciary duties, albeit that these are likely to be few, given the mainly ministerial functions to be performed. In general, however, the common law demands that, for there to be a fiduciary relationship, there must be a reposing of confidence by one party in another—a reasonable expectation on the part of a

---

[64] [1984] QB 713, 728.

[65] J. Lehane, 'Role of Managing and Agent Banks', in D. Pierce *et al.* (eds.), *Current Problems in International Financial Law* (Singapore, Butterworths, 1985); R. Tennekoon, *The Law and Regulation of International Finance* (London, Butterworths, 1991), 56.

[66] e.g. *In re Continental Resources Corp.*, 799 F 2d 622 (10th Cir. 1986); *Chemical Bank* v. *Security Pacific National Bank*, 20 F 3d 375 (9th Cir. 1994); *Banque Arabe et Internationale d'Investissement* v. *Maryland National Bank*, 57 F 3d 146 (2nd Cir. 1995).

syndicate member that the lead/agent bank will put its interests ahead of its own.[67] In the normal syndicate the banks are at arm's length and are not entitled to relax their vigilance or independent judgement. Even if *UBAF* is correct, members of a bank syndicate have arguably consented to the lead/agent bank acting in breach of most of its fiduciary duties. After all they will be sophisticated enough to know whether it has an established banking relationship with the borrower/issuer, that it will be extracting additional fees, and generally that it will be ploughing its own furrow.

In any event the modern view is that fiduciary duties are moulded by their contractual setting.[68] This can be in the way a role is defined. It can also be done expressly, as by absolving a fiduciary of its duty to avoid or disclose conflicts of interest and 'secret profits'. Thus the typical syndicated loan agreement makes clear that the lead/agent bank need not disclose or account to any other bank for sums or fees received for its own account. To obviate conflict-of-interest problems standard clauses will also enable the lead/agent bank to engage in banking or other business, such as a financial adviser to the borrower. Further, a clause may protect the lead/agent bank if in its judgement it decides not to disclose to the syndicate certain of the confidential information it has obtained from the borrower. Freely negotiated at arm's length between banks, such a clause is not unreasonable.[69] The lead/agent bank thus avoids being placed in the impossible position where to disclose is in breach of its duty of confidentiality to the borrower, but not to disclose is in breach of its fiduciary duties to the syndicate. Finally, the agreement may provide explicitly that nothing in it constitutes the lead/agent as a fiduciary of the syndicate.[70]

(iv) An Arm's-Length Relationship

Does this mean that the fourth characterization of a bank syndicate, that it is an arm's-length relationship governed by the terms agreed, is thus the most persuasive?[71] Yes, but this does not preclude claims against a lead bank by members of the syndicate for negligence or breach of contract, for example, for failing to use reasonable care when valuing the borrower's assets.[72] Another example is in selecting lawyers to draft the documentation, for example, the lead will need to act, as with any person providing a service, with reasonable care and skill. This is an easily satisfied standard if it chooses a reputable law firm, and in any event there

---

[67] *LAC Minerals Ltd.* v. *International Corona Resources Ltd.* (1989) 61 DLR (4th) 14, 29, 40, 61 (SCC), and the academic and other authorities there cited. See 187 below.

[68] *Kelly* v. *Cooper* [1993] AC 205, 213–15; *Henderson* v. *Merrett Syndicates Ltd.* [1995] AC 145, 206; *Hospital Products Ltd.* v. *United States Surgical Corporation* (1984) 156 CLR 41, 96–7.

[69] *National Westminster Bank plc* v. *Utrecht-America Finance Co.* [2001] EWCA Civ. 658, [2001] 3 All ER 733.

[70] Loan Market Association, Multicurrency Term and Revolving Facilities Agreement, §§26.4–26.5, 26.12.

[71] L. Clark and S. Farrar, 'Rights and Duties of Managing and Agent Banks in Syndicated Loans to Government Borrowers' [1982] *U Ill. LR* 229. See also J. O'Sullivan, 'The Roles of Managers and Agents in Syndicated Loans' (1992) 3 *JBFLP* 162; A. Mugasha, 'A Conceptual-functional Approach to Multi-bank Financing' (1995) 6 *JBFLP* 5.

[72] *Banque Bruxelles Lambert SA* v. *Eagle Star Insurance Co. Ltd.* [1997] AC 191, [1996] 3 All ER 365 (HL). See also *Sumitomo Bank* v. *Banque Bruxelles Lambert SA* [1997] 1 Lloyd's Rep. 487.

may be an express exclusion of lead liability in the documentation. The lead will need to have systems in place to ensure that its officers do not make negligent or fraudulent statements to members of the syndicate, for these may give rise to liability.

E. THE AGENT BANK

If the lead takes on the position of agent bank once a syndicated loan agreement is in force, it will be liable for breach of its duties in that role. But even if not described as such, these duties will be mainly of a mechanical or administrative nature. The agent bank will receive the documents constituting the conditions precedent and other information from the borrower, but in all likelihood will be expressly excused from checking their accuracy and completeness on behalf of the syndicate. The agent bank will be the conduit for drawdown and payment, yet the agreement may say that it does not hold any funds on trust, nor does it have any fiduciary obligations.[73] In particular it will have no obligation to provide any bank with credit information about the borrower, and the syndicate members must continue to make their own independent appraisal.

Under the general law it is arguable that an agent bank must exercise care and skill in monitoring the condition of the borrower, in particular whether any event of default has occurred. In practice any such duty will be negated by the agreement, which will also provide that the agent is not deemed to have constructive knowledge of any event of default. If it does have actual knowledge of default it will simply need to inform the syndicate; it is the syndicate which must decide to act either by majority or unanimously as provided for in the agreement. Absent gross negligence or wilful misconduct, the agreement will give little scope for any liability on the part of an agent bank to syndicate members.

F. THE LEAD'S LIABILITY FOR THE INFORMATION MEMORANDUM

A particularly difficult issue is the liability of the lead for misstatements and omissions in the information memorandum. Certainly the borrower will be liable for them since the information memorandum is its document, designed to be distributed to potential members of the syndicate. There will be remedies against it at common law or under the agreement, since there the borrower will typically represent that the information memorandum is not misleading, does not omit material facts, and that there has been no material adverse change since its issue. Breach will be an event of default. But what if these remedies are illusory because the borrower is insolvent and the only deep pocket is the lead's? If the lead bank has acted purely as a conduit pipe from the borrower to syndicate members, it is arguable that there is no assumption

---

[73] Cf. the position if the agent bank is insolvent: *Re Japan Leasing (Europe) plc* [2000] WTLR 301.

of responsibility to found an action in negligent misstatement.[74] Treating the lead
bank as the borrower's agent does not advance matters, since an agent acting purely
ministerially can avoid liability.

In fact in many cases the lead bank will be intimately involved in the preparation of
the information memorandum. In these circumstances it will be liable if it has not
used reasonable care to ensure that the information is accurate—if in the American
phraseology it has not carried out due diligence. English law will regard the lead as
having assumed the requisite responsibility, and as far as potential syndicate members
are concerned there will be the necessary proximity for an action in negligent misstatement as well. In extreme cases fraud (deceit) is also a possibility. Yet the lead bank
may yet triumph. First, the syndicate member will have to demonstrate reliance—
that it entered the agreement with the borrower in reliance on the information
memorandum. As a factual matter it may not have done so.

Moreover, a syndicate bank will find it difficult to surmount the usual exclusion
clauses and disclaimers inserted in the documentation. The information memorandum itself will state that all information in it comes from the borrower, that the
lead is not making representations or warranties about the information or undertaking to review it, and that each bank should make its own assessment of its
relevance and accuracy. This will be backed up by similar clauses in the relevant
agreement. There can be no question that these exclusions and disclaimers are
enforceable. Controls such as the Unfair Contract Terms Act 1977 can have no application in arm's-length, commercial contracting between financial institutions. It is
only in the unlikely event that the lead is fraudulent, or knows that the borrower is
making a false statement but decides to stand by, that English law will ignore an
exclusion clause.

[74] e.g. *Royal Bank Trust Co. (Trinidad) Ltd.* v. *Pampellonne* [1987] 1 Lloyd's Rep. 218, PC. But see 211 below.

3

BANK REGULATION

Monetary policy—discussed in the next chapter—was once an important reason for regulating banking and financial institutions, but prudential, investor-protection, anti-crime, and consumer-protection reasons now loom larger. Section I of this Chapter examines the wide range of reasons behind bank regulation.[1] Somewhat paradoxically in an era of financial liberalization, the legal regulation of banking and finance has been tightened significantly in recent years.[2] In fact the appropriate response to financial liberalization, with the greater risks banks consequently take and the more aggressive marketing involved, is a tightening of regulation. Then in section II particular attention is given to the techniques involved in the prudential regulation of banks. Not only must banks be authorized, but there are a range of controls on their structure, operations, management, and activities, all designed to underpin their soundness. Some of these controls are sketched in this section of the Chapter. Sections III and IV of the Chapter turn to, respectively, the prudential regulation of multi-functional banks and of international banking. With multifunctional ('universal') banking prudential regulation of a bank is needed in respect not only of core banking, but other activities as well—securities, insurance and so on—where they threaten contagion of the financial system. International banking is the focus of the last part of the book, but the discussion in section IV of this Chapter touches on the dimension of its prudential regulation.[3] How can home and host regulators act to ensure the soundness of an international bank?

Perhaps the most characteristic feature of banking regulation these days is convergence: countries around the world are moving closer in terms of the content of prudential regulation and the techniques used. As we shall see throughout the Chapter, the work of the Basle Committee on Banking Supervision (formerly the Committee on Banking Regulations and Supervisory Practices) has been especially important. The committee consists of the central banks and (where different) banking regulators

---

[1] Securities regulation, for investor protection reasons, is dealt with elsewhere in the book, especially in ch. 12.

[2] W. Blair, 'Liberalisation and the Universal Banking Model: Regulation and Deregulation in the United Kingdom', in J. Norton, C.-J. Cheng, and I. Fletcher (eds.), *International Banking Regulation and Supervision* (Dordrecht, Martinus Nijhoff, 1994); J. Alworth and S. Bhattacharya, *The Emerging Framework of Bank Regulation and Capital Control*, LSE, FMG Special Paper No 78, 1996, 13–16.

[3] See J. Norton, 'Banking Law in the 21st Century', in R. Cranston (ed.), *Making Commercial Law. Essays [for] Roy Goode* (Oxford, Clarendon, 1997).

of the G10 countries (plus Switzerland and Luxembourg). Its purpose is to foster co-operation between banking regulators and to establish agreed minimum standards for the supervision of international banking groups. The standards are not set out in the form of international instruments: they are 'soft law' *par excellence*. Its Core Principles for Effective Banking Supervision are especially important.[4] The prestige and power of the committee's members have meant, however, that in practice many other countries adopt its standards. Banking supervisors in other parts of the world have formed parallel committees.[5]

Within Europe, convergence in bank regulation has been given a great impetus by the European Community, in particular its single market programme. Banks author-ized in one Member State are entitled to establish branches, and to provide services, in other Member States, without needing authorization there.[6] In other words, there is mutual recognition by each Member State of the others' licensing processes. However, mutual recognition is coupled with harmonized minimum standards. If Member States are to have confidence in banks licensed in other Member States, they must be assured that they comply with certain minimum standards. Capital adequacy is a key harmonized standard,[7] but others include investment in non-financial entities,[8] deposit protection,[9] the ownership and control of banks,[10] large exposures,[11] and consolidated supervision.[12]

Despite convergence, it seems useful in the Chapter occasionally to contrast the regulatory position between jurisdictions, in particular between Britain and the United States. Not least, this demonstrates how two free-market economies, with similar legal traditions, have developed different legal tools for regulating the same area of economic activity. Traditionally what must have struck the outside observer of banking regulation in Britain was that in important areas the task was left to self-regulation. Moreover, where there was legal regulation, it tended, when compared with that in other countries, to be nominal, informal in its implementation, and administered by bodies the regulatory functions of which were muted. Under European and international influences, and as a result of banking crises and changing institutional and market conditions, much of this older approach has been transformed.

---

[4] (Basle, BIS, 1997). See G. Walker, *International Banking Regulation. Law, Policy and Practice* (London, Kluwer, 2001), 443ff; L. Lee, 'The Basel Accords as Soft Law' (1998) 39 *Virginia JIL* 1.

[5] C. Hadjiemmanuil, 'Central Bankers' "Club Law" and Transitional Economies', in J. Norton and M. Andenas (eds.), *Emerging Financial Markets and the Role of International Financial Organisations* (London, Kluwer, 1996), 183–5.

[6] 85 below.   [7] 89 below.   [8] 35 above.   [9] 78 below.
[10] 86 below.   [11] 91 below.   [12] 105 below.

I. REASONS FOR REGULATION

The reasons behind the range of regulation facing banking can be analysed in various ways. One approach is historical, which usefully brings out the contingent nature of bank regulation. In the United Kingdom a great deal of prudential regulation has been triggered by particular crises. While the first general regulatory measure for banks, the Banking Act 1979, was a response to the EC First Banking Directive, it was primarily a result of the secondary banking crisis of the early 1970s.[13] Prior to that, the 'secondary' or 'fringe' banks were unregulated. The Banking Act 1979 brought the secondary banks within the supervisory control of the Bank of England through a system of licensing for institutions taking deposits. The Banking Act 1987 was designed to improve prudential control. The committee set up after the collapse of Johnson Matthey Bankers Ltd. in 1984 recommended that the dual system of control in the Banking Act 1979, which distinguished between recognized banks and licensed deposit-takers, should be abandoned. Not only were there bureaucratic-administrative reasons for this, such as the problems of applying the criteria fairly between institutions, but prudential reasons as well. For example, to become a recognized bank, which had a higher status than a licensed deposit-taker, some institutions diversified and expanded in ways which were 'artificial and, at worst, could be counter-prudential'.[14] Subsequently the collapses of Bank of Credit and Commerce International (BCCI) and Barings led to modifications of the 1987 regime. Barings in particular focused attention on multifunctional banking, since it was fraud in its securities arm which led to the collapse of the bank as a whole. This gave added impetus to regulatory rationalization. The Financial Services and Markets Act 2000 transferred bank regulation from the Bank of England to the Financial Services Authority, and treats core banking as just one more financial service to be regulated (see discussion in Part III of this Chapter).

In the United States an historical account explains how a system of banking regulation has grown up which almost defies logic. Nineteenth-century populism is one factor. 'Free banking'—the notion that banks could incorporate without a special charter—emerged in the late 1830s as an egalitarian philosophy. Federal chartering of banks emerged in the 1860s because of the financial exigencies of the Civil War: national banks were required to buy bonds to finance the war.[15] Self-interest has also been important. At state level, for example, the exclusion of out-of-state banks has been an obvious manifestation. More generally, the securities and insurance industries have fought a running battle, one weapon being litigation, against the

---

[13] J. Cooper, *The Management and Regulation of Banks* (London, Macmillan, 1984), 245.

[14] *Report of the Committee set up to Consider the System of Banking Supervision*, Cmnd. 9550, HMSO, 1985, 4.

[15] E. White, *The Regulation and Reform of the American Banking System 1900–1929* (Princeton, NJ, Princeton UP, 1983), 11.

expansion of banks into these areas.[16] Furthermore, social objectives have been more important in United States bank regulation, as compared with that in Britain. For example, one aspect of regulation has been to channel bank credit in certain socially desirable directions.

Another approach to the topic is to look at the emergence and form of bank regulation. It is necessary to distinguish between the motives and purposes underlying regulation on the one hand, and the rationale offered by its proponents on the other. A study of the way regulation emerges is also important, because it throws light on its efficacy. For example, despite the intentions of its proponents, bank regulation may be deficient because of the form it eventually takes, the resources given to those entrusted with its implementation, or the effort devoted by the regulated to avoiding its impact. There is no necessary congruence between the reasons given for bank regulation and the resources to implement it.

There is not the space here to pursue a sophisticated analysis of these matters. Rather, this section sets out in a fairly straightforward manner the reasons behind the different ways banking is regulated.[17] Its aim is to give some flavour of the range of regulation facing banks and banking. Section II of the Chapter then focuses at greater length on one particular type of regulation, the prudential regulation of banks, and in so doing contains some discussion on whether the methods of regulation are adequate in the light of the reasons behind it.

A. SYSTEMIC RISK

Systemic risk looms large in the regulation of banking and financial institutions. While there is a concern to protect depositors against loss through default by individual institutions, public policy is also concerned with confidence in the system as a whole. Part of the conventional wisdom in banking is that default by one institution can spread to undermine other institutions. This is systemic risk. It is separate from the other risks facing individual banks—credit risk, market risk, political risk, and so on.[18] There is now firm empirical evidence that if systematic risk becomes a reality, and there is a banking crisis, the costs of its resolution and output loss in the economy can be some 15–20 per cent of GDP.[19]

Systemic risk derives in part from the interbank linkages examined in Chapter 2. If

---

[16] G. Benston, 'Federal Regulation of Banking: Historical Overview', in G. Kaufman and R. Kormendi (eds.), *Deregulating Financial Services* (Cambridge, MA, Ballinger, 1986), 11.

[17] Cf. M. Möschel, 'Public Law of Banking', *International Encyclopedia of Comparative Law. Commercial Transactions and Institutions*, 1991, ix.

[18] e.g. E. Gardener, *UK Banking Supervision* (London, Allen & Unwin, 1986), ch. 1; V. Polizatto, 'Prudential Regulation and Banking Supervision', in D. Vittas (ed.), *Financial Regulation: Changing the Rules of the Game* (Washington, DC, World Bank, 1992), 283–4; E. Davis, *Debt, Financial Fragility, and Systemic Risk* (Oxford, Clarendon, 1992); R. Lastra, *Central Banking and Banking Regulation* (London, LSE Financial Markets Group, 1996), 81–6.

[19] G. Hoggarth and V. Saporta, 'Costs of Banking System Instability', *Bank of England Financial Stability Review*, June 2001, 148.

banks have large interbank deposits with a failed bank, for example, they may in turn suffer illiquidity or, in extreme cases, insolvency. Because the exposures which banks have to other banks can be enormous, techniques such as loss-sharing are impractical. However, exposure on the interbank market is less extensive than it was: banks use the interbank market for basic funding needs, but derivatives for hedging and position-taking. The credit exposure is less than with deposits, since the loss on derivatives is confined to the replacement value.[20] Indeed, sophisticated institutions close to the market generally anticipate bank failure and thus protect themselves by reducing their exposure on the interbank market to the suspect bank.

Partly also, systemic risk derives from the linkages between banks through the payment system.[21] We examine these in Chapters 8 and 10. Briefly, with net settlement systems, banks send innumerable payment instructions to other banks during the course of a day. At the end of the day, the instructions are netted and settled. If a bank fails and is unable to settle the payment obligations it has accumulated to other banks during the day, those other banks are in jeopardy of defaulting on the payment obligations they have in turn contracted. Fear of contagion through the payment system has been a major factor in the move to real-time gross settlement, where each payment obligation is settled immediately.[22]

Then there is systemic risk because of the public perception that other banks are in the same position as the suspect or failed bank. There is a run on these other banks as the public moves to banks perceived to be the very strongest, or there is a flight to cash. These banks may be perfectly healthy, but will face a liquidity crisis if there is a rush to withdraw deposits.[23] There is an asymmetry in the maturity of a bank's deposits on the one hand (payable on demand or usually within a short period) and their assets on the other (loans and other investments which cannot be readily liquidated). In normal times this does not matter, because banks will have sufficient liquidity to deal with withdrawals. In times of crisis, banks will have to call on the lender-of-last-resort facilities of the central bank. As we shall see in the following chapter, these may be refused.

There are a range of prudential techniques designed to prevent systemic crises arising in the first place. These are as varied as ensuring that banks are prudently run, with adequate capital and liquidity, to restricting their activities and operations. Moreover, there are also protective techniques once a crisis arises. The safety net of deposit insurance is one; regulatory rescue is another.[24] Section II of this Chapter gives attention to some of them.

---

[20] 97 below.

[21] See H. Scott, 'Deregulation and Access to the Payment System' (1986) 23 *Harv. J Legislation* 331.

[22] 277 below.

[23] See E. Baltensperger and J. Dermine, 'European Banking: Prudential and Regulatory Issues', in J. Dermine (ed.), *European Banking in the 1990s* (2nd edn., Oxford, Blackwell, 1993); I. Michael, 'Financial Interlinkages and Systematic Risk', *Bank of England Financial Stability Review*, Spring 1998, 26; G. Kaufman, 'Bank Contagion. A Review of the Theory and Evidence' (1994) 8 *J. Fin. Services Research* 123.

[24] H. Zhu, *Bank Runs. Welfare and Policy Implications* (Basle, BIS Working Paper No 107, 2001).

B. PREVENTION OF FRAUD, MONEY-LAUNDERING, AND TERRORISM

Even the most ardent free marketeer accepts the need for controls to minimize fraud. Markets cannot work smoothly unless persons can deal with each other in the knowledge that fraud is an exceptional, rather than a regular, feature of the environment.[25] As well as this more theoretical justification, there are the enormous costs of banking fraud. Bank failures through fraud are a direct economic cost. There are also social costs, such as those caused by the criminals who could not operate, at least on the same scale, without being able to launder and transfer their ill-gotten gains through the banking system. It is difficult to escape the conclusion that fraud prevention is as important as prudential supervision.

(i) Insider and Outsider Fraud

Bank fraud may involve either insiders or outsiders to a bank. The collapse of the international bank, the Bank of Credit and Commerce International (BCCI), highlighted the problem of insider fraud. This was not a unique example: insider fraud has featured in the collapse of banking institutions around the world.[26] Insider fraud was in many ways facilitated by the financial liberalization of the 1980s. It manifests itself in various ways—loans to phoney borrowers, or borrowers which are nominees of an insider, are two examples. Insider fraud underlines the point about the considerable overlap of fraud prevention and prudential supervision.

Legally, insider fraud can be combatted in a variety of ways. There is the obvious vetting of those who are controllers of banks.[27] Large exposure limits can reduce the opportunities for insiders to siphon off funds to phoney or nominee borrowers.[28] A bank's auditors now have an enhanced role in monitoring what goes on in a bank. The report by Bingham LJ on BCCI identified as one weakness of UK bank regulation that, while a bank's auditors could voluntarily disclose wrongdoing to the regulators, they were under no duty to do so.[29] Since 1994 a bank's auditors have been obliged to report to the regulators anything which gives the auditors reasonable cause to believe that the minimum criteria for authorization are not being fulfilled and which is likely to be material to the exercise of the regulators' functions.[30]

Fraud by outsiders may be at the expense of the bank—cheque, credit card, and mortgage fraud are simple examples[31]—or may involve fraudsters using banks and the

---

[25] See R. Posner, *Economic Analysis of Law* (5th edn., Boston, Aspen, 1998).

[26] See C. Goodhart and D. Schoenmaker, 'Institutional Separation Between Supervisory and Monetary Agencies', in C. Goodhart, *The Central Bank and the Financial System* (London, Macmillan, 1995), 372–410; R. Clark, 'The Soundness of Financial Intermediaries' (1976) 86 *Yale LJ* 1, 12–13; P. Swire, 'Bank Insolvency Law now that It Matters Again' (1992) 42 *Duke LJ* 469, 505–12.

[27] 86 below.   [28] 91 below.

[29] *Inquiry into the Supervision of the Bank of Credit and Commerce International*, HC 198, 1992, 189–90.

[30] See M. Stewart and J. Dunn, 'The Role of Auditors in Protecting against Bank Fraud', in J. Norton and G. Walker (eds.), *Banks: Fraud and Crime* (2nd edn., London, LLP, 2000).

[31] e.g. R. Goldspink and J. Cole, *International Commercial Fraud* (London, Sweet & Maxwell, 2001); M. Levi, *The Prevention of Cheque and Credit Card Fraud* (Crime Prevention Unit Paper No 26, London, Home Office, 1991).

banking system to facilitate their schemes or to secrete their gains. As regards the first, England has yet to emulate some other common law jurisdictions by enacting a general offence of fraud, i.e. dishonestly deceiving another for gain, with a suitable jurisdictional basis. It is necessary to draw on a range of disparate provisions such as theft, deception, false accounting, forgery, and conspiracy.[32] The lacunae in the law are illustrated by the dishonest misrepresentation which leads one bank to make payment by credit transfer to another. Payment in this way does not involve any transfer of property.[33] Consequently, it was held that it is not caught by section 15(1) of the Theft Act 1968, which refers to obtaining the property of another by deception, and the Theft (Amendment) Act 1996 was necessary to introduce the new offences of obtaining a money transfer by deception and dishonestly retaining a wrongful credit.[34] By contrast there is an arsenal of offences in the United States: for example, at the federal level there is the specific offence of defrauding a bank.[35] The width of American provisions contains a threat of implicating professionals like lawyers who may be regarded as aiders and abetters, or co-conspirators, to banking fraud.[36] The European Union has adopted a Framework decision requiring all Member States to have a wider range of criminal offences relevant to banking fraud.[37]

Perhaps it is no bad thing to create one more police force against such fraud. Certainly that role is being forced on banks. The old attitude of being reluctant to report fraud must go, even if the bank has not suffered directly, despite the embarrassment and inconveniences, such as the interruption to business. Welcome in this regard, for example, is the view of the British Bankers' Association that corruption by a head of state or a public sector official is fraud and should be reported as such.[38] One of the great advantages which fraudsters have had is being able to disguise suspicious transactions in jurisdictions which offer a high degree of bank secrecy. At various points in the book we see the incursions on traditional bank secrecy in the interests of detecting and prosecuting fraud and criminal practice.[39]

(ii) Money-laundering

Fraud and other crimes by outsiders can involve the use of the banking system to facilitate criminal purposes. No bank need suffer direct loss. Money-laundering is the best example.[40] In broad terms it is the dishonest concealment of the true source of moneys, although these may later reappear in 'legitimate' investments, as phoney loan

---

[32] A. Smith, *Property Offences* (London, Sweet & Maxwell, 1995); D. Kirk and A. Woodcock, *Serious Fraud—Investigation and Trial* (2nd edn., London, Butterworths, 1996).

[33] 235 below.

[34] *R. v. Preddy* [1996] AC 815 (HL); cf. Law Commission, *Criminal Law: Conspiracy to Defraud*, Working Paper No 104, 1994.

[35] 18 USC §1344.

[36] P. Coggins and J. Norton, 'The United States Perspective on "Bank Fraud"', in J. Norton and G. Walker (eds.), *Banks: Fraud and Crime* (2nd edn., London, LLP, 2000).

[37] Council Framework Decision 2001/413/JHA, [2001] OJ L149/1.

[38] House of Commons, International Development Committee, *Corruption*, HC 39, 2001, v.1, para. 139.

[39] 178, 449 below.

[40] e.g. B. Rider (ed.), *Money Laundering Control* (Dublin, Round Hall, 1996), especially chs. 1–3.

repayments and so on. Money-laundering is increasingly seen to be within the sphere of responsibility of central banks and bank regulatory authorities: it adversely affects public confidence in, and the stability of, the banking system. In broad terms, money-laundering legislation encourages banks to put in place effective procedures to ensure that all persons conducting business with them are properly identified, and that transactions which do not appear to be legitimate are reported. In 2000, representatives of the international banking industry launched the Global Anti Money Laundering Guidelines for Private Banks. These underline legal obligations on banks to know their customers, including beneficial owners, and their source of wealth. There are no sanctions behind these so-called Wolfberg principles.

International co-operation is central to measures to control money-laundering and to enforce money-laundering laws. After all, concealment typically involves cross-border transfers, especially through jurisdictions with strong bank secrecy laws. The association of money-laundering with drug trafficking was recognized in the first significant international step to encourage the criminalizing of money-laundering. The UN Convention against illicit traffic in narcotic drugs and psychotropic substances of 1988[41] obliges adherents to criminalize intentional money-laundering in relation to various offences of drug trafficking.[42] Moreover, adherents to the treaty must take steps to ensure that bank secrecy does not act as a barrier to national and cross-border enforcement efforts.[43]

Within Europe, the extension of intentional money-laundering beyond its association with drug trafficking is required by the Council of Europe convention on the matter in 1990.[44] Under it, not only can money-laundering be of the proceeds of any criminal offence (the predicate offence), but this offence need not have occurred within the jurisdiction.[45] But neither the UN nor Council of Europe convention grapples with the issue of corporate, as distinct from individual, liability for money-laundering. Neither obliges adherents to cover money-laundering which is not intentional (although the Council of Europe convention permits negligent money-laundering to be criminalized and the matter is addressed in jurisdictions like the UK).[46] Thus neither convention properly addresses the role of banks in money-laundering.

A partial answer is given by the EC Directive on money-laundering, recently amended.[47] Article 2 of the Directive provides that Member States shall ensure that it

---

[41] UN Document E/Conf.82/15 of 19 Dec. 1988. Reprinted in (1989) 28 *ILM* 493; W. Gilmore, *International Efforts to Combat Money Laundering* (Cambridge, Grotius, 1992), 75–97. See also B. Rider and C. Nakajima, *Anti Money Laundering Guide* (Bicester, CCH, 1999), para. 80–000ff.

[42] Art. 3(1)(b).   [43] Arts. 5(3), 7(5).

[44] Council of Europe Convention on Laundering, Search, Seizure and Confiscation of the Proceeds of Crime, *Europ.TS*, No 141, 1990, Art. 6.

[45] Art. 6(2)(a).

[46] Art. 6(3). See W. Gilmore, 'International Initiatives' in R. Parlour (ed.), *Butterworths International Guide to Money Laundering Law and Practice* (London, Butterworths, 1995), 20.

[47] [1991] OJ L166/77. See K. Magliveras, 'Banks, Money Laundering and the European Communities', in J. Norton and G. Walker (eds.), *Banks: Fraud and Crime* (2nd edn., London, LLP, 2000).

is 'prohibited'. Drug-related money-laundering was all that was covered by the Directive, but now the predicate offences include serious criminal activities such as organized crime, corruption, and fraud involving substantial proceeds. While the UK was early in the field in criminalizing the laundering of proceeds of crimes additional to drug offences, there was unnecessary complexity because the legislation differed depending on the predicate offence. The Proceeds of Crime Act 2002 consolidates the money-laundering offences in the Criminal Justice Act 1988 and the Drug Trafficking Act 1994. Moreover, the Act covers conduct abroad which would be an offence in the UK if it occurred there.

Reflecting in important parts the forty recommendations in 1990 of the inter-governmental Financial Action Task Force on Money Laundering,[48] the Directive goes on to require customers and beneficial owners to be identified when entering into business relations, particularly when opening a bank account or safe-custody facil-ities, and otherwise when transacting business involving at least €15,000 in a single transaction or series of transactions which seem to be linked.[49] Where the customer is another bank subject to the Directive, the identification obligation does not apply.[50] (The United Kingdom extends this identification exemption to non-member-country banks subject to equivalent money-laundering laws.[51]) Records must be kept, and special attention given to any transaction which appears particularly likely, by its nature, to be related to money-laundering.[52] As a result of an adverse report of FATF, there are now UK money-laundering controls for bureaux de change, money transmission agencies, and those cashing cheques.[53] In 2000 a FATF report identified a number of jurisdictions—the non-co-operating jurisdictions—where the anti-money laundering controls had serious systemic problems. Some jurisdictions have subsequently been removed from the list. UK banks must take into account FATF conclusions of inadequacy regarding particular jurisdictions in entering transactions.

Perhaps the cornerstone of the Directive is the obligation placed on banks to co-operate with the authorities: in particular they must of their own initiative inform the authorities of any fact which may be indicative of laundering.[54] In the UK this embraces an objective test—a bank must disclose not only if it knows or suspects, but also if it has reasonable grounds for knowing or suspecting that a person is engaged in money-laundering.[55] (Money-laundering is defined, in general terms, as concealing, transferring, or facilitating the holding of criminal property.[56]) No offence is com-mitted if the bank has reasonable excuse not to disclose: no doubt it will be said that this includes the case of a branch of a UK bank in a foreign jurisdiction with bank secrecy legislation, which has knowledge or suspicion, or ought to have, about

---

[48] See G. Walker, *International Banking Regulation. Law, Policy and Practice* (London, Kluwer, 2001), 431ff; T. Bennett, *International Initiatives Affecting Financial Havens* (London, Tolley, 2001).

[49] Art, 3.   [50] Art. 3(7).

[51] Money Laundering Regulations 1993, SI 1993 No 1933, r. 9(5).   [52] Arts. 4–5.

[53] Money Laundering Regulations 2001, SI 2001 No 3641.

[54] Art. 6. See also Art. 10 (duty of co-operation on prudential regulators).

[55] Proceeds of Crime Act 2002, s. 330(2).   [56] Ss. 327–9.

money-laundering on an account. In deciding whether a bank has met the objective standard, the Act mandates the court to take into account whether the bank complies with the Guidance Notes of the Joint Money Laundering Steering Group.[57] A bank must not disclose to customers and third parties that a disclosure has been made if this is likely to prejudice a possible investigation (the tipping off offence), and immunity for breach of confidence is given to timely disclosures of information by banks to the authorities.[58]

One study of a considerable volume of disclosures which the duty has produced found that they could be more effectively winnowed to assist the police.[59] Perhaps this is one explanation for the observation by the government's Performance and Innovation Unit that, despite the high number of disclosures, prosecutions are low compared with some other countries.[60] Money-laundering controls also require the identification of customers and the keeping of records.[61] Identity must be verified when customers open accounts, together with the expected origin of funds so that this can be monitored. As part of the other procedures, bank staff must be trained to detect money-laundering, and reporting is through a designated 'money laundering reporting officer'. Guidance notes in the United Kingdom recommend that these requirements of verification of identity and record-keeping be applied as well to all overseas branches and subsidiaries, unless the standards demanded by the host country are higher.[62] Having proper procedures in place to prevent money-laundering is now a continuing requirement for a bank to be authorized to conduct business under the FSMA 2000.[63] Associated with the money-laundering rules is the obligation on a bank to freeze an account on suspicion of money-laundering.[64] It is said that there is dilemma for banks if they freeze an account: in effect this will tip off the customer. The answer is that the bank will not have the necessary *mens rea* for that offence.

(iii) Terrorist Financing

In the eyes of policy-makers, the financial system is a crucial battleground in the war against terrorism. Choking off funds for terrorists, and if possible confiscating those funds, are goals pursued legally by a variety of techniques—for example, disclosure obligations on banks about terrorist financing, freezing orders against terrorist funds held by banks, and prohibitions on banks making funds available to terrorists. These legal controls are outlined below. In as much as terrorists use cash, or informal money transfer systems, to avoid such legal controls, anti-terrorist legislation also contains

---

[57] S. 330(8).   [58] Ss. 333, 337.

[59] M. Gold and M. Levi, *Money Laundering in the UK: An Appraisal of Suspicion-based Reporting* (London, Police Foundation, 1994).

[60] *Recovering the Proceeds of Crime* (London, 2000), paras. 9.7–9.8.

[61] e.g. Money Laundering Regulations 1993, SI 1993 No 1933, rr. 7–13.

[62] Joint Money Laundering Steering Group, *Guidance Notes*, December 2001, para. 3.30.

[63] FSA Handbook, Money Laundering Rules, r.2.1.1. See also FSA, Money Laundering: The FSA's New Role: Policy Statement on Consultation and Decisions on Rules, 2001.

[64] Proceeds of Crime Act 2002, s. 41.

powers to seize cash and other financial instruments.[65] These fall outside the scope of the present discussion. The regulation of informal money transmission systems has been noted.[66] The major difference between the reality addressed by money-laundering and terrorist funding regulation is that by comparison with money-laundering, only small amounts are involved in terrorist funding. Moreover, terrorist funding sometimes derives from legitimate sources such as business or charities. Both factors make detection all the more difficult.

As with money-laundering, there are international legal instruments in the case of terrorist funding. Most notably the UN International Convention for the Suppression of the Financing of Terrorism in 1999 was the culmination of General Assembly concern in the mid-90s about the need for measures to counteract the movement of funds suspected of terrorist purposes, without impeding free capital movements. In force in April 2002, the Convention obliges states to create various offences relating to the funding of terrorism and to take measures for the identification, detection, freezing, and seizure of such funds and proceeds. In the particular case of the Taliban in Afghanistan, the Security Council imposed a freeze on its funds by Resolutions 1267 of 1999 and 1333 of 2000.[67] This was in recognition of the sanctuary provided by the Taliban to Osama bin Laden, and followed the embassy bombings in Africa in 1998.

The events of September 11th have further galvanized the international community in relation to terrorist funding. Acting under Chapter VII of the UN Charter, the Security Council decided that all states should criminalize the funding of terrorism (the International Convention obligation) and should 'freeze without delay funds and other financial assets or economic resources' of terrorists, entities owned by terrorists and those acting for them (Resolution 1373 of 28 September 2001). The UK government was able to take immediate implementing action by Order in Council under the United Nations Act 1946 in early October.[68] It was not until 27 December that the European Community passed the necessary Council Regulation.[69] Promoted by the events of September 11th, the UK government also enacted the Anti-Terrorism, Crime and Security Act 2001, which amended in important respects the Terrorism Act 2000. As a result there is now an armoury of legal provisions relevant to banks in the United Kingdom.

First, a bank commits a criminal offence if it fails to disclose to the police that it knows or suspects, or that it has reasonable grounds for knowing or suspecting, that someone has committed one of the terrorist offences, broadly described, of raising,

---

[65] Anti-terrorism, Crime and Security Act 2001, s. 1, Sched. 2. The power is analogous to that in the Proceeds of Crime Act 2002, pt. 5, ch. 3.

[66] 71, above.

[67] See also Council Regulation (EC) No 467/2001, [2001] OJ L67/1, Art. 2; Afghanistan (United Nations Sanctions) Orders 2001, SI 2001 No 396; SI 2001 No 2557, replaced by the Al-Qa'ida and Taliban (United Nations Measures) Order 2002, SI 2002 No 111.

[68] The Terrorism (United Nations Measures) Order 2001, 2001 SI No 3365.

[69] Council Regulation (EC) No 2580/2001, [2001] OJ L334/70.

providing, or money-laundering funds for terrorism.[70] Knowledge includes turning a blind eye; suspicion is something less than belief but something more than speculation, and may arise because of unexplained movements on a bank account (even if this raises a suspicion of wrongdoing other than the terrorist offences). The objective standard demanded of a bank for reporting terrorist offenders—reasonable grounds for knowing or suspecting—parallels that for money-launderers. In both cases the objective standard is justified for banks (part of the so-called 'regulated sector' defined in the legislation) because they are expected to exercise a higher level of diligence in handling transactions than other businesses. In recognition that the standard for disclosure is objective, the legislation provides that the court must take any Treasury approved guidance into account in determining whether any offence has been committed.[71] A bank does not commit an offence if it has reasonable excuse for not disclosing: no doubt it will be argued that a United Kingdom bank with a branch or subsidiary abroad has a reasonable excuse for not disclosing if the criminal law of the jurisdiction where it is located protects bank secrecy.[72] A disclosure pursuant to the section is a 'protected disclosure', and does not breach bank confidentiality or other restrictions on disclosure.[73]

Outside the regulated sector—and the representative offices of foreign banks in the United Kingdom would not fall within the regulated sector—the standard for disclosure is subjective: the bank must actually know or suspect. That a bank acquires a knowledge or suspicion in the course of its business outside the regulated sector means that it is not subject to the higher, objective standard.[74] As far as terrorist property, as opposed to a terrorist offence, is concerned, a bank has a discretion, not an obligation, to disclose its suspicion or belief 'that any money or other property is terrorist property or is derived from terrorist property', or the matter on which that suspicion or belief is based.[75] Terrorist property is both property likely to be used for terrorism and the proceeds of acts of terrorism.

Secondly, a bank must comply with freezing orders of what are suspected to be terrorist funds. The juristic basis of freezing orders in the United Kingdom is three-fold. Freezing orders by Order in Council under the United Nations Act 1946, giving effect to United Nations Security Council Resolutions, have already been mentioned. So, too, have freezing orders implementing European Community Regulations: here the UK statutory instrument needs simply to criminalize breach of the EC Regulation.[76] A third source of freezing orders is domestic law. In the UK section 4 of the Anti-terrorism, Crime and Security Act 2001 empowers the Treasury to make such orders in the event of threats to the economy, or life or property of UK nationals or residents,

---

[70] Terrorism Act 2000, s. 21A(2). A person is taken to have committed a terrorist offence if what was done abroad would be an offence in the UK.

[71] S. 21A(b). See Joint Money Laundering Steering Group, *Guidance Notes*, December 2001, paras 2.5–2.6, 2.32–2.37.

[72] S. 21A(5).   [73] S. 21B.   [74] S. 21A(3).   [75] S. 20(1)(a).

[76] Of course neither UNSCR nor EC Regulation freezing orders are limited to terrorist funds: e.g. Council Regulation (EC) No 2488/2000, [2000] OJ L287/19, freezing the funds of Milosevic and his associates.

by foreign governments or residents. It is then a criminal offence for a bank to make funds or securities available to those identified in the freezing order.[77] However, although the offices of foreign banks in the UK are covered, the criminal offence does not extend to branches of UK banks abroad, which are treated as if they were incorporated there.[78]

To the issue of whether freezing orders will be recognized by foreign jurisdictions we will return.[79] Of more immediate concern is what banks need to do when presented with a freezing order. There may be problems of identification, as to whether a customer is the person specified under the freezing order. Under the Anti-terrorism, Crime and Security Act 2001, a bank has a defence if it can prove that it did not know and had no reason to suppose that a person to whom or for whose benefit funds were made available was the person specified.[80] In the absence of this sort of defence being set out in other freezing instruments, a bank would need to contend that *mens rea* was required and that it did not exist in the particular instance. As a practical matter a bank would check personal details about the customer and review movements on the account and linked accounts for anything not fitting the profile of the customer or for unusual activity.

Associated with bank disclosure obligations and freezing orders are other powers such as production orders, which a judge can make ordering a bank to produce information about accounts to the police for the purposes of a terrorist investigation.[81] In addition, account monitoring orders can require real-time disclosure by a bank that a transaction on a specified account has occurred.[82] Failure of a bank to comply with a production order or account monitoring order is contempt of court. Finally, the Terrorism Act 2000 enables restraint orders to be made any time after an investigation has started, which freezes assets so as to prevent their dissipation.[83]

(iv) Enforcement Action

Uncovering fraud, money-laundering or terrorism, is only the start of the process of seizing the proceeds and bringing the wrongdoers to book. Confidentiality is often an obstacle to investigation: while many jurisdictions confer powers on regulatory authorities to compel banks to disclose information, some trumpet the ability of their banks to hold moneys in secret. This underlines the point that there is typically a cross-border dimension to enforcement action in these areas. Mutual assistance arrangements facilitate investigations by enforcement agencies outside a jurisdiction.[84]

If the cross-border dimension is put to one side, bank regulators and others investigating these matters, and other regulation matters, have wide powers conferred on

---

[77] S. 5(6), Sched. 3, paras. 2, 7.   [78] Ss. 5(2), 9(4).
[79] 443 below.   [80] Sched. 3, para. 7(5).
[81] Terrorism Act 2000, Sched. 5, paras. 5–10.
[82] Terrorism Act 2000, Sched. 6A. Cf. Proceeds of Crime Act 2002, s. 370.
[83] Schedule 4, Part 1; Anti-terrorism, Crime and Security Act 2001, Sched. 2, pt. 2.
[84] See G. Stessens, *Money Laundering. A New International Law Enforcement Model* (Cambridge, CUP, 2000), pt. IV.

them to demand answers to questions and to obtain relevant documents. The duty of confidentiality is overriden. Indeed, in England a demand by bank regulators may trump an injunction against disclosure previously granted in favour of a bank's customers.[85] Rights such as those against self-incrimination, and legal professional privilege, may also be overridden.[86] A bank's employees may disclose confidential information to the bank regulators in cases of serious malpractice. Despite their general duty of confidentiality, the public interest justifies their whistle-blowing.[87] However, there are still outstanding legal issues to be resolved such as the human rights ramifications of confiscating bank accounts.[88]

C. CONSUMER PROTECTION AND DEPOSIT INSURANCE

Specific consumer-protection law for core bank customers has been a rarity. By contrast investor protection has generated detailed provisions for over half a century at least; the subject matter falls mainly within the compass of Chapter 12. However, consumer protection is now one of the four regulatory objectives for the Financial Services Authority (FSA) set out in FSMA 2000—it applies to the whole range of activities falling within the remit of the FSA—so it may be that core banking will attract greater attention than in the past. Moreover, Britain led the way with a specific banking ombudsman, which other countries emulated.[89] Some of the more general ombudsmen in other jurisdictions handle banking complaints. Several EC initiatives on electronic funds transfers have led to consumer-protection measures in the Member States. Use by the EC of the device of the Recommendation, rather than the Directive, has guaranteed a tardy response in this regard.[90] The United States has long had an Electronic Funds Transfer Act as a consumer-protection measure.[91] A more recent EC initiative is designed to ensure price control for consumers when they send moneys cross-border.[92] Resort must also be had to general consumer-protection law. For example, control of standard-form banking contracts was given an impetus by the EC Directive on unfair contract terms.[93]

At the bank regulatory level, it can be argued that prudential supervision ensures a sound banking system, and thus protection for customers. In particular, deposit insurance schemes give some comfort to customers in the event that banks fail. Competition law may also be said to have a role in furthering the consumer interest, although the entry of foreign competitors may be a more effective stimulus to price and service competition. Usury laws, which limit interest charged on loans, have

---

[85] *A* v. *B Bank (Governor and Company of the Bank of England Intervening)* [1993] QB 311.

[86] e.g. *Bank of England* v. *Riley* [1992] Ch. 475 (CA); *Price Waterhouse (a firm)* v. *BCCI Holdings (Luxembourg) SA* [1992] BCLC 583.

[87] Public Interest Disclosure Act 1998. See M. Brindle and G. Dehn, 'Confidence, Public Interest and the Lawyer', in R. Cranston (ed.), *Legal Ethics and Professional Responsibility* (Oxford, Clarendon, 1995).

[88] e.g. *R* v *Rezvi* [2002] 1 All ER 801 (HL).

[89] 158 below.   [90] 268 below.

[91] 15 USC §1693.   [92] 41 above.   [93] 150 below.

disappeared in Europe, although disclosure of interest and charges feature prominently in the consumer-credit laws of the different countries.[94] In the United States
consumer-credit controls tend to be more extensive than elsewhere: for example,
there are detailed provisions on discrimination in the provision of credit.[95]

(i) Marketing Regulation

Controls over the price of money to the consumer have a long history in Western
countries. Usury was at first unlawful, although later specific controls were placed on
interest rates. Usury laws continued much later in the United States than in many
other jurisdictions. It was only in 1980 that federal legislation of general application
displaced an important number of state usury laws, on the ground that they were
discouraging savings and creating inequities. In the late 1970s, as a result of interest
rates that went above state usury ceilings, lending for home loans was said to have all
but ceased in many areas. In broad terms, the counterpart in Islamic societies of usury
controls is the prohibition of interest (*riba*) in favour of profit-sharing.[96]

In England, under the Moneylenders Act 1927, moneylenders had to be licensed,
and interest greater than 48 per cent was regarded as *prima facie* excessive, and the
courts could reduce it.[97] But banks and many other financial institutions fell outside the
ambit of the Moneylenders Acts. The rate regulation of the Moneylenders Acts was
abandoned in the Consumer Credit Act 1974, and all that remains is a power for a
court to reopen an extortionate credit bargain if the payments required are grossly
exorbitant.[98] There is a similar power in insolvency law.[99]

However, the Consumer Credit Act 1974 instituted controls over those financial
institutions, including banks, which grant consumer credit. These are reflected in the
provisions of the Consumer Credit Directives of the European Community.[100] In
broad outline they include controls on the advertising of consumer credit and on the
content, form, and termination of consumer-credit agreements. However, there are
some variations and exemptions for banks because of the peculiar nature of consumer
credit advanced by way of overdraft on a current account. For example, bank transmission charges for operating a current account are excluded from the total charge for
credit, since the charge varies according to use of the account.[101]

The counterpart of consumer-credit disclosure—disclosure by a bank of interest
and charges payable on an account—is rudimentary in most jurisdictions. In the
United Kingdom the Banking Codes oblige banks to disclose information about

---

[94] 77–78 below.

[95] Equal Credit Opportunity Act, 15 USC §1691; Community Reinvestment Act, 12 USC §2901.

[96] e.g. N. Saleh, *Unlawful Gain and Legitimate Profit in Islamic Law* (London, Graham & Trotman, 1992);
H. Shirazi, Islamic Banking (London, Butterworths. 1990), 7–10; S. Chinoy, 'Interest-free Banking' [1995]
12 *JIBL* 517; M. Iqbal, 'Islamic and Conventional Banking in the Nineties' (2001) *Islamic Economic
Studies*, v.8(2).

[97] C. Scott and J. Black, *Cranston's Consumers and the Law* (3rd edn., London, Butterworths, 2000), 255.

[98] Ss. 137–40. See, e.g., *Coldunnel Ltd. v. Gallon* [1986] 1 QB 1184.

[99] Insolvency Act 1986, s. 244.

[100] Dir. 87/102/EEC [1987] OJ L42/48; Dir. 90/88 EEC [1990] OJ L61/14.

[101] See R. M. Goode, *Consumer Credit Legislation* (London, Butterworths, looseleaf), para. 966.

the interest rates which apply to an account, when interest will be deducted or
paid, and charges on the account.[102] There is some regulatory action in relation to
advertising and marketing bank deposits. In essence it only applies if the financial
promotion of deposit taking does not involve an authorized bank, and if it concerns a
'non-real time communication'. Even then all that is required is that the communication be accompanied by detailed information about the bank's nature and any dispute resolution procedure.[103] The obvious fear is of unscrupulous or incompetent
banking institutions which are beyond the reach of UK regulators and of the redress
mechanisms otherwise open to UK depositors.

(ii) Deposit Insurance

Protecting depositors from bank failure can take various forms. One approach is a
state guarantee, although when this has been used it has tended to be confined to
small savers. A second approach is to confer on depositors a priority over other
creditors on a bank's insolvency. Depositors may still rank, however, after preferred
creditors such as employees. A third approach is a deposit insurance or guarantee
scheme, well established in the United States and Britain, and now universal in the
European Community as a result of the 1994 Directive on the matter.[104]

In the United States deposit insurance was designed not so much to compensate
individual depositors after a failure, but to prevent instability through the mass withdrawal of funds from the banking system in the first place. If depositors were
generously protected, the argument ran, they should not be a source of systemic risk
because there was no reason for them to panic. The rationale was a reaction to the
1930s, when there were runs which threatened even conservatively managed banks.[105]
Elsewhere, as in the United Kingdom, deposit insurance is justified primarily as an
investor-protection measure. Unsophisticated investors are at an informational disadvantage in judging the soundness of banks and should not lose their savings if these
are in a bank which fails. Many ordinary people are likely to have a disproportionate
part of their wealth (other than in housing) in deposits, as opposed to private
pensions, securities, or other investments.

There is an argument that deposit insurance has undermined the incentive of
depositors to monitor excessive risk-taking by banks. Bank managers are thus free,
it is said, to pursue excessively risky strategies—perhaps attracting an influx of
funds—since depositors simply rely on the safety net. The economists call this 'moral

---

[102] Banking Code, Jan. 2001, §4–5; Business Banking Code, Mar. 2002, §4–5.

[103] Financial Services and Markets Act 2000 (Financial Promotion) Order 2001, SI 2001 No 1335, paras.
22–23.

[104] Deposit-guarantee Directive, 94/19/EC [1994] OJ L135/5.

[105] E. White, 'Deposit Insurance', World Bank Policy Research Working Paper 1541, Nov. 1995;
J. Arrigunaga, 'Deposit Insurance Schemes', in M. Giovanoli (ed.), *International Monetary Law* (Oxford,
OUP, 2000), 324–7; G. García, *Deposit Insurance. A Survey of Actual and Best Practices* (IMF Monetary and
Exchange Affairs Dept., WP 99/54, 1999); Financial Stability Forum, *Guidance for Developing Effective Deposit
Insurance Schemes* (Basle, FSF, 2001).

hazard'.[106] This type of analysis is somewhat removed from the real world. Unsophisticated depositors are in no position to be vigilant. Even if the information is available it will generally require expertise to interpret it. Moreover, a reason for the insolvency of some banks is dishonesty, and that by its nature tends to be concealed. If a reasonably large bank appears on the surface to be successful, ordinary depositors will have no reason to withdraw funds, even though the bank may have been adversely judged by other banks, so that it is unable to raise money on the interbank market, or has to pay a substantial premium.

The European Community Directive imposes an obligation on a home Member State—where a bank is authorized—to ensure that a deposit guarantee scheme is introduced and officially recognized.[107] Authorized banks must be members of a scheme. (The Directive leaves it for Member States to decide whether branches of non-member-country banks must join the scheme.) The obligation has been imposed on home, rather than host, Member States because of the link with prudential supervision: there would be less of an incentive on home Member States to supervise banks rigorously if they did not have to bear the cost of their own inadequacies. Consequently, a scheme must cover depositors not only at branches in the home Member State, but also at branches established elsewhere in the Community. Claims must generally be paid within three months of deposits becoming unavailable to avoid depositors, who will often have pressing commitments, having to wait for a winding up order to be made.

Because as a matter of law deposit insurance is determined by the home country, this means that banks in any one jurisdiction (say London) will be subject in this area to a range of different laws. To minimize this problem, certain minimum standards of coverage are laid down in the Directive. The Directive also establishes the principle that in general the cost must be borne by the banks themselves. This is aimed at reducing the distortions which could arise if states underwrote their schemes. Under the Directive, non-EU currency deposits need not be covered, nor those of large companies.[108] Because Member States could not agree on coverage, the Directive permits them to provide a higher ceiling than the minimum level of coverage set out in the Directive—not less than 90 per cent of a deposit or deposits with the one bank, with a payout of up to €20,000.[109] Less than full protection is thought to address the moral hazard problem, for it creates some incentive for depositors to be vigilant about their banks.

That approach is continued in the current UK deposit protection scheme, which is administered by the Financial Services Compensation Scheme, established under the

[106] See C. Goodhart, 'Bank Insolvency and Deposit Insurance: a Proposal', in P. Arestis (ed.), *Money and Banking* (London, Macmillan, 1993).

[107] Art. 3(1). See M. Andenas, 'Deposit Guarantee Schemes and Home Country Control', in R. Cranston (ed.), *The Single Market and the Law of Banking* (2nd edn., London, LLP, 1995); S. Key, 'Deposit-guarantee Directive', in M. van Empel, *Banking and EC Law* (Hague, Kluwer, looseleaf); D. Schoenmaker, 'Internationalisation of Banking Supervision and Deposit Insurance' [1993] 8 *JIBL* 106.

[108] Art. 7(2), Annex 1, para. 14.   [109] Art. 7(1),(4).

FSMA 2000. The Scheme is responsible, as the name suggests, for administering compensation for a range of other financial services (notably, losses on insurance and investments).[110] The level of cover for bank deposits is currently 100 per cent of the first £2,000, and 90 per cent of the next £33,000, with a maximum payment of £31,700.[111] For reasons already given, it is unlikely that many ordinary depositors, if they exceed this limit, will engage in any sophisticated practice of deposit-splitting— placing deposits within the limits with different institutions. Given the interpretation the House of Lords has placed on 'depositor' in the legislation—that it means the person who makes the original deposit with a bank—this figure cannot be avoided by depositors assigning part of their deposits, beyond the maximum, to other individuals.[112] However, there seems no objection to depositors maximizing their compensation by using set-off—provided they are able, by contract, to do so.

Germany objected to the Directive on the grounds of subsidiarity—that there was no need for a Community measure and national steps were sufficient. It specifically opposed the top-up provisions, whereby branches of banks in states other than the home state are entitled to join the host state scheme, so that depositors there can obtain a greater degree of protection. Topping-up is not only complicated, but in German eyes exposes its generous scheme to losses consequent on the inadequate prudential supervision of non-German banks by their home-country authorities. The European Court of Justice rejected Germany's objections.[113] All Member States have introduced topping up, although no payments have yet been made under such arrangements. A report by the European Commission concludes that it would be premature to abolish topping up especially because of the benefits in EC enlargement to accession countries as they establish branches of their banks elsewhere in Europe.[114]

The EC deposit guarantee Directive for banks is mirrored by the EC Directive for investor compensation schemes covering investment firms (including banks). Clearly this is important in protecting customers as regards moneys placed with banks other than as deposits.[115]

D. COMPETITION (ANTITRUST) POLICY

The application of competition (antitrust) policy to bank mergers has already been noted.[116] Yet mergers are only one context in which banks and banking are regulated for reasons of competition (antitrust) policy. In the European Community, Article

---

[110] FSMA 2000, Part XV; Financial Services Compensation Scheme, *How we handle your claim for compensation. Deposit and Investment Claims* (London, no date).

[111] FSA Handbook, Compensation, r.10.2.3.

[112] *Deposit Protection Board* v. *Dalia* [1994] 2 AC 367.

[113] Case C-233/94, *Germany* v. *European Parliament and the Council of the European Union* [1997] ECR I-2405.

[114] *Report from the Commission on the Operation of the 'topping-up' provision,* COM (2001) 595 final.

[115] Investors Compensation Directive 97/9/EC [1997] OJ L84/22.

[116] 16 above.

81(1) of the Treaty prohibits agreements between undertakings which have an anticompetitive effect within the Community and which may affect trade between Member States. The European Commission has long rejected the notion that banking is somehow different and does not fall within this rule.[117] Thus it has applied Article 81(1) to various interbank agreements. One example is that the Commission objected to certain provisions in agreements between European savings banks, under which they undertook not to enter each others' geographical territories, or agreed that banks in their home territories had certain exclusive rights to market and distribute common products.[118] Another example is that the Commission has used competition policy to ensure access for banks to certain payment systems.[119] The Commission has also monitored the Target system, the real-time gross settlement system operated for the euro by the European Central Bank, since it competes with the euro payment scheme of the European Bankers' Association.[120]

One particular aspect of EC competition policy is the restriction on state aid in Article 87(1) of the Treaty, in so far as it 'distorts or threatens to distort competition by favouring certain undertakings'. In the last decade the European Commission has intensified its examination of the application of state aid to banks. In doing so, it takes into account the special nature of banks, in particular systemic risk, and may approve state intervention to restore confidence in the banking sector or to protect the proper functioning of the payments system. Legally this is justified under Article 87(3) of the Treaty, as aid to remedy a serious disturbance in the economy of a Member State.[121] In the *Crédit Lyonnais* decision, the Commission agreed to the French government providing financial support to that bank, but on conditions—that to avoid conflicts of interest there had to be a clear division between Crédit Lyonnais and the entity to which the bad assets were spun off, that those assets could only be repurchased by Crédit Lyonnais on strict conditions, and that the cost of aid be kept under certain levels.[122] More recently, Germany agreed that state guarantees for its Landesbanks would be phased out over a four-year period. The European Commission argued that the guarantees were anticompetitive state aid, in enabling the Landesbanks to borrow and lend on more favourable terms than commercial banks.[123]

[117] *Züchner* v. *Bayerische Vereinsbank* [1981] ECR 2021 is the seminal case. See J. Usher, *The Law of Money and Financial Services in the European Community* (2nd edn., Oxford, Clarendon, 2000), ch. 3; M. Dassesse, S. Isaacs, and G. Penn, *EC Banking Law* (2nd edn., London, LLP, 1994), pt. V.

[118] European Commission, *21st Report on Competition Policy* (EC Commission, Brussels, 1991), 34. See also *Banque Nationale de Paris/Dresdner Bank* [1996] OJ L188/37.

[119] e.g. Notice on the application of the EC competition rules to cross-border credit transfers [1995] OJ C251/3. See also Case No COMP/29.373—*Visa International* [2001] OJ L293/24.

[120] Commissioner van Miert, 'EU Competition Policy in the Banking Sector', Speech to Belgian Bankers' Association, 22 Sept. 1998.

[121] M. Dassesse, 'State Aid and Banking Activities' (1996) 4 *JFR & C* 349.

[122] Commission notice [1995] OJ C121/4; European Commission press release 1P/95/829, 26 July 1995.

[123] K. Soukup and S. Moser, 'Germany—Further Developments on State Guarantees for German Public Banks', *European Commission Competition Policy Newsletter*, Oct. 2001, No 3, 75.

II. TECHNIQUES OF PRUDENTIAL REGULATION

A useful distinction in prudential regulation is between preventive and protective techniques.[124] Preventive regulation involves those techniques which are designed to forestall crises by reducing the risks facing banks. These include vetting the controllers and monitoring the management of banks, capital, solvency, and liquidity standards, and large exposure limits. Protective techniques, on the other hand, provide support to banks once a crisis threatens. Lender-of-last-resort facilities are of immediate benefit, but ultimately rescue operations may be necessary, as well as payments under deposit insurance schemes.

Clearly preventive and protective techniques overlap. For example, if moral hazard is associated with deposit insurance, the greater risks banks take may demand stronger preventive techniques. Moreover, the division between preventive and protective techniques does not always highlight issues of legal significance. Thus historic factors clearly influence the style of bank regulation. For example, the crucial role the Bank of England played in regulating City affairs is explained partly by the close ties among persons and institutions which have been situated there. These acted as a justification both for abnegation by government and for the informal and non-legal manner in which the Bank has purported to police bank behaviour. That the Bank of England was nationalized as late as 1946 is a partial explanation for its independent stance from government, even in the relatively recent past, in relation to prudential supervision. Probably as important in this regard was the Bank's dual role as both representative of City interests before government on one hand, and the regulatory arm of government on the other.[125] In 2001 the role of the Bank as prudential supervisor was assumed by the Financial Services Authority.

A. MACHINERY OF PRUDENTIAL REGULATION

Before we examine some of the more specific techniques of prudential regulation, its general machinery warrants some discussion. Clearly we put to one side the other regulators of banks and banking alluded to—the police, consumer-protection agencies, competition authorities, securities regulators, and so on—to focus on the prudential regulators of core banking. Who are the prudential regulators of core banking; how, as a matter of legislative technique, do they regulate; and to what controls are they in turn subject?

---

[124] R. Dale, *The Regulation of International Banking* (Cambridge, Woodhead-Faulkner, 1984), 55–68. Cf. OECD, *Banks Under Stress* (OECD, Paris, 1992), 33.

[125] See J. Norton, 'The Bank of England's Lament: The Struggle to Maintain the Traditional Supervisory Practices of "moral suasion"', in J. Norton (ed.), *Bank Regulation and Supervision in the 1990s* (London, LLP, 1991); K. McGuire, 'Emergent Trends in Bank Supervision in the United Kingdom' (1993) 56 *MLR* 669; C. Hadjiemmanuil, *Banking Regulation and the Bank of England* (London, LLP, 1996), ch. 1.

(i) The Bank Regulators

Identifying the regulators of core banking is not as straightforward as might be thought. First, some jurisdictions hive off the prudential regulation of specified banks into separate regulatory bodies with their own legislative regime—co-operative banks in some continental European jurisdictions, credit unions in the United States.[126] Secondly, federal systems such as the United States and Germany have prudential regulation divided between state and central governments.[127]

Thirdly, in many jurisdictions prudential regulation is entrusted to the central bank. Where prudential regulation is entrusted to an agency or agencies independent of the central bank, whatever the legal position the central bank is still likely to have a role in prudential regulation.[128] It will have a large hand in supervising the payment system, it will be in possession of important information for prudential regulation, and it will be the body which in a crisis makes available lender-of-last-resort facilities. The statute of the European Central Bank leaves responsibility for prudential supervision with the national authorities.[129] However, the Bank has argued the case for central bank control over bank supervision on the basis that a central bank is in a better position to assess quickly and effectively the potential for a systemic crisis, in particular because of its closeness to payment and settlement systems. A separate regulator, it argues, concentrates overly on the investment and consumer protection agenda, with a minor role for systemic risk monitoring.[130]

The trend has been the other way, notably the establishment of the Financial Services Authority in the UK, and the amalgamation in Germany of bank, securities, and insurance supervisors with a single financial markets supervisory authority.[131] In broad outline the argument for an integrated supervisor is to reflect the reality of financial institutions and markets, where commercial banks, investment banks, and insurance companies are increasingly multifunctional and marketing similar products.[132] Ancillary advantages include bureaucratic effectiveness, not least the representative role with national audiences and internationally. The ECB concern about systemic risks being overlooked is met partly by internal specialization and partly by close co-ordination with the central bank. In the UK the latter is effected by removing legal impediments to the exchange of information between the FSA and the Bank of England and by a Memorandum of Understanding between the two bodies setting out matters such as their respective responsibilities for systemic stability:

[126] e.g., Act on Membership Banks 1996 (Sweden); 12 USC §1757.

[127] e.g. M. Gruson and U. Schneider, 'The German Landesbanken [1995] *Col. BLR* 337, 378–9.

[128] C. Goodhart and D. Schoenmaker, 'Institutional Separation Between Supervisory and Monetary Agencies', in C. Goodhart, *The Central Bank and the Financial System* (London, Macmillan, 1995).

[129] C. Hadjiemmanuil, 'European Monetary Union, the European System of Central Banks, and Banking Supervision: A Neglected Aspect of the Maastricht Treaty' (1997) 5 *J. Int'l & Comp. L.* 105.

[130] *The Role of Central Banks in Prudential Supervision* (Frankfurt, ECB, 2001).

[131] Gesetz über die integrierte Finanzaufsicht 2001.

[132] D. Mohamed, 'A Single Regulator for the EC Financial Market' [2001] *JIBL* 203; M. Blair, L. Minghella, M. Taylor, M. Threipland, and G. Walker, *Financial Services and Markets Act 2000* (London, Blackstone, 2001), 16.

while the Bank is responsible for overall stability, and the FSA for specific institutions, markets, and clearing and settlement systems, the Bank is permitted to undertake financing operations in exceptional circumstances in order 'to limit the risk of problems in or affecting particular institutions spreading to other parts of the financial system'.[133]

The position becomes more complicated with cross-border banking. If a bank operates in a foreign (host) jurisdiction it will generally be subject to some sort of prudential regulation in both home and host jurisdictions. The minimum standards for international banking groups established by the Basle Committee on Banking Supervision require all international banks to be supervised by a home-country regulator which capably performs consolidated regulation. However, host-country regulators may impose restrictive measures to satisfy their prudential concerns, including refusal of a licence to establish there.[134] There are, however, important qualifications to this. Under the EC Credit Institutions Directive banks authorized in one Member State can freely establish branches and provide services in other Member States. The home jurisdiction of a bank exercises the important prudential tasks in relation to the branches thus established, and services offered, elsewhere in the Community. The host jurisdiction has some regulatory authority under the Directive, but this is mainly in the non-prudential sphere.

Notably, there is a general power of EC host states 'to take appropriate measures to prevent or to punish irregularities committed within their territories which are contrary to the legal rules they have adopted in the interest of the general good'.[135] The width of this power is undefined. The Economic and Social Committee gave its opinion that host countries have the right to legislate to promote consumer protection and prevent distortions of competition.[136] Some have argued that this interpretation would render illusory the freedom to establish branches and to provide services.[137] In other contexts the European Court of Justice has indicated that it will not allow host-country restrictions to operate on services if they discriminate, duplicate home-jurisdiction rules, or are not objectively justified or proportionate to the result to be achieved.[138] The same restriction applied in the interest of the general

---

[133] Memorandum of Understanding between HM Treasury, the Bank of England, and the Financial Services Authority, para. 2(iv) in M. Blair, R. Cranston, C. Ryan, and M. Taylor, *Bank of England Act* (London, Blackstone, 1998), App. 5. See C. Kahn and J. Santos, *Allocating Bank Regulatory Powers, Working Paper No. 102* (Basle, BIS, 2001).

[134] 105 below.

[135] Credit Institutions Directive 2000/12/EC [2000] OJ L126/1, Art 22.5.

[136] ESC 287/88 [1988] OJ C318/42, para. 1.6.3.

[137] M. Dassesse, S. Isaacs, G. Penn, *EC Banking Law* (2nd edn., London, LLP, 1994), 42.

[138] e.g. Case 205/84 *Commission* v. *Germany* [1986] ECR 3755; Case C–384/93 *Alpine Investments BV* v. *Minister van Financiën* [1995] ECR I–1141; Case C-233/94 *Germany* v. *European Parliament and the Council of the European Union* [1997] ECR I–2405; *Société Civile Immobilière Parodi* v. *Banque H Albert De Barg et Cie* [1997] All ER (EC) 946. See E. Lomnicka, 'The Home Country Control Principle in the Financial Services Directives and the Case Law' [2000] EBLR 324; P. Nielsen, *Services and Establishment in European Community Banking Law* (Copenhagen, DJØF, 1994), 238ff; European Commission, *Commission Communication, Freedom to provide services and the interest of the general good in the Second Banking Directive* [1997] OJ C209/6.

good may be adjudged proportionate in respect of a branch, but disproportionate in respect of a banking service. In the banking context, the court should be slow to strike down host-state regulations on the ground that they are not for the general good. The fact is that host states have a legitimate concern in regulating the branches of banks from other Member States. Despite the harmonization of certain prudential standards, host states may incur substantial costs if branches prove not to be sound.[139] Admission to payment and settlement systems is one means whereby failure of a branch from another Member State could expose a central bank or host-state banks to systemic risk.

(ii) Legislative Technique: Authorization

Authorization (licensing) is central to the prudential regulation of banking. It has been mandatory in Europe since the First Banking Directive of 1977.[140] The notion is of preventing undesirable activity by obliging those who provide banking services to meet a range of standards and threatening to withdraw approval in the event of any breach of standards.[141] While authorization can be a very powerful tool of control, its success depends on the thoroughness of the vetting, its effectiveness in practice, the extent to which the behaviour of those authorized is monitored, and the capacity of the regulatory authority to take disciplinary action against those who infringe standards. There can also be a tension between effective authoritization on the one hand and the monopoly effects produced by preventing entry on the other.

Since the Banking Act 1987 there has been only one category of authorization. In 2001 the authorized population was 664—185 were UK-incorporated banks, and 124 were branches of banks incorporated outside the European Economic Area. Thus a significant number, 355, were authorized elsewhere in Europe but were carrying on business in the UK under the Credit Institutions Directive.[142] In addition to refusing, varying, or cancelling permission, the FSA can restrict a bank's permission by imposing such limitations and requirements as are thought appropriate.[143]

The threshold conditions for authorization include measurable factors such as solvency, liquidity, provisioning, and initial capital. As well there are other relatively objective factors, such as the business to be directed by at least two individuals and the bank to have adequate records, systems, and internal controls. These are set out in considerable detail in the FSA's Handbook on Threshold Conditions and the Interim Prudential Handbook for Banks. Both contain the rules and evidential provisions made under the FSMA 2000 and the guidance setting out the FSA's expectation of how banks should comply: where a bank follows the guidance the FSA will normally hold it to be in compliance with the relevant threshold conditions and other rules.

---

[139] And in respect of other matters as well, such as conflicts of interest.
[140] Dir. 77/780/EEC [1977] OJ L322/30.
[141] A. Ogus, *Regulation* (Oxford, Clarendon, 1994), ch. 10.
[142] Financial Services Authority, *Annual Report 2000/01*, 26.   [143] FSMA 2000, ss. 42(7)(a)(b), 43(1).

Unlike some jurisdictions, however, where there is a reluctance to entrust wide discretion to regulators, FSMA 2000 contains a number of open-textured criteria for authorization. In important respects these reflect the historical development of banking regulation in the United Kingdom. First, there is a catch-all provision, enabling the FSA to include in its permission such requirements as it considers appropriate, so as to require a bank to take or refrain from specified action, even in relation to activities which are not regulated.[144] Secondly, the duty to ensure initial and continuing compliance of a bank with the threshold conditions does not prevent the FSA 'having due regard to that duty, from taking such steps as it considers are necessary, in relation to a particular authorized person, in order to secure its regulatory objective of the protection of consumers'.[145]

Thirdly, there is the requirement for directors, controllers, and managers to be fit and proper persons.[146] This very British control has been transplanted into the European Community generally. There is a similar requirement for those who attain certain specified thresholds of shareholding or voting power of the bank or its parent—for UK-authorized banks 10 per cent, 20 per cent, 33 per cent, and 50 per cent, together with shareholdings of less than 10 per cent where the person is in a position to exercise a significant influence over the management of the bank or its parent.[147] Despite the attempt to spell out aspects of what fit and proper means—for example, ability, probity, judgement, breach of relevant laws and codes, reputation, and record—at the end of the day a wide discretion is entrusted to the FSA as the responsible regulatory authority. Finally, the FSA has a wide discretion to cancel permission. Not only may the FSA do this if the threshold conditions are not fulfilled, but it may act if it is desirable in the interests of consumers or potential consumers.[148]

Open-textured discretion, along these lines, demands legal review. Under the FSMA 2000, when the FSA refuses permission, incorporates limitations, or imposes requirements in relation to permission on its own initiative, it must give the bank notice.[149] This triggers the bank's right to be given reasons and, in some cases, access to material on which the notice was based.[150] Ultimately a bank can have a matter decided by a specially constituted body, the Financial Services and Markets Tribunal, and after consideration by it a point of law can be referred to the courts. A special tribunal is justified on the basis of the special nature of financial services regulation and the consequent need for expertise. In fact in reaching a decision the Tribunal has considerable leeway: it may consider any evidence, whether or not available to the FSA at the time of its decision, must determine what action the FSA must take, and may also make recommendations as to the FSA's regulatory provisions or procedures.[151] Those unhappy with the Bank's decision must generally follow the appellate path laid down

---

[144] S. 43.   [145] S. 41(3).

[146] Sched. 6, para. 5. See also FSA Handbook, The Fit and Proper Test for Approved Persons.

[147] Ss. 179–180, Sched. 186(2).

[148] Ss. 45(1), 54.   [149] Ss. 52(6)–(7), (9), 53(4), (7)–(8), 54(2).

[150] Pt. XXVI.   [151] S. 133.

in the Act: a direct approach to the courts though judicial review will generally not be available.[152]

The authorization provisions cannot work without information and monitoring. Under FSMA 2000 banks are obliged to provide information to the regulators on a periodic basis or on demand.[153] Historically the Bank of England eschewed the on-site inspection visits of US bank regulators and many others in favour of discussions with management, although that changed as a result of the collapse of BCCI and Barings and the advent of the FSA. Monitoring of the performance of authorized institutions under FSMA 2000 depends also on use of an institution's auditors. Confidentiality restrictions under the general law have been removed, enabling direct communication between supervisors and auditors.[154]

(iii) Accountability—Negligence and Judicial Review

The appeal mechanisms just considered raise the broader issue of the accountability of banking regulators. In any system there will be political accountability of some sort or another. The activities of the FSA are thus reviewed by the Treasury Select Committee of the House of Commons. In some cases political accountability can be very attenuated. For example, if regulatory responsibility over European banks were to be transferred to the European Central Bank the guarantees on political independence would apply. As for legal accountability, there is first the legislative setting. For example, the FSMA 2000 obliges the FSA to consult practitioners and consumers, in particular through the establishment of two independent panels, one made up of practitioner representatives and one of consumer representatives, each of which reports publicly on its work. Should the FSA disagree with a view or proposal of either panel, it must give a written statement explaining its reasons.[155] In addition, the FSMA 2000 provides for an independent Complaints Commissioner, whose role is to scrutinize complaints against the FSA in relation to any instance of mistake, unprofessional conduct, unreasonable delay, bias, or lack of integrity on the Authority's part. Complaints about policy or regulatory decisions are not covered. The Complaints Commissioner can recommend that the FSA take remedial action, including paying compensation, and has power to publish his or her reports and to require the FSA to do likewise with its response.[156]

Whether bank regulators are accountable depends partly also on the general law. It might be said that the regulators should never have licensed a bank in the first place, that they failed to monitor it adequately, that they should have closed it earlier, and so on. With hindsight it will often be possible to say that some things were done inadequately, or could have been done differently. But in everyday practice regulatory decisions can turn on fine and difficult judgements. In times of crisis decisions have to

---

[152] Cf. *R. v. Bank of England, ex p. Mellstrom* [1995] CLC 232.
[153] FSMA 2000, s. 165. See also s. 398 (offence to provide false or misleading information).
[154] Ss. 342(3), 343(3).
[155] FSMA 2000, ss 8–11; Financial Services Authority, *Annual Report 2000/01*, 56–61.
[156] FSMA 2000, Sched. 1, paras. 7–8.

be made on limited information, in a short space of time. In fact the weight of English authority is against making regulators liable for losses suffered by individual depositors and investors. There is a not unnatural judicial reluctance to second-guess the regulators. Moreover, since this is the realm of pure economic loss, the English courts hesitate in awarding damages because of the large, unquantifiable amounts which may be involved.

Doctrinally, when presented with negligence actions against bank regulators the courts have held that no duty of care exists. Reference has been made to the delicate nature of decision-making and the fact that imposing a duty would, in effect, be making bank regulators liable for the default of a bank's management, over which they cannot in practice exercise great control.[157] In addition, one of the current conceptual prerequisites for duty—'proximity' between the regulators and those suffering loss—has been found wanting. Breach of statutory duty has not fared any better as a foundation for a claim for damages, even though some of the regulatory powers of the FSA are expressed to be exercisable in the interest of consumers—for example, granting, varying, or cancelling permission; making rules—consumers in broad terms being those using banking services.[158]

Finally, there needs to be a causal link between the negligence and the loss suffered. This again presents difficulties for prospective litigants. In the case of the fraudulently run bank, the more direct cause of the claimant's loss can generally be said to be the behaviour of the managers as compared with that of the regulators.

If bank regulators are in general immune from actions in negligence, there are at least two other possibilities.[159] First, there is the tort of misfeasance in public office. Since this entails bad faith, it is not affected by the immunity provision of the FSMA 2000.[160] Misfeasance in public office involves a deliberate and wrongful use of powers entrusted to a public officer. This could involve *mala fides*. Alternatively, with untargeted malice it would have to be shown that the regulators knew that an act or omission was unlawful, and that the act or omission would probably cause damage to the claimant or were reckless whether this was the case.[161] Just to state the elements of the tort is to give an inkling of the hurdles a claimant will face in establishing a claim, quite apart from the issue of causation—that the acts or omissions of the regulators were the effective cause of the claimant's losses. Thus the majority decision of the House of Lords, not to sanction the strike out of a misfeasance claim against the Bank

---

[157] *Yuen Kun Yeu* v. *Attorney-General of Hong Kong* [1988] AC 175 (PC); *Davis* v. *Radclife* [1990] WLR 821, [1990] All ER 536 (PC); *Three Rivers DC* v. *Governor and Company of the Bank of England (No 3)* [2000] UKHL 33, [2000] 2 WLR 1220, [2000] 3 All ER 1 (HL). See M. Andenas and D. Fairgrieve, 'To Supervise or to Compensate?' in M. Andenas and D. Fairgrieve (eds.), *Judicial Review in International Perspective* (London, Kluwer, 2000). See generally P. Craig and D. Fairgrieve, 'Barrett, Negligence and Discretionary Powers?' [1999] *PL* 626.

[158] FSMA 2000, ss. 41(3), 45(1)(c), 138(1)(7).

[159] A third possibility—that depositors have rights conferred by the EC First Banking Dir.—was rejected in *Three Rivers DC* v. *Bank of England (No 3)* [2000] UKHL 33, *supra*.

[160] Sched. 1, para. 19.

[161] *Three Rivers DC* v. *Bank of England (No 3)* [2000] UKHL 33, *supra*.

of England in relation to its supervision of BCCI, is surprising to say the least, when no document was produced to support the claim.[162]

Secondly, the regulators' decisions may be judicially reviewable. In other words, the regulators may be ordered by a court to reconsider their decision on grounds such as acting *ultra vires* their legislative power, taking irrelevant factors into account or overlooking relevant factors, and acting as no reasonable regulator would act. Procedural impropriety, such as breaching the rules of natural justice, is also a ground for review. However, there are a number of obstacles to obtaining judicial review of the decisions of bank regulators. One is that courts tend to defer to the regulators' judgement.[163] Another is that where there is a remedy provided in the legislation, a party will be obliged to pursue that first. Even if an application for judicial review is successful, the remedy will usually be to reconsider a decision: the remedy of damages in English public law is under-developed.

B. CAPITAL ADEQUACY

Illustrative of the standards imposed on banks which want authorization are those concerning capital adequacy (dealt with in this section) and those relating to large exposures (dealt with in the next section). As indicated there are a range of other standards with which banks must comply relating, on the financial side, to matters such as liquidity, provisioning, and foreign exchange position risk. Space precludes any discussion of them.[164] Ownership rules, deposit-protection arrangements, and some of the other criteria for authorization are mentioned elsewhere.[165]

Capital adequacy rules are perhaps the outstanding example of convergence at the international level in bank regulation. The international standards on capital adequacy grew out of the work of the Basle Committee on Banking Supervision. They were prompted by concern over the deteriorating capital levels of international banks from the early 1980s, as a result of increased competition and the debt crisis in developing countries. Capital adequacy standards are to provide a cushion of capital which may protect depositors' funds in the event of a bank incurring significant loss. International standardization was also believed desirable to ensure a level playing field for international banks from different jurisdictions with different capital requirements.[166]

In the final formulation of the Basle Capital Accord, the work of the European Commission was important. Once capital could move freely within the European

---

[162] *Three Rivers DC* v. *Bank of England* [2001] UKHL 16, [2001] 2 All ER 513 (HL).

[163] e.g. *A* v. *B Bank* [1993] QB 311, 326–8.

[164] See e.g. M. Hall, *Handbook of Banking Regulation and Supervision* (2nd edn., London, Woodhead-Faulkner, 1993), chs. 16, 17, 19.

[165] 32, 78, 86 above.

[166] C. Goodhart, 'Comment' (1995) 9 *J Fin. Services Res.* 421; H. Scott and S. Iwahara, *In Search of a Level Playing Field. The Implementation of the Basle Capital Accord in Japan and the United States* (Washington, DC, Group of Thirty, 1994).

Community, European-wide minimum capital adequacy standards were seen as crucial, if banks were to be empowered to move freely within a European single market. However, unlike the Basle Capital Accord, the EC standards are legally binding. Moreover, they apply to all banks, not just internationally active banks, and there are some differences in terminology and substance.

In formulating the Basle Capital Accord many issues had to be resolved. What should count as the capital of a bank (or owners' own funds) other than paid-up share capital? To what should that capital be related? Deposit liabilities or asset values? Deposit liabilities are more indicative of liquidity, but simply choosing the nominal value of a bank's assets would provide a poor reflection of the risks a bank faces.[167] What of the growth of off-balance-sheet instruments and techniques? Banks were using these, partly to avoid the pressure of national regulators to improve their capital position.

Ultimately the Basle Capital Accord, and later the Solvency Ratio Directive of the European Community, adopted the 8 per cent solvency (or risk asset) ratio for banks as indicative of minimum acceptable capital adequacy—capital as the numerator and assets, suitably adjusted in value to reflect their varying risk characteristics (risk weighted), as the denominator. In brief, capital is divided into Tier 1, core capital (notably permanent shareholder equity and disclosed reserves), and Tier 2, supplementary capital (notably, undisclosed and revaluation reserves, preference shares, and subordinated debt). Tier 2 capital must not exceed 100 per cent of Tier 1 capital. As for assets, they have attached to them, 0, 10, 20, 50, or 100 per cent risk weightings, depending mainly on the category of counterparty. To take just a few examples, cash, bullion, and claims on Zone A (OECD) central governments and central banks have a 0 per cent risk weighting; house mortgage finance a 50 per cent risk weighting; and claims on the non-bank private sector a 100 per cent risk weighting. Off-balance-sheet exposures are converted to on-balance-sheet equivalents by a factor which varies in accordance with the category of liability in question.[168]

The criticisms of these capital adequacy standards are various. First, it is said that they are overly complex, the complexity increasing as the regulators have responded to criticisms of existing standards, to attempts at their circumvention, and to market realities on matters such as netting.[169] A corollary of complexity is a loss of transparency.[170] Secondly, it is said that the standards can distort a bank's activities. Regulation of any kind produces a reaction by the regulated, as these seek to diminish its impact. Raising new capital has not been a practical possibility for many banks, so

---

[167] J. Norton, *Devising International Bank Supervisory Standards* (Dordrecht, Martinus Nijhoff, 1995), 12–13.

[168] Basle Committee on Banking Supervision, *International Convergence of Capital Measurement and Capital Standards*, July 1988; EC Dir. on the own funds of credit institutions, 89/299/EEC [1989] OJ L124/16; EC Dir. on a solvency ratio for credit institutions, 89/647/EEC [1989] OJ L386/14. These various instruments have been consolidated in the Credit Institutions Directive 2000/12/EC [2000] OJ L126/1.

[169] e.g. J. Pierce, *The Future of Banking* (New Haven, Conn., Yale UP, 1991), 96.

[170] J. Norton, *Devising International Bank Supervisory Standards* (Dordrecht, Martinus Nijhoff, 1995), 40.

there is a temptation to move their business in favour of lower risk-weighted assets, rather than having a diversified portfolio of assets. Thirdly, it is said that the standards are insufficiently precise to measure accurately the risks a bank faces. The original capital adequacy instruments focused largely on credit risk, rather than on some of the other types of risk in banking such as market risks. Fourthly, the risk weightings are crude: for example, a 100 per cent weighting is given to corporate lending, whereas in some cases this is less of a risk than mortgage lending (which carries the lower 50 per cent weighting under the Directive).[171] Finally, it is said that there are variations in the way the standards have been adopted in different jurisdictions. This involves the danger, possibly not great, of the migration of banks to 'low-cost' regulation states.

The upshot is that the Basle Capital Accord is under review. The overall aim of the proposed Basle II is to ensure that a bank's capital is more closely calibrated to the risks it faces, rather than resting on the comparatively crude yardsticks in the current rules (pillar 1). This is coupled with incentives for banks to adopt their own internal risk assessment procedures, which go to determining the denominator of the required capital ratio. In addition to the requirement to hold capital against credit and market risk, banks will need to provide against operational risk, i.e. losses which may result from inadequate procedures, control systems, or inside fraud. Pillars 2 and 3 of Basle II are respectively the supervisory review process, under which supervisors will have more discretion in assessing a bank's capital adequacy, and market exposures, which is to work through information disclosure to a bank's stakeholders.[172] The proposals have been fiercely contested. Among the criticisms are that the proposals are so complex and costly that enforcement will be more difficult and arbitrage encouraged.[173] It is also said, notably by the German government, that the proposals oblige too much capital to be set aside for lending to small and medium sized businesses— an obvious disincentive for banks and raising the cost of bank debt capital to this type of borrower. More generally even proponents acknowledge concern that the new provisions will make economic cycles more pronounced by encouraging lending during economic expansion and causing banks to withdraw funds during downturns. At the time of writing it appears that Basle II will not take effect until 2005 at the earliest.

C. LARGE EXPOSURE REGULATION

Experience is that bank failure can sometimes be attributable to over- exposure to one borrower or corporate group. For more than a century US national banks were

---

[171] M. Hall, 'Capital-adequacy Assessment', in C. Stone and A. Zissu (eds.), *Global Risk Based Capital Regulations* (Ill., Irwin Publishers, 1994), i, 271.

[172] Basle Committee on Banking Supervision, *The New Basle Capital Accord. Consultation Document* (Basle, BIS, 2001). The European Community's proposals, in line with Basle II, are: European Commission, Internal Market DG, *A Review of Regulatory Capital Requirements. Consultation Document of the European Union*, MARKT/1000/01.

[173] Centre for the Study of Financial Innovation, *Bumps on the Road to Basle. An Anthology of Views on Basle 2* (London, CSFI & SUERF, 2001).

forbidden to lend more than 10 per cent of their capital to a single borrower. While some argue that this was a populist measure, to force banks to spread their benefits, the better view is that it had as its rationale the soundness of banks.[174] Eventually other countries have followed suit, in one form or the other. Thus Britain adopted a policy on large exposures in the early 1980s, but statutory limits were eschewed. Guidelines were issued and later legislation obliged banks to report large exposures to the bank regulators.[175] The rather spurious objections to set ceilings were that they would encourage banks to avoid them and possibly also to trade up to them as the norm.[176] In fact the real objection was probably a fear of the competitive disadvantage if British, but not other European, banks were subject to compulsory thresholds.

Now large exposure limits are mandated by a European Community Directive.[177] It is based on the assumption, obviously correct, that even if a bank satisfies the capital adequacy requirements, that will do little good if its asset base is concentrated on particular borrowers which fail. It replaces a less onerous recommendation dating from 1986 which, in Community law, lacked any binding force. The Directive defines exposure, broadly speaking, in terms of the assets and off-balance-sheet items set out for the solvency ratio (but not risk weighted).[178] In other words, it covers not only a bank's exposure to borrowers but also through certain dealings in derivatives.

Exposure is caught by the Directive if it is to a single customer or to a group of connected customers. Here the Directive uses the familiar test for identifying a corporate group—the power of control of one company over another (e.g. voting power, power to appoint directors, dominant influence). Given the reason for the exposure limits, however, it sensibly takes contagion into account by adding another test—whether customers are to be regarded as constituting a single risk, in that if one of them were to face financial problems the others would encounter repayment difficulties.[179]

The key limit in the Directive is in Article 49(1): generally speaking a bank must not incur an exposure to a customer or group of connected customers the value of which exceeds 25 per cent of its capital. Article 49(2) reduces that to 20 per cent, where exposure is to members of the bank's own corporate group. There is an overall limit on large exposures—defined as equal to or exceeding 10 per cent of a bank's capital—which in the aggregate must not exceed 800 per cent of a bank's capital: Article 49(3).

These various limits can be exceeded only in exceptional circumstances, although bank regulators must fix a deadline for banks to regularize the position. Moreover, as well as generous transitional provisions, there are extensive potential exemptions in

[174] 'The Policies Behind Lending Limits' (1985) 99 *Harv. LR* 430.
[175] Banking Act 1987, s. 38.
[176] *Report of the Committee [on] the System of Banking Supervision*, Cmnd. 9550 (London, HMSO, 1985), para. 5.4.
[177] Credit Institutions Directive 2000/12/EC [2000] OJ L126/1, consolidating Dir. on the monitoring and control of large exposures of credit institutions, 92/121/EEC [1993] OJ L29/1. See P. Pearson, 'Large Exposures Directive', in M. van Empel (ed.), *Amsterdam Financial Services* (Hague, Kluwer, looseleaf).
[178] Art.1(24).   [179] Art. 1(25).

the Directive. These reflect in part the risk-weighting process for assets set out for the solvency ratio for banks. On the surface this seems unsatisfactory. First, it undercuts the earlier provision against risk weighting and, secondly, it seems to confuse the aim of the solvency ratio, which is with counterparty risk, with the policy on large exposures, which supposedly addresses the separate problem of concentrated risk. The Directive also contains a system for reporting large exposures to bank regulators.[180] Member States are given a choice of how reporting is to be effected. The various large exposure provisions will generally be supervised on a consolidated basis by the home regulator of a banking group.[181]

The law on large exposures addresses the risks incurred by banks because they are exposed to the one customer or corporate group. Yet history is clear that banks can face grave crises when they are over-exposed in particular markets, geographic areas, or economic sectors.[182] The difficulty for the law in this regard is said to lie in defining with any degree of precision the assets subject to common risks. Large exposures of this nature must thus be regulated informally. However, it is as well to note the provision in the banking laws of some jurisdictions prohibiting an over-exposure to real estate, given its historical association with bank failure.[183] Admittedly, restrictions on the real-estate activities of banks in the United States were based on the ideological belief that, since the individual ownership of land was a necessary precondition for political independence, banks should not be able to own land, especially that purchased at distress prices in foreclosure sales. Nonetheless, the point remains that the EC Directive addresses only part of the problem of risk exposure.

D. CRISIS MANAGEMENT—BANK RESCUES

Bank failures are not a new phenomenon, but in recent years they have been a feature of the financial scene in many countries. Financial liberalization leading to competitive pressures; bad loans and proprietary trade losses; economic recession; over-exposure to property and other cases of insufficient asset diversification; fraud and gross negligence—these seem to be the major features in bank failures.[184] The threat of failure is unlikely to fall, given the increasing risks which banks are assuming, in particular their dependence on trading income in securities and derivatives. This has given new life to the concept of the 'narrow bank': in return for confining its funds to high-quality, marketable assets, only the narrow bank would be permitted access to the payments system and to the deposit guarantee fund. The concept runs against the strong current in favour of universal banking and financial liberalization.

---

[180] Art. 48(2).   [181] Art. 50.

[182] C. Hadjiemmanuil, *Banking Regulation and the Bank of England* (London, LLP, 1996), 224.

[183] e.g., Banking Act, ch. 19, s. 33 (Singapore).

[184] A. Demingue-Kunt and E. Detragiache, *The Determinants of Banking Crises in Developed and Developing Countries*, IMF Staff Papers, 45, 1998, 81; W Blair, 'Dealing with Banks in Distress', in R. Effros (ed.), *Current Legal Issues Affecting Central Banks* (Washington DC, IMF, 1998), 252ff.

Rescuing banks is usually justified on the ground of preventing contagion in the banking sector. If a solvent yet illiquid bank is not rescued, there may be a run on other banks. However, there is a fine balance in any decision to rescue a bank. Moral hazard is an obvious problem: unless some banks are permitted to fail, then risk is eliminated from the banking system, together with the necessary market disciplines on operating banks. Yet the extreme position that there is no difference between the damage caused by a bank failure and an ordinary business failure is untenable as a guide to policy. In some cases bank regulators cannot take the chance of systemic risk and must intervene.[185]

Which banks should be rescued? The distinction between the bank with a temporary liquidity problem and the insolvent bank may be difficult to draw in the short time in which the decision to rescue must be made. If a bank is illiquid, this generally indicates that its solvency is suspected by the market, for otherwise it would be able to obtain liquidity on the interbank market. On the other hand, the history of banking is the history of many banks being brought back from the brink because a central bank provided lender-of-last-resort facilities to overcome temporary illiquidity.

The advent of deposit insurance may incline bank regulators to be less willing to mount a rescue than in the past. Moreover, the threat of contagion these days comes not only from core banking but also from other financial activities. Securities and derivatives trading, for example, can create enormous exposures. In circumstances where this has caused the loss, bank regulators may be less willing to intervene or, if they do, they may be willing only to hive off and rescue the core banking parts of a business. There is the additional problem that, where banks are multinational, contagion may cross borders. Co-operation between different bank regulators to rescue an international bank may not be easy.

(i) The UK Approach

The approach of the Bank of England to rescues evolved before 1946, when the City was more like a club and the Bank was a private company without statutory backing. Rescues were co-operative affairs, and although they were underpinned by law, this was the ordinary private law, not public law. Two examples suffice. Barings was rescued in 1890; a large number of banks gave guarantees to make good any loss which might appear at the final liquidation, in consideration of the Bank of England making advances to enable Barings to meet its liabilities. The Bank also took security over Barings' assets.[186] The guarantees were never called and Barings survived—for another century at any rate. William Deacon's, a clearing bank, was rescued in 1930, first by the Bank guaranteeing repayment of its advances to some forty cotton-spinning companies (which were in no position to repay because of economic recession). The Bank then arranged for the Royal Bank of Scotland to take it over,

---

[185] C. Goodhart, *The Evolution of Central Banks* (London, MIT Press, 1988), 62–6, 100.
[186] J. Clapham, *The Bank of England 1797–1914* (Cambridge, Cambridge UP, 1944), ii, 334.

transferring to the Royal Bank as a sweetener the Bank's redundant 'Western' branch in fashionable Burlington Gardens (in the West End of London).[187]

The Bank of England Act 1946 contained nothing about bank rescues: it should not be surprising that the approach to rescue after nationalization followed the pattern already set. In the secondary banking crisis of 1973–5, the Bank formed a committee with the clearing banks to provide support for those considered worthy of rescue (the so-called 'lifeboat'). The clearing banks (and some pension funds and insurance companies) lent to those being rescued, in effect recycling the funds which had been withdrawn from the latter in a 'flight to quality'. The funds provided were subordinated to other deposits, thereby reassuring holders of the latter. Security was sometimes taken. When the position got worse, and the clearing banks felt that to go further was to raise doubts about their own soundness, the Bank provided support by itself, facilitated the reconstruction or absorption of some institutions, and acquired one as a wholly-owned subsidiary.[188]

Acquisition by the Bank was again necessary in 1984, when no other purchaser could be found for Johnson Matthey Bankers. As with the secondary banking crisis there was a fear of systemic risk, but this time because of the possibility of contagion of other banks in the London gold market. The Bank made a non-negotiable offer to acquire JMB for £1, conditional on its parent company injecting capital. The Bank then indemnified it against certain losses, and the major private banks gave the Bank counter-indemnities for half this amount. This example usefully illustrates the Bank of England policy that rescues must not involve a public subsidy to private shareholders. When losses occur, they must first fall on the shareholders. Conversely, any benefit from the rescue accrues to the Bank. It will be virtually impossible for the former shareholders of a rescued bank later to reopen the bargain on the grounds that the selling price was too low. There is no support in English law for the proposition that, because of its unique position in the world of banking, the Bank of England owes a duty of fair dealing.[189] The ordinary rules of contracting apply, and in the commercial sphere the proposition that 'Chancery mends no man's bargain' applies in its full force.[190]

Then in the early 1990s some small banks failed, and the Bank of England judged there was systemic risk as funds were moved from smaller to larger banks. The problem was accentuated by the collapse of BCCI and the recession in the property market. Consequently, the Bank provided widespread liquidity support. The clearing banks provided loans (at least one syndicate was arranged) but they were no longer prepared to bear any risk themselves, and the Bank was obliged to guarantee them fully. In effect the Bank was conducting the rescue by itself, with the clearers being used only so that there could be a pretence to the public that normal credit lines were being

---

[187] R. Sayers, *The Bank of England 1891–1944* (Cambridge, Cambridge UP, 1976), i, 253–9.
[188] M. Reid, *The Secondary Banking Crisis, 1973–75* (London, Macmillan, 1982).
[189] *Burmah Oil Co. Ltd.* v. *Governor of the Bank of England* (1981) 125 *Sol. J* 528.
[190] 213ff. below.

extended to those being rescued. Again the Bank ended up acquiring one of the rescued banks.[191]

The banking community now refuses to prop up its members in temporary difficulty, even when there is a risk of contagion. The responsibility falls on the shoulders of the Bank of England. Apart from the issue of whether a bank must be given notice of the rescue efforts which the Bank intends to undertake,[192] there are also nice legal questions about the *vires* of the Bank's rescue efforts, especially where public moneys are being used. There is no power of rescue in the Bank of England Acts 1946 and 1998 or the FSMA 2000, although the Bank's charters give the Bank full power of contracting, which must include bank rescues. The Memorandum of Understanding between the Bank and the FSA recognizes the responsibility of the Bank to support operations, when there is a genuine threat of systemic disturbance, although in other cases the FSA has lead responsibility (e.g. facilitating a market solution such as the introduction of new capital into a troubled firm by a third party).[193]

(ii) The Approach in the United States

By contrast with Britain, the approach to bank rescues in the United States is legalistic, the banking community is not as greatly involved, and the task of rescue is entrusted to federal agencies, notably the Federal Deposit Insurance Corporation (FDIC), rather than the central bank (i.e. Federal Reserve system). Partly this reflects the more legalistic nature of American society, partly the fragmentation of its banking markets, partly the scale of bank failures, and partly also an attempt to reduce the political pressures to rescue particular banks.

The National Bank Act of 1864 empowered the Comptroller of the Currency to rescue a failed national bank. Many bank failures in the Great Depression led to the creation of the FDIC in 1933 as a receiver of failed national banks and, very soon after, state banks.[194] At times the FDIC has concentrated on liquidating the assets of failed banks and paying off depositors. However, amendments to the legislation have opened up a range of other techniques, notably 'open bank assistance' and 'purchase and assumption' transactions. The first involves financial assistance to keep a bank open. Legislative change in 1982 expanded this possibility as the FDIC was enabled to purchase a bank's bad loans and to inject capital.[195] 'Purchase and assumption' involved financial assistance to enable a healthy bank to take over a failed bank's deposit liabilities and assets. The legislation gave the FDIC considerable flexibility to determine the structure and terms of a transaction.

However, the costs of purchase and assumption led to legislative change. As a result the FDIC is now obliged to pursue the avenue which imposes least cost on the deposit

---

[191] R. Dale, 'Bank Crisis Management' [1995] 8 *JIBL* 326, 329–30.
[192] *Century National Merchant Bank and Trust Co. Ltd. v. Davies* [1998] AC 628 (PC).
[193] n. 133 above, paras. 3(iii)(b), 11.   [194] 12 USC §191.
[195] J. Macey and G. Miller, 'Bank Failures, Risk Monitoring, and the Market for Bank Control' (1988) 88 *Colum. LR* 1153, pt. III; E. Hüpkes, *The Legal Aspects of Bank Insolvency* (Hague, Kluwer, 2000), 98–100.

insurance fund.[196] Thus the FDIC cannot now facilitate the transfer of a failed bank, even though this may protect against contagion in interbank markets, if the effect is to increase loss to the deposit insurance fund. Only if large numbers of banks are threatened can the FDIC so act, and then only with the authorization of the Secretary of the Treasury, in consultation with the President and notice to the Congress—not an easy avenue. The result is that the disruptive effects of a bank failure on interbank and other markets are no longer as well addressed by US legislation. Nor are the social costs of bank failure, which only make a liquidation more expensive overall.[197] The price of legalism is greater inflexibility.

III. REGULATING THE MULTIFUNCTIONAL BANK

A world-wide tendency is for banks to become multifunctional institutions ('universal banks'). In addition to core banking, banks now engage in other activities, notably securities and derivatives transactions, and insurance. This combination of activities raises various regulatory issues. The focus of the present discussion is on the control of risk as banks conduct operations in securities and derivatives.[198] The risks of combining core banking and insurance are put to one side.[199]

As a matter of policy the law must address the different risks facing core banking and securities business—credit risk with the former, market risk with the latter.[200] In addition core banking involves deposits, which can be easily moved. On its own, the case for regulating securities activity focuses mainly on investor protection. This was the basis of securities regulation in the United States in the 1930s, which has provided a general model for many other countries, in the case of Britain embodied in the Financial Services Act 1986 and subsequently the FSMA 2000.

In combination with banking, the case for regulating securities activity is founded largely on risk. Historically the issue has been seen as whether core banking ought to be combined with riskier activities such as dealing, underwriting, and investing in securities. Even if, as many argue, securities and derivatives activity is no riskier than core banking, there is the potential for contagion if the different activities are mixed. Whereas the independent securities firm which collapses can probably be wound up in an orderly fashion by selling off its mainly marketable assets, if the securities side of a bank collapses this may mortally wound the banking side. The funding base (deposits) of core banking is inherently volatile and may evaporate on the slightest hint of trouble in a banking group as a whole.

[196] 12 USC §1823(c).
[197] H. Garten, 'United States Bank Failure Policy' (1993) 1 *Int.J Reg.L & Practice* 239.
[198] On the conflict of interest problems: 21 above.
[199] See U. Schneider, 'The Supervision of Financial Conglomerates', in G. Ferrarini (ed.), *Prudential Regulation of Banks and Securities Firms* (London, Kluwer, 1995), 28.
[200] R. Dale, 'The Regulation of Investment Firms in the European Union', in *ibid.* 28.

Arguably derivatives raise no new risk concerns compared with securities, although the traditional concerns may take more acute form. It is said that derivatives are just one aspect of the financial changes of recent decades along with interest-rate volatility, high debt, and deregulation: they are not so much a cause, but a consequence, of instability in interest and exchange rates, and achieve stability in these.[201] On the other hand, end-users have suffered considerable losses, and there is the example of the Barings bank collapse through derivatives activities.[202] Competition leads banks into even more complex derivatives deals, indeed riskier deals because they give higher returns. A less benign international economic environment than in recent times could accentuate the problems. Derivatives are often traded on OTC markets rather than regulated exchanges. Sudden change is a characteristic of the derivatives markets. In particular, the amount of credit exposure a bank has on a swap, unlike the credit exposure it has on a loan, constantly fluctuates in size with the movements in interest rates and exchange rates.[203]

A fear of excessive risk, when core banking is combined with securities business, led the United States, and later Japan, to impose a strict separation on the different activities. In the United States this took legal form in the famous Glass–Steagall Act, the first topic discussed here. At the other end of the spectrum German law has long sanctioned universal banking—banks being able to engage in securities and other activities. Britain has fallen between the extremes, although not unusually the law has been silent on the matter. As a matter of tradition the clearing (commercial) banks were separated from the merchant (investment) banks, partly because it was thought risky for the former to engage in dealing in shares and debentures.[204] But that tradition evaporated in the 1960s and 1970s as clearing banks, unimpeded by law, acquired or established merchant-bank subsidiaries. The trend was accentuated by the financial liberalization of the 1980s. Universal banking is now legally sanctioned in the European Community. The risks associated with it are next discussed. Thirdly in this section, there is some account of recent measures to address the problem of derivatives. Finally, there is a note on regulatory co-ordination.

---

[201] See H. Hu, 'Misunderstood Derivatives: The Causes of Informational Failure and the Promise of Regulatory Incrementalism' (1993) 102 *Yale LJ* 1457. Cf. A. Shah, 'Regulating Derivatives: Operator Error or System Failure?' (1996) 4 *JFR&C* 17.

[202] W. Blair, 'Liability Risks in Derivatives Sales' [1996] 11 *JIBL* 18; *Report of the Board of Banking Supervision Inquiry into the Circumstances of the Collapse of Barings*, HC 673, 1995; *The Report of the Inspectors Appointed by the Minister for Finance: Baring Futures (Singapore) Pte. Ltd. Investigation Pursuant to Section 231 of the Companies Act (Chapter 50)* (Singapore, Ministry of Finance, 1995).

[203] H. Hu, 'Swaps, the Modern Process of Financial Innovation and the Vulnerability of a Regulatory Paradigm' (1989) 138 *U Pa. LR* 333, 385.

[204] E. Perkins, 'The Divorce of Commercial and Investment Banking: A History' (1971) 88 *Banking LJ* 483, at 486.

A. COMMERCIAL–INVESTMENT BANK SEPARATION IN
THE UNITED STATES AND JAPAN

The separation of commercial and investment banking in the United States was first embodied in law in the form of the National Bank Act 1864. The prohibition on banks' dealing in non-government securities applied to federally chartered, not state, banks, and national banks were able to avoid the restriction by forming state affiliates. Consequently, in 1913, the Federal Reserve Act removed the restriction on national banks as well. By the late 1920s, banks and bank affiliates were underwriting, distributing, and facilitating the issue of securities on a large scale.[205]

However, the 1929 collapse led to the revival in the Glass–Steagall Act of a legal separation of banking from securities business.[206] That some 9,000 banks failed between the collapse and the end of 1933 was thought to be caused partly by banks or bank affiliates engaging in the riskier business of distributing and underwriting issues of securities. Banks should never again be exposed to the dangers of this involvement in securities activities. Risk, and conflicts of interest leading to risk, would be avoided by a legally mandated institutional separation.[207] The separation was later adopted in Article 65 of the Securities and Exchange Law of Japan, as a result of the American occupation. There are differences between the two measures, however: for example, Article 65 of the Japanese law gives greater scope for banks to affiliate with securities firms through cross-shareholding or contract.[208]

The Glass–Steagall Act was under enormous pressure for years. Considerable effort was put into debunking the historical underpinning of the Glass–Steagall Act and to showing that the risks and abuses were not as great as its proponents claimed.[209] American banks were able to avoid its prohibition, to varying degrees. Legally this was accommodated by the relevant regulators adopting a more liberal interpretation of the legislation, and to some extent through judicial approval of those decisions.[210] The protagonists of the abandonment of the Glass–Steagall prohibition argued that banks' lending activities had proved at least as risky as securities activities. Economic efficiency, greater competition, and customer convenience, they contended, demanded removing this restriction on banks. The upshot was the Gramm–Leach–Bliley Act of 1999, which repealed part of the Glass–Steagall Act. Banks are still prohibited from acquiring securities and engaging in underwriting and dealing with securities, and securities firms must not accept deposits. However, banks which are members of the

---

[205] V. Carosso, *Investment Banking in America* (Cambridge, Mass., Harvard University Press, 1970), 98, 368.

[206] Banking Act of 1933, §§16, 20, 21, 32, consolidated in 12 USC, §§24, 78, 377, 378 (1994). See also Bank Holding Company Act 1956, 12 USC §1843(a)(2).

[207] *Investment Company Institute* v. *Camp*, 401 US 617, 630–3 (1971).

[208] J. Norton and C. Olive, 'Regulation of the Securities Activities of Banks', in E. Gardener and P. Molyneux (eds.), *Investment Banking* (2nd edn., London, Euromoney, 1995), 61; M. Hall, *Banking Regulation and Supervision. A Comparative Study of the UK, USA and Japan* (Aldershot, Edward Elgar, 1993), 227–35.

[209] e.g. G. Benston, *The Separation of Commercial and Investment Banking* (New York, OUP, 1990).

[210] See K. Fisher, 'Reweaving the Safety Net' (1992) 27 *Wake Forest LR* 123.

Federal Reserve System can now be affiliated with securities firms in the one holding group.[211] In Japan, in line with the general liberalization of financial markets, the Financial System Reform Act 1992 permitted an expansion in banks' securities activities (e.g. as in the United States through securities subsidiaries).

B. UNIVERSAL BANKING IN THE EC

The thrust of the Credit Institutions Directive and its predecessor, the Second Banking Directive, is to liberalize banking service.[212] This is due to the fact that banks with a single licence may engage in the activities subject to mutual recognition, through branches or across borders, if authorized to provide them in their home state. The activities subject to mutual recognition are listed in Annex 1 to the Directive and include participation in securities issues. There is no requirement of segregation for securities activities. Insurance, however, is not included in the Annex, although the quite separate limitation in the Directive on investments in non-bank entities does not apply to insurance, so that banks can have insurance subsidiaries.[213] Clearly the extended nature of the list in the Annex puts pressure on a Member State, which does not permit its banks to engage in such activities, to do so. Otherwise the latter will be at a competitive disadvantage in competing with banks from other Member States, which can.

This universal banking model, inherent in the Credit Institutions Directive, has operated successfully for many years, notably in Germany. But that does not mean that it will necessarily be an unqualified success in all Member States. The business of securities can be risky, and banks tend to use expanded investment opportunities to increase their risk-taking. Universal banking can, therefore, create dangers for the financial system, since risks in one part of a financial institution can infect other parts.[214] Central banks are likely to refuse to provide lender-of-last-resort facilities for all the activities of an institution, especially those not traditionally regarded as banking. What, then, are the solutions?

'Firewalls' to segregate risks, such as those associated with securities activities, are said to be one answer to the contagion problem. To be effective they should insulate the banking side from calls for financial support when the securities side is in serious difficulty. The parent should be able to walk away from the securities subsidiary without fear that the corporate veil will be pierced. Indeed, with a true firewall the parent would be obliged to do this. This is because in practice it is difficult to separate

---

[211] 13 Stat. 1341–2, 1346 (1999). See J. Macey, 'The Business of Banking: Before and After Gramm–Leach–Bliley' (2000) 25 *J Corp L* 691.

[212] Credit Institutions Directive 2000/12/EC [2000] OJ L126/1, consolidating the Second Banking Directive Dir. 89/646/EEC [1989] OJ L386/1.

[213] 36 above.

[214] R. Dale, *International Banking Deregulation* (Oxford, Blackwell, 1992), 171, 179.

the two sides in the public mind, which is never overly concerned with legal niceties. Even if the legal position is that there is no obligation to the securities subsidiary, public pressure will be for the parent to assist it.

Some commentators have pointed out that 'funding firewalls' have their own dangers in forbidding financial support precisely when it is needed, and that firewalls seeking to limit confidence crises, such as fully capitalizing an insulated securities subsidiary, defeat the very economies of scope on the marketing side which combining the activities was designed to achieve. It may be that there is no answer to the questions whether and how banking and other activities like securities business should be combined. It is troublesome, however, that although the Credit Institutions Directive approves the combination of activities, little consideration seems to have been given to how the potential contagion of risks can be handled. Moreover, there is the additional point that the European Community and United States may be moving in different directions on segregation.[215] The European tradition is in favour of universal banking, and firewalls are not even on the agenda. The United States now imposes certain firewalls on bank holding companies and their subsidiaries. Thus the latter are at a competitive disadvantage as a result of the different regulatory approach.

A major EC measure, ostensibly designed to counteract market risks associated with securities and other activities, was the Capital Adequacy Directive (the CAD).[216] In fact the CAD had as much to do with competitive concerns as with addressing problems of risk. In particular, there was the fear that universal banks, with the capital requirement imposed on them by the Solvency Ratio Directive, would be at a competitive disadvantage against non-bank securities firms if these were subject to no such demands. The CAD thus sought to impose a level playing field.[217] There was much criticism of this approach for protecting the universal bank from competition from non-bank securities firms, and overlooking that these firms can use sophisticated risk management techniques which demand little capital.[218]

In relation to the multifunctional bank, the CAD imposes its capital adequacy requirements by segregating the securities 'trading book' of a bank and applying more liberal capital adequacy rules to it than those for core lending activities (the 'banking book'). It does this by identifying 'financial instruments'—such as transferable securities, money market instruments, and derivatives. The capital adequacy requirements of the CAD apply to such financial instruments held for short-term trading

---

[215] *Ibid.*, 186.

[216] Directive on the capital adequacy of investments firms and credit institutions, 93/6/EEC [1993] OJ L141/1. See M. Hall, 'The Measurement and Assessment of Market Risk: a Comparison of the European Commission and Basle Committee Approaches', *BNL Quarterly Rev.*, no 194, Sept. 1995, 183; G. Walker, 'The Law of Financial Conglomerates' (1996) 30 *Int'l. L* 57.

[217] B. Scott-Quinn, 'EC Securities Markets Regulation', in B. Steil (ed.), *International Financial Market Regulation* (Chichester, J. Wiley, 1994), 121.

[218] e.g. E. Dimson and P. Marsh, *The Debate on International Capital Requirements* (London, City Research Project, Subject Report 8, 1994).

purposes, with the aim of benefiting from actual or expected price differences or price and interest-rate variations, and to those positions which hedge an exposure on the trading book. An amendment to the Directive in 1998 gives scope for banks to reduce capital requirements on the basis of their own internal risk management models.[219]

C. THE SPECIAL PROBLEM OF DERIVATIVES

Generally speaking central banks and bank regulators have taken the view that, since the benefits flowing from the markets in derivatives are considerable, a wholesale regulation would do more harm than good. However, some steps have been taken. These have involved bank regulators working with securities and other regulators within particular jurisdictions, and with regulators in other jurisdictions. Basically the regulatory moves have been four-fold.

First, there has been the effort to strengthen individual banks to withstand shocks. The traditional approach, reflected in capital adequacy requirements, has had to be modified in the light of the growth of derivatives. It will be recalled that the Basle Capital Accord for banks requires risks associated with off-balance-sheet items to be taken into account in calculating a bank's solvency ratio.[220] In 1995 the Capital Accord was modified in the light of risks associated with OTC derivatives contracts. The matrix of factors taken into account for potential off-balance-sheet exposure has been expanded. At the same time, however, the Accord now recognizes netting in these calculations: the rationale is that forward-exchange contracts and interest-rate swaps improve efficiency and stability in interbank settlements. Thus bilateral netting can be accepted where national supervisors are satisfied that agreed minimum legal requirements are met and that the netting is legally enforceable in each of the relevant jurisdictions.[221]

Secondly, there has been the attempt to improve the flow of information about derivatives. Several reports of the Bank for International Settlements have emphasized the need for more information about derivatives, and this has been underpinned by the work of the Basle Committee on Banking Supervision.[222] For example in November 1995, the committee and IOSCO (International Organization of Securities Regulators) published a report with recommendations for further improvements in banks' and securities firms' public disclosures about their trading and derivatives activities.[223] A third dimension of the regulatory response has been

---

[219] Directive 98/31/EC amending Council Directive 93/6/EEC on the capital adequacy of investment firms and credit institutions [1998] OJ L204/13, Annex, para. 5, adding Annex VIII.

[220] 90 above.

[221] See also Dir. 98/31/EC amending Council Directive on the capital adequacy of investment firms and credit institutions [1998] OJ L204/13, Annex, paras. 1, 3.

[222] G. Walker, 'Financial Derivatives—Global Regulatory Developments' [1996] *JBL* 66.

[223] *Public Disclosure of the Trading and Derivatives Activities of Banks and Securities Firms* (Basle Committee on Banking Supervision/IOSCO, Nov. 1995).

to encourage the strengthening of risk management within banks and the strengthening of financial infrastructures generally to prevent individual shocks spreading. At one level these steps are basically non-legal in character. Thus the Basle Committee on Bank Supervision has tried to encourage internal systems which ensure appropriate oversight by boards of directors and the senior management of banks, adequate risk-management processes and limits, sound measurement procedures and information systems, continuous risk monitoring, as well as comprehensive internal controls and audit procedures.[224] Related in this regard has been the movement in favour of banks' own internal models for evaluating and managing risk.[225]

Strengthening risk management and financial infrastructure also had a legal counterpart in private law. In particular bank regulators have encouraged banks to strengthen the legal underpinnings of derivatives transactions. This ranges from improving the standard-form documentation, through vetting whether a transaction is *intra vires* a counterparty, to taking better security in support of a transaction from a counterparty.[226] At the level of infrastructure netting is one key factor, since credit exposure of a bank trading derivatives is mitigated if netting with counterparties is firmly in place. Efficient clearing systems are another, since they reduce settlement risk.[227] Both netting and clearing need a well-founded legal basis in all the relevant jurisdictions.

D. FINANCIAL CONGLOMERATES

The consolidation of the financial services industry, and the intensification of links between financial markets, has impelled the European Commission to propose a directive for financial conglomerates as part of its Financial Services Action Plan. Inconsistencies between the sectoral directives on banks, investment firms, and insurance companies, and any regulatory arbitrage to which these give rise, are to be addressed by common prudential standards. Specific problems dealt with in the proposed directive are multiple gearing, where the same capital is counted twice over for different entities in the same corporate groups and excessive leveraging, when the parent is in debt and downstreams the proceeds as equity to its subsidiaries to meet capital adequacy requirements. Intra-group transactions are also addressed, not by quantitative limits but by ensuring that there is internal monitoring and reporting to regulators. The Directive also envisages a designated authority responsible for each corporate group on the one hand to avoid gaps and on the other duplication in

---

[224] *Risk Management Guidelines for Derivatives* (Basle, Bank for International Settlements, July 1994).

[225] See H. Scott, 'Models Based Regulation for Bank Capital', in R. Cranston (ed.), *The Making of Commercial Law* (Oxford, Clarendon, 1997).

[226] e.g. J. Golden, 'Setting Standards in the Evolution of Swap Documentation', 13 *IFLR*, May 1994, 18–19. See A. Hudson, *The Law on Financial Derivatives* (3rd edn., London, Sweet & Maxwell, forthcoming).

[227] A. Corcoran, 'Prudential Regulation of OTC Derivatives—Lessons from the Exchange-traded Sector' (1995) 2 *EFSL* 274, 279.

prudential supervision.[228] The European Community proposal must be seen against a backdrop of international measures in relation to financial conglomerates.[229]

IV. REGULATING INTERNATIONAL BANKS

Elsewhere in this book there is some discussion of international banking, in particular how international banks may be subject to special regulatory regimes.[230] Here the concern is with the special regulation to which international banks are subjected for prudential reasons: in other words, with the measures specially adopted by both home and host jurisdictions to ensure the soundness of these banks, and in the interests of limiting systemic risk. Given the risky international environment for banks, and the links between world financial centres, the dangers of collapse and contagion are not to be underestimated.

A. NATIONAL MEASURES

At a national level, bank regulators have grappled with the problems of prudential regulation of international banks for a considerable time. In some jurisdictions bank regulators have required that a foreign bank establishing a subsidiary there should stand behind it, for example, by means of a comfort letter.[231] This has the obvious advantage that the whole of the capital of the international banking group will be available if the subsidiary runs into difficulty. With a branch, it will be the home country of the bank which will be exercising primary control over its soundness. The host country to the branch will have little influence, for example, over its capital adequacy, although the Basle Capital Accord should be of some comfort if the home country is applying it properly.

Consequently, some host jurisdictions have enhanced regulation of the branches of foreign banks established there. One approach is to require the foreign bank to establish a subsidiary, or a joint venture with a local bank, which can then be regulated in the same way as local banks. Another approach, falling short of this, is to require that the foreign branch have a minimum, endowment capital—as an assurance against a crisis.[232] In the European Community, the Second Banking Directive obliged Member States to remove capital endowment requirements for branches of banks from other Member States, as being inconsistent with the single market.[233] This encourages cross-border establishment by way of branches.

---

[228] Proposal for a Directive on the supplementary supervision of credit institutions, insurance undertakings and investment firms in a financial conglomerate, COM (2001) 213 final.

[229] 105–8 below.   [230] 438 below.   [231] 13 above.

[232] e.g. F. Malan, 'Contemporary Influences on the Development of South African Banking Law', in J. Norton and M. Andenas (eds.), *Emerging Financial Markets and the Role of International Financial Organisations* (London, Kluwer, 1996).

[233] Art. 6. Now Credit Institutions Directive 2000/12/EC [2000] OJ L126/1, Art. 13.

B. CONSOLIDATED SUPERVISION

At an international level the Basle Committee on Banking Supervision has been addressing the prudential concerns about international banking for the last quarter century. In 1975 it drew up a set of principles—the 1975 Concordat—to guide the division of responsibilities in regulating international banks.[234] In brief these were that the supervision of foreign banking establishments should be the joint responsibility of host- and home-country regulators. No foreign banking establishment should escape regulation, each country ensuring that it is supervised, and each judging that regulation by both it and the other is regular and adequate.

The 1975 Concordat was replaced by the 1983 Concordat which reformulated and supplemented the earlier principles,[235] in particular to take account of the subsequent acceptance of the principle that the soundness of an international bank cannot be fully evaluated unless regulators can examine the totality of its business worldwide, through the technique of consolidation. The principle of consolidated supervision, as the Concordat explained, is that parent banks and parent supervisory authorities monitor the risk exposure of the banks or banking groups for which they are responsible, as well as the adequacy of their capital, on the basis of the totality of their business, wherever conducted. This principle does not imply any lessening of host authorities' responsibilities for supervising foreign bank establishments which operate there. The 1983 Concordat noted that adequate supervision of a bank's foreign establishment calls not only for an appropriate allocation of responsibilities between home and host regulators, but also for contact and co-operation between them.

As with other Basle pronouncements, the 1983 Concordat was soft law. It has depended for its implementation on jurisdictions adopting it and giving it force. Within the European Community, the principle of consolidated supervision became a legal requirement as a result of the First Consolidated Supervision Directive.[236] Consolidated supervision extended to all credit and financial institutions in which the credit institution had a participation—ownership of 25 per cent or more of its capital. (In the 25 to 50 per cent range, there was discretion whether and how consolidation should be implemented.) The Directive imposed the responsibility for consolidated supervision on the home regulator where a parent credit institution (bank) had its head office. However, the Directive applied only where a credit institution (bank) was the ultimate holding company. To ensure that home regulators could perform effective consolidated supervision, the Directive obliged Member States to ensure that the necessary information could be exchanged.

---

[234] These were not publicly available until published in International Monetary Fund, *International Capital Markets: Recent Developments and Short-term Prospects*, Occasional Paper No 7, Aug. 1981, 29.

[235] Committee on Banking Regulations and Supervisory Practices, *Principles for the Supervision of Banks' Foreign Establishments*, Basle, May 1983, reprinted (1983) 22 ILM 901.

[236] 83/350/EEC [1983] OJ L193/18.

C. MAKING CONSOLIDATED SUPERVISION MORE EFFECTIVE

The collapse of the international bank, BCCI, pointed up the inadequacies of cross-border bank regulation, in particular the gaps in the existing system of consolidated supervision. Luxembourg was the home country, but 98 per cent of BCCI's activities occurred elsewhere. Consistently with the 1983 Concordat there was a college of regulators to co-ordinate regulation of the separately incorporated subsidiaries operating in different countries, but BCCI's complex structure enabled it to disguise the real character of important transactions.[237] Moreover, the BCCI affair exposed how international banks could take advantage of the inadequate banking regulation in particular jurisdictions. Indeed, there was an element of the well-known phenomenon in regulation of a 'race to the bottom', since at least some of the jurisdictions in which BCCI operated promised bank secrecy and, at least implicitly, a lax regulatory regime, in order to attract international banking operations.[238] Clearly the Basle Concordat had not worked in requiring host countries to discourage, or forbid, foreign banking operations if the home regulator was inadequate, nor in requiring the home country to extend its supervision or to discourage operations if host-country regulation was ineffective.

The response to BCCI in the Basle Committee on Banking Supervision was to issue in 1992 a supplement to the 1983 Concordat.[239] While the 1983 Concordat was still viewed as sound, the committee recognized that a greater effort was necessary to ensure that its principles were applied in practice. One step was that the committee adopted the view that supervising authorities should undertake an affirmative commitment to co-operate, on a best-effort basis, with supervisors from other countries on all prudential matters pertaining to international banks. More importantly, the committee reformulated certain of the 1983 principles as minimum standards which its members expected each other to observe, and which it hoped all bank regulators would adopt. The minimum standards were designed to provide greater assurances that in the future no international bank could operate without being subject to effective consolidated supervision. In brief, these minimum standards were: (1) all international banks and banking groups should be supervised by a home-country regulator which capably performs consolidated supervision; (2) a cross-border banking establishment must receive the prior consent of both the host-country regulator and the bank's (and if different, banking group's) home-country regulator; (3) home-country bank regulators must have the right to gather information from the cross-border banking establishments of a bank or banking group; and (4) if a host

---

[237] R. Dale, 'Reflections on the BCCI Affair' (1992) 26 *Int'l. L* 949, 950–1; 'Bank Regulation after BCCI' [1993] 1 *JIBL* 8, 11–12.

[238] Cf. C. Bradley, 'Competitive Deregulation of Financial Services Activity in Europe after 1992' (1991) 11 *Oxford J Leg. Stud.* 545.

[239] Basle Committee on Banking Supervision, *Minimum Standards for the Supervision of International Banking Groups and their Cross-border Establishments* (Basle, June 1992).

regulator determined that any one of these minimum standards is not met it could ultimately restrict or prohibit an international bank from operating.

The Basle committee said, in the press release accompanying the 1992 supplement, that groups of countries might apply the minimum standards through negotiated agreements for the harmonization of supervisory rules and mutual recognition. In its view, this had already been achieved in the European Community's banking legislation 'which is fully in keeping with these standards'. Otherwise EC banking law is inconsistent with the minimum standards. Under the Credit Institutions Directive a Member State cannot prevent a bank from another Member State establishing a branch there. This is hardly consistent with minimum standards (2) and (4). Of course the Directive assumes that each Member State of the European Community is capably performing consolidated supervision of its banks, and has full access to information in other Member States, within minimum standards (1) and (3), so that minimum standards (2) and (4) are redundant. History suggests that these are large assumptions.

In the light of the 1992 Basle supplement, and of the more general concerns about the state of bank regulation in Europe following the BCCI collapse, the European Community took several steps. First, it adopted a new Consolidated Supervision Directive.[240] In broad outline, this extends consolidated supervision to non-bank financial holding companies and ensures host-country control where most activity occurs outside the home country. The first is achieved by applying consolidated supervision where a bank (a credit institution) has another bank or a financial institution as a subsidiary, or has a participation in such an institution, or where the parent undertaking of a bank is a financial holding company.[241] A 'financial institution' is an institution, other than a bank, involved in the activities subject to mutual recognition under what is now the Credit Institutions Directive. A 'financial holding company' is a financial institution the subsidiary undertakings of which are either exclusively or mainly bank or financial institutions, one at least of such subsidiaries being a bank. 'Participation' means ownership, directly or indirectly, of 20 per cent or more of the voting rights or capital of an undertaking.[242] In the result, consolidation is not required for banks that are subsidiaries of companies which are neither banks nor financial institutions. Nor is it required for a so-called 'mixed-activity holding company', which is defined as a parent undertaking, other than a financial holding company or a bank, the subsidiaries of which include at least one bank. However, bank regulators must require mixed-activity holding companies and their subsidiaries to supply any information which would be relevant for the purposes of supervising the bank subsidiaries.[243]

The second is achieved by entrusting the task of consolidated supervision to the state which authorizes a parent undertaking, where the parent of a bank is another

---

[240] 92/30/EEC [1992] OJ L110/52. See G. Walker, 'Consolidated Supervision' [1996] *BJIBFL* 74 (pt.1), 132 (pt.2).
[241] Art. 3(1)–(2).   [242] Art. 1.   [243] Art. 6(1).

bank.[244] Where the parent of a bank is a financial holding company, the task of consolidated supervision is given to the Member State which authorized the bank. However, where a financial holding company has bank subsidiaries in more than one Member State, supervision on a consolidated basis is entrusted to the Member State where the financial holding company and one bank have been set up. If the financial holding company has been set up in a Member State in which there is no bank subsidiary, the regulators of a subsidiary (and those in the state in which the financial holding company was set up) must seek an agreement on which is to undertake consolidated supervision. In the absence of such agreement, the matter is delegated to the bank regulators who authorized the bank with the greatest balance sheet total.[245]

Secondly, in 1995, various directives were amended by the post-BCCI Directive to reinforce prudential supervision of international banking groups.[246] Under the Directive the conditions for licensing a bank are expanded: bank regulator must only authorize a bank if the links between it and others are transparent so as to permit the exercise of regulatory functions. Moreover, Member States must require that any bank have its head office in the Member State which has authorized it, and in which it actually carries on its business.

The Basle Core Principles of 1997 codify the current wisdom on supervising international banking groups. On the allocation of responsibilities between bank supervisors it recommends that the home jurisdiction be responsible for supervising all aspects of the bank world-wide, but that those of the host jurisdiction must apply the same high standards as are required of domestic institutions. It also recommends as a key component of consolidated supervision contact and information exchange between host and home supervisors.[247] Moreover, since 1996 a Joint Forum of the Basle Committee on Banking Supervision, the International Organization of Securities Commissioners, and the International Association of Insurance Supervisors has met regularly to discuss supervision of financial conglomerates, primarily those whose large-scale activities cross national boundaries. The joint forum is not a standard setting body but it has made a number of recommendations to the parent bodies on matters such as the sharing on information cross-border (specifically, on the management and key shareholders of individual estates) and identifying a lead supervisor ('co-ordinator') in particular circumstances, but not according to any template.

D. REGULATING INTERNATIONAL BANKS AND THE FUTURE

Prudential regulation of international banks demands effective steps by both home and host countries. Consolidated supervision is one aspect, since it means that a home

---

[244] Art. 4(1).   [245] Art. 4(2).

[246] Prudential Supervision Dir. 95/26/EC [1995] OJ L168/7. For the UK, Financial Institutions (Prudential Supervision) Regulations 1996, SI 1996 No 1669.

[247] *Compendium of Documents Produced by the Joint Forum* (Basle, BIS, 2001). See P. Follack, 'International Harmonisation of Regulatory and Supervisory Frameworks', in M. Giovanoli (ed.), *International Monetary Law* (Oxford, OUP, 2000), 303–5.

country regulator can monitor compliance by an international bank with prudential standards on matters such as capital, large exposures, and investment in the non-financial sector. Consolidated supervision is a brake on banks escaping the prudential standards of a home jurisdiction by moving business into subsidiaries abroad. However, it is no excuse for laxity on the part of host regulators, as the Basle Core Principles make clear. Recent experience shows just how difficult it is to control activities abroad. Host regulators must act boldly against international banks in the event that there are prudential concerns.

Minimum international standards are another aspect of the prudential regulation of international banks. They counter the temptation for home jurisdictions to impose a less burdensome regulation on their banks. This may be designed to avoid their banks facing competitive disadvantages internationally, or it may be positively to foster that jurisdiction as a financial centre. Whatever the reason, it can impose costs on host jurisdictions if these banks fail or, worse, are a source of systemic risk in the host country. Minimum international standards are some assurance to host jurisdictions that home-country regulators are not excessively lax in the standards being imposed.

Yet international prudential standards do not provide a guarantee at present to host countries. First, there is their limited nature and scope. Second is the argument that they need to be put on a sounder legal footing 'than a gentlemen's agreement among central banks'.[248] This, of course, is done within the European Community. Thirdly, and perhaps most importantly, is the question mark over their application in practice. There needs to be some mechanism to provide the assurance that prudential regulation, by both home and host countries, is effective in practice. Co-operation, and now co-ordination between bank regulators in different jurisdictions is only one element of this. Some have argued for a measure of centralization, at least in the European Community, where direct responsibility for the control of larger banks may be placed in the hands of a European-wide regulator.[249] Even if politically feasible, this does not address the problem of the truly international banks. For these a World Financial Authority has been proposed, performing the tasks of authorization, surveillance, guidance, and enforcement, but acting through national regulators as agents.[250] This touching idea has as much chance of realization as pigs have of flying.

---

[248] H. Scott, 'Supervision of International Banking Post-BCCI' (1992) 8 *Georgia SULR* 487. See also S. Key and H. Scott, *International Trade in Banking Services: A Conceptual Framework* (Washington DC, Group of Thirty, Occasional Paper 35, 1991), 37–43.

[249] J.-V. Louis *et al.*, *Banking Supervision in the European Community* (Brussels, Editions de l'Université de Bruxelles, 1995).

[250] J. Eatwell and L. Taylor, *Global Finance at Risk. The Case for International Regulation* (Cambridge, Polity, 2000), 220–4, 228–38.

4

CENTRAL BANKING

Banking lawyers have often taken little interest in central banks. Central banking law, at least in the common law countries, has been regarded as a specialized subject, mainly for public lawyers. But the public lawyers have generally done little, although the debate about the European Central Bank generated a greater interest on their part. There is hardly any literature about central banking law, although that published by the International Monetary Fund is an important starting point for any student.[1] The importance of currency boards in some jurisdictions has also produced a limited legal literature.[2] In a modest way this Chapter attempts to redress the balance. It begins with the obvious point—a central bank stands at the centre of a country's banking system because ultimately it is the central bank which provides liquidity to the commercial banks and thus to the economy as a whole.

I. BANKER TO THE BANKS AND TO GOVERNMENT

A central bank is at the heart of the banking system. This is not only, or even mainly, because the central bank may be entrusted with administering the system of banking regulation discussed in the previous chapter. Rather it is because the central bank is the banks' bank and the government's bank.

A. THE BANKS' BANK

There are various dimensions to this. The first is that in exceptional cases the central bank acts as the lender of last resort to the banks. One aspect which we saw in Chapter 3 was that where a particular institution faces difficulties the central bank may rescue it. Another aspect of a central bank acting as lender of last resort is where there is a shock to the system as a whole, and cash is withdrawn from a range of banks which is not redeposited with other banks (a 'flight to cash'). Such a widespread loss of

---

[1] e.g. R. Effros (ed.), *Current Legal Issues Affecting Central Banks* (Washington, DC, International Monetary Fund, 1992(i), 1994(ii), 1996(iii), 1997(iv), 1998(v)).

[2] e.g. C. Ho, *A Survey of the Institutional and Operational Aspects of Modern-day Currency Boards*, BIS Working Papers, No 110, 2002, 17–19.

confidence is rare, but if it occurs the central bank will provide extra reserves to the banks to avoid a collapse of the system.

Secondly banks, or at least the leading banks, need to have operational accounts with the central bank because, apart from the use of cash (which is impractical), this is the only acceptable way of settling certain obligations.[3] One such obligation is if a bank needs to make payments to government (e.g. for it or its customers' tax bills) and government has its account at the central bank. This involves a flow from the banking sector and thus a movement on the accounts which banks have with the central bank. Another example is if a bank, after netting payments due to other banks against those due to itself, still owes the other banks. Again, only settlement by adjustments to the accounts which banks have with the central bank is acceptable. That the banks have accounts with the central bank for this purpose provides an avenue, as we shall see, for it to administer monetary policy.

Thirdly, banks use the central bank as ordinary customers use their banks, as a source of notes and coins. Indeed the most basic function of a central bank is the issue of currency. Generally the central bank will have the sole right to issue banknotes, although in Britain for historical reasons certain banks in Scotland and Northern Ireland still have a limited right to do so.[4] The right to issue coins may be entrusted to the central bank or, as in Britain, to another body (the mint). In the Eurozone, the European Central Bank has the exclusive right to authorize the issue of banknotes although both the Bank and the national central banks may actually issue the notes— and only such notes have the status of legal tender within the Eurozone. Member States of the Community may issue coins subject to approval of the European Central Bank as to volume. A central bank makes a profit (seigniorage) on the issue of the currency because government deposits securities with the bank to back the issue (hence the usage of the term 'fiduciary issue'). (In Britain all such profits of the Bank of England go to the Treasury under the Currency and Bank Notes Act 1928. By section 2 of the Currency Act 1983 there are some limits on the fiduciary note issue, although these can be varied by a Treasury directive and ultimately a statutory instrument.) These days 'printing money' is a function of the public need for a certain amount of currency, neither a source of revenue for the government nor an instrument of monetary policy. Nonetheless a currency is a potent symbol of a polity's unity, integrity, and perhaps strength. Governments interfere with it at their peril.

B. GOVERNMENT BANKER

As well as being the banks' bank—a point to which we return—the central bank is typically the government's banker. In other words the central bank performs for the

---

[3] Bank of England Act 1998, s. 6, Sched. 2.

[4] Bank Charter Act 1844, s. 10. The last time that a bank could issue banknotes under that section, now repealed, was in 1921. See also Currency and Bank Notes Act 1954, s. 1. There are various statutes for Scotland and Northern Ireland.

government the services a bank ordinarily provides for customers with a current account, notably receiving and making payments and advising and assisting in the operation of the account. In England the Exchequer (which is the central account of the government) is kept by the Treasury at the Bank of England, along with the National Loan Funds (which is the account of the Treasury at the Bank used for loans and advances by government) and various subsidiary accounts.[5] Government departments and agencies may also keep accounts at the commercial banks to facilitate payments to and from the public without breaching the statutory provisions establishing the accounts with the Bank. Government accounts with commercial banks lessen the impact on their liquidity requirements of the large and unpredictable payments from and to the government by the central bank, and hence in and out of the banking sector. This in turn reduces the need for open-market operations.[6]

But the relationship of a central bank to government is not simply that of banker and customer. A central bank may perform a variety of tasks for government which vary in kind from the ordinary relationship. For example the central bank may manage the public debt—issuing, servicing, and redeeming it. Under the National Debt Act 1870 the Bank of England acted in this capacity by advising the government on the issue of its securities (called 'gilts' and Treasury bills in Britain). The Bank was not typical in this regard in Europe; debt management is usually performed elsewhere such as by the ministry of finance. In 1998 the Debt Management Office, which is an executive agency of the Treasury, assumed responsibility for carrying out the government's debt management policy.[7]

In relation to foreign exchange the central bank may be the source of rules: it might license foreign-exchange dealers, administer foreign-exchange controls, and be the compulsory depository of the foreign-exchange earnings of residents.[8] More importantly these days a central bank will be subject to rules, albeit fairly minimal, as it engages in foreign-exchange transactions, either on its own account or as agent of government. For example the Bank of England holds the exchange equalization account on behalf of the Treasury; it is through this that the government could act in the foreign-exchange markets to try to manage the exchange rate of sterling.[9]

The most important role of a central bank *vis-à-vis* government is in giving advice on national economic policy and, significantly, conducting one aspect of it, monetary policy. This part of a central bank's work occupies much of the remainder of this Chapter. The particular prism through which the topic is viewed is the conventional wisdom that central-bank independence is a prerequisite to sound monetary policy.

[5] Exchequer and Audit Departments Act 1866, ss. 10, 18–19; National Loans Act 1968, s. 1 (1).
[6] See N. Schnadt, *European Monetary Union and the Sterling Money Market* (London, City of London Corporation, 1994), 45–7.
[7] United Kingdom Debt Management Office, *Annual Report and Accounts, 2000–01* (London, 2001).
[8] e.g. H. Aufricht, *Comparative Survey of Central Bank Law* (London, Stevens, 1965), 189ff. See *Camdex International Ltd.* v *Bank of Zambia* [1998] QB 22.
[9] Exchange Equalization Account Act 1979, s. 1.

II. THE LEGAL REGIME FOR CENTRAL BANKING

The European Central Bank is strongly independent; the European Community Treaty obliges Member States to bring their central banks into line (although under Protocol II Britain has the option whether to be bound by this); and the International Monetary Fund has pushed the cause of central-bank independence world-wide. The current popularity of the notion has various origins. One lies in the public-choice literature, which sees politicians using monetary expansion as a means of stimulating the economy in the interests of short-term electoral popularity. An independent central bank, it is said, would deprive politicians of the temptation to take this easy path. In fact the evidence that monetary policy follows the electoral cycle is thin.

More important are two strands of the mainstream economic literature. One is the evidence suggesting that in the medium to long term inflation does not contribute to positive economic performance.[10] In other words, the Phillips curve, which shows an inverse relationship between inflation and unemployment, does not hold in the medium to long term. In the short term, however, it is clear that the relationship does hold—recessions have repeatedly followed tighter monetary policy and output has been stimulated by accelerating monetary growth. Primarily it seems that this occurs because wages and prices are sticky, i.e. it is difficult to reduce nominal levels.[11] The policy recommendation which follows, however, is that to deliver economic growth monetary growth must be stable and the best way of ensuring this is through an independent central bank. The other string to the argument is the evidence that the average rate of inflation has tended to be lower in countries with an independent central bank.[12] Correlation is not causation, so that the relationship (such as it is) may reflect third factors, such as fiscal restraint and political stability.[13] As well, there is the way hyper-inflation seared itself into the public consciousness in Germany, which led both to the creation of an independent Bundesbank and to the almost universal determination to keep inflation low. Clearly changes on the supply side of the economy are also critical.

With these various matters as background let us turn to the legal regime for central banks. Various dimensions are examined: the status of the central bank, its structure and the goals set for it, and the extent to which the central bank must fund the government deficit.

---

[10] See especially C. Goodhart, *The Central Bank and the Financial System* (London, Macmillan, 1995), 60ff.

[11] S. Fischer, 'Modern Central Banking', in F. Capie *et al.*, *The Future of Central Banking* (New York, Cambridge University Press, 1994), 269.

[12] e.g. A. Cukierman, *Central Bank Strategy, Credibility, and Independence: Theory and Evidence* (Cambridge, Mass., MIT Press, 1992), chs. 19–23; C. Briault *et al.*, 'Central Bank Independence and Accountability: Theory and Evidence', *Bank of England Q Bull.*, v.36, No 1, Feb. 1996.

[13] R. Lastra, *Central Banking and Banking Regulation* (London, FMG, 1996), 22.

A. STATUS

In its narrow sense the legal status of a central bank is not explicitly relevant to its functioning. For example, the Bank of England is constituted a body corporate by its 1694 charter. The 1946 legislation nationalizing it transferred all its shares to a person nominated by the Treasury (in fact, the Treasury Solicitor),[14] and constituted as members of the body corporate not only that person, but also the governor, the deputy governor (both appointed for five-year terms) and the directors (appointed for four-year terms) even though they hold none of the capital.[15] These peculiar arrangements cannot be said of themselves to cause the Bank to conduct monetary and other policy any differently than if the Bank were like many other central banks, a body corporate constituted by statute.

In broader terms the legal status of a central bank indicates its place in the scheme of government. Near one end of the scale was the Bank of England before 1998.[16] It was quite explicitly subject to political direction: the Treasury was empowered under section 4(1) of the 1946 Act to give such directions to the Bank as it thought necessary in the public interest. Albeit that this very wide discretion could only be exercised after consultation with the governor of the Bank, and that a direction under this section had never been given, the legal position reflected the fact that the Bank lacked autonomy in the formulation and implementation of monetary policy. Yet the long history of the Bank and its pre-eminent position in the City of London meant that its views had an authority and weight belied by the legal position.

Contrast the position of those central banks near the other end of the scale, the independence of which is constitutionally guaranteed. Constitutions are generally speaking less readily amendable than statutes. Under the Constitution in South Africa the Reserve Bank's primary objective is protecting the value of the currency in the interests of balanced and sustained economic growth. In pursuit of this objective, the Bank must:

perform its functions independently and without fear, favour or prejudice, but there must be regular consultation betwen the Bank and the Cabinet Minister responsible for national financial matters.[17]

Section 225 says that the powers and functions of the South African Reserve Bank are those customarily exercised and performed by central banks.

Equally well protected is the independence of the European Central Bank, since the Member States of the European Community have undertaken by treaty to respect its independence. Article 108 of the EC Treaty reads:

When exercising the powers and carrying out the tasks and duties conferred upon them

---

[14] Bank of England (Transfer of Stock) Order 1946, S.R. & O. 1946, No 238.
[15] Bank of England Act 1946, ss. 1(1)(a), 2(1), 3(2).
[16] See also G. Miller, 'Decision-Making at the Bank Japan' (1996) 28 *L & P Int'l Bus* 1.
[17] Constitution of the Republic of South Africa, 1996, s. 224(2). See J. Leape, M. Ramos, and L. Thomas (eds.), *Central Bank Independence in Emerging Economies* (London, Macmillan, 1997).

by this Treaty and the Statute of the ESCB, neither the ECB, nor a national central bank, nor any member of their decision-making bodies shall seek or take instructions from Community institutions or bodies, from any government of a Member State or from any other body. The Community institutions and bodies and the governments of the Member States undertake to respect this principle and not to seek to influence the members of the decision-making bodies of the ECB or of the national central banks in the performance of their tasks.

This independence is underpinned by the eight-year terms of appointment for the president, vice-president, and other members of the executive board of the Bank coupled with the protection that they can be removed only for cause found by the European Court of Justice.[18] To amend a multilateral treaty like the EC Treaty is as difficult to amend as a constitutional provision.

Along the scale lies the Bank of England. As a result of the Bank of England Act 1998, it has what has been described as 'operational independence'. Economists sometimes call this 'instrument independence', in that the Bank has discretion in the use of monetary policy instruments to reach its goal. Monetary policy instruments are used to influence short-term interest rates, which in turn have an effect (with time lags) on inflation. The Bank does not have 'goal' or 'target independence'. Section 11 of the Act specifies the objectives of the Bank in relation to monetary policy. Under the Act the Treasury are obliged to give notice to the Bank as to what these objectives entail. Within these constraints, however, the Bank is free from the political direction to which it was theoretically subject under the 1946 Act: the power to give a direction under section 4(1) of the 1946 Act may not be used in relation to monetary policy. There is an exception for emergency situations, where the Treasury have a reserve power to direct the Bank with respect to monetary policy if satisfied that such action is required by the public interest and by extreme economic circumstances. The reserve power is exercisable only after consultation with the Governor of the Bank and in accordance with the special procedures applying to an order under the section. These overarching powers are one reason that, as a matter of law, the legislation is not compatible with the criteria for independence in the EC Treaty. However, the reserve power will be rarely exercisable. Extreme economic circumstances include war or a major catastrophe which affect the nation and have an impact on economic circumstances, or a major catastrophe which affects another economy closely related to the British economy. There have not been extreme economic circumstances, within the terms of the Act, in the previous 25 years: neither the Gulf War nor the cessation of British membership of the European exchange rate mechanism in 1992 qualify.

A central bank's status, in the broad sense of this term, inevitably raises the issue of

---

[18] EC Treaty, Art. 112; Statute of the ESCB and ECB (contained in EC Treaty as Protocol 18 and hereafter ECB Statute), Arts. 11.2, 11.4, 23. See R. Smits, 'Central Bank Independence and Accountability in the Light of EMU', in M. Giovanoli (ed.), *International Monetary Law* (Oxford, OUP, 2000); C. Zilioli and M. Selmayr, *The Law of the European Central Bank* (Oxford, Hart, 2001). Cf. R. Torrent, 'Whom is the European Central Bank the Central Bank Of?' (1999) 36 *CMLR* 1229.

accountability.[19] At the least it should justify its policies to the public and the public should be able to monitor its performance and call it to account in the event of its failure to achieve its goals (which can be called 'narrow accountability'). Transparency can occur through explicit goal setting, information disclosure, and appearances before parliamentary committees. Given the important economic and distributional consequences of central-bank action there is an argument for an additional dimension to accountability, a capacity on the part of the public to override existing monetary policy in the event that its consequences become unacceptable (what can be called 'broad accountability').

Few central banks which are formally independent have explicit mechanisms for accountability in either its narrow or broad sense. Under the EC Treaty the position of the European Central Bank is that it must present an annual report to the Council of Ministers and the European Parliament, which may hold a general debate on it.[20] But otherwise there are a range of institutional provisions insulating the Bank from controls.[21] There has been criticism of the lack of transparency of the Bank, although it is fair to note that it is more transparent than the Bundesbank ever was.[22] By contrast with the European Central Bank, transparency in decision-making is a notable feature of the Bank of England Act 1998. The Bank must publish, as soon as practicable after a meeting of the Monetary Policy Committee, a statement as to what action was decided on (s. 14(1)). The exception is if the decision is to meet the monetary policy objectives through interventions in financial markets, and immediate publication would impede or frustrate such intervention. Nonetheless, as soon as practicable after the Committee has decided that publication would no longer have that market-sensitive quality, the Bank must publish details of its decision on such intervention.

As well as publication of decisions, the Act also provides for publication of minutes of meetings of the Monetary Policy Committee, no more than six weeks later, with members' voting preferences indicated (s. 15(1)). The delay of up to six weeks is to prevent financial markets pre-empting the Committee's decisions by using the minutes of one meeting to draw conclusions about what will be decided at the next. Again there is an exception in the case of market-sensitive information about intervention in financial markets, although in line with section 14 this information must be published within six weeks of any statement of the relevant decision under that section. The policy behind the section is greater accountability: observers and commentators will be able to see the reasoning behind particular decisions on monetary policy and how each member voted.

---

[19] See T. Daintith, 'Between Domestic Democracy and an Alien Rule of Law. Some Thoughts on the "Independence" of the Bank of England' [1995] *PL* 118.

[20] Art. 113; ECB Statute, Art. 15.3; P. Magnette, 'Towards "Accountable Independence"? Parliamentary Controls of the European Central Bank and the Rise of a New Democratic Model' (2000) 6 *ELJ* 326.

[21] See H. Hahn, 'The European Central Bank: Key to European Monetary Union or Target?' (1991) 28 *CML Rev.* 783, 803–10.

[22] See A. Blinder, C. Goodhart, P. Hildebrand, D. Lipton, and C. Wyplosz, *How Do Central Banks Talk?* Geneva Reports on the World Economy No 3 (London, CEPR, 2001).

Unusually for an independent central bank the Reserve Bank of New Zealand Act of 1989 contains detailed provisions for accountability. Narrow accountability is based on the agreed targets, described below. The legislation places a statutory duty on the governor to ensure that the actions of the Bank in implementing monetary policy are consistent with the targets.[23] Most significantly the governor can be removed from office if his performance is inadequate in ensuring that the Bank achieves its targets or if a policy statement is inconsistent with the Bank's primary function or the targets.[24] Broad accountability turns importantly on the override mechanism set out in the legislation: the government can direct the Bank to formulate and implement monetary policy for an objective other than price stability for renewable periods up to a year. The relevant order must be published.[25] Presumably the drafters contemplated that the power would be used sparingly, perhaps if serious foreign exchange problems arose, because of the crisis it would probably provoke.

B. STRUCTURE OF CENTRAL BANKS

In a narrow sense the structure of a central bank can contribute indirectly to its accountability (what can be called 'indirect accountability'). For example its board of directors could include representatives of different economic, social, or regional interests. The more representative the board the more likely that its pursuit of monetary policy will win acceptance in the community. As a matter of law there is no pretence that the directors of the Bank of England are representative. Appointments are in the government's discretion—government ministers and civil servants cannot be appointed directors; nor can the directors be full-time employees of the Bank except for the Governor and two deputy Governors; and there are certain formal disqualifications (e.g. insolvency).[26] As a matter of practice, apart from the Bank itself the directors are drawn mainly from the banks and from commerce and industry. The justification for appointing bankers and business people is, of course, the expertise which such directors bring.[27] (The 1998 Charter provides for the disclosure of a director's conflicting interests and his or her abstention.) The director of the Consumers' Association was appointed in 1998. A leading trade unionist had been appointed after 1946, none was appointed 1994–8, but the practice was revived in 1998. At the time of writing four of the nine directors are women.

Contrast the legal position elsewhere. The constitutive laws for the European Central Bank guarantee regional representation. Under Article 112 of the EC Treaty the governing council of the European Central Bank will comprise members of the executive board and the governors of each of the national central banks. Interestingly, the European Parliament must be consulted about appointments to the executive

[23] S. 11. See D. Flint, 'Central Bank Reform: The Reserve Bank of New Zealand', in M. Giovanoli (ed.), *op cit.*

[24] S. 49(2)(d), (f).   [25] S. 12(6).

[26] Bank of England Act 1998, Sched. 1.

[27] e.g., *Committee on the Working of the Monetary System*, Cmnd. 827, 1959, para. 783.

board; however board members must be persons of recognized standing and professional experience in monetary or banking matters.[28] In the United States legislation goes beyond regional to emphasize social and economic representation. For example, in appointing the seven governors of the Federal Reserve System, with the advice and consent of the Senate, the president 'shall have due regard to a fair representation of the financial, agricultural, industrial, and commercial interests, and geographical divisions of the country'.[29] Of the directors of each federal reserve bank three are chosen by and are representative of the stock-holding banks, and the six others represent the public and are elected with due, but not exclusive, consideration to the interests of agriculture, commerce, industry, services, labour, and consumers.[30]

In the UK the Bank exercises its operational independence through a specially constituted Monetary Policy Committee. Section 13 of the Bank of England Act 1998 establishes the Committee, which comprises the Governor, the two Deputy Governors, and six other members, two of whom are the Bank officials responsible for monetary policy analysis and monetary policy operations respectively. These two are appointed by the Governor, after consultation with the Chancellor. The Chancellor appoints the remaining four members of the Committee. Before appointing these persons, the Chancellor must be satisfied that they have knowledge or experience which is likely to be relevant to the Committee's functions. The appointment of these outsiders ensures that a broader range of opinion and expertise determines monetary policy than if the decisions were left within the Bank alone.

Schedule 3 sets out details relating to its membership and operations. The Committee must meet at least once a month (para. 10) and decisions are taken by a majority vote (para. 11). A Treasury representative may attend and speak at any meeting of the Committee (para. 13), an efficient method of conveying the government's latest views on the economy. Section 16 obliges the sub-committee of the court of directors of the Bank, constituted under section 3 of the Act, to keep under review the procedures followed by the Committee. In particular they must determine whether the Committee has collected the regional, sectoral, and other information necessary for the purposes of its monetary policy functions. There is no doubt that in making monetary policy, central banks need an extensive network of information gathering. Information must not only come from the banking sector, but from companies and elsewhere. The Bank's agents around the country collect such information.

C. CENTRAL BANK OBJECTIVES

The contemporary wisdom is that a central bank should have a single objective for monetary policy—price stability. This anti-inflation objective is coupled with the cause of central-bank independence. With this clear objective, it is said, an independent central bank will promote confidence in its monetary policy and dampen inflationary expectations. The European Central Bank, following the Bundesbank

---

[28] Art. 112.2(b).   [29] 12 USC §241.   [30] 12 USC §302.

model, has as its primary objective the maintenance of price stability, although, without prejudice to that objective, it shall support the general economic policies in the Community with a view to contributing to the broad goals which the Community has set for itself.[31] The objectives of the Bank of England's monetary policy set out in section 11 of the Bank of England Act 1998 are to maintain price stability (the primary objective) and, subject to that, to support the government's economic policy, including its objectives for growth and employment (the secondary objective). Price stability as a goal concentrates on the domestic value of the currency: it connotes low inflation. One justification for this these days is that while monetary policy is an important factor in the nominal exchange rate, as a result of speculative attacks in international markets the external value of a currency may not be clearly related to a country's economic performance. While desirable, then, a stable and competitive exchange rate is not a primary goal for the Bank, although as part of the government's economic policy it may be a secondary goal. Price stability as the primary objective is something to be achieved over the medium to long term. Pursuing short-term inflation targeting could destabilize the real economy. For example, were there to be very high inflation it is clear that the Bank might not be able to reduce it immediately. Similarly, if there were to be an external shock to the economy, such as a dramatic rise in oil prices or a fall in the stock market, it might be damaging to deflate the economy in order to achieve quickly the goal of price stability. Price stability is the primary goal. The goal of supporting the government's economic policy is 'subject to that'. In essence, the Bank must pursue price stability, and in so far as this is not inconsistent with the government's economic policy, must act in a way supportive of that. Were there to be an incompatibility between the objectives of price stability and supporting government economic policy, as a matter of law the latter would need to give way. In practice the two are inextricably linked: the government sees price stability as a precondition of high and stable levels of growth and employment, which in turn will help to create the conditions for price stability on a sustainable basis.

Three comments can be made about the notion of a central bank having the single objective of price stability. First, some well-established central banks moulded by the Keynesianism of the immediate period after World War II, place an emphasis on goals additional to price stability, such as maximum employment.[32] Where a central bank has such multiple goals there is a potential difficulty that in particular circumstances they may be in conflict, at least in the short run. One consequence is that it becomes more difficult to call the bank to account for a failure to achieve its goals, unless the goals have been placed in some sort of hierarchy. Even if the legislative mandate does not establish a priority between different goals, inevitably the central bank will need to do so. As a matter of law there is no necessary obstacle to this since, as so widely expressed, the goals are exhortatory rather than justiciable.

That leads to the second point, that without more specification even the single goal

---

[31] Art. 105(1). See also Protocol 3, Arts. 2, 3a.
[32] 12 USC s. 225a (US Federal Reserve); Reserve Bank Act 1959 (Australia), s. 10(2).

of price stability is incapable of any sort of enforcement or, to put it another way, the bank cannot be held accountable for not achieving it. For accountability to occur there needs to be an elaboration of the goal, taking into account that what others do may have a bearing on price stability; that in any event there will be time lags; and that there may be uncertainties in determining whether price stability has been achieved. There also needs to be a mechanism for calling to account in the event that it is not achieved. Under the Bank of England Act 1998 the government must specify for the Bank what it means by 'price stability' and what its 'economic policy' is taken to be. The government has set an inflation target, which the Bank must meet by setting short-term interest rates, as 2½ per cent, defined by the 12-month increase in the retail price index excluding mortgage interest payments. The target is symmetric, in the sense that inflation below the target is as undesirable as inflation above.

Under section 12 the government must set the inflation target once every 12 months. In this sense the Bank does not have the goal or target independence of some central banks e.g. the European Central Bank. The arguments against goal independence relate to democratic accountability. Rather the Bank has operational independence to reach the inflation target set by government. By virtue of the section, however, the government can reset the target in its discretion. Were it to do this too frequently—in fact, it has not—the Bank's operational independence would be affected. Thus time lags before changes in short-term interest rates take effect in the economy would mean uncertainty about whether the Bank had ever hit the government's targets.

Thirdly, even if price stability is the primary goal of a central bank, to which all other goals are subordinate, that is not the end of the story. A central bank must be concerned with other goals quite apart from any responsibility it has for bank regulation. Financial stability is one, for without a sound financial system the bank's monetary policy, such as price stability, will not be effective. Aspects of financial stability include an efficient system for payments and settlement, efficient and reliable financial markets, and sound financial intermediaries.[33] A sound financial system also means that a central bank can economize on its acting as lender of last resort.

III. INSTRUMENTS OF MONETARY POLICY

Let us turn to the modern instruments of monetary policy. Even if central banks lack goal independence—central banks such as the European Central Bank have their goal of price stability set for them, although, because that concept needs elucidation, we have seen how they may have some flexibility in setting the requisite targets—they might have a choice of the avenues available to reach it ('instrument independence').

---

[33] 'The Financial Stability Conjuncture and Outlook', *Bank of England Financial Stability Review*, June 2001, 97–101.

Fashion has a role in the use of monetary instruments; the trend has been away from regulatory to market instruments.

Regulatory instruments can be characterized as direct or indirect. Direct regulation seeks to control directly the amount of money and credit provided through the banking system. Thus, in the past the Bank of England required the banks to adopt particular deposit-taking and lending policies. Quantitative requirements were used at one time—that a bank's rate of growth for interest-bearing deposits should not exceed a maximum, or that a bank's new lending over the next six months (say) should not exceed a specified amount, whatever the increase in the bank's deposit base. Qualitative directives have also been used, advising the banks to lend to some sectors of the economy rather than others. Direct regulation is transparent and quickly effective, although it will soon lead to distortions.

Reserve requirements are an indirect regulatory instrument: the banks must maintain minimum reserves, notably in cash and liquid assets with the central bank, which the latter can vary in the light of monetary conditions. The size of the reserves clearly determines the volume of money in circulation and the extent to which a bank can itself extend credit to its customers. In England the legal basis for minimum reserves, as with direct regulation, lies in the power of the government under section 4(3) of the 1946 Act to approve the issue of directives supporting recommendations made by the Bank of England to bankers. In fact no order has ever been made defining banker for the purposes of the section and no directive issued. Nonetheless banks have complied when the Bank has laid down reserve ratios.[34] Elsewhere the law is much more explicit in endowing central banks with the power to set minimum reserves, for example as a ratio of designated liabilities.[35] Non-compliance is visited by the levying of penalty interest rates and other sanctions. Although the European Central Bank has the potential to use minimum reserves as an instrument of monetary policy once the Council of Ministers has defined the basis for doing so, indicative of the current trend is that the Reserve Bank of New Zealand Act has been shorn of the power to use them. Certainly reserve requirements cannot regularly be varied because of the disruption which would be caused to banks, and they can also lead to distortions: for example a bank may book deposits in its branches in jurisdictions with lower or no reserve requirements. This was one reason that the Euromarkets developed, to avoid US reserve requirements.

Contract provides the legal basis for the primary method used these days in most developed countries to implement monetary policy (these methods are less effective in countries without developed financial institutions). Recall the nature of commercial banking—largely illiquid loans as assets but depositors who are entitled fairly readily to pay away or otherwise withdraw funds. At any particular time a bank will find it impossible to predict precisely whether, as a result of banking activities, it will be in a net credit or debit position. Banks in a net debit position can borrow from

[34] See *Monetary Control*, Cmnd. 7858 (London, HMSO, 1980).
[35] e.g. ECB Statute, Art. 19.

other banks on the interbank market, but can also seek liquidity from the central bank. This a central bank provides by engaging in money-market transactions with the banks, for example purchasing (discounting) commercial bills selling and repurchasing government securities (repos), or providing credit directly by way of an advance. A central bank can affect monetary conditions by varying the rates for these transactions (e.g. the discount for purchasing instruments) or the type of transactions it will contemplate (e.g. what is eligible for sale/repurchase; the security required for credit). Thus in England when the government announces that interest rates are being lowered or raised—the main tool these days to implement monetary policy—it is primarily the discount rate which is being changed. This will typically, in turn, produce a change in the base rates of the banks.

Modern open-market operations, developed in the United States in the 1920s, rely heavily on the buying and selling of government securities. In purchasing them a central bank makes payments to the sellers, which, when deposited with banks, enable the latter to create more money by increasing lending. Conversely, when a central bank sells government securities the money supply contracts. The technique is almost infinitely flexible. For example switching short-term with longer-term securities can lead to a contraction in the money supply if longer-term debt is held more outside the banking sector. The Statute for the European Central Bank contemplates that it will conduct open market operations

by buying and selling outright (spot or forward) or under re-purchase agreement and by lending or borrowing claims and marketable instruments, whether in Community or in non-Community currencies, as well as precious metals.[36]

IV. FINANCING GOVERNMENT

Limiting the extent to which a central bank can finance the government acts as a brake on the latter's budgetary policies, and encourages economic rectitude. If the terms of such financing are more favourable than those available on domestic or foreign markets, this implies a lower cost for the government in funding its budget but a burden (perhaps losses) for the central bank. Easier finance for government may lead to financial imprudence on its part. Moreover, a central bank which must finance government will be tempted to do so by printing money. There is an obvious inflationary potential in doing so.

Legal controls on a central bank financing the government are thus a common feature of banking and finance law.[37] To be effective all forms of loans to and other credit transactions with government need to be covered by the law. For example if the

---

[36] Art. 18.1. See European Central Bank, *The Monetary Policy of the ECB* (Frankfurt, ECB, 2001), ch. 4.

[37] A. Leone, 'Effectiveness and Implications of Limits on Central Bank Credit to the Government', in P. Downes and R. Vaez-Zadeh (eds.), *The Evolving Role of Central Banks* (Washington, IMF, 1991).

central bank purchases government securities this may have the same economic effect as lending government the money, although, as a matter of law, it has a quite different character. However, purchasing government securities may be an aspect of open-market operations rather than to fund government. Limits on the former may therefore be expressed to exclude open-market operations. To the extent that the law limits a central bank financing government through cash advances or the purchase of its securities, the bank's independence is enhanced. Its financial position is more secure and it is able to pursue monetary policy more independently of fiscal policy.

The strictest limit on a central bank financing government is an absolute prohibition; it is incorporated in Article 101.1 of the EC Treaty for the European Central Bank (the ECB):

Overdraft facilities or any other type of credit facility with the ECB or with the central banks of the Member States (hereinafter referred to as 'national central banks') in favour of Community institutions or bodies, central governments, regional, local or other public authorities, other bodies governed by public law, or public undertakings of Member States shall be prohibited, as shall the purchase directly from them by the ECB or national central banks of debt instruments.

The use of 'directly' in this Article is designed to exempt open-market operations. Unfortunately this was not done explicitly, for as it is expressed one can easily conceive of schemes which, while in breach of its spirit, would not be in breach of its letter (for example warehousing a purchase by a central bank through a commercial bank).

At the other end of the spectrum are laws which impose few, if any, limits (although as a matter of practice there may be quite definite limits). At one time loans by the Bank of England to the Crown required the authority of Parliament,[38] but under section 12 of the National Loans Act 1968 the Bank may lend the Treasury any sums which the latter has power to borrow.[39] If Britain moves to the third stage of European monetary union then, consistently with Article 101.1 of the EC Treaty, the government will have to abandon this possibility.

Intermediate between these two positions are those laws which permit a central bank to advance cash to, or purchase the securities of, government, but impose limits on amount, maturity, or conditions. Explicit limits on the amount advanced can be expressed variously as a proportion of the central bank's own capital or liabilities or as a percentage of government expenditure or (most commonly) revenues. The Federal Reserve system in the United States provides an illustration of how maturity conditions can be controlled: unless they are purchased on the open market, a federal reserve bank cannot purchase US government securities having a maturity from the date of purchase exceeding six months.[40] Among the important conditions attached to advances to a government is whether it must pay market rates.

---

[38] Bank of England Act 1819, s. 1.

[39] S. 12(7). Most loans and advances by government to bodies (e.g. local authorities) are financed from the National Loans Fund, which is an account of the Treasury at the Bank of England.

[40] 12 USC §355.

V. CONCLUSIONS

By comparison with many other jurisdictions, there is in Britain less law governing central banking.[41] Partly it is history. Partly it is attributable to the success of the Bank of England in achieving its goals through a combination of economic power and moral suasion. The exercise of economic power is most obvious with open-market operations. Moral suasion derives from the authority which the Bank has acquired over the centuries, and possibly also from a belief on the part of some that non-compliance with the Bank's wishes may be visited by sanctions either formal (e.g. the exercise of powers under FSMA 2000) or informal (e.g. a denial of lender-of-last-resort facilities). Ultimately of course the Bank has had the long-stop of its powers under section 4(3) of the 1946 Act to direct the banks. That it has never done so probably weakens the threat, because to invoke it now would be seen as very drastic.

That leads naturally to the much discussed issue of independence for central banks, independence coupled with the goal of price stability. Without reaching a definite conclusion on this issue a number of points can be made. First, there is the vexed issue of what independence means. Secondly, there is the obvious recognition that, even if a central bank is independent as a matter of law, in fact, because of, say, the way appointments to its board are made it can hardly be said to be independent of government. Thirdly, independence must in a democratic society be coupled with mechanisms of accountability.[42] Information disclosure (transparency) is but one aspect of accountability; it enables the activities of the bank to be monitored. The New Zealand override provisions are another aspect, in recognizing that price stability at all costs is not a virtue. It is fair to point out that in this respect there have been override provisions in other central-bank laws for some considerable time.[43] Yet a third aspect of accountability is when the board of directors has some pretensions to represent different interests in the community, rather than, as used to be the case of the Bank of England, being a closed shop for merchant bankers. A more representative board, as with the other dimensions of accountability, can be justified on the basis, not only that in a democratic society accountability is to be expected of powerful institutions such as the central bank, but also because it means that monetary policy is more likely to be effective by winning public acceptance.

Apart from the question of independence is the matter of the objectives set for monetary policy. Price stability is, as we have seen, the fashionable, sometimes even the only, goal. Yet as a goal it needs spelling out. Hence the popularity of targets. The monetary aggregates used in the 1980s are no longer considered valid and replaced by inflationary targets. Let us put aside the desirability of inflationary targets, or at least

---

[41] See the seminal article by Professor Daintith, 'The Functions of Law in the Field of Short-term Economic Policy' (1976) 92 *LQR* 62.

[42] L. Gormley and J. de Haan, 'The Democratic Deficit of the European Central Bank' (1996) 21 *EL Rev.* 95.

[43] e.g. Bank of Canada Act, RS, 1985, c. B-2, s. 14.

the figures chosen, to examine implementation. The monetary instruments are ready to hand, although in countries with underdeveloped financial systems and financial institutions, regulatory controls rather than market techniques are still necessary (e.g. open-market operations). But how is implementation to be better guaranteed? Partly we return to the scene of accountability—central banks must be monitored in their task of achieving targets and called to account for incompetence in doing so. But can it be said that the legalism of the New Zealand model is more effective in ensuring competence than more traditional central-bank laws? Attaching personal responsibility to the governor of a central bank if targets are not achieved has surely only a symbolic function. Moreover, as important as the competence of the central bank in whether targets are reached are the actions of government. One relevant aspect examined is the extent to which a central bank is expected to fund the government's deficit. More generally, monetary policy needs to be co-ordinated with fiscal and budgetary policies, for a failure in the latter can subvert the former.

PART II

BANKS AND
THEIR CUSTOMERS

5

THE BANK–CUSTOMER
RELATIONSHIP

So far the focus of attention has been on the banks themselves and on bank regulators and the central bank. This Chapter introduces another character into the plot, the customer, and brings a change of scene, the services which banks offer customers. Consistently with our theme, however, that banking law must align itself with modern banking practice, the customer in this book plays many roles and the services which banks provide are painted with a broad brush.

The Chapter begins by filling in some of the details about the customers of banks and modern banking services. In this context it gives attention to how the relationship between banks and their customers may be characterized as a matter of law. Contract emerges from this as the overarching feature of the relationship, and so the second and third sections of the Chapter are given over to banking contracts and their regulation. The final part of the Chapter turns to a specific banking service, the taking of deposits. Historically this has been the core banking service, and we have seen how deposit-taking features in any definition of banking. However, the private law governing deposit-taking is well established and largely uncontroversial. Those desirous of knowing more about its finer points must look elsewhere.

I. BANK CUSTOMERS AND BANKING SERVICES

A. MATTERS OF DEFINITION

The concept of customer is used in this book in a wide sense to describe anyone who deals with a bank in relation to a banking service. Those with accounts are customers, but so too are borrowers and those using the bank for financial advice, fund management, securities and derivatives dealings, and so on. Customers can be other banks and market counterparties, commercial customers, and private customers. The relationship of banks to other banks was considered in Chapter 2: the focus of this Chapter is on the second and third categories of customers.

The conventional view is that 'customer' has a technical meaning, which leads to lengthy discussions of who is or is not a bank's customer. In fact the only reason that

English courts have thought that question to be legally relevant is because of the protection given in the Bills of Exchange Act 1882, and subsequently in section 4 of the Cheques Act 1957, when banks collect cheques to which a 'customer' has a defective title. Customer is undefined in the legislation, and it has been necessary to decide whether the rogues and others who bank such cheques fall within the ambit of the term. If not, the banks are exposed to actions in conversion by the true owners of the cheques. Ultimately the courts have decided that anyone who opens an account, rogue or angel, is a customer for the purposes of statutory protection.[1] A foreign bank sending a cheque to a bank for collection within the jurisdiction is also a customer for these purposes.

Whether a person is a customer in the sense of having an account with a bank is legally irrelevant to the many other, and more important, issues discussed in this book. The duty of confidentiality is certainly not confined to account holders. Nor is bank liability for faulty advice or breach of fiduciary duty. Having an account with a bank indicates a contractual relationship, which can obviously found remedies, but so too can the myriad of other contracts which banks make with customers. It is a trite point, but worth making, that banks can enter these many other contracts with customers who do not have an account with them.

The concept of the multi-functional bank immediately conjures up the image of a bank providing many different types of service. Deposit-taking is basic, albeit mundane. Coupled with deposit-taking is giving effect to customers' payment instructions, the subject matter of Part III of the book. Bank financing (Part IV) encompasses a variety of techniques, from the simple overdraft through trade finance to sophisticated project financings. Already we have seen how important are the securities and derivatives activities of modern banks. In this regard banks conduct much business for their own account, but they also act for customers on securities and derivatives markets, as investment managers and as custodians.

The legal ramifications of banks providing these various services are dealt with throughout the book. However, some general points ought to be mentioned here. First, unless contractually bound banks are free in the main to decide whether or not they will provide a particular service to customers. As a matter of English law customers with current accounts are entitled by implied contract to demand cash over the bank's counter and to have cheques honoured and collected. Banks habitually provide other services to account customers—standing orders, direct debits, letters of credit, and so on—but it is not clear whether they are legally obliged to do so. A sensible rule would be to say that banks are obliged to provide modern payment services functionally equivalent to cheques, but that is all. Secondly, if a bank provides a service to customers it is entitled to reasonable remuneration, if that has not been agreed. This principle derives from the general law.[2]

The third general point concerns the scope of banking business. There are

---

[1] e.g. *Commissioner of Taxation* v. *English, Scottish and Australian Bank Ltd.* [1920] AC 683 (PC).
[2] Supply of Goods and Services Act 1982, s. 15.

authorities, in the nineteenth and early twentieth centuries, which suggest that investment advice falls outside the scope of banking business.[3] A leading banking law text still contains the statement, attributable to its original author, that an arrangement like that examined in a 1920 decision,[4] whereby the bank would supervise the customer's business, especially the financial side, and take all reasonable steps to maintain his credit and reputation, while he was away on war service, 'can hardly be said to be within the scope of banking business'.[5] In fact it cannot be said as a matter of law whether or not a particular service is within the scope of banking business. What is or is not a matter constituting banking business must always be a question of fact, depending on what the bank has agreed to do. It is quite clear nowadays, and it was probably the case in 1918, that investment advice is the common practice of bankers. Supervising a customer's business may be unusual, but not impossible. In these days of the multifunctional bank the scope of banking business seems, as a matter of practice, to be infinitely elastic.

B. CHARACTERIZING THE BANK–CUSTOMER RELATIONSHIP

Foley v. *Hill*[6] was a historical breakthrough when, in 1848, the House of Lords held that the banker–customer relationship was essentially a debtor–creditor relationship. This characterization was obviously crucial, for it enabled banks to treat money deposited with them as their own. All they were obliged to do was to return an equivalent amount. Rival characterizations—bailment, trust, or agency—would have precluded this. Bailment would in the nineteenth century have obliged the return of the very things deposited and would have had no application with payments into a customer's bank account by book entry. Trust and agency would have limited how the moneys could be employed. Instead, as Lord Cottenham LC noted, the characterization of the bank as debtor meant the

money placed in the custody of a banker is, to all intents and purposes, the money of the banker, to do with it as he pleases; he is guilty of no breach of trust in employing it; he is not answerable to the principal if he puts it into jeopardy, if he engages in a hazardous speculation; he is not bound to keep it or deal with it as the property of his principal; but he is, of course, answerable for the amount, because he has contracted, having received that money, to repay to the principal, when demanded, a sum equivalent to that paid into his hands.[7]

In the modern day, the characterization of the customer's claim as debt has also been proffered as a basis for enabling it to be traced at common law into its product (e.g. money taken out by a fraudster).[8]

Yet it was quickly apparent that the debtor–creditor characterization was only part

---

[3] *Banbury* v. *Bank of Montreal* [1918] AC 626 (HL) is the leading case.

[4] *Wilson* v. *United Counties Bank Ltd.* [1920] AC 102 (HL).

[5] M. Hapgood (ed.), *Paget's Law of Banking* (11th edn., London, Butterworths, 1996), 130.

[6] (1848) 2 HLC 28, 9 ER 1002.   [7] At 1005–6.

[8] *Lipkin Gorman* v. *Karpnale Ltd.* [1991] 2 AC 548, 574, *per* Lord Goff.

of the story. As was acknowledged in *Foley* v. *Hill* itself, a bank can in particular circumstances also be trustee and fiduciary. We return to this in the next Chapter. Moreover, in some circumstances a bank can act in yet another capacity, for example as agent for the customer.

Even on its own terms the debtor–creditor characterization did not accord 100 per cent with the reality. Unlike the ordinary debtor, it was unrealistic to oblige the bank to seek out its creditor, or to repay the loan immediately it was due, in other words, directly after the customer had had the money paid into its account. Conversely, it was also unrealistic to permit the customer, like any ordinary creditor, to demand repayment of the deposit at any time and place. Rather, it was established in a number of cases that the obligation of the bank was not a debt pure and simple, such that the customer could sue for it without warning, but rather a debt for which demand had to be made, and at the branch at which the account was kept.

The jurisprudential basis of all this lies in practical business necessity, and at the end of the day the leading authority found it necessary to fall back upon the course of business and custom of bankers to explain the deviations from ordinary debtor–creditor law.[9] More recently, 'the basis on which banks invite and get money deposited with them' was invoked as an explanation of why a bank was not to be treated like other debtors, this time when summary judgment was sought against it for return of a deposit which it resisted on the basis of the equitable interest which someone else might have had in the moneys.[10] In practical terms such decisions are obviously sensible. For the purposes of the present argument, however, the fact that the ordinary law of debtor–creditor must be bent to accommodate the bank–customer relationship suggests caution in becoming too wedded to it as a characterization of the relationship, even for the narrow sphere of deposit-taking in which it was developed.

Indeed, the excessive attention given to the debtor–creditor side of *Foley* v. *Hill* obscures the fact that the case had an important contractual basis. Chorley probably goes too far in suggesting that if modern contract law had been better developed in 1848 the judges would not so readily have grasped at the long-established cause of action in debt as a method of explaining the bank–customer relationship.[11] But he is certainly correct to highlight the decision's contractual dimensions, for example Lord Cottenham's recognition, in the passage quoted earlier, that the banker had contracted to repay the customer. In terms of the 'superadded obligations' which the decision also involves, including the duty to honour a customer's payment instructions, clearly their basis is in contract. Contract, in fact, dominates the law relating to the deposit of a customer's moneys with a bank. As the US Supreme Court put it on one occasion: 'The relationship of bank and depositor is that of debtor and creditor, founded upon contract'.[12]

---

    [9] *Joachimson* v. *Swiss Bank Corporation* [1921] 3 KB 110 (CA).
    [10] *Bhogal* v. *Punjab National Bank* [1988] 2 All ER 296 (CA).
    [11] Lord Chorley, *The Law of Contract in Relation to the Law of Banking* (Gilbart Lectures on Banking, London, 1964), 6–7.
    [12] *Bank of Marin* v. *England*, 385 US 99, 101 (1966).

Once we go beyond the role of the bank as a depository, debt rarely, if ever, raises its head. Contract is pervasive—oral contracts made by bank employees, standard-form contracts in different shapes and sizes, and tailor-made written contracts for particular purposes. Even if the bank is potentially liable in negligence, as a fiduciary, or by statute, contract typically enters the fray so as to modify its duties or exculpate it entirely.[13] No apology is needed for placing the banking contract centre stage. We have already seen its importance in the banking networks in which banks enmesh themselves with other banks. As we saw in Chapter 2, these interbank contracts may be legally binding on customers. However, this Chapter is concerned with those contracts which banks enter directly with commercial and private customers.

II. BANKING CONTRACTS

Central to the bank–customer relationship is contract. The bank–customer relationship is rarely reduced to the one document, however, but instead comprises a variety of written forms, supplemented by terms implied by law. Often, a standard-form contract will govern specific aspects of the bank–customer relationship, whether it be the account, payment, borrowing, security (including guarantees), and securities and derivatives dealing. Associations of banks have had a hand in drawing up standard-form contracts. The role of the International Swaps and Derivatives Association (ISDA) and the International Primary Markets Association (IPMA) is mentioned elsewhere. In countries like Germany, the Netherlands, and Switzerland there are general business conditions for accounts, drawn up by associations of banks. Historically in Britain banks have not had a standard-form contract for accounts and the parameters of the relationship have been set by a series of terms which the courts have implied over the years. Banks have now adopted codes of practice when dealing with personal customers. These are not themselves legally binding, but the courts may well use them as a basis for implying terms into the bank–customer relationship. We return to these later in the Chapter.

There are efficiency and marketing advantages to a bank in the standardization of contracts, reflected in the language of 'banking products'. Standard terms also enable a bank to set parameters to their liability (or at least to attempt to do so)—for example by terms which represent that counterparties are not relying on advice from the bank, confirm that the written contract is the entire agreement between the parties, and exempt the bank from specified liabilities. Over the years the introduction of new services such as electronic funds transfers has led banks to prepare standard terms for their customers. The securities laws now demand written agreements with private customers in areas such as fund management.[14] Yet banking contracts are still tailor-made. Particular terms in financing documents or a securities issue can be

---

[13] 147, 188 below.   [14] FSA Handbook, Conduct of Business, r.4.2.7.

negotiated at length. With derivatives there may not be a 'battle of the forms' which are standardized, but a 'battle of the schedules', which contain the key terms about price and nature.

This part of the Chapter examines four general matters concerning a bank's contracts with customers: first, identifying who, precisely, is the customer; secondly, determining whether there is an enforceable contract; thirdly, deciding what are the bank's duties when a customer instructs it to act in a particular way under a banking contract; and fourthly, determining the terms of a particular banking contract.

A. IDENTIFYING THE CUSTOMER

'Know your customer' is now a widely accepted obligation on banks. The Financial Action Task Force on Money Laundering, established by the G7 summit in 1989 and based in Paris, has done much to promote the idea as a prerequisite to effective money-laundering controls and it has been given legal force in many jurisdictions.[15] The more recent concern with terrorist financing has given 'know your customer' added impetus. Indeed, the Basle Committee on Banking Supervision regards 'know your customer' as part of the minimum standards which banks should have in place to enable them to manage risks.[16] Questioning about the costs to banks of 'know your customer' rules and their possible adverse effects on access by the whole community to financial services,[17] has led to a greater emphasis on the quality of information as to identity, rather than its quantity. Where a bank has reasonable grounds to conclude that an individual is not able to produce detailed evidence (e.g. a driving licence or utility bills) and cannot reasonably be expected to do so, it may accept instead a statement from a person in a position of responsibility as to a new customer's identity.[18]

Apart from situations where the customer conceals its real identity, there are also circumstances where the bank may be unsure who, precisely, is its customer. A good example is where a bank is dealing with a fund manager. Fund managers typically do not take positions as principals, but sell their expertise in return for a fee.[19] Thus a fund manager may be acting on behalf of the trustees of a fund, an investment company, or rich individuals (the fund). The particular fund or company may be clear, and the fund manager as agent drops out of the picture. However, while the bank may be aware that the fund manager is acting as agent it may not be told which fund is involved, at least until after the contract is made. The fund manager may not disclose this information for commercial reasons; or because it enters a block transaction,

---

[15] 71 below.

[16] Basle Committee on Banking Supervision, *Customer Due Diligence for Banks* (Basle, BIS, 2001).

[17] D. Cruickshank, *Competition in UK Banking. A Report to the Chancellor of the Exchequer* (London, 2000), xiv–xv.

[18] Joint Money Laundering Steering Group, *Guidance Notes*, Dec. 2001, para. 4.101–4.110.

[19] Financial Law Panel, *Fund Management and Market Transactions. A Practice Recommendation* (London, Financial Law Panel, 1995).

where the securities, foreign exchange, and so on are allocated to particular funds only after the transaction is complete.

In such cases of an unnamed principal, the bank faces the practical problem of not being able to assess the creditworthiness of the customer. There are also the difficulties of knowing whether the transaction is *intra vires* the principal, and whether rights of set-off and netting will be effective. Moreover, in calculating a bank's capital adequacy, we saw in Chapter 3 how different risk weightings attach to different types of counterparties. A bank with an unknown counterparty will be in a difficult position calculating its capital requirements. Also on the regulatory side is that a bank dealing with unnamed counterparties may find itself in breach of the large exposure limits. To reflect these greater risks, the Financial Services Authority requires that banks deal with only regulated, not unregulated, fund managers and that there be in place documentation which sets out clearly matters such as whether the fund manager is acting on its own behalf or on that of undisclosed clients, their *vires*, the obligation of the fund manager to inform the bank immediately if circumstances change, and the right of the bank to close out trades straight away in the event of default or a material adverse change.[20] Although the money-laundering controls in general terms require identification of a bank's customer, there is an important exception if the transaction is conducted with a party (in our example, the fund manager) which is itself subject to the controls or their equivalent.[21]

Legally, a customer will be liable on a contract with an unnamed principal, at least if the customer authorized the fund manager (to continue that example) to transact. A difficult question is whether the fund manager is liable also if, say, the transaction is *ultra vires* the customer (the fund). There are various arguments that the fund manager, as agent, may be—for example, trade usage, collateral contract, suretyship, and undisclosed (rather than unnamed) principal—but there is no clear authority.[22] Another difficult question concerns the bank settling with an agent (the fund manager), which defaults before it in turn has settled with the unnamed principal (the fund). The bank may be liable to settle again unless the agent had express authority to settle from the principal, or there is a trade usage for settlement with the agent which can be implied in the contract between bank and principal.[23]

The problems are compounded where there are a number of unnamed principals, for example the case of the bank transacting with a fund manager in a block transaction of securities, foreign exchange, and so on, which are subsequently allocated to various funds for which the fund manager acts. First, there must be doubts whether with a block transaction the bank is brought into contractual relations with the different funds. Doctrines such as ratification, novation, and assignment are probably not available. It would be different if there were separate contracts which were

---

[20] FSA Handbook, Prudential Sourcebook Banks, ch. LE, §§13.2.1–13.2.2.

[21] 71 above.

[22] *Bowstead and Reynolds on Agency* (17th edn., London, Sweet & Maxwell, 2001), 469–71.

[23] See O. Lando and H. Beale (eds.), *Principles of European Contract Law* (Dordrecht, Martinus Nijhoff, 1995), art. 3.302.

subsequently allocated, rather than a block transaction, but this is not always market practice. If the funds refuse, or are unable, to settle with the bank, can it look to the fund manager? Various arguments for making the fund manager, as agent, personally liable were touched on in the previous paragraph, and may be applicable here as well. The Financial Law Panel argued that standard documentation, which imposes a duty on the fund manager promptly to allocate trades, can deem a contract between the bank and each customer to exist, binding both, and relieving the fund manager of liability.[24]

So far we have been concerned with the position where there is a principal—it is just that it is unnamed. However, there are situations where the bank deals with a counterparty and it is uncertain whether it is acting as either principal or agent. An example is the multifunctional bank which does not have separate departments and which sometimes transacts on its own account but at other times for, say, the funds which it manages.[25] English law has the peculiar doctrine of undisclosed principal, under which an undisclosed principal can not only sue but also be sued on a contract entered into within its agent's actual authority. The fund manager, as agent, is also liable on the contract if, for example, the undisclosed principal (the fund) does not settle.

But if the doctrine of undisclosed principal can be applied when one fund is involved, what of a block transaction, subsequently allocated to various funds (i.e. various undisclosed principals)? The doubt whether there can be a contract between the bank and each fund, discussed in the context of unnamed principals, applies here as well. Dual capacity is undesirable, and it is better if a bank segregates its activities— proprietary trading, fund management, and so on—and so makes clear to others on what basis, principal or agent, it is entering a transaction. Not only does this overcome some of the problems arising from the law of agency, it can also mitigate some of the conflicts of interest discussed in Chapter 1.

B. VALIDITY OF A BANKING CONTRACT: AUTHORITY AND CAPACITY

For a bank and its customers to be able to enforce a contract, it must obviously be recognized as having been validly effected in law. The topic can be examined in various ways, but here the analysis proceeds by examining, first, the authority of the persons contracting and, secondly, the capacity of those purporting to contract. A first line of defence raised in many cases is that the person who contracted lacked authority to do so, or that the contracting party itself lacked capacity to enter the particular contract.

[24] Financial Law Panel, n. 19 above, 32, 40.
[25] Financial Law Panel, *Legal Uncertainties in Fund Management* (London, unpublished, 1993), 19–20, 24–8; Financial Markets Lawyers Group, *Fund Managers Acting as Agents and Market Transactions* (New York, FMLG, 1996), 11–14, 21–5.

(i) The Persons Contracting—Authority

Say A negotiates a financing contract with a bank. It deals with the manager of an important branch of the bank. Subsequently the bank reneges, claiming that the manager lacked authority to enter into the particular contract.[26] Conversely, take the situation where a bank negotiates with A, a 'manager' of a company, and agrees to advance money to a third party on the company giving certain undertakings. Subsequently, when the bank claims under the undertakings, the company contends that A never had its authority to give them.[27] Both examples are illustrative of the problems which arise because organizations, including banks, must of their nature act through human agents.

Agency is a key concept in whether a commercial organization is to be bound by those such as directors and other employers acting in its name. An agent can by virtue of his or her authority bind a principal in relation to a third party. If an agent has express actual authority to negotiate a banking contract, then its principal is bound. Even where an agent acts without express, actual authority, it is generally open to the principal subsequently to ratify the transaction. The problem arises where, in this situation, the principal instead wants to renege on the transaction.

English law has two answers. First, if the agent has implied, even if not express, actual authority, the principal is bound. So too with usual authority. Usual authority is authority which is objectively determined—what is normal or customary in the particular business or profession. For example, where companies appoint managing directors, they impliedly authorize them to do such things as fall within the usual scope of that office.[28] Limitations on their authority do not count unless the third party is aware of them. The difficulty with usual authority is in determining what is normal or customary: for example, what is normal or customary for the managing director of an international bank may not be normal or customary for the person occupying that position in a small trading company with which the bank contracts. For this reason usual authority can rarely be invoked.

A second answer provided by English law is that, because of the principal's own conduct or the way it has allowed the agent to act, it may be estopped from denying the latter's authority if the third party has acted in reliance upon the apparent position. The agent is said to have apparent or ostensible authority; sometimes the result is described, not always accurately, as agency by estoppel. Unfortunately the law is in a tangle, and causes injustice to third parties dealing with a body, by making the issue of the binding nature of transactions turn on matters which are purely internal to that body. This is because of the rule, which tends to be treated as if it had statutory force, that the representation that the agent had authority to enter a transaction must be

---

[26] *First Energy (UK) Ltd.* v. *Hungarian International Bank Ltd.* [1993] 2 Lloyd's Rep. 194 (CA).

[27] *British Bank of the Middle East* v. *Sun Life Assurance Co. of Canada (UK) Ltd.* [1983] 2 Lloyd's Rep. 9 (HL).

[28] e.g. *UBAF Ltd.* v. *European American Banking Corporation* [1984] 1 QB 713, 724 (CA); *Equiticorp Finance Ltd. (in liq.)* v. *Bank of New Zealand* (1993) 11 ACSR 642 (CA).

made by someone within the body who has *actual* authority to manage its business, either generally such as the board of directors, or in respect of matters to which the particular contract relates.[29] Consequently, however reasonable it may be for third parties to do so, they cannot rely on an agent's own representations as to his or her authority, or even on representations by a superior lacking actual authority.

Fortunately, in several cases, the Court of Appeal has been able to reach a commercially sensible result and has upheld transactions which the third party plausibly regarded the agent as having authority to enter.[30] This, however, has involved intellectual gymnastics to maintain the principle that any representation must be made by someone with actual authority. A distinction has been drawn between those with actual authority representing an agent's authority, and representing that someone is in a position to communicate decisions from those with actual authority. Thus a body may confer apparent authority on an agent to convey, falsely, its approval of a transaction, even though the agent is not clothed with apparent authority to enter into it on behalf of the body. More intellectually satisfying would be a new approach to the issue of apparent authority, which gave effect to the reasonable expectations of third parties, and which recognized the commercial realities, for example that given constraints such as time, third parties cannot penetrate too far behind institutional facades.

(ii) The Bodies Contracting—Capacity

Agency is a doctrine which has a wide application in determining whether organizations are bound by the actions of their officials. However, it is not universally applicable. The legal relationship between a public body and those acting on its behalf is generally one of delegation, although there will be cases where apparent authority can be established in the ordinary way. Indeed, the juridical nature of a body has a series of consequences for its capacity to enter transactions. What follows is a sample.

Until relatively recently, those entering contracts with companies were bedevilled by the *ultra vires* rule and the doctrine of constructive notice. Thus a bank might subsequently find that the company with which it had contracted was acting beyond the scope of its constitution.[31] It was deemed to have constructive notice of a company's constitution, along with its other 'public documents'. Since *ultra vires* contracts are void, a bank was unable to enforce them, although it might be able to recover money advanced by restitution or subrogation to other creditors. Statute has largely abrogated the *ultra vires* rule and the doctrine of constructive notice in relation to corporate contracts.[32] A company now has full capacity as regards third parties. In dealing with a company in good faith third parties are not affected by any constitutional limitations on the authority of the board of directors. Good faith is presumed.

---

[29] *Freeman & Lockyer* v. *Buckhurst Park Properties (Magnal) Ltd.* [1964] QB 480, 506, *per* Diplock LJ.

[30] *First Energy (UK) Ltd.* v. *Hungarian International Bank Ltd.* [1993] 2 Lloyd's Rep. 194; *Egyptian International Foreign Trade Co.* v. *Soplex Wholesale Supplies Ltd.* [1985] 2 Lloyd's Rep. 36 (CA).

[31] e.g. *Introductions Ltd.* v. *National Provincial Bank* [1970] Ch. 199 (CA).

[32] Companies Act 1985, ss. 35, 35A, 35B, 711A.

Moreover, not only are third parties under no duty to investigate whether a transaction is contrary to the company's constitution, they are not to be regarded as acting in bad faith by reason only of knowledge that an act is outside the board's powers.

Quite apart from *ultra vires* and constructive notice, whether a third party who deals with someone representing a company is entitled to assume that the board has authorized that person to bind the company depends on the principles of agency already mentioned. There is also a rule of company law relating to matters of procedure—the rule in *Turquand's case*.[33] As a result of this, unless third parties have been put on inquiry, they are entitled to assume that there has been due compliance with all matters of internal management and procedure. This is especially helpful if they are dealing with those other than the board or persons authorized by it, since the statutory protections discussed in the previous paragraph do not apply in respect of their acts and transactions.

Finally in relation to companies, mention should be made of section 37 of the Companies Act 1985, whereby bills of exchange, cheques, and promissory notes are deemed to be drawn, accepted, or endorsed on behalf of a company if done so in the name of the company, or if the person with authority signs 'by or on behalf of' or 'on account of' the company. Those not so signing may be personally liable on the instrument.[34] For present purposes, however, the more interesting question is whether this provision gives greater protection than the common law to, say, banks discounting an instrument. Take the position if the person in signing it is fraudulent. At common law, constructive knowledge that the person is acting in his or her own interests will defeat the bank. But in discounting a bill the bank might argue that not only is constructive notice anathema as a matter of policy, since a commercial transaction is involved, but also that the section 'deems' the instrument to be drawn etc. by the company, with the result that the bank is protected.

Ultra vires is still alive and well when it comes to transactions involving bodies other than companies, such as local authorities and industrial and provident societies. Banks are generally protected in lending to a local authority, since they are absolved by statute from inquiring into whether it has power to borrow, and they are not prejudiced by the absence of any such power.[35] Similarly, the Local Government (Contracts) Act 1997 establishes a safe harbour for a limited category of local government contracts, notably, a guarantee given to a bank which is financing a third party constructing facilities for the local authority.[36] But moneys paid over to a local authority may be for purposes *ultra vires* its powers, such as a derivatives transaction, albeit that the moneys may be recovered as unjust enrichment of the local authority.[37] Moreover, the statutory comfort for banks does not extend to trans-

[33] *Royal British Bank* v. *Turquand* (1856) 6 El. & Bl. 327, 119 ER 886.
[34] Companies Act 1985, S. 349(4).
[35] Local Government and Housing Act 1989, s. 44(6).
[36] Ss. 2(1), 4(3), 4. Cf. *Crédit Suisse* v. *Allerdale BC* [1997] QB 306 (CA). See also National Health Service (Private Finance) Act 1997.
[37] See 249 below.

actions with foreign local authorities: that depends on the law of their own jurisdiction.[38]

A final example relates to dealings with trustees. Banks may transact with trustees including trustees of investment funds, or themselves be trustees of funds or of securities issues. Because a trust is not a legal entity, a counterparty must transact with the trustees of a trust or, in the case of a corporate trustee, that corporate trustee. The counterparty must satisfy itself that the trust instrument permits the trustees to enter into the transaction in question. This is because, for the trustees to be indemnified out of trust assets—and thus, in turn, for the counterparty to have an effective claim against the assets by way of subrogation to the trustees' indemnity—the trustees must have incurred the liability properly and in the due administration of the trust. Even if the trustee is empowered to enter a transaction, there is authority that a trustee may lose its right of indemnity for an unrelated breach of trust. A counterparty is likely to be ignorant of this and unable to discover it by inquiry.[39] A separate problem arises where a trustee is acting in relation to a number of trusts, for example, as trustee of various investment funds. In each transaction it is necessary to identify on behalf of precisely which investment fund the trustee is acting, for its right of indemnity is confined to those assets alone.

C. THE BANK'S MANDATE

Civil lawyers have sometimes used the concept of mandate to categorize the relationship between customers and their bank. No practical consequences seem to flow from this categorization in France, Belgium, and the Netherlands. In fact other classifications have also been used, for example, a relationship for rendering a service. German law, however, contains a number of specific consequences if the relationship is subsumed under the heading of mandate, flowing from the provisions of the civil code governing this type of contract.[40]

English banking law has taken the concept of mandate, but has given it no precise meaning. Sometimes bankers use it as a general term applying to the contract with their customers governing particular banking services (e.g. the mandate for a joint account).[41] We can put mandate in this first sense to one side. At other times mandate is used in a second, narrower sense, as the authority for a bank to act in a particular way, for example a mandate authorizing a third party to draw on an existing account. This may not constitute a contractual variation, at least until acted upon. Once a mandate is binding on a bank, however, it must act or be in breach of contract. Thus a mandate

---

[38] *Merrill Lynch Capital Services Inc. v. Municipality of Piraeus* [1997] CLC 1214.

[39] R. Russell, 'Impact of Recent Corporation Collapses on Negotiating and Drafting Syndicated Loans', in J. Norton, C.-J. Cheng, and I. Fletcher (eds.), *International Banking Operations and Practices* (Dordrecht, Martinus Nijhoff, 1994), 239–40.

[40] BGB, ss. 662–5.

[41] Lord Chorley, 'Opening the Account, and Other Problems', Gilbart Lectures in Banking, London, 1955, 43.

in this second sense leads to an order, rather than a request. If the bank acts outside any authority so conferred, this will not be binding on the customer and the bank will be liable for any loss. If the mandate is withdrawn, the bank must comply.[42]

Where a mandate is given in this second sense, there is a duty on the customer to exercise care to make the mandate clear and unambiguous, so that the bank will not suffer loss while executing it with reasonable care and skill. 'The banker, as a mandatory, has a right to insist on having his mandate in a form which does not leave room for misgivings as to what he is called upon to do.'[43] If the mandate is ambiguous it has been said that the bank is not in default if it adopts a reasonable meaning.[44] This is now subject to the caveat that when the ambiguity is patent, the bank should have the instructions clarified by the customer, before acting on them.[45] Saying that the customer is authorizing the bank to act in a particular way should not be taken to mean that the bank automatically then acts as agent. In acting with a customer's authority it may well be, and often is, doing so as principal.

Mandate is sometimes used, thirdly, in a yet narrower sense, as the authentication under the contract for the bank to act for the customer in a particular way, for example, to make payment, to release securities held by it as custodian, to transfer investments, and so on. Signature is a typical form of authentication but there may be other avenues such as a PIN, a so-called electronic signature, tested telex, or SWIFT message.[46] Banking practice will be important in this regard, but not determinative. Because of the possibility of fraud, certain forms of authentication ought not to be acceptable (e.g. faxed signatures). In general terms, the authentication ought to be a commercially reasonable method of security against unauthorized orders.[47]

In this third sense mandate is analytically distinct from authorization. In practice the consequences of disobeying a mandate in this third sense are often expressed as an issue of authority: not having authentication, the bank had no authority to act and is liable for the customer's loss. However, mandate in this third sense is contractual in character, either as a term of the contract governing the particular service, or the method of performance contemplated by the contract. The bank acting without proper authentication is breaching its contract.

What a customer has authorized (mandate in the second sense) or what authentication is required (mandate in the third sense) may be a matter of interpretation of the contract. Thus a bank's agreement in relation to a joint account to honour only those instructions signed by both account holders carries with it a duty not to honour

[42] *American Express Services Europe Ltd.* v. *Tuvyahu*, CA, 12 July 2000.

[43] *London Joint Stock Bank Ltd.* v. *Macmillan* [1918] AC 777, 784, *per* Lord Haldane. See also UCP, art. 5a.

[44] *Midland Bank Ltd.* v. *Seymour* [1955] 2 Lloyd's Rep. 147, 168, *per* Devlin J; *Commercial Banking Co. of Sydney Ltd.* v. *Jalsard Pty. Ltd.* [1973] AC 279 (PC).

[45] *European Asian Bank AG* v. *Punjab & Sind Bank (No 2)* [1983] 1 WLR 642, [1983] 2 All ER 508 (CA); *Patel* v. *Standard Chartered Bank* [2001] Lloyd's LR Banking 229.

[46] See 278 below. See Electronic Signatures Directive 1999/93/EC [2000] OJ L13/12, implemented in the UK by Electronic Communications Act 2000, s. 7.

[47] Cf. UNCITRAL Model Law on International Credit Transfers, Art. 5(2)(a).

instructions which are not signed in that manner—a duty incidentally owed to the account holders severally.[48] Say that the written contract with the bank says that particular services (e.g. release of securities in custody) will be performed 'on the customer's written instructions only'. This type of clause should be read as obliging the bank to act only when it has received instructions in writing (rather than orally), and provided that they are suitably authenticated. Sometimes the mandate on its face appears clear, but in the light of background circumstances must be interpreted differently (e.g. the director signatories have not been validly appointed).[49]

Once the nature of the mandate is determined, the approach of the English courts is strict. The bank must do exactly what the customer requires of it. This is a general contractual principle—whenever anyone undertakes to secure a particular end, failure to do so is breach of contract. Almost achieving the goal, even exercising reasonable care and skill, is insufficient. Thus the bank straying beyond its authority, however slightly, and despite herculean efforts, will be in breach of mandate.

So, too, if a bank acts on faulty authentication, however close it may be to the contractual authentication, and although reasonable care and skill would not have detected the deviation. A common instance is the forged cheque which, however expertly done, does not entitle the bank to debit a customer's account. However, banks are free to specify the authentication they will accept in their standard-form contracts. In retail electronic funds transfer systems, for instance, if all they require is the use of a card and a PIN, this exposes customers to a greater chance of loss when compared with the use of signatures on cheques.[50] Customers suspecting that their mandate is being abused must notify the bank so it can take preventive action. Failure to do so may estop them from denying that it is proper and authentic.

A strict approach to mandate protects customers. So, too, does the recognition in English law that there are some limits on a bank's entitlement to treat a mandate as absolute. Thus a bank receiving a valid order from a customer, properly authenticated, is generally bound to execute it. But if the bank knows it to be dishonestly given, if it shuts its eyes to the obvious fact of dishonesty or if it acts recklessly in failing to make such inquiries as an honest and reasonable bank would make, then it will be liable for the customer's loss as a result of it so acting.[51] The situations in which a bank must not act, even if the instructions conform with its mandate, will be unusual.[52] The test is, however, whether any reasonable bank would suspect fraud. Partly this may be a matter of banking practice. Primarily, however, whether a bank is 'put on inquiry' is a matter of fact. Apart from the clear indicia of fraud, matters to be taken into account in determining the factual issue seem to include the bank's course of dealing with the

---

[48] *Catlin* v. *Cyprus Finance Corp. (London) Ltd.* [1983] QB 759.

[49] *Sierra Leone Telecommunications Co. Ltd.* v. *Barclays Bank plc,* [1998] 2 All ER 821.

[50] 268, below.

[51] *Barclays Bank plc* v. *Quincecare Ltd* [1988] FLR 166, [1992] 4 All ER 363; *Verjee* v. *CIBC Bank and Trust Co. (Channel Islands) Ltd.* [2001] Lloyd's LR Banking 279.

[52] As a result of legislation this may be required in the case of suspicions of money-laundering or terrorist financing.

customer, the amount involved, the need (or otherwise) for prompt action, the status of any person purporting to act as the customer's representative, the relative ease in making inquiries, and any unusual features.

D. CONTRACT TERMS

As we have seen, standard-form contracts, sometimes drawn up by associations of banks, are a feature of the bank–customer relationship. By definition these are in writing. Because of their nature, tailor-made contracts are typically also in writing. Yet despite a written contract, parties may argue that there are additional terms which should be implied. The English courts are nowadays loath to do this.

A leading decision is *Tai Hing Cotton Mill Ltd. v. Liu Chong Hing Bank Ltd.*[53] There the banks argued that the account relationship gave rise to a contractual or tortious duty on the part of the customer to exercise reasonable internal controls to prevent forged cheques being presented to the bank, or at least to check its periodic bank statements to uncover unauthorized items. The Privy Council held that the customer had no such duties. To have held otherwise would have been inconsistent with principle. In the absence of express terms, English courts will imply terms in contracts only if previous decisions so demand, if there is some compelling reason ('business efficacy'), or because of custom or usage. In the present case, previous decisions were against the implied duties suggested, that customers take precautions or check bank statements. Precedent quite specifically limits the implied duties of customers to exercising reasonable care in executing written orders, such as cheques, so as not to mislead the bank or to facilitate forgery,[54] and to notifying the bank of forgeries of which they actually (not constructively) know.[55] Moreover, the implied terms suggested by the banks were not a necessary incident of the bank–customer relationship, nor did they have any basis in banking practice.

If the banks wanted protection, said the Privy Council, they could have specified it in written contracts with the customer, or have the legislature change the law. Besides, it noted, the existing law spreads losses which, for an individual customer, could be very serious. It was also argued that the customer had duties in tort to take precautions or to check its bank statements. There is no reason why, on ordinary principles, tortious and contractual duties should not co-exist. The Privy Council held, however, that a tortious duty could not be wider than a contractual duty in relation to the same matter, and for this reason it held that tort could not assist the banks by imposing duties on the customer not arising out of the contract.

Tai Hing involved a recurrent theme in commercial law decisions—which of two

---

[53] [1986] AC 80. See also *Canadian Pacific Hotels Ltd. v. Bank of Montreal* (1987) 40 DLR (4th) 385 (SCC); *National Australia Bank Ltd. v. Hokit Pty. Ltd.* (1996) 39 NSWLR 377 (CA); *BNZ v. Auckland Information Bureau (Inc.) Ltd.* [1996] 1 NZLR 420 (CA).

[54] *London Joint Stock Bank Ltd. v. Macmillan* [1918] AC 777.

[55] *Greenwood v. Martins Bank Ltd.* [1933] AC 51; R. Goddard, 'Banking Law: the *Greenwood* Duty Revisited' (2001) 151 *NLJ* 958.

relatively innocent parties should suffer from the fault of the third? It might be thought on the facts that the customer was more to blame for the loss than the bank in not exercising adequate control over its fraudulent employee. But to have held the customer liable the Privy Council would have had to distort significantly the general law of contract and tort in order to place liability on it. In any event, a bank could always place the liability on customers through express terms, subject to the common law rules and the unfair contract terms legislation. That none have done so suggests a fear of adverse customer reaction. Otherwise, if there is a case for sharing the loss between the two innocent parties in such cases, it must be introduced through legislative, not judicial, change.

In response to the *Tai Hing* decision, a UK government-appointed committee on banking services recommended that there should be a statutory provision whereby, in an action against a bank in debt or for damages arising from payment in breach of contract, the bank would be able to raise contributory negligence as a defence if it were sufficiently serious and inequitable for the bank to be liable for the whole amount.[56] Nothing has been done to give effect to this recommendation, perhaps not surprisingly when, with private customers at any rate, it would have put the banks so firmly in the driving seat. The committee rejected the approach elsewhere in Europe of general business conditions for banks, on the rather tenuous grounds that this would mean inflexibility. Its support for a code of banking practice did, however, bear fruit.[57]

In *Tai Hing* the judicial refusal to imply terms benefited the customer. And only exceptionally will an English court bind a customer to standard banking practice to its disadvantage.[58] Generally the courts refuse to add to those few duties traditionally imposed on customers in relation to an account. That existing implied terms in this context are favourable to customers may be explained by the fact that they evolved at a time when bank customers were principally traders and the professional middle class.[59] In other contexts, however, the refusal to imply terms may be to the benefit of the bank. Examples are dealt with in Chapter 7, where customers were unsuccessful in their attempts to impose liability on banks through the doctrine of implied terms.

III. REGULATING BANKING CONTRACTS

Once a bank offers services to the public, the relationship of bank and customer is potentially subject to regulation. The state acts as a surrogate for the customer and compels banks to meet standards purportedly in the customer interest. By contrast

---

[56] *Banking Services*, Cm. 622 (London, HMSO, 1989), 43. See also B. Geva, 'Allocation of Forged Cheque Losses—Comparative Aspects, Policies and a Model for Reform' (1998) 114 *LQR* 250, 288–91.

[57] 158 below.

[58] e.g. *Emerald Meats (London) Ltd. v. AIB Group (UK) plc* [2002] EWCA Civ. 460 (CA).

[59] G. Borrie, 'Estate Agents and Bankers—Regulation or Self-regulation?' [1990] *CLP* 15, 28–9.

with elsewhere, the bank–customer relationship in the United States is heavily influenced by regulation.[60] This is not to say that regulation is unknown elsewhere. In Sweden, for example, the Finance Inspection Board has made important rulings relevant to aspects of the basic relationship.[61]

Regulation varies with the type of customer: thus consumer customers are especially protected by general legislation on unfair contract terms and by specific legislation on consumer credit.[62] The subject matter is also relevant. Discrimination on grounds such as race and sex is prohibited in banking as in other services. Securities dealings are quite heavily regulated in the interest of investor protection, as we see in Chapter 12. Yet another variable is the regulatory style of a jurisdiction. In the United Kingdom self-regulation is sometimes favoured so that matters which in other places like the United States are dealt with by regulation and the courts, in Britain are resolved through the banking codes and the operation of the Financial Ombudsman Service.

From the range of relevant provisions, this section selects for discussion the general statutory controls on unfair contract terms, as they relate to banking services. Reference is also made to the common law and banking codes. The approach is illustrative, rather than exhaustive.

A. THE COMMON LAW

Legislative control of unfair contract terms was enacted against a background of common law rules, which were thought to be inadequate in protecting contracting parties. That does not mean the common law rules should be overlooked. There is, however, the fundamental problem in English law that once customers sign a contract they are generally bound, even if they have not read its terms.[63] The justification for this rule focuses on form, not substance. Signature of a document is a formal device, and means that parties can treat a contact as concluded. Another, ancillary, justification is that a party obtaining a signature relies on it as conclusive of the other party's agreement. The rule is subject to a number of limited exceptions: *non est factum*; fraud and misrepresentation; undue influence and unconscionability; and that the document did not appear to be contractual. It may also be that there is an exception where the signature was otherwise written in circumstances in which it did not signify the customer's assent to be bound. In some other common law jurisdictions the signature rule has not always been applied.

Absent signature, however, customers may be able to argue that the bank's written terms have not become part of the contract.[64] The bank has to establish that customers were given adequate notice of them. This is a question of fact and a court will give attention to all the circumstances of a case. The burden is heavy if unusually wide or

---

[60] See J. Norton and S. Whitley, *Banking Law Manual* (New York, Matthew Bender, 1989), ch. 11.
[61] K. Moberg, 'Sweden', in R. Cranston (ed.), *European Banking Law* (2nd edn., London, LLP, 1999), 150.
[62] R. Goode, *Consumer Credit Legislation* (London, Butterworths, looseleaf).
[63] *L'Estrange* v. *Graucob* [1934] 2 KB 394.
[64] e.g. *Burnett* v. *Westminster Bank Ltd.* [1966] 1 QB 742.

onerous conditions are to become part of the contract. In one case Denning LJ said: 'Some clauses which I have seen would need to be printed in red ink on the face of the document with a red hand pointing to it before the notice could be held to be sufficient.'[65] That approach was applied in another leading Court of Appeal decision, where nothing was done to draw the customer's attention to the relevant condition: it was merely one of four columns' width of conditions printed across the foot of the delivery note. Consequently the court held that it never became part of the contract between the parties.[66]

As far as their reasoning is concerned, such cases usually involve a consideration of what is customary in a trade, or what are the reasonable expectations of a party, in order to determine whether a clause is unusually wide or onerous. For example, it could never be argued these days on behalf of customers that they would always expect a fixed or maximum rate of interest. Bank customers are used to floating interest rates. What, arguably, they do not expect is a change in the method of calculating interest rates which results in a rate being substantially greater than under the previous method of calculation. Were a variation clause to permit this, it should arguably be treated as unusually wide or onerous and needing the 'red-hand' treatment before being incorporated in the bank–customer contract.

Even if clauses are found to have been incorporated in a contract, they may be construed against a bank. The *contra proferentum* rule is applied in cases of ambiguity or where other rules of construction fail. If it is applicable, it results in a contract being construed against its maker. Particular types of clause may be construed against a bank. Clauses imposing bank charges, for example, must be very clear about the obligation of the customer to pay. Exclusion clauses are another example, and must explicitly state that they extend to a bank's oral, as well as written, misrepresentations, include its failure to exercise reasonable care and skill and cover both direct and consequential losses.

Variation clauses regularly appear in UK banking contracts. They may be void for uncertainty.[67] Moreover, there is authority that clear words are necessary if a contract is to entrust one party with power unilaterally to vary its terms.[68] The reason behind this is fairly obvious. As a matter of legal analysis, it can be treated as one of the various rules of construction—of which the *contra proferentum* rule is another—used by courts to discover the intention of the parties to a contract. There is English Court of Appeal authority that discretion to vary interest rates during the term of a variable-rate mortgage is subject to an implied term that it is not to be exercised for an improper purpose, dishonestly, arbitrarily, or so unreasonably that no reasonable lender would act in that way.[69] The decision muddies public and private law; in any event such a term would only bite in the most extraordinary circumstances.

---

[65] *Spurling (J) Ltd* v. *Bradshaw* [1956] 1 WLR 461, 466.

[66] *Interfoto Picture Library Ltd.* v. *Stiletto Visual Programmes* [1989] 1 QB 433.

[67] *Kabwand Pty. Ltd.* v. *National Australia Bank* (1989) 11 ATPR 40–950.

[68] *Lombard Tricity Finance Ltd.* v. *Paton* [1989] 1 All ER 918 (CA); *Paragon Finance plc* v. *Nash & Staunton* [2001] EWCA Civ. 1466, [2002] 2 All ER 248.

[69] *Paragon Finance plc* v. *Nash & Staunton* [2001] EWCA Civ. 1466, [2002] 2 All ER 248.

Entire agreement clauses typically provide that the written contract sets out the entire agreement between the parties and that the customer cannot rely on any misrepresentation unless contained in it. In several decisions the English courts have found the wording of such clauses was not effective in excluding liability for a pre-contractual misrepresentation.[70] A very explicit entire agreement clause will be sufficient at common law, for example, to deprive a collateral warranty of its legal effect. However, it would still run the gauntlet of the reasonableness test demanded by section 3 of the Misrepresentation Act 1967 of exclusions or restrictions on liability for misrepresentation.[71]

B. UCTA

Despite these common law rules, additional protection was thought necessary. As far as the Unfair Contract Terms Act 1977 (UCTA) is concerned, the important general point to note is that it is not confined to consumer contracts. Indeed the majority of reported cases under UCTA have been commercial cases. This is especially relevant to the provision of banking services.

(i) Negligence

The result of section 2(2) of UCTA is that a bank cannot, by reference to any contract term, or to a notice given to customers generally or to particular customers, exclude or restrict its liability for negligence, unless the term or notice satisfies the requirements of reasonableness. Negligence is defined to mean the breach of any obligation, arising from the express or implied terms of a contract, to take reasonable care or exercise reasonable skill in the performance of a contract, or of any common law duty to take reasonable care or exercise reasonable skill (e.g. as an agent).[72] Throughout the book there are frequent references to the obligation of a bank to act with reasonable care or skill. Section 2(2) applies.

(ii) Contractual Performance

Section 3 of the 1977 Act applies to contracts in which a person deals as consumer or— and here commercial contracts are potentially caught—on another's written standard terms of business. The latter are not defined in the Act. If section 3 applies, a bank (in our case) cannot by reference to any contract term, except insofar as it satisfies the requirement of reasonableness, 'claim to be entitled to . . . render a contractual performance substantially different from that which was reasonably expected' of it.[73] The subsection can apply where there is no breach of contract at all, as with a clause enabling the bank to terminate a facility 'on demand', or with a variation clause.

---

[70] e.g. *Thomas Witter Ltd.* v. *TBP Industries Ltd.* [1996] 2 All ER 575.
[71] See also Unfair Terms in Consumer Contracts Regulations 1999, SI 1999 No 2083, Sched. 2(q).
[72] S. 1(1).
[73] S. 3(2)(b)(i). S. 3(2)(a) deals with excluding or restricting liability when a bank is in breach itself and s. 3(2)(b)(ii) with claims not to perform at all.

As its wording indicates, the focus is on the reasonable expectations of the customer. It would seem that the presence of the clause is itself a factor to be taken into account in deciding what were the reasonable expectations of the customer. In other words, to continue with the examples of a termination or variation clause, if the customer actually knew that a bank had an unlimited power to terminate or to vary the contract, it might be difficult in practice to establish that its reasonable expectations were other than the mode of performance set out in the written terms signed at the time the contract was first made. However, there is a plausible argument against this: in the absence of 'red-hand' treatment, or of evidence that particular customers knew of the existence of the clause, can it be said that, simply because they signed the terms, their reasonable expectations were other than that the bank would perform in accordance with the general terms of the contract, or of the accompanying material, unless they were seriously in default, or with perhaps some minor variation of the contract, for example in matters such as interest rates?

(iii) General Matters

Section 13 of the Act extends the scope of section 2(2) beyond exclusion clauses proper to duty-defining clauses, i.e. those which purport to limit or exclude the relevant duty of care. Also caught in relation to sections 2(2) and 3 are attempts to subject liability in its enforcement to restrictive or onerous conditions; excluding, restricting, or prejudicing rights or remedies; and using the rules of evidence or procedure to avoid liability. A clause in a banking contract excluding or restricting a right of set-off would thus be subject to the UCTA tests.[74]

The reasonableness test pervades the Act and applies in particular to the provisions already considered. It is determined at the time the contract is made so that the extent of any loss cannot of itself be taken into account.[75] The term must have been a fair and reasonable one to include having regard to the circumstances which were, or ought reasonably to have been, known to or in the contemplation of the parties at that time. In other words, reasonableness is decided between these parties, not in the abstract. The onus is on the bank to establish that the test is satisfied.[76] In decisions examining the reasonableness of contractual terms, the courts have had regard to a wide range of factors (including those set out in Schedule 2 to the Act, although strictly speaking these are confined to the application of those parts of the Act relating to the sale of goods and analogous matters). Thus the respective bargaining power of the parties; whether the terms were negotiated (not necessarily between the parties but between representatives, say, of the banks and of the consumer interest); the degree of notification to the customer; and the length of the contract—these have all been taken into account. Section 11(4) directs attention to resources and insurance as factors to be considered in the reasonableness of limitations on the amounts payable on liability for damages. As would be expected, the courts are more prepared to declare clauses in

---

[74] *Stewart Gill Ltd. v. Horatio Myer & Co. Ltd.* [1992] QB 600 (CA).
[75] S. 11(1).   [76] S. 11(5).

contracts involving consumers to be unreasonable than clauses in contracts involving commercial parties like banks of equal bargaining strength.[77]

By contrast with the Unfair Terms in Consumer Contracts Regulations 1999, UCTA is not confined to consumer contracts. Attempts to exclude negligence (section 2), and standard terms affecting contractual performance (section 3), are caught, even if between a bank and commercial customer. But some of UCTA's protections are confined to those dealing as consumer. Thus if a banking contract is tailor made—it is not the bank's written standard terms of business—section 3 applies only to a customer dealing as consumer.

'Dealing as consumer' is defined in terms of neither making a contract in the course of a business nor holding oneself out as doing so. Moreover, the onus in UCTA is placed explicitly on the party claiming that another party does not deal as consumer to show that.[78] 'Dealing as consumer' has been considered by the courts on a number of occasions and a wide view taken. In one case the Court of Appeal was persuaded that a company which was in the business of shipping brokers and freight forwarding agents was dealing as a consumer in purchasing a motor car, which was to be used by the owners of the business partly for business and partly for pleasure.[79] The somewhat questionable reasoning was that the company was not in the business of buying motor cars, and indeed had bought only one or two previously. Clearly if this reasoning were to be applied, the customer of a bank using its services for both business and private purposes may well be said to be dealing as consumer.[80]

(iv) Exclusions

Specific exclusions of UCTA's application are set out in the legislation. Schedule 1 provides that sections 2 and 3 do not extend to a variety of contracts, including any contract so far as it relates to the creation or transfer of securities or of any right or interest in securities. In a banking context this exclusion in UCTA covers certain contracts, such as one to carry out a customer's instructions to sell securities. Thus excluding the bank's duty in a securities sale to provide best execution, to avoid conflicts of interest, and to account for all profits made, may not fall within the UCTA net. (Financial services law may, however, apply.[81]) Clauses excluding liability for advice in relation to securities would not be as fortunate.

Where commercial parties choose as the governing law of a banking contract a law other than that of England, the UCTA does not apply[82] (UCTA does apply where the governing law clause has been imposed by one party to evade the operation of the Act, or if one of the parties is dealing as consumer, is habitually resident in the UK, and the

---

[77] *National Westminster Bank plc* v. *Utrecht-America Finance Co.* [2001] EWCA Civ. 658, [2001] 3 All ER 733 (CA); J. Adams and R. Brownsword, *Key Issues in Contract* (London, Butterworths, 1995), 263–9.

[78] S. 12.

[79] *R & B Customs Brokers Co. Ltd.* v. *United Dominions Trust Ltd. (Saunders Abbott (1980) Ltd.) (third party)* [1988] 1 WLR 321, [1988] 1 All ER 847.

[80] 150 below.   [81] 351 below.

[82] S. 27(2); *Centrax Ltd.* v. *Citibank NA* [1999] EWCA Civ. 892, [1999] All ER (Comm) 557.

contract was made there). UCTA is also excluded from applying to contracts, when English law is the proper law of the contract by choice of the parties but the law of some other country would, in the absence of that choice, have been the proper law.[83] This is an unusual provision for UK legislation, as generally it will be only as a matter of implication that UK statutory law does not apply in such circumstances. It is especially important in banking, since financing contracts having no connection with England will often have English law as the proper law: UCTA does not apply in such cases.

C. THE UNFAIR TERMS IN CONSUMER CONTRACTS DIRECTIVE

The Unfair Terms in Consumer Contracts Regulations 1999 (the UTCC Regulations)[84] implement in the United Kingdom a European Community directive on the matter. The Regulations add a layer of regulation to consumer banking contracts, while leaving the existing law in place. The Regulations are at once both narrower and broader in scope than the Unfair Contract Terms Act 1977. They are narrower in being confined to consumer contracts; UCTA applies to both consumer and commercial contracts. On the other hand the regulations extend well beyond exclusion clauses: they specifically mention clauses which occur in a financing context—set-off clauses, forfeiture clauses, and clauses which arguably infringe the rule against penalties.[85] Moreover, the regulations do not have the same exclusions written into them as UCTA, such as the exclusion of contracts for carrying out a customer's instructions to sell shares. There is also the important provision that the written terms on which (in our case) a banking service is provided must be in plain, intelligible language.[86] Note that plain, intelligible language does not necessarily go as far as plain English. If there is any doubt about a written term, the interpretation most favourable to the consumer prevails.

(i) Consumer Contracts

The UTCC Regulations apply to any term in a contract concluded between a supplier and a consumer. The meaning of supplier is examined shortly. 'Consumer' is defined as a natural person who is acting for purposes which are outside his or her business, trade or profession.[87] This is language different from the meaning of the term 'consumer' in other UK legislation, notably UCTA. The point arises of the individual contracting partly for business, partly for other purposes. In the banking context there are obvious examples—the small trader with just one current account for his business and personal matters; the professional borrowing for home renovations which are to include a new study so that she need not travel every day to work; and a wife, who just happens to be a shareholder in her husband's business, giving the bank security over

[83] S. 27(1).
[84] SI 1999 No 2083, replacing earlier regulations: SI 1994 No 3159.
[85] Sched. 2, para. 1(b), (d), and (e).   [86] R. 7(1).   [87] R. 3(1).

her share in the domestic home for that business. Since the regulations do not require a consumer to be acting 'wholly' outside the business, it seems arguable that, so long as one purpose or more was outside the person's business, he or she could still be a consumer despite there being a business purpose. A more restrictive test, while still recognizing that having some business purpose will not disqualify a person from being a consumer, is to read the definition as requiring the consumer to act *primarily* for purposes which are outside his or her business. This would be consistent with other areas of the common law. Focusing on the primary purpose or purposes to determine whether a person is acting outside a business seems also consistent with European Union law.[88]

(ii) Standard Terms

The Directive strikes only at standard terms; despite earlier drafts the Directive as adopted does not apply to every term in a consumer contract, nor indeed to a consumer contract at all if every term has been individually negotiated. However, the definition of terms which have not been individually negotiated is very broad. Thus the UTCC Regulations apply to any term in a contract concluded between a bank and a consumer where the term has not been individually negotiated.[89] Notwithstanding that a specific term or certain aspects of it have been individually negotiated, the regulations apply to the rest of the contract if an overall assessment of it indicates that it is a pre-formulated standard contract.[90] Under the regulations the onus of establishing that a term was individually negotiated is on the bank.[91]

The distinction between standard and individually negotiated terms derives from German law; the Standard Contract Terms Act 1976 provides that there are no standard contract terms where the conditions of the contract have been negotiated in detail. The approach differs from UCTA, where section 3 applies if a party deals on the other party's written standard terms of business. Under the UTCC Regulations a party could be dealing in that way but not be able to attack a particular term in the contract as unfair because it was individually negotiated. Obviously the key issue is to identify the individually negotiated term.

Reflecting the Directive, the Regulations provide that a term is always to be regarded as not having been individually negotiated when it has been drafted in advance.[92] Clauses from precedents, manuals, or even one previous agreement would be drafted in advance. Consequently, even if a consumer negotiates hard over such a term, but at the end of the day fully accepts a pre-formulated term, that is not an individually negotiated term and can be attacked as unfair. Similarly, if a consumer is given a choice of a number of pre-formulated terms, say in relation to different methods of repaying a mortgage (repayment, endowment, etc.), those terms are not individually negotiated. But if there are gaps in a pre-formulated term, which are filled in after negotiation, then the term should be an individually negotiated term.

[88] e.g. *Guiliano–Lagarde Report on the Convention on the Law Applicable to Contractual Obligations* [1980] OJ C282/1, 23.
[89] R. 5(1).   [90] R. 5(3).   [91] R. 5(4).   [92] R. 5(2).

Take a hypothetical case, the bank genuinely wants the guarantee to cover £15,000 but eventually agrees to a limit on the surety's liability of £10,000. It is easy in this context to conclude that the term has been individually negotiated. It should, however, be possible to conclude that the clause has been individually negotiated where the consumer finally agrees to the figure being £15,000. In the Directive, a term is always regarded as not being individually negotiated when it has been drafted in advance 'and the consumer has not been able to influence the substance of the term'.[93] If the bank is genuinely open to persuasion, but at the end of the day the consumer agrees to the bank's position, the term is arguably still individually negotiated. It will be necessary to examine the circumstances surrounding the negotiation of the term. The difficulty facing the bank will be in establishing that it was open to persuasion— and the onus is, as indicated, on it.

(iii) Exclusion of Core Provisions

A very significant limit on the reach of the UTCC Regulations is that the core provisions of a contract cannot be questioned.[94] In other words, it is only the subsidiary terms of a contract which can be attacked as unfair. Nonetheless, the UTCC Regulations provide that in assessing the fairness of a particular contract term, the courts may refer to all the other terms of the contract, including core terms.[95]

This limitation on the scope of the UTCC Regulations reflects the position ultimately agreed for the Directive, that consumers should not be able to reopen a bad bargain. Any control of the essence of the business–consumer relationship, it is said, would be in breach of the fundamental tenets of the free market and consumers would no longer shop around for the best banking terms. The first point is purely rhetorical, since the fundamental tenets of the free market are constantly adulterated. The argument about moral hazard, that consumers would be less careful if the substance of the contract were reviewable, even if only at the margin, would seem counterbalanced by other considerations. However, the Directive accords with the English common law reluctance to examine the value of consideration. The result is, however, that the title of the Directive is a misnomer, as is that of the 1977 Act. At most these core terms may fall foul of the requirement in the regulations that all terms in a consumer contract be clearly expressed, or of provisions in the general law such as those against extortionate credit bargains.[96]

The unfair terms which are not capable of review under the regulations are those which relate to 'the definition of the main subject matter of the contract' or to 'the adequacy of the price and remuneration'. Inevitably there will be quibbles about what is encompassed by the main subject matter of the contract.[97] Take a basic banking contract, the customer opening an account. Is the main subject matter of the contract

---

[93] R. 3(2).   [94] R. 6(2).   [95] R. 6(1).

[96] R. 7; Consumer Credit Act 1974, s. 137.

[97] R. Brownsword and G. Howells, 'The Implementation of the EC Directive on Unfair Terms' [1995] *JBL* 243, 248–9.

the simple undertaking of the bank to accept deposits and to repay, say, on demand? Or does it extend to the bank's willingness to provide cheque facilities, since in the English context a current account implies a willingness to accept deposits *and* provide such facilities? In theory it should not be possible for a bank to inflate the main subject matter of a deposit contract by qualifying the description of the facility. The bank agrees to open a 'premium account' for the customer—but there is still the issue of whether the main subject of a contract to open a premium account is everything which distinguishes a premium account from an ordinary account.

The 'adequacy of the price and remuneration'—words taken from the Directive—is referred to as the 'quality/price ratio' in its preamble. The terms, 'price' and 'remuneration', arguably differ between themselves. Neither is equivalent to the English concept of consideration which encompasses money and money's worth. There seems little doubt that the interest rate in a loan agreement is a core provision, a conclusion strengthened by the specific exemption built into the list of potentially unfair terms relating to variable interest rates but not a term providing for default interest to be paid until the borrower repays. That is an ancillary provision—it relates to the exceptional case of default—and not one concerned with the adequacy of the bank's remuneration as against the services provided.[98]

(iv) Mandatory, Statutory, or Regulatory Provisions/International Conventions

Excluded from the scope of the regulations is a term incorporated in a consumer contract in order to comply with or which reflects (i) mandatory statutory or regulatory provisions of the United Kingdom or European Community; or (ii) the provisions or principles of international conventions to which the Member States or the Community are party.[99]

'Statutory provisions' are straightforward and would include terms inserted in consumer credit agreements in line with the Consumer Credit Act 1974 and its attendant regulations. 'Regulatory provisions' are also fairly readily identifiable and include terms inserted in an agreement as required by the rules of the Financial Services Authority. In both cases the justification, set out in the Preamble to the Directive, for excluding such terms from the test for unfairness is met, namely that the legislator or regulator in performing its public functions will presumably take the consumer interest into account in formulating such terms.

What of self regulation, for example the terms required by the Banking Codes—do they reflect regulatory provisions? If there were a substantial input into that code by, or if a public body such as the FSA or the Office of Fair Trading had a veto power over its contents, the question may have some force. Even then it might be said that the substantial public input or veto would have to have consumer-protection purposes behind it. In other words, it would not be enough for the FSA or Office of Fair Trading to have primarily in mind prudential or competition reasons.

---

[98] *Director General of Fair Trading* v. *First National Bank plc* [2001] UKHL 52, [2002] AC 481 (HL).
[99] Sched. 1(e).

The exclusion of provisions demanded by or reflecting international conventions has a narrow ambit. All Member States would seem to have to be party, or the Community itself has to be a party. Were the United Kingdom to be an adherent of an international convention, however, implementing legislation would most likely have been passed so that the regulations would not apply by reason of statutory provision.

(v) Banking and Financial Services

As indicated, the UTCC Regulations apply to any term in a contract concluded between a supplier and a consumer. A supplier is defined as a person who acts for purposes related to his or her business, trade, or profession.[100] The definition does not require that the service be provided to the consumer. Thus a guarantee is covered, albeit that the bank is providing the service (i.e. finance) not to the consumer guarantor, but to the borrower, and that the borrower is not a consumer. Where a consumer borrower is providing the security, it is arguable that the security forms part of a financing package—indeed there will be cross-referencing—so that it must be read together with the loan contract, and both together involve a service.[101]

'Services' is not defined, but clearly banking and financial services are covered. Core banking—taking deposits and making loans—obviously involves the provision of services. Effecting a customer's payment orders is also a service. So, too, are financial advice, securities dealing, fund management, and so on. The indicative list of unfair terms in the Directive, and in Schedule 2 to the Regulations, refers to clauses which regularly feature in financing contracts. For example, jurisdiction clauses are covered by paragraph 1(q), since their object or effect could be to exclude or hinder the consumer's right to take legal action.[102] Indeed financial services are specifically mentioned in Schedule 2.

Paragraphs 1(g) and (j) refer to terms which enable a supplier to terminate a contract of indeterminate duration without reasonable notice (except when there are serious grounds for doing so), or to alter the terms of the contract unilaterally without a valid reason which is specified in the contract. Paragraph (l) refers to a term which allows a supplier of services to increase its price without giving the consumer the corresponding right to cancel the contract if the final price is too high in relation to the price agreed when the contract was concluded. Then paragraph 2 of the Schedule goes on to state expressly that the indicative clauses in paragraphs 1(g) and (j) are without hindrance to suppliers of financial services, which terminate a contract of indeterminate duration unilaterally, or which reserve the right to alter the interest rate or other charges, provided in both cases the consumer is required to be quickly notified and, in the case of unilateral alteration, the consumer is also free to dissolve the contract.

---

[100] R. 3(1).

[101] Department of Trade and Industry, *The Unfair Terms in Consumer Contracts Regulations 1994. Guidance Notes*, 1995, 8.

[102] *Oceano Grupo Editorial SA v. Quintero* Cases C240/98 to C244/98 [2001] ECR I–4941.

On demand termination is a feature of some bank financings. It would seem to be a core provision and not subject to attack, unless in unintelligible language. However, this is subject to notifying the customer, and arguably this demands individual notification, not general advertising. Variation clauses in banking contracts have already been mentioned: often general clauses empower the bank to vary the contract at will, and there may be specific clauses, such as those in guarantees, enabling a bank to increase the borrowings without informing the guarantor. The effect of paragraph 2 seems to be that there are no problems for a bank in varying interest rates. Varying other charges must be for a valid reasons.

In addition paragraph 2 states that paragraph 1(g), (j), and (l) do not apply to transactions in transferable securities, financial instruments, and other products or services where the price is linked to fluctuations in a stock exchange quotation or index, or a financial market rate that the seller or supplier does not control. Clearly this paragraph would cover the sale or purchase of securities on an exchange where the bank is to sell or buy at the market price. In an objective sense an undertaking to sell or buy at the best price is also at a financial market rate 'which the supplier does not control', although whether the best price is obtained turns, in fact, on the care and skill of the bank. Likewise, the paragraph would fit easily with perpetual securities, which usually are redeemable at will (paragraph 1(g)), and pay a floating interest rate (the words of description in paragraph 2(c)). The terms of their redemption would thus fall outside the UTCC Regulations.

Paragraph 2(c) also says that the indicative terms in paragraph 1(g), (j), and (l) do not apply to '[a] contract for the purchase or sale of foreign currency, travellers' cheques and international money orders denominated in foreign currency'. It will be a sophisticated consumer, and an esoteric financial product, for paragraph 1(g) to apply. One can see more readily how indicative terms 1(j) and 1(l) apply, since the supplier will retain the right to vary, say, the time or price at which an exchange occurs.

(vi) Unfair Terms

English lawyers, in particular banking lawyers, are not unfamiliar with the task of assessing whether credit bargains require a payment which is grossly exorbitant or which grossly contravenes the ordinary principles of fair dealing, and whether a transaction is manifestly disadvantageous or at a considerable undervalue. Testing terms in consumer contracts for their unfairness under the Directive and UTCC Regulations is not conceptually very different, albeit that the definition of unfairness is new and invokes the notion of good faith which, familiar to lawyers from civil law systems and the United States, does not have an everyday ring to English ears.

To be unfair under the UTCC Regulations a term must, contrary to the requirement of good faith, cause the significant imbalance specified in the Regulations.[103] The language, lifted from the Directive, indicates that the question is whether the term

---

[103] R. 5(1).

causes the significant imbalance (a) against the customer; (b) in a manner or to an extent which is in breach of good faith.

The requirement of good faith in this context is one of fair and open dealing. Openness requires that the terms should be expressed fully, clearly and legibly, containing no concealed pitfalls or traps. Appropriate prominence should be given to terms which might operate disadvantageously to the customer. Fair dealing requires that a supplier should not, whether deliberately or unconsciously, take advantage of the consumer's necessity, indigence, lack of experience, unfamiliarity with the subject matter of the contract, weak bargaining position or any other factor listed in or analogous to those listed in Schedule 2 to the Regulations. Good faith in this context is not an artificial or technical concept . . . [104]

In other words, good faith in UTCC demands a dedication to the interests of consumers on the part of a bank in both the making and substance of the contract. For this reason the concept in particular contexts may not coincide with the standard of reasonableness in UCTA. While a similar result is in many cases likely to be achieved when applying the two concepts, this will not always be the case. The factors which the courts have addressed in applying the reasonableness standard need not necessarily involve an inquiry into whether a bank has dealt fairly and taken into account a consumer's interests.

The lack of good faith must cause a significant imbalance in the parties' rights and obligations under the contract, to the detriment of the consumer. Thus the fairly obvious imbalance between a bank and a consumer customer is not the immediate focus of inquiry, although it may be the reason for the imbalance in rights and obligations. This contrasts with an important factor in determining reasonableness under UCTA, whether or not there is an inequality of bargaining power. The natural imbalance between bank and consumer need not necessarily lead to an imbalance in contractual rights and obligations; in any particular contract this will be a matter of inquiry. In assessing, say, a default clause in a loan agreement the dimensions of the bank's rights must be assessed in terms of the clause itself (is it unambiguously expressed? is it simply default in payment or in other serious matters? is there a grace period, e.g. thirty days, and a materiality test?) and other aspects of the facility (e.g. is the loan unsecured? is the interest rate a market rate or one which is grossly exorbitant?).

One difficulty is the meaning to be attached to 'significant' in the description of the imbalance in rights and obligations. One connotation of the term is that the imbalance must be really serious or exceptional. This would accord more with the traditional approach of English law to upholding bargains but enabling hard cases to be upset in a consumer context outside the specific doctrines of unconscionability, undue influence, and duress. Another connotation of 'significant' is important; the term has been inserted in recognition that imbalances permeate consumer contracts,

---

[104] *Director General of Fair Trading v. First National Bank plc* [2001] UKHL 52, para. 17, [2001] AC 481, 494, *per* Lord Bingham.

so that there is a need to filter out those which are trivial. But as long as the balance is non-trivial it satisfies the definition of unfairness. There is support for this approach in the exclusion from UTCC of the core provisions of a contract. The justification for this exclusion is that consumers should not be able to reopen a bad bargain. To require a serious imbalance in subsidiary terms before unfairness can be invoked would be to extend the protection to bad bargains well beyond the core terms. Moreover, the indicative list has unfair terms which do not all seem to contain a serious imbalance.

Finally, there has been some discussion of the phrase 'to the detriment of the consumer' in the context of the imbalance. One argument is that the words have no operative effect but are simply words of description—the imbalance has to be to the detriment of the consumer, not the bank.[105] On the other hand, since the phrase is unnecessary to indicate the direction of the imbalance, the words must be given some independent effect. If this is the case how is effect to be given to a requirement that the imbalance be to the detriment of the consumer? The first, and obvious, point is that the words of the regulations do not require that the detriment be significant (as the imbalance must be); we are not looking for a serious detriment comparable to the manifest disadvantage which the applicant in an undue-influence action must presently demonstrate.[106] Secondly, it would seem that the test must be objective, rather than being geared to the character of the consumer in any particular case, especially since the regulations are confined to standard-form contracts. Thirdly, there must be few terms causing a significant imbalance in rights and obligations which are not simultaneously to the detriment of the consumer. A default clause enabling a loan to be called in for a trivial breach is to the detriment of the consumer, and no less obviously so because the terms governing interest and repayment are generous.

Determining whether a term is unfair demands an inquiry into the matters so far considered, taking into account 'context'—the nature of the banking or financial service and referring to the circumstances attending the conclusion of the contract, other contractual terms, and other contracts on which it is dependent.[107] Since the regulations are concerned only with standard-form contracts, the relevant inquiry into context would seem to be less wide-ranging than were all contracts to be subject to the Directive. Generally speaking, if a standard term in a particular type of banking contract (e.g. a guarantee) were to be fair for one consumer, it would be a recipe for uncertainty were it to be unfair for another. Exceptionally a consumer might belong to a particular class of consumers so that in the context the term is unfair—a standard banking contract proffered, say, to a member of a non-English speaking ethnic

---

[105] *Director General of Fair Trading* v. *First National Bank plc* [2001] UKHL 52, para. 36, [2001] AC 481, 499, *per* Lord Steyn. See R. Brownsword, G. Howells, and T. Wilhelmsson, 'Between Market and Welfare: Some Reflections on Article 3 of the EC Directive on Unfair Terms in Consumer Contracts', in C. Willett (ed.), *Fairness in Contract* (London, Blackstone, 1996).

[106] 215 below.

[107] R. 6(1).

minority. In the case of security or a guarantee, cross-reference could be made to the loan agreement. The assessment of context is to be made at the time of the conclusion of the contract. In this respect the Regulations reflect the approach of UCTA.

D. THE BANKING CODES AND FINANCIAL SERVICES OMBUDSMAN SERVICE

In 1991 UK banks introduced a voluntary code of banking practice for dealing with personal customers. The current edition of *The Banking Code*, dated January 2001, was joined in March 2002 by *The Business Banking Code* for sole traders, partnerships, and limited companies with an annual turnover of under £1 million, as well as associations, charities, and clubs with an annual income under the same amount. There was a considerable incentive to introduce the code in 1991, since the government-appointed committee on banking services had recommended a statutory code should the banks fail to act or introduce an inadequate code.[108] Similarly, the Business Banking Code was introduced at a time when the Competition Commission reported that a complex monopoly existed in the market of banking services to small and medium sized companies which meant they were being overcharged for banking services.[109] The codes are drawn up by the Banking Code Standards Board, funded by the banks, but with a majority of independent directors. Although the codes are voluntary in nature the government established a review body in November 2000 which made certain recommendations on content, but also for biennial reviews by an independent person and for closer monitoring of code compliance.[110]

The codes are addressed to banks dealing with their customers. Their governing principles require that banks act fairly and reasonably in dealings with customers. In relation to banking services and products, the codes oblige banks to give information in plain language and to offer help if anything is not understood. Despite the governing principles, however, there is no general requirement that the terms and conditions be fair.

The codes cover a range of matters from information to be provided to customers to standards of service. These are referred to at various points in the book, and need no repetition here.[111] Two general points, however, are in order. The first is the relationship of the codes to the law. Even if the codes are not accepted as evidence of trade usage, and thus a basis for implying terms in a bank–customer contract, it is apparent that courts will have regard to the provisions in formulating legal principles.[112] Secondly, at the level of policy, there is some discrepancy between common law protections and provisions of the codes.[113] There is no need for a disquisition on

---

[108] *Banking Services*, Cm. 622 (London, HMSO, 1989), 141.

[109] *Supply of Banking Services by Clearing Banks to Small and Medium-Sized Enterprises*, Cm. 5319, 2002.

[110] Banking Services Consumer Codes Review Group, *Cracking the Codes for Banking Customers* (London, 2001).

[111] 166, 182, 208.   [112] *Barclays Bank* v. *O'Brien* [1994] 1 AC 180, 197–8.

[113] Especially 220 below.

the advantages and disadvantages of self-regulation as a technique for channelling business behaviour.[114] However, attention needs constantly to be given to customer input into the codes' periodic revision. At present that is done through the presence of the independent directors on the Banking Code Standards Board and consultation with consumer organizations but, as mentioned, there is the prospect of biennial review by an independent reviewer. In the Netherlands, representatives of consumers negotiate directly with the banks over the Dutch general banking conditions. In Germany consumer groups have successfully challenged the general banking conditions before the courts.

Separate from the Banking Codes is the statutory Financial Services Ombudsman Service, encompassing eight previous private and public ombudsmen within the financial services sector.[115] The objective is to establish dispute-resolution mechanisms which are accessible, speedy, and inexpensive. Complaints from individuals and small companies about the provision of banking services and products are included. Decisions are binding on banks, but not on complainants who can further pursue matters in court.[116] The Ombudsman determines matters by reference to what is, in his opinion, fair and reasonable in all the circumstances.[117] In doing so he will take into account the relevant law, the FSA's rules, guidance and standards, the Banking Codes, and good industry practice. But since he need only take into account these matters, it seems that the Ombudsman could go beyond a rule or relevant judicial decision to achieve what he regards as fair and reasonable in all the circumstances.

IV. THE BANK AS DEPOSITORY — THE ACCOUNT

The most basic service a bank can provide to members of the public is to act as a depository for their moneys. This is the essence of commercial banking; it provides a legal definition for banking.[118] The public generally holds its deposits with banks in the form of accounts, the subject matter of this final section of the Chapter.

These days, multifunctional banks hold the public's moneys in other forms as well — in various collective investment schemes, funds, and insurance products. In many senses these are functionally equivalent to bank accounts, and may be economically more advantageous for customers. As a matter of law, however, they are quite distinct from bank accounts. They are often regulated under the securities laws.

---

[114] C. Scott and J. Black, *Cranston's Consumers and the Law* (3rd edn., London, Butterworths, 2000); G. Roberts, 'The British Penchant for Self-regulation: The Case of the Code of Banking Practice' [1995] *BJIBL* 385; J. Black, 'Constitutionalising Self-regulation' (1996) 59 *MLR* 24.

[115] C. Clarke, 'The Banking Ombudsman Scheme' (1994) 2 *JFRC* 195; P. Morris, 'The Banking Ombudsman—Five Years On' [1992] *LMCLQ* 227; M. Seneviratne, R. James, and C. Graham, 'The Banks, the Ombudsman and Complaints Procedures' (1994) 13 *CJQ* 253; R. James, *Private Ombudsmen and Public Law* (Aldershot, Ashgate, 1997); P. Cartwright, *Consumer Protection in Financial Services* (London, Kluwer, 1999).

[116] FSMA 2000 s. 228(5).   [117] S. 228(2).   [118] 6 above.

Banks also issue certificates of deposit (CDs). These are debt instruments of high value, payable to bearer, and sold in the wholesale markets. CDs are negotiable instruments as a matter of market practice, if they are not also promissory notes under the Bills of Exchange Act 1882. In the United Kingdom they are regarded as debentures, but not always in other jurisdictions.

A. THE CURRENT ACCOUNT

Bank accounts have varying characteristics. The most basic account is the savings account. Savings accounts cannot be overdrawn, and generally notice has to be given of withdrawal. Current accounts are payable on demand, either by withdrawal or by the customer instructing the bank to make payment to a third party. They can be overdrawn, by way of overdraft. Then there are trust accounts, foreign currency accounts, 'flexible' accounts (combining current and mortgage accounts) and any other number of accounts with different features and services. We focus on the current account. Account holders vary as well, from individuals through to multinational enterprises and governments. The special rules relating to account-holding by unincorporated associations, partnerships, executors, minors, the mentally ill, and so on are beyond the scope of this book. Banks hold accounts at other banks as a result of the system of correspondent banking, and because one bank may act as the agent of another when, for example, it is a member of a payment system and the other is not.[119]

The relationship between customer and bank in relation to the current account is fundamentally that of creditor and debtor. Consequently, banks can be served by the judgment creditors of customers with third party debt/garnishee orders, which purport to attach the balance in the account. The effect of a third party debt/garnishee order is that the bank will pay the judgment creditor rather than the customer what is owed.[120] In addition to the obligations derived from the debtor–creditor relationship, an account also gives rise to important obligations in contract. The classic statement of these at common law is contained in the judgment of Atkin LJ in *Joachimson* v. *Swiss Bank Corp.*:[121]

The bank undertakes to receive money and to collect bills for its customer's account. The proceeds so received are not to be held in trust for the customer, but the bank borrows the proceeds and undertakes to repay them. The promise to repay is to repay at the branch of the bank where the account is kept, and during banking hours. It includes a promise to repay any part of the amount due against the written order of the customer addressed to the bank at the branch, and as such written orders may be outstanding in the ordinary course of business for two or three days, it is a term of the contract that the bank will not cease to do business with the customer except upon reasonable notice. The customer on his part undertakes to exercise reasonable care in executing his written orders so as not to mislead the bank

---

[119] 40 above; 235 below.
[120] *Société Eram Shipping Co. Ltd.* v. *Cie Internationale de Navigation* [2001] EWCA Civ. 1317, [2001] 2 All ER (Comm) 721 (CA).
[121] [1921] 3 KB 110, 127.

or to facilitate forgery. I think it is necessarily a term of such contract that the bank is not liable to pay the customer the full amount of his balance until he demands payment from the bank at the branch at which the current account is kept. Whether he must demand it in writing it is not necessary now to determine.

Thus a bank must collect its customers' bills of exchange and cheques. Failure to do so, or delay in doing so, constitutes breach of contract. The passage in *Joachimson* can be generalized to oblige a bank to gather into its customers' accounts payments owing to them through other mechanisms such as direct debts—quite apart from express contract. In Chapter 8 we see, however, that customers are obliged to accept the normal incidents of particular payment mechanisms, for example delays. The delay associated with gathering in certain payments means that banks need not pay on a customer's instruction until payments in have been cleared.

Moreover, a bank has a duty to effect payment on the order of the customer. There are many decisions where banks have been held liable for wrongful dishonour—for not paying a customer's cheque—but these are simply illustrative of the principle that banks have a contractual duty to pay on demand when they hold a customer's current account. Conversely, there are many decisions where banks have been held liable for paying out on forged cheques: again these are simply illustrative of how a bank is liable for paying without its customers' mandate. In law the bank is treated in these circumstances as having paid away its moneys, and it has no entitlement to debit the customer's account.

However, payment as a matter of law is not effected through assignment.[122] Thus a bank is obliged to make payment—to meet its customer's demand—only if the balance or overdraft is sufficient to cover the amount. If the balance or overdraft falls short of doing so, even by a penny, the bank is entitled to ignore the instruction completely.[123] At common law a bank has no obligation to combine a customer's accounts held at different branches if there are insufficient funds in the account to which the payment instruction is directed. It is unclear whether in these circumstances the bank must combine accounts at the same branch, although for reasons of consistency this would seem to be the sensible rule. On hearing of the position the customer can easily enough transfer moneys from one account to the other.

Overdrafts must generally be agreed. As a matter of law giving a payment order when there are insufficient funds constitutes a request for an overdraft on the bank's standard terms, for example as to charges.[124] Much more difficult is to establish that a bank is bound by a term implied in the contract to permit the customer to operate the overdraft in excess of the agreed limit.[125] A bank which honours payment instructions in these circumstances, over a period, may be bound by its course of conduct and find itself to be in breach of its waiver should it finally decide, on a particular occasion, and

---

[122] 233 below.
[123] *Bank of New South Wales* v. *Laing* [1954] AC 135, 154 (PC).
[124] *Lloyds Bank plc* v. *Voller* [2000] 2 All ER (Comm) 978 (CA).
[125] *Narni Pty. Ltd.* v. *National Australia Bank Ltd.* [2001] VSCA 312 (CA Victoria).

without notice, to refuse payment. Even in the absence of written agreement, banks may charge compound interest on outstanding amounts on current accounts.[126]

The current account has been analogized to a stream, in the sense that it is flowing or running, although it seems more accurate to use the metaphor of a pond on a stream, with payments flowing in and out of the pond. Even here there are difficulties, since the flows are by a variety of diverse payment sources. The pond, as we know, belongs to the bank—moneys in the hands of a bank are its moneys, not moneys held as bailee, trustee, or agent.

The notion of flow is useful, however, when it comes to the rule in *Clayton's Case*,[127] which establishes a presumptive rule for the order in which individual credit and debit transactions occur in a current account. The first sum paid in is regarded as the first drawn out, and the first debit in the account is reduced or extinguished by the first sum paid in. One result of the rule is that, subject to any term in the documentation, if a customer gives security in relation to a specific, overdrawn amount, it is discharged as soon as the equivalent has been paid into the account, even though with further drawings the account has not been brought into balance.

The rule in *Clayton's Case* is a presumptive rule only. A customer can appropriate a payment in for a specific purpose, provided this is communicated clearly to the bank and the bank assents. Moreover, the 'first in-first out' rule of *Clayton's Case* applies only as between the bank and its customer: if persons mix moneys held in their capacity as fiduciary with their own moneys, payments are presumed to come first from their own moneys, leaving as much as possible for the beneficiaries.[128] However, the difficulty arises where they have mixed moneys in a current account from two claimants, who can both trace into the account. Applying the rule in *Clayton's Case* would work an injustice, for it would mean that withdrawals from the account would be presumed to be made on the 'first in-first out' basis, rather than rateably from the amounts attributable to each claimant. The English Court of Appeal has refused to apply the rule in the case of a collective investment scheme, because of the injustice it would work between different investors,[129] but there needs to be a more ready judicial repudiation of the rule in other situations as well.[130] The securities laws now provide that a firm must segregate its customers' moneys and hold them in a separate client account. In the event, say, of the firm's default, the moneys are consequently not available to the firm's creditors. Instead, the moneys are pooled and distributed to customers in proportion to their entitlement.[131] The rule in *Clayton's Case* has no application.

[126] *National Bank of Greece SA v. Pinios Shipping Co. (No 1)* [1990] 1 AC 637 (HL).
[127] *Devaynes v. Noble; Clayton's Case* (1816) 1 Mer. 572, 35 ER 767.
[128] 255 below.
[129] *Barlow Clowes International Ltd. v. Vaughan* [1992] 4 All ER 22 (CA). See also *Ontario Securities Commission v. Greymac Credit Corp.* (1987) 55 OR (2d) 673 (CA); *Re Registered Securities* [1991] 1 NZLR 545 (CA).
[130] A. Oakley, 'Proprietary Claims and their Priority in Insolvency' (1995) 54 *CLJ* 377, 416–20.
[131] FSA Handbook, Conduct of Business, r.9.5.7.

Banks are not bound to open an account, and indeed to comply with money-laundering and terrorism law they are obliged to take various steps before they do so.[132] On the other side of the coin banks must give sufficient notice of their intention to close a customer's account, which probably turns on the time needed for the customer to make alternative arrangements. The appropriate remedy in English law for closing an account without sufficient notice is damages, rather than an injunction.

With a corporate customer in financial difficulty, the bank is in a dilemma. To close (or freeze) the account is equivalent to signing a death warrant for the customer's business. But not to do so is to expose a bank to liability under the Insolvency Act 1986, which seeks to preserve for creditors generally the assets which are available. In particular, section 127 provides that any disposition of a company's property after a winding-up petition is presented is void, unless validated by a court order.[133]

If a company's account is overdrawn, payments in either by credit transfer or the bank collecting payment (e.g. by cheque) are dispositions to the bank within the meaning of section 127.[134] Payments in when the account is in credit may also be said to be a disposition of the company's property, in that the bank substitutes as debtor for the third party payee. On policy grounds creditors generally would not benefit from such payments in, if the bank was in a position to combine that account with another in debit. Payments out, in favour of third parties, do not involve the bank in dispositions of the company's property but simply in adjustments to the account.[135] However, banks may still exercise caution in such cases, not least because any increase in the liability of the company to the bank in the period between notice to the bank of the petition and the winding-up order will not be available for set-off against any credit balance on another account.[136]

B. STATEMENTS OF THE ACCOUNT

Banks generally provide the balance of an account on request. Full statements of an account are also available on request, but otherwise at regular intervals. If a bank pays out money for a customer by mistake, this may be because its records about the customer are inaccurate. The bank must set the customer's record straight. Whether it can reclaim the moneys from the payee is a different matter. When the customer is the payee an account balance or bank statement may be relevant in such a claim to any defence on the part of the customer of change of position.

The Uniform Commercial Code of the United States imposes a duty on customers to examine bank statements and accompanying 'items'—in the United States banks return their customers' cheques with bank statements—with reasonable care and promptness, to discover any unauthorized signature or material alteration, and to

---

[132] 71 above.   [133] See also s. 129(2).

[134] *In re Gray's Inn Construction Co. Ltd.* [1980] 1 WLR 711, [1980] 1 All ER 814 (CA).

[135] *Hollicourt (Contracts) Ltd. v. Bank of Ireland* [2001] 2 WLR 290, [2001] 1 All ER 289 (CA).

[136] N. Frome and C. Hanson, 'The Hollicourt Case—Are Banks off the Hook or on the Horns?' (2001) 3 *JIBFL* 126, 130.

report any discrepancy promptly.[137] Failure to comply precludes customers from asserting forgeries against the bank, unless the bank itself has been negligent in paying the items. The General Business Conditions for German banks produce the same result as a matter of contract.[138] In Canada the Supreme Court has held to similar effect if customers agree in writing to verify the correctness of statements on the account, and to notify the bank of any mistakes within a short period.[139] However, the decision was at a time when Canadian banks returned customers' cheques with their statements, and in the absence of a verification agreement Canadian law follows English law.[140]

English law approaches the matter from the other end. Apart from contract, there is no limit on customers contesting the wrongful debit of their accounts just because they have received a bank statement identifying the payment. *Tai Hing* emphatically rejected the bank's argument that customers owe an implied contractual duty to check their periodic statements so as to be able to notify the bank of any debits which they have not authorized. It also held that failure by customers to notify the bank does not constitute an estoppel against it. Mere silence or inaction could not constitute the representation necessary for an estoppel in the absence of a duty to disclose or act. As a matter of policy the decision is obviously sensible: customers may reasonably expect when they are sent a statement that it is to assist them and not in the interests of the bank. As far as private customers are concerned, there seems to be no public interest in requiring them to conduct their private affairs efficiently. Nonetheless, in deciding what is fair in all the circumstances, the banking ombudsman has attributed an element of contributory negligence to complainants who do not check their statements to identify errors.[141]

As for express contract, if banks are to insert terms in their standard-form contracts binding customers who do not query their bank statements to the debit items set out there, *Tai Hing* also held that they must do so clearly and unambiguously. The burden of the obligation, and of the sanction imposed, must be brought home to customers. The test is rigorous. Such a 'conclusive evidence' clause is also subject to attack under the unfair contracts regime considered in section III of the Chapter. In balancing the different factors to be considered in deciding whether such a clause is unfair, the courts would no doubt be concerned with whether customers receive back their cheques (so as better to check payments), whether payees are identified on their bank statements, the time allowed for customers to challenge inaccuracies, and whether customers are precluded from doing so even if the bank has been negligent.

---

[137] UCC, §4–406.

[138] §7.

[139] *Arrow Transfer Co. Ltd.* v. *Royal Bank of Canada* (1972) 27 DLR (3d) 81 (SCC). See K. Perrett, 'Account Verification Clauses' (1999) 14 *BFLR* 245; F. Malan, J. Pretorius, and C. de Beer, *Malan on Bills of Exchange, Cheques and Promissory Notes in South African Law* (2nd edn., Durban, Butterworths, 1994), 350–1.

[140] *Canadian Pacific Hotels Ltd.* v. *Bank of Montreal* (1988) 40 DLR (4d) 385 (SCC).

[141] *The Banking Ombudsman Scheme, Annual Report 1994–95* (London, Office of the Banking Ombudsman, 1995), 28.

C. COMBINATION OF ACCOUNTS

The common law confers on banks a privilege not available to a customer's other creditors—the right of combination. This enables it to apply a credit balance in favour of the customer on any account against a debit balance on the customer's other accounts with the bank. A bank can thus recoup itself without any thought of litigation. The bank must give notice, for until the customer knows that the right is to be exercised it is entitled to have its payment orders effected. It may be that the term combination is a misnomer: no matter how many accounts there are, these are but entries in the bank's books. All that is happening is a calculation of the overall debt existing at any one time between bank and customer, by taking into account all credits and debits that have not been expressly or impliedly excluded from the ambit of the relationship. In short, combination is really only an accounting procedure.[142] That a customer's accounts are in different currencies should not be an objection.[143]

The courts have been generous to banks concerning the right of combination. Banks can, but need not, combine accounts at different branches.[144] It may be that the arrangements between a customer and bank exclude the right of combination, as where an account in debit is frozen and a new account opened for trading operations. But if circumstances materially change, as with a decision by the customer to wind itself up, the right of combination in such cases revives.[145] Similarly, the right of combination does not extend to loan accounts—it would not be sensible if a customer's payment orders from a loan account could be arbitrarily blocked because of a deficiency in the current account—but only so long as the customer is able to carry on business. Insolvency will clearly enable the bank to combine: after all, set-off operates under ordinary principles of insolvency law.

In the multifunctional bank the right of combination does not extend to moneys paid to the bank for particular purposes, such as to the fund management or securities-dealing arms. It may be difficult for a customer to resist combination, however, if such moneys are co-mingled in the customer's ordinary accounts. English law takes a strict view of the separateness of members of a corporate group, so that at common law the combination of their different accounts is impossible.[146] Contractually, however, members of a corporate group may bind themselves to inter-group combination and set-off.

---

[142] See S. McCracken, *The Banker's Remedy of Set-Off* (2nd edn., London, Butterworths, 1996); R. Derham, *Set-Off* (2nd edn., Oxford, Clarendon, 1996).

[143] B. Horrigan, 'Combining Bank Accounts in Different Currencies' (1991) 65 *ALJ* 14.

[144] 9 above.

[145] *National Westminster Bank Ltd.* v. *Halesowen Presswork and Assemblies Ltd.* [1972] AC 785 (HL).

[146] *Royal Bank of Scotland* v. *Wallace International Ltd.* [2000] EWCA Civ. 16(CA).

D. BANK CHARGES

In many countries there has been a considerable consumer controversy over bank charges for accounts. The UK banking codes have introduced greater transparency: published tariffs are to be available, charges outside the tariff are to be advised on request or at any time the service is offered, fourteen days' notice is to be given of deductions for interest and charges on accounts, and details of interest charges are to be given. But there are no controls on charges and they can also be varied by the bank with immediate effect. Likewise, the German general business conditions for banks do not require the notification of any change in interest or charges, but if customers decide to terminate the service the bank cannot apply the increase to the terminated service. There is little law relevant to bank charges. If a charge is imposed because a customer has breached the contract (e.g. by overdrawing an account) then the rule against penalties has a potential application. With commercial customers, banks may take an indemnity against all charges and costs incurred.

6

THE DUTY OF CONFIDENTIALITY

The legal duty of confidentiality (or secrecy) which banks owe their customers is not difficult conceptually, although I will argue that the common law has got it muddled. The real problems are in the application of the doctrine in practice. These are basically two-fold. First, confidentiality has a habit of getting in the way of commercially (but not necessarily socially) acceptable practices. We have already come across examples such as the potential breaches of confidentiality involved in multifunctional banking. Indeed, one reason confidentiality is under attack is that banks would like to distribute information throughout the corporate group so that the whole range of bank services can be marketed to customers. As well as the situations described in this Chapter we see that confidentiality raises its head later in the book. For instance, if a bank assigns its mortgage accounts as part of a securitization deal, unless its agreement with its customers permits release of the information there will be a breach of the duty of confidentiality. Secondly, confidentiality frequently acts as a cloak for wrongdoing, often on a massive scale. Political leaders who have exploited their people, drug barons, and fraudsters in many shapes and sizes have used the banking system to spirit away their ill-gotten gains. Bank confidentiality has then acted as a barrier, sometimes an impenetrable barrier, to bringing the culprits to book and recovering the booty.[1] Confidentiality provides one of the explanations of how international terrorists have transferred their financing round the world without detection.

International instruments sometimes recognize the duty of confidentiality which banks owe to customers under national law. Thus the Annex on Financial Services to the General Agreement on Trade in Services (the GATS) provides that nothing shall be construed to require a Member State to disclose information relating to the affairs and accounts of individual customers. In the main, however, the trend is for international instruments to require that bank confidentiality be overridden in the interests of enforcement.[2] The Protocol to the European Union Convention on Mutual Assistance provides an example: a Member State must not invoke banking secrecy as a reason for refusing co-operation regarding a request for mutual assistance for a

---

[1] R. Naylor, *Hot Money* (London, Unwin Hyman, 1987).

[2] G. Stessens, *Money Laundering* (Cambridge, CUP, 2000), 333.

Member State.[3] As a consequence, Member States must have in place legislation enabling them to override bank confidentiality in such cases. The Criminal Justice (International Co-operation) Act 1990 contains the relevant power in the United Kingdom.

I. AN OUTLINE OF THE DUTY

A. NATURE AND JUSTIFICATION OF THE DUTY

In Germany it has been said that bank confidentiality is protected by provisions of the federal constitution such as Article 2 (the freedom to choose and exercise one's profession).[4] Whether or not this is correct as a matter of German law, an English lawyer would say that provisions such as that in Article 8 of the European Human Rights Convention (respect for a person's private and family life, home, and correspondence) do not bear directly on the law of bank secrecy although it may be used to underpin it.[5] The argument of this Chapter is that even that goes too far, for both as a matter of law and of public policy the duty of confidentiality which a bank owes its customers is a duty which frequently is, and should be, trumped by the countervailing public interests recognized in Article 8.

It is as well to start historically. For it was not until the much cited decision of *Tournier* v. *National Provincial and Union Bank of England*[6] that English law firmly placed an obligation of confidentiality onto banks. When the matter had been litigated some half a century previously, the courts implied that, while expected, the observance of secrecy by a bank was a matter of moral, not legal, obligation.[7] Not surprisingly the *Bankers' Magazine* applauded this approach as entirely in harmony with common sense and common usage—bankers would responsibly exercise the trust reposed in them and there was no need for a legal duty.[8] And if the relative absence of litigation is any guide, there was something to that. Then came Mr Tournier, or rather Mr Fennell, the manager of a branch of the National Provincial Bank. Concerned that one of his customers, Tournier, was not paying off his some £10 overdraft as agreed, indeed had endorsed one cheque in his favour to a bookmaker,[9]

---

[3] [2001] OJ C326/1, Art. 7.

[4] O. Sandrock and E. Klausing, 'Germany', in R. Cranston (ed.), *European Banking Law* (London, LLP, 1999), 91. Cf. 'Germany', in *ibid.*, 2nd edn., 1999, 74. There seems to be no protection for bank customers under the US constitution: *United States* v. *Miller*, 425 US 435 (1976).

[5] See D. Feldman, *Civil Liberties and Human Rights in England and Wales* (2nd edn., Oxford, Clarendon, 2002), 622.

[6] [1924] 1 KB 461.

[7] *Hardy* v. *Veasey* (1868) LR 3 Ex. 107. See also *Tassell* v. *Cooper* (1850) 9 CB 509, 137 ER 990. Cf. *Foster* v. *Bank of London* (1862) 3F & F 214, 176 ER 96.

[8] 'Bankers and their Customers' (1868) 28 *Bankers' Magazine*, 218–19.

[9] Normally of course Fennell would never have seen the cheque, but as luck would have it the drawer was another of his customers. When it reached his hands he was able by inquiry of the collecting bank to discover what Tournier had done with it.

Fennell revealed all to Tournier's employers, who decided not to employ him after his probationary period. Like many of the figures who move briefly into the spotlight of the common law, Tournier's ultimate fate at the hands of the courts is unknown, for the Court of Appeal ordered a new trial. But the latter's decision spread as authority for the duty of bank confidentiality throughout the common law world, albeit that it took some decades to reach US shores.[10]

Although *Tournier* is probably the most-cited decision in banking law, it helps little in understanding the nature of a bank's duty of confidence. Moreover, these days it may mislead in relation to the qualifications to the duty. The fact is that the general law of confidence, of which bank confidentiality is a part, has moved on. However, many banking lawyers latch immediately onto *Tournier* if a problem of confidentiality arises, rather than using it against a backdrop of general principle.

Before elaborating this theme, it is necessary to say a few words about the public-policy justifications for the duty of confidentiality, in particular that imposed on banks. *Tournier* itself is of little assistance. The only reason given in the judgments for implying into the bank–customer contract a duty of confidentiality was a suggestion by Bankes LJ that '[t]he credit of a customer depends very largely upon the strict observance of that confidence'.[11] But credit does not depend on concealing the state of one's bank account; even in the 1920s traders obtained this information by means of a banker's references without, it might be said, the express consent of a customer. Indeed, there is possibly something to Professor (now Judge) Posner's argument that concealing vital financial information from creditors, which if known would impair the person's reputation, is equivalent to the fraud of a producer concealing defects in its products.[12]

Posner is concerned that confidentiality (or privacy) is not always economically efficient. Whatever the validity of this view there are at least two arguments which can be marshalled in favour of imposing a duty of confidentiality on banks. The first relates to the commercially sensitive nature of business information. Information about a business has a market value, and doubly so if it is confidential information. It is not difficult to envisage situations where disclosure by a bank of confidential information about a business would place it in jeopardy from a competitor or predator. The second is perhaps the major argument for the duty of bank confidentiality—its value to the individual in protecting personal autonomy. In the commercial context this overlaps with the first argument for, in a sense, the common concern is with reducing exploitation and domination by others. At a very practical level commercial and private customers value keeping their finances

---

[10] *Peterson v. Idaho First National Bank*, 367 P 2d 284 (1961) appears the first clear decision: see also 92 ALR 2d 891, 901.

[11] At 474.

[12] R. Posner, 'The Right of Privacy' (1978) 12 *Georgia LR* 393; 'Privacy, Secrecy and Reputation' (1979) 28 *Buff. LR* 1. Cf. K. Scheppele, *Legal Secrets* (Chicago, Ill., Chicago UP, 1988), 36ff.

confidential. A bank which acquired a reputation for not doing this would lose the public's trust.[13]

If there are public interests in the law obliging banks to keep customers' financial information confidential, so too are there public interests on the other side of the equation. The modern state could not properly function if its members could keep banking information secret. Some would unfairly avoid paying the proper amount of tax.[14] The integrity of markets would be threatened if insiders and manipulators had one more avenue of evasion. Drug traffickers and others engaged in heinous crimes would be able to launder and secrete their gains. Over-indebtedness is a major social problem, and financial institutions should have access to the fullest information about the credit history of applicants for credit. These are just some instances of the public interests which are to be placed in the balance with confidentiality. The modern technology of banking and its internationalisation—matters dealt with in Chapter 17—give added weight to these factors. The law does not ignore them, although often their full import for the duty of bank confidentiality is not appreciated.

B. BASIS OF THE DUTY

In some jurisdictions the banker's duty of confidentiality is based in the criminal law. Well-known is Article 47 of the Swiss Federal Banking Law, which was enacted in 1934 at a time when the Nazis had begun confiscating the property of persons because of their race or beliefs. A banker breaching Article 47 is liable to imprisonment or a fine, although if it is done negligently then only a fine can be imposed. While originally designed to protect legal behaviour from illegitimate investigation, the Swiss law became notorious as a barrier to law-enforcement agencies from other jurisdictions tracing the proceeds of wrongdoing. The difficulties have been mitigated by the steps taken by Swiss banks to observe care in accepting funds (know your customer), changes in the Swiss Criminal Code, the introduction of the Money Laundering Act, action by the Swiss Banking Commission, and the mutual-assistance agreements between Switzerland and other jurisdictions.[15] As a result of the first three measures a bank, or at least its senior management, must know the identity of the beneficial owners of deposits and the economic background of transactions. To the mutual assistance agreements we return.

Yet just as the Swiss banking system was rendering itself less attractive to money launderers and others, a number of jurisdictions were successfully transforming themselves into offshore financial centres, a major attraction being a duty on banks,

---

[13] R. Wacks, *Personal Information* (Oxford, Clarendon, 1989), 11–12; 'International Banking Secrecy' (1990) 23 *Vand. J Trans. L* 653, 656–8.

[14] OECD, *International Tax Avoidance and Evasion* (Paris, OECD, 1985), 108–12.

[15] D. de Montmollin, 'Are Recent Developments in International Cooperation Incompatible with Swiss Banking Secrecy?' (2001) 2 *JIBFL* 72; M. Giovanoli, 'Switzerland', in R. Cranston (ed.), *European Banking Law* (London, LLP, 1993); F. Taisch, 'Confidentiality at the Bank Counter—Protection of Personality in the Banking Business: Liechtenstein–Swiss Aspects' (1996) 3 *EFSL* 201.

enforceable by the criminal law, to observe confidentiality.[16] These jurisdictions purportedly distinguish between acting as a safe haven for funds from what they regard as legitimate reasons on the one hand (e.g. flight capital from exchange-control or fiscal laws), and illicit purposes on the other. In practice it does not work that way: while bank-secrecy jurisdictions will attract legitimate moneys, they will also be used by drug traffickers and other criminals who will take advantage of bank secrecy to prevent the creation of an 'audit trail', which investigators can follow.[17]

By contrast with those jurisdictions which place the banker's duty of confidentiality on a statutory or even constitutional basis, many jurisdictions, of which England is one, found the duty in the common law. A leading commentator on the English law of breach of confidence has suggested that its precise jurisdictional source in the common law is secondary to the underlying notion; he argues for the existence of a *sui generis* action.[18] In *Tournier* the bank's duty of confidentiality was implied in the bank–customer contract.[19] These days there must be doubts whether this conclusion would follow, given the unnecessarily stringent test (at least in England) for the implication of contractual terms. In any event contract is not the whole story for otherwise it would be difficult to uphold the duty in the case of a potential customer, or a partner or business associate of a customer. Nor would protection be afforded against a third party to whom the confidant bank had either inadvertently or with consent disclosed information. Equity must and does have a role in protecting confidences in these situations independently of contract. Equity also provides assistance through its remedy of the injunction to underpin any contractual duty. Moreover there are other possibilities than contract and equity. For example a third party might be sued in tort for inducing a confidant bank to disclose information to it in breach of a contractual duty. Perhaps the precise jurisdictional basis of breach of confidence in the common law is secondary to the underlying notion.

C. SCOPE OF THE DUTY

The starting point in examining the scope of the duty is not any special law of bank confidentiality (such as laid down in the *Tournier* case) but the general principles governing breach of confidence. We must look to these, moulded by the banking context, to fathom the scope of the duty. Lord Goff stated these general principles in the leading English decision on the subject:

---

[16] e.g. D. Campbell (ed.), *International Bank Secrecy* (London, Sweet & Maxwell, 1992); B. Rider, 'The Practical and Legal Aspects of Interdicting the Flow of Dirty Money' (1996) 3 *J. Fin. Crime* 234, 236.

[17] G. Hilsher, 'Banking Secrecy', in E. Effros, *Current Legal Issues Affecting Central Banks* (Washington DC, IMF, 1992), i, 239–40.

[18] F. Gurry, *Breach of Confidence* (Oxford, Clarendon, 1984), 58ff. See also R. Goff and G. Jones, *The Law of Restitution* (5th edn., London, Sweet & Maxwell, 1998), 751–4.

[19] Two historical footnotes: (1) there was an express term of secrecy in Tournier's passbook; and (2) since damages were not thought to be available in equity at the time of the decision the court was impelled in the direction of contract.

a duty of confidence arises when confidential information comes to the knowledge of a person (the confidant) in circumstances where he has notice, or is held to have agreed, that the information is confidential, with the effect that it would be just in all the circumstances that he should be precluded from disclosing the information to others ... To this broad general principle there are three limiting principles ... The first ... is that the principle of confidentiality only applies to information to the extent that it is confidential ... The second limiting principle is that the duty of confidence applies neither to useless information, nor to trivia ... The third limiting principle ... is that, although the basis of the law's protection of confidence is that there is a public interest that confidences should be preserved and protected by the law, nevertheless that public interest may be outweighed by some other countervailing public interest which favours disclosure ...[20]

It is at once obvious that it is not only banks which have imposed on them a duty of confidentiality. This book is concerned with banks, but we can note in passing that the non-banking members of a banking group—the securities arms, the insurance subsidiary, and so on—might also be subject to obligations of confidentiality. More-over, it is also obvious that the duty of confidence in the context of banking is not confined to information provided by the customer: any information generated by the confidant bank, including impressions and assessments, or any information which comes to it relating to the customer, is protected if it has a confidential quality and the circumstances are such as to import the duty of confidence.[21]

The details of transactions (e.g. the names of those whom customers pay or from whom they receive payment), the state of customers' accounts, personal information such as their employment—all are clearly covered. There is no reason in principle that information of a negative character should not also be covered: that a customer has not used the account recently, has not drawn on a credit line, or has not sought advice in relation to a takeover bid. For this reason the protection can extend to information acquired by the bank in the course of providing non-banking services. Clearly also the duty does not depend on the capacity of the customer. The New York rule, which recognizes an implied duty of confidentiality between a bank and its depositors, but not between a bank and its borrowers, makes no sense in the English context.[22] As with breach of confidence generally, the duty of a confidant bank applies to pre-contractual dealings and also survives the termination of the bank–customer relationship.

Once bank confidentiality is located in general principle it is possible to solve what have been thought of as puzzles.[23] Thus the very existence of A's relationship with bank X is potentially subject to the duty. It is non trivial information—for one reason creditors might wish to freeze or attach any account—having a generally inaccessible quality, of which the confidant (the bank) has notice. Information which is common

---

[20] *Attorney-General* v. *Guardian Newspapers Ltd.* (*No 2*) [1990] 1 AC 109, 281–2.

[21] It will be recalled that in *Tournier* the duty was held (Scrutton LJ *contra*) to cover the information obtained from another bank.

[22] *Graney Development Corporation* v. *Taksen*, 400 NYS 2d 717, 720, aff'd. 411 NYS 2d 756 (App. Div. 1978); *Sharma* v. *Skaarup Ship Management Corp.*, 699 F. Supp. 440 (SDNY 1988).

[23] A number of these were raised in R. Goode, 'The Banker's Duty of Confidentiality' [1989] *JBL* 269.

knowledge is not, however, subject to the duty.[24] An example is information recorded in a land or securities registry.[25] But just because A writes cheques on his current account with Bank X does not make it common knowledge that that is A's bank. As credit and debit transfers become more popular, however, then, as in Germany, customers will routinely inform creditors of details of an account so that payments can be made to them. The information could be published on documents such as invoices. In these circumstances the fact that A has an account with Bank X would not be subject to the duty.

A bank must have notice that the information has a confidential quality. That, generally speaking, will be obvious. What of the bank's state of mind with respect to the breach of duty? What, for example, of the situation where a hacker accesses the bank's computer and the confidential information stored there? Is it relevant that the bank has installed the best security system available on the market? In principle liability for misuse of confidential information is strict, and the confidant should take steps to protect against it. Negligence is not relevant to this type of duty, whether grounded in contract (where strict performance is generally demanded) or equity (which looks rather to good faith). Whether an adequate security system is installed goes, however, to the issue of whether the bank has misused the information: it cannot be said to have done so if it has done everything it could to protect the confidences.

Third parties who acquire information from a confidant are also bound, as we have seen, to respect the confidence. Moreover, in sanctioning the release of confidential information for a particular purpose a person is not relinquishing any claim to general protection. Finally, it is well to note that in addition to the duty of confidence is the related duty not to profit from use of confidential information.[26] This is underpinned by the view of the Information Commissioner that, without consent, it is unlawful for a bank to use information on its own databases to market the services of third parties (including other members of the banking group), even though no data are actually disclosed to them and customers are simply placed in certain broad categories.[27]

As far as remedies are concerned breach of confidentiality, if serious, would justify a customer in terminating the banking relationship (if that could not be done in any event). Breach of the duty of confidentiality can give rise to damages (as in *Tournier's* case) or an injunction. Damages are for breach of contract (if there is a contract) or under Lord Cairns's Act (in lieu of an injunction). Damages will have a strong pecuniary element in a commercial context, but if a personal confidence is breached, the claim will involve a non-pecuniary element covering matters like distress. A trivial disclosure may lead to only nominal damages. Not all loss to a customer will be

---

[24] Some civil lawyers argue that specific, rather than general, financial information is more likely to be covered by the duty of secrecy; but in English law there is no reason to think that it is any more likely to have a confidential quality or not be common knowledge.

[25] *Christofi v. Barclays Bank plc* [2000] 1 WLR 937, [1999] 4 All ER 437 (CA).

[26] *Guertin v. Royal Bank of Canada* (1983) 1 DLR (4th) 68, aff'd. 12 DLR (4th) 640n (Ontario CA).

[27] Data Protection Registrar, *Personal Data held by the Finance Industry*, Jan. 1994, para. 20.

compensated. For example, if a customer is obliged to pay tax because of confidential information which a bank need not have revealed to the revenue authorities, that is not recoverable because the customer is obliged to pay it in any event. Conceivably there are circumstances where a bank would be liable for an account of profits for misusing a customer's confidential information.

D. DUTY NOT TO USE CONFIDENTIAL INFORMATION

Closely related to the duty of secrecy attaching to confidential information is the duty not to misuse it. Banks are sometimes bound by express contract not to use confidential information provided by a customer or potential customer for any purpose other than evaluating a proposed transaction.[28] Moreover, misuse of confidential information without the customer's consent is actionable in equity and in blatant cases may constitute the tort of unlawful interference with the customer's business interests.[29] In extreme cases an injunction may issue against the bank pursuing a course of conduct triggered by the acquisition of the confidential information. One difficulty, however, is that the duty continues only so long as the information remains confidential: if publicly available there can be no objection to the bank using it. Perhaps the greatest obstacle facing a customer is to demonstrate how the bank misuse occurred. A significant lapse of time may negate the causal link. Moreover, it is not enough that the bank is galvanized into action by its knowledge of the confidential information unless it takes a course of action it would otherwise not have contemplated, or unless it uses the actual details of the information to its advantage.[30]

II. QUALIFICATIONS TO THE DUTY

The qualifications to the duty of confidentiality are invariably treated as those spelt out in the judgment of Bankes LJ in *Tournier*: (1) where disclosure is under compulsion of law; (2) where there is a duty to the public to disclose; (3) where the interests of the bank require disclosure; and (4) where the disclosure is made by the express or implied consent of the customer. Almost universally these are regarded in the jurisprudence as exceptions to the duty and as if they had statutory force. They are incorporated as section 13.1 of the Banking Codes. Indeed, some common law jurisdictions have given them statutory force.[31] The advantage of the approach is that it is easily understood; unfortunately it can mislead.

---

[28] Financial Law Panel, *Confidentiality Agreements in Corporate Finance Transactions* (London, FLP, 2001), 12.

[29] *Indata Equipment Supplies Ltd. (t/a Autofleet)* v. *ACL Ltd.* [1997] EWCA Civ. 2266, *The Times*, 14 Aug. 1997; *United Pan-Europe Communications NV* v. *Deutsche Bank* [2000] EWCA Civ. 166, [2000] 2 BCLC 461 (CA).

[30] *Arklow Investments Ltd.* v. *Maclean* [2000] 1 WLR 594 (PC).

[31] e.g. Banking and Financial Institutions Act 1989, ss. 97, 99 (Malaysia).

If the law compels the disclosure of information otherwise confidential—the first qualification—it is hardly accurate to say that this is an 'exception' to the duty of confidentiality. Rather, disclosure is the duty and that duty overrides duties which would otherwise obtain. As Diplock LJ put it in one case, the overriding duty to disclose is a duty to comply with the law of the land.[32] Calling this an 'exception' reflects, of course, the view which common lawyers have of statutory law, the main derivation of the first qualification. It is a pity that banking lawyers have not retained Bankes LJ's term, 'qualification'. As a matter of law, if one of the qualifications applies the duty no longer exists.

But there are more serious problems than that of faulty conceptualization. One has been the tendency of banks to read certain of the qualifications too liberally: notably banks have detected the implied consent required by the fourth qualification when, had customers known that confidential information was to be disclosed, they almost certainly would have vetoed it. Another error has been to overlook the general principle that, apart from legal compulsion and contract, the duty of confidentiality can be trumped only by a countervailing public interest, as indicated in Lord Goff's judgment, quoted previously. Bankes LJ's second qualification is thus firmly grounded, although his example of the banker not being permitted to disclose a customer's accounts to the police investigating fraud can no longer be good law, quite apart from statute.

Most importantly the third qualification—disclosure in the interests of the bank—does not survive developments in the law of confidence. Bankes LJ gave as an example of the third qualification where a bank issues a writ claiming payment of an overdraft stating on the face of the writ the amount.[33] Perhaps in ordinary parlance this is disclosure of confidential information in the interests of the bank. As a matter of law, however, it is a disclosure in the public interest that justice be administered effectively. The very phraseology, disclosure in the interests of the bank, is apt to mislead, and courts have had to resist the suggestion that just because disclosure is an advantage to the bank does not bring it within the qualification.[34]

Sunderland v. *Barclays Bank Ltd.*[35] is regularly cited to support this third qualification; the case has never been officially reported, and this is as it should be. There du Parcq LJ, sitting at first instance, upheld the defendant bank's argument that it was justified in informing the plaintiff's husband that most of the cheques passing through the account were for bookmakers. As pleaded the defence was that the disclosure was with the wife's implied consent (the fourth qualification), and thus was the main ground for the decision. Implied consent is a tricky notion, as we shall see; in any event it can be argued that it did not extend to what was said about the gambling when referring simply to the balance on the account would have sufficed. Without, it

---

[32] *Parry-Jones* v. *Law Society* [1969] 1 Ch. 1, 9.
[33] At 473. See also 479, 481, *per* Scrutton LJ.
[34] *X AG* v. *A Bank* [1983] 2 All ER 464, 479.
[35] (1938) 5 LDAB 163.

seems, referring to *Tournier*, du Parcq LJ added that, given the implicit demand of the husband for an explanation of what seemed to him to be discourteous treatment of his wife by the bank, the manager was entitled to 'give the information which explained what the bank, rightly or wrongly, had done . . . the interests of the bank required disclosure'.[36] Consistent with general principle, the correct interpretation of this passage is that it might be in the public interest that potentially damaging statements be immediately refuted by a limited release of confidential information.

Failure to recognize that Bankes LJ's third qualification cannot stand in the light of principle led the Jack Committee to consider under this head the practices of passing of confidential information about customers within a banking group and to outside credit-reference agencies. Unhappy with these developments, the committee recommended legislation to confine the 'interests of the bank' qualification.[37] In fact, consistent with general principle, such practices can be justified only if in the public interest (apart from statute or contract). We return to these matters shortly. Relying on *Tournier* to the exclusion of general principle also led the committee to conclude that, in the light of the many statutory obligations on banks to disclose confidential information, disclosure under the second qualification—where there is a duty to the public to disclose—'will require a very special justification'.[38] In fact public interest lies at the heart of the doctrine of confidentiality; it is the lens through which any qualification to the duty must be considered.

A. COMPULSION OF LAW

The classic example of compulsion of law is associated with court proceedings. The public interest in the administration of justice has demanded that banks produce information regardless of breach of confidence. The disclosure of the whole truth is essential to judicial decision-making. What confidence would the public have if important, relevant evidence were withheld? Banks receiving a subpoena directed to them must therefore produce the information required about a customer. Not to do so places them in contempt of court.

If the evidence is sufficiently cogent, section 7 of the Bankers' Books Evidence Act 1879 may be also used. This enables a litigant to obtain an *ex parte* order to inspect entries in a bank's records which might be relevant. But the courts do not permit the section to be used 'for fishing expeditions', and neither will they make orders against those who are not closely connected with a case. There is a raft of case law on the section: 'bankers' books' has been given a narrow interpretation. Mention should also be made of so-called 'Bankers Trust' orders, which are based on the inherent jurisdiction of the court to obtain information about bank accounts to facilitate the

---

[36] At 164.
[37] *Banking Services: Law and Practice*, Cm. 622 (London, HMSO, 1989), 31–3, 35–6.
[38] At 30.

use of *Mareva* injunctions.[39] Finally there is the so-called *Shapira* order, which enables a victim of fraud to obtain disclosure against a bank of confidential information concerning customers involved in the fraud.[40]

When disclosure is mandatory, a bank has no obligation to its customer to contest an apparently lawful and proper request for access. It is neither part of the duty of confidentiality (which *ex hypothesi* no longer exists) nor capable of being implied as a matter of necessity or efficacy in the bank–customer contract. These considerations also lead to the conclusion that a bank is under no general obligation to inform the customer that such a request has been made. Public policy also points in this direction, since notification of a customer might hinder a lawful inquiry or actually constitute an offence (the tipping off offence).[41] At most it may be arguable in particular circumstances that a bank has breached its general duty to exercise care and skill in its handling of the request. In particular circumstances failing to use its best endeavours to notify the customer might constitute such a breach.[42]

Despite the multitude of statutory obligations on banks to disclose confidential information, each can be supported on public-interest grounds. Banking supervision, tax evasion, company fraud, insider dealing, drug trafficking, terrorism—these are just some of the legitimate public concerns to which (as the committee recognized) bank confidentiality must give way.[43] It would be tedious to go over the details of even a few of the many statutory provisions. A few general remarks are, however, in order.

First, there is no need for the statute specifically to refer to the bank–customer relationship, although in practice it often will. If in its terms it compels the production of the particular information covered a court will give it full effect despite the banker's duty of confidence. To require the legislation to spell out the large class of relationships involving contractual duties of confidentiality, of which that in the bank–customer relationship is but one, would be to impose a quite unsupportable judicial restraint upon legislators.[44]

Secondly, the statutory provisions do not override confidentiality completely. Information, when disclosed, does not become available to the public generally. In the main access to information disclosed is limited. Indeed those who obtain the information might be under quite separate statutory duties not to disclose it further. This is the position, in general, with banking regulators.[45] As with others under such a duty banking regulators might be required to disclose information in court proceedings,

---

[39] See N. Clayton, 'Problems of Self-incrimination in Seeking to Obtain Bank Records' [1996] 4 *JIBL* 162, 164–8.

[40] *Bankers Trust v. Shapira* [1980] 1 WLR 1274, [1980] 3 All ER 353 (CA); *C v. S* [1999] 1 WLR 1151, [1999] 2 All ER 1506 (CA).

[41] Proceeds of Crime Act 2002, s. 333. See J. Wadsley, 'Banks in a Bind: Implications of the Money Laundering Legislation' (2001) 16 *JIBL* 125.

[42] Cf. *Robertson v. Canadian Imperial Bank of Commerce* [1994] 1 WLR 1493; [1995] 1 All ER 824 (PC).

[43] e.g. Terrorism Act 2000, s. 21B(1), Sched. 6, para 2(b); Companies Act 1985, ss. 434, 443, 447, 452(1A); Insolvency Act 1986, s. 236.

[44] *Smorgan v. Australia and New Zealand Banking Group Ltd.* (1976) 134 CLR 475, 489.

[45] FSMA 2000, s. 348.

for example, where the interest in establishing the truth outweighs the interests in maintaining the confidentiality.[46]

Thirdly, instead of mandating the disclosure of specific information, legislation sometimes places the responsibility of deciding whether to disclose on banks themselves. The legislation is permissive, not mandatory. Section 20 of the Terrorism Act 2000 is an example of the permissive approach: it protects a bank from breach of confidentiality if it discloses to the police a 'suspicion or belief' that funds are derived from terrorism. If there is no obligation on the bank to disclose, it might well decide not to risk alienating a customer or, worse, being successfully sued because a court later decides that the disclosure was not protected by the relevant section or by any other countervailing public interest. If in serious doubt a bank can seek a declaration from the court: if the court takes the view that it should disclose, then it would be able to resist a subsequent action by its customer.[47]

B. PUBLIC INTEREST

The second qualification mentioned by Bankes LJ is 'where there is a duty to the public to disclose'. Examples of this qualification given in the books are when during time of war a customer's dealings indicate trading with the enemy. Analogous is notice of terrorist connections. Disclosure could be to the police, to regulatory authorities such as the banking supervisors, to an official inquiry into regulation of banking, and to those, even in other jurisdictions, involved in winding up a multinational bank.[48] There is of course a clear distinction between the public interest and what the public may be interested to know. Historically the qualification was based on the iniquity rule, that there is no confidence as to the disclosure of an iniquity. In modern formulation, this extends to crime, fraud, and misdeeds, both those actually committed and those in contemplation. It is clear that in English law the public-interest defence to breach of confidence potentially involves a range of public interests. Ironically some Australian courts remain wedded to the nineteenth-century English position that the balancing is limited to the public interest in detecting or protecting wrong-doing.[49] The public-interest qualification is underpinned now by a number of provisions obliging a bank to disclose particular information to regulators or law enforcement bodies. Already discussed is that banks commit an offence if they fail to disclose a knowledge or suspicion—or indeed reasonable grounds for knowledge or suspicion—that a customer is engaged in money-laundering or terrorist offences.[50] Disclosure must be to the police or in accordance with established procedures within the bank, as soon as

---

[46] S. 349. See *Municipality of Hillegom v. Hillenius* [1985] 3 ECR 3947, [1986] 3 CMLR 422.

[47] *Governor and Company of the Bank of Scotland v. A. Ltd.* [2001] EWCA Civ. 52, [2001] 1 WLR 751, [2001] 3 All ER 58 (CA).

[48] *Libyan Arab Foreign Bank v. Bankers Trust Co.* [1989] QB 728, 770–1; *Price Waterhouse v. BCCI Holdings (Luxembourg) SA* [1992] BCLC 583; *El Jawhary v. BCCI* [1993] BCLC 396.

[49] See P. Finn, 'Professionals and Confidentiality' (1992) 14 *Syd. LR* 317, 323.

[50] Proceeds of Crime Act 2002, s. 330; Terrorism Act 2000, s. 21A.

practicable after the information or other matter comes to the bank. Most importantly for present purposes, the legislation provides that such disclosure is a 'protected
disclosure'—it 'is not to be taken to breach any restriction on the disclosure of
information (however imposed)'.[51] Thus by statutory provision banks can avoid
liability for breach of the duty of confidentiality.

Just because legislation now requires the disclosure of information by bankers in a
range of circumstances does not mean that the public-interest exception is redundant.[52]
The disclosure of confidential information is always permitted at common law if in
the public interest. The public interest in preserving the confidentiality is balanced
against other public interests favouring disclosure. The bank may be in a dilemma:
namely to disclose will adversely affect its reputation in some circles, but to be seen
providing a shield for unsocial activities will damage public confidence. It seems that
the onus would be on the bank to establish the qualification, although whether disclosure is in the public interest will, at the end of the day, be a matter of judicial
impression rather than evidence. That impression will be influenced by social trends,
for example the steps taken around the world against money laundering. Tax avoidance is a different matter, and it will take a considerable shift of opinion if bank
secrecy is not to be regarded as a legitimate shield for the proceeds.[53] The public interest
qualification will generally be confined to the type of disclosure which would be of
interest to a proper authority such as the banking regulators. For example, it would
not be in the public interest for a bank to warn other customers of the potential
insolvency of one of its customers: if the customer steps back from the brink then its
reputation may have been fatally wounded in the longer term; if it proceeds to its fate
then those customers who were warned may be able to steal a march on the creditors
of the insolvent.

C. CUSTOMER'S CONSENT

Express consent to disclosure by a customer clearly absolves a bank from responsibility for breach of confidence. As a matter of prudence the bank will be advised to
obtain the consent in writing. For example, consumer loan documentation may contain an express-consent clause to the customer's bank passing on information about
any default under the loan to credit-reference agencies. Express consent can be general
or qualified. The latter is limited to the purposes for which it is given. In theory
express consent can be of infinite duration, but the circumstances may change so
much that an express consent, once given, becomes stale. An example is the written
consent which banks require before releasing information to a customer's auditors
about the state of its bank accounts, any security, and contingent liabilities. That needs
to be periodically renewed.

---

[51] Ss. 337(1), 21B(1) respectively.

[52] Cf. Banking Act c. 19 (rev. edn.), s. 47 (Singapore), which contains no general public-interest
qualification but only specific permitted disclosures.

[53] OECD, *Improving Access to Bank Information for Tax Purposes* (Paris, OECD, 2000).

Is there, halfway between express and implied consent, a notion of compelled consent, whereby A is compelled by law to give her consent to the disclosure of information by her bank? Within any particular jurisdiction the notion is redundant, at least in common law jurisdictions. If a bank is compelled by law to disclose, it matters not whether this is effected as a matter of juristic technique by compelling either A or her bank. Where two jurisdictions are involved, however, the issue acquires some relevance. Say A in New York is compelled by a New York court to consent to the disclosure of information by her bank, Bank X, in the Cayman Islands.[54] In an oft-quoted decision the Grant Court of the Cayman Islands has held that in this situation A would not have given her genuine consent and thus Bank X would be in breach of the Confident Relationship (Preservation) Law 1976 as amended, which makes it an offence to divulge confidential information without the express or implied consent of the relevant principal.[55] The reasoning is unconvincing. It is trite law that the confidence is of the customer, not the bank. Once the customer has consented to the disclosure it should not matter to a court whether this was voluntarily or under compulsion of law, since ipso facto the consent dissolves the confidence. The customer's bank has no independent right to maintain the confidence.

In limited circumstances customers will be treated as having given their implied consent to a disclosure by their bank. Giving one's bank as a referee is an example. Similarly, if A gives B a payment instrument (e.g. a cheque) A is giving implied consent to B to ask A's bank whether it will be paid. Another case which appears to fall under this head is when guarantors seek information on the extent of their liability. The bank must tell them of their existing and continuing liabilities, although if the amount of the debt is greater than the limit of the guarantee, they need simply be told that they are liable for the full amount. The guarantor is not entitled to examine the customer's account or to have access to details of specific transactions.

It is difficult to see how the disclosure of information by a bank to other companies in the same banking group can be justified on the basis of implied consent, especially if disclosure is so that those other companies can market non-banking services such as insurance and investment opportunities. In principle, the duty of confidentiality is breached if a bank discloses to other companies within the same banking group. Although the economic reality may be that the bank and the other subsidiary are one, the law treats them in many respects as separate entities.[56] Similarly, disclosure of information to credit-reference agencies regulated by the Consumer Credit Act 1974 seems not to be justified, although there is a good argument that the latter falls within

---

[54] See *United States* v. *Ghidoni*, 732 F 2d 814 (11th Cir. 1984); *Doe* v. *United States*, 487 US 201 (1987); *In re Grand Jury Proceedings (Marsoner)*, 40 F 3d 959 (9th Cir. 1994).

[55] *In re ABC Ltd.* [1984] CILR 130. See M. Alberga, 'Cayman Islands: Privacy—A Balancing Act in Changing Times' (1998) *J. Fin. Crime* 176.

[56] *Bank of Tokyo* v. *Karoon* [1987] AC 45n, 53–54 (CA). Two caveats: (1) passing personal data abroad, even if to a branch, i.e. within the same entity, is caught by the Data Protection Act 1998; (2) disclosure of information within a banking group may be justified under the other exceptions, for example, in order to comply with a bank's obligation to report large exposures.

the public interest exception in the case of 'black' information (information about default). Express authorization or, if that is impossible or impracticable, variation of the banking contract, seems to be the best avenue open to the bank. This is especially so in the light of the Data Protection Act 1998, which, generally speaking, makes unlawful the use of personal data for a purpose other than that for which it was provided. Consent makes that use lawful, but the Information Commissioner takes the view that proper consent must be voluntary, and not coerced, that individuals must be fully aware of what they are consenting to, and that it is impossible to infer assent from silence alone.[57]

Bankers' opinions in response to so-called status inquiries were well-established in the nineteenth century in the context of taking bills of exchange in payment. As a leading nineteenth-century writer on banking noted:

If [a trader should] take the bill to the banker's, at whose house it is made payable, and say, 'Gentlemen, I will thank you to inform me if the accepter of this bill be a respectable man— May I safely give goods or money in exchange for it?' They will reply, 'Sir, we never answer such questions to strangers.' But if the holder of this bill keeps an account at a banker's he has only to ask his banker to make the inquiry for him, and he will easily obtain the most ample information. Among nearly all the bankers in London, the practice is established of giving information to each other as to the respectability of their customers. For as the bankers themselves are the greatest discounters of bills, it is their interest to follow this practice; it is indeed the interest of their customers also, of those at least who are respectable.[58]

Bankers' opinions do not disclose precise details of accounts and contain coded language. The legal justification for breaching the confidence of customers was never satisfactorily addressed. While mentioning the practice, the judgments in *Tournier* remained largely neutral. Books on banking law eventually developed the rationale that customers impliedly consented to the practice or that it was a trade usage. Only Lord Chorley's amongst them was prepared to call the banks' bluff.[59] The Court of Appeal has finally accepted that Chorley was right: while status inquiries are acknowledged and understood as between banks, they are unknown to customers whose consent cannot be implied as a result of banking practice.[60] What is now required, therefore, is for banks not to give a banker's reference without the express consent of the customer concerned.[61] Moreover, so long as consent is given, there seems no reason why opinions should not be given direct to inquirers, rather than routed through their bankers.

---

[57] *Personal Data held within the Finance Industry*, Jan. 1994, para. 10. Similarly, the Banking Codes, para. 8.3. See G. Howells, 'Data Protection, Confidentiality, Unfair Contract Terms, Consumer Protection and Credit Reference Agencies' [1995] *JBL* 343.

[58] J. Gilbart, *A Practical Treatise on Banking* (5th edn., London, Longman, 1849), 10–11.

[59] Lord Chorley, *Law of Banking* (6th edn., London, Sweet & Maxwell, 1974), 24.

[60] *Turner v. Royal Bank of Scotland plc* [1998] EWCA Civ. 529, [1999] 2 All ER (Comm) 664 (CA).

[61] Banking Code, January 2001, §13.7; Business Banking Code, March 2002, §13.7.

III. INTERNATIONAL DIMENSIONS

Despite the duty of confidentiality, banks in the jurisdiction, even branches or sub-sidiaries of foreign banks, can be compelled by law to disclose information about customers, including their transactions with a foreign connection.[62] But what about customers or banks abroad? A standard method of obtaining information across borders is by a letter of request (or a letter rogatory): a court or tribunal in one country requests the assistance of a court in another county to obtain information. The procedure is regulated internationally by the Hague Convention of 1970 on the Taking of Evidence Abroad in Civil and Commercial Matters.[63] English courts will readily comply with letters of request, although bank confidentiality is not overlooked in the balancing exercise of deciding whether to give effect to the public interest of assisting the foreign court.[64]

An understandable temptation is to avoid the delays and limitation inherent in the letter-of-request procedure and to obtain a court order directed at the local offices of a multinational bank which has the information in its branches elsewhere. Thus A in England seeks a subpoena or other order (e.g. a *Shapira* order; an order under the Bankers' Books Evidence Act 1879) from an English court directed at X bank in London to produce information held at its office in another jurisdiction. In the past English courts have been cool about issuing such orders themselves; the duty of confidentiality and comity have weighed heavily in the balance.[65] For the same reasons the English courts have enjoined the operation of such orders issued by foreign courts.[66] Banks then find themselves in the invidious position of being in contempt of the English court if they comply with the order or of being in breach of the law in the jurisdiction where the order was issued if they fail to do so. From the point of view of English law it can well be argued that confidentiality has been given too much weight, and other public interests too little, in the reluctance to issue such orders, or to respond positively to such orders when issued by other jurisdictions.

The third avenue to obtaining information is by international co-operation. We consider this in the context of international banking in Chapter 17. For example, mutual-assistance treaties provide for the law-enforcement machinery of one country to be made available to assist investigations in other countries. The procedures under the treaties are not exclusive. Mutual legal-assistance treaties may permit disclosure other-wise in breach of local bank-secrecy laws. Mutual legal-assistance treaties have been heavily criminal, however, so that they do not necessarily cover regulatory offences. Nor are they oriented towards the preliminary inquiries before an offence can be pros-ecuted. Here, however, a memorandum of understanding (MOU) may be available.[67]

---

[62] *Clinch* v. *Inland Revenue Commissioners* [1974] QB 76.   [63] Cmnd. 6727, 1976.
[64] *In re State of Norway's Application (Nos 1 & 2)* [1990] 1 AC 723, 810–11; see Criminal Justice (International Co-operation) Act 1990, s. 4.
[65] *Mackinnon* v. *Donaldson Lufkin and Jenrette Securities Corp.* [1986] Ch. 482.
[66] *X AG* v. *A Bank* [1983] 2 All ER 464.   [67] 456 below.

7

ADVISORY AND TRANSACTIONAL LIABILITY

A recurrent theme of this book is the changing role of banks and the implications of this for the law. It is an especially pertinent theme when considering the advisory and transactional liability of banks. The fact is that banks now enter, on their own behalf and for customers, a range of transactions which, even comparatively recently, have been regarded as unusual even within the universal banks. Banks also market to customers or prospective customers their own financial products, some of considerable complexity. The opportunities for incurring transactional liability are thus much greater, including liability for what is said in relation to them. Additionally, banks have promoted themselves as financial advisers to customers although, since they are often advising on financial products of their own devising, they cannot be regarded as independent advisers in the traditional sense. Again there is a source of potential liability, independent perhaps of any transaction entered into.

The Chapter opens with a discussion of the general principles governing a bank's liability. The topic can be approached in various ways. One involves a consideration of the relevant doctrines in English law whereby banks can incur liability. Section I of the Chapter selects just a few such doctrines. Another approach considers the various factual matters which feed into legal decisions about bank liability. The same factors recur across different legal doctrines: indeed, they arise for consideration as well in other systems of law. This is the focus of section II of the Chapter.

Next, the Chapter considers advisory liability (section III). This can arise in two ways—a failure to advise where the law imposes a duty to do so, and a failure to advise adequately when a bank assumes the task of advising a customer or third party. Then in section IV the Chapter turns to the English law doctrines—undue influence, unconscionability, and duress—which have a particular application to transactions involving those the law regards as vulnerable. In the main these doctrines need not trouble a bank dealing with commercial parties.

Finally, these particular themes are examined in the specific context of 'lender liability' (section V). This is generally taken to cover situations in which banks may be liable to borrowers and potential borrowers, to the shareholders, directors, creditors, and guarantors of borrowers and potential borrowers, and even to other lenders. Institutional and cultural features of the legal system in the United States—jury trial for civil cases, contingent fees, the propensity to litigate, and so on—have spawned a variety of claims falling within this description. While there has not been the same range of claims in other jurisdictions, there has been some notable litigation. The drive behind much of this is to find a deep pocket when borrowers fail. However, the possibility of a claim may have the important practical effect of thwarting a bank seeking summary judgment against a borrower. There is no specific head of lender liability, but in particular instances traditional legal doctrines maybe mobilized.[1]

I. DOCTRINAL BASES OF LIABILITY

In the past, partly because of the heavy emphasis on bills of exchange, and partly because it was not generally taught in an academic environment, banking law has been perceived as being significantly independent of the general law. In fact the opposite is the case: banking law draws heavily on the general law, and no more so than in this area of a bank's potential liability. To understand banking law at the doctrinal level, then, demands a consideration of general law principles. Rooted in contract, the relationship between a bank, its customers, and third parties is overlaid with a range of rights and obligations having their derivation in tort (delict), equity, restitution, and statute. Indeed, as we shall see, some of the leading cases in these areas of substantive law were banking cases, in that they involved banks or banking transactions.

It would be otiose to set out the basic principles of contractual and tortious liability, even if it were possible within the limited space available. Indeed, important aspects of the law of contract as it affects banks appear throughout the book. One obvious issue is the nature of the duties to which a bank has contractually bound itself. Express terms in any contract must be interpreted. *Barclays Bank plc v. Quincecare Ltd.*[2] does not break any new ground in this regard, but it does remind us that a bank may waive any term for its benefit, and that in considering whether a party has acted in accordance with the terms of a banking contract, reference can be made to the contextual background without infringing the parol evidence rule. As we saw in the previous chapters many of a bank's contractual duties are strict (e.g. breach of mandate). Fault is not typically an element of a bank's contractual liability. In some cases, however, the customer's claim will be that the bank failed to exercise the duty of reasonable care and skill implied in the contract. To that duty we shortly return.

In attempting to attach liability to banks, customers may contend (i) that the express terms of a contract with a bank subsume wider duties than are immediately

---

[1] This chapter is concerned with bank liability. Of course banks and other financial institutions are not only victims: for example in recent times in England they have successfully sued others for losses attributable to a negligent overvaluation of property taken as security: e.g. *Banque Bruxelles Lambert SA v. Eagle Star Insurance Co. Ltd.* [1997] AC 191 (HL); *Smith New Court Securities Ltd. v. Scrimgeour Vickers* [1996] 4 All ER 225, 769, [1997] AC 254 (HL); *Platform Home Loans Ltd. v. Oyston Shipways Ltd.* [2002] 2 AC 190 (HL).

[2] [1992] 4 All ER 363.

apparent from the words themselves; (ii) that these wider duties can be implied into the contract; or (iii) that in any event the bank assumed these wider duties.[3] The first argument will turn importantly on the expert evidence of bankers—what does it mean to employ a bank in a particular capacity; the second on whether it is possible to satisfy the onerous tests of usage, obviousness, or business efficacy for implying terms in English law; and the third on the evidence in the case itself, such as any claims made by the bank in its advertising literature and other marketing endeavours.[4] The third claim may be a contractual claim (notably in collateral contract) or a tortious claim under the *Hedley Byrne* doctrine.

Indeed tort constantly features in banking claims.[5] That part establishing liability for negligent misstatement is dealt with in section III of this Chapter. *Hedley Byrne & Co. Ltd.* v. *Heller & Partners Ltd.*[6] is the leading case which, as is often forgotten, revolved around the liability of a bank for the reference it gave about one of its customers through another bank to the claimant. The defendant bank avoided liability only because of the standard disclaimer in bank references. The *Hedley Byrne* principle raises in one context the general issue of how the courts are to impose limits in tort on what could be the indeterminate or enormous liability for pure economic loss. In the case of negligent misstatement, they have done this by making liability turn on the assumption of responsibility towards a particular party, giving rise to a special relationship. In *Hedley Byrne* the bank assumed a responsibility towards the claimant by answering the inquiry made on its behalf by its bank. *Hedley Byrne* has been extended beyond advice-giving to other services where the defendant has assumed a responsibility to the claimant and the latter has reasonably foreseeably suffered financial loss as a result of the defendant's failure to exercise care.[7] The boundaries and implications of this development—which blur the line between statements and other acts, as well as between acts and omissions—are still being worked out. One such boundary in the context of banking is that contract often defines the relationship, including any assumption of responsibility, as between a bank and other parties.

This part of the Chapter confines itself to three areas of doctrine of importance to banks. The first concerns the general standard of care the law expects, once a duty of care has been established, whether that be in contract, tort, or fiduciary law. Then the potential liability of a bank is explored as a fiduciary, constructive trustee, or an accessory. This area is singled out because, if given an expanded interpretation, it could lead to extensive liabilities being imposed on banks. Finally, there is brief mention of some emerging standards of liability which have primarily a statutory base.

---

[3] e.g. *Eagle Trust plc* v. *SBC Securities Ltd.* [1995] BCC 231; *Fennoscandia Ltd.* v. *Clarke* [1999] EWCA Civ. 591 (CA); *McEnvoy* v. *Australia and New Zealand Banking Group Ltd.* [1990] Austn. Torts R 81–014 (NSW CA).
[4] 49 above.   [5] e.g. 41, 87 above, 222, 263 below.   [6] [1964] AC 465.
[7] See *Henderson* v. *Merrett Syndicates Ltd.* [1995] 2 AC 145; *White* v. *Jones* [1995] 2 AC 207; *Spring* v. *Guardian Assurance plc* [1995] 2 AC 296; *Marc Rich & Co. AG* v. *Bishop Rock Marine Co. Ltd.* [1996] 1 AC 211 (HL); *McFarlane* v. *Tayside Health Board* [2000] 2 AC 59 (HL).

A. REASONABLE CARE AND SKILL

A duty of reasonable care and skill for anyone providing a service (including giving advice) runs through contract, tort, and fiduciary law. Very occasionally it is stated explicitly as a standard, as in the *Uniform Customs and Practices for Documentary Credits*, which are regularly incorporated by reference into letter-of-credit contracts.[8] Section 13 of the Supply of Goods and Services Act 1982 implies a term to this effect in contracts for the supply of a service in the course of a business. Mostly, however, the duty of reasonable care and skill is a duty imposed as a matter of common law.

After a mass of conflicting case law, notably the challenge to concurrent liability in contract and tort posed by the banking case, *Tai Hing*,[9] it is now settled that a claimant may seek compensation for economic loss caused through the failure to exercise reasonable care and skill in both contract and tort.[10] It may be that the contract, in accordance with ordinary principles, limits or excludes a claim. Of course it does not matter in many cases if a claim is brought in tort rather than contract. However, there are two main situations where it does matter. First, contract's limitation period is six years from breach whereas the six-year limitation period for negligently caused economic loss may not begin to run until some time after the transaction.[11] Secondly, the rules about remoteness of damage in contract are more restrictive than in tort.

As for fiduciary law, it has long been the position that a fiduciary (including a trustee) must act or advise with reasonable care and skill. That fiduciary duty, along with other fiduciary duties, may be modified by the terms of an underlying contract.[12] It is unclear whether aspects of fiduciary liability, such as causation and damages, will continue to be more generous to claimants than their counterparts in contract and tort.

Whatever be its conceptual base, what does the duty of reasonable care and skill of a bank encompass? It is easy enough to state in theory. The duty is to exercise the care and skill of a reasonable bank in carrying out the particular activity concerned. The law does not impose liability for what turns out to be an error of judgement, unless the error was such that no reasonably well informed and competent bank would have made it. Moreover, two reasonable banks can perfectly reasonably come to opposite conclusions on the same set of facts without forfeiting their title to be regarded as reasonable. 'Not every reasonable exercise of judgment is right, and not every mistaken exercise of judgment is unreasonable.'[13]

Sometimes it will be obvious that a bank is in breach of duty. When there are two ways of doing a thing, and one is clearly right and the other doubtful, it will not be exercising reasonable care and skill to follow or advise the latter course. On a more

---

[8] UCP 500, Art. 13(a). See 385 below.
[9] *Tai Hing Cotton Mill Ltd.* v. *Liu Chong Hing Bank* [1986] AC 80, 107.
[10] *Henderson* v. *Merrett Syndicates Ltd.* [1995] 2 AC 145.
[11] Law Commission, *Limitations of Actions*, Law Com No 270, 2001, 8–11.
[12] *Henderson* v *Merrett Syndicates Ltd.*, at 206. See 187 below.
[13] *Re W (an infant)* [1971] AC 682, 700, *per* Lord Hailsham LC.

practical level, the officer of a bank selling insurance to a private customer will be in breach of duty in advising in relation to a proposal that a serious medical condition need not be disclosed. In more complex cases much will depend on the evidence, in particular the expert evidence of what should have been done in accordance with good practice in the particular circumstances. It requires strong evidence of a want of care and skill on the part of a bank in a case where a customer has incurred a loss on one of many securities, derivatives, or foreign-exchange transactions. Such transactions are inherently risky and losses are to be anticipated.[14]

There is long-established authority, in the context of bills of exchange, that a bank can be in breach of its duty of reasonable care and skill in failing to make inquiries. Certain transactions are so out of the ordinary course that they ought to arouse doubts and put the bank on inquiry. If the bank fails to inquire, it cannot be said to have acted without negligence in converting a bill.[15] The *Quincecare* case[16] applies the principle in another context—the care and skill the bank should exercise in paying money away from a customer's account: it will be liable if it does so knowing that the instruction is dishonestly given by, for example, fraudulent directors of the borrowing company, shutting its eyes to the obvious fact of dishonesty, or acting recklessly in failing to make such inquiries as an honest and reasonable bank would make. Factors such as the standing of the customer, the bank's knowledge of the signatory, the amount involved, the need for prompt transfer, the presence of unusual features, and the scope and means for making reasonable inquiries may be relevant.

B. FIDUCIARY LAW

(i) Fiduciary Duties and Their Negation

The common law (or at least equity) imposes fiduciary duties in certain situations. Relationships in certain established categories are automatically fiduciary in character (trustee–beneficiary; principal–agent; director–company). Otherwise the law imposes fiduciary duties in special circumstances only. Fiduciaries do not all owe the same duties in all situations. The type of fiduciary, the nature of the relationship between fiduciary and beneficiary, and the contractual context all bear on the nature and extent of the duties imposed by law. Apart from the duty of care key prescriptions are that fiduciaries (1) should not permit their private interests to conflict with their duty to a beneficiary of the duty; (2) should not permit their duties to one beneficiary to conflict with their duties to another; (3) should not make a secret profit, i.e. a profit from their position which is undisclosed to their beneficiaries; and (4) have a duty of

---

[14] 205 below

[15] e.g. *Morison v. London County and Westminster Bank Ltd.* [1914] 3 KB 356, 369, *per* Buckley LJ; *A. L. Underwood Ltd. v. Bank of Liverpool and Martins Bank* [1924] 1 KB 775, 795, *per* Atkin LJ. See 264 below.

[16] *Barclays Bank plc v. Quincecare Ltd.* [1992] 4 All ER 363. See also *Lipkin Gorman (a firm) v. Karpnale Ltd.* [1989] 1 WLR 1340, [1992] 4 All ER 409 (CA); *Sansom v. Westpac Banking Corporation* [1996] Austn. Torts R. 63, 315 (NSW CA).

confidentiality. The law can be as much concerned with the possibility of a breach of fiduciary duty as with an actual breach.[17] A breach of fiduciary duty can lead to an injunction, damages, or to the fiduciary having to account for any profits made. The obligation to account for profits does not depend on the customer suffering a loss, nor is it material that the customer him- or herself could not have made the profit (although an allowance from the profit may be made for the fiduciary's exercise of skill and expertise, and its expenses).

The beneficiaries of these duties may release their fiduciaries provided they fully understand what they are doing, what their rights are, and that they are surrendering them. In traditional language, fiduciaries must make full disclosure and obtain the informed consent of their beneficiaries to their acting inconsistently with their duties. It is difficult to see how a generalized disclosure in advance could meet these tests. Moreover, in theory neither contract nor trade practice ought to exempt fiduciaries from their duties. However, the trend of modern English jurisprudence is that contract may define a relationship so that it is not fiduciary in character, or so that the fiduciary duties are limited in scope. For example, if under the particular contract there is clearly no duty on the bank to advise a customer on a matter, the customer cannot claim to be owed any fiduciary duty to be given that advice.[18] An example of such a contract is a clause whereby customers accept that they are not entitled to information on the other side of a Chinese wall in a multifunctional bank, or given in breach of duty.

While contracts may modify the scope of fiduciary duties, however, it cannot be that contract can be invoked to negate them regardless of the circumstances. The relative sophistication of the customer is one factor in determining whether contract has successfully modified fiduciary obligations, the way the fiduciary has held itself out another. Thus, since many private customers will not necessarily expect their bank to be conducting conflicting corporate-finance business, it will be difficult to imply a contract term negating the undivided loyalty the bank may owe if it is a fiduciary. Moreover, courts are likely to construe strictly contractual provisions which attempt to modify the normal incidents of a particular fiduciary relationship. Such provisions are also likely to have to meet the standards of reasonableness and fairness established under the unfair contract terms legislation.[19]

(ii) Trustees and Agents

Fiduciary duties are clearly imposed on trustees and agents. The position with trustees is relatively straightforward. In acting as a trustee of an estate or investment fund a bank must, generally speaking, not invest with itself. That would breach its fiduciary duty because of the conflict between its duty to the beneficiaries and its duty to its shareholders.[20] A bank can always make deposits with other banks or invest with other

---

[17] *Phipps* v. *Boardman* [1967] 2 AC 46, 103–4.
[18] *Kelly* v. *Cooper* [1993] AC 205 (PC); *Clark Boyce* v. *Mouat* [1994] 1 AC 428 (PC).
[19] 147ff., above.
[20] *Marley* v. *Mutual Security Merchant Bank & Trust Co. Ltd.* [1995] CLC 261 (PC).

financial institutions. But a bank will not be in breach of its fiduciary duties if the trust instrument empowers it to open accounts or make deposits or investments with itself, despite its being the trustee. Beneficiaries are then on the same plane as customers in the event of the bank's insolvency.[21] In fact these days in the commercial arena the traditional duties of a bank acting as trustee will often be modified by the contractual setting. The example of a trustee of a securities issue is examined in Chapter 12. Another example of a divergence from the traditional law of trusts occurs when a bank acts as a nominee (a bare trustee). Then the bank may not be obliged to maintain the integrity of the trust assets—the traditional rule—but simply to compensate the beneficiary for any loss caused by its breach of duty.[22]

The position with agents is slightly more complicated, not least since agency is a malleable concept. (Just because in many securities and derivatives markets banks act on a principal to principal basis does not change their status as agents *vis-à-vis* their customers.) In fact treating a bank as a fiduciary because it is an agent may add little to the analysis. For example, the implication of a bank being an agent in effecting a customer's payment instructions may be nothing more than it must act with reasonable care and skill. That duty is already inherent in the contract for the provision of a service like payment. Whether the duty derives from an agent's position as fiduciary or from contract becomes relevant only when considering ancillary matters such as causation, the measure of damages, and limitation periods. In some contexts, however, fiduciary analysis can advance the argument. For example, agents must not use their position to acquire benefits for themselves at the expense of their principals. Therefore the bank instructed by a customer to buy certain securities cannot buy on its own behalf or move the market against the customer before it buys. If it does, it must account for the profits.

The fiduciary duties attaching to an agent vary, as already mentioned, with the nature of the agency. Thus, the bank instructed simply to buy or sell securities has fewer fiduciary duties than if it is the manager of a discretionary fund. Since, for example, multiple retainer is contemplated on the part of securities dealers, it has been suggested that they cannot be obliged to disclose to a customer inside information given to them in confidence by another customer for whom they also act.[23] While this may be true as between the different customers for whom a bank is acting as broker, or even fund manager, to be consistent with the well established principles of fiduciary law it can have no application as between such customers and customers dealing with the bank in a completely different capacity, e.g. with its corporate-finance arm.

(iii) Banks as Financial Advisers and Facilitators

As indicated, fiduciary duties are also imposed outside the law of trust and agency. A duty of confidence between A and B, or an assumption of responsibility to act in B's

---

[21] *Space Investments Ltd.* v. *Canadian Imperial Bank of Commerce Trust Co. (Bahamas) Ltd.* [1986] 1 WLR 1072 (PC); Trustee Act 2000, s. 3(1)

[22] *Target Holdings Ltd.* v. *Redferns (a firm)* [1996] 1 AC 421 (HL).

[23] *Kelly* v. *Cooper* [1993] AC 205, 214.

interests, have been suggested as the basis for doing so.[24] Thus, if A makes clear to B that it does not accept the obligation of selflessness, then a fiduciary duty cannot generally arise, and B is not justified in relaxing its self-interested vigilance or independent judgement. Applying these rather vague tests would not generally pro-duce a fiduciary relationship between a customer and a bank acting, say, as a deposi-tory, financial adviser, or financier.[25] Generally speaking, a bank is not undertaking to prefer the customer's interest to its own. Moreover, as a matter of policy there is a reluctance to overlay ordinary, arm's-length commercial relationships with fiduciary duties.[26] This is because the parties in these situations are said to have an adequate opportunity to prescribe their own mutual obligations, and the contractual remedies available to them to obtain compensation for any breach of those obligations should be sufficient.[27] It is for this reason that it is unlikely that there are fiduciary duties within a banking syndicate.[28] Typically the bank–commercial customer relationship is also arm's-length.

In broad terms there are two situations where common law courts have imposed fiduciary duties on banks outside trust and agency. The first is when a bank has assumed the role of financial adviser as promoter of a particular scheme. As indicated previously, a fiduciary relationship does not arise simply because a bank gives an explanation or proffers advice. After all, in doing so it is not generally purporting to act selflessly. But the situation may be different if the bank has positively assumed the role of financial adviser as promoter of a particular scheme of providing investments, and the customer relies on the decisions being made by the bank, to the bank's knowledge, and indeed has placed complete faith in the bank.[29]

If in this situation the bank, as investment adviser, proposes to offer the customer an investment in which it has a financial interest—and this is the context in which fiduciary liability tends to be imposed for financial advice—it will be held to the fiduciary standard proscribing conflicts of interest. Then its duty is to furnish the customer with all the relevant knowledge which it possesses, concealing nothing which

---

[24] e.g. *White v. Jones* [1995] AC 207, 270, *per* Lord Browne-Wilkinson. See P. Finn, 'Fiduciary Law and the Modern Commercial World' in E. McKendrick (ed.), *Commercial Aspects of Trusts and Fiduciary Obligations* (Oxford, Clarendon, 1992); L Glover, 'Banks and Fiduciary Relationships' (1995) 7 *Bond LR* 50; D. Waters, 'Banks, Fiduciary Obligations and Unconscionable Transactions' (1986) 65 *Can. Bar Rev.* 37; K. Curtis, 'The Fiduciary Controversy: Injection of Fiduciary Principles into the Bank–Depositor and Bank–Borrower Relationships' (1987) 20 *Loyola LALR* 795.

[25] e.g. *Guardian Ocean Cargoes Ltd.* v. *Banco do Brasil SA (Nos 1 & 3)* [1994] 2 Lloyd's Rep. 152, 160 (CA).

[26] Leading cases outside banking include *Kelly* v. *Cooper* [1993] AC 205 (PC); *Hospital Products Pty. Ltd.* v. *United States Surgical Corporation* (1984) 156 CLR 41; *LAC Minerals Ltd.* v. *International Corona Resources Ltd.* (1989) 61 DLR (4th) 14 (SCC); *DHL* v. *Richmond* [1993] 3 NZLR 10 (CA); *Pilmer* v. *Duke Group Ltd. (in liq.)* (2001) 180 ALR 249. See Sir P. Millett, 'Equity's Place in the Law of Commerce' (1998) 114 *LQR* 214. Recent Canadian law is different: J. McCamus, 'Prometheus Unbound: Fiduciary Obligation in the Supreme Court of Canada' (1997) 28 *CBLJ* 107.

[27] Kennedy J, 'Equity in a Commercial Context', in P. Finn (ed.), *Equity and Commercial Relationships* (Sydney, Law Book Co., 1987), 15.

[28] 58 above.

[29] *Daly* v. *Sydney Stock Exchange Ltd.* (1986) 160 CLR 371; *Hodgkinson* v. *Simms* [1994] 3 SCR 377.

may reasonably be regarded as relevant to the making of the investment decision; to give the best advice which it can give; if not it, but a third party, has the financial interest in the investment to be offered, to reveal fully that financial interest; and to obtain for the customer the best terms which the customer would obtain from a third party if the bank were to exercise due diligence on behalf of its customer in such a transaction.[30]

Closely related is the second situation where banks have been held to fiduciary standards. Here a bank has led a customer, A, to believe that it will act in the customer's interests in advising it on an investment. In fact the bank is also acting for B and is promoting B's interests, to the detriment of A's interests. Conceptually the decisions in this area are not always satisfactory, as courts seem to reason back from certain consequences (e.g. a conflict of interest; A has confidential information) to the existence of a fiduciary duty. *Woods* v. *Martins Bank Ltd.* [31] is an old authority, where the bank advised A to invest in B, which was heavily indebted to it. It is still good law although, since it predated *Hedley Byrne*, it was necessary to find a fiduciary relationship if liability was to be imposed for negligent advice. The Court of Appeal has held that there was a seriously arguable case that a bank was in breach of its fiduciary duty to one of its large commercial customers, where the bank itself had acquired another company (A) after discussions with the customer about a takeover bid for A.[32] The customer advanced a separate head of claim in relation to misuse of confidential information it had provided to the bank because of the latter's involvement in its initial public offering, several syndicated loans, and the proposed bid for A.[33]

In one sense this decision goes too far, because it was an arm's-length, commercial relationship between customer and bank. A fiduciary relationship cannot exist if a bank has no reason to believe that the customer is placing trust and confidence in it and relying on it to put the customer's interests above all else. Only in very special circumstances will this occur in the banking context. In any event, when B has acted for A, or promoted A's interests in the past, the fact that dealings are complete will ordinarily mean that its duties are at an end. Any issue of misuse of confidential information is quite separate from the existence of a fiduciary relationship. Of course if a relationship is fiduciary in character, candour is necessary if a bank is to avoid liability for putting interest above duty, or duty to one customer above that to another. Candour may be impossible because it would involve breach of a duty of confidence not to reveal the affairs of the other customer, and in these circumstances the bank should decline to act.

---

[30] *Daly* v. *Sydney Stock Exchange Ltd.* (1986) 160 CLR 371, 385, *per* Brennan J.

[31] [1959] QB 55. See also *Commonwealth Bank of Australia* v. *Smith* (1991) 102 ALR 453 (FC); *Hayward* v. *Bank of Nova Scotia* (1984) 45 OR (2d) 542, (1985) 51 OR (2d) 193 (CA); *Standard Investments Ltd.* v. *Canadian Imperial Bank of Commerce* (1986) 22 DLR (4th) 410.

[32] *United Pan-European Communications NV* v. *Deutsche Bank AG* [2000] EWCA Civ. 166, [2000] 2 BCLC 461 (CA).

[33] See *Indata Equipment Supplies Ltd.* v. *ACL Ltd.* [1997] EWCA Civ. 2266, *The Times*, 14 Aug. 1997 (CA); *Arklow Investments Ltd.* v. *Maclean* [2000] 1 WLR 594 (PC); 174 above.

C. KNOWING RECEIPT, INCONSISTENT DEALING, AND ASSISTANCE

Banks may sometimes be implicated in a breach of trust or fiduciary duty. A not unusual situation is where moneys held with a bank on trust are used in breach of trust. In this situation the bank may simply be acting on what it treats as its customer's mandate. Similar is the position on insolvency, where a bank combines a number of the debtor's accounts although some turn out to contain trust moneys. These days, the problem not infrequently arises when a director or officer of a company, in breach of fiduciary duty to his or her company, misuses its assets, e.g. by paying a bank for services or, more likely, siphoning the assets off through the banking system for personal use. Typically the wrongdoer has disappeared or is insolvent, so the bank is sued. Even if available, the victim may be reluctant to sue the wrongdoer, and so suit is brought against the bank. (In this latter situation the bank may be able to obtain contribution from the wrongdoer.)

To what extent is the bank in these situations liable in law for any loss of funds experienced by their owner? Occasionally the answer will turn on the tort of conversion, if a bank has handled negotiable instruments of one sort or the other. However, resort is often had to the law of trusts and of restitution. First, a bank may be liable as a trustee de son tort, in other words, it is treated as a trustee (even though not formally a trustee) because it has intermeddled in trust matters.[34] No more need to be said of this very special situation. Secondly, if a bank has knowingly received funds which have been misappropriated in breach of trust or fiduciary duty, it may be liable ('knowing receipt'). This is a form of secondary liability; the wrongdoer is primarily liable. Closely related is a third liability: this arises if a bank receives funds properly but then applies them for its own benefit. Inconsistent dealing in this way is a form of primary liability. However, as with the knowing-receipt head, the bank must have handled the funds. Both are personal, not proprietary, claims. Importantly, the bank no longer need have the funds.

Fourthly, a bank may also be liable as an accessory, even if it has not handled the funds, where it has assisted a breach of trust or fiduciary duty ('assistance'). This is just one possible form of accessory liability. The better view is that a bank liable in this way is simply being made to compensate the victim for any loss and is not to be regarded as a constructive trustee. In instances of bank insolvency, if the owner of the funds can have a constructive trust imposed, then it would be in a stronger position than if it has a claim only to compensation, since the latter ranks with other unsecured claims. As a matter of policy, there do not seem to be strong reasons for giving the claimant a priority in an insolvency for this, but not other, forms of accessory liability.[35]

---

[34] Cf. *DFC (New Zealand) Ltd.* v. *Goddard* [1992] 2 NZLR 445 (CA).

[35] *Governor and Company of the Bank of Scotland* v. *A Ltd.* [2001] 1 WLR 751, 764; [2001] 3 All ER 58, 70. See C. Mitchell, 'Assistance', in P. Birks and A. Pretto (eds.), *Breach of Trust* (Oxford, Hart, 2002), 147–8; A. Oakley, 'Proprietary Claims and their Priority in Insolvency' [1995] *CLJ* 377, 382.

(i) Knowing Receipt

For this form of liability it must be shown, first, that the funds have been disposed of in breach of trust, fiduciary duty, or as a result of some other unconscionable dealing. Moneys held on trust and misapplied are obviously caught. So, too, are misapplied corporate moneys, since historically directors have been treated as if they were trustees of the property of the company under their control, so that any wrongful disposition is a breach of trust. Analysing the disposition in terms of a breach of fiduciary duty is the more modern approach, and has the advantage that it extends beyond directors to employees, who have duties of loyalty to their company. However, when there is no trust or fiduciary relationship at all, as with an outside thief of corporate funds who disposes of them through the banking system, English law does not accord a remedy to the company in knowing receipt. The bank may be liable on other grounds, however, for example as an accessory.

The second prerequisite to an action in knowing receipt is that the bank must have received the claimant's funds for its own benefit. Tracing has a role here: the bank must have beneficially received funds which are traceable as representing those of the claimant.[36] However, the law on whether a bank has received funds beneficially is hopelessly confused and sits ill with legal principle and banking practice.

Thus it is said that neither a paying nor a collecting bank will normally receive funds beneficially, since it is acting as agent (ministerially).[37] Similarly, where a fraudulent fiduciary pays the principal's moneys into his or her account and then pays it away, that is said not to constitute beneficial receipt by the bank because (it is said) the bank is merely acting as a conduit or agent for its customer in passing on the funds. None of this accords with basic principle, that as soon as money is paid into a bank it is, generally speaking, the bank's, to use as it wishes. That is the case whether money is paid in as a consequence of collecting a negotiable instrument or otherwise or whether it is the customer or a third party paying the money into the customer's account. Conversely, when money is paid out, however shortly after payment in, that is the bank's own money.

The analysis is similarly flawed when it is said that if a bank exchanges funds into other currency, that constitutes beneficial receipt, since the bank can use the original currency as its own.[38] A bank can generally use all money paid in for its own purposes, whether for foreign exchange or not. There is authority that a bank receives money for its own benefit for the purposes of the knowing-receipt doctrine if it exercises a right of set off or reduces the customer's indebtedness with it (e.g. by applying it to an overdraft).[39] As a matter of banking reality, however, reducing the indebtedness of a

---

[36] 252 below.

[37] *Agip (Africa) Ltd.* v. *Jackson* [1990] Ch. 265, 292 *per* Millet J, impliedly approved on appeal: [1991] Ch. 547.

[38] *Polly Peck International* v. *Nadir (No 2)* [1992] 4 All ER 769, 777, *per* Scott LJ; cf. *Polly Peck International plc* v. *Nadir* [1993] 2 Bank LR 344, 347, *per* Hoffmann LJ.

[39] e.g. *Stephens Travel Service International Pty. Ltd.* v. *Qantas Airways Ltd.* (1988) 13 NSWLR 331 (CA). *Citadel General Assurance Co.* v. *Lloyds Bank Canada* (1997) 152 DLR (4th) 411.

solvent customer is not necessarily for the bank's benefit, since to that extent the bank does not earn interest (although it may have reduced its credit exposure to that customer and be able to lay the money out immediately in equally profitable ways).

There is a need to bring the legal analysis of beneficial receipt into line with banking practice. There is also a need to bear in mind that if 'beneficial receipt' is widely defined, banks are exposed to huge potential liabilities if, as discussed below, the knowledge requirement is not dishonesty—apart from any other liabilities they have as accessories. Beneficial receipt cannot be equated with the bank being benefited in the ordinary way through a payment in. Confining it to receipt by a bank when not acting as agent ('ministerially') does not assist, since banks receive beneficially even when acting as agents. It must be confined to situations of real benefit, for example, to the bank pressing the customer to reduce its indebtedness under a facility when the customer is of doubtful solvency.[40] Provided the payment to the bank is not later upset in the insolvency as a preference, the bank is in this situation clearly benefited.

Thirdly, liability for knowing receipt demands knowledge on the part of the bank that there has been a payment in breach of trust, fiduciary duty, etc. The first aspect of this issue—already addressed in Chapter 1[41]—is whether the knowledge of a bank's officers or agents is regarded as a matter of law as the bank's knowledge. The only point to note here is that the officers and agents must have the requisite knowledge when the bank still holds the money or its proceeds. The second aspect has to do with the quality of the requisite knowledge. Here the law is a mess. The classic division is between actual and constructive knowledge. Subsequently, it became popular to refer to five categories of knowledge—actual knowledge on the part of the bank; wilfully shutting its eyes to the obvious; wilfully and recklessly failing to make such inquiries as an honest and reasonable bank would make; knowledge of circumstances which would indicate the facts to an honest and reasonable bank; and knowledge of circumstances which would put an honest and reasonable bank on inquiry.[42] The five-fold test has been disapproved from on high, although it is still invoked by judges at the coalface. Now the Court of Appeal has said that all that is required is that the bank's state of knowledge be such as to make it unconscionable to retain the benefit of the receipt.[43] But what does all this mean in practice?

An earlier view, that knowledge for knowing receipt must fall at the dishonesty end of the scale, no longer attracts much support.[44] But it is not self-evidently wrong. Often overlooked is that policy issue which permeates commercial law—which of two

[40] See M. Bryan, 'When Does a Bank Receive Money?' [1996] JBL 165, 173; C. Rickett, 'The Banker's Liability for Receipt in Equity and at Common Law' (1995) 16 Co.L 35, 40.

[41] 22 above.

[42] *Baden Delvaux and Lecuit v. Société Générale pour Favoriser le Développement du Commerce et de l'Industrie en France SA* [1983] BCLC 325, 407, [1992] All ER 161, 235. See S. Gardner, 'Knowing Assistance and Knowing Receipt: Taking Stock' (1996) 112 LQR 56, 58–9.

[43] *Bank of Credit and Commerce International (Overseas) Ltd. v. Akindele* [2001] Ch. 437 (CA); P. Birks, 'The Burden on the Bank', in F. Rose (ed.), *Restitution and Banking Law* (Oxford, Mansfield, 1998); M. Bryan, 'Recovering Misdirected Money from Banks', in *ibid.*

[44] But see Arden J in *Eagle Trust plc v. SBC Securities Ltd.* [1995] BCC 231.

parties must carry the loss as the result of a third party's wrongdoing. Why should a bank, if it has not been dishonest, be accountable for the loss when the company (say) whose funds have been plundered has not instituted adequate controls to prevent the wrongdoing? Certainly banks these days have to put in place controls to address wrongdoing such as money laundering and terrorist financing and can be criminally liable for failure to take reasonable care to detect and report it. But in our system of law civil liability has never followed automatically from criminal breach, since the policies behind each can differ.[45] (A separate policy issue of why the company—to continue with the example—should trump the ordinary creditors of an insolvent constructive trustee, does not loom large in the banking context, as it does elsewhere, since bank insolvencies are a relatively infrequent occurrence.[46]) In other words, why should the bank bear the loss unless it knew it was the company's money, or was probably the company's money, which the person was misusing, or it wilfully shut its eyes to the obvious fact, or knowingly and recklessly failed to make inquiries which a reasonable bank would have made?

The dominant approach is that something akin to negligence suffices for liability in knowing receipt—for example, knowledge of circumstances in which the honest and reasonable banker would have concluded that the moneys were probably misapplied and would have refused them, or segregated them, until the true position was ascertained.[47] Such an approach enables the court to balance in any particular case the various factors bearing on liability. The inquiry thus tracks that which arises when a bank acts in breach of its duty to exercise reasonable care and skill. Liability does not arise through a failure to speculate, the mere possibility that a breach of duty is involved, or the wisdom of hindsight.[48]

In the past the courts have been mindful that to fix banks too readily with knowledge would impede the smooth running of the banking system.[49] The sheer scale and speed of payments through the system means that it is commercially impractical to inquire deeply into what, on the face of it, are ordinary and authorized transactions. This is especially the case if the owner of the funds is not even a customer of the bank. Until alerted to the possibility of dishonesty, the bank is entitled to assume it is dealing with the honest. Recall, as well, that a bank is in breach of mandate if it fails to act promptly on a customer's instructions. However, large payments into an account with previous small balances should put a bank on inquiry. If a bank makes inquiry and a reasonable answer is given, then it has fulfilled its duty. Whether a bank has

---

[45] D. Fox, 'Constructive Notice and Knowing Receipt: An Economic Analysis' (1998) *CLJ* 391, 398–400.

[46] See R. Goode, 'The Recovery of a Director's Improper Gains: Proprietary Remedies for Infringement of Non-proprietary Rights', in E. McKendrick (ed.), *Commercial Aspects of Trusts and Fiduciary Obligations* (Oxford, Clarendon, 1992).

[47] *Eagle Trust plc* v. *SBC Securities* [1991] BCLC 438; *Bank of Credit and Commerce International (Overseas) Ltd.* v. *Akindele* [2001] Ch. 437, 450, 452 (CA); *Criterion Properties plc* v. *Stratford UK Properties LLC* [2002] EWHC Ch. 496, paras. 36–8.

[48] *Lipkin Gorman (a firm)* v. *Karpnale Ltd.* [1989] 1 WLR 1340, [1992] 4 All ER 409 (CA). The claim against the bank was not pursued in the House of Lords: [1991] 2 AC 548.

[49] C. Harpum, 'The Stranger as Constructive Trustee' (1986) 102 *LQR* 267, 276.

complied with regulatory requirements (e.g. on money-laundering) is also obviously a relevant factor in terms of its failure to know.[50]

There is a strong academic literature favouring strict liability for knowing receipt, subject to defences of change of position and *bona fide* purchaser.[51] Change of position must not be dishonest, although it is available as a defence if negligent. Strict liability, it is said, would be to recognize the restitutionary nature of the claim. At first glance a supporting argument from a banking perspective would be that strict liability is imposed on banks if they convert negotiable instruments.[52] However, banks have long had a statutory defence to an action in conversion if they have acted in good faith and without negligence, even if they have not provided value. Apart from the onus being on the bank to establish this defence, this means in effect that the law of conversion for banks is more in line with the existing authorities requiring knowledge at the negligence end of the scale for liability in knowing receipt than it is with an approach focusing on strict liability. Moreover, change of position, which is the central restitutionary defence, is not a defence to conversion. *Bona fide* purchaser has, however, a long history in the law of money. The owner of notes and coins, or negotiable instruments, cannot recover them from one providing valuable consideration and acting in good faith.[53] In short, the negotiable-instruments analogy points to negligence, rather than strict liability, as the standard of liability for knowing receipt.

(ii) Inconsistent Dealing

As indicated, a bank receiving funds in circumstances which do not constitute knowing receipt can still be liable if those funds are subsequently applied for its own benefit ('inconsistent dealing'). At that point the bank must know that the funds involved are subject to a trust or fiduciary duty and that what it is doing with them is in breach of that. It need not know the exact terms of the trust or fiduciary duty. Knowledge at the dishonesty end of the scale is, however, necessary.[54] Thus the bank is not accountable if it failed to appreciate, albeit negligently, that it was acting inconsistently with the trust or fiduciary duty. Because dishonesty is involved, this form of liability is akin to accessory liability, to which we now turn.[55]

(iii) Assistance

Even if a bank is not liable for knowing receipt, it may be liable as an accessory for dishonest assistance. For example it may have received funds, but not beneficially as

---

[50] *Westpac Banking Corp. v. MM Kembla (New Zealand) Ltd.* [2001] 2 NZLR 298, 317.

[51] See P. Birks, 'Receipt', in P. Birks and A. Pretto (eds.), *Breach of Trust* (Oxford, Hart, 2002); Lord Nicholls, 'Knowing Receipt: The Need for a New Landmark', in W. Cornish, R. Nolan, J. O'Sullivan, and G. Virgo (eds.), *Restitution: Past, Present and Future* (Oxford, Hart, 1998). See also *Grupo Torras SA v. Al-Sabah (No 5)* [2001] Lloyd's Rep. (Banking) 36, 62.

[52] 263 below.   [53] *Miller v. Race* (1758) 1 Burr. 452, 97 ER 398.

[54] *Neste Oy v. Lloyds Bank plc* [1983] 2 Lloyd's Rep. 658.

[55] C. Harpum, 'The Basis of Equitable Liability', in P. Birks (ed.), *The Frontiers of Liability* (Oxford, Clarendon, 1994), i, 16.

this concept is interpreted for the purposes of the knowing-receipt doctrine. Assistance is a form of accessory liability, which sits alongside other forms of accessory liability in equity, such as the receipt of information in breach of confidence, and inducing breach of trust or fiduciary duty.[56] There is a parallel with accessory liability in the economic torts, such as knowing participation in a fraud or inducing breach of contract.[57] Indeed, in particular circumstances it may be possible to proceed against a bank on the basis of both these economic torts and assistance. Unlike the economic torts, however, the accessory in equity is unable to reduce its liability by arguing that the claimant was contributorily negligent in the loss. Powerful voices argue that assistance ought to be assimilated to other forms of accessory liability or abolished completely.[58] In the United States the problem is dealt with as a form of common law aiding and abetting liability.[59]

What are the prerequisites for this form of accessory liability? First, there has to be a breach of trust or fiduciary duty. That has already been examined in the context of knowing receipt. However, one gloss in this context is the suggestion in the oft-cited case of *Barnes* v. *Addy*[60] that for assistance there has to be 'a dishonest and fraudulent design on the part of the trustee'. This may be defended as a way of narrowing the potential liability of accessories such as banks. However, it is now clear that there is no need to establish fraud on the part of the trustee or fiduciary, and an innocent breach of duty is sufficient.

The second element in assistance is fault. Although knowledge at the negligence end of the scale had been thought to be adequate,[61] it is now clearly the case that this type of accessory liability is founded on dishonesty on the part of the bank.[62] The test of dishonesty is subjective: did the bank to its knowledge act as an honest and reasonable bank would have in the circumstances known at the time? To put it another way, was the bank's behaviour commercially unacceptable in the particular circumstances and known to be such? An objective standard of dishonesty, in which the bank does not appreciate that it was acting dishonestly, is not enough, even if it knows all the facts making it wrongful to act. The standard of proof, which is not as high as the criminal standard, demands a high degree of probability that the bank was dishonest.

As a matter of legal policy, dishonesty is the preferable approach for founding this

---

[56] P. Finn, 'The Liability of Third Parties for Knowing Receipt or Assistance', in D. Waters (ed.), *Equity, Fiduciaries and Trusts* (Toronto, Carswell, 1993).

[57] *John Shaw (Rayners Lane) Ltd.* v. *Lloyds Bank Ltd.* (1944) 5 LDAB 396, 413; 319 below.

[58] P. Birks, 'Civil Wrongs: A New World', *Butterworth Lectures for 1990–1* (London, 1992), 99–101; L. Hoffmann, 'The Redundancy of Knowing Assistance', in P. Birks (ed.), *Frontiers of Liability* (Oxford, Clarendon, 1994).

[59] J. Barist, 'Financial Institution Aiding and Abetting Liability' (2001) 3 *JIB Reg.* 155.

[60] (1874) LR 9 Ch. App. 244.

[61] *Agip (Africa) Ltd.* v. *Jackson* [1991] Ch. 547, 567 (CA).

[62] *Royal Brunei Airlines Sdn. Bhd.* v. *Tan* [1995] 2 AC 378 (PC); *Twinsecta Ltd.* v. *Yardley* [2002] 2 WLR 802(HL). Cf. W. Blair, 'Secondary Liability of Financial Institutions for the Fraud of Third Parties' (2000) 30 *HKLJ* 74, 83; P. Millett, 'Tracing the Proceeds of Fraud' (1991) 107 *LQR* 71, 84.

type of accessory liability. Recall that in the banking context it is a matter of imposing a loss on one of the parties, when the wrongdoer has disappeared or is insolvent. As a matter of legal practice, however, the full implications of adopting dishonesty as the basis for assistance liability are yet to be worked out. Of particular importance is how easily will the dishonesty of employees and agents be attributable to banks? Is an accessory dishonest for the purposes of liability if it believed that it was involved in a different type of breach (e.g. breach of exchange-control regulations) rather than a breach of trust or fiduciary duty? Is it dishonest where there is a genuine doubt whether there is a breach of duty but the bank decides to go ahead having received favourable legal advice? As with knowing receipt, a breach of a regulatory provision or a recognized code of practice will no doubt assist in the decision whether a bank has acted honestly. In many common law countries, with the abolition of civil juries it is no longer possible simply to leave issues of dishonesty to a jury, as it can conveniently be left in criminal matters.

D. EMERGING STANDARDS: DUE DILIGENCE, SUITABILITY, GOOD FAITH

Due diligence as a standard emerged from securities law: in the United States a bank involved in a public offer of securities must make its own investigations (in relation to statements for which it takes responsibility), in other words it is obliged to undertake 'due diligence' in relation to the issuer and the issue.[63] Under the UK Financial Services and Markets Act 2000 a bank is unlikely ever to be responsible for the listing particulars relating to an issue of securities, but if it is, and these are false or there are omissions, it will be exempted from civil liability to those incurring loss only if it demonstrates, *inter alia*, that it reasonably believed, having made reasonable inquiries, that the listing particulars were true and not misleading, or that the omission was properly made.[64] As a result of the authorization provisions of the Act, those carrying on a regulated activity in breach of the general prohibition commit an offence unless they prove that they exercised all due diligence and took all reasonable precautions to avoid doing so.[65] The same defence applies under the Act in the case of breach of the market abuse rules.[66] The 'know your customer' rules are sometimes said to impose a duty on banks to carry out proper due diligence on their counterparties and customers. This seems to be part of a growing trend to make banks statutorily liable for unlawful activities which they facilitate by their operations, unless they can demonstrate due diligence.[67]

Due diligence seems also to have an emerging base outside regulatory law, and thus

---

[63] e.g. *In re Software Toolworks Inc. Securities Litigation*, 38 F 3d 1078 (9th Cir. 1994).
[64] FSMA 2000, s. 90, Sched. 10, para. 1.
[65] FSMA 2000, s. 23(3). See 70 above.
[66] S. 123(2)(b).
[67] *Due Diligence* (ICC Publication No 534, London, 1994).

to be capable of giving rise to civil liability.[68] It has been seen that the duty of reasonable care and skill can imply a responsibility to act in accordance with good practice and to make inquiries. Failure to do so can also give rise to liability where there has been a breach of duty by a trustee or fiduciary. As a result, a bank may fail its common law duties—whatever the position under the statutory law—if it has not investigated the customers it is representing, checked the information it is passing on, or reviewed the services or products it is marketing. Omitting to do so may lead to civil liability in contract, tort, equity, or restitution. The possibility of such liability is underpinned by a number of extra-legal standards. Just one instance is the recommendation of the International Primary Markets Association that lead or arranging banks in the Euromarkets should consider the appropriate level of due diligence.[69]

Suitability, too, is a concept most developed in the area of securities regulation. It imposes a liability on those marketing securities which are incompatible with the needs of customers. First developed in the United States,[70] it is now part of securities law elsewhere. For example, there is a general principle of 'know your customer' laid down by the FSA in the United Kingdom, which is coupled with obligations imposed on firms to make suitable recommendations and to effect suitable transactions.[71] The general view is that suitability is somewhere along the spectrum between 'not unsuitable' through 'reasonable suitable' to 'positively and indisputably the most suitable available'.[72] There is also a role in the rules for the related concept of best advice.[73] Breach of such rules grounds a claim under FSMA 2000 by private investors suffering loss as a result of the breach. Compared with due diligence it is not as easy to see any broad counterpart to the suitability standard in the general law.

Good faith is a more general doctrine than either due diligence or suitability. There is a considerable jurisprudence behind the doctrine in civil law systems.[74] US courts have applied a requirement that parties negotiate and perform contracts in good faith, and have limited the exercise of contractual rights in bad faith.[75] The duty to perform contractual undertakings in good faith derives from section 1–203 of the Uniform Commercial Code and, more importantly because of its applicability to all contracts, from section 205 of the *Restatement of Contracts, Second*: 'Every contract imposes upon each party a duty of good faith and fair dealing in its performance and its enforcement.' In general terms, the more recent commentaries closely associate good

---

[68] See W. Duncan and S. Travers, *Due Diligence* (Sydney, LBC, 1995); C. Davis, *Due Diligence: Law and Practice* (London, Sweet & Maxwell, looseleaf), chs. 1–2.

[69] R. Foster, 'Due Diligence', 15 *IFLR*, Mar. 1996, 23. See also Department of Trade and Industry, *House of Fraser Holdings plc* (London, HMSO, 1988), 510–11.

[70] e.g. *Brown v. E. F. Hutton Group Inc.*, 991 F 2d 1020 (2nd Cir. 1993).

[71] FSA Handbook, Conduct of Business, rr. 5.2, 5.3.

[72] M. Blair, *Financial Services. The New Core Rules* (London, Blackstone, 1991), 94.

[73] 209 below.

[74] e.g. R. Zimmerman and S. Whittaker (eds.), *Good Faith in European Contract Law* (Cambridge, CUP, 2000).

[75] e.g. E. Farnsworth, 'Good Faith in Contract Performance', in J. Beatson and D. Friedmann (eds.), *Good Faith and Fault in Contract Law* (Oxford, Clarendon, 1995).

faith with notions such as fairness, honesty, and reasonableness. In other words, it means simply that in the performance of a contract both parties are assumed to agree not to do anything to impede its performance, or to injure the right of the other to receive its benefit. The good-faith doctrine has been invoked in the context of banking, requiring a bank to disclose material information to a commercial counterparty.[76]

There are straws in the wind that some common law courts outside the United States may adopt the doctrine, as well as the special application it has in insurance and mortgage law as a result of statutory law, for example in the United Kingdom as a result of the Unfair Terms in Consumer Contracts Directive.[77] In other words, they may demand a standard of fair dealing by banks, and that banks do not use their contractual powers excessively or oppressively, or in a manner which is beyond the purpose intended. Proponents argue that good faith would be a useful, intermediate standard between the demands of selflessness in fiduciary law, and the wide scope for self-interested behaviour which the law otherwise permits (short of the 'long-stop' doctrines of undue influence, unconscionability, and duress examined in section IV of this Chapter). On the other hand critics contend that good faith in the commercial context would lead to the uncertainty which English courts, at least, have always deprecated.[78]

II. DETERMINING THE CONTENT OF LIABILITY STANDARDS

The standards of behaviour the law expects vary in stringency. In some cases these are fairly tightly drawn and it is relatively clear what must be done. Thus a bank must perform the duties it has contractually undertaken, for example to pay from the customer's account on demand, to pay the beneficiary of a letter of credit on presentation of conforming documents, or to execute immediately its customer's purchase or sale orders in relation to investments. Of course even here there can be some argument—whether 'on demand' means straight away, whether a document actually conforms to the letter of credit, whether immediately gives some latitude, and so on. On the other hand, the law's standards can be open-textured and it is not immediately obvious what is required. The duty in contract, tort, and fiduciary law to exercise reasonable care and skill is an obvious example.

---

[76] e.g. *Banque Arabe et Internationale d'Investissement* v. *Maryland National Bank*, 57 F 3d 146 (2nd Cir. 1995); *Procter and Gamble Company* v. *Bankers Trust Company*, CCH Fed. Sec. L Rep. §99, 229 (1996). See T. Kitada, 'Emerging Theories of Bank Liability—the Breach of the Covenant of Good Faith and Fair Dealing' (1986) 103 *Banking LJ* 80; J. Norton, 'Lender Liability in the United States', in W. Blair (ed.), *Banks, Liability and Risk* (3rd edn., London, LLP, 2001), 364–5, 386–88.

[77] 155 above. See A. Mason, 'Contract, Good Faith and Equitable Standards in Fair Dealing' (2000) 116 *LQR* 66; J. Stapleton, 'Good Faith in Private Law' (1999) 52 *CLP* 1.

[78] See P. Finn, 'The Fiduciary Principle', in T. Youdan (ed.), *Equity, Fiduciaries and Trusts* (Toronto, Carswell, 1989), 4; J. Thompson, 'Good Faith in Contracting: A Sceptical View', in D. Forte (ed.), *Good Faith in Contract and Property Law* (Oxford, Hart, 1999).

Between tightly-drawn and open-textured standards are intermediate situations: the law's expectations are not necessarily definite, nor completely flexible. For example, the duty of a fiduciary to avoid conflicts of interest may be as strict as saying 'disclose or desist', but can also be less onerous as a result of contract. Equitable fraud, such as undue influence and unconscionability, is clear about certain forms of behaviour—for example, oppressive conduct—but until fairly recently contained fewer guidelines for banks about how to avoid responsibility for the equitable fraud of others.[79]

The focus of this section of the Chapter is how, as a practical matter, the law gives content to its various standards. Put to one side are the jurisprudential aspects of the issue, although it is worth commenting that what is essentially practical reasoning is sometimes mistakenly elevated into something more. Three tangible sources of the law's practical reasoning are banking practice, banking codes, and bank manuals. Pertinent to a standard's content in particular circumstances are the type of banking transaction in issue and the relative sophistication of the customer.

A. BANKING PRACTICE

Common law courts draw on a variety of sources to give expression to the general behaviour expected of banks if they are to comply with the relevant legal standards. Of long standing is the practice of referring to what banks do.[80] This, however, is variously expressed in the English cases—the ordinary practice of bankers, the practice of reasonable bankers, and the practice of careful bankers. Sometimes it will be obvious that a bank is in breach of duty. In more complex cases much will depend on the evidence, in particular the expert evidence on what should have been done by the bank in the particular circumstances.

There can be confusion here as the standard the law demands becomes entangled with its contents. Analytically the two are distinct, although in particular cases they may merge. Thus a practice may be so clearly established and well known in the area in which it is alleged to exist that the banks which conduct that type of business may be treated as contracting with that practice as an implied term.[81] The standard of reasonable care and skill, to take another example, tells little about the behaviour the standard requires. While the standard is objective, this does not preclude a court from examining the practice of banks to assist in deciding what they *should* do. A third example comes from fiduciary law: the practice of banks in relation to customers may

---

[79] 216 below.

[80] e.g. *Bank of England* v. *Vagliano Brothers* [1891] AC 107; *Cornish* v. *Midland Bank plc* [1985] 3 All ER 513, 523, *per* Kerr LJ; *Royal Bank of Scotland plc* v. *Etridge (No 2)* [2001] UKHL 44, para. 51, [2001] 3 WLR 1021, 1039 (HL); *Sansom* v. *Westpac Banking Corporation* [1996] Aust. Torts R. 63, 315, 328 (NSW CA).

[81] 52 above.

indicate that the behaviour of a particular bank gave rise to no conflict of interest on the occasion in issue.[82]

Clearly what banks ordinarily do may not be sufficient for the law's purposes. While the existence of a common practice over an extended period by persons habitually involved in a particular business is strong evidence of what the law demands, a court will not regard itself as bound by that practice if it constitutes lax behaviour.[83] In this situation it may be that a few banks do engage in acceptable behaviour—the 'reasonable banks', or the 'careful bankers' used in some judicial formulations[84]—and it is this which is expected of all banks. In some circumstances none of the banks may be conducting themselves to accord with what the court decides is desirable, and so the court must formulate its own guidance as to good behaviour.

B. INDUSTRY AND REGULATORY CODES

Acceptable practice is sometimes found in the codes of conduct drawn up by an industry ('industry codes'). Important incentives for an industry to draw up these codes are public concern about a matter and governmental pressure to do something (backed by the threat that if nothing is done legislative action is on the cards.) In the retail area the Banking Codes are an obvious example. Illustrative in the wholesale area is the International Code of Conduct and Practice for Financial Markets, concerned with foreign exchange dealings, which was drawn up in 2000 by ACI—The Financial Markets Association, based in Paris. Because of its nature, the code is not primarily concerned with a bank's relations with customers, but with how banks should organize themselves and act in relation to banks.[85] Earlier, reference was made to the wholesale industry code for London, the Non-Investment Products Code.[86]

Codes of conduct lay down acceptable standards of behaviour. Some of these may relate to matters such as the internal controls a bank should introduce, or to the information it should disclose in its financial statements. But some may be directly relevant to its dealings with customers, such as what information it should disclose or advice it should give to them. There is no one answer to whether breach of these latter standards will give rise to civil liability. As with banking practice, in exceptional cases the provisions of a code may constitute trade usage, or otherwise as a matter of English law constitute an implied contractual term with a customer. Breach then obviously gives rise to the ordinary contractual remedies. At the other extreme a court may treat the code's standards as having nothing to do with whether a customer can

---

[82] *SCF Finance Co. Ltd.* v. *Masri (No 2)* [1986] 1 All ER 40, 47, affirmed [1987] QB 1002.

[83] *Deeny* v. *Gooda Walker Ltd.* [1994] CLC 1224, 1255; *Turner* v. *Royal Bank of Scotland plc* [1998] EWCA Civ. 529, [1999] 2 All ER (Comm) 664 (CA).

[84] *Marfani & Co.* v. *Midland Bank* [1968] 1 WLR 956, 970, *per* Diplock J.

[85] Cf. H. Scott, 'Liability of Derivatives Dealers' in F. Oditah (ed.), *The Future for the Global Securities Market* (Oxford, Clarendon, 1996), 276.

[86] 103 above.

claim against its bank for the way the bank has conducted itself. In other words, a code of practice is treated as precisely that, an indication of how a bank is expected to behave, but in formulating it an industry is treated as being unable to alter the ordinary principles of legal liability. Therefore, non-compliance with any code provision cannot give rise to a claim against a bank for a customer's losses; conversely, compliance with the code will not necessarily discharge a bank from responsibility for those losses.

A third possibility, which has attracted the English courts in recent times, is to use an industry code in a non-formulary way in the enunciation of behavioural standards. The code is mined for appropriate conduct, which is then said to reflect legal policy. Alternatively, the standards laid down in the code are invoked to fortify conclusions said to follow as a matter of legal analysis.[87] Either way, the code is not determinative of standards but assists in their formulation. From the point of view of public policy it would be wrong to take standards formulated by the industry as conclusive of what is desirable.

In addition to industry codes are the rules of conduct prepared by those regulating an industry ('regulatory codes'). As a matter of legislation, breach may automatically give rise to civil liability, as with rules drawn up under FSMA 2000. A private person (essentially an individual or a person not acting in the course of a business) who suffers loss as a result of the breach of specified rules has a right to sue for damages, in addition to any cause of action at common law.[88] The clear advantage is that the person needs to demonstrate only breach of the rule and resultant loss, not something additional such as negligence or breach of fiduciary duty. Often, however, a breach of regulatory rules is primarily for other purposes, such as disciplining aberrant banks. Indeed, under FSMA, a regulatory rule may specifically provide that it is not to found civil liability.[89] If there is no provision in a regulatory code one way or the other, can breach of itself give rise to civil liability?

Just as in the case of industry codes, regulatory codes may found civil liability if they are implied as a term of the bank–customer contract, although the difficulties in this should not be underestimated given that they are designed with other purposes in mind.[90] They may also be used in the interpretation of a bank–customer contract or because they assist a court to give content to a legal standard.[91] Moreover, under the doctrine of breach of statutory duty some regulatory codes may give rise to civil liability when breached. The test for this is easy enough to state—as a matter of construction of the relevant statute, are the provisions of the code made under it for

---

[87] e.g. *Barclays Bank plc* v. *O'Brien* [1994] 1 AC 180, 197; *Turner* v. *Royal Bank of Scotland plc* [1998] EWCA Civ. 529, [1999] 2 All ER (Comm) 664 (CA).

[88] S. 150(1); Financial Services and Markets Act (Rights of Action) Regulations 2001, SI 2001 No 2256. See G. McMeel and J. Virgo, *Financial Advice and Financial Products* (Oxford, OUP, 2001), 193–209.

[89] Ss. 149(1), 150(2). See e.g., FSA Handbook, Principles for Business, r.3.4.4.

[90] *Clarion Ltd.* v. *National Provident Institution* [2000] 1 WLR 1888, [2000] 2 All ER 265.

[91] *Investors Compensation Scheme Ltd.* v. *West Bromwich Building Society* [1998] 1 WLR 896, 912–3, [1998] 1 All ER 98, 114–5 (HL).

the protection of a limited class of the public, and is it intended to confer a private right of action for damages for their breach? However, the precise application of the test in particular circumstances is difficult to rationalize or predict. It is fair to say that outside the area of the statutory codes relating to health and safety at work, the law is sparing in vesting in those adversely affected by a breach of a statutory duty a right of action for damages.[92] Something more must be established, such as a common law duty of care or, as indicated, a clear provision indicating that a breach of the code constitutes civil liability towards persons who incur loss as a result.

C. BANK MANUALS

The rules and statements contained in the internal manuals of a bank may be indicative of the behaviour the law will demand. The legal analysis parallels that which applies in the case of industry codes. It is clear that the rules and statements are not a direct measure of the legal liability of a bank. Breach of them is not conclusive proof of the bank failing in its legal duty. They may well fall short of, or they may exceed, what the courts regard as the bank's duty in a particular case.[93] Customers cannot require a bank to comply with its own internal rules. Yet the rules and statements in bank manuals afford a valuable criterion of the obvious risks against which the banks think it is their duty to guard. Breach of them is a matter to which a court will give close attention. Indeed, it may well be said that if they are disregarded that would be evidence of negligence, since they indicate what may be reasonably expected of the bank.

D. TYPE OF TRANSACTION AND CUSTOMER

Rarely will the type of transaction which a bank enters into for a customer have direct doctrinal significance. Thus a loss on a risky transaction or on a volatile market will not of itself be evidence of a want of care and skill on the part of a bank under the doctrine *res ipsa loquitur* or give rise to an equitable presumption. The loss will not be under its complete control since a foreign-exchange or derivatives transaction is obviously at the mercy of unpredictable movements in exchange and interest rates, albeit that protective action can be taken.[94] Nor does the common law rule about things dangerous in themselves—which imposes a peculiar duty to take precautions, and under which it is no excuse to say that the accident would not have happened without intermeddling by another—have direct application here. Foreign-exchange and derivatives transactions may result in considerable loss, depending on whether certain

---

[92] e.g. *Aldrich v. Norwich Union Life Assurance Company Ltd.* [1999] EWCA Civ. 2042, [1999] 2 All ER (Comm) 707 (CA).

[93] *Lloyds Bank Ltd. v. E. B. Savory & Co.* [1933] AC 201, 212.

[94] *Stafford v. Conti Commodity Services* [1981] 1 All ER 691, 697; *Merrill Lynch Futures Inc. v. York House Trading* (1984) 81 L.Soc. Gaz. 2544 (CA); *Ata v. American Express Bank Ltd.* [1998] EWCA Civ. 1015 (CA).

contingencies occur, but they are not dangerous, let alone dangerous in themselves, merely because this possibility exists.[95]

Yet as a practical matter the type of transaction feeds into judicial decision-making. Even when a bank provides a standard service to all customers, a court will bear in mind its nature in reaching a decision about what conduct on the bank's part the relevant legal standard requires. The type of transaction weighs more heavily in the balance as it becomes tailor-made for the particular customer, the risks associated with it increase, or the matter becomes more complex. This does not necessarily mean that the conduct expected of a bank becomes more demanding. English courts sometimes take the hard-headed view that, in the absence of express contractual terms, customers cannot expect their banks to take protective action on their behalf, or to advise them that they are not going to do so, in areas such as 'the man-made jungle of the commodity markets, red in tooth and claw'.[96] Yet if customers are unlikely to appreciate the risks associated with a particular type of transaction, or to understand what they are letting themselves in for, the courts are more likely to expect a bank to advise them.

So, too, if customers are relatively unsophisticated. This can result from their personal qualities or because they have never before made an investment or entered this type of transaction. Vulnerability features in some cases in the identification of a fiduciary relationship, and in undue influence and unconscionability.[97] If the bank's customer is commercially experienced, or its counterparty is a large financial institution, however, it does not need the law's protection.

The contract was negotiated at arm's length by two large banks, both of which were advised by skilled commercial lawyers. Each bank knew that the other might have information of the type described in the clause which would affect the price if it were disclosed. Yet each bank expressly agreed that there would be no duty on the part of either bank to disclose the information. It was thus agreed by each that the other could deliberately keep to itself information which it knew would assist it to negotiate the price or indeed to decide whether to enter into the contract at all.[98]

Those aware of the risks faced, or capable of discovering them, are on the whole confined to the contractual claims they may have.

---

[95] *David Securities Pty. Ltd* v. *Commonwealth Bank of Australia* (1990) 93 ALR 271, 291 (Fed. Ct., Full Ct.), on appeal on a different point: (1992) 175 CLR 353; *Commercial Bank of Australia* v. *Mehta* (1991) 23 NSWLR 84 (CA).

[96] *Drexel Burnham Lambert International NV* v. *El Nasr* [1986] 1 Lloyds Rep. 356, 366. See also the Singapore decision: *Banque Nationale de Paris* v. *Tan Nancy* [2002] 1 SLR 29 (CA).

[97] See *National Westminster Bank plc* v. *Amin* [2002] UKHL 9 (HL).

[98] *National Westminster Bank plc* v. *Utrecht-America Finance Co.* [2001] EWCA Civ. 658, para 49, [2001] All ER (Comm) 7, 23–4. See also *Lloyd* v. *Citicorp Australia Ltd.* (1986) 11 NSW LR 286, 288.

III. ADVICE

Some situations clearly involve a bank in giving advice. Advice on reorganization, mergers and acquisitions financing, and so on is the staple diet of investment (merchant) banking. In other situations a bank may assume the role of financial adviser. However, many banking services are not associated with giving advice. The legal issue is whether there is any obligation on a bank to proffer advice in this situation. That is the first matter dealt with in this section of the Chapter. The second matter addressed is a bank's liability if it actually does give advice, the advice is faulty, and the customer incurs a loss.

A. DUTY TO ADVISE

(i) The General Rule

Generally speaking, one party will be under no obligation to advise another about the nature of the transaction, its prudence, or other features. There has been an historical reluctance in common law systems to impose liability for omissions, and the nineteenth-century liberal assumption that dealings are between equal and equally knowledgeable parties dies hard, whatever the reality. Circumstances must be special before a failure to act becomes culpable. In countless cases English law has taken the robust view that there was no obligation on one party to reveal matters to the other, even though highly relevant to the transaction.

So, too, in banking. English courts have held that the bank providing an account for a customer need not advise on the risks, or on the tax implications, of certain payments in relation to it.[99] Nor need it advise customers of a more advantageous type of account it is now providing.[100] In the lending context, a bank is not under any contractual or tortious duty to advise on the wisdom of commercial projects for the purpose for which it is asked to lend money. If the bank examines the details of the project for the purpose of deciding whether or not to make the loan, it does that for its own prudent purposes as lender, and not for the benefit of the proposed borrower.[101] The same analysis would apply to assessing the capacity of a borrower to repay.

However, there is a rather clear difference between these and some of the other services and transactions of the modern multifunctional bank. Take the bank selling its own products—be they derivatives to commercial customers, or insurance policies, or interests in a collective investment scheme to private customers. If the large commercial customer does not understand the risks associated with, say, a swap transaction, it has the capacity to find out. Legal and other advice can easily be taken. *Caveat*

---

[99] *Redmond* v. *Allied Irish Bank* [1987] 2 FTLR 264; *Schioler* v. *Westminster Bank Ltd.* [1970] 2 QB 719.

[100] *Suriya & Douglas (a firm)* v. *Midland Bank plc* [1999] EWCA Civ. 851, [1999] 1 All ER (Comm) 612 (CA). But see Banking Code, Jan. 2001, §4.11; Business Banking Code, Mar. 2002, §4.11.

[101] *Lloyds Bank plc* v. *Cobb*, unreported, 1991 (CA).

emptor is the appropriate legal response if it subsequently claims that things were unexplained (unless, of course, it was actually misled by the bank's officers). For those without this capacity to understand, however, the law should be more willing to oblige the bank positively to advise the customer, especially if the bank's own products are involved.

In some situations English law has recognized a duty to speak, a duty to advise. It has acknowledged that silence is meaningful; in other words, can mislead. Unfortunately the matter has not been approached in a systematic way, either doctrinally, or taking into account the cost of providing advice on one side of the balance, and the knowledge of the other party, that other party's reasonable expectations and the risks associated with any transaction on the other side. English law on the duty to advise is a collection of single instances.

(ii) Situations Imposing a Duty to Advise

The first situation where the law imposes a duty to advise is where there is a misrepresentation—a failure to speak or act can constitute conduct which misleads. Thus a half-truth may constitute a misrepresentation, as where a bank canvasses the advantages, but not the risks, of a transaction with a customer. The bank must tell the whole story. A bank's advertising may be relevant in this respect. So, too, with a statement which is later discovered to be faulty, or which subsequent events falsify— the bank must speak and correct it before the transaction is closed. Conduct capable of giving rise to an estoppel may also found a claim for misrepresentation. Reliance is essential to a misrepresentation claim, however, and a customer may not be able to show that it was led to believe that a representation was being made and that it relied on it.

Secondly, there can be liability for a failure to disclose in precontractual negotiations if there has been a voluntary assumption of responsibility to do so and reliance by the customer.[102] In some cases, having regard to the special circumstances and the relationship between the parties, a voluntary assumption of responsibility may be deemed to have been undertaken. Ordinarily this will not occur in precontractual negotiations between a bank and a customer, even if there is an established relationship between the two.

Thirdly, in *Cornish* v. *Midland Bank*,[103] Glidewell LJ said that once a bank enters upon the task of advising a customer, it is obliged to 'explain fully and properly' about the nature of the borrowing. Fulfilling the duty may thus demand a full account of the attendant risks and the disadvantages of the particular transaction. In several Australian decisions this dictum has been applied.[104]

Fourthly, if a relationship is fiduciary in character, then disclosure is necessary if a person is to avoid liability for putting interest above duty, or duty to one above duty to

---

[102] *Hedley Byrne & Co. Ltd.* v. *Heller & Partners Ltd.* [1964] AC 465.

[103] [1985] 3 All ER 513, 520.

[104] e.g., *Chiarabaglio* v. *Westpac Banking Corporation* (1989) ATPR 40–971.

another. Recall the potential conflicts of interest in the multifunctional bank. Make
full disclosure of any conflict to the customer, and the bank is absolved of any wrongdoing. Yet disclosure of a conflict of interest may be in breach of a duty of confidentiality to another customer. If disclosure is a breach of duty to another, it may be
that the bank must desist completely from acting.[105]

Fifthly, at common law a bank which takes a guarantee is bound to disclose unusual
features in the transaction which has been guaranteed.[106] That the bank is unhappy
with the borrower's credit and that the borrower is in grave financial difficulties and
consistently exceeding its facility limit have been held not to be unnatural features
requiring disclosure. However, where the facility letter changes the arrangement in a
way potentially disadvantageous to a guarantor, and not naturally expected, the bank
must disclose, or the surety will be in a position to rescind.[107] More needs to be
disclosed to a guarantor under the O'Brien and Etridge decisions, considered below.[108]

Finally, the duty to advise can be imposed as a result of regulation. The UK Banking
Codes adopt as a governing principle that banks will seek to give customers a good
understanding of banking services and products. Information must be given on the
operation of an account and regular statements of the account provided.[109] Other,
more specific, information must be given on matters such as account charges.[110]
Under the Business Banking Code there is an additional obligation to explain, if
requested, a refusal to provide a loan or credit and debit card facilities.[111] In relation to
foreign exchange and international payment services, an explanation must be given
under both codes on aspects like charges.[112] Customers must be told of a bank's
internal complaints procedure and of external mechanisms such as the Financial
Services Ombudsman.[113] The advice which banks must give under the codes in
relation to guarantees and other types of third-party security is referred to below.[114]
So, too, are the information obligations in relation to payment cards.[115]

The Banking Codes are, of course, self-regulation, without statutory force. Despite
a suggestion that if the practice of banks is to advise, the law will impose an obligation
to do so,[116] the only basis in English law for this is if a term can be implied as trade
usage, or there has been an assumption of responsibility under the Hedley Byrne
principle. By contrast, in areas such as investments and consumer credit the duty to
advise is backed by law.

Of particular importance under the UK Financial Services and Markets Act 2000,

[105] 23 above.
[106] Commercial Bank of Australia Ltd. v. Amadio (1983) 151 CLR 447, 457; Crédit Lyonnais Bank Nederland
v. Export Credit Guarantee Department [1996] 1 Lloyd's Rep. 200.
[107] Levett v. Barclays Bank [1995] 1 WLR 1260, [1995] 2 All ER 615; Westpac Banking Corporation v.
Robinson (1993) 30 NSWLR 668 (CA).
[108] 217 below.
[109] Banking Code, Jan. 2001, §§3.2, 9.2; Business Banking Code, Mar. 2002, §§3.2, 9.3.
[110] §§5.1, 5.3, §§5.1, 5.4 respectively.   [111] §11.1.
[112] §12; §12 respectively.   [113] §17; §17 respectively.
[114] 220 below.   [115] 267 below.
[116] Cornish v. Midland Bank plc [1985] 3 All ER 513, 522–3, per Kerr LJ.

for example, is the requirement not to recommend transactions to private customers, not to act as a discretionary manager for them, not to arrange deals in warrants and derivatives for them, and not to engage in stock lending with them, unless reasonable steps have been taken to enable them to understand the risks involved.[117] Information about the investment firm (the bank in our case) must be given: in particular, when advising a private customer to buy a 'packaged product'—a life policy, an interest in a collective investment scheme or a stakeholder pension—the customer must be adequately informed about the firm's polarization status, i.e. whether it is advising about only its own products or acting as an independent intermediary. Indeed, in relation to packaged products there are specific obligations to give details so private customers make informed decisions.[118] Breach of these rules gives private investors a statutory right to sue for losses.[119]

(iii) The Advice Required (If Any)

So far the concept of a duty to advise has been used fairly loosely, as in everyday language where 'advice' encompasses both the short risk warning and the extended legal opinion. As a matter of law the advice which needs to be given by banks under the various heads referred to in (ii) varies in its length. Advice may translate into the legal concept of notice, as where the bank must give notice in relation to a conflict of interest. In fact, this is a demanding standard, since the beneficiaries of the fiduciary duty must give their fully informed consent. Complete disclosure of all relevant facts known to the fiduciary is required.[120] In some situations, advice may take the form of disclosing limited and specific information. In the case of misrepresentation, for example, the half truth may be readily corrected by full disclosure, and what is stale information may be fairly simply updated. But not always. As for mandatory advice under legislation such as the FSMA 2000, this ranges from the short risk warning to the detailed disclosures which few private customers will fully digest. Generally speaking, a duty to advise will never involve an obligation to make recommendations, except possibly the recommendation to seek legal advice.

As well as how detailed any advice must be, there is the question of its character. Advice must, of course, be honestly given—otherwise it is fraudulent. Generally speaking it must also be accurate. If honestly given and accurate, the common law offers little comfort to the customer who enters a disadvantageous transaction on the basis of it. Regulation goes further, however, and prescribes in greater detail the nature of the advice required. Some such advice involves highlighting the terms of the contract being entered (or at least some of them). Another approach is to require advice about the alternatives on offer—in terms, say, of repayment methods, interest rates, charges, and commissions. One step further would be 'best advice': this involves a

---

[117] FSA Handbook, Conduct of Business, r. 5.4.3.
[118] R. 6. At the time of writing this is under review.
[119] 346 below.
[120] *Phipps* v. *Boardman* [1967] 2 AC 46.

prior, conscientious search for available services and then, in any particular transaction, recommending the service which is believed to be the best, or at least as good as any other available, for that customer. Coupled with best advice are concepts such as suitability.[121] Perhaps the most effective advice in relation to some banking transactions is advice about the attendant risks. The standard demanded here may be objective, although it could also be associated with an obligation on the bank to take steps to ensure that *this* particular customer understands the risks.

B. LIABILITY FOR ADVICE GIVEN

Advice can be given to customers or to third parties. At one time, liability to third parties—such as those seeking credit assessments of another through their own banks—foundered on the absence of contract. Now tortious (or delictual) liability enables third parties to sue banks for negligent advice, as well as for fraudulent advice. A contractual nexus may still be necessary, however, in the case of misrepresentation. Fraudulent advice is uncommon, but not unknown. Little need be said about it, except that in the United States there seems to be no reluctance to allege fraud against banks. Neither is this the place for an analysis of the law of misrepresentation, except to reiterate the point that, because of what is omitted, what is said may constitute a misrepresentation.

At one time it was said that a bank could not be liable for negligent advice given by its officers, since it was not a banking function to give advice.[122] But even before banks began to promote themselves as financial advisers it was probably unrealistic to divorce advice from banking. In that event, the reasoning was flawed if grounded on the law of agency: a principal is liable for the wrongs of an agent if the agent does what is within his or her apparent authority even if, unbeknown to the third party, it is prohibited from doing so.[123] A more serious legal obstacle has been the reluctance to impose non-contractual liability for economic loss disassociated with physical injury. The potential amount of recoverable damages is not surprisingly perceived as the major obstacle. Whatever the general problem with 'pure' economic loss, however, the extent of the liability consequent on negligent advice is limited—the money itself and the profit which may have been generated through its employment elsewhere. It is not surprising, therefore, that negligent advice has been carved out as the major exception to the rule that, generally speaking, there is no liability in English law for pure economic loss.

The seminal case recognizing the tort of negligent advice, *Hedley Byrne & Co. Ltd.* v. *Heller & Partners Ltd.*,[124] involved advice given about a customer's credit-worthiness in a bank reference. As subsequently interpreted, *Hedley Byrne* liability depends importantly on an assumption of responsibility by (in our case) a bank, a sufficiently

---

[121] 119 above   [122] *Banbury* v. *Bank of Montreal* [1918] AC 626.
[123] *Bowstead and Reynolds on Agency* (17th edn., London, Sweet & Maxwell, 2001), 420–34.
[124] [1964] AC 465.

proximate relationship between the bank and the customer or third party, and on there being reliance on the statement. Assumption of responsibility and proximity are, in large part, legal fictions, and in practice a court will have regard to factors such as the purpose for which the statement was made and communicated, the bank's knowledge that the advice was needed for a particular purpose, the relationship between the bank and the person relying on the advice, and the size of any class to which the latter belongs.

Thus all the circumstances, including the bank's promotional material, may lead to the conclusion that it has taken on the responsibility of the borrower's financial adviser.[125] There is a greater chance of liability when the bank advises unsophisticated customers: in several cases the English courts have held that a bank was liable when its bank manager failed to explain clearly to a wife the effect of a charge taken over joint property to secure a husband's borrowings.[126] Not surprisingly, a court will be reluctant to conclude that the bank has assumed a responsibility to the world at large. It is clear that a bank can be negligent not only in what it advises, but also as a result of what it omits to advise. Liability for negligent advice is imposed irrespective of whether it is given gratuitously. Of course the reality is that, while a bank may not make a specific charge for advice, it is not done without benefit to the bank: the bank may provide one of its services as a result of the advice or, at the other end of the spectrum, may retain a satisfied customer.

Negligent advice can obviously occur in the range of matters in which banks become involved. Examples include credit references; failure to pass on information when a bank enters upon the task of advising a potential borrower about the attendant risks of a particular facility; statements by a bank that it will make available to a customer adequate funds to enter a contract with a third party; advice about investments; and assurances that workout plans are heading in the right direction, and that the bank is optimistic about an agreement being reached.[127]

Analytically there is a distinction between a bank simply passing on information about, say, a potential investment, and a bank actually giving advice on that investment.[128] Liability is not imposed in the case of the former, unless there is a duty to do so under, say, the bank–customer contract. The justification is that a conduit should not be made responsible for what is transmitted through it. The reasoning is fallacious: the retailer has long been held liable in contract for defective mass-produced goods, even though it does not have the opportunity of examining them as they pass along the distribution chain started by the manufacturer. Moreover, the bank passing on information is not analogous to a telephone line: there can be no strict dichotomy

---

[125] e.g. *Verity and Spindler* v. *Lloyds Bank plc* [1995] CLC 1557.

[126] e.g. *Cornish* v. *Midland Bank plc* [1985] 3 All ER 513 (CA).

[127] *Turner* v. *Royal Bank of Scotland plc* [2001] EWCA Civ. 64, [2001] 1 All ER (Comm) 1057; *British & Commonwealth Holdings plc* v. *Quadrex Holdings Inc.* [1995] CLC 1169 (CA); *VK Mason Construction Ltd.* v. *Bank of Nova Scotia* (1985) 16 DLR (4th) 598 (SCC); *Richter SA* v. *Bank of America National Trust & Savings Assoc.*, 939 F 2d 1176 (5th Cir. 1991).

[128] *Royal Bank Trust Co. (Trinidad) Ltd.* v. *Pampellonne* [1987] 1 Lloyd's Rep. 218 (PC).

between passing on information and giving advice. At the least a bank passing on information is giving some imprimatur to the contents, unless this is expressly disclaimed. This does not mean that the bank's negligence is necessarily to be equated to the negligence (if there be any) of the person preparing the information. Depending on the circumstances, its responsibility may arise in law only in its choice of the source, or in its failure to warn the party not to rely on the information without further investigation. As with a duty to pass on information, liability will not necessarily flow for all the foreseeable consequences of action taken in reliance on it.

In *Hedley Byrne* the bank avoided liability because of a disclaimer in the reference. It would seem right as a matter of policy for a bank to be able to avoid the consequences of giving negligent advice by suitable notice to those receiving it. As a matter of policy, whether this is regarded conceptually as aborting liability or as exempting from liability already begotten is beside the point. The central issue in practice should be whether the disclaimer of, or exemption from, liability has been made clear to those being advised so they are in no doubt that the bank is washing its hands of the consequences if the advice proves inappropriate or wrong. A small print clause in a document given to those being advised is unlikely to satisfy this test. In English law the matter is handled by applying the unfair contract terms legislation.[129]

IV.　VITIATING FACTORS IN BANKING TRANSACTIONS

Developed systems of law have techniques for upsetting contracts which are in a general sense unfair because of the nature of their terms or the conduct of one of the parties. Freedom of contract gives way to an attempt to produce a result which is in a sense more just than the product of market exchange. Whether this constitutes a transformation of nineteenth-century contract law to the standards of the social market is a source of debate.[130] What is clear is that, while inequality of bargaining power may not itself provide the conceptual basis for vitiating contracts, it is often the occasion for its exercise. The law more readily interferes to protect the vulnerable, the unsophisticated, and the consumer than if the counterparty is, too, a commercial organization.

At least in English law, a major burden in countering inequality of bargaining power has been carried by the legislation on unfair contract terms, discussed in Chapter 5. Occasionally, a vulnerable person may be able to invoke other legislation, as where there is not a sufficient memorandum of a contract under section 4 of the Statute of Frauds and its successors. Alternatively, specific legislation relating to

[129] See *Smith* v. *Bush* [1990] 1 AC 831 (HL).
[130] e.g. H. Collins, *The Law of Contract* (3rd edn., London, Butterworths, 1997).

consumer credit or financial services regulation may not have been satisfied. The statutory provisions for reopening extortionate credit bargains have been mentioned earlier.[131]

There are, however, a range of discrete common law doctrines, of different historical derivation, which can be invoked in limited circumstances to vitiate contracts which are procedurally or substantively unfair. Thus in relation to the signature of contracts there is *non est factum*, although English law is reluctant to overturn transactions which have been signed, on the basis both that signature indicates assent and that others may rely on a signed document. For procedural unfairness there is also misrepresentation, mistake, undue influence, unconscionability, and duress. Substantive unfairness has been less tested by the common law. However, there is some potential for doing this by the implication of terms, and there are also isolated doctrines such as the rule against penalties.[132] This section of the Chapter outlines a few of these doctrines, before turning to how banks can have their transactions vitiated because they are infected by the wrongful conduct of others.

A. UNDUE INFLUENCE, UNCONSCIONABILITY, AND DURESS

Undue influence and unconscionability have featured regularly in common law countries as vitiating factors in the formation of banking contracts. Their popularity at any particular moment may reflect the turn of the economic cycle, as customers seek to mitigate the consequences of economic failure. Duress is conveniently considered alongside these doctrines, although in practice it has not been as frequently invoked.

Functionally these three doctrines are often interchangeable. Conceptually, however, they are distinct. In the banking context undue influence and duress are concerned with the impairment of the customer's judgement by some handicap. To put in another way, they are customer-sided in their application. By contrast, unconscionability is bank-sided in its focus, in that the bank must be shown to have behaved badly towards the customer, or to have notice of such behaviour on the part of others.[133]

(i) Undue Influence

It has become conventional to divide undue influence into actual and presumed undue influence.[134] Actual undue influence is analogous to duress, since it is necessary for the person seeking to have the contract set aside to establish affirmatively the exertion of excessive pressure.[135] Presumed undue influence falls into two categories.

---

[131] 77 above.   [132] 323 below.

[133] P. Birks and N. Y. Chin, 'On the Nature of Undue Influence', in J. Beatson and D. Friedmann (eds.), *Good Faith and Fault in Contract Law* (Oxford, Clarendon, 1995), 62.

[134] *Royal Bank of Scotland v. Etridge (No 2)* [2001] 3 WLR 1021; *Barclays Bank plc v. O'Brien* [1994] 1 AC 180. See also *Lough v. Diprose* (1992) 175 CLR 621; *Geffen v. Goodman Estate* (1991) 81 DLR (4th) 211 (SCC).

[135] e.g. *Bank of Montreal v. Stuart* [1911] AC 120 (PC).

The first involves established relationships where undue influence is irrebuttably presumed—parent and child, solicitor and client, trustee and beneficiary, but not husband and wife. The justifications for there being no such presumption of undue influence of a husband over his wife are said to be commercial reality, domestic harmony, and the ordinary expectation that wives will make gifts, and transfer property, to their husbands. Even if there is no established relationship, there is a second category of presumed undue influence where, for instance, the person proves a relationship as a result of which he or she has generally reposed trust and confidence in the other party or in which the other party has acquired an ascendancy. There is no reason that this other party cannot be a bank.[136] The circumstances in which this can occur are multiplied as the modern multifunctional bank holds itself out to customers as financial adviser, planner, and confidant.

Coupled with a transaction which is not readily explicable, the reposing of trust and confidence enables the court to infer, in the absence of a satisfactory explanation, that the transaction has been procured by undue influence. There is an evidential rebuttable presumption which the court draws, although it will consider the whole of the evidence, and it may be that the person in whom trust and confidence has been reposed can counter the inference which would otherwise be drawn. The presumption may survive the relationship. Rebutting the presumption means showing that despite the relationship the first person has been in a position to decide freely what to do. It is not sufficient for the second person to demonstrate proper behaviour on its part. The most usual way to try to show a free exercise of independent will is to establish that the transaction was entered into after its nature and effect were fully explained by some independent and qualified person.[137]

Dominating influence has been said from time to time to be a prerequisite for presumed undue influence.[138] There is no such requirement. What is necessary is that the degree of trust and confidence be such that parties in whom it is reposed are in a position to influence the other party in effecting a transaction, either because they have become an adviser of the other, because they have been entrusted with the management of the other party's affairs or everyday needs, or for some other reason. The presumption is not perfected and remains inoperative until the party who has ceded the trust and confidence makes a gift so large, or enters into a transaction so improvident, as cannot be reasonably accounted for on the grounds of friendship, relationship, charity, or other ordinary human motives.[139]

Apart from cases of actual undue influence, it is still necessary that a person seeking to vitiate a transaction establish that it is seriously enough disadvantageous to require evidence to rebut the presumption. At one point this had the label 'manifest advantage' attached to it,[140] but that term has been deprecated as giving rise to

---

136 *Lloyd's Bank v. Bundy* [1975] 1 QB 326 (CA).
137 *Inche Noriah v. Shaik Allie Bin Omar* [1929] AC 127 (PC).
138 e.g. *National Westminster Bank plc v. Morgan* [1985] AC 686 (HL).
139 *Goldsworthy v. Brickell* [1987] Ch. 378 (CA).
140 *National Westminster Bank plc v. Morgan* [1985] AC 686.

misunderstanding.[141] In this respect, the court is looking not only at procedural, but also at substantive, unfairness. The test is an objective test—whether any independent and reasonable person who considered the transaction at the time, with knowledge of all the facts, would have regarded it so obviously disadvantageous that it was only explicable on the basis that undue influence had been exercised. It seems necessary to balance the seriousness of the risk of the transaction being enforced in practical terms with the benefits gained by the person in accepting the risk.[142]

In the frequently litigated situation of a wife guaranteeing her husband's business debts, misrepresentation is often coupled with undue influence as a basis for seeking to set the guarantee aside. We return shortly to that dimension involving the liability of the third party bank. What, however, of the relationship between the spouses? The English courts are realistic in expecting florid descriptions by husbands about their business prowess so do not treat exaggerated forecasts of success as misrepresentation. As to undue influence, in the ordinary course this will not be the type of transaction which, failing proof to the contrary, will be *prima facie* evidence of its exercise by husbands. While there is an obvious risk to wives in undertaking such transactions, the English courts take the view that there are inherent reasons why they are for their benefit, when ordinarily the fortunes of both spouses are bound up together.

It has been held that a transaction impugned on the basis of undue influence must be rescinded completely, without conditions. Consequently, in the case, say, of misrepresentation, it is not open for a court to set aside a transaction, such as the giving of security, on terms that the person acknowledges that it is valid for the amount which was represented. Although in principle recision in equity can be moulded to the particular circumstances, and terms imposed, in this context it is said to be an 'all or nothing process'.[143] Like public policy, a discretion to grant relief on terms has the potential for being an unruly horse. Yet its careful application would enable a court, without rewriting the parties' bargain, to achieve practical justice for both parties. Distinctions would need to be drawn, for instance, between different kinds of legal wrong, undue influence as opposed to misrepresentation, fraudulent rather than innocent misrepresentation, and so on. Using equity's flexibility in this way in granting rescission would also accord with the evolving law of restitution.

(ii) Unconscionability

There is a functional overlap between undue influence and unconscionable dealing, although analytically the doctrines are distinct. The requirements for the latter are, first, that there be circumstances of special disadvantage which affect a person's ability to judge self-interest, such as poverty, illness, ethnic origin, ignorance, or lack of advice. It is clear that in ordinary circumstances in the modern age, a wife is not in a

---

[141] *Royal Bank of Scotland v. Etridge (No 2)* [2001] UKHL 44, [2001] 3 WLR 1021.

[142] *Bank of Credit and Commerce International SA v. Aboody* [1990] 1 QB 923 (CA).

[143] *TSB Bank plc v. Camfield* [1995] 1 WLR 430; [1995] 1 All ER 951 (CA); *Dunbar Bank plc v. Nadeem* [1998] 3 All ER 876 (CA).

position of special disadvantage for the purposes of the doctrine. Secondly, this weakness of the one party must have been exploited by the other in some morally culpable manner. In other words, the disadvantage must have been sufficiently evident to the latter, and he or she must have taken advantage of it unfairly and unconscientiously. Thirdly, the resulting transaction must be one which is not just, fair, or reasonable.

Unconscionability may be presumed by weakness on one side and exploitation of that by the other side.[144] The doctrine does not give relief for what is simply an unfair bargain—it has to be an unconscionable one, the terms of which show conduct shocking the conscience of the court.[145] Unconscionability has been fairly dormant in England in recent times. Its work has been done for it by undue influence although, as we have seen, the two are doctrinally distinct.

(iii) Duress

Economic duress is unlikely to lead to the vitiation of banking transactions. The prerequisites for economic duress are pressure to induce the victim to enter into a contract, and that the pressure be illegitimate. The illegitimate pressure need not be the sole reason for the person to enter into the contract. It was the absence of causation which led the New South Wales Court of Appeal to hold in one case that economic duress was not made out. There the bank refused to hand over moneys unless the security document was signed. Although the court regarded the pressure which the bank applied as being unlawful, it concluded that it had played no part in the execution of the mortgage, which had occurred before the pressure was applied.[146] Subsequently, the same court has drawn a bright line between, on the one hand, pressure which consists of unlawful threats, or amounts to unconscionable conduct and, on the other, commercial pressure which is not of itself unlawful or unconscionable, even to the point where the party the subject of the pressure has little choice but to act as it did.[147] Thus when a borrower is in financial difficulties, it is not objectionable for the bank to press for repayment or better security if it is not to call default.

B. VITIATION AND THIRD PARTY BEHAVIOUR

It will be unusual for a bank itself to have exercised undue influence, acted unconscionably, or exerted illegitimate pressure. If it has, or if, as is more likely, it has misrepresented a transaction to a customer (however innocently), the law may disable

[144] *Commercial Bank of Australia Ltd.* v. *Amadio* (1983) 151 CLR 447.

[145] *Burmah Oil Co. Ltd.* v. *The Governor of the Bank of England, The Times,* 4 July 1981; *Credit Lyonnais Bank Nederland NV* v. *Burch* [1997] 1 All ER 144, 151, 152 (CA); *Portman Building Society* v. *Dusangh* [2000] EWCA Civ. 142, [2000] 2 All ER (Comm) 221. See D. Capper, 'Undue Influence and Unconscionability: A Rationalisation' (1998) 114 *LQR* 479, 494.

[146] *Crescendo Management Pty. Ltd.* v. *Westpac Banking Corporation* (1989) 19 NSW LR 40.

[147] *Equiticorp Finance Ltd. (in liq.)* v. *Bank of New Zealand* (1993) 32 NSW LR 50. See also *CTN Cash and Carry Ltd.* v. *Gallaher Ltd.* [1994] 4 All ER 714 (CA); A. Phang, 'Economic Duress' (1997) 5 *RLR* 53.

it from enforcing the transaction. Misrepresentation may also result in an award of damages against it.

More typically litigated has been the situation where a party argues that a banking transaction is tainted by the behaviour of a third party and so cannot be enforced. In England the way that banking transactions are affected by the wrongdoing of third parties is under the guidelines laid down in *Barclays Bank* v. *O'Brien* and *Royal Bank of Scotland* v. *Etridge (No 2)*.[148] In essence a bank is put on inquiry whenever a wife offers to stand surety for her husband's debts, by a combination of two factors, the transaction on its face is disadvantageous and there is a substantial risk that it could be as a result of the misrepresentation, undue influence, or other wrong of the husband. So stated the test is less onerous than for the presumption of undue influence as between the spouses themselves. All that is required is that the wife offer to stand surety for the husband's business debt. The same approach applies where A and B are cohabiting or otherwise tied together emotionally, sexually, or economically, and the bank knows this.

A typical situation giving rise to the problem which the cases address has been where women have given a bank security over their property, such as their share in the domestic home, to support their partner's business debts. The law has been concerned on the one hand to protect the women, who may still in the modern day be misled or pressured, or whose judgement may be emotionally clouded, so that they agree to give the bank security without bringing an informed or independent mind to bear. On the other hand, there has been a reluctance to upset such common transactions, especially since the bank itself has had no hand in the wrongdoing. Moreover, in the case of security given over domestic property, the courts are as concerned that such an important form of wealth in modern British society should not be economically sterile, but should be available to underpin business, especially small business enterprises.

(i) Possible Approaches

In various jurisdictions the law has grappled with these contending policy considerations using a variety of legal tools. In the decade before *O'Brien* English courts analysed the problem in terms of 'agency'—had the third party been the agent of the bank? In cases of true agency there can be no doubt that a bank is liable. The bank as principal is vicariously liable for the acts of its agent. Agency, however, acquired a particular meaning in the context of the English decisions, and was said to encompass situations where the bank had left it to the third party to obtain the security.[149] *O'Brien* deprecated this artificial use of agency principles.

A second possible approach, which became known as 'Lord Romilly's heresy', also lurked in the common law.[150] This was to the effect that whenever anyone made a

---

[148] [1994] 1 AC 180, [2001] 3 WLR 1021 respectively. See also *Barclays Bank plc* v. *Boulter* [1999] 1 WLR 1919; [1999] 4 All ER 513 (HL).

[149] *Turnbull & Co.* v. *Duval* [1902] AC 429 (PC); *Bank of Credit and Commerce International SA* v. *Aboody* [1990] 1 QB 923 (CA).

[150] Cf. S. Gardner, 'A Confused Wife's Equity' (1982) 2 *OJLS* 130.

large, voluntary gift or the like (e.g. a guarantee), the burden was thrown on the party benefiting (the bank) to justify it. Although Lord Romilly laid it down as a rule in the mid-nineteenth century, it was rejected by contemporaneous commentators, rarely invoked in subsequent case law, and emphatically rejected on a number of occasions. It no longer seems a possible argument.

Another line of authority, which took root in Australia,[151] meant that security might be unenforceable, notwithstanding that the bank had no knowledge of, and was not responsible for, B's wrongdoing. In cases falling within the protected class (initially married women), this occurs if the relationship and the consequent likelihood of influence and reliance were known to the bank, and if the class member lacked an adequate understanding of the nature and effect of the transaction, and the bank failed to take reasonable steps to ensure that she did and that her consent was true and informed. So notice of the likely relationship of trust and confidence is the key. In *O'Brien* the Court of Appeal adopted this approach, but it was emphatically repudiated when the case was appealed to the House of Lords. The approach contained a minor conceptual contradiction: wives are not a protected class if the bank exercises undue influence directly, but are if a bank obtains security from them as a result of their husband's undue influence.[152]

The approach which has ultimately come to prevail as a result of *O'Brien* and *Etridge* supposedly turns on the constructive notice a bank is said to have when a wife and others act as surety. It derives from a strand of authority in all common law jurisdictions that a person is adversely affected if he or she has notice of the wrongdoing of a third party—the husband in our typical case.[153] If notice provides the doctrinal foundation, however, it says little about the law's practical application in this area. It requires, first, that A's consent to the security be obtained by misrepresentation, undue influence, or other wrong on the part of B. This is fairly obvious: if A cannot upset a transaction in the absence of wrongdoing by the bank, why should it be able to do so in the absence of wrongdoing by anyone else? For the bank, however, it is almost an impossible task to do this, and indeed there is no obligation on it to discover whether there has, in fact, been wrongdoing. So in practice this first requirement need not be proved. Secondly, the bank must know that the relationship between A and B is of a close, emotional, or economic nature. In policy terms this is because the informality of business dealings in such a relationship raises a substantial risk of misrepresentation, or the fear of damaging it makes the ties a ready weapon for undue influence. This type of relationship is assumed with wives. Otherwise,

[151] Notably in Dixon J's judgment in *Yerkey* v. *Jones* (1939) 63 CLR 649 and *Garcia* v. *National Australia Bank* (1998) 194 CLR 395. See Justice Kiefel, 'Guarantees by Family Members and Spouses: Garcia and a German Perspective' (2000) 74 *ALJR* 692; Justice Santow, 'Sex, Lies and Securities—Touching the Conscience of the Creditor' (1999) 10 *JBFLP* 7.

[152] See S. Cretney, 'Mere Puppets, Folly and Imprudence' [1994] *RLR* 3.

[153] *Bainbrigge* v. *Browne* (1881) 18 Ch.D 188, 197 *per* Fry J is by no means the earliest authority. Elsewhere e.g. *Weitzman* v. *Hendin* (1989) 69 OR (2d) 678 (CA); *Contractors Bonding* v. *Snee* [1992] 2 NZLR 157 (CA); US Restatement on Security, §119. Cf. Restatement on Contracts, Second, §164(2). Cf. J. Mee, 'Undue Influence, Misrepresentation and the Doctrine of Notice' [1995] *CLJ* 536.

the relationship can be heterosexual or homosexual, need never have involved cohabitation, and can also be between parent and child or employer and employee.[154]

Thirdly, the transaction on its face must be one which benefits the wrongdoer, B, at the expense of the other party, A, or which, to the bank's knowledge, is intended to do so, even though on its face it appears to be for their joint benefit. A guarantee or security given by A to support the debts of B or B's business (where A has no interest in the business) on its face benefits B at the expense of A. By contrast, a joint loan has been held not to do so, even if in fact it is for B's own purposes unless the bank actually knows. If all joint loans put banks on inquiry, it is said, they would be disinclined to grant facilities to couples, or would need to become excessively intrusive.[155] Yet the distinction between suretyship and joint loans could be artificial, for what is effectively a loan to the husband could be structured into a separate joint loan account, and thus avoid liability, unless the bank actually knew that the loan was for the one party only. What of the situation where A has an interest in B's business? In some cases in the common law world, the wife's interest in the company being guaranteed has been used as the basis for insulating the bank from B's wrongdoing.[156] As a result of *Etridge*, however, English law puts a bank on inquiry, even when the wife is a director or secretary of the company. This can be justified because A's shareholding in B's business, if small, even A acting, say, as company secretary, might not prevent A's security benefiting B and only B. A could be regarded as not having a financial interest in the company, since the shares are unlikely to be saleable, a dividend will probably never be declared, and any remuneration from the position as secretary can hardly be characterized as direct.

(ii) The Guidelines

If the doctrinal foundations of *O'Brien* and *Etridge* are rather unsure, what a bank must do is relatively straightforward. In general terms, it must take reasonable steps to satisfy that A has brought home, in a meaningful way, the practical implications of the proposed transaction.

A number of decided cases had shown that written warnings of themselves are often not read and are sometimes intercepted by the other party (B). So one approach is for the bank to conduct a personal interview. In the interview the advice would be about the risks, not the wisdom, of the transaction. However, advising on the risks would not seem confined to advising on the general effect of this type of transaction (general risk) but on the effect of this particular transaction in the light, say, of A's financial position (specific risk). As we have seen, once a bank embarks on giving such advice, there is a chance that it will be inadequate or negligently given. It is not surprising,

---

[154] e.g., *Massey* v. *Midland Bank plc* [1995] 1 All ER 929 (CA). *Banco Exterior Internacional SA* v. *Thomas* [1997] 1 WLR 221 (CA); *Credit Lyonnais Bank Nederland NV* v. *Burch* [1997] 1 All ER 144 (CA).

[155] *CIBC Mortgages plc* v. *Pitt* [1994] 1 AC 200 (HL). See A. Lawson, 'O'Brien and its Legacy' [1995] CLJ 280, 282.

[156] e.g. *Warburton* v. *Whiteley* (1989) NSW Conv. R. 55–453, (CA); *North-West Life Assurance Company of Canada* v. *Shannon Height Developing Ltd.* (1987) 12 BCLR (2d) (CA).

then, that banking practice is not to conduct such interviews. Instead banking practice, approved by the courts, is to ensure that A is advised by a solicitor, acting solely for A, in a face-to-face meeting.[157] The bank will generally be able to rely on confirmation from the solicitor that the advice about the practical implications of the proposed transaction has been given. English courts place great faith in solicitors. They expect that, regardless of who is paying the fee, solicitors will regard themselves as owing an exclusive duty to the person being advised (A), and that the advice they give will be appropriate.

(iii) The Policy Issue

There is no doubt that bank and other mortgage lenders have improved their procedures as a result of *O'Brien* and related decisions.[158] Whether the law in this area addresses the fundamental problems has been raised by a number of commentators. Advice may counter a misrepresentation or misunderstanding. But where A is emotionally or financially dependent on B, advice is highly unlikely to stem the sources of undue influence. Typically, advice about the risks will not dissuade A from entering the transaction. A will go ahead anyhow, her judgement clouded by the relationship.[159] Some jurisdictions have tackled the problem head on. In the context of family property there are legislative restrictions on the extent to which one party can encumber it other than in the context of acquiring it ('homestead' legislation).[160] There may also be an effective prohibition under anti-discrimination legislation, in that it is said to be discrimination against a married applicant for credit, who is unquestionably creditworthy, to require that his or her spouse guarantee the loan.[161] There may be a case for addressing the discrepancy between the regulation of consumer and small business credit.[162]

   At the least there is a strong case for following the *O'Brien* and *Etridge* guidelines whenever an individual acts as surety, and on the face of it obtains no benefit from doing so. In other words, as in the Banking Codes there should be no distinction between sureties who are in some close emotional relationship, and others. All need warning about general and specific risks, and all need counselling about the benefits of independent legal advice. Indeed the Codes are more onerous than the guidelines in that taking unlimited (all moneys) guarantees from individuals is generally forbidden under both codes.[163]

---

[157] *Royal Bank of Scotland* v. *Etridge (No 2)* [2001] UKHL 44; [2001] 3 WLR 1021 (HL).

[158] M. Pawlowski and S. Greer, 'Constructive Notice and Independent Legal Advice' (2001) 65 *Conv.* 229.

[159] G. Fehlberg, *Sexually Transmitted Debt. Surety Experience and English Law* (Oxford, Clarendon, 1998); Law Reform Commission (Australia), *Equality before the Law: Women's Equality*, Report No 69 (Sydney, LRC(A), 1994), pt. II, 257–8.

[160] N. Gravells, 'Creditors and the Family home' (1985) 5 *OJLS* 132.

[161] A Farley, 'The Spousal Defense—A Ploy to Escape Payment on Simple Application of the Equal Credit Opportunity Act' (1996) 49 *Vand. LR* 1287.

[162] R. Graycar, R. Johansson, and J. Lorrie, 'Guaranteeing Someone Else's Debts' (2001) 12 *JBFLP* 181.

[163] Banking Code, Jan. 2001, §11.2; Business Banking Code, Mar. 2002, §11.3.

V. LENDER LIABILITY

'Lender liability' is an elastic term, which can cover a range of liabilities, based on a variety of legal doctrines. Clearly it could cover the liability which would arise because a bank gives negligent advice, does not exercise reasonable care and skill, is liable in knowing receipt or dishonest assistance, etc. But what of more novel claims—of a bank failing to advise on the imprudence from the borrower's perspective of a loan, negligently processing a loan application, failing to negotiate in good faith following a commitment letter, refusing to lend, negligently administering a loan, and improperly calling payment of a demand loan or accelerating and cancelling a facility? And what about insolvency and environmental liability? A narrow definition of lender liability focuses on the liability of banks: (i) in, say, administering or terminating a loan; (i) when involved in a work-out or the insolvency of a borrower; and (iii) as a result of legislation, in particular environmental legislation.

A difficulty in fully understanding international developments in lender liability is trying to find a pattern amongst developments in a variety of jurisdictions with different legal orders. One aspect of this is the simple matter of legal reporting: it is not uncommon in England for important banking cases, which do not go on appeal, not to be reported. Thus the most important pure lender-liability case in England, *Barnes* v. *Williams and Glyn's Bank Ltd.* has never been fully reported.[164] By contrast, the commercial imperatives of law publishers in the United States means that every conceivable lender-liability case is reported. The result may be to give a quite misleading impression of the incidence of lender-liability cases between different jurisdictions.

There are some common patterns in the lender-liability case law in jurisdictions with quite different legal systems. In a way this should not be surprising, given the similar social and economic contexts of the litigation. Much of the recent litigation in this area is a product of economic downturn coupled with the changed behaviour of banks from the 1980s. Financial liberalization and competition led banks to engage in activities which in the past should have warned them against. It is not unnatural for those who are swept by the economic winds of change to seek a deep pocket for the losses that have been incurred. Often these claims by borrowers are driven along by the internal logic of the legal system, as liquidators of insolvent borrowers look around to maximize the assets available to other creditors.

There is a pattern across jurisdictions to the type of factual circumstances giving rise to lender-liability claims. In the Anglo-American system the legal doctrines used to advance them are quite basic. Let us focus on some different sets of factual circumstances.

---

[164] There is a limited report in [1981] Com. LR 205.

A. PROMOTING RISKY LOANS

Generally speaking banks cannot be said to be negligent in concluding a facility with a borrower, or in advancing moneys under it. A bank will conduct due diligence for its own purposes, but it would be remarkable in a commercial context for an English court to treat a bank as being in breach of duty to the borrower because it failed to carry out sufficient inquiry into its capacity to service the debt. This is not undermined in any way by the decisions in England, where banks have been held to be contributorily negligent in the actions they have brought against surveyors for negligently valuing property the banks took as security for loans. When some borrowers defaulted, the banks found that they could not recover fully against the property, which surveyors had overvalued. In some of these cases the banks' damages against the surveyors have been reduced, on the basis that the banks were contributorily negligent in, for example, making inadequate inquiries of borrowers, or in lending too high a proportion of the value of the property without taking the status of the borrower into account.[165] Yet these cases say nothing about any duty which banks have to borrowers: the essence of contributory negligence is a failure to take reasonable care of one's own interests and does not necessarily connote any failure to take reasonable care in relation to others.

Exceptionally, if a bank promotes lending which is inherently risky, especially if the borrowers are relatively unsophisticated, the courts are likely to look more sympathetically when things turn sour and borrowers sue. The factual circumstances most likely to generate successful claims are where lenders, in the case of an unusually risky type of facility, have not explained to borrowers the grave risks involved. A good illustration is provided by the raft of litigation in Australia and New Zealand in relation to the foreign-currency loans, which banks promoted to customers in the 1980s. Their advantage was said to be the low interest rates. In a number of these cases the courts have held the banks to be liable, mainly because of a specific statutory requirement that corporations not engage in misleading or deceptive conduct.[166] Borrowers have successfully argued that it was misleading or deceptive conduct for the banks not to explain to unsophisticated borrowers, such as farmers and small business people, that foreign-currency loans entail great risks, and that it was advisable to enter a forward-exchange contract to hedge the exchange risk.

Common law claims have also been advanced. Borrowers have contended that the bank had contracted to manage the foreign-currency loan by analysing foreign-exchange trends and advising hedging when necessary. In the absence of express terms to this effect, however, courts have been reluctant to imply this duty as part of a facility agreement. Even if there were a contractual duty to manage a foreign-currency loan, the standard expected of the bank has been held to vary with the commercial

---

[165] e.g., *Banque Bruxelles Lambert SA* v. *Eagle Star Insurance Co.* [1995] 2 All ER 769, 820, [1994] 31 EG 68, on appeal on a different point. [1997] AC 191.

[166] Trade Practices Act 1974, s. 52 (Aust.); Fair Trading Act 1986, s. 9 (NZ).

experience of borrowers and not to extend to protecting them against all adverse currency movements.[167]

Negligence has also been advanced in relation to the information (or lack of it) provided prior to a foreign-currency loan being entered. We have seen that *Hedley Byrne* liability is possible for a failure to advise, if there has been a voluntary assumption of responsibility to do so. Ordinarily this will not occur in precontractual negotiations between a bank and a potential borrower, but in a few cases the Australian courts have held that there were special circumstances giving rise to a duty to advise because of the new and complex nature of foreign-currency facilities.[168]

B. MANAGEMENT AND TERMINATION OF A FACILITY

During the lifetime of a facility, its terms will obviously determine much of the relationship between the bank and the borrower. What the terms mean is a matter of construction, although a bank may waive any term for its benefit (for example, a stipulation for so many days' notice to draw down). Courts will only reluctantly imply additional duties into contracts, such as a duty to increase the facility, or to give adequate notice of a refusal to do so.[169] Although there will be general reluctance on the part of courts to imply terms as against a bank, this does not mean that the words of the written agreement are the only repository of a bank's obligations during the facility's lifetime. First, the contract may be partly oral and partly written, or there may be a side letter; secondly, the bank may be under a duty to exercise due care and skill in effecting some of its contractual obligations; and thirdly, the bank is under a duty not to make misrepresentations or to proffer negligent advice.

The duty to exercise care and skill may arise in the performance of the terms of the loan. Much depends, however, on the particular terms involved and on what the lender has undertaken to do (if anything). For example, has the bank assumed a responsibility to respond immediately to any inquiry, or has it undertaken only to give more general views about market trends, if asked? Generally speaking, a duty of care and skill in managing a loan will have a limited ambit. For example, the bank should exercise care and skill in paying over money on draw-down: if it executes the request for draw-down knowing that it is dishonestly given by, for example, fraudulent directors of the borrowing company, shutting its eyes to the obvious fact of dishonesty, or acting recklessly in failing to make such inquiries as an honest and reasonable lender would make, it will be liable.

The possibility of lender liability increases if the bank acts inconsistently. In English law the doctrine of estoppel may prevent a bank exercising certain rights, despite the very clear terms of the loan documentation.[170] A factual example is provided by a

---

[167] *Lloyd* v. *Citicorp Australia Ltd.* (1986) 11 NSWLR 286.

[168] P. Nankivell, 'The Liability of Australian Banks for Swiss Franc Loans', in W. Blair (ed.), *Banks, Liability and Risk* (3rd edn., London, LLP, 2001), 323; J. O'Donovan, *Lender Liability* (Sydney, LBC, 2000), 223–4.

[169] *Barnes* v. *Williams and Glyn's Bank Ltd.* [1981] Com. LR 205, 209.

[170] e.g. *Lombard North Central plc* v. *Stobart*, *The Times*, 2 Feb. 1990 (CA).

decision of the German Federal Supreme Court. There a bank had financed the construction of warehouses which were later to be sold by the borrower. The loan agreement set out the purpose of the loan and its terms, including the security (collateral) required. In the course of the continuing business relationship, the bank conducted an audit of the borrower and discovered that its financial situation was worse than originally thought. It thus demanded additional security which the borrower refused. The Düsseldorf Court of Appeal held that the bank had waived its right to demand additional security, although on appeal the Supreme Court held that despite mention of specific security in the agreement, this did not preclude the bank from taking advantage of its right to demand more security, pursuant to the German banks' General Terms and Conditions. However, the Supreme Court recognized that the bank's behaviour was contradictory and therefore violated the principle of good faith.[171]

Termination of a loan facility has given rise to litigation in many jurisdictions; the borrower claims that despite any clear right given in the loan documentation to take this course, the bank should not have done so, and is thus liable for the losses incurred. The English courts have been unsympathetic to this sort of argument, except in certain limited situations. Thus a bank cannot vary or withdraw a facility in breach of contract. In particular circumstances it may be estopped from withdrawing a facility without reasonable notice. And if the language of the facility is unclear, on ordinary principles an English court will be reluctant to imply in favour of the bank a right (say) to terminate without notice.[172]

General speaking, however, banks take a right to terminate and the plain words of the lending contract are given effect.[173] At most the borrower will be given a 'reasonable time' to repay, and a reasonable time is not the time it takes to refinance from another lender, but the short time it takes to set the mechanics of the repayment system in operation.[174] In relation to third parties, there would seem to be no duty on a bank not to terminate so as to prevent loss to, say, a guarantor of the borrower. The bank's business is to lend; the guarantor is not, in the ordinary course, in a sufficiently proximate relationship to be the beneficiary of such a duty.

Other jurisdictions have been more generous. The oft-quoted American decision, *KMC Co. Inc.* v. *Irving Trust Co.*,[175] arose after the insolvency of KMC. Irving Trust had extended a line of credit and had been requested to advance additional moneys, which the bank had originally agreed. Subsequently, however, Irving reneged on this agreement. The Sixth Circuit Court of Appeals concluded that Irving Trust owed

---

[171] U Schäfer, 'Lender Liability Towards Financially Troubled Borrowers in German Law', in W. Blair (ed.), *Banks, Liability and Risk* (3rd edn., London, LLP, 2001), 225—6.

[172] e.g. *Crimpfil Ltd* v. *Barclays Bank plc* [1995] CLC 385 (CA).

[173] *Socomex Ltd. (in administrative receivership) & Ors* v. *Banque Bruxelles Lambert SA* [1996] 1 Lloyd's Rep. 156.

[174] *Bank of Baroda* v. *Panessar* [1987] Ch. 335; *Sheppard & Cooper Ltd.* v. *TSB Bank plc* [1996] 2 All ER 654; *Lloyds Bank plc* v. *Lampert* [1998] EWCA Civ. 1840, [1999] 1 All ER (Comm) 161.

[175] 757 F 2d 752 (6th Cir. 1985).

KMC an implied obligation to give a period of notice to the company to enable it to obtain alternative financing. It affirmed a very significant monetary judgment against the bank on the basis of the latter's breach of its duty of good-faith performance. Significantly, the court indicated that even though the loan agreement gave the bank a discretionary right to make advances, the lender was nonetheless under an obligation of good faith. There are cases in other jurisdictions like Germany and Canada, where a similarly sympathetic view was taken when banks abruptly terminated lending facilities.[176]

C. WORKOUTS, RECEIVERSHIPS, AND INSOLVENCIES

The Anglo-Saxon view is that banks lend moneys and business people run their businesses. In other words, the business of banks is lending and not to become involved in the business decisions of their borrowers. This contrasts with the position in other countries, such as Germany, where banks appoint directors to the boards of their borrowers and become involved with business decisions. There are advantages to this in that banks are forced to take a long-term view of the relationship, and are therefore more inclined to see a borrower over a difficult patch. However, even in the Anglo-Saxon world there are situations where banks do interfere more with business decisions—typically when things start going wrong, or in a formal 'workout'. Indeed, there is some official encouragement of a 'rescue culture', in which banks are more willing to help borrowers over temporary difficulties.

Banks will have inserted in their facility agreements representations and warranties, and covenants, as devices to protect themselves in the event of a borrower's decline, and to control potential misbehaviour on its part.[177] The law has no objection to borrowers agreeing, say, to pass on detailed financial information to the banks, and to do and not do certain things. In the case of a financially distressed borrower, however, banks must exercise some care in what they do. In a workout a bank has an obvious and legitimate interest in aiding the struggling borrower. Indeed, there is a larger public interest in banks nursing borrowers back to good health. Yet other creditors, and the borrower's administrator or liquidator (if insolvency ensues), may claim that the bank gained an improper leverage in doing so, which damaged them or the company.

In a workout the formal default mechanism in the loan agreement will not have been invoked, and thus the express protections set out there not enjoyed by the bank. Banks thus seek to reduce the risks associated with a workout by entering a workout agreement with the borrower. This must document any extension of time and reserve the right to accelerate and terminate.[178] Otherwise, a bank may be held to have waived its rights under the facility agreement to a greater extent than intended. Even then a bank may still be exposed to the risk of liability to persons other than the borrower,

---

[176] 306 below.   [177] 313 below.
[178] G. Olson, 'Bank in Distress—Non-Performing Loans', in W. Blair (ed.), *Bank and Remedies* (2nd edn., London, LLP, 1999).

particularly to creditors and potential creditors of the borrower, and perhaps even in some circumstances to its shareholders. This is a real threat in other jurisdictions. For example, in the United States banks have been found liable on various bases, including the so-called instrumentality theory—they have controlled and dominated a borrower and it has become their mere instrumentality. Banks have been held responsible in these circumstances for debts which a borrower has incurred to other creditors.[179]

The duty of care to the borrower required of a holder of security, such as a bank, in exercising a power of sale, is well known, although there is some disagreement about whether it lies in tort or equity.[180] The administrative receiver or administrator must use care to obtain a proper price for the property being sold. Liability for loss on a sale at an undervalue is otherwise imposed.[181] However, some recent decisions mark off in an artificial way this from other liability in the exercise of rights to security. Thus the creditor can decide in its own interests whether, and when, to sell the security, and it owes no duty in this regard to a borrower or guarantor. The duty to obtain a proper price if there is a sale, however, remains.[182] Moreover, it is said that there is no duty of care to continue trading in any circumstances—a real threat to the 'rescue culture', and unnecessary if liability were only imposed were a decision not taken reasonably.[183] If trading is carried on, however, there is a duty to manage with due diligence in doing so.[184]

As a matter of practice banks can also avoid liability as 'shadow directors'. From the viewpoint of public policy this is desirable, if banks are to be encouraged to nurse ailing companies back to health. The legal issue arises in Britain as a result of the wrongful-trading provisions of the insolvency legislation. Directors—including shadow directors—of a borrower at a time when they knew, or ought to have concluded, that it had no reasonable prospect of avoiding liquidation, may be liable to contribute to its assets.[185] (Shadow directors are those in accordance with whose directions or instructions the directors of the borrower are accustomed to act.) Provided a bank refrains from too great an involvement in management decisions, it should not be regarded as a shadow director. Thus it should not be drawn into the detail (e.g. on how the borrower is to schedule payments when experiencing difficulties), and more generally should avoid leaning on the directors to follow any advice it gives. If a bank simply lays down certain conditions to ensure the continuance of a lending facility, the company then has a choice whether or not to comply with the conditions.[186] Even

---

[179] J. Norton, 'Lender Liability in the United States', in W. Blair (ed.), *Banks, Liability and Risk*, (3rd edn., London, LLP, 2001), 351, 379–80.

[180] J. O'Donovan, *Lender Liability* (Sydney, LBC, 2000), 672–3.

[181] *Cuckmere Brick Co. Ltd.* v. *Mutual Finance Ltd.* [1971] Ch. 949 (CA).

[182] *China and South Sea Bank Ltd.* v. *Tan* [1990] 1 AC 536 (PC).

[183] *Downsview Nominees Ltd.* v. *First City Corpn. Ltd.* [1993] AC 295 (PC).

[184] *Medforth* v. *Blake* [2000] Ch. 86 (CA).

[185] Insolvency Act 1986, s. 214.

[186] *Re PTZM Ltd.* [1995] BCLC 530. See Financial Law Panel, *Shadow Directorships* (London, Financial Law Panel, 1994); P. Millett, 'Shadow Directorship—a Real or Imagined Threat to Banks' (1991) *Insol. P.* 14. Cf. M. Markovic, 'Banks and Shadow Directorships' (1998) 9 *JBFLP* 284.

when a bank has appointed directors to the board, it does not follow automatically that the company will be accustomed to act on their suggestions, quite apart from whether these suggestions can be sheeted home to the bank as a matter of law.[187]

To what extent will non-statutory duties be imposed on banks in a workout because of their active intervention in the borrower's affairs? The argument was considered by the English Court of Appeal in the *Pinios* case.[188] In that case the bank, instead of calling default, entered into a tripartite agreement with Pinios and a manager, whereby the manager was appointed as sole and exclusive agent to manage and conduct the activities of the vessel, the construction of which was being financed. The manager was obliged to do this in the best interests of Pinios and the bank, but failed to insure adequately. The vessel was lost. After failing to obtain payment from the manager, despite a successful judgment of the House of Lords, Pinios now counter-claimed against the bank, arguing that it was under a duty to see that the manager did not under-insure the vessel. The Court of Appeal refused to imply such a term into the contract. An additional argument was that the bank owned Pinios a duty of care, because it actively intervened in the procuring of the insurance. In the result, the Court of Appeal was prepared to accept the proposition, but held that Pinios could not succeed on the facts: although entitled to do so under the workout agreement, the bank had not directed and interfered with the manager's activities.

D. ENVIRONMENTAL LIABILITY

Lender-liability for environmental damage might be imposed as a result of statute, as with the Superfund legislation in the United States, or at least the way the courts have interpreted it. *United States* v. *Fleet Factors*[189] heightened concerns, since the court there held that a lender could be liable, even if it took no active part in the management of the business of a troubled borrower, so long as it had the 'capacity to influence' management decisions. As a result of that decision, however, the Environmental Protection Agency promulgated a rule setting out a number of 'safe harbours' from Superfund liability. That EPA rule was overturned later by the courts which held that it did not have the power to limit a party's liability but that such determinations were the exclusive province of the federal courts. Nonetheless, since the *Fleet Factors* case a number of other federal decisions have limited very much the extent to which lenders are liable in a workout situation. These decisions of district courts show that, although lenders must continue to act cautiously where real property transactions

[187] *Kuwait Asia Bank* v. *National Mutual Life Nominees Ltd.* [1991] 1 AC 187 (PC); cf. M. Hobson, 'The Law of Shadow Directorships' (1998) 10 *Bond LR* 184, 195.

[188] [1989] 3 WLR 185. This aspect was not dealt with on appeal: [1990] AC 637 (HL).

[189] 901 F 2d 1550 (1990). In later proceedings in the case the lender was held to be liable for its actions in foreclosing against the borrower: 819 F Supp. 1079 (1993). See M. Jeffery, 'Environmental Liability: A Continuing Concern for Lenders', in A. Boyle (ed.), *Environmental Regulation and Economic Growth* (Oxford, Clarendon, 1994), 52; J. Enoch, 'Environmental Liability for Lenders after *United States v. Fleet Factors Corp.*' (1991) 48 Wash & Lee LR 659.

are involved, they will be able to avoid liability as long as they do not cross the line into 'participation in management'. This approach has been confirmed by the Asset Conservation, Lender Liability and Deposit Insurance Protection Act 1996 which confines impermissible participation in management under the Superfund legislation to actual involvement.

So far environmental liability outside the United States has been mainly a fear, rather than a reality. Banks do not generally satisfy the 'triggers terms' of environmental legislation such as carrying on, causing, knowingly permitting, or consenting to and conniving in environmental damage.[190] They do not have sufficient control over the offender and it cannot be said they are under any duty to prevent such damage. Banks are most vulnerable if they exercise their rights to security and occupy or foreclose against polluted land or a polluting facility.[191] The European Commission White Paper on Environmental Liability takes the same approach: 'Lenders not exercising operational control shall not be liable'.[192] These days banks are on guard, and take steps, such as obliging environmental audits of potential borrowers, contacting relevant regulatory authorities direct, and including environmental covenants in the loan documentation.

---

[190] J. Jarvis and M. Fordham, *Lender Liability. Environmental Risk and Debt* (London, Cameron May 1993); J. Marks, 'Domestic Environmental Liability' in W. Blair (ed.), *Banks, Liability and Risk* (3rd edn., London, LLP, 2001), 146–52.

[191] R. Hooley, 'Lender Liability for Environmental Damage' [2000] *CLJ* 405, 405–8. Cf. *Panamericana de Bienes y Servicios* v. *Northern Badger Oil & Gas Ltd.* (1991) 81 DLR (4th) 280 (Alta. CA); M. Ogilvie, 'Environmental Lender Liability in Canada' [19961] *JBL* 94.

[192] European Commission, *White Paper on Environmental Liability*, COM (2000) 66 final, 18.

PART III

PAYMENT AND PAYMENT SYSTEMS

8

PRINCIPLES OF PAYMENT

Payment and banking go hand-in-hand. Except for small-value transactions, where cash, credit cards, and e money are used, payments are typically made through the banking system. This does not mean that banks are essential to payment, just that the alternatives are at present inconvenient, not secure, or impractical in larger commercial transactions. For some time now central banks have had the integrity of payment systems high on their agenda. The banking system is threatened if that integrity comes into question—a bank's inability to pay may lead to systemic risk in the system as a whole. A central bank may not be able or willing to provide sufficient liquidity in the event of a bank's insolvency, a system failure, or significant fraud. The speeding up of payments, the internationalization of payment mechanisms, and the sheer volume of payments (resulting, in particular, from foreign exchange, securities, and derivatives deals) accentuate the problem.

What this Chapter aims to do is to analyse at a general level some of the legal problems arising with payment through the banking system. Specific payment methods are examined in Chapter 9, and settlement and netting dealt with in Chapter 10. The first section of the present Chapter sketches the basic elements of payment and the way banks make payment. Then the second section turns to some specific issues—how payment obligations are discharged, whether payment instructions can be countermanded, the availability of funds to payees, and the completion of payment as between banks. The third section of the Chapter examines the particular problem of mistaken and void payments. Finally, there is an outline of the law of tracing, which is basic to exercising a right, or invoking a remedy, to money paid through the banking system, or its product.

At the outset it should be emphasized that the law is not always clear on the matters discussed. Nor does it always provide guidelines on how issues are to be determined. There is some conflict in the English authorities about whether the resolution of disputes in the area is an issue of law or of banking practice.[1] The better view is that both must be considered. Banking practice will in turn be influenced by a range of factors. For example, if payee banks are not satisfied as regards a method of transfer, or the creditworthiness of paying banks, a banking practice may evolve that payment

---

[1] See *Momm v. Barclays Bank International Ltd.* [1977] QB 790, 799 (a matter of law). Cf. view adopted by *Banking Services: Law and Practice. Report by the Review Committee*, Cm. 622 (London, HMSO, 1989) (Jack Committee), 104.

of the payee occurs only after banks have settled between themselves. In the court decisions in this area, matters of practice such as these are mentioned, and presumably influence the conclusions of law. The method of payment, the terms of transfer, the relationship between the banks—all have been commented on by the judges. Law and practice are intertwined.

There have been attempts to place the law of payment on a firmer and clearer foundation. At the international level the International Chamber of Commerce has had Uniform Rules for Collections since 1956, designed to codify good banking practice in relation to documentary collection.[2] UNCITRAL has drawn up a Model Law on International Credit Transfers (1992), which runs parallel to Article 4A ('Funds Transfer') of the Uniform Commercial Code of the United States, adopted in 1989. Both attempt to define the rights and obligations which arise on what is called here a credit transfer. The European Community's Settlement Finality Directive is designed to reduce the risks associated with the insolvency of a participant in the payment system.[3] At present with international credit transfers, different systems of law may govern different parts of the transaction—for example, the law of the payor bank, the law of any intermediate banks, the law of settlement systems, and the law of the payee.[4]

Finally, a note on terminology. This book tends to use the terms 'payor' (Pr) and 'payee' (Pe), and 'payor bank' (PrB) and 'payee bank' (PeB) as the most general available. Many discussions use the alternatives 'creditor' and 'debtor', but these terms are not always appropriate. Take a bank making moneys available under a syndicated facility; it pays the agent bank, which in turn pays the borrower. Draw-down by the borrower imposes an obligation on the bank to pay, but in this scenario it would be confusing to call the borrower the creditor rather than the debtor. The terms 'transferor' and 'transferee' are awkward and, as explained shortly, misleading. Some legislative instruments, such as the UNCITRAL Model Law on International Credit Transfers, use the terms 'originator' and 'beneficiary'. Not only are these terms unfamiliar as yet in banking practice, but the term 'beneficiary' has a well-established meaning in other contexts (a beneficiary under a letter of credit; in common law jurisdictions, a beneficiary under a trust). The Model Law complicates matters yet further by referring also to the 'sender' and the 'receiving bank'.

I. BASIC ELEMENTS AND MECHANISMS

Certain fundamentals of banking law, relevant to payment, have already been canvassed. One is mandate.[5] These days banks make many payments on their own initiative, resulting from their own dealings in foreign exchange, securities, and

---

[2] Currently ICC 522, 1995.   [3] 243, 245, 283–4 below.

[4] See especially C. Proctor, *International Payment Obligations. A Legal Perspective* (London, Butterworths, 1997).

[5] 140 above.

derivatives. When customer-driven, however, mandate is central to payment. If a bank acts within the mandate, it may claim reimbursement from the payor (for example, by debiting its account if it has one). If it acts outside the mandate, for example paying on a forged mandate, it has no authority to claim reimbursement, although the payor may ratify what the bank has done, or it may be estopped from denying the bank's right to reimbursement. It is sometimes said that the payor's bank must comply strictly with the terms of the mandate, but this means only that it must act within its terms. A bank is not necessarily to be regarded as guaranteeing any particular result, for example, discharge of a payment obligation. So long as it exercises reasonable care and skill in carrying out its instructions, it may be regarded as fulfilling its mandate. But acting with reasonable care and skill means paying on time: if a bank accepts a mandate to pay by a specified date, it cannot excuse non-performance on its own part.

Another fundamental addressed earlier, the relationship between banks, is also relevant. Banking networks are necessary to most payments.[6] Banks often act through correspondents in effecting payment. Banking networks, and the role of correspondents, were examined in Chapter 2. Also discussed there was the liability of banks to customers when payment is wrongly effected through a banking network. The payment network may be bilateral or multilateral. Correspondent banks clearly enter bilateral contracts with each other. Settlement systems are often governed by multilateral contracts.[7]

A. BASIC ELEMENTS

Three basic elements of making payment through the banking system deserve to be highlighted. The first is the payment message. Payment messages in this context are unconditional instructions to effect payment in favour of a payee. They may facilitate a credit or debit transfer. It is on receipt of a payment message that banks effect payment. In practical terms, a payment message may be divided between the customer's mandate to its bank to pay and any instructions which that bank then sends to another bank (e.g. the payee's bank or a correspondent). In fact, if in effecting payment the customer's bank sends a message to one of its correspondent banks, the customer's bank, as the customer of its correspondent, is in the same position as a matter of law in giving instructions as its customer is in instructing it. Traditionally payment messages were paper-based, but outside the realm of cheques and payment cards are now conveyed electronically. As part of an anti-terrorism measure, banks must include on both domestic and international payment messages information on the organization's name, address, and account number.[8]

A second basic element of payment through the banking system is that it simply involves movements on accounts. Obviously the customer's account is debited, and the payee's credited. In addition, as we will see on closer examination of payment

---

[6] 45 above.   [7] Ch. 10 below.

[8] Financial Action Task Force, *Special Recommendations on Terrorist Financing*, Oct. 2001, VII.

mechanisms below, other accounts may also be debited and credited, such as those
which the customer's bank has with its correspondent.[9] Thus payment is not effected
by the assignment of any debt the payor's bank owes the payor. This is made explicit
in the case of bills of exchange, where statute provides that a bill does not constitute
any assignment of a debt claim which the customer has against the bank, nor of any
moneys of the bank.[10] Despite occasional suggestions to the contrary, this is clearly also
the case with other methods of payment.[11] Consequently, a payor may be able to revoke
after giving instructions to its debtor (that is, its bank), which would not be possible if
payment was by way of assignment. Moreover, payees have no contractual claim on
the basis of assignment against a payor bank, but only in contract against their own
bank. Exceptionally, however, there may be special arrangements giving rise to a
contract between the payor bank and the payee. A letter of credit provides an
example.[12] But this has nothing to do with assignment.

  That payment involves a movement on accounts cannot be emphasized too much.
The language sometimes used, such as 'funds transfer', conjures up an image of the
physical movement of funds or property. Legal analysis which touches on the payment system, such as that relating to tracing, has been bewitched in the past by this
image of money or property moving along a chain.[13] Payment through the banking
system—whether by credit transfer, direct debit, cheque, or the other means considered in the next chapter—involves a movement on accounts effected, of course,
following receipt of a payment message.

  A third basic element of payment through the banking system is settlement. By
'settlement' is meant payment between the banks themselves of their obligations *inter
se*, arising out of a payment. Settlement may follow each payment (gross settlement),
or it may occur periodically through the netting of a series of payments—either
between two banks (bilateral netting) or among a number of banks (multilateral
netting). Settlement can be effected by a movement on accounts which both banks
have with a third bank, but is typically effected by a movement on the accounts which
banks have with a central bank.[14] This is yet another example of how payment through
the banking system involves a movement on accounts. Settlement is dealt with at
greater length in Chapter 10. The important point for present purposes is that, since
settlement is typically across the books of the central bank, payments involving a
particular currency are usually routed through the country of that currency. Thus US
dollar payments are usually settled in New York, sterling payments in London, yen
payments in Tokyo, and so on. With the euro, payment messages are exchanges
bilaterally between the two central banks of the countries of the payor and payee
concerned, using reciprocal accounts for debiting and crediting.

---

  [9] 236 below.

  [10] Bills of Exchange Act 1882, s. 53(1); *Deposit Protection Board* v. *Dalia* [1994] 2 AC 367, 400 (HL).

  [11] *Libyan Arab Foreign Bank* v. *Bankers Trust Co.* (1989) QB 728, 750; *R.* v. *Preddy* [1996] AC 815, 834 (HL).
Cf. *R.* v. *King* [1992] QB 20 (CA); *Delbrueck & Co.* v. *Manufacturers Hanover Trust Company*, 609 F 2d 1047,
1051 (1979).

  [12] 384 below.   [13] 253 below.   [14] 110 above.

B. PAYMENT METHODS: CREDIT/DEBIT TRANSFERS

The sequence of banking operations involved in payment turns, in part, on whether there is a credit transfer or debit transfer. With a credit transfer the payor instructs its bank to pay, and the payor's bank responds in a variety of ways. One response is to debit the payor's account. If the payee has its account at another bank, the payor's bank will send a payment message to that bank (perhaps indirectly, as we shall see). Ultimately the payee's account will be credited. Funds are often said to be 'pushed' to the payee, but the language is apt to mislead when all that payment entails is at most messages, movements on accounts, and ultimately settlement between different banks. Credit transfers are widely used for commercial payments, but also feature in payments of employee's salaries, company dividends, and social welfare benefits.

With a debit transfer the sequence begins with the payor authorizing its bank to pay, but actual payment is initiated when the payee presents a debit instrument (e.g. a cheque) or debit instruction (e.g. under a direct debit) to the payor's bank. Typically this will be through the payee's bank. For example, with non-paper-based systems the payee's bank will send a debit message to the payor's bank. With a paper-based system such as cheques, the payee's bank will 'collect' the instrument—hence the term debit collection—by presenting it to the payor's bank, in most cases through an organized clearing system. The payee's account will probably be credited, albeit provisionally, before the payor's account is debited. This is, of course, the reverse of what happens with a credit transfer. Overall it is sometimes said that with a debit transfer funds are being 'pulled' from the payor.

Different types of credit-transfer and debt-transfer payment systems are examined at greater length in the next chapter.

C. IN-HOUSE, DOMESTIC, CORRESPONDENT, AND COMPLEX PAYMENT

Payment through the banking system can be broadly categorized as 'in-house', domestic, correspondent, and complex.[15] An *in-house payment* occurs when both payor and payee have accounts at the same bank. The payor's account is debited, and the payee's credited. No other bank is involved (diagram 8.1).

Typically the payment either creates or increases a debt owed by the payor to the bank, or discharges or reduces an existing debt the bank owes to the payor. At the same time payment discharges the payor's obligation to the payee. The bank is now obliged to the payee, or the payee's debt to the bank is reduced. Additional parties do not affect this basic method of how payment is effected.

---

[15] R. Goode, *Payment Obligations in Commercial and Financial Transactions* (London, Sweet & Maxwell, 1983), ch. 4; B. Geva, *The Law of Electronic Funds Transfers* (New York, Matthew Bender, looseleaf), chs. 2–4; H. Scott, 'Where are the Dollars?—Off-shore Funds Transfers' [1988–89] 3 *BFLR* 243; B. Geva, *Bank Collections and Payment Transactions* (Oxford, Clarendon, 2001), 109, 127–8, 186–200.

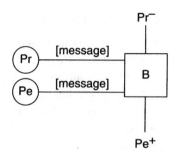

Diagram 8.1: In-house payment

Where payor and payee have accounts at different branches of the same bank, an internal clearing office may be used. This is typically the case where cheques have been used. Note that payment need not be in-house, even if payor and payee have accounts at the same bank. Thus where the different branches are in different jurisdictions (say London and Singapore), and payment is in the currency of a third country (say dollars), payment may involve the bank's correspondent in New York—this is because settlement is across the books of the New York Fed. We return to payment involving correspondents shortly.

By *domestic payment* is meant payment in the local currency between banks in the same country. In this case settlement can be across the books of that country's central bank. With a credit transfer, the payor instructs its bank, which sends a payment message to the payee's bank. With a debit transfer the payor has authorized its bank to pay when the payee presents a debit instrument or otherwise sends a debit instruction. In both cases the payor's bank debits its customer's account. Conversely, the payee's bank credits its customer's account (diagram 8.2).

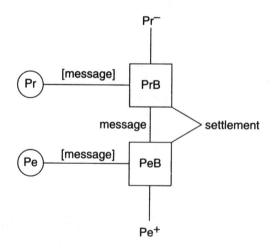

Diagram 8.2: Domestic payment

The banks themselves settle by making payment across the books of the central bank, either immediately in the case of real-time gross settlement, or periodically in the case of net settlement. Where a bank does not have an account with the central bank, it must settle through a bank which does.

Traditionally, *correspondent payment* has occured because of payment between those in different jurisdictions. With a credit transfer the payor's bank will send a payment message to its correspondent in the jurisdiction of the payee's bank. The correspondent will, in turn, send a payment message to the payee's bank. (In the case of a debit collection, the payee's bank will usually forward the instrument to its correspondent for collection through its local clearing system.) The payor's bank and correspondent will settle pursuant to the correspondent arrangements between them; the correspondent and the payee's bank will probably settle though their accounts with the central bank in that jurisdiction (diagram 8.3, for a credit transfer).

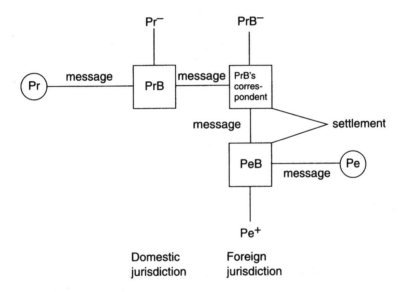

Diagram 8.3: Correspondent payment

However, correspondent payment can involve payment between two banks in the same jurisdiction, if payment is to be in foreign currency. The banks need to use their correspondents in that foreign country, since settlement facilities need to be available in that currency. (In some international financial centres this may be unnecessary if there are local facilities for settling in foreign currencies.) If both banks share the same correspondent, settlement can be across its books. Otherwise settlement will involve movements on the accounts which those correspondents have with the central bank of that foreign country.

In fact, we are now in the realm of *complex payment*, where payment is in a foreign currency and there is a string of banks. An intermediary bank may be needed where, for example, the payor's bank does not have a correspondent in the jurisdiction of the payment currency. Banks in three countries may be involved, as where the payor in London wants to make payment in US dollars to the payee in Singapore. One way of doing this is for the payor's bank to send a payment message to its correspondent in New York, which in turn contacts the payee bank's correspondent there. Settlement between the two correspondents may be through the CHIPS system and then over the books of the New York Fed.[16] Ultimately the payee's account with its bank in Singapore is credited (diagram 8.4).

There are any number of permutations and combinations with complex payment.

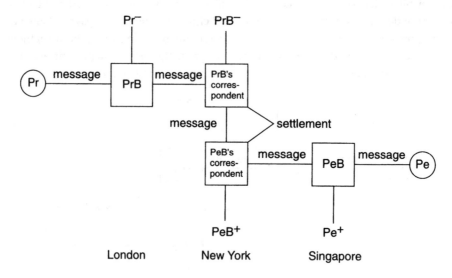

Diagram 8.4: Complex payment

II. DISCHARGING PAYMENT OBLIGATIONS, COUNTERMAND, FUNDS AVAILABILITY, AND COMPLETION

This section of the Chapter examines four different aspects of payment made through the banking system. The first is the discharge of an underlying payment obligation. This concept involves the payor and payee and applies to any system of payment, whether or not through the medium of the banking system. A second aspect is countermand, the stage of the process up to the point when the initiator of a payment has the right to countermand (or revoke) it. A third aspect relates to availability of funds—when does a payee have access to the proceeds of a payment? Fourthly, there is the point which in some accounts is described as when payment is complete. This is

---

[16] 279 below.

not necessarily identical to the discharge of the obligation between the payor and payee, but relates to the position of the banks *inter se*. None of these points necessarily coincide, although some (e.g. countermand) cannot be later than others (e.g. availability of funds). Let us examine each in turn.

A. DISCHARGE OF UNDERLYING PAYMENT OBLIGATION

This may be a matter of contract between the parties. There may be an express provision, or it may be possible for it to be implied. The consequences of a late payment may turn, as well, on the underlying contract. Payment by the pay date may be a condition of the contract, enabling the payee to terminate the contract if it is not met. The parties may expressly or impliedly agree that payment is made if dispatched to the payee by a specified date. Generally, however, payment must have reached the payee by the pay date. However, it is a well-established common law rule that, so long as payment arrives before midnight in the relevant time zone on the pay date, that is sufficient in the absence of an express provision to the contrary. Where banks are involved, the midnight rule is based on the consideration that, since banks close their business at different times, to use close-of-business as the crucial point would be too uncertain a test, given the drastic consequences which may follow late payment.[17]

(i) Payment into a Bank Account

Commercial contracts often provide that payment is to be made by having immediately available (or 'same day') funds in a specified account in a specified bank on a specified day. For example, a charterparty may read: 'Payment of hire is to be made in New York in United States currency to X bank [address], for the credit of the account of Z re [ship], on the first day of each month.' Thus by contract, payment to the payee's bank is being treated as equivalent to payment directly to the payee. Legally, the payor's obligation is being discharged by the payee accepting a claim against its bank.

The English courts have said that this type of clause cannot mean that payment occurs at the point when the payee bank receives a payment message from the payor's bank; rather the payee bank must have at least made the decision unconditionally to credit the payee's account, even if it has not actually credited it.[18] The law treats the payee as having been paid, even if it cannot draw on the funds that day: this derives from the midnight rule, already referred to. The payee does not need to have been notified, although if the payee were to contact its bank it would be told of the unconditional decision to credit.[19] Although, generally speaking, the payee will be

---

[17] *Afovos Shipping Co. SA* v. *Pagnan* [1983] 1 WLR 195, [1983] 1 All ER 449 (HL); *Mondial Shipping and Chartering BV* v. *Astarte Shipping Ltd.* [1995] CLC 1011.

[18] Cf. 'Payment is deemed to be made at the moment when the amount due is effectively put at the disposal of the creditor': *Model Rules on the Time of Payment of Monetary Obligations* (Warsaw, International Law Association, Report of the Sixty-Third Conference, 1988).

[19] *Tenax Steamship Co. Ltd.* v. *Reinante Transoceania Navegacion SA (The Brimnes)* [1973] 1 WLR 386, 402; approved on appeal [1975] 1 QB 929, 950–1, 963–4, 968.

treated as having been paid, despite not being notified, if payment to the payee bank is late, in the wrong currency, or of a lesser amount than specified in the contract, the payee will have to be contacted, and waive breach of contract, if it is to be regarded as having been paid.[20]

Since the key point is the unconditional decision to credit, the payment obligation will not be discharged by a provisional crediting of the account.[21] Moreover, there is no unconditional decision to credit if payment to the payee is subject to a condition precedent (e.g. arrival of the 'pay date') or condition subsequent (e.g. payment 'under reserve' under a letter of credit). Nor, at the other end of the spectrum, does it matter that after the decision to credit, there are other administrative processes (for example, the overnight processing of data by computer). The precise point of the decision to credit will not always be clear, but will depend on the evidence of practices within the particular bank. For example, it may be that debits and credits are made to accounts during each day, but that final decisions are made only at the end of the day. The test is an objective test: were the payee to contact its bank, at what point would it have been told that it had made an unconditional decision to credit (what could be termed 'the hypothetical positive response test')?

The key aspect, as already mentioned, is that an unconditional decision to credit must have been made. In a decision which can be criticized as adopting an unduly narrow interpretation of whether payment has been made, the House of Lords held that a credit transfer had not been effected when funds, although available, were subject to an interest liability.[22] The decision involved a credit transfer from a charterer to the owner's account with an Italian bank. On 22 January the owner's bank credited the owner's account with the amount, and the owner had immediate use of the money, although the evidence was that if it had withdrawn the sum then it would probably have incurred a liability to its bank to pay interest until 26 January. The court's reasoning was that the book entry made by the owners' bank on 22 January in the owners' account was not the equivalent of cash, nor was there any reason why the owners should have been prepared to treat it as such. It followed that on 22 January there was no 'payment in cash' by the charterers of the hire then assumed to be due, and accordingly the owners were entitled to withdraw the ship. The case may have turned on the express provision for payment 'in cash': certainly it is undesirable that a payor does not obtain a good discharge because of some local quirk of banking practice affecting the payee's account, or the relationship it has with its bank.

A payee cannot sue the payor if its bank fails after it has been paid. That occurs in the case of a credit transfer, as we have seen, as soon as there is an unconditional decision to credit the payee's account. The payee's remedy is against its bank in the insolvency. The payee must take the credit risk of its bank's failure if it accepts

---

[20] *Mardorf Peach & Co. Ltd.* v. *Attica Sea Corpn. (The Laconia)* [1977] AC 850. Cf. R. King, 'The Receiving Bank's Role in Credit Transfer Transactions' (1982) 45 *MLR* 369.

[21] Cf. B. Geva, 'Payment into a Bank Account' [1990] 3 *JIBL* 108, 110.

[22] *A/S Awilco of Oslo* v. *Fulvia SpA di Navigazione of Cagliari (The Chikuma)* [1981] 1 WLR 314 (HL).

payment by credit transfer, just as it takes the credit risk of depositing its money with that bank.

(ii) No Specified Method of Payment

So far we have considered situations where the contract provides expressly that a payment obligation is to be discharged by payment into a specified bank account. The contract may provide for payment in a variety of other ways: at a straightforward level by cash or cheque; in a more complex manner by novation discharging existing indebtedness and replacing it with a new payment obligation, by set-off or account stated, or by the exchange of goods as in countertrade.[23] What if there is no express provision in the contract?

Legal tender is what the payee must accept in discharge of a payment obligation. It is usually limited to cash, but in the Netherlands now extends to payment via credit transfer.[24] As for what a payor must proffer in discharge of a payment obligation, the fundamental principle in English law is that a monetary obligation must be discharged in cash, unless the right to cash has been waived by the payee.[25] Waiver could be by the payee stipulating another method, or by so acting after receipt of payment by another method that it could be said to have accepted it. It does not seem necessary that the payee should contact the payor to indicate such acceptance. It seems that in the absence of any reference in the contract to cash, English courts will fairly readily find that a commercial payee intended to accept other than cash.

If a person has a fundamental right to be paid in cash, but he or she accepts payment by credit transfer into a bank account, it follows that the obligation is not discharged until there is an unconditional decision to credit. In other words, the same approach applies as under an express clause requiring payment into a bank account. There is one caveat: normally the payee does not need to be contacted for a credit transfer to constitute an effective discharge. However, that may be necessary where it is not possible on other grounds to decide that the payee has accepted this mode of payment.

(iii) Conditional Payment

Conditional payment may mean nothing more than that a party has made payment for a particular purpose, or conditional on a certain event occurring, such as a refinancing agreement being reached. In other words, the payment is not an irrevocable outright payment and must be repaid if the purpose or condition is not met.[26] Moreover, under English law it may be possible to spell out an intention of a bank, say,

---

[23] R. Goode, *Commercial Law* (2nd edn., London, Penguin, 1995), 501–2; M. Brindle and R. Cox (eds.), *Law of Bank Payments* (2nd edn., London, Sweet & Maxwell, 1999), 1–10.

[24] Dutch Civil Code, B. 6, Art. 114.

[25] *Libyan Arab Foreign Bank* v. *Bankers Trust Co.* [1989] QB 728; *TSB Bank of Scotland Ltd.* v. *Welwyn Hatfield DC* [1993] 2 Bank LR 267. See F. Mann, *The Legal Aspect of Money* (5th edn., Oxford, Clarendon, 1992), 75–6.

[26] e.g. *Guardian Ocean Cargoes Ltd.* v. *Banco do Brasil* [1994] CLC 243 (CA).

that moneys lent should not become the general property of the borrower, but should be kept separate and applied exclusively for a particular purpose. The moneys are then impressed with a trust for that purpose, so that if the purpose fails the money is returnable to the bank. This is the famous *Quistclose* trust, about which much has been written.[27]

There is another sense of conditional payment. The English courts generally treat payment by a bill of exchange or other negotiable instrument as conditional payment. In other words, payment is subject to a condition subsequent that the instrument be paid on presentation. The payor is not in default if this occurs. If the instrument is dishonoured, the underlying payment obligation revives. If the instrument is paid, the better view is that the time of payment is back-dated to the time when it was given to the payee.[28] This accords with the nature of the condition as a condition subsequent (so that if the instrument is paid it ranks as actual payment from that date); and with the fact that the instrument changes the legal relationship between the parties, giving the payee a legal right to sue on it for a sum of money. Similar rules apply to payment by means of a letter of credit. If the seller does not receive payment under the letter of credit, then generally speaking the buyer is still liable to pay the price.

In re Charge Card Services Ltd.[29] considered whether there is a general principle of English law that whenever a method of payment is adopted which involves a risk of non-payment by a third party, there is a presumption that the acceptance by the payee of payment through a third party is conditional on the third party making the payment. The Court of Appeal decided that there is no such general principle. Each method of payment has to be considered in the light of the consequences and other circumstances attending that type of payment. With the type of charge card involved in that case, and it would seem as well with credit cards, debit cards, and e money, the payment obligation is discharged when the card is handed over, and the payment authenticated. If for some reason a retailer is not paid by the card issuer, it must not look to the customer who used the card to pay.

B. REVOCATION

Revocation (or countermand) involves the obligation of a bank to comply with its customer's instructions (or mandate) to cancel a payment instruction. Subject to any contractual provisions, if the bank's mandate is withdrawn, it must comply with the instruction and stop the process if this is practicable. Of course it will charge the customer for this. Notice of revocation must be clear, brought to the attention of

---

[27] *Barclays Bank Ltd.* v. *Quistclose Investments Ltd.* [1970] AC 567; *Twinsectra Ltd.* v. *Yardley* [2002] UKHL 12, [2002] 2 WLR 802, [2002] 2 All ER 377. See, e.g., S. Worthington, *Proprietary Interests in Commercial Transactions* (Oxford, Clarendon 1997), 43–70; R. Chambers, *Resulting Trusts* (Oxford, Clarendon, 1997), 68–89; L. Ho and P. Smart, 'Re-interpreting the *Quistclose* Trust' (2001) 21 *OJLS* 267.

[28] Cf. J. Vroegop, 'The Time of Payment in Paper-based and Electronic Funds Transfer Systems' [1990] *LMCLQ* 64, 66–9, 86.

[29] [1989] Ch. 497.

the bank (constructive revocation is not recognized in English law), and, subject to other arrangements, given to the branch of the bank where the account is kept.[30]

In the absence of express contract, the English authorities seem to establish the following propositions relevant to revocation of a credit transfer. First, a customer who instructs its bank to hold funds to the disposal of a third party can countermand, at least until the time when credit has been given to the payee. Secondly, a customer who instructs its bank to pay a third party cannot revoke from the moment the bank incurs a commitment to the third party. Thirdly—and this is the typical case—a customer who instructs its bank to pay another bank to the order of a third party cannot revoke once the payee bank has acted on the instructions. This may be a point prior to the crediting of the payee's account.[31] In all these cases, it is irrelevant, from the point of view of revocation, whether the third party has been informed of the payment.

However, revocation is often a matter of express contract between the customer and the bank. The customer agrees by contract not to revoke. Alternatively, the rules of a payment system may provide that revocation is impossible, for example, once there has been a 'logical acknowledgment' of the payment message by the payee bank. Designated payment systems under the Settlement Finality Directive must have a definite rule on revocation by customers and must prohibit revocation beyond the point specified.[32] Payors whose banks use these systems are bound to these rules, on the legal grounds considered earlier.[33] Under the UNCITRAL Model Law, a payment order cannot be revoked beyond a time sufficient to afford the intermediary or payee bank a reasonable opportunity to act before the later of the time when funds are placed at the disposal of the payee, or the beginning of the pay date.

C. AVAILABILITY OF FUNDS

Discharge of a payment obligation turns on the payee bank deciding unconditionally to credit the payee's account. In terms of the hypothetical positive-response test, the payee would be told, if it contacted the bank, that its account was credited. There are a number of reasons, however, that this point may not coincide with the point at which the payee can get access to funds. For example, a payee may still be indebted to the bank after a payment and have agreed with its bank not to draw on its account until its indebtedness is reduced still more, or possibly eliminated altogether. Payment has been made, but by agreement the payee does not have access to moneys. There are also

---

[30] *Westminister Bank Ltd.* v. *Hilton* (1926) 43 TLR 124 (HL); *Curtice* v. *London City and Midland Bank Ltd.* [1908] 1 KB 293 (CA).

[31] *Astro Amo Compania Naviera SA* v. *Elf Union SA (The Zographia M)* [1976] 2 Lloyd's Rep. 382; *Dovey* v. *Bank of New Zealand* [2000] 3 NZLR 641, para 24.

[32] Settlement Finality Directive 98/26/EC [1998] OJ L166/45, Art 5, implemented in UK by Financial Markets and Insolvency (Settlement Finality) Regulations 1999, SI 1999 No 2979, Sched., para. 5(1). See 283–4 below.

[33] 51 above.

a variety of reasons why, despite being paid itself, the payee's bank may delay a decision unconditionally to credit the payee's account—the payment message needs to be checked, money-laundering may be suspected, there may be a freeze order against paying nationals from the payee's country, and so on.[34]

Conversely, the payee may by arrangement with its bank obtain access to funds in anticipation of a payment being made. This may be before it, the bank, is paid. In this case the bank is not simply crediting the account provisionally—it is making an advance in the customer's favour in anticipation of being reimbursed by later payment. A third situation is if the bank has been paid, but the pay date specified is some time in the future. Again the bank is advancing its own moneys by paying early. The payor's payment obligation is not discharged, in law, until the pay date, and it may be that the payor could still revoke prior to that date.

D. COMPLETION OF PAYMENT

Completion of payment is the term used to describe the position between the banks themselves. It is relevant where they are making payment both on behalf of customers and on their own account. One reason it is relevant is if there is a loss, for example, through an insolvency of one of the banks. If a payment has been completed it may be said that the payor bank cannot reverse a transfer to the bank which has become insolvent.

English common law is rather sparse on the matter. There is some authority, however, for both in-house payments (when both payor and payee have accounts at the same bank) and interbank payments (when they have accounts at different banks). With an in-house payment, payment is complete when the entries are made in the bank's books debiting the payor and crediting the payee, or on the day when entries are made in the computer for debiting or crediting. The payee need not have received notification of the transfer.[35] With an interbank transfer between a bank and its correspondent, there is authority that payment is complete when the payee bank is notified that funds are made available for the credit of the customer's account. Consequently, the payor has no claim against its bank for not effecting the transfer if the payee bank ceases trading after such notification, since the transfer is complete at that point.[36] With an interbank transfer through a clearing house, a transfer is complete when the rules so provide. This may be as late as when movements are made on the accounts of the respective banks with the central bank, i.e. settlement.

Outside insolvency, the notion of completion of payment has also been applied to whether the payor bank can stop a payment if it decides that there are insufficient funds, discovers that the payor will not reimburse it, or for other reasons such as a freeze order.[37] The Jack Committee broached legislative change. Its reasoning was that

---

[34] 72, 74–5 above.   [35] *Momm v. Barclay's Bank International Ltd.* [1977] QB 790.

[36] *Royal Products v. Midland Bank* [1981] 2 Lloyd's Rep. 194.

[37] e.g. *Libyan Arab Foreign Bank v. Manufacturers Hanover Trust Co. (No 2)* [1989] 1 Lloyd's Rep. 608.

there is a risk with a sudden failure of a bank involved in a transaction so large as to have repercussions on payment systems generally. Error and fraud were also thought to be risks. Clarifying the law would not prevent a crisis, but would assist its resolution. Jack's specific recommendation was that the rules should provide that with interbank transfers, payment should be regarded as complete at the point where the payee's bank accepts a transfer of funds from the paying bank for the payee's account, provided that the transfer is or has become unconditional.[38] The UNCITRAL Model Law obliges the payor's bank to refund the payor if a credit transfer is not complete, completion turning on whether the beneficiary's bank accepts a payment order for the benefit of the beneficiary.[39] Although the Settlement Finality Directive does not mandate any particular rule, it requires designated payment systems to have a definite rule specifying the point beyond which a participant bank cannot cancel a payment order and prohibiting breach of it.[40]

III. MISTAKEN AND VOID PAYMENTS

A. MISTAKEN PAYMENTS

Mistaken payments may occur for a variety of reasons. Clerical or technological error within a bank may lead to payment being made twice, to payment being made despite a countermand, or to money going into the wrong account. There may be fraud, either by an officer of the bank or by some third party. Fraud can lead to payment being made by a bank when it does not have the authority of the account party. The mistake may be because a payment instrument or payment instruction is fraudulently altered, forged, or given, or because the bank pays to an imposter.

The focus of the present discussion is on mistaken payments by banks, although the same principles apply to the converse situation, where a customer mistakenly pays a bank, and indeed to mistaken payments generally. The recipient of a mistaken payment by a bank may well be another bank. Once the mistake is uncovered the recipient will often simply make a reverse payment. Sometimes, and especially where fraud is involved, that is resisted, for money has been paid on. Thus the essence of many of the legal claims in this area is which of two parties must bear the loss as a result of the wrongdoing of another.

The bank making a mistaken payment has a number of possible legal claims. Attention here is on the restitutionary claims, when property in the money has invariably passed to the recipient. However, in some cases the bank may be able to argue that the mistake meant property in a payment instrument never passed. For example,

---

[38] *Banking Services: Law and Practice. Report by the Review Committee*, Cm. 622 (London, HMSO, 1989), 109.

[39] Arts. 14(1), 19(1).

[40] Settlement Finality Directive 98/26/EC [1998] OJ L166/45, Art. 5.

a mistake about identity of a recipient can lead to title to a payment instrument not passing to it, although this needs to be at least a mistake as to an attribute which identifies the person (for example, as a result of a false pretence of agency). Indeed, it may be that unless it is fundamental to the bank that a person has a particular identity, this sort of mistake can never prevent title passing.[41]

Moreover, the recipient of a mistaken payment may also be liable for knowing receipt or assistance,[42] or for conversion of a negotiable instrument.[43] If the recipient knew of the mistake at the time when it received the money, there may well be a claim in fraud on the basis that the recipient deliberately induced the mistake by a positive false representation, or by the concealment of relevant facts. In such cases the bank may waive the tort (i.e. the fraud) and instead make a restitutionary claim. The recipient's knowledge does not prevent the restitution claim, although it may bear on its defence.

(i) Money Paid Under Mistake

Money paid under mistake of fact is *prima facie* recoverable by the bank. It does not matter that it was a careless mistake. However, the mistake must be as to a specific fact and not be a misprediction as to the nature of the transaction which would come into effect once payment was made (e.g. a loan rather than the purchase of foreign exchange).[44] In England, the mistake may now also be of law. In other words, the bank may be able to recover if it has paid because it is mistaken as to the general law, or as to the legal effect of the circumstances under which the money is paid, if it has a full knowledge of the facts.[45] Even where it is possible to claim for payments made under mistake of law, however, there is still a case that payments should be irrecoverable if made regardless of the risk whether they are legally enforceable.

The common law action for money had and received to the use of the claimant, on the ground of mistake, grew out of assumpsit (the old common law form of action to recover damages for breach of a contract not under seal). The starting point for a consideration of the action is an oft-quoted passage of Parke B in *Kelly* v. *Solari*:[46]

I think that where money is paid to another under the influence of a mistake that is, upon the supposition that a specific fact is true, which would entitle the other to the money, but which fact is untrue, and the money would not have been paid if it had been known to the payor that the fact was untrue, an action will lie to recover it back, and it is against conscience to retain it; though a demand may be necessary in those cases in which the party receiving may have been ignorant of the mistake.

There has been much debate about the requirements laid down in this passage. At one time it was thought that the claimant could not succeed unless, on the facts

---

[41] *Midland Bank plc* v. *Brown Shipley & Co. Ltd.* [1991] 1 Lloyd's Rep. 576.
[42] 192 above.   [43] 263 below
[44] *Dextra Bank and Trust Co. Ltd.* v. *Bank of Jamaica* [2001] EWPC 26 (PC).
[45] *Kleinwort Benson Ltd.* v. *Lincoln CC* [1999] 2 AC 349.
[46] (1841) 9 M & W 54, 58, 152 ER 24, 26.

as supposed, it would have been under a legal liability to the recipient ('upon the supposition that a specific fact is true, which would entitle the other to the money'). However, there are cases of the highest authority in which claimants were given recovery of money paid under mistake of fact, despite the absence of any legal obligation on the facts as supposed. This is clearly relevant to bank payments for, as we have seen, the payor bank will generally have no legal obligation to a payee.

A further requirement has been said to be that the mistake must be 'fundamental'. 'Fundamental' mistake does not require either that the bank's mistake be shared by the recipient, or that the mistake be as to the existence of a fact which, if it had existed, would have resulted in the bank being under a legal obligation to make the payment. It seems that the requirement that the mistake be fundamental does not involve any more than that, without the mistake, the payment would not have been made.[47] Clearly any mistake as to the customer's mandate, or as to the true payee is causal in the relevant sense. So, too, if the recipient concedes that it would have had to repay the money if notified immediately of the mistake.

It has been held that a payment under mistake constituted the recipient as a trustee of the money. This gave the claimant an equitable proprietary claim, so that in the particular insolvency it benefited over other creditors.[48] However, there is no basis in principle for the contention that, in the ordinary course, a person can retain an equitable, or indeed any, interest in money paid away. It may be that, once a recipient learns of the mistake and retains the money, equity will act on conscience and impose a constructive trust.[49] Moreover, in special circumstances a bank lending money to enable the borrower to reduce a first mortgage on its assets may, if acting under mistake as to the priority of its loan, be subrogated in a way giving it priority over a party having a second mortgage over the assets.[50] In the ordinary case, however, there is a strong policy in favour of an ordinary restitutionary claim. This leads us to the defences to a claim for mistaken payment.

(ii) Defences

Among the defences to an action for money paid under mistake are change of position, ministerial receipt, passing on, good consideration, and estoppel. What follows is an illustrative, rather than a full, account.

What change of position will justify the defence? Payment of a debt by the recipient which would have had to be paid sooner or later is not generally sufficient; reliance expenditure is thought to be necessary.[51] The difficulty is whether this is the case where the recipient is another bank, it credits its customer's account in accordance with the

---

[47] e.g. *Barclays Bank Ltd.* v. *W. J. Simms Ltd.* [1980] QB 677; *Banque Financière de la Cité* v. *Parc (Battersea) Ltd.* [1999] 1 AC 221 (HL); *David Securities Pty. Ltd.* v. *Commonwealth Bank of Australia* (1992) 175 CLR 353; *Royal Bank of Canada* v. *LVG Auctions Ltd.* (1985) 12 DLR (4th) 768 (Ont. CA).

[48] *Chase Manhattan Bank NA* v. *Israel-British Bank (London) Ltd.* [1981] Ch. 105.

[49] *Westdeutsche Landesbank Girozentrale Bank* v. *Islington LBC* [1996] AC 669, 705, *per* Lord Browne-Wilkinson.

[50] *Bank Financière de la Cité* v. *Parc (Battersea) Ltd.* [1999] 1 AC 221 (HL).

[51] *Scottish Equitable plc* v. *Derby* [2001] EWCA Civ. 369; [2001] 3 All ER 818 (CA).

payment instruction, but the money is then paid away beyond recall. In policy terms
this should, in general, give the recipient bank a defence. One way of analysing this
situation legally is in terms of ministerial receipt: where the person to whom payment
is made receives it as an intermediary, its *prima facie* liability is displaced where it has
handed the money to the person for whom it receives it. If the principal (the customer) has effectively received the benefit of the payment, *prima facie* liability moves
from the agent (the recipient bank) to it.[52]

This analysis sits somewhat uncomfortably with the way payment is effected
through the banking system, but it at least protects the recipient bank. Another
approach is to invoke an underlying rationale of restitutionary payments and to say
that it would be unjust in this situation to insist on the recipient bank making
restitution, given its payment away beyond recall. It certainly seems unjust that
where the sending, not the recipient, bank has made the mistake or is the victim of
fraud, and the recipient bank has simply made payment in accordance with the
payment message received, it should have to make restitution when the payment is
beyond recall. Making legal consequences turn on whether something is 'unjust' is,
however, difficult, especially in a commercial context where certainty is rightly
valued.

Assume that a recipient of a mistaken payment has a *prima facie* defence of change
of position. Several technical problems arise. The first is if there is payment away from
an account by a series of transactions. *Prima facie* the rule in *Clayton's Case*[53] will apply
to determine how these various payments away are to be attributed. The second
problem occurs because of the suggestion that a change of position must follow
receipt.[54] There is now good authority that anticipatory reliance is a defence to a
restitution claim so long as the recipient acts in good faith and the change of position
is factually related to the anticipated payment.[55] Were it to be otherwise the change-of-
position defence would often sometimes not apply in situations involving interbank
payments. Outside real-time gross settlement systems, banks take a risk and pay their
customers, even though they themselves have not been paid.

The third technical problem concerns the bank making payment on a countermanded cheque. In English law this is treated as a case of mistaken payment, in which
the bank can recover the amount from the payee. Can the payee defend on the basis
that it changed its position detrimentally, since it gave up the cheque (for collection),
which means it is confined to suing the drawer on the underlying transaction?[56] The
detriment to the payee is that if it could sue on the cheque it could seek summary

---

[52] *ANZ Group Ltd.* v. *Westpac Banking Corp. Ltd.* (1987) 164 CLR 662.
[53] (1816) 1 Mer. 572; 35 ER 781.
[54] Cf. the much-criticized *South Tyneside MBC* v. *Svenska International plc* [1995] 1 All ER 545. See
P. Birks, 'Overview', in P. Birks (ed.), *Laundering and Tracing* (Oxford, Clarendon, 1995), 329.
[55] *Dextra Bank and Trust Co. Ltd.* v. *Bank of Jamaica* [2001] EWPC 26 (PC).
[56] R. Goode, 'The Bank's Right to Recover Money Paid on a Stopped Cheque' (1981) 97 LQR 254;
H. Luntz, 'The Bank's Right to Recover on Cheques Paid by Mistake' (1968) 6 *Melb. ULR* 308. It might also be
argued that in giving up the cheque the payee has a defence of *bona fide* purchaser.

judgment, without the drawer raising any counterclaims.[57] (One response to this is said to be that the cheque may be returned to the payee, to enable it to sue the drawer on it. But the section of the Bills of Exchange Act 1882 governing negotiable instruments cancelled under a mistake, section 63(3), does not impose any obligation on the bank to return the cheque to the payee.)

A recipient must change its position as a result of the payment received. Thus if a bank mistakenly pays another bank, and the recipient bank then pays money away beyond recall, its change of position will not be on the faith of the receipt if it has relied, not on the instruction in the payment message, but on its customer's representations (fraudulent or otherwise) that that is payment for it.[58] This is sound policy, because the proper working of the payment system turns on a recipient bank following exactly the terms of a payment instruction, and inquiring of the sending bank if there is any gap or doubt in the message.

Change of position can only be invoked if the recipient acts *bona fide* and is not a wrongdoer.[59] Clearly if the recipient of a payment knows that it is not entitled to it, it is generally not acting bona fide.[60] The recipient who has fraudulently induced the payment is also unable to use change of position. There is some authority that a simply careless recipient is also barred from using change of position.[61] In the commercial context this has little to recommend it. Why should the recipient's carelessness be brought into account, when it is irrelevant whether the payor acted carelessly? In deciding which of two parties should suffer there is no merit in demanding that a recipient take reasonable precautions, when a payor can claim restitution of a mistaken payment, whether or not made through its own fault. There is also a great deal to be said for protecting the integrity of the payment system by upholding the position of banks, which rely on payment messages received in the ordinary course of business.

A claim by a bank paying under mistake may also be met by the defence of estoppel—that it is estopped from denying that the recipient has good title to the money. Estoppel as a defence bars recovery completely, whereas change of position operates *pro tanto*, i.e. only to the extent to which the recipient has changed its position, so that some money may be repayable, even though the restitutionary claim is partially barred. For this reason estoppel as a defence to mistaken payment is becoming unpopular and a recipient would most likely be permitted to retain only its reliance losses.[62] Yet if a paying bank has made a definite representation that payment

---

[57] 381 below.

[58] *State Bank of New South Wales Ltd.* v. *Swiss Bank Corp.* (1995) 39 NSWLR 350 (CA).

[59] *Lipkin Gorman (a firm)* v. *Karpnale Ltd.* [1991] 2 AC 548, 580.

[60] *Goss* v. *Chilcott* [1996] AC 788 (PC). Cf. the special circumstances of *National Bank of New Zealand Ltd.* v. *Waitaki International Processing (NI) Ltd.* (1996) 6 NZLBC 102, 646 (CA), noted (1999) 115 *LQR* 198 (P. Watts).

[61] *South Tyneside MBC* v. *Svenska International* [1995] 1 All ER 545, 569.

[62] *National Westminster Bank plc* v. *Somer International (UK) Ltd.* [2001] EWCA Civ. 970, [2001] Lloyd's Rep. Banking 263.

is genuine the recipient bank may have expectation losses, beyond its reliance losses, so that no windfall is involved.

Mere payment cannot, of itself, constitute the representation required for an estoppel. What is required is, for instance, that the paying bank make a collateral representation to the recipient bank, on the latter inquiring, that payment is authorized and in order. As well as a representation by the bank, estoppel also requires reliance by the recipient on the representation to its detriment, and that the recipient not be at fault. Detriment for a recipient bank would be paying the money away, on instructions, beyond recall.[63] Fault would occur if the recipient realized the mistake and did nothing about it, or somehow induced it, possibly even through innocent misrepresentation. A recipient is also precluded from invoking estoppel, if it has failed to reveal to the sending bank facts which would have put it on its guard about making the representation.

(iii) Good Consideration and the *Liggett* Doctrine

A recipient providing good consideration has a defence to an action for mistaken payment.[64] What of the paying bank, which in making payment discharges a debt its customer owes the recipient: has the latter given good consideration so the bank cannot recover? The authorities say that for the bank to be unable to recover, payment must be made with the customer's actual authority, or the customer must subsequently ratify the payment. Thus if, say, the customer has countermanded payment or the mandate is inadequate (e.g. one signature instead of two) but the bank mistakenly pays, and the customer does not ratify, expressly or impliedly, payment does not discharge the debt and the bank can recover. Any argument that the bank in this case has apparent authority to pay has been rejected. However, when the customer clearly authorizes payment but the bank mistakenly pays because it wrongly assumes that it is in funds, payment discharges the customer's debt and the money is irrecoverable from the recipient.[65]

That leads to the position of the customer under the *Liggett*[66] doctrine which has been described as a last resort of a bank unable for practical or legal reasons to claim for a mistaken payment against the payee. As explained in the *Liggett* decision by Wright J, if the bank by paying has discharged genuine debts of its customer, it would be inequitable if it were not able to debit its customer's account, despite a lack of authority (e.g. as a result of a countermand, or an inadequate mandate).

Despite its practical appeal the doctrine cannot stand in the light of the authorities, that without the authority of or ratification by its customer mistaken payment by a bank to a third party does not discharge any debt owed by the customer to the third

[63] See the old case *Deutsche Bank v. Beriro & Co.* (1895) 73 LT 669.
[64] There is a separate defence of *bona fide* purchaser: *Dextra Bank and Trust Co. Ltd. v. Bank of Jamaica,* [2001] EWPC 26 (PC).
[65] *Lloyds Bank plc v. Independent Insurance Co. Ltd.* [2000] QB 110 (CA).
[66] *B. Liggett (Liverpool) Ltd v. Barclays Bank Ltd* [1928] 1 KB 48. See E. Ellinger and C. Lee, 'The Liggett Defence' [1984] *LMCLQ* 459.

party.[67] Consequently, the bank cannot debit its customer's account. The unjust enrichment of the customer which *Liggett* addressed remains open, for the bank will frequently be unable to reclaim from third parties—they will have changed their position in reliance on the payment and so have a good defence to the bank's action. The customer is thus unjustly enriched, with his account intact but debts to third parties discharged. Restitution should be available to the bank in such cases.[68]

B. VOID PAYMENTS

A contract entered by a bank may be void or avoided for a variety of reasons: for example, a vitiating factor may operate;[69] the contract may be *ultra vires* the counterparty;[70] or there may be invalidating legislation.[71] It could be said that payments under void or avoided contracts are made on the basis of a failure of consideration. Failure of consideration in this sense means contractual performance which was expected but did not occur—payments under a gross-up clause in a loan contract (*David Securities*), payments by a swap counterparty (*Westdeutsche Landesbank*), and so on. Restitution is justified in these cases because of the failure of an expected, future event. On this analysis if the contract runs its full course, despite being void or voidable, restitution is impossible—the parties get what they expected. Conversely, if it does not, to the extent that performance falls short of what was expected, a restitutionary claim would be possible *pro tanto*.

In fact, in English law restitutionary claims can be made for payments under void contracts, but on the basis of no consideration.[72] No consideration relates to the consideration necessary in English law for the formation of a contract (the exchange of a promise for a promise, or a promise for an act). Failure of consideration in the sense discussed in the preceding paragraph is different: it refers to performance on the contract, not the promise. There are conceptual problems with basing restitution on no consideration, rather than failure of consideration, not least that it renders redundant the carefully defined categories of restitutionary claims, such as that of mistaken payments examined earlier.[73] There are practical consequences as well. Thus restitution is probably only possible in relation to void, not voidable, contracts: with voidable contracts, there is arguably some consideration. Moreover, if a void contract has been completely performed restitution is still possible—there is no

---

[67] e.g. *Crantrave Ltd.* v. *Lloyds Bank plc* [2000] QB 917.

[68] R. Pedley, 'Repent Not That You Should Lose Your Friend And He Repents Not That He Pays Your Debt' [2001] *JIBL* 169.

[69] 212 above.

[70] *Westdeutsche Landesbank Girozentrale* v. *Islington LBC* [1996] AC 669 (HL).

[71] *David Securities Pty. Ltd.* v. *Commonwealth Bank of Australia* (1992) 175 CLR 353.

[72] Especially the *Westdeutsche Landesbank* case [1994] 1 WLR 938, [1994] 4 All ER 890 (CA).

[73] e.g. P. Birks, 'No Consideration: Restitution after Void Contracts' (1993) 23 *UWALR* 195; W. Swadling, 'Restitution for No Consideration' [1994] *RLR* 73.

consideration—even though both parties obtained the performance expected.[74] As well, restitution could not operate *pro tanto.*

In recognizing restitutionary claims on void contracts, English law accepts change of position as a defence. As for remedies, it is now clear that when money passes under a void contract, although the payor (such as a bank) has a restitutionary claim, this is not of a proprietary nature.[75] To give the payor an equitable proprietary claim would be to confer on it rights against third parties, and a priority in the insolvency of a recipient. Moreover, a payor is confined to simple interest—it cannot obtain compound interest—on the amount recovered as a result of a successful restitutionary claim.

IV. THE IDENTIFICATION RULES—TRACING

It is common to refer to 'tracing assets' on behalf of commercial organizations such as banks or governments, when these have been misappropriated, or they are otherwise unlawfully withheld (e.g. tax payments). Tracing assets in this wide sense involves investigators, auditors, and lawyers, and a range of legal tools from criminal, civil, procedural, and international law.[76] Sometimes the assets are what English lawyers call choses in possession (goods, money *in specie*) and documentary intangibles (e.g. negotiable securities), but often what is involved is a right to money, which has been transferred through the banking system, albeit that it may later be used to acquire tangible assets. Tracing the movement of money in this sense is a matter of evidence. The term 'following the audit trail' is sometimes used. The trail may be lost in other jurisdictions. Wrongdoers often seek to transfer their gains to foreign jurisdictions, with strong laws on bank secrecy.

In English law there are special rules about tracing, i.e. when the law permits the owner of the original property to assert title to the traceable product in its place.[77] The modern view is that these are rules for identifying value, and are neither a claim nor a remedy.[78] Once a claimant has identified value as having reached the defendant's hands, whether or not it is still there, it will need to found a claim. As a matter of English law, and depending on the circumstances, that claim may be a personal claim in money had and received, or knowing receipt or restitution.[79] It may also be a

---

[74] E. McKendrick, 'Local authorities and Swaps' in R. Cranston (ed.), n. 85 below, 254.

[75] *Westdeutsche Landesbank Girozentrale* v. *Islington LBC* [1996] AC 669 (HL).

[76] e.g. K. Houston, 'The Asset Tracer's Armoury' (1996) 3 *J Financial Crime* 373; M. Ashe, A. Keltie, N. Pearson, and B. Rider, *International Tracing of Assets* (London, Sweet & Maxwell, looseleaf).

[77] See R. Grantham and C. Rickett, 'Tracing and Property Rights' (2000) 63 *MLR* 905; P. Birks, 'Property and Unjust Enrichment' [1997] *NZL Rev.* 623.

[78] *Boscawen* v. *Bajwa* [1996] 1 WLR 328, 334, [1995] 4 All ER 769, 776, *per* Millett LJ; *Foskett* v. *McKeown* [2001] 1 AC 102, 128, *per* Lord Millett.

[79] 246, 193 above.

proprietary claim, for example, it may be an equitable proprietary claim in trust money which has been misappropriated,[80] enforced by a lien, so that in the event of insolvency the claimant obtains a priority over the insolvent's unsecured creditors.[81]

Of course there may be a defence to the claim. Change of position is now recognized as a defence to restitutionary claims, including the common law claim for money had and received. In commercial transactions, an equitable claim will often be defeated by the defence of *bona fide* purchaser. *Bona fide* purchaser defeats common law claims as well. The holder in due course of a negotiable instrument is an example.[82] More relevant for present purposes, banks typically give consideration for payments to them—the provision of banking services coupled with the promise to pay on the customer's instructions in the case of a customer paying money into an account which then has a positive balance. Equitable claims may also be met by the defences such as laches (delay) and acquiescence.

The tracing rules are rules which operate when, as a matter of evidence, a claimant cannot locate value beyond a particular point. Tracing establishes the connection between the value which left the claimant and that received by the defendant, even though it passed through different hands and took different forms.[83] Take the fraudulent company officer, siphoning off funds from the company's bank account into a bank account in another jurisdiction. As we saw in section 1 of this Chapter, this will typically occur by a movement on bank accounts and will probably involve a clearing system. No property is transferred—payment does not involve assignment.

As a matter of evidence, it may be relatively simple to follow the movements on the various bank accounts and to locate value in the foreign account. But what if the fraudster has paid the stolen money into an account with other money in it, or used funds in the account to pay someone else, or to purchase some form of property? It is here that the presumptions in the English law of tracing become relevant, in enabling the company to found an action.

Unfortunately, the law of tracing through bank accounts has been bedeviled by a misunderstanding of how payment is effected. As we have seen this is by transmitting payment messages, and a consequent movement on accounts. Unfortunately, some legal discussions in effect have analogized payment to a piggy bank, where a person's physical money is paid in, possibly mixed, and then extracted. Even if A pays notes and coins into an account—typically not the case—it is basic law that that money is the bank's own, to use as it wishes. The bank is, of course, subject to its obligation to make payment on the customer's instructions. If A pays money into an account with a positive balance, moneys are not being 'mixed'—the phrase invariably used—but rather A's debt claim against the bank is enhanced. If the account is overdrawn, the bank's claim against A is reduced, or A obtains a debt claim against the bank.

[80] *Foskett* v. *McKeown* [2001] 1 AC 102 (HL).
[81] *Space Investments Ltd.* v. *Canadian Imperial Bank of Commerce Trust Co.* [1986] 1 WLR 1072 (PC).
[82] 380 below.
[83] P. Birks, 'Overview', in P. Birks (ed.), *Laundering and Tracing* (Oxford, Clarendon, 1995), 289–92.

Another difficulty in the authorities has been an assumption that, whenever an electronic clearing system is involved in payment, this somehow acts as a block on identifying whether value has passed. By contrast, if the clearing system is paper-based the payment can be traced.[84] The distinction is metaphysical. First, it rests on the faulty premise that, at every point in tracing, it is necessary to point to a chain of property substitutes. Secondly, it overlooks how payment systems work. The movement on accounts at the recipient bank occurs in both cases because the bank receives an instrument, or more typically a payment message, and thus knows to adjust a customer's account.

The English law of tracing has also been badly affected by the distinction between common law and equitable tracing. This still survives in the authorities, although there are powerful voices for a rationalization and reformulation.[85] Common law tracing founds common law actions, notably an action for money had and received— a strict liability action. Equitable tracing can only be used for equitable claims, and with an equitable proprietary claim the court has no discretion as to whether to allow it to be asserted. A claim in knowing receipt is not a strict-liability claim and probably requires the claimant to show that the recipient, if it had behaved reasonably, would have known that the moneys were being paid in breach of trust or fiduciary duty.[86]

While not impossible, tracing at common law through mixed accounts and clearing systems is said to face difficulties. Thus it is said that a claimant's money may cease to be identifiable in the eyes of the common law when it becomes mixed with that of another, or is paid away through a clearing system. If a company's money is misappropriated by a director and paid into a bank account with a nil balance, however, tracing is possible. Common law tracing is also possible into property purchased out of that bank account.[87] If the director pays the money from that account away to X, then common law tracing may still be possible.[88] But if the director or X has mixed the company's with his or her own money, it is generally said to be impossible at common law to say that it was the company's money which X received. And common law tracing through a clearing system is also said to be impossible.[89]

Tracing in equity is generally acknowledged to be more extensive than at common law. Thus tracing through a bank account with mixed moneys does not face difficulties, nor does tracing through a clearing system. Tracing through back-to-back credits is possible. There is some authority in favour of 'backward tracing', as when a credit

---

[84] *Agip (Africa) Ltd.* v. *Jackson* [1991] Ch. 547, 563.

[85] *Foskett* v. *McKeown* [2001] 1 AC 102, 128–9, *per* Lord Millett; L. Smith The *Law of Tracing* (Oxford, Clarendon, 1997) 120–30, 342–7; P. Birks, 'The Necessity of a Unitary Law of Tracing', in R. Cranston (ed.), *Making Commercial Law* (Oxford, Clarendon, 1997).

[86] 194 above.

[87] *Lipkin Gorman (a firm)* v. *Karpnale Ltd.* [1991] 2 AC 548; *F. C. Jones & Sons* v. *Jones* [1996] 4 All ER 721 (CA).

[88] *Banque Belge pour l'Etranger* v. *Hambrouck* [1921] 1 KB 321. See P. Matthews, 'The Legal and Moral Limits of Common Law Tracing', in P. Birks (ed.), *Laundering and Tracing* (Oxford, Clarendon, 1995), 47–66.

[89] *Agip (Africa) Ltd.* v. *Jackson* [1991] 1 Ch. 547, 566; E. McKendrick, 'Tracing Misdirected Funds' [1991] LMCLQ 378, 384.

entry on a recipient's bank account, although first in time, is identified with a debit on the sender's bank account. Of particular relevance, because payments are often made cross-border, is that equity's ability to trace is not dependent on each successive recipient being within the jurisdiction—it is sufficient if the defendant is.[90]

Yet there are drawbacks to tracing in equity. There is the rule, which seems to have a precarious future, that there must be a fiduciary relationship between the claimant and the defendant, or between the claimant and the third party through whose account the money passed. (In this sense common law tracing has an advantage.) Clearly in the example above a company director is in a fiduciary relationship with the company, and the requirement is satisfied. So, too, with employees of the company. But it is not the case in English law with an outside thief of the company's moneys. Other common law jurisdictions overcome this problem by stretching the law and treating the thief as the owner's (company's) fiduciary. The trouble with this is that it attenuates the notion of being a fiduciary.

The equitable rules of tracing enable a claimant to take property bought with money traced, unless the property has been purchased from an account with mixed funds, although in this case the claimant can obtain a proportional share of the property (including any increase in value). It is presumed that, if some money is drawn from a mixed account and dissipated, what is left is the claimant's moneys. It is also presumed that if some money is drawn from a mixed account and an investment purchased, with the remainder being dissipated, it was the claimant's money which went into the investment.

Yet equity cannot trace into an overdrawn account: the money is treated as ceasing to exist. Similarly, there is the rule about the 'lowest intermediate balance'. This is that if it is possible to identify a credit balance, x, at time t_1, in a bank account, and the balance decreases to y at t_2, the intermediate balance (y) is all that can be traced even if, at t_3, the balance has risen.[91] If at t_2 the account has a nil balance, or it is in debit, then under the rule nothing traceably survives in any later credit balance. As we have seen, it may be possible to trace into property acquired—in this case, say, property acquired by the payment which left the intermediate balance, and indeed through those assets back into the account. A limited exception to the lowest intermediate balance rule is where the balance has risen at t_3 as a result of an intention to reimburse the claimant. This must be a real, not a fictitious, intention, so it hardly arises in the case of a fraudster. The rights of the claimant in this case are derived through intentional transfer, not tracing.[92]

---

[90] *El Ajou* v. *Dollar Land Holdings plc* [1993] 3 All ER 717, 736, [1994] 2 All ER 685 (CA).

[91] *Bishopsgate Investment Management Ltd. (in liq.)* v. *Homan* [1995] Ch. 211 (CA).

[92] L. Smith, 'Tracing Swollen Assets and the Lowest Intermediate Balance' (1994) 8 *Trusts L Int'l.* 102, 103.

9

PAYMENT METHODS

Payment methods are the instruments, procedures, and institutions which enable users to meet payment obligations. Traditionally, payment methods have been classified as credit or debit transfers, depending on whether the payor's payment instructions are given direct to its bank (credit transfer) or pass via the payee (a debit transfer). Payment methods are either paper based, electronic, or a combination of both. An additional classification divides payment systems into small- and large-value systems. This Chapter examines some common payment methods. It is illustrative, rather than exhaustive. Cheques have a range of legal peculiarities because of their association with bills of exchange and merit special attention. Attempts to apply all their rules to other payment methods are misplaced.[1] Rather methods such as credit transfer and direct debit turn on their own contractual and institutional arrangements. Their general operation should be clear from the previous discussion[2] and there is some discussion of large-value payment systems in Chapter 10. After cheques this Chapter turns to payment cards and the hot topic of e money.

I. CHEQUES

In some jurisdictions, cheques have never been a popular method of payment. Elsewhere, as in the United Kingdom, France, and the United States, they have. However, it is clear that even in these places the traditional cheque will, with time, disappear, for its processing costs are a deadly disadvantage in a cost-conscious world. As in Darwin's theory of natural selection, a species must adjust to survive. Payment cards are definitely in the ascendency.

As mentioned, the use of the cheque varies enormously across countries. In countries like France cheques have been used in around 40 per cent of non-cash transactions. By contrast, in Germany they have constituted less than 5 per cent of such transactions: credit transfers and direct debts have dominated. The trend is away from

---

[1] Cf. *Esso Petroleum Co. Ltd.* v. *Milton* [1997] 1 WLR 938, [1997] 2 All ER 593 (CA) (payment by direct debit equivalent to payment by cheque, thus precluding set off: unfortunately an appeal was not pursued [1997] 1 WLR 1060).

[2] Especially 39–44; 235–8 above. See M. Brindle and R. Cox (eds.), *Law of Bank Payments* (2nd edn., London, Sweet & Maxwell, 1999).

the use of the cheque in all jurisdictions, although it still remains a not insignificant feature of non-cash transactions in some, involving millions both in terms of volume and value. These features of the use of the cheque compared with other non-cash payment instruments are summarized in Table 1 for three jurisdictions, France, Britain and Germany.[3]

Table 1 Comparative use of cashless payment instruments: percentage by volume, 1999

	Cheques	Credit/Debit cards	Credit Transfers	Direct Debits	e money
Germany	4.0	5.2	50.5	40.3	0.14
France*	44.0	23.9	17.8	14.4	—
Britain	29.0	34.6	17.6	18.9	—

* 1998 figures.

The proportionate volume of cheque transactions exceeds their value, in other words the cheque is used mainly for retail transactions as an alternative to cash and payment cards. The sharp decline in the average value of cheques in Britain over the last decade reflects the encouragement for the commercial world to make wholesale payments by paperless credit transfer, rather than by cheque.

A. THE NATURE OF CHEQUES

(i) The Law of Cheques

A further variation across countries regarding the cheque concerns the different legal regimes governing its use. One divide is between the common law, represented by the Bills of Exchange Act 1882, and the civil law, represented by the Geneva Convention on Cheques of 1931.[4] Another divide is within the civil law itself, because even where the Geneva Convention was adopted domestic peculiarities continued because of reservations to the convention, or because the convention was silent on particular points. These consequent differences between the laws of different European countries have various manifestations. In English law, for instance, a customer can stop or countermand a cheque, whereas in France the owner of a cheque acquires rights when

---

[3] *Payment and Securities Settlement Systems in the European Union* (the Blue Book) (Frankfurt, ECB, 2001), Table 12. See also D. Hancock and D. Humphrey, 'Payment Transactions, Instruments, and Systems' (1998) *JB&F* 1573, 1592.

[4] Three conventions were signed at Geneva on the unification of the law relating to bills of exchange on 7 June 1930 and three further conventions on the unification of the law relating to cheques on 19 Mar. 1931: *League of Nations Treaty Series*, v. CXLIII, Nos 3301, 3313–17. The most important for our purposes is the Uniform Law for Cheques. This has been introduced into the municipal legislation of various countries.

the cheque is issued so that the cheque cannot be stopped.[5] A related point concerns the concept of *provision* or cover. In French law one cannot issue a cheque without adequate *provision* (i.e. the drawer must be in funds), and the issue of the cheque transfers the right to *provision* to the payee. The concept gives a payee a direct right of recourse against the drawee bank, although if there are no funds then generally the drawee does not have to pay. There is nothing comparable in English law: a cheque does not operate as an assignment of funds and the payor's bank is not liable on the instrument.[6]

Cheques in English law are undoubtedly bills of exchange—bills of exchange, drawn on a banker, payable on demand, says the Bills of Exchange Act 1882.[7] In practice, however, cheques have little in common with the bills of exchange examined in Chapter 14. In practice cheques these days are hardly ever transferred to third parties, beyond the payee. UK banks have taken advantage of the change brought about by the Cheques Act 1992, printed their cheques 'account payee', with the result that the cheque is valid only as between the parties to it.[8] As a practical matter, therefore, negotiability and indorsement do not arise now in relation to the typical cheque and much of the old learning is redundant.

These days, then, cheques are better thought of as payment instructions by customers to their bankers, and analysed along with other payment methods in the context of the ordinary law governing the relationship between banks and their customers. Clearly reference needs to be made to the Bills of Exchange Act 1882, but it is simply not accurate, at least in relation to the typical account-payee cheque, to have bills of exchange law dominate the discussion. Indeed, it is high time the law of cheques was shorn off from the Bills of Exchange Act 1882 and located in separate legislation, such as with the Australian Cheques and Payment Orders Act 1986.

(ii) Cheques as Payment Instructions

Important parts of the law, relevant to cheques as payment instructions, have already been considered. In a valid cheque the instrument must have the customer's signature: a forged cheque is not a valid mandate, and the bank cannot debit the customer's account.[9] There are the limited exceptions where the customer is estopped from raising the forgery against its bank, for example, because it has facilitated the fraud in the way it has drawn the cheque, or because it has failed to contact the bank, despite suspecting that its cheques were being fraudulently used.[10] Of course, if the customer has properly drawn the cheque, but its account is not in funds, or if paying the cheque would take the account beyond an agreed overdraft, the bank is not obliged to pay it: a bank is generally not under any obligation to provide financial accommodation to its customers.[11]

[5] Bills of Exchange Act 1882, s. 75(1); B. Geva, *Bank Collection and Payment Transactions* (Oxford, OUP, 2001), 184.
[6] Bills of Exchange Act 1882, s. 53.   [7] S. 73.   [8] Bills of Exchange Act 1882, s. 81A.
[9] 140 above.   [10] 143 above.   [11] 130 above.

Crossings are another dimension to cheques as payment instructions. These have a long, and interesting, history: today they serve mainly to thwart fraud.[12] For present purposes it is sufficient to mention the typical crossings. First, there may be two parallel transverse lines across the face of the cheque: this is a general crossing within the terms of the Act[13] and directs the customer's bank to pay only to another bank. The customer's bank is liable to the true owner of the cheque for any loss it sustains, owing to the cheque not having been so paid.[14] (The less common special crossing involves the two parallel transverse lines, with the addition of the name of a bank, i.e. the payee's bank. Payment other than to that bank means that the payor's bank is liable to the true owner for any loss.[15]) In practice banks may sometimes pay a low-value cheque across the counter, despite a general crossing. Some people still do not have bank accounts and so cannot get a bank to collect their cheques. There is no sanction in the Act for banks which do this. If payment is made to the true owner, the customer who drew the cheque would only be entitled to nominal damages for breach of mandate. If payment is made to someone other than the true owner and the bank is liable, the loss to the bank is unlikely to be great, given that it will only pay across the counter with low-value cheques.

Secondly, there is the addition to the general crossing of the words 'account payee' or 'a/c payee', with or without the word 'only'. As mentioned already, this means the cheque is not transferable and is valid only as between the parties to it, i.e. the customer (drawer) and payee.[16] Thus an indorsee of the cheque could not claim payment under it. There is the disadvantage that those without bank accounts cannot indorse cheques to others for payment. However, the policy decision favouring non-transferable cheques, embodied in the Cheques Act 1992, is the need to reduce fraud.[17] Certainly the law reports are replete with decisions where fraud has occurred because cheques were fraudulently indorsed.[18]

Thirdly, there may be added to the general crossing the words 'not negotiable'. This does not affect the transferability of the cheque but means that the person taking it cannot get a better title to it than the title of the person from whom it took it.[19] However, assume the cheque is a typical cheque and non-transferable because of an 'account payee' crossing. What additional protection does the 'not negotiable' crossing afford? In special circumstances there is some benefit. Take a situation where an employee of a company fraudulently makes one of its properly signed cheques payable to a third party. As a result of the 'not-negotiable' crossing the third party does not obtain a good title to the cheque.[20]

The crossings are a material part of the cheque, and in general it is not lawful for

---

[12] J. Holden, *The History of Negotiable Instruments in English Law* (London, Athlone Press, 1955), 229ff.

[13] S. 76(1).   [14] S. 79(2).   [15] Ss. 76(2); 79(2).   [16] S. 81A(1).

[17] *Banking Services: Law and Practice*, Cm. 1026 (London, HMSO, 1990), 22–3. See also J. Macleod, 'The Plight of the Unbanked Payee' (1997)113 *LQR* 133.

[18] As well as the standard texts see F. Kessler, 'Forged Indorsements' (1938) 47 *Yale LJ* 863; W. Vis, 'Forged Indorsements' (1979) 27 *Am. J Comp. L* 547.

[19] S. 81.   [20] 378 below.

any person to alter them.[21] Alteration, as with bills of exchange generally, will avoid the cheque.[22] However, the customer (drawer) can vary a crossing, which is simply to vary its instructions, and subsequent holders can make a crossing more restrictive (e.g. by adding 'account payee' to a general crossing).[23]

Countermand (revocation) is yet another dimension to cheques as payment instructions. Cheques can be countermanded under section 75 of the Bills of Exchange Act 1882. The section tells us nothing about what countermand requires and what are its implications. However, we have seen that countermand must be explicit and generally given to the branch of the bank where the account is kept.[24] We have also seen that if a bank mistakenly pays, despite countermand, it may be able to reclaim from the payee in limited circumstances, but if that is impossible the restitutionary grounds for debiting its customer's account are unclear.[25]

Section 75 is also of no assistance in identifying the point up to which countermand is possible: it simply indicates that the duty and authority of a bank to pay a cheque drawn upon it are terminated by countermand. As a matter of principle, it would seem that if the bank's mandate is withdrawn, it must comply with its principal's instruction and stop the process, if this is practicable. In other words, countermand must be received by the branch of account in time to enable it reasonably to refuse payment. This leads to the following propositions:

- countermand is possible at any time before close of business where a customer has paid in a cheque drawn on the same branch of the same bank (as long as that customer has not been told before close of business that it has been paid).

- countermand is possible where a cheque is presented through the clearing system up until the point defined by the clearing rules as that when the paying bank can return the cheque. This is an example of how customers can take the benefit of the clearing rules although, in general, they cannot incur obligations under them.[26]

In jurisdictions where a cheque can be backed by a guarantee card, there cannot be countermand. A customer undertakes not to countermand as a matter of contract.[27] Moreover, a customer may be sued by a holder in due course, despite countermand of a cheque, although there cannot be a holder in due course of an 'account payee' cheque.[28] Finally, countermand is too late if there has been special presentation or certification of a cheque (in jurisdictions where cheques are certified).[29]

Post-dated cheques are sometimes used by customers where the debt owed to the payee has not yet matured, or where the customer is awaiting funds to cover the

[21] S. 79.   [22] S. 64.   [23] S. 77(2)–(6).

[24] 242 above. S. Magnet, 'Inaccurate or Ambiguous Countermand and Payment over Countermand' (1979) 4 Can. BLJ 297.

[25] 251 above.   [26] 53 above.   [27] 242 above.   [28] 263 below.

[29] Special presentation (or clearance or collection) is the accelerated presentation of a cheque by sending it direct to the branch on which it is drawn, rather than through the clearing system. On certified cheques: J. Reynolds, 'Countermand of Cheques' (1981) 15 UBCLR 341, 344.

cheque. There are no difficulties if the post-dated cheque is paid on or after the specified date, or even if it is paid before then and the customer does not object. But what if the bank has paid the cheque before the specified date and the customer now countermands payment? Clearly the bank is in breach of mandate in paying before the date has arrived, and on the face of it cannot debit its customer's account.[30] Of course, it may have a claim in restitution against the payee if there is no change of position.[31] What if the bank pays before the specified date, between that date and the specified date another cheque is presented for payment, but the bank refuses to pay it because there are now insufficient funds? It is clear that the bank's dishonour of the second cheque is wrongful.[32]

B. COLLECTION OF CHEQUES

Cheques, as we know, are debit instruments. With our typical cheque, the payee will give it to its bank, which will present it for payment to the payor (drawer's) bank. The process is known as collecting the cheque. The payee's bank is known as the collecting bank, and the payor's bank as the paying bank. Given their volume, cheques are typically collected in bulk, through the bank's clearing office if collecting and paying bank are branches of the same bank, or through a clearing house if they are different banks.[33] There is a definite economic incentive in favour of replacing the manual clearing of cheques by the use of electronic systems in which data on cheques are exchanged by magnetic media or via a telecommunications system.

Cheque truncation describes the system whereby each cheque is no longer sent physically from the collecting to the paying bank, but instead its details or an image are sent electronically. Not only does cheque truncation reduce the cost of the collection process but it also has the potential for speeding up the collection cycle and cutting cost. Cheque truncation was thought to be impermissible in Britain, because the Bills of Exchange Act 1882 requires that a cheque be 'presented' for payment at the branch on which it is drawn, and presentment has been interpreted to mean physical presentment.[34] The Bills of Exchange Act 1882 was amended in 1996 to remove that duty from collecting banks and to permit cheque truncation.[35]

---

[30] *Brien* v. *Dwyer* (1978) 141 CLR 378. CLR 378. See C. Craigie, 'Post-dated Cheques' (1983) 11 *Aust. BLR* 107.

[31] 250 above.   [32] *Keyes* v. *Royal Bank of Canada* [1947] 3 DLR 161 (SCC).

[33] Neither clearing office nor clearing house need be involved if payor and payee have accounts at the same branch.

[34] Bills of Exchange Act 1882, s. 45; *Barclays Bank plc* v. *Bank of England* [1985] 1 All ER 385. See J. Vroegop, 'The Legal Implications of Cheque Truncation' [1990] *LMCLQ* 244; B. Geva, 'Off-premises Presentment and Cheque Truncation under the Bills of Exchange Act' [1989] *BFLR* 295. Under the Geneva Convention on Cheques presentment at a clearing house is permitted: Convention providing a Uniform Law for Cheques, Signed at Geneva, 19 Mar. 1931, *League of Nations Treaty Series*, v. CXIII, No 3316, Art. 21; Annex II, Art. 15.

[35] Deregulation (Bills of Exchange) Order 1996, SI 1996 No 2993.

(i) The Paying Bank

When a cheque is presented for payment the paying bank, as we know, must comply strictly with its customer's mandate. The bank must not pay if the cheque is forged or materially altered, if it is drawn without authority, or if it has been countermanded. In paying the cheque it must also exercise a degree of care in the event that the payment instruction is improper.[36] If payment is in accordance with the customer's mandate, however, it can debit the customer's account.

A paying bank may dishonour the cheque—refuse to pay it—if the customer is not in funds, or if there is not a sufficiently agreed overdraft at the time it is presented. The customer's account or agreed overdraft must cover the entire amount of the cheque. The customer may have made payment in to cover the cheque, but unless payment in is complete[37] the bank is entitled to dishonour the cheque. Just because the bank has credited the customer's account with a cheque paid in, but not yet cleared, does not oblige the bank to pay the customer's own cheque.[38] This may be expressly stated and part of the customer's contract with the bank.[39] Nonetheless, the bank may agree to a customer drawing against an uncleared cheque. Whether there is a course of dealing to this effect (in respect of a particular customer) would be a matter of inquiry.

A bank wrongfully dishonouring a cheque is in breach of contract. There is a presumption of fact that every customer suffers some injury to its credit and reputation when its cheque is wrongfully dishonoured.[40] The damages payable will reflect the type of customer, the transaction involved, and the size of the cheque. Moreover, the bank may also be liable in defamation if the reason given, albeit mistakenly, is insufficient funds. It has sometimes been said that 'refer to drawer' is not defamatory, meaning 'go back to the drawer and ask him to pay', but today it is generally accepted that the phrase may imply a lack of funds.[41]

There is nothing in the Act about when the paying bank must decide whether or not to pay a cheque. Nor is the current version of the clearing rules explicit on the point.[42] However, the paying bank will be bound by the practice of bankers: by not responding within that period the paying bank can be said to make a representation to the collecting bank that the cheque will not be dishonoured. If the collecting bank acts on the representation and suffers loss of the amount advanced to the customer, it will be able to claim that from the paying bank.[43]

The typical cheque these days is an account-payee cheque, paid in by the named payee. There are no indorsements. We thus pass by the prodigious learning in the standard texts about the paying bank's liability when a cheque has been indorsed.

---

[36] 186 above.   [37] 243 above.

[38] A. L. Underwood v. Bank of Liverpool [1924] 1 KB 775 (CA). See A. Campbell and N. Kibble, 'Dishonoured Cheques. A Comparative Analysis' [2001] JBL 77.

[39] Westminster Bank Ltd. v. Zang [1966] AC 182 (CA, HL).

[40] Kpohraror v. Woolwich Building Society [1996] CLC 510 (CA).

[41] M. Hapgood, Paget's Law of Banking (11th edn., London, Butterworths, 1996), 338–9.

[42] Automated Debit Clearing Rules and Procedures, r.10. Cf. r.12 of a previous version of the rules in Butterworths Banking Law Handbook (1st edn., London, Butterworths, 1989).

[43] Parr's Bank v. Ashby (1898) 14 TLR 563.

(ii) The Collecting Bank

In collecting a cheque, the collecting bank will act as agent for its customer. This means that it must act with reasonable care and diligence: for example, it must collect the cheque promptly. It also means that once the cheque is collected, the collecting bank comes under an obligation to credit the customer's account with the amount. Once it has done this it must not reverse a credit to the customer in the event that it has repaid the paying bank, but that bank does not have a valid claim. Take as an example the situation where the paying bank has dishonoured the cheque, not in accordance with the clearing rules or the practice of bankers, but nonetheless the collecting bank decides to repay it. The customer would be entitled to succeed in an action against its bank, because its bank as agent has reversed a payment without authority and without any obligation to do so.

In theory, a bank may be a holder for value of a cheque. It then collects the cheque on its own behalf, at least to the extent of the value given. It can become a holder for value by permitting its customer to draw against an uncleared cheque. Provisional crediting of the account, pending collection, is not, however, enough. A bank also becomes a holder for value to the extent of an existing overdraft: section 27(3) of the Act constitutes as a holder for value anyone with a lien on a cheque, and as matter of common law a bank has a lien on uncollected cheques in relation to an overdraft.[44] As a holder for value the collecting bank may also be a holder in due course.[45] It thus has the best title to the amount collected. It is thus able to sue the drawer on the cheque: this can be a valuable right if the drawer has countermanded the cheque, the drawer's bank has mistakenly paid, but the collecting bank's own customer is unable, or unwilling, to repay amounts drawn on the basis of it.[46]

In practice, however, the result of the Cheques Act 1992 is that banks do not now collect cheques as holders for value. This is because the typical cheque is an account-payee cheque, and an account-payee cheque is valid only as between the drawer and payee. None, including the collecting bank, can become a holder for value of an account-payee cheque. Even if banks have permitted drawings against the cheque, they will not be able to sue the drawer on a dishonoured cheque in the event of being unable to recover from their own customer.[47]

In collecting a cheque, a bank exposes itself to liability if it does so for the wrong party. It may collect for the wrong party if the signature is forged or without authority or if the cheque is stolen and altered. Of course the collecting bank may be able to pass on the losses arising from its liability to others: thus, it may have an indemnity against its customer, although in practice this may be worthless. In English law one source of the collecting bank's liability is the tort of conversion: by legal fiction, a series of

---

[44] *Barclays Bank Ltd.* v. *Astley Industrial Trust Ltd.* [1970] 2 QB 527; *National Australia Bank Ltd.* v. *KDS Consturction Services Pty. Ltd. (in liq.)* (1987) 163 CLR 668.

[45] 380 below.

[46] e.g., *Midland Bank Ltd.* v. *R. V. Harris Ltd.* [1963] 1 WLR 1021, [1963] 2 All ER 685.

[47] R. Hooley, 'Prevention of Fraud by Non-transferable Cheques' [1992] *CJL* 432.

decisions treated 'the conversion as of the chattel, the piece of paper, the cheque under which the money was collected, and the value of the chattel converted as the money received under it'.[48] Conversion is a strict liability tort.

One answer which the collecting bank has in a case where a cheque has been stolen and the payee's name fraudulently altered is that this is a material alteration which avoids the cheque. Thus it is a worthless piece of paper and any action in conversion is not for its face value but for nominal damages only. A fraudulent change in the amount of the cheque will also be a material alteration. However, this does not assist in the case of the forged or unauthorized signature, which is not a material alteration under the terms of the Act. Once the potential liability of collecting banks became obvious in this sort of case, however, legislation was introduced to give them some protection.[49]

The current provision, section 4 of the Cheques Act 1957, protects a banker (undefined)[50] against liability to the true owner of a cheque, when it collects the cheque for a customer who has no title, or who has a defective title. Collection can be in either of the capacities mentioned—when the bank collects for a customer or when, having credited a customer's account with the amount of the cheque, it receives payment for itself on a cheque which is not crossed 'account payee'. 'Customer' in this context has a technical meaning: anyone for whom a bank has opened, or agreed to open, an account, including another bank.[51] The section does not confer on the bank a right to the proceeds, but it will not be liable to the true owner of the cheque in conversion. Nor, if it has given value, will it be liable under the general law in restitution. Thus, if the bank satisfies the prerequisites in the section the true owner must bear the loss if the bank has allowed its fraudulent customer to draw against the cheque.

Crucially, the bank must have acted with good faith and without negligence if it is successfully to invoke the statutory protection. Good faith is not the civil law, or US, concept, but means honesty in fact, whether or not negligent.[52] Negligence means falling below the standard of reasonable care expected of a bank. The concept has already been examined.[53] In this context, the considerable body of case law requires the bank to take steps, in both the opening and operation of the account, to thwart the fraudulent customer. There must be checks on the identity and suitability of new customers, a duty now underpinned by the money-laundering laws, with their requirement, for example, that prospective customers produce satisfactory evidence of identity, and that a bank have procedures in place, and take steps in accordance with them, as will do likewise.[54] If identification is clear, there are still traps, as where directors or employees pay company cheques into their own account.[55] This may be

---

[48] *Lloyds Bank Ltd.* v. *Chartered Bank of India, Australia and China* [1929] 1 KB 40, 55–6, *per* Scrutton LJ. See also *Arrow Transfer* v. *Royal Bank of Canada* (1972) 27 DLR (3d) 81 (SCC).

[49] J. Holden, *The History of Negotiable Instruments in English Law* (London, Athlone Press, 1955), 222ff.

[50] 5 above.   [51] 127 above.

[52] Bills of Exchange Act 1882, s. 90.   [53] 186 above.

[54] 72, 134 above. Cf. *Marfani & Co. Ltd.* v. *Midland Bank Ltd* [1968] 1 WLR 956.

[55] *Lloyds Bank Ltd.* v. *E. B. Savory & Co.* [1933] AC 201 (HL).

perfectly proper, but a bank may need to demonstrate that, given the nature of the payment, it has taken sufficient steps to ensure that nothing is untoward. If such a payment is dishonestly made, if the bank is liable to the true owner, and if it cannot invoke section 4, the bank may be able to claim against the company in contributory negligence.[56]

The claim against the collecting bank will be brought by the true owner of the cheque. There is no definition of true owner in the statutory or case law. Normally, where A hands a cheque to B as payee, B becomes the true owner. What if A posts the cheque to B and it is stolen in transit: is B the true owner? What if a third party fraudulently induces A to make a cheque payable to B, by inducing A to think that he is buying something from B? Does B become the true owner, so as to be able to sue the fraudster's bank in conversion for having collected the cheque? To answer these questions, courts have invoked a variety of concepts. In the decisions from which these facts are taken, reliance was placed, respectively, on the absence of delivery and any implied request to send the cheque by mail, and the absence of a real business transaction despite the intention of the drawer.[57] In such situations, where one of two innocent parties has to bear the loss of fraud, it may be better if the court is empowered to apportion the loss. In the absence of such discretion, however, it is necessary to determine the true owner.

The owner of a thing is the person who has the greatest interest in it.[58] Among the standard incidents of ownership are the right to exclusive physical control, the right to use it, the right to decide how and by whom it is to be used, and the right to alienate it. Most important for the present discussion is that ownership can generally only be acquired or lost with the consent of the parties. Exceptionally, English law recognizes that in a limited number of cases third parties may acquire a good title to property, even though they obtain the property from someone not having a good title. This occurs without the consent of the owner, and indeed so as to divest the owner of the incidents of ownership.

This analysis of ownership is consistent with the reasoning used by the court which considered the first fact situation posited above. Since the Post Office is the drawer's agent, the drawer remains the owner of a posted cheque until the payee receives it, unless the payee has requested him to post it, expressly or by implication. But it is not consistent with the approach of the court which decided the second case. There, the court disregarded the intention of the parties, and said simply that the payees were never the true owners of the cheque because the whole thing was a fraud and a sham.[59] In fact, the reason that the payee never became the true owner of the cheque was that

---

[56] Banking Act 1979, s. 47.

[57] *Channon* v. *English Scottish & Australian Bank* (1918) 18 SR (NSW) 30; *Smith and Baldwin* v. *Barclays Bank Ltd.* (1944) 5 LDAB 370. See also *Honourable Society of Middle Temple* v. *Lloyds Bank plc* [1999] 1 All ER (Comm) 193 (cheque apparently stolen in post; common ground that drawer was the owner).

[58] See A. Honoré, 'Ownership', in A. G. Guest (ed.), *Oxford Essays in Jurisprudence* (Oxford, Clarendon, 1961).

[59] *Smith and Baldwin* v. *Barclays Bank Ltd.* (1944) 5 LDAB 370, 373.

the payee never consented to it, although the drawer had intended it. That the whole thing was a sham was only relevant in as much as it meant that the payee never knew about it, and therefore could not consent to becoming owner.

II. PAYMENT CARDS

There is no need to underline the importance of payment cards for the discharge of retail payment obligations. Apart from credit cards, there are a range of payment cards: the debit card, which permits the customer to pay for goods and services at the point of sale (the so-called EFTPOS transaction); the cheque guarantee card, which is used in conjunction with a cheque book and guarantees the payment of a cheque up to a specified amount; and the e money card, which the customer can use to pay for small value items and which can be used independently of a bank account. Of course, any one card may be multifunctional. Payment cards also may enable the customer to obtain cash and access other bank services from an automated teller machine (ATM).

A. THE CONTRACT NETWORKS

Rather than examining each particular type of card, this part seeks to analyse the legal framework for payment cards in general. This is primarily provided by contract law. Credit cards are subject to extensive regulation, but that is a special topic and put to one side.[60] Generally speaking, payment cards other than credit cards and e money have escaped close regulatory scrutiny in most jurisdictions. In Europe, Denmark seems to be the only country with special legislation.[61] The United States has had its Electronic Funds Transfer Act since 1978.[62]

One advantage of payment cards is that they can fairly readily be used across borders. In terms of the various contracts governing their use, there may be an issue about which system of law governs. Some of the formal contracts may provide expressly for a governing law. If not, the governing law must be determined under the rules of private international law. The governing law determines, of course, the meaning and effect to be given to particular contractual provisions. Even if there is a governing law for a particular contract, use of a payment card can involve another system of law. For example, local consumer law could require that customers be provided with certain information when they use their payment cards. Clearly persons in using a payment card could also commit criminal offences in a state other than that of the governing law.[63]

---

[60] See, e.g., G. Stephenson, *Credit, Debit and Cheque Cards* (Birmingham, Central Law Publishing, 1993).
[61] Act on Certain Payment Instrument, No 414 of 31 May 2000.
[62] D. Baker and R. Brandel, *The Law of Electronic Funds Transfer Systems* (revd. edn., Boston, Warren, Gorham & Lamont, 1996), pt. II.
[63] 440 below.

(i) Customer-Issuing Bank

Until recently, a contract between a customer and the issuing bank was thought essential. How else was a customer to pay what was spent on use of a payment card? Now e money cards (sometimes known as prepaid cards or electronic purses) are in the offing. These are cards where value is loaded onto a microchip contained within the card. Such cards are equivalent in a way to cash and facilitate relatively small value payments. There is no need for any contract between customer and issuer.

At the time of writing e money cards are not fully operational, and so payment cards still typically involve a relationship with an issuer. Despite a traditional reluctance to use formal contracts in relation to the account, UK banks seek to impose standard terms and conditions on customers granted a payment card. The conditions of use are governed by English law. Typically, they cover the matters which could be anticipated for any method of payment. For example, the conditions permit the bank to debit the customer's account for payments and charges. Yet some clauses give banks considerable power. The cards may largely be withdrawn in the bank's discretion. Generally the terms of the contract may be varied with or without notice. The bank may exempt itself from liability if unable to perform any of its obligations.

Such provisions raise well-known legal issues associated with adhesion contracts. Did they become part of the contract? Usually customers must sign and return them, so there is little scope for argument that they are not bound.[64] Can the customer argue that the bank's marketing gave rise to a collateral contract, which has precedence over a written term? This argument is theoretically possible, but difficult to succeed with in practice.[65] Is it possible to construe the terms against the bank or to negate them entirely under the controls in unfair contract terms legislation? Perhaps this is the best avenue for success.[66] Public concern at the one sided nature of some of the terms used by banks has led to specific provisions in the Banking Codes about payment cards. These relate particularly to liability for loss of a card or its fraudulent use.[67]

(ii) Bank–Bank; Bank–Retailer

Agreements between banks enable customers to use their payment cards at bank outlets other than their own.[68] Within the system each bank member may be able to seek authorization on a card issued by any other member. Each member may be able to clear and settle financial data with other members. Moreover, banks may enter direct contractual relationships with retailers for EFTPOS transactions.[69] The retailer may need to obtain authorization if the amount is over limit and to check whether

---

[64] *L'Estrange* v. *F. Graucob Ltd.* [1934] 2 KB 394.
[65] Cf. *Mendelssohn* v. *Normand Ltd.* [1970] 1 KB 177; *Burnett* v. *Westminster Bank Ltd.* [1966] 1 QB 742.
[66] 147 above.
[67] e.g., *Banking Code*, Jan. 2001, §§14.6–14.12. See C. Reed, 'Consumer Electronic Banking', in C. Reed, I. Walden, and L. Edgar (eds.), *Cross-Border Electronic Banking* (2nd edn., London, LLP, 2000).
[68] H. Rowe, 'Legal Issue Between Banks Sharing Networks' [1990] 7 *Computer L & P* 2.
[69] *Commissioner for Customs and Excise* v. *FDR* [2000] BTC 5277, paras. 6–18 (CA); A, Arora, *Electronic Banking and the Law* (2nd edn., London, Banking Technology, 1993), 71.

the card is on a stop list as stolen or whether the customer is within a credit limit. The contracts will also provide for the reimbursement by the retailer's bank of amounts paid to the retailer and the collection by that bank of the amount from the card issuer's bank (if the retailer's bank is not the issuing bank). The bank–bank contract will provide for chargebacks of amounts wrongly paid by the issuing to the retailer bank. We have seen that the customer is treated as having paid the retailer on using the card, although the customer will only pay the issuing bank on a periodic basis for all such transactions.[70]

(iii) Issuing Bank–Payee

Payment is not effected by the assignment of any debt the issuer's bank owes the payor. Consequently, payees have no contractual claim on this basis against an issuer's bank. However, the payee may have a direct contractual claim for payment against their bank, as in the EFTPOS situation just mentioned. More difficult legally is the cheque guarantee card. In English law, the conditions of the card would seem to be an offer to the world, which particular payees accept when they take a cheque in accordance with them.[71] Alternatively, the customer could be regarded as conveying the bank's offer as agent. The conditions are that the cheque must be signed in the presence of the payee; that the signature must agree with that on the card; that the name of the bank and account on the cheque and on the card must agree; that the number of the card is written on the back of the cheque; and that the cheque is issued and dated before the expiry date on the card. Non-compliance with the conditions means that the bank cannot be sued on the guarantee. Under these conditions, if the cheque is used by an imposter, who forges the signature, the signature does not coincide with that on the card, and the payee cannot invoke the guarantee.

B. REGULATING PAYMENT CARDS

Apart from credit cards and e money cards, payment cards tend not to be directly regulated in most jurisdictions. Their terms and conditions may be subject to the general unfair contract terms legislation, as we have seen. Moreover, there is a body of 'soft law' in a number of jurisdictions controlling their use: the UK Banking Codes have already been mentioned in relation to the unauthorized and fraudulent use of payment cards. There has been concern about the adequacy of these measures, and their implementation, and some demands for greater legal regulation.[72]

In the European Community the Commission has adopted a Recommendation on a European code of conduct for electronic payment.[73] The code governs the relationship between financial institutions, traders and service establishments, and

---

[70] 241 below.

[71] The classic authority is *Carlill v. Carbolic Smoke Ball Co.* [1893] 1 QB 256.

[72] See, e.g., S. Gutwirth and T. Joris, 'Electronic Funds Transfer and the Consumer' (1991) 40 *ICLQ* 265; M. Sneddon, 'A Review of the Electronic Funds Transfer Code of Conduct' (1995) 6 *JBLFP* 29.

[73] 87/598/EEC [1987] OJ L365/72.

consumers. In particular it is designed to ensure fair practice, and that payment systems are as inter-operable as possible. As regards contracts between issuers and traders, and issuers and consumers, the code says that they should be in writing and the result of prior application. Presumably the latter is directed, in part, at the unsolicited mailing of payment cards. The contract must set out in detail the conditions of the agreement, which shall be freely negotiable and clearly stipulated in the contract. The standard form of contracts used by banks are hardly 'freely negotiated', although it would be a surprising result if the code were intended to be directed against these. More specifically, the code says that any scale of charges must be determined in a transparent manner, taking account of the actual costs and risks and without any restriction on competition. Moreover, conditions specific to termination of the contract must be stated and brought to the notice of the parties prior to the contract being concluded. Since the code mentions only the termination clause in this context, it seems that at the least it requires the 'red-hand' treatment in any conditions of use.[74]

The code then says that inter-operability in the Community 'shall be full and complete, so that traders and consumers can join the network[s] or contract with the issuer[s] of their choice with each terminal being able to process all cards'.[75] Inter-operability is defined as a state of affairs whereby cards issued in one Member State and/or belonging to a given card system can be used in other Member States and/or in the networks installed by other systems. The code continues that traders must be able, if they wish, to install a single, multi-card terminal. Moreover, they must be free to choose which point-of-sale terminal they will install. Under 'fair access to the system', it also says that irrespective of their economic size, all service establishments must be allowed fair access to the system of electronic payment. In addition, the code says that there must be no unwarranted difference in the remuneration for services concerning transactions within one Member State, and the remuneration for the same services concerning transactions with other Community countries. Two supplementary provisions on the relations between issuer and traders are, first, that there must be no exclusive trading clauses requiring the trader to operate only the one system; and secondly that compulsory provisions in trader–issuer contracts must be limited strictly to technical requirements for ensuring the system functions properly. The code contains an important principle under the heading 'data protection and security', that payments 'are irreversible. An order given by means of a payment card shall be irrevocable and may not be countermanded.'[76] The code purports thereby to overcome the difficult question of the reversibility of payments.

In addition to the code on inter-operability, the Commission has taken separate consumer-protection initiatives in relation to electronic payment instruments, including remote access and e money instruments.[77] Under them issuers must provide written terms of contract, expressed in easily-understood language. In the interests of

---

[74] 146 above.   [75] Cl. III 2.   [76] Cl. III 4(a).

[77] 'Commission Recommendation concerning payment cards, and in particular the relationship between cardholder and card issuer' [1988] OJ L317/55; 'Commission Recommendation concerning transactions by electronic payment instruments' [1997] OJ L208/52.

transparency holders must also be given specified written information relating to each transaction using the instrument. The issuer is liable for the consequences of defects in the system (liability may be limited to exclude consequential losses). The issuer is liable for the consequences of defects in, or a failure in the operation of, the system. (The liability may be shared by others such as the retailer or the network assembler.) Holders should be liable for damages arising from the loss of a card until the consumer notifies the issuer. That liability may not exceed the equivalent of €150 unless consumers have committed an act of extreme negligence or behaved fraudulently. Issuers must provide a means whereby their customer may at any time notify the loss of their payment instrument.

Recommendations do not, of course, have any direct binding force under the EC Treaty.[78] The legal justification for recommendations, rather than a binding instrument, is that the latter is not essential to the internal market. Consumers have a choice of payment systems within any one Member State, and uniform conditions throughout the Community for all electronic payment instruments is not necessary to the internal market. Of course it may be that there are independent reasons for a Community consumer protection measure separate from the steps necessary for the success of the internal market. In any event, under some systems of domestic law, the Community Recommendation may be admissible as a matter of law to show good custom and practice.

III. E MONEY

So far the use of e money is very small, hardly matched by the paper devoted to the issue.[79] e money is defined broadly by a European Community Directive as monetary value as represented by a claim on the issuer, stored in an electronic device and accepted as a means of payment by undertakings other than the issuer.[80] This includes e money cards (sometimes known as electronic purses) and prepaid software products for use on the internet (sometimes known as digital cash). Excluded, however, are products which enable consumers to use conventional payment services, for example, paying by credit card on the internet.

So far the legal focus has been on regulation: in the European Community those issuing e money, if not banks, have been brought within the regulatory frameworks for banks, although they are not subject to the whole panoply of controls.[81] The

---

[78] Art. 249.

[79] Committee on Payment and Settlement Systems, *Survey of Electronic Money Developments* (Basle, BIS, 2001), 100–4, Table B.

[80] Community Directive on [e money] 2000/46/EC, OJ L275/39. See M. Vereecken, 'Electronic Money: EU Legislative Framework' [2000] *EBLR* 417.

[81] Community Directive on e money, *ibid.*, implemented in the UK by the Electronic Money (Miscellaneous Amendments) Regulations 2002, SI 2002 No 765; Financial Services and Markets Act 2000 (Regulated Activities) Order 2002, SI 2002 No 682.

primary concern here has been with monetary policy, since institutions other than banks are issuing the equivalent of money. The impact on money supply has thus far been minimal, given both the low number and low average value of e money transactions. For the future, however, other regulatory concerns such as the use of e money for money laundering is likely to loom larger.

In terms of non-regulatory issues e money is governed by the written terms and conditions governing its issue. We have just seen this in relation to e money payment cards, but the same applies to digital cash.[82] The Banking Codes provide that in the event of the loss of an e money card, the consumer must bear the losses. However, unless the issuer can show that customers have acted fraudulently or without reasonable care, they are not liable for any value transferred from their account to their e money card after they have informed the issuer that it has been lost or stolen or that someone else knows the PIN. Prior to that the maximum they are liable for under the Codes is £50 if their card is credited with unauthorized withdrawals prior to the issuer being informed of the loss, theft, or misuse.[83] A recommendation of the European Community is that issuers should generally be liable for lost value and for defective payment when either is attributable to a malfunction of the e money card or instrument.[84] This seems eminently possible.

IV. PAYMENT METHODS CROSS-BORDER

Credit transfers are a vital means of payment cross-border: their features were effectively examined in the last chapter. At the retail level payment cards, which have just been considered, are also prominent in cross-border payment. In this part of the Chapter we supplement the previous discussion by addressing a number of miscellaneous issues. The eurocheque, which featured in the last edition of this book, has passed into the dustbin of history.

A. THE USE OF CHEQUES AND DRAFTS

Cheques and drafts are used internationally, but not extensively. The statistics relate mainly to retail payments. First, we know that retail cross-border payments are a small proportion of all retail payments. The European Banking Federation reported that in 1991 cross-border payments effected in European Community Member States constituted only 1.3 per cent of the total number of payment transactions. There is a clear variation between Member States, determined in part by geography. Thus while on

---

[82] Cf. A. Tyree, 'The Legal Nature of Electronic Money' (1999) 10 *JBFLP* 273.

[83] Banking Code, Jan. 2001, §§14.9–14.12; Business Banking Code, Mar. 2002, §§14.9–14.12.

[84] Commission Recommendation of 30 July 1997 concerning transactions by electronic payment instruments [1997] OJ L208/52, Art. 8.4.

average there are only 1.2 payments per inhabitant across the Community, for Luxembourg the figure is 17. The bulk of cross-border retail payments are face-to-face with cash or payment cards. In terms of remote payments cards and credit transfers dominate.

What of larger payments for commercial transactions? Writing in 1960 one eminent banking lawyer said that payment by cheque in international transactions was significant.[85] Presumably he was writing of the commercial use of cheques. An Italian banker has said: 'Bank-to-bank payment orders are not the only way to move money around the world; there are also cheques and bank drafts. . .'.[86] There is a dearth of statistics but at the present day the use of cheques for cross-border commercial payments seems to be getting smaller (although the amounts involved are still considerable). Some importers will still try to pay by cheque to unsophisticated counterparties because of the 'float' they receive until the cheque is presented and their account debited. Under systems like Citibank's 'Worldlink System' subscribers using a computer link to the bank, print and draw cheques in numerous foreign currencies on branches of the bank, its affiliates, or correspondents.[87]

In commercial transactions cross-border payment may also be by foreign draft, which is a cheque drawn by the payor's bank on a bank in the beneficiary's country. For the payor the foreign draft may be more convenient if more control is required over the release of a payment, or if documents or messages must be sent with payment. Because a foreign draft is drawn by a bank on another bank, it is almost equivalent to cash, and some businesses like the comfort of being paid that way. Although a transfer by electronic means will be cheaper, the payor will probably need to know the details of a beneficiary's bank account (although it is possible to send instructions to pay cash to a person who supplies correct identification). For a recipient the disadvantage of transfer by electronic means is that, unless it has a direct link with its bank, it is not assured that payment has been made unless it contacts the bank or vice versa. Especially with a foreign draft, a recipient knows it has been paid.

The declining number of cross-border payments by ordinary cheque is not for any legal reason. Indeed, the European Court of Justice has held that national law cannot require prior approval before moving bearer cheques between Member States.[88] The Court has derived this not from Article 28 or 49 of the Treaty, but from the Capital Movements Directive, designed to abolish restrictions on capital movements.[89] The Court's reasoning seems to apply *a fortiori* to non-bearer cheques. Rather the reason for the relatively insignificant use of ordinary cheques across borders is

---

[85] H. Harfield, 'Checks in International Trade' (1960) 15 *Bus. L* 638, 638.

[86] R. Polo, 'Netting Arrangements' in C. del Bustro (ed.), *Funds Transfer in International Banking* (Paris, ICC, 1992), 40. For use of cheques in association with bills of exchange: R. Welter, 'Bills of Exchange in International Trade', in P. Sarcevic and P. Volken (eds.), *International Contracts and Payments* (London, Graham & Trotman, 1991), 100.

[87] *Centrax Ltd. v. Citibank NA & ANR First* [1999] EWCA Civ. 892, [1999] 1 All ER (Comm) 557 (CA).

[88] *Aldo Bordessa and Vincente Mari Mellado* [1995] ECR I–0361.

[89] Dir. 88/361/EEC [1988] OJ L178/5, art. 1, 4. See now in the EC Treaty, Art. 56.

purely practical, mainly that the bank charges are disproportionate to the amount transferred.

The process for use of an ordinary cheque in a cross-border transaction is, in theory, simple. A in Britain draws a cheque on its bank, the drawee (paying) bank, and gives it or sends it to B in Germany. B takes it to its, the remitting bank. The remitting bank sends it for collection to a bank in Britain, probably its correspondent bank.[90] That collecting bank will then present the cheque for payment through a domestic clearing system (assuming A's bank is not the correspondent of B's bank, which makes things simpler).[91] The collecting bank will obtain value in the currency of the drawer's country, pounds, but will then convert it into euros.

In processing the cheque, B's bank may negotiate it, in other words purchase it from B and then collect it on its own behalf. B will then have its account credited fairly quickly, although its bank will retain the right to take the payment back if the cheque is not paid when presented to the foreign bank. B's bank may not be prepared to negotiate a foreign cheque if B is not an established customer or if the risk is otherwise considered too high—because of the country on which it is drawn, its value, and sometimes the bank on which it is drawn. Then the cheque will be collected on behalf of B. Typically collection on behalf of a customer is governed by the Uniform Rules for Collection issued by the International Chamber of Commerce.[92] The current, the 1995, uniform rules, are adhered to by banks in many jurisdictions and are widely used.[93] The rules apply because they are incorporated specifically by reference. Alternatively they may apply to a collection as a result of a course of conduct between B and his bank, or as a matter of trade usage (commercial custom).[94] Cheques are among the 'financial documents' which can be collected under the uniform rules.[95] While banks under the rules must act in good faith and exercise reasonable care, in utilizing the services of other banks such as a correspondent a remitting bank does so for the account of and at the risk of the customer.[96] The English courts have held that a collecting bank (the correspondent bank) is entitled to an indemnity in its favour, as against the remitting bank (B's bank) as well as to the benefit of an implied warranty from the latter that its customer is entitled to the proceeds of any cheque paid in.[97]

While simple in theory, the cost of processing foreign cheques means that it is uneconomic when they are of modest value. Indeed, some banks may simply refuse to arrange the collection of foreign cheques for customers (and indeed will be obliged to refuse if exchange control prohibits payment to non-residents). This is quite apart from other disadvantages in using this method—the lack of transparency and the

---

[90] 39 above.   [91] Individual presentment is ignored in this account.

[92] ICC publication no 522. See E. Ellinger, 'The Uniform Rules for Collection' [1996] *JBL* 382. The uniform rules apply to both retail and wholesale collections but, because of the amounts involved, seems to have a greater relevance to the latter.

[93] E. Schinnerer, 'Collection by Banks and its Documents', in N. Horn (ed.), *The Law of International Trade Finance* (Deventer, Kluwer, 1989), 188.

[94] *Harlow and Jones Ltd. v. American Express Bank Ltd.* [1990] 2 Lloyd's Rep. 343.

[95] Art. 2(b)(i).   [96] Arts. 9, 11(a).

[97] *Honourable Society of the Middle Temple v. Lloyds Bank plc* [1999] 1 All ER (Comm) 193.

time that effecting final payment takes. A knows the cost of sending the cheque but does not know the conversion rate which will be used or the fees which the other banks will levy.[98] Neither does B necessarily know what time it will take before definitely receiving funds, which may be considerable if a correspondent bank has to be involved. Delays between a bank giving or receiving value and either debiting or crediting a customer's account can also result in 'an indirect and non-transparent remuneration (in addition to the commission for international payment that it will charge . . .)'.[99]

The process for foreign drafts is simpler. A obtains a foreign-currency bank draft from its bank, in other words a cheque drawn by its bank on a bank in Germany where it has an account, probably its correspondent bank. A gives it or sends it to B. B's bank will present it to the German bank on which it is drawn, through the German domestic payment system. That bank will debit A's bank with the amount.[100]

B. LONDON CURRENCY CLEARINGS

In some financial centres there are special clearing systems which expedite the clearing of payments drawn in a foreign currency. These may be instruments given by A to B where they are both in that jurisdiction, or where B is in a different jurisdiction. Such a system is the Tokyo Dollar Clearing in Japan.[101] Another such system is the so-called Currency Clearings in London, and is illustrative of this type of arrangement. This clears and settles unconditional paper-based currency payments such as cheques and bank drafts, provided they are drawn on or payable at participants in the United Kingdom.[102] In the year to December 2001 the total number of items cleared in all these currencies was about 330,600, of which 40 per cent was in US dollars. In the scheme of international payments the amounts were not large.[103]

Currency Clearings originated as the London US Dollar Clearings in 1975, to enable dollar cheques and drafts in London to be cleared on a same date basis. Clearing now extends to the euro, the Japanese yen, and the Canadian and Australian dollar. The Currency Clearings was conceived as excluding large interbank and Eurocurrency payments. Indeed in June 1981 a 'Working Party on Wholesale Dollar Clearing', set up with the Bank of England and representatives from the banking

---

[98] Typically collection charges are for the account of the payee (B in our example): see Uniform Rules for Collection, Art. 21.

[99] M. Dassesse, 'Cross-border Payments: A Need to Reassess Priorities' [1993] 5 *JIBL* 169, 172.

[100] Unlike 'bank cheques' (or cashier's cheques in American terminology) bank drafts are in law, cheques; 'bank cheque', which is a cheque drawn by a bank on itself, is not a cheque in English law: Bills of Exchange Act 1882, s. 73. In England the term 'bank draft' is used confusingly to cover both bank drafts and bank cheques.

[101] B. Geva, *The Law of Electronic Funds Transfers* (New York, Matthew Bender, looseleaf), para. 4.02(3).

[102] There is an account of the scheme in *Libyan Arab Foreign Bank v. Bankers Trust Co.* [1989] QB 728.

[103] *Annual Review of the Association for Payment Clearing Services 2001* (London, 2001), 13.

associations, concluded that there should not be a wholesale dollar clearing in London. The credit risk of a wholesale clearing was one consideration in this conclusion. Now the rules of the Currency Clearings specifically exclude instruments drawn in settlement of interbank foreign exchange deals and for principal amounts of interbank Eurocurrency transactions.[104]

Direct access to the Currency Clearings is limited to settlement banks, but there are other participating banks which have agency arrangements with a settlement bank. Not all participating banks participate in all currencies. Each settlement bank nominates a branch to act as its co-ordinating branch and as agent for the participating banks. Among settlement banks one bank acts as settlement agent for the other settlement banks for each currency. Settlement between the settlement agent and the others is effected through specified correspondent banks in the country of the currency: settlement members having to pay the settlement agent instruct their correspondent in sufficient time for value to be obtained in cleared funds according to the timetable. Similarly, the settlement agent instructs its foreign correspondent to pay the receiving settlement members in sufficient time for value to be obtained in cleared funds according to the timetable.[105]

C. TRAVELLERS' CHEQUES

Travellers' letters of credit can be traced back to those given in 1201 by King John to two emissaries to the Pope. As evolved in subsequent centuries, they were letters addressed by the issuing bank to specified correspondents abroad, which the traveller called upon to obtain advances.[106] The modern-day travellers' cheque varies with the issuer, but at base the issuer (which may be a bank) sells the cheques to the traveller, who can then obtain cash from, or make payment abroad to, a third party prepared to accept them. A travellers' cheque contains a promise by the issuer to pay a third party, or to the order of a third party, provided the countersignature, added in its presence, coincides with the signature already placed there by the traveller at the time of purchasing the cheques.

Travellers must pay for their travellers' cheques in advance of their use, as with e money cards, by contrast with cheques, debit cards, and, of course, credit cards. However, the advantage of travellers' cheques is said to be that if they are stolen, the traveller will be reimbursed by the issuer. Arguably there is implied right to this effect in the contract with the customer.[107] There may also be a collateral contract resulting, for example, from the claims made in the issuer's marketing material. However, the express written contract may be especially onerous, obliging the traveller to

---

[104] Clearing House Rules for the Currency Clearings, r.4.
[105] R.7(d)(e).
[106] E. P. Ellinger, 'Travellers' Cheques and the Law' (1969) 19 *U Tor. LJ* 132, 132–4.
[107] *El Awadi v. Bank of Credit and Commerce International SA Ltd.* [1990] 1 QB 606.

demonstrate, as a precondition of obtaining reimbursement, that he or she has safeguarded, without negligence, each travellers' cheque against loss or theft.[108]

D. EUROPEAN COMMUNITY REGULATION

The high cost of cross-border payments to individuals and small- and medium-sized enterprises led to a European Community Directive in 1997, which imposes transparency requirements and minimum obligations on payments between European countries not exceeding €50,000.[109] In summary, the transparency requirements are that banks must provide a written indication of the time needed for payment to be credited to the payee's bank; the time needed from receipt by the payee bank for the payment to be credited to the payee's account; the manner of calculation of any commission, fees, and charges; the value dates (when respective accounts of payor and payee are debited and credited); and details of the complaint and redress procedures. Subsequent to payment, the Directive sets out certain information to be provided to customers—a reference identifier, the amount, the charges etc., the value date, and any exchange rate—but this is not mandatory and banks can avoid having to do this by their standard terms. Among the minimum obligations set out in the Directive are execution of payment within the time agreed: in the absence of agreement the payor bank must pay the payee bank within five business days, and the payee bank must credit the account by the end of the following day. Generally speaking, the full amount must be paid to the payee, without any deduction, and there is a money back guarantee if payment goes astray.

   As well, the European Commission has been attempting to accelerate smaller cross-border payments in Europe and to reduce the charges. At one time it had instituted proceedings against more than 130 banks for colluding to keep prices high. After the introduction of the euro, the Commission was especially concerned that within the eurozone charges for cross-border payments continued to be higher than for domestic payments. As a result the European Community has adopted a regulation imposing price control on smaller cross-border payments in euro.[110] The UK has not extended the approach to sterling denominated payments on the grounds that competition will be inhibited.

---

[108] *Braithwaite* v. *Thomas Cook Travellers Cheques Ltd.* [1989] QB 553.

[109] Cross-Border Credit Transfers Directive, 97/5/EC [1997] OJ L43/25, implemented in UK by Cross-Border Credit Transfer Regulations 1999, SI 1999 No 1876. See R. Hooley, 'EU Cross-Border Credit Transfers—The New Regime' [1999] *BJIBFL* 387. Cf Banking Code, Jan. 2001, §12; Business Banking Code, Mar. 2002, §12.

[110] Regulation (EC) No 2560/2001 on Cross-Border Payments in Euros [2001] OJ L344/13.

10

SETTLEMENT, CLEARING, AND NETTING

From some general principles of payment in Chapter 8, we moved in Chapter 9 to some particular methods of payment. At various points in these chapters, and at other points in the book, settlement, clearing, and netting have been touched on. We have noted that settlement between banks could be through a settlement account maintained for that purpose, or across the books of the central bank. With international payments, we saw that each bank may maintain a correspondent account for the other.[1] Where the banks are not linked in this way, they may well use a third, correspondent bank to this end. Moreover, they may be linked to a network providing clearing and settlement facilities: these are discussed in general terms in the first section of this Chapter.

Netting reduces the amount of value and the volume of transfers necessary to discharge payment obligations. It has been important for payment systems, and is thus conveniently dealt with in this Chapter as well. However, two points should immediately be made about netting. First, netting in large-value payment systems is no longer to be recommended. The systemic risks are so great that the Working Group on EC Payment Systems adopted as a principle that, as soon as feasible, every Member State should have a real-time gross-settlement system (RTGS) through which as many large-value payments as possible should be channelled.[2] The United Kingdom implemented this recommendation in 1996.[3] Real-time gross settlement is a feature of the Target system—the payment system arrangement for the euro operated by the European Central Bank. Core Principle IV of the G10 report on systemically important payment systems means that in most countries it should be the goal for at least one payment system to provide real-time final settlement during the day, and that this is especially desirable in countries with large volumes of high value payments and sophisticated financial

---

[1] 40 above.

[2] See Ad Hoc Working Group on EC Payment Systems, Issues of Common Concern to EC Central Banks in the Field of Payment Systems (1992), 58–9; Working Group on EC Payment Systems, *Minimum Common Features for Domestic Payment Systems* (1993), Principle 4; Working Group on EU Payment Systems, *Developments in EU Payment Systems 1995* (Frankfurt, EMI, 1996), 9; D. Schoenmaker, *A Comparison of Net and Gross Settlement* (LSE Financial Markets Group, Special Paper No 60, 1994).

[3] See 'The Development of a UK Real-time Gross Settlement System' (1994) 34 *BEQB* 163.

markets.[4] As well as cost, real-time gross-settlement systems have their own problems, notably 'gridlock'—the risk that if one or more participants have their performance deferred, until they have built up sufficient credits from others, this will glue up the whole system.[5]

Secondly, netting has a relevance for banking well beyond payment systems. It features as well with interbank deposits, foreign exchange, securities, and derivatives. It operates in OTC and exchange markets. It is now a recognized concept in regulatory laws.[6] In all, it is central to the safety and efficiency of financial systems, even if there is a trend towards real-time gross settlement in payment systems.[7]

Finally, mention should be made of message systems, which are analytically distinct from payment and clearing system. These are designed to provide a secure method for transferring payment instructions between banks. SWIFT, based in Brussels, is the best-known of the international message systems and it can be noted that in 2001 it conveyed 926 million payment messages.[8] Its operation is beyond the scope of this book. One obvious legal issue is its liability if somehow messages between banks go wrong.

I. SETTLEMENT AND CLEARING

A. SETTLEMENT AND CLEARING SYSTEMS

Settlement is the transfer of value to discharge a payment obligation. In theory legal tender may be used, but in a modern economy movements on bank accounts are the most frequently accepted substitute. A party can discharge a payment obligation to its own bank by having the bank debit its account. If the settlement of a payment obligation between two parties is effected by the debiting and crediting of their accounts, the bank (or banks) are intermediaries in the payment process. Important to their role as intermediaries is that banks can provide credit to their customers in the expectation of the transfer of value.

As for the settlement of payment obligations between banks themselves, a bank must send a payment message to a bank with which it has settlement facilities. In the case of domestic payments, i.e. within the one jurisdiction, these facilities will often be because both have accounts with the central bank. (In England such banks are

---

[4] Committee on Payment and Settlement Systems, *Core Principles for Systemically Important Payment Systems* (Basle, BIS, 2001), para. 3.4.2.

[5] M. Giovanoli, 'Legal Issues Regarding Payment and Netting Systems', in J. Norton, C. Reed, and I. Walden (eds.), *Cross-border Electronic Banking* (London, Lloyd's of London Press, 1995).

[6] 91 above.

[7] P. Wood, *Title Finance, Derivatives, Securitisations, Set-off and Netting* (London, Sweet & Maxwell, 1995), 151.

[8] e.g. SWIFT, *Annual Report 2002* (Brussels, 2002), 6.

called clearing banks.) Otherwise a bank will need to send payment messages through a bank which has such an account: settlement between the non-clearing and clearing bank will be as between correspondent banks. In the case of correspondent payments, i.e. between different banks in different jurisdictions, the settlement facilities will be provided by the correspondent arrangements between the banks. As for the correspondents themselves, settlement will typically involve a movement on the accounts which they as local banks have with the central bank in that foreign jurisdiction.

The timing of settlement can be immediate, during the same day, at the end of the banking day, or on a later day (the 'value' day). Settlement can be gross, in that value is transferred for each individual payment obligation. Net settlement is where payment obligations are off-set against similar counter-obligations. With netting, gross obligations are discharged by the transfer of the net amount of value due from each obligor.

In practice, therefore, settlement involves information being conveyed from one bank to another, often through intermediate banks, and to the central bank. Organizing, and possibly recording such information centrally, is sometimes called clearing (hence the notion of a clearing house).

In its narrow sense, 'clearing system' is a mechanism for the calculation of mutual positions within a group of participants ('counterparties') with a view to facilitate the settlement of their mutual obligations on a net basis. In its broad sense, the term further encompasses the settlement of the obligations, that is, the completion of payment discharging them.[9]

Each jurisdiction has its various clearing and settlement systems for payment. For example, each has a system for clearing cheques and for retail debit and credit transfers. The extent and operation of these varies considerably. Moreover, at the heart of each jurisdiction's payment system is a large-value payment (or transfer) system (LVTS) for the relevent currency—CHIPS and Fedwire in the United States (dollars), TARGET in the European Community (euros), CHAPS in the United Kingdom (pounds), and so on.[10] These domestic systems have international implications. If, say, a German bank wants to pay sterling to a Chinese company it will probably instruct its London correspondent to pay the Chinese company's bank through the latter's London correspondent. The transfer between the London corespondents will probably be effected through London's large-value payment system, CHAPS.[11] Similarly, if the German bank had wanted to pay euros, the euro payment system, TARGET, might have been used. Because of the importance of the US dollar, perhaps the most important clearing system, used on an international basis, is the CHIPS

---

[9] B. Geva, 'The Clearing House Arrangement' (1991) 19 *Can. BLJ* 138, 138. See also F. Andrews, 'The Operation of the City Clearing House' (1942) 51 *Yale LJ* 582.

[10] The systems are described in European Central Bank, *Payment and Securities Settlement Systems in the European Union* (ECB, Frankfurt, 2001) (the 'Blue Book') and in regular reports of the Committee on Payment and Settlement Systems, published by the Bank for International Settlements in Basle.

[11] In the event that both the German and Chinese banks have the same London correspondent, there will be no need, of course, to use a payment and clearing system. See 236 above.

system in New York. If the German bank had wanted to pay US dollars the CHIPS system would probably have been used.[12]

While domestic systems may have international implications, there are clearing systems which are cross-border in character. First, at the retail level, there are the global credit and debit card systems. Giro systems are also used.[13] Secondly, in addition to TARGET, there is a private euro clearing and settlement system set up by the Euro Banking Association and involving banks from both within and outside the European Community. Thirdly, there are the clearing systems for the international trade in securities which work on a delivery against payment basis. As well as handling securities transfers, they also provide cash management services through an extensive network of correspondent banks.[14]

B. THE RULES OF CLEARING SYSTEMS

Clearing systems are governed by rules. The rules are not the whole story, for there are also institutions and technical mechanisms which are basic to a clearing system, and indeed to payment systems in general.[15] At its simplest, banks bind themselves by contract to comply with the rules. Non-compliance with the rules could result in disciplinary action, and ultimately exclusion from a clearing system. The binding effect of the rules, on the banks themselves, and on other parties such as bank customers, has been explored at some length in Chapter 2.[16]

The rules may be overlaid by statutory law. A good example is the European Community Settlement Finality Directive, to which we return shortly. Another is in the relationship in the United States of Article 4A of the Uniform Commercial Code—which deals with 'funds transfers'—to CHIPS. The origins of Article 4A are explained in the abandonment of the Uniform Payment Code project, which was designed to cover all payment systems, just as Article 9 of the UCC had brought together the different types of secured transactions under the same umbrella.[17] Article 4A has been widely adopted in US jurisdictions, including New York. Article 4A can be varied by agreement.[18] It does not cover all aspects of electronic funds transfers: for example, it does not cover conditional payment orders, such as payment against delivery of documents or securities.[19] Article 4A also excludes debit transfers.[20]

---

[12] These various systems are analysed in B. Geva, *The Law of Electronic Funds Transfers* (New York, Matthew Bender, looseleaf).

[13] H. Verkoren, 'Eurogiro: Transparency in Cross-border Payments', *Payment Systems Worldwide*, Winter 1993–4, 28.

[14] See *Committee on Payment and Settlement Systems, Recommendations for Securities Settlement Systems* (Basle, Bank for International Settlements, 2000).

[15] B. J. Summers, 'The Payment System in a Market Economy', in B. J. Summers (ed.), *The Payment System* (Washington, DC, IMF, 1994), 1.

[16] 51 above.

[17] See H. Scott, 'Corporate Wire Transfers and the Uniform New Payments Code' (1983) 83 *Colum. LR* 1664.

[18] UCC §4A.501(a).   [19] UCC §4A.103(a)(1)(i).   [20] UCC §4A.103(a)(1)(ii).

CHIPS is governed by Article 4A and its own rules, the latter prevailing except as otherwise provided in Article 4A. One difference between the CHIPS rules and Article 4A is that payment orders under the latter can be cancelled or amended if notice is received at a time and in a manner affording the receiving bank a reasonable opportunity to act before it accepts the order.[21] Under CHIPS rules release of a payment message to the receiving bank marks the point at which the message cannot be revoked.[22] In effect, Article 4A has extraterritorial effect, since most US dollar payments are routed through CHIPS, even though the parties may have no other connection with the United States.

The rules of a clearing system will provide for a range of matters. Cheque-clearing rules may contain straightforward provisions, for example, how and when cheques must be returned by a paying bank as dishonoured. By not complying with the rules about dishonour, a paying bank may be obliged to pay the collecting bank in any event.[23] With high value clearing systems, the rules may be more complex. The rules about revocation must be certain, for unless it is clear that a payment order can no longer be withdrawn, further payment orders on the back of it are at risk. A major problem is settlement risk—the failure of a member to settle and the consequent disruption as other members, in turn, have difficulty in settling. One solution to this is the introduction of real-time gross settlement as in CHAPS. Since each payment is immediately settled, systemic risk is eliminated. However, with real-time gross settlement banks need resources before making payments, and so the rules may provide for what liquidity members must have.[24]

With net settlement the clearing rules need to be clear about finality—when a bank sending a payment order has settled the associated obligation to transfer value. The rules need also to provide limits on the exposure of the members to each other: these may be limits on the exposure of each member to each other member, together with limits on the exposure of the whole membership to any one member. Moreover, the rules need to provide for an actual failure of one of the banks to settle. Thus there may be a loss-sharing arrangement whereby each participant provides a portion of the funds necessary to complete settlement, should a participant be unable or unwilling to meet its settlement obligations. The agreement will be secured by collateral sufficient to cover a default by a system net debtor.

Clearing-system rules obviously need to be interpreted. Clearly this must be done against the background of the manner and operation of the particular system in question. A legalistic interpretation of the rules would be fatal. To avoid this the CHAPS rules provide that they must be construed in accordance, not only with the law, but also to take into account 'banking practices current in England and

[21] UCC §4A.211(b).

[22] CHIPS Rules and Administrative Procedures, Jan. 2001, r.2(a). See *Delbrueck & Co.* v. *Manufacturers Hanover Trust Co.*, 609 F 2d 1047 (2nd Cir. 1979).

[23] e.g., *Parr's Bank (Ltd.)* v. *Thomas Ashby & Co.* (1898) 14 TLR 563.

[24] D. Schoenmaker, *A Comparison of Alternative Interbank Settlement Systems* (London), LSE Financial Markets Group, 1995.

Wales'.[25] Construing the rules needs also to accord with the nature of the rules themselves. The rules for London clearings are largely operational in nature, and tend to avoid defining the rights and duties of the parties.

Informal settlement of disputes between banks over the rules of a payment clearing system is usually encouraged. At the end of the day, however, the courts may become involved in construing the rules if the members of the system cannot agree. The rules may deal with a particular matter expressly. If not, a solution may be readily implied. In some instances the rules may be rules of imperfect obligation, although evidence, perhaps the best evidence, of the practice of bankers.[26]

Sometimes, the courts will need to construe the clearing rules because they arise in disputes between non-members and a member. Customers may in some circumstances be able to invoke the clearing rules for their benefit. The converse situation—the extent to which non-members of a clearing system (or market) are bound by its rules—was discussed earlier.[27] Although '[one] who employs a banker is bound by the usage of bankers',[28] this is only if the clearing rules are usages, and if they are reasonable. Bingham J said in a London arbitration on the London clearing rules:

If it is to be said that the drawer loses [a] right as a result of a private agreement made between the banks for their own convenience, the very strongest proof of his knowledge and assent would be needed, not only because of the general rule that an individual's rights are not to be cut down by an agreement made between others but also because, in this particular case, the rights of additional parties (such as indorsers) could be affected.[29]

C. REGULATING CLEARING SYSTEMS

Countries differ in the manner in which regulatory law intrudes onto payment-clearing systems. Partly it is a matter of legal culture; partly of how the problems are perceived; and partly also of the structure of the banking and financial sector.

(i) Prudential Regulation

Three examples illustrate the range of approaches to regulating payment-clearing systems for prudential reasons. First, in the United Kingdom there is no need for prior authorization of a payment-clearing system, nor are they recognized clearing houses under the Financial Services and Markets Act 2000. The only direct statutory power is that the Bank of England can designate payment clearing systems under the settlement finality regulations so their rules take precedence over normal insolvency law if a member is subject to insolvency proceedings.[30] Secondly, with the Eurosystem, Article 105(2) of the European Community Treaty defines as a basic task the

---

[25] R9.1.   [26] e.g. *Ryan* v. *Bank of New South Wales* [1978] VR 555.

[27] 52 above.   [28] *Hare* v. *Henty* (1861) 10 CBNS 65, 142 ER 374, 379.

[29] *Barclays Bank plc* v. *Bank of England* [1985] 1 All ER 385, 394.

[30] 283 below. In May 2000 the Bank of England designated the CHAPS Sterling and CHAPS Euro systems. Banks of England, *Oversight of Payment Systems* (London, 2000), 20.

promotion of the smooth operation of payment systems. To this end Article 22 of the European Central Bank Statute gives the European Central Bank a power to make regulations, which are directly applicable in the Member States which adopt the euro.[31] So far, the Eurosystem has relied as in the UK on informal tools (e.g. moral suasion) and on the powers of Member States' national central banks.[32] Finally, Canada has enacted a Payment Clearing and Settlement Act 1996. It allows the Bank of Canada to designate clearing and settlement systems which may be operated in such a manner as to pose systemic risk. The Bank can then take supportive action to facilitate the operation of a system, but the other side of the coin is that it becomes subject to directives issued by the Bank, it must give the Bank notice of any significant change to the system (e.g. in its rules), and it can be audited and inspected by the Bank.

In general, the operation of payment-clearing systems is not subject to the same extensive legal regulation as banks. There is of course indirect regulation, since the members—the banks themselves—are strictly regulated. The systemic consequences have been the main prompt for payment system regulation. The Settlement Finality Directive of the EC is illustrative.[33] In essence it suspends the ordinary rules of insolvency in relation to the failure of a participant in a designated clearing system in favour of the rules of that system, including the default arrangements set out in the rules. Designation turns on the systemic risks posed by a failure in the system and whether the system has adequate resources, rules (e.g. on revocation), and default arrangements. Thus payment orders and netting are legally enforceable against third parties, and netting cannot be unwound, so long as the payment orders were entered into the system before the moment when insolvency proceedings were opened. There is a limited exception that a payment order can still be binding after that moment, if the order is carried out on the same day and the settlement agent, central counterparty, or clearing house was not aware, nor should it have been aware, that insolvency proceedings had commenced.[34] (The UK implementing regulations put the latter in terms of the settlement agent, central counterparty, or clearing house not having notice of the commencement of insolvency at the time of settlement of the payment order, but been deemed to have such notice 'if it deliberately failed to make enquiries as to that matter in circumstances in which a reasonable and honest person would have done so'.[35]) The moment of entry of a payment order into the system is defined by the rules of the system.[36] So, too, is the moment beyond which a transfer order cannot be revoked. In jurisdictions where it operates, the midnight rule has no effect. Finally, the

---

[31] 'The Role of the Eurosystem in Payment and Clearing Systems', *ECB Monthly Bulletin*, Apr. 2002, 49–53.

[32] *Blue Book*, 20.

[33] Directive on settlement finality in payment and securities settlement systems 98/26/EC [1998] OJ L166/45.

[34] Art. 3.1.

[35] Financial Markets and Insolvency (Settlement Finality) Directive Regulations 1999, SI 1999 No 2979, r.20(2), (3).

[36] Art. 3.3.

Directive provides that the law governing the payment system determines the rights and obligations of a participant in the system in the event of insolvency proceedings being commenced against it.[37] Specifically, it insulates collateral security in the system from the insolvency law of a participant.[38] Neither provision can be fully effective against the insolvency law of a participant from a state not bound by the Directive, a point recognized in the UK implementing regulations.

Typically, then, the legal framework of the systems is principally a matter of the contract between the parties in the rules. Particular payment methods, such as cheques, may be governed by legislative provisions which have implications for clearing. However, the actual operation of the systems is largely a matter of private rule-making. Even the Canadian legislation leaves the rules of a payment system largely to its members. The exception to private rule-making is where the government itself runs the system, where by definition public rule-making is involved. Thus in the United States, the Federal Reserve's Regulation J defines the rights and responsibilities of those using its Fedwire system.[39]

Whatever the legal position, however, there is governmental oversight of payments systems, including their rules. The integrity of payment systems is high on the agenda of central bankers. The risks can be categorized as:

Credit risk:	the risk that a counterparty will not ever meet an obligation.
Liquidity risk:	the risk that a counterparty will not settle an obligation, when due.
Operational risk:	the risk of system failure (e.g. computer systems), human error, or fraud, giving rise to exposure and possibly loss.
Legal risk:	the risk of an unexpected application of the law or of legal uncertainty, leaving the payment system or its members with unforeseen financial exposure and causing possible loss.

A failure in a payment system could have serious repercussions for the banking system as a whole. It could also result in calls on the central bank to provide liquidity through lender-of-last-resort facilities.[40] Thus central banks want to be assured of the quality of those participating in a system and about the management and operation of the system itself. Since the central bank ultimately enables settlement to be made between banks on the back of clearing, and since banks want assurance that lender-of-last resource facilities are in place, a central bank will have plenty of leverage in ensuring that its prudential concerns are met, albeit without having to take explicit legal steps.

---

[37] Art. 8.   [38] Art. 9.1.

[39] T. Baxter, 'Core Legal Principles across Major Large-value Credit Transfer Systems', in M. Giovanoli (ed.), *International Monetary Law* (Oxford, OUP, 2000), 362.

[40] 110 above.

(ii) Competition Law

Access on the part of banks to payment and clearing systems has been a matter of some controversy. With some clearing systems, for example, existing members have taken the view that open access is unfair since they have invested the money and effort in establishing them. But there are larger issues as well, in broad terms the operational and financial integrity of the system. Compliance with the rules of the system, such as those about the timetable and the accuracy of work, is just one aspect. Another is the extent to which members, or any lender of last resort, can be exposed to credit and liquidity risks if one member is unable to meet a debit position on settlement.

In the UK an inquiry into bank competition noted the impact for payment systems of 'network effects', each user of a payment system gains from the addition of new users, such as the advantages to customers as more retailers join a payment card system. That means established payment systems have a benefit because customers faced with a choice prefer to use the larger system, other things being equal, and existing users have invested in equipment relevant to the existing system and may be reluctant to duplicate it for a rival system. The inquiry conceded that with a high value payment system the credit and liquidity risks meant that there was little scope for non-banks to join. With low value payment systems, however, it concluded that the operational risks could not justify the existing restrictions on membership. Legislation furthering competition in this area is to be introduced.[41]

Among the activities in Annex 1 to the EC Credit Institutions Directive, which banks (credit institutions) can freely undertake in other Member States, as well as their own, by the establishment of branches or the supply of services, are 'money transmission services' and the 'issuing and administering [of] means of payment (e.g. credit cards, travellers' cheques, and banker's drafts)'.[42] Thus a bank established in one Member State can open an account and issue a payment card or cheque book to someone in another Member State, and a bank established in one Member State can open an ATM terminal in another state for use of its customers or others when in that state. But can a bank established in one Member State demand membership of a payment-clearing system in another Member State? It would seem not, unless the payment and clearing system operated a discriminatory policy against banks of another Member State. This seems to follow because, although the Directive ensures that a bank does not need authorization apart from its home-country authorization to engage in money-transmission services and the means of payment, it does not overcome access barriers unless these are in breach of the general principles of Community law. The same analysis seems to apply with the right of free establishment under the EC Treaty itself.[43]

However, competition law also is relevant to the question of access. Thus in the European Community a bank denied access to the payment-clearing system in

[41] D. Cruickshank, *Competition in UK Banking* (London, TSO, 2000), ch. 3; HM Treasury, *Competition in Payment Systems* (London, 2001).
[42] 83 above.   [43] 434 below.

another state, or to that of a more general European system, could argue that this is in breach of Articles 81 and 82. Where a cross-border credit-transfer system constitutes an 'essential facility' it must be open for further membership, provided that candidates meet appropriate membership criteria. An essential facility is a facility or infrastructure without access to which competitors cannot provide services to their customers.[44] The membership criteria must be non-discriminatory and justifiable. The outcome will be a matter of assessing whether the rules of the clearing system are designed to exclude potential competitors, whether they can be justified because the applicant lacks the standing to guarantee the operational and financial integrity of the system, and so on. It may be said that a bank without direct access to a payment system can always use a member bank as agent.

Again we are in the area of soft law. The central banks of the European Union have committed themselves to a principle of no discrimination in access: in other words, no discrimination can be made between home-based banks (credit institutions) and banks licensed in other EC countries which ask to participate in local interbank payment systems, either through their local branches or directly from another Member State. Applicants, however, may be required to establish that they can meet the relevant legal provisions of the host country. They also have to comply with the necessary technical requirements of the system, although these requirements must not be discriminatory. Access criteria must be transparent and may additionally include adequate financial strength of the institution; a minimum number of transactions; the payment of an entry fee; the approval (on technical or creditworthiness grounds) of either the controller of the system or the direct participants; and the approval of the central bank (if this is legally possible under the law of the country).[45] Core Principle IX of the G10 report on systemically important payment systems is that there should be objective and publicly disclosed criteria for participation, which permit fair and open access. Access criteria based on risk measures may be justified under this principle as can those ensuring operational efficiency such as minimum payment amounts. However, the concern about risk may be addressed by controls over credit and liquidity risk rather than access. Criteria which are motivated by a desire to retain the benefits of the investment in establishing the system are not justified, and that concern can be addressed in other ways such as pricing policy.[46]

---

[44] Notice on the application of the EC competition rules to cross-border credit transfers, [1995] OJ C251/3, paras. 25–6.

[45] Working Group on EC Payment Systems, *Minimum Common Features for Domestic Payment Systems* (1993), Principles 1–3; *Blue Book*, 20–1.

[46] Committee on Payment and Settlement Systems, *Core Principles for Systemically Important Payment Systems* (Basle, BIS, 2001), 51–2.

II. NETTING

Before proceeding further it is useful to rehearse the benefits of netting. Because netting reduces the extent to which value must be transferred, it directly lowers transaction costs.[47] With n participants in a netting system the volume of transfers is a maximum of $n(n - 1) \div 2$ with bilateral netting, and a maximum of n with multilateral netting.[48] Netting also reduces transaction costs indirectly by standardizing procedures and producing operational savings. From the point of view of the banks themselves netting therefore has advantages, although it is fair to say that in so reducing transactions netting also means that there is not the same capacity to generate income by providing certain services. It is the impact of netting in reducing risk, however, which explains its importance to banks and other financial intermediaries.

Netting can be classified along various dimensions.[49] As indicated, one possibility is whether netting is bilateral or multilateral. Bilateral netting has a significant impact only between active counterparties, but multilateral netting can provide benefits even if a party has only occasional transactions with a counterparty. Building on the distinction one can analyse the extent to which different bilateral or multilateral systems control the behaviour of participants: for instance, individual participants may be responsible for controlling their risks *vis-à-vis* counterparties, or risks may be controlled centrally by obliging a participant to establish a bilateral credit limit with every other participant and maybe a net debit position *vis-à-vis* all participants.

Central control may also be imposed by a clearing house being substituted as the counterparty for each transaction. Legally this can occur by the rules of the clearing house providing that a contract between counterparties is extinguished and replaced by a contract between each counterparty and the clearing house.[50] Alternatively a contract between the clearing house and each party could result automatically when the parties transact: legally the clearing house makes an open offer to act as principal which is accepted by the conduct of the parties transacting.[51] The contracts between each member and the clearing house could be continuously netted and novated. Since until final settlement the clearing house still has an exposure as principal, it must monitor credit and liquidity risk *vis-à-vis* each member for every transaction.

---

[47] e.g. R. Polo, 'Netting Arrangements' in C. del Busto, *Funds Transfer in International Banking* (Paris, ICC, 1992).

[48] D. Schoenmaker, *Externalities in Payment Systems: Issues for Europe* (LSE Financial Markets Group Special Paper No 55, 1993), 11.

[49] See e.g., W. Hartmann, 'Aspects of International Netting and Settlement Arrangements', Paper delivered to the 8th Annual Seminar on International Financial Law (Vienna, 1991); F. Nassetti, 'Basic Elements in the Maze of Netting' [1995] 4 *JIBL* 145; P. Wood, *Title Finance, Derivatives, Securitisations, Set-off and Netting* (London, Sweet & Maxwell, 1995), 152–9.

[50] M. Hains, 'Reflections on the Sydney Futures Exchange Clearing House: The Rise of the Mirrored Contract Theory' (1994) 5 *JBFLP* 257, 273–80.

[51] G. Duncan, 'Clearing House Arrangements in Foreign Exchange Markets', in *Symposium Proceedings. International Symposium on Banking and Payment Services* (Washington DC, 10–11 Mar. 1994).

Members may be capped as to what transactions they can enter. Moreover, they may be required to provide adequate credit support, for example through security (collateral), cash, or lines of credit.

A second classification of netting is according to the nature of the underlying transactions—payment-system netting, foreign-exchange netting, derivative-contracts netting, and so on. Banks enter such transactions on their own behalf or provide payment services for those of their customers who have done so. Thus netting has been a common feature of national payment systems, although with large-value payment orders we have seen that central banks are tending to insist on gross settlement.[52] The sheer magnitude of foreign-exchange transactions between banks has led to bilateral and multilateral netting systems, mainly run by consortia of banks. Foreign-exchange netting reduces transaction costs and risk. These netting arrangements involve standard agreements and computer systems.

A third way of classifying netting, the one used here, attempts to highlight its legal nature. *Position (or payment) netting* is the simplest, in that parties agree by contract to settle net their various obligations, which fall due on the same day and which are of the same type or in the same currency. The original gross obligations remain until settlement brings about an effective discharge. *Close-out netting* takes effect on a defined event of default of a counterparty: future obligations of the parties are thereupon terminated, and the gains and losses of the parties calculated and then off-set (netted) against each other. Close-out netting can therefore apply to obligations with different value dates and a different character. Close-out netting can be coupled with novation, so that it applies not to the parties' gross obligations but to their novated net obligations. Novation can be automatic and continuous until any final net amount is settled.[53] Neither of these different forms of netting are terms of art.

A. NETTING AND RISK

A party entering into transactions with a counterparty obviously faces a credit risk— that the counterparty will be unable to meet its payment obligations. Related to credit risk is sovereign risk, whereby a counterparty is unable to meet its obligations because of an action of its government (e.g. exchange control). In addition a non-defaulting party may face a liquidity risk: to meet its own payment obligations, which it was anticipating doing from the settlement of the counterparty's obligations, it now faces temporary difficulties as it borrows or liquidates assets. If it is unable to do the latter there is systemic risk—the inability of the counterparty to settle places others in the same position.

Netting lowers credit risk in the event that a counterparty fails, since all of the losses and gains on the parties' contracts are off-set against each other. A lower credit

---

[52] 277 above.

[53] Common lawyers tend to think of novation as tripartite, but there is clear authority that only two parties need be involved: *Scarf v. Jardine* (1882) 7 App. Cas. 345, 351.

risk means that bank supervisors need less capital for a bank.[54] Banks are also less likely to be in breach of the large exposure limits *vis-à-vis* their customers, which banking regulators set for prudential reasons. So, too, with systemic risk.

Yet netting does not address all risks which arise on settlement in the same way as it reduces liquidity needs by reducing the amounts to be settled on each value day. So-called Herstatt risk occurs in the foreign-exchange market because of the need to settle different legs of a single transaction in different markets, and in different markets, and in different times zones.[55] Say Bank A and Bank B have netted all the yen and dollar obligations for a particular value day, so that Bank A owes Bank B dollars, and Bank B owes Bank A yen. If the settlement of yen is through FEYCS (the foreign exchange yen clearing system of Japan), and that of dollars through CHIPS in New York, Bank B incurs a credit risk because the settlement of the net yen obligation becomes final up to some fourteen hours before the net dollar obligation.[56] An analogous risk to Herstatt risk in securities transactions is that delivery of the securities might not coincide with payment—hence the need for so-called delivery versus payment (DVP) mechanisms.[57]

In fact foreign-exchange settlement risk is not simply because of the need to settle different currencies in different markets and time zones but also a product of the timing of settlement and of reconciliation procedures. For example, the exposure in settling a yen–dollar spot trade could be reduced by paying out yen as late as possible, but this might not occur because of a bank's operating procedures for issuing and cancelling yen payment instructions, and the procedures used by its correspondent bank for yen. In the result the yen payment instruction might become irrevocable well before the yen payment system even opens. At the other end of the settlement process, the bank's procedures and correspondent banking arrangements may mean that it takes a day or two to confirm that the counterparly paid the dollars.[58]

A failure by a participant to settle in accordance with the rules has particular repercussions in a netting system because of the inevitable time-lag to settlement, and because of the temptation to rely in the meanwhile on the net position in anticipation that settlement will occur. At one level a failure may simply constitute a liquidity problem, but at another level there is systemic risk if other participants have planned to use the proceeds of settlement to cover their own obligations, or in expectation of settlement have made payments or have advanced credit to their customers.[59] That

---

[54] 90–1 above.

[55] C. Borio and P. van den Bergh, *The Nature and Management of Payment System Risks* (Basle, BIS Economic Papers No 36, 1993), 21–7.

[56] B, Summers, 'Clearing and Payment Systems: The Role of the Central Bank' (1991) 77 *Federal Reserve Bulletin*, 81, 85n.

[57] Bank for International Settlements, *Delivery Versus Payment in Securities Settlement Systems* (Basle, BIS, 1992).

[58] New York Foreign Exchange Committee, *Reducing Foreign Exchange Settlement Risk* (New York, NYFEC, 1994).

[59] G. Juncker, B. Summers, and F. Young, 'A Primer on the Settlement of Payments in the United States' (1991) 77 *Federal Reserve Bulletin*, 847, 853.

netting might disguise risks and concentrate them so as to increase the likelihood of one participant's failure undermining the financial condition of others has attracted the attention of bank supervisors.[60] It is the impetus behind the move to real-time continuous gross settlement for high value payment systems. In 2001 CHIPS adopted a halfway house, moving from traditional net end of day settlement to a process involving repeated settlements throughout the day of batches of bilaterally and multilaterally off-setting payments.

In the event of default by a participant in a netting system, the other participants are most likely to suffer some losses. If the netting agreement proves to be legally unenforceable, those losses may be the gross amount of credit exposure to the defaulter. Moreover, surviving participants may find that the liquidator of the defaulter engages in so-called cherry picking of executory contracts: instead of netting the unrealized gains and losses on all, it chooses to enforce those contracts which are profitable to the estate of the defaulter, but disaffirms the remainder. The losses in relation to the latter are the gross amounts of credit exposure to the defaulter. As we have seen, the EC Settlement Finality Directive prevents such cherry picking.

B. LEGALITY OF NETTING

The legal enforceability of netting against a defaulting participant is thus a constant concern for public policy. It is the first of the minimum standards laid down in the Lamfalussy Report for the design and operation of cross-border and multi-currency netting schemes. It features prominently in the conditions proposed by the Basle Committee on Banking Supervision and the EU if bank supervisors are to recognize for capital-adequacy purposes the risk-reducing effect of bilateral netting. And it has led to the promotion of recent legislation in the United States and Europe to overcome doubts about netting's efficacy in an insolvency.[61]

(i) Position Netting

Position (payment) netting, in the absence of insolvency, depends on contract. Parties agree to accept a net amount in discharge of the settlement obligations which would otherwise arise on the same value day. Legally the gross obligations may remain, but the means by which they are discharged is modified. Credit risk is therefore not affected. A transfer by one of the parties of its claims would not disadvantage

---

[60] e.g., Bank for International Settlements, *Report of the Committee on Interbank Netting Schemes of the Central Banks of the Group of Ten Countries* (Basle, 1990) (The Lamfalussy Report).

[61] Financial Institutions Reform, Recovery and Enforcement Act 1989, and amendments in 1990 to the Bankruptcy Code, had primary importance for swaps netting. Title IV of the Federal Deposit Insurance Corporation Improvement Act 1991 had its genesis in protecting multilateral netting in CHIPS: H. Cohen and M. Wiseman, 'Legal Issues Relating to Netting', International Symposium on Banking and Payment Services, Washington, DC, Mar. 1994; D. Cunningham and W. Rogers, 'Netting is the Law' [1990] *BJIBFL* 354.

In fact English lawyers do not in general see insolvency law problems with netting: see Financial Law Panel, *Guidance Notice. Netting of Counterparty Exposure*, 19 Nov. 1993; City of London Law Society. Banking Law Sub-Committee, *Netting of Foreign Exchange Transactions. Guidance Note*, 28 Sept. 1994.

the counterparty who would still be able to net claims against either the transferor or transferee. Contract may provide for 'cross-product' netting, whereby foreign exchange and derivatives contracts (say) are netted.

In a pure multilateral netting system the parties may by contract have agreed to delete a party's obligations if it has defaulted, and to recalculate the net positions. If this does not achieve settlement, then the parties may also have agreed to unwind all obligations, leaving the parties to achieve individual settlement independently of the system. In either event there remain the obligations between each non-defaulting party and the defaulting party. In the absence of other provisions insolvency law governs their discharge, although close-out netting may avoid its rigours. In a multi-lateral netting system, where the clearing house is principal with each member, the failure of one does not affect the others directly. Under the rules, however, the clearing house will be able to call on its members to cover any losses it suffers. The rules may allocate these losses between members in the same way as would have occurred with pure multilateral netting.

(ii) Close-out Netting

Close-out netting, as the term suggests, enables a non-defaulting party to terminate ('close out') executory contracts between itself and a defaulting party. Termination occurs when specified events happen, such as adverse action by a regulator, or the initiation of rescue procedures or insolvency. Terminating the contracts prevents 'cherry picking' by the liquidator of the defaulting party. In the main, only executory contracts are capable of being terminated—forward contracts (e.g. commodities, currency, securities), swaps, and so on. With non-executory contracts termination is not generally possible, for example if prior to insolvency a non-defaulting party has already transferred foreign currency or securities to the defaulter. After termination the next prong to close-out netting is for the non-defaulting party to calculate the gains and losses to itself.[62] In relation to terminated contracts a present value must be given to future claims. The method is to calculate losses and gains on the basis of a notional purchase of a substituted performance in the market.

Finally the gains and losses have to be allocated. One approach is that a defaulter should pay any loss suffered by a non-defaulter, but that a non-defaulter need not pay any gains. Such one-way payment or walkaway clauses are disapproved by some standard-form contracts and also by bank regulators who, for capital-adequacy purposes, require two-way payments, so that the defaulter pays losses but also receives profits. This is because in some jurisdictions for the insolvent to be deprived of gains under a walkaway clause would be regarded as void because it reduces the assets available to the general creditors. Two-way payments are required, for example, by the

---

[62] There are examples in the standard-form contracts used in the markets: e.g., 1992 ISDA Master Agreement (Multicurrency-Cross Border); British Bankers Association, The 1997 International Foreign Exchange Master Agreement Terms (IFEMA). See generally R. Gilbert, 'Implications of Netting Arrangements for Bank Risk in Foreign Exchange Transactions' (1992) 74 *Federal Reserve Bank of St. Louis Monthly Review* 3.

IFEMA Terms. Gains and losses are offset in a base currency and a net figure is payable either by the non-defaulting or defaulting party. The Basle Committee in April 1993 justified requiring two-way payments because not paying a defaulter its gains would introduce an element of 'instability and uncertainty . . . in a netting environment'.[63] English lawyers say, however, that, as a matter of common law, it has never been the rule that an innocent party who accepts a repudiation of a contract must pay the defaulter any gains.[64]

How well does close-out netting stand up to insolvency law? A few jurisdictions look on it with disfavour because it prevents the liquidator or trustee in bankruptcy from swelling the assets with profitable contracts, to be available for creditors generally. There is also a problem in jurisdictions with a 'midnight hour' rule, i.e. one which invalidates all transactions beginning from midnight of the day prior to insolvency.[65] Elsewhere it seems that it is only transactions after the commencement of the insolvency which are at risk. The legal justification of close-out netting is that a non-defaulting party is simply exercising its contractual right to terminate on an event of default; is mitigating its losses by immediately calculating them (since movements in the market are a potential risk for both parties);[66] and is doing so by resort to what is *prima facie* a reasonable method.[67] One aspect is that if the method involves a genuine pre-estimate of losses, the English rule against penalties is not a threat.

For close-out netting the Basle Capital Accord amendments for bank capital demand that the netting constitute a single legal obligation. And the ISDA Master Agreement 1992 purports to transform all transactions into a single agreement, although *quaere* whether this results, given the separate documentation contemplated for each transaction. Presumably the rationale of the one single legal obligation is to prevent cherry picking. It is not a prerequisite to netting in English law that there be one single contract.

(iii) Insolvency

There is a conflict between jurisdictions which permit mutual claims and obligations to be set off and those which generally forbid a set-off.[68] In jurisdictions such as England, which mandate insolvency netting, a bank can measure its exposure to

---

[63] Basle Committee on Banking Supervision, *The Supervisory Recognition of Netting for Capital Adequacy Purposes*, Apr. 1993, 3.

[64] The matter is discussed e.g., E. Coleman, 'Netting a Red Herring' (1994) 9 *BJIBFL* 391. See also P. Wood, *English and International Set-off* (London, Sweet & Maxwell, 1989).

[65] P. Wood, *Title Finance, Derivatives, Securitisations, Set-off and Netting* (London, Sweet & Maxwell, 1995), 195.

[66] For this reason the ISDA Master Agreement 1992 has been questioned, at least as a matter of English law, in permitting the parties' exposure to be calculated by reference to market prices at a date other than the termination date: D. Turing, 'Set-off and Netting: Developments in 1993 Affecting Banks' [1994] 4 *JIBL*, 138, 139.

[67] B. Crawford, 'The Legal Foundations of Netting Agreements for Foreign Exchange Contracts' (1993) 22 *Canadian BLJ* 163, 172–3.

[68] P. Wood, *Title Finance, Derivatives, Securitisations, Set-off and Netting* (London, Sweet & Maxwell, 1995), 200–1 has a list.

counterparties, not by the sum of the gross amounts (which is the 'at worst' case), but by the net of individual transactions.[69] Netting in such cases occurs irrespective of any agreement or not between the parties, happens automatically on insolvency, and cannot be affected by any subsequent assignment of a claim.[70] It applies to all mutual dealings, including executory contracts where the losses and gains are estimated. Mutuality goes to the capacity in which parties hold claims, not to the connection between them. Parties must be the beneficial owners of claims owed to them and personally liable on claims owed by them. Transactions by a party with a parent company are not mutual with transactions with a subsidiary;[71] nor are transactions between brokers acting as agents on behalf of customers. But mutuality does not demand that the claims arise, for example, under the same master agreement, or on the same market.

C. MULTI-JURISDICTIONAL AND MULTILATERAL NETTING

So far we have examined how these various forms of netting operate in terms of the law of a single jurisdiction. Of course cross-border netting must hold up in all relevant jurisdictions. The proper law of the netting agreement is clearly crucial, as is any other jurisdiction which the parties to the agreement have chosen for dispute-resolution. But there may be other jurisdictions where, for example, a non-defaulting party can be sued for gross amounts despite the netting, or where the defaulting party can be subjected to insolvency rules which do not recognize the netting. Thus a non-defaulting party may be sued elsewhere because the underlying obligations to be netted have a proper law, or place of performance in, or other nexus with, a jurisdiction different from that of the netting agreement. Clearly the courts of a party's incorporation have jurisdiction to wind it up, but other courts may claim to be able to do so, for example where a party has a place of business or assets.[72] Netting of particular transactions needs to be tested against the law of each of these various jurisdictions.

The prudential considerations regarding multi-jurisdictional netting have been addressed by requiring written legal opinions that, in the event of a legal challenge, the relevant courts and administrative authorities will find the bank's exposure to be a net amount under (1) the law of the jurisdiction in which the counterparty is incorporated and, if the foreign branch of a counterparty is involved, also under the law of the jurisdiction in which the branch is located; (2) the law that governs the individual transactions; and (3) the law that governs any contract or agreement necessary to effect the netting. In other words, the netting must be enforceable under the laws of each of the relevant jurisdictions. Moreover, procedures must be in place to ensure that the legal characteristics of netting arrangements are kept under review in the light of possible changes in relevant laws. Yet firm legal opinions about the soundness of netting are not sufficient. Practical steps must also be taken, for example, in relation to

---

[69] R. 4.90 of the UK Insolvency Rules 1986.
[71] Cross-guarantees may, however, result in mutuality.
[70] *Stein v. Blake* [1996] AC 243.
[72] e.g. UK Insolvency Act 1986, pt. V.

cross-border and multi-currency transactions. There are a number of options, from a modest lengthening of opening hours (to address Herstatt risk) to the establishment by central banks through a 'common agent' of multi-currency accounts and settlement facilities.[73]

As we have seen, what appears to be multilateral netting may well be bilateral netting, in that the clearing house becomes the principal in each transaction between clearing-house members. Each contract between the parties is replaced by a contract between each party and the clearing house. There are two contracts, where previously there was one.[74] True multilateral netting involves net balances being struck. If effective it can substantially reduce liquidity and credit exposures in aggregate, although, depending on how losses are allocated, it may cause a participant which had few dealings with a defaulting counterparty to bear a greater burden than would occur with bilateral netting.

Yet multilateral netting is most vulnerable to insolvency law. In jurisdictions whose insolvency law demands mutuality, multilateral netting can be challenged because it involves the set-off of non-mutual claims.[75] Making a clearing house the principal in each transaction is one way of overcoming this problem. There is then mutuality between the clearing house and each member of the system. The clearing house is made the principal in some financial and commodity markets and in some foreign-exchange netting systems.

There are a number of well-used techniques to reduce the risks in multilateral netting. The Lamfalussy Report identified a number in the minimum standards it postulated for netting systems.

III. Multilateral netting systems should have clearly-defined procedures for the management of credit risks and liquidity risks which specify the respective responsibilities of the netting provider and the participants. These procedures should also ensure that all parties have both the incentives and the capabilities to manage and contain each of the risks they bear and that limits are placed on the maximum level of credit exposure that can be produced by each participant.

IV. Multilateral netting systems should, at a minimum, be capable of ensuring the timely completion of daily settlements in the event of an inability to settle by the participant with the largest single net-debit position.[76]

The credit limits mentioned in standard III can be bilateral limits in relation to each other participant and net debit limits in relation to all other participants collectively.

---

[73] Bank for International Settlements, *Central Bank Payment and Settlement Services with respect to Cross-Border and Multi-Currency Transactions* (Basle, 1993). See D. Cunningham and C. Abruzzo, *Multibranch Netting—A Solution to the Problems of Cross-Border Bank Insolvencies* (London, International Bar Association, 1995).

[74] B. Hills *et al.*, 'Central Bank Counterparty Clearing Houses and Financial Stability', *Bank of England Financial Stability Review*, June 1999.

[75] *British Eagle International Airlines Ltd.* v. *Compagnie Nationale Air France* [1975] 1 WLR 758, [1975] 2 All ER 390 (HL).

[76] *Report of the Committee on Interbank Netting Schemes of the Central Banks of the Group of Ten Countries* (Basle, Bank for International Settlements, 1990) (Lamfalussy Report), 5.

The implementation strategy for Core Principle V of the G10 report on systemically important payment systems demands that additional financial resources be available to meet the liquidity risk arising from an inability to settle on the part of one or more participants. These will usually involve a combination of committed lines of credit and a proof of collateral, large enough in relation to the maximum settlement obligation, and whether the system is designed to withstand an inability to settle by the participant with the largest single settlement obligation or a more widespread inability to settle.[77]

[77] Committee on Payment and Settlement Systems, *Core Principles for Systemically Important Payment Systems* (Basle, BIS, 2001), 33.

PART IV

BANKS AND FINANCE

11

LENDING

Lending is central to a bank's business. In bankers' jargon, loans are a bank's assets. Depending on their nature, and in the absence of repayment problems, they can produce a steady stream of income. Under the Credit Institutions Directive of the European Community, lending is one of the two elements defining a bank (or credit institution as banks are called)—'an undertaking whose business is to receive deposits or other repayable funds from the public and to grant credits for its own account'.[1] But just as some financial institutions are able to lend money without raising it by means of deposits from the public—for instance, they use the wholesale markets—so banks need not necessarily lend to make a profit. The tragedy in some countries has been that banks have sometimes found it more profitable to buy government bonds, thereby funding presidential palaces, bloated armies, and so on, rather than to provide credit to small businesses, farmers, and consumers.

Commercial lending by banks can take various forms.[2] Bankers often use the generic term 'facility' to describe them all. The most basic is the term loan, where a specified maturity date sets the time for ultimate repayment. Term loans vary from the short term (bridging finance, working capital, trade finance) through the medium term (two to five years for working capital, some capital expenditure), to the long term (project finance, capital expenditure). A term loan can have a fixed repayment schedule. It can also be a revolving facility, in that during its term the borrower can repay amounts but then reborrow, so long as the overall limit of the facility is not exceeded. Thus the revolving credit facility is akin to the overdraft, which is a loan facility enabling a customer of a bank to make payments from its account not in excess of a set ceiling. But there is a vital difference: while a revolving credit facility is for a fixed period—indeed powerful borrowers might negotiate them for five to ten years for general corporate purposes—the overdraft is generally speaking repayable on demand. It has been a criticism of British banks that, unlike the German and Japanese banks, they have favoured overdraft lending at the expense of providing more certain, and longer-term financial backing for business.[3]

These, then, are the basic forms of bank lending—term loans, revolving facilities,

---

[1] 8 above.

[2] This Chapter is not primarily concerned with banks lending to individuals. Much personal credit is provided by point-of-sale credit.

[3] See generally, e.g., M. Collins, *Banks and Industrial Finance in Britain 1800–1939* (London, Macmillan, 1991); P. Marsh, *Short-Termism on Trial* (London, Institutional Fund Managers' Association, 1990).

and overdrafts. We need note only that there are a variety of other facilities which are built on these, and that a range of credit possibilities may be combined in the one, aptly named, multiple-option facility. The main aim of this Chapter is to examine the fundamentals of agreements establishing a commercial loan facility. In practice lending agreements vary greatly in detail: for a simple overdraft the facility letter may be short or non-existent; for a multiple option facility it may be 100 pages or more. Yet there are common features which are directed at mitigating the credit risk any bank faces in advancing moneys and, in the more elaborate and international facilities, other risks such as those arising from currency fluctuations, market disruptions, and governmental action which interferes with the performance of the borrower's obligations (performance risk). First, however, a few words about whether there is a loan agreement, and how its terms are identified.

I. IDENTIFYING THE AGREEMENT

A. INFERRING AN AGREEMENT AND AGREEMENTS TO AGREE

Once a bank has discussions with a potential borrower, there is the possibility of liability as a result of what is said (or not said) or done (or not done). Various dimensions to this were examined in Chapter 7. As a matter of contract, the law of agency determines whether the bank's officials had actual or apparent authority to bind the lender in purporting to approve a loan.[4] In exceptional cases moneys may be paid over before a loan agreement is finalized. In those circumstances it may be that a contract can be inferred from the conduct of the parties. On the other hand there may be a common understanding that the payments are contingent upon the conclusion of a loan agreement, so that they are immediately repayable if negotiations are to no avail. If ultimately a contract is agreed in this type of situation, then it may have retrospective effect.

A second possible, but again unusual, situation is where a loan document is signed but requires further agreement on particular matters. The latter does not necessarily make it void, but it is generally said that English law does not countenance agreements to agree, to negotiate, or to negotiate in good faith.[5] Other systems of law embody varying precontractual duties to negotiate in good faith.[6] In reaching its conclusion English law works on the assumption that negotiations are inherently adversarial, whereas in fact there may be elements of co-operation. It also overlooks the commercial reality that business people are sometimes comfortable with an agreement to agree or to negotiate and that, in any event, commercial contracting these days is frequently a process, necessarily completed in stages.

---

[4] 137 above.   [5] *Walford* v. *Miles* [1992] 2 AC 128 (HL).   [6] 199 above.

B. VARYING THE AGREEMENT

There may be more than one agreement. One example is where a lending agreement is accompanied by a side letter. Side letters can constitute a variation of the main agreement or a collateral contract with terms distinct from those in the main agreement. Alternatively, a side agreement may simply evidence a likely course of conduct by a bank (e.g. on default), rather than one to which it is contractually bound.[7]

Another example is where there is a later, seemingly inconsistent, provision, for example in the security agreement contemplated by the loan agreement. A court may be able to reconcile the provisions; in the case of an incompatibility, it may find that the original loan agreement has been varied. A rescheduling agreement—yet another example—will quite clearly vary the original loan agreement.

C. COMMITMENT LETTERS

A regular product of negotiations between a bank and a prospective borrower is a document which sets out the nature of the contemplated loan, and some or all of the terms to which it will be subject. Various terms are used to describe such documents, such as offer documents, heads of agreement, and commitment letters (the term used here).[8] To what extent are such documents legally binding? This may become important where a borrower refuses to pay, or a bank refuses to repay, a fee referred to in the document, or where one of the parties refuses to complete the more formal documentation contemplated by it. Generally speaking, as a matter of contract law, just because parties contemplate further terms to be agreed, or the execution of a more formal document, does not mean that they do not intend to be bound immediately. Failure to reach agreement or execute the formal document does not of itself invalidate the earlier agreement.

There are as many types of commitment letter as there are prospective loans. In general the legal character of commitment letters depends on their individual nature. With some, however, the authorities suggest a formulary approach. A commitment letter 'subject to contract' will automatically be regarded as not being binding. In exceptional circumstances the parties may subsequently agree to convert such a letter into a contract, there may be representations giving rise to a collateral contract, or some form of estoppel may arise to prevent the parties from denying the terms and effect of transactions envisaged by it. The phrase 'subject to documentation' does not have the same conclusive quality. 'Documentation satisfactory to us [the bank]' is clear; it is for the bank to determine whether the final documentation is satisfactory (a subjective test), not some reasonable person (an objective test). So long as the bank acts honestly, the commitment letter is not uncertain. Even if the test is objective—for

---

[7] *Lloyds Bank plc* v. *Lampert* [1998] EWCA Civ. 1840, [1999] 1 All ER (Comm) 161 (CA). See M. Furmston, T. Norisada, and J. Poole, *Contract Formation and Letters of Intent* (New York, Wiley, 1999).

[8] Cf. in other contexts the letter of intent: R. Lake and V. Draetta, *Letters of Intent and Other Precontractual Documents* (2nd edn., New Hampshire, Butterworths, 1994).

example 'subject to usual documentation'—that will not necessarily make the matter too indefinite for the court, knowing the circumstances, may be able to decide what the terms should be.

Otherwise, the test is whether the commitment letter was intended to be binding (the traditional approach of English law), or whether a binding letter is consistent with the reasonable expectations of the parties (the approach of some modern writers). In determining this issue, reference ought to be made to all the circumstances, not just to the letter itself. The following may be relevant:

(i)   How the document is described is some indication. For example, a document expressed as an 'agreement' and containing a sentence 'this is a provisional agreement until a fully legalized agreement is drawn up' may well indicate an intention to be bound. 'Offer document' seems to suggest less of an intention to be bound than 'commitment letter'. However, provision is sometimes made for the offer document to be signed as 'accepted' by a prospective borrower and returned. At that point the description 'offer' would become irrelevant in determining the issue. In some financial contexts the term 'commitment' itself does not connote a binding commitment, only a definite interest.[9]

(ii) Whether the commitment letter contains a reasonably complete statement of the proposed terms is a good indication, but not determinative. Documents which do not contain all the terms which ordinarily occur in such agreements may still, in the light of the surrounding circumstances, be intended to be binding.[10] This is because the law regards it as a matter for the parties to decide the terms by which they are to be bound. If a term typically regarded as important is omitted, the less likely it is that a court can regard them as having agreed to all the terms. A commitment letter may contain so few of the terms which would be expected in the formal documentation that it cannot be said that the parties intended to be bound. Omission of the interest rate, the currency (in the case of an international loan), or the terms of repayment would be fatal in the absence of custom or commercial usage. At the other end of the spectrum, even though the terms appear complete, other circumstances may negate the parties' intention to be bound.

(iii) Reference may be made to the steps preceding, and subsequent to, the completion of the commitment letter. Protracted discussions about the proposed contents of the letter, a considerable degree of formality, a belief by the parties that it will be binding, and subsequent conduct such as payment of the commitment fee pursuant to the letter, are some limited indications that the parties intended it to be binding.

---

[9] *Governor and Company of the Bank of Scotland* v. *3i plc* [1993] BCLC 968, 1022–7.

[10] See the Canadian appellate decisions: *First City Investments Ltd.* v. *Fraser Arms Hotel Ltd.* (1979) 104 DLR 3d 617, [1979] 6 WWR 125; *Accord Holdings Ltd.* v. *Excelsior Life Insurance* (1983) 44 AR 368, (1985) 62 AR 234. See M. Ogilvie, 'Canadian Bank-Lender Liability', in W. Blair (ed.), *Banks, Liability and Risk* (3rd edn., London, LLP, 2001), 287–9.

Just because a commitment letter is not binding does not mean that the expenses and fees mentioned in it are not payable. The fees may be characterized as fees payable for considering whether to grant the proposed loan, for an 'in-principle' commitment to lend, or for the issue of the commitment letter itself. The first is straightforward: the fees are a sort of processing cost. The second and third suggestions will no doubt be met by the objection that fees are not payable for what is not legally binding (an in-principle commitment, or the letter itself), but it is a question of the parties' intention. The commercial world often places a high value on what is legally un-enforceable. It is suggested that the non-binding commitment letter, especially from a reputable financial institution, is in the same category. Of itself it might be of great value to a prospective borrower in relation to third parties, e.g. in a takeover situation where the bidder can use it in negotiations over control of the target.

D. THE ADVISER-ARRANGER

This section addresses the position when a bank acts as a financial adviser to a customer, but subsequently assumes the role as an arranger of finance for it. This may, but need not be, through a syndicate of banks.[11] Is it caught by any conflict of interest because of the two roles it performs? In other words, can a borrower subsequently claim that, in advising on the structure of the finance, negotiating with sources of finance, developing or reviewing documentation, and so on, the bank acted in a manner which precluded the customer from obtaining a better deal?

In dealing with other potential sources of finance as arranger, the bank is acting as the borrower's agent. It is thus subject to fiduciary duties: one aspect is that it must avoid a conflict between its own interest in providing the finance itself, and its duty to the borrower in obtaining the best terms. However, it may be possible to imply a term into a written contract if there is some 'trade usage', not inconsistent with the written terms. The position whereby a bank acts in both roles—as adviser and as arranger—is common in the market, so that it is arguable that 'trade usage' supports the assump-tion by a bank of a dual capacity. Perhaps the simplest solution from the bank's perspective is an explicit contractual term, enabling it to recommend itself as the source of funds.

As agent, the bank also must act honestly, with the reasonable care, skill, and diligence of a banker in its position. Say that the borrower claims subsequently that the bank's advice was deliberately couched in such a way that only it, the bank, could be awarded the mandate. That would be an allegation of fraud, i.e. dishonesty. English lawyers are reluctant to allege fraud, and English courts reluctant to find it proven. Otherwise, subject to any contractual provision to the contrary, the bank is not guaranteeing the most competitive terms. As indicated above, it is enough that it uses the care, skill, and diligence of a reasonable banker to obtain such terms. Thus the bank is not obliged to do more than is ordinarily expected of a financial adviser in

[11] 304 below.

notifying the market and potential financiers of a possible financing. It is not concerned primarily with getting the finest terms available, but rather with conducting the process so that the goal of adequate financing is achieved. For example, a potential financier offering the finest terms may also be the institution which is too inexperienced or over-confident in its ability to put a bank syndicate together, if that is how the financing is to be effected.

E. MANDATE OF LEAD BANK IN FORMING BANK SYNDICATE

Bank syndicates have been dealt with at some length in Chapter 2. However, in the context of the relationship between a bank and a borrower—the focus of this Chapter—it is worth mentioning the obligation of the arranging, or lead, bank once it is given the mandate to form a syndicate for the financing. Under the so-called 'letter of mandate', the lead bank will usually undertake to use reasonable or best endeavours to effect the customer's aims. English law does not regard a contract to use reasonable or best endeavours as too uncertain, although the object to be achieved must be definite. An agreement to put a bank syndicate together would be definite enough, and thus an enforceable legal obligation. The test of reasonable endeavours is objective. As for best endeavours, one interpretation is that that demands a greater effort—a near absolute commitment. The more generally accepted interpretation is that contained in the Unidroit Principles of International Commercial Contracts,[12] that under a duty of best endeavours in performance of an activity, a party must make such efforts as would be made by a reasonable person of the same kind in the same circumstances, but that there is no obligation to achieve a particular result. Thus best endeavours requires the bank to place itself in the shoes of the customer, but not so as to tarnish its image as a bank. For example, in using best endeavours to put a syndicate together a lead bank would need to leave no stone unturned, but would not be obliged to engage in such tactics as would alienate other banks.

II. THE FACILITY AND ITS REPAYMENT

Assume there is a binding loan agreement. From the commercial viewpoint, the terms relating to the type of facility and its repayment are central. When can the facility be drawn upon? Is the borrower obliged to borrow, or the bank to lend? For what purpose can the facility be used? When and how must it be repaid? What interest is payable? Can default interest be imposed for late payment?

---

[12] (Rome, Unidriot, 1994), Art. 5.4(2): see L. Gorton, 'Best Efforts' [2002] *JBL* 143, 152–62.

A. DRAW-DOWN AND DEMAND FACILITIES

Generally, a term loan can be drawn down during a limited period after the agreement is signed (sometimes called the commitment period). If it can be drawn down in tranches, these may be of a specified minimum amount. A number of days' notice of a draw-down will be provided for, so a bank can make arrangements to have the funds available. At the end of the commitment period the obligation to lend lapses. By contrast, an overdraft or revolving facility can be drawn upon at any time. In other words, the bank is obliged to advance funds during the life-time of the facility. This has implications for the assignability of revolving facilities.[13]

The difference between the overdraft and revolving facility is that the overdraft is, of its nature, repayable on demand by the bank. So too with an uncommitted, 'on-demand' facility—the bank has a right to make immediate demand for repayment. A bank needs no reason, let alone a breach by the borrower, for it to require repayment of an on-demand facility. It may be that the demand character of an overdraft or facility is negatived by particular words or circumstances, for example if it were granted for a period of twelve months for a specific purpose. Moreover, English courts will not imply a term to give reasonable notice before a bank refuses further finance under an overdraft or demand facility.[14]

The law in other jurisdictions has been more generous to borrowers with a demand facility. In *KMC Co. Inc.* v. *Irving Trust Co.*,[15] it was held that the implied obligation of good faith may impose on lenders the duty to give notice to a borrower, before refusing to advance further funds under a financial agreement with a demand provision. A Canadian court has applied a reasonableness test (seven days in that case) to termination of a line of credit.[16] But other Canadian cases have drawn the distinction between enforcing security (reasonable notice required), and termination of an on-demand line of credit (no surprise, and hence no need for notice). In Germany termination of the lending contract—as with continuous contracts generally—requires the bank to show cause. Objectively banks must show that there has been an impairment of the loan or a material deterioration of the borrower's status. Moreover, the demands of good faith and fair dealing also have an impact here. There is some recognition of the principle German courts that lenders may have become so involved with a borrower that they owe a duty of loyalty to stand by them during temporary financial difficulties.[17] There is no such duty in English law, except that in particular circumstances a bank by its behaviour towards the borrower may be estopped from withdrawing credit without reasonable notice.[18]

---

[13] 357 below.   [14] 223–4 above.

[15] 757 F 2d 752 (6th Cir. 1985).

[16] *Whonnock Industries Ltd.* v. *National Bank of Canada* (1987) 42 DLR 4d 1 (CA).

[17] U. Schäfer, 'Lender Liability Towards Financially Troubled Borrowers in German Law', in W. Blair (ed.), *Banks, Liability and Risk* (3rd edn., London, LLP, 2001) 220–34.

[18] Cf. *Bank of Ireland Ltd.* v. *AMCD (Property Holdings) Ltd.* [2001] 2 All ER (Comm) 894.

B. THE OBLIGATION TO LEND, *FORCE MAJEURE*, AND REMEDIES

The borrower will not, generally speaking, be obliged to draw on a facility. What of the bank: is it obliged to lend once a notice of draw-down is given? Assume a significant and sudden change in the condition of the borrower or in the general economic climate. As we shall see shortly, there may be an illegality clause in the agreement, which enables the bank to terminate. Moreover, an event of an extraordinary nature which, in the opinion of the bank, will materially and adversely affect the ability of the borrower to perform its obligations may constitute an event of default, enabling the bank to cancel the facility. In the absence of such specific contractual provision, what rights does the common law give the borrower if the bank refuses to lend because of the changed situation?

Specific performance, the authorities say, is not generally available to a borrower to compel the bank to lend. Damages are an adequate remedy, especially in the case of an unsecured loan: specific performance would create a position of inequality, since the borrower would get the money but the lender would have only the hope of repayment. The Privy Council has said, without elaboration, that in 'exceptional cases' specific performance might be awarded in the case of an unsecured loan agreement.[19] Possibly this would be if there were necessarily difficult questions about the measure and remoteness of damages or obviously great delay and expense in obtaining them.

The rules for damages are easy enough to state. The general rule is that only nominal damages are available, since it is assumed that a borrower can always obtain money in another quarter.[20] If money is obtainable only at less advantageous rates, damages can be awarded to cover the difference. This is fairly straightforward— quotations can be obtained, say, for a loan on similar terms, albeit at a higher interest rate. But there are difficulties. Is it correct to assume that the borrower would have satisfied all the conditions precedent, if it has not done so at the time the bank pulls out? There is a case for saying that some discount should operate on its damages, because it may not have been able to borrow anyhow under the existing facility.

Clearly the administrative expenses in obtaining the money elsewhere can be recovered as consequential losses, but what of the loss of profit because, without the money, a borrower is unable to enter into or complete some other transaction? To be recoverable, the expenses or loss must be within the contemplation of the parties at the time of the agreement—a difficult test at the best of times. Of course in commercial transactions, the parties must be taken to understand the ordinary practices of the other's business, but in a non-project-related loan, the bank should not be taken to know the profit-making purposes of a borrower, just because there is a typically vague purpose clause.

---

[19] *Loan Investment Corporation of Australasia* v. *Bonner* [1970] NZLR 724 (PC).
[20] *South African Territories Ltd.* v. *Wallington* [1898] AC 309 (HL).

C. PURPOSE CLAUSES, ILLEGALITY, AND *VIRES*

The purpose of the lending shapes the transaction. It will influence whether the lending has a commercial logic, whether it is consistent with the bank's policy, and what the documentation must contain to protect its position. The facility agreement may contain a purpose clause. If its violation is obvious, the borrower will be in default and exceptionally may hold the moneys subject to a *Quistclose* trust, giving the bank an advantage in the event that insolvency follows default.[21] Again exceptionally, others holding or paying away the borrowed moneys and knowing of the purpose clause may be in breach of trust or liable for dishonestly assisting breach of trust.[22] More likely, a purpose clause in practice may be so vague that it is impossible to say that it has been breached (e.g. the funds must be 'used towards the borrower's working capital requirements'). Banks wanting to exercise control over the borrower's use of the funds will need to build in other mechanisms, e.g. a project certificate about the successful completion of each stage can be required before the next stage is funded.

If a bank knows that a facility is illegal—say it is in breach of exchange control, a moratorium, or freeze regulations—English law will treat it as void and disallow any action seeking recovery of what has been advanced. Subsequent illegality in relation to an initially lawful agreement is regarded differently, and the bank can recover, although any remedy may be blocked in cross-border lending by the action of the other jurisdiction in enforcing its law. In international loan agreements banks try to insist on an illegality clause whereby, if it becomes unlawful for them to continue with a loan—their governments impose a freeze on dealings in the borrower's country, or their regulators oblige them to reduce their exposure there—the borrower must immediately repay. Borrowers may seek a variation of this clause to oblige a bank so affected to use reasonable endeavours to seek a substitute bank to continue with the loan.

Banks must also make checks on the *vires* of organizations to whom they lend. At common law *ultra vires* transactions are void *ab initio*. The 'swaps litigation' in Britain brought this point home sharply to international financial markets. There it was held that local authority swaps transactions were *ultra vires* under the relevant legislation.[23] Subsequently other cases involving local authorities have hammered the point by holding that other (non-swaps) financial transactions were *ultra vires* their powers.[24] However, in a further wave of litigation it has been held that the banks could recover sums advanced on restitutionary principles.[25] It would be highly unusual if borrowing, of itself, was *ultra vires* a commercial organization.

---

[21] 242 above.

[22] *Twinsectra Ltd.* v. *Yardley* [2002] UKHL 12, [2002] 2 WLR 802, [2002] 2 All ER 377.

[23] *Hazell* v. *Hammersmith and Fulham LBC* [1992] 2 AC 1 (HL).

[24] 139 above.

[25] *Westdeutsche Landesbank Girozentrale* v. *Islington LBC* [1996] AC 669 (HL); *Guiness Mahon and Co. Ltd.* v. *Kensington and Chelsea LBC* [1999] QB 215 (CA). See 251 above.

D. REPAYMENT

(i) Time of Repayment

With à demand facility, or one expressed as repayable on demand, we have seen that there is no concept in English law of a reasonable time to pay, once demand is made. A debtor required to pay money on demand is allowed only such time as is necessary to implement the mechanisms needed to discharge the debt, before being in default. In view of modern methods of communication and payment systems, the available time needed is exceptionally short. Thus, as little as one or two hours will generally be sufficient, at which time the bank can exercise its remedies, for example proceeding under the security it has taken. The justification of the English approach is that banks will make demand only when the situation of a borrower is out of hand. Then, because the borrower is most likely insolvent, speed is of the essence in the exercise of default remedies.

Payment of a term loan will be on a specified date or specified dates. Payment by instalments during the lifetime of the loan provides a bank with a greater degree of assurance than payment of the whole amount at the end (the so-called 'bullet' loan). The latter very often leads to refinancing. As a general rule in English law, there is no need to give notice if a sum of money is payable on a particular day. The agreement may, however, expressly oblige the bank to make demand before it can call default. Again there is no need for a reasonable time to pay. English law does not seem to require that the demand notice be entirely accurate. The rationale is that the borrower should know what it owes. This is not a compelling reason when the claim is against a guarantor, and in such cases the demand should specify a failure to pay and the amount of the debt.

Some common law jurisdictions such as the United States, Canada, and Australia oblige lenders to give a reasonable period within which to meet a demand for repayment, under an on-demand facility or otherwise.[26] They take the view that the law cannot stand aloof, but must provide some outer boundaries to the conduct of lenders. Maybe, the reasoning seems to go, if borrowers had a reasonable time, some might be able to retrieve the situation. Reasonable time depends on the circumstances, but at its most generous may involve sufficient time for the borrower to refinance. So too in many civil law jurisdictions. The justification is that in particular circumstances the principles of good faith and fair dealing demand it, especially if a bank seeks to contradict the reasonably generated expectations that it will give significant advance notice.

(ii) Early Repayment

There is no right at common law to pay early, but the agreement may permit early repayment (prepayment) 'without premium or penalty'. However, a bank may be concerned about early repayment of a term loan, since if there are no credit problems

---

[26] 224 above.

that can cut short the life of an attractive asset. Under the agreement a borrower may be required, in the event of prepayment, to make an additional payment. This may be simply to compensate the bank, but in some cases it may seem to be designed to discourage prepayment. The rule against penalties would not apply, since the obligation to make additional payment does not arise on breach of contract.

When prepayment is of only part of the total amount outstanding, banks will prefer the agreement to treat this as shortening the overall life of the loan, rather than simply relieving the borrower of the obligation to make scheduled repayments at the front end of the loan. For this reason the agreement will provide that any amounts prepaid will be applied against repayment instalments in inverse order of their maturity.

(iii) Other Matters

With overdrafts and revolving facilities, drawings and repayments will be from time to time. The parties will need to ensure that any particular drawing does not take the borrower over any limit on borrowings. This could be in breach of financial ratios in this or other agreements. Moreover, there is the technical difficulty raised by the rule in *Clayton's Case*: repayments are deemed to discharge the borrower's indebtedness in the chronological order in which it was incurred, in other words the earliest element first.[27] *Clayton's Case* establishes a legal presumption, which can be displaced by express contractual agreement. This will need to be done to avoid the rule adversely affecting any security or guarantee given to support the loan facility, since these may otherwise be discharged once the borrower has repaid a total amount equivalent to the overall limit of the facility.

The agreement will lay down when and how the borrower is to repay the principal, interest, and other amounts, e.g. for value on the due date at a specified time (e.g. 12.00 noon) in cleared funds. Cleared (or same-day funds) are immediately available funds. Moreover, the agreement will require payment free and clear of any present or future taxes, duties, charges, fees, or withholdings, and without any set-off or counter-claim by the borrower. If clearly expressed, there is no doubt that the buyer's right of set off can be excluded.[28]

Along with these prohibitions on the range of deductions will be a gross-up obliga-tion on the borrower: if it is compelled by law to make any deduction or withholding, it must gross up what it does pay, so that the bank receives the full amount it would have received had no deduction or withholding been made. In some jurisdictions this type of clause might be unlawful in shifting a lender's tax liabilities to the borrower.[29] A powerful borrower may be able to negotiate a modification of the standard gross-up clause if the bank is capable of recovering the full amount of any tax deduction or withholding from another source (e.g. its tax office). In addition to grossing up, the borrower may have to indemnify the bank for any increased cost it (the bank) incurs

---

[27] (1816) 1 Mer. 572, 35 ER 781.
[28] *Coca-Cola Financial Corporation* v. *Finsat International* [1996] CLC 1564 (CA).
[29] See *David Securities Pty. Ltd.* v. *Commonwealth Bank of Australia* (1992) 175 CLR 353.

as a result of a change in the law or government policy. Under this type of provision a borrower might find itself called upon to compensate the bank, because of a change in banking regulations or monetary policy, reducing the bank's effective return under the loan, or on its capital.

E. INTEREST

Interest is one element of a bank's profit on a loan agreement. It is payment for the use of money or compensation for being kept out of it. Thus in the absence of clear language in an agreement, interest is not payable for moneys which have not been drawn down or which have been repaid. In addition, a bank may be entitled under the agreement to a front-end fee for arranging the loan, a commitment fee—theoretically for having the moneys available even if not drawn—and an indemnity for any costs and expenses e.g. in negotiating, amending, and enforcing the agreement.

Much commercial lending is at a variable rate of interest. Britain is unusual in that much lending to individuals (e.g. home mortgagees) is also at a variable, rather than a fixed, rate. A variable interest rate will be at a specified margin over, for example, the bank's base (or prime) rate, or over a market rate, such as the cost of funds on the interbank market.[30] The former is the base (or prime) rate from time to time.[31] Choice of the latter requires elaboration in the agreement of how it is to be calculated (when in the day; which are to serve as the reference banks from which quotations are to be obtained; is the average of the rates quoted to be rounded up and how?). Out of an abundance of caution a 'market disaster' clause may be inserted into the agreement in the event that it is not possible to obtain any, or realistic, quotations on the interbank market. This is because there is no right in English law to interest in the absence of a source for determining it. The market-disaster clause may oblige the parties to use their best endeavours to negotiate a new mechanism, failing which the bank has discretion to set the rate, coupled with the right of the borrower to repay. The borrower will be able to choose the period for which a particular floating rate will obtain (e.g. one, three, six months). The determination by the bank of the rate of interest may be treated by the agreement as conclusive. Despite the approach of the courts to conclusive evidence clauses in other areas of banking,[32] in this context it is difficult to see how it is challengeable, in the absence of manifest error.

F. DEFAULT INTEREST AND THE RULE AGAINST PENALTIES

Interest will be payable at the end of the specified interest periods. If a borrower fails to pay on time the agreement will probably provide for default interest, in other words

---

[30] 45 above. Thus LIBOR (London Inter-Bank Offered Rate), which can be US$ LIBOR, Euro LIBOR, £ LIBOR, etc.

[31] *Provincial North West plc v. Bennett* [1999] EWCA Civ. 676, *The Times*, 11 Feb. 1999.

[32] 165 above.

a higher rate of interest than normal. Is such a stipulation unenforceable as a penalty, being an additional amount payable on breach? Civil law systems and international restatements such as the UNIDROIT Principles do not find penalty clauses objectionable, although they may provide for a power of reduction where the amount payable is disproportionately high.[33] On the other hand, Anglo-American law will strike down a stipulated payment as a penalty, primarily if it is extravagant or unconscionable in relation to the other party's greatest loss, or if it is not a genuine pre-estimate of that loss.[34] Default-interest clauses have been treated as penalties when the higher rate is payable for *both* the interest period and the period of default from the due date. Yet there is no penalty if the clause provides for a reduction of interest on punctual payment[35]—demonstrating just how technical the law in this area has become. Moreover, there is no objection if the default rate is modest and is confined simply to the period from the due date: the increased rate payable by the borrower is justified because, being in default, it is now a worse credit risk.[36] This is a variant of compounding, to which English law also has no objection.[37] But whereas the borrower can always avoid the default rate by bringing its payments up to date, with compounding a borrower will be paying interest on interest for the remainder of the loan.[38]

In modern conditions, however, the common law does not seek to extend the rule against penalties. Contracting parties are given considerable latitude, consistent with the doctrine of freedom of contract. A sum has to be quite extravagant or unconscionable to be struck down. There must be a considerable disproportion between the sum set out in the agreement and the likely loss, if the parties are of roughly equal bargaining power. Morever, if a clause provides for payment of a sum of money on a specified event other than breach of contract—for example, under an indemnity for losses—the rule has no application.[39]

---

[33] G. Treitel, *Remedies for Breach of Contract* (Oxford, Clarendon, 1988), 220–8; H. Beale, A. Hartkamp, H. Kötz, and D. Tallon (eds.), *Contract Law* (Oxford, Hart, 2002), 865–72.

[34] *Dunlop Pneumatic Tyre Co.* v. *New Garage & Motor Co. Ltd.* [1915] AC 79 (HL).

[35] *Wallingford* v. *Mutual Security* (1880) 5 App. Cas. 685, 702.

[36] *Lordsvale Finance plc* v. *Bank of Zambia* [1996] QB 752; *Citibank* v. *Nyland and the Republic of the Philippines*, 878 F 2d 620 (2nd Cir. 1989); *David Securities Pty. Ltd.* v. *Commonwealth Bank of Australia* (1990) 93 ALR 271 (Fed. Ct., Full Ct.) (on appeal on different grounds: see n. 29). Cf. *Hong Leong Finance Ltd.* v. *Tan Gin Huay* [1999] 2 SLR 153 (CA).

[37] *National Bank of Greece SA* v. *Pinios Shipping Co.* [1990] 1 AC 637 (HL).

[38] R. Pennington, *Bank Finance for Companies* (London, Sweet & Maxwell, 1987), 15–17.

[39] *Export Credits Guarantee Department* v. *Universal Oil Products Co.* [1983] 1 WLR 399, [1983] 2 All ER 205 (HL).

III. CONDITIONS PRECEDENT, REPRESENTATIONS AND WARRANTIES, COVENANTS

A. CONDITIONS PRECEDENT

A facility agreement may contain conditions precedent. These may be that certain documents be produced to the bank, for example the company's constitutional documents, a resolution of its board approving the facility, a written consent of the authorities and, in the case of a cross-border transaction, legal opinions from relevant lawyers on its validity. Depending on the bargaining power of the parties, the bank may have a wide discretion to determine which documents must be produced as conditions precedent. It may also be a condition precedent to each drawing under the facility that the representations and warranties are correct, and that no default is outstanding or will result.

Several legal issues arise in relation to the conditions precedent. The first is whether they are conditions precedent to the agreement coming into effect, or conditions precedent to the bank's performance under the facility. The better view is that there is a binding contract as soon as the parties agree the terms but that, until the conditions precedent are fulfilled, the bank need not make the funds available. This accords with the contractual language of even the simplest facility letter. It also has the practical advantage that the bank can claim the fees and expenses set out in the agreement, since at least in that respect it has come into effect. If there is no agreement under which the fees can be claimed, English law does not recognize an action for reliance losses in anticipation of a contract. It may be that the bank can claim for a *quantum meruit* for services performed, although there is some authority that it would need to show that the potential borrower has somehow benefited. Even if the bank is successful with a *quantum meruit* claim, this will not necessarily be equivalent in amount to the fees and expenses set out in the agreement.

A second issue is whether the bank need co-operate so that the conditions precedent can be satisfied. Of course some conditions precedent will turn on the actions of third parties (e.g. whether a regulatory body approves), and satisfying many of the conditions precedent will be solely in the hands of the borrower itself.[40] Occasionally, however, unless the bank acts, a borrower may be unable to fulfil a condition precedent. If such a condition precedent can be construed as an agreement to agree, an English court will not oblige the bank to act. Nor will it readily imply a term that the bank co-operate so that the borrower can meet the condition. However, the bank will need to be careful that it is not, as a result of its behaviour, deemed to have waived compliance by the borrower with that condition precedent. Moreover, if the condition precedent can be construed as imposing on the bank a duty to act, by preventing

---

[40] Cf. *Total Gas Marketing Ltd.* v. *ARCO British Ltd.* [1998] UKHL 22, [1998] 2 Lloyd's Rep. 209 (HL).

fulfilment of the condition the bank will not only be liable in damages, but may also be precluded from claiming that the condition has not been satisfied.

B. REPRESENTATIONS AND WARRANTIES

There is some overlap between the conditions precedent and the representations and warranties (if any) in a facility agreement. Both concern the borrower's status, the lawfulness of its entering the agreement, and the absence of any default. In addition to the representations on these matters, however, the borrower will make representations in the agreement on other matters, for example that its accounts are accurate and have suffered no material adverse change since they were drawn up, and that there are no legal proceedings in the pipeline which may have a material adverse effect on it. Where there is a syndicate of banks there will also be representations about the accuracy of the information memorandum sent to potential members. The representations will go further than the common law in covering omissions as well as changes since the memorandum was distributed. The other advantage over the common law is that the misstatement, omission, or failure to update will constitute default, even in the absence of any reliance on the part of the syndicate bank.

It has been rightly said that representations and warranties perform an investigative role.[41] The representations may relate not only to the borrower but also to its parent guarantor and to subsidiaries. Borrowers need to consider whether they can realistically make representations about other companies in the group, especially those in other jurisdictions. The agreement will probably deem the representations to be repeated on each draw-down (the so-called evergreen provision).

C. COVENANTS

The representations and warranties concern, in the main, existing facts. In effect they act as a checklist of concerns which a bank must have about the financial condition of the borrower and the legal validity of the agreement. By contrast the covenants (variously described) are undertakings by the borrower as to what it will or will not do in the future—that it will regularly provide specified financial and other information to the bank; that it will maintain certain financial ratios (e.g. gearing, minimum tangible net worth); that it will maintain regulatory consents; and that it will not dispose of its assets, change its business, or enter into an amalgamation, merger, or reconstruction. The latter is designed to preserve the entity and its income-producing assets, against which the bank lent. Other important covenants are the *pari passu* and negative-pledge clauses, designed to achieve an equal ranking for this indebtedness, and considered shortly. Which covenants appear in a facility turns on factors such as its nature and size, the position of the borrower and its financial needs, the purpose

---

[41] P. Wood, *International Loans, Bonds and Securities Regulation* (London, Sweet & Maxwell, 1995), 29.

of the loan, the existence of other indebtedness, and competition from other banks.[42]

D. BREACH BY THE BORROWER

With both the representations and warranties, and the covenants, the first legal issue is their interpretation. For example, is a financial ratio limiting the borrower's indebtedness breached because it is exceeded in a short period of time between the issuance of new bonds and the retirement of old ones?[43] If the anti-disposal covenant prohibits the borrower from selling, transferring, leasing, etc. all or any substantial part of its assets, is this triggered by a transaction in which 51 per cent of the total book value of the assets is sold?[44] Is the anti-merger clause wide enough to cover a change in the ownership of the borrower's shares (over which, in the case of a hostile takeover, the borrower will not have ultimate control)?

Secondly, there are the legal consequences of the borrower breaching the representations and warranties, and the covenants. Broadly speaking these are two-fold. First, both the representations and warranties and the covenants will be part of the default clause, so that their breach will enable the bank to cancel any outstanding commitment and accelerate repayment. Secondly, a breach also gives rise to certain consequences under the general law. As a practical matter this becomes important when there is a syndicate of banks and the majority are not prepared to invoke the default clause (perhaps it is a situation where they favour rescheduling). Although individual banks are not able to call default, they can, generally speaking, exercise their general-law remedies against the borrower. In English law these are to sue for what is owing them and for any damages. If the particular representation and warranty or covenant goes to the root of the contract, or if its breach constitutes a serious failure in performance, then a bank will also have a right to terminate the agreement and thus be released from any further obligation under it. Failure to act may constitute a waiver of the breach and, in certain circumstances, a variation of the agreement.

---

[42] E. Ferran, *Company Law and Corporate Finance* (Oxford, OUP, 1999), 471–2; J. Day and P. Taylor, 'Evidence on the Practices of UK Bankers in Contracting for Medium-term Debt' [1995] 9 *JIBL* 394; J. Day and P. Taylor, 'Bankers' Perspectives on the Role of Covenants in Debt Contracts' [1996] 5 *JIBL* 201.

[43] *Kelly* v. *Central Hanover Bank & Trust Co.*, 11 F Supp. 497, 504–5 (SDNY 1935).

[44] *Sharon Steel Corp.* v. *Chase Manhattan Bank NA*, 691 F 2d 1039 (2nd Cir. 1982), cert. denied 460 US 1012 (1983).

IV. THE NEGATIVE PLEDGE AND
PARI PASSU CLAUSES

A. NEGATIVE PLEDGE LENDING

The term 'negative-pledge' clause is a misnomer. In its basic form it is simply a promise by a borrower that it will not grant security to a third party (the 'basic negative pledge'). In another form there may be a promise on the part of the borrower to grant equal and rateable security in the same asset to the bank, or matching security in other assets, if it does grant security to a third party (the 'equivalent security' negative pledge). Some negative-pledge clauses go further and provide that the bank shares in any security the borrower grants in breach of the clause, or that security is automatically conferred in the same asset should breach occur (the 'automatic security' negative pledge).

This discussion concentrates on (i) the ambit of the negative-pledge clause; (ii) the remedies the bank has against the borrower should it breach the clause; and (iii) the remedies the bank has against a third party taking security from the borrower in breach of the clause. The discussion focuses on unsecured lending, although in jurisdictions such as England which recognize the floating charge, the bank may insert a negative-pledge clause, with the intention of preserving its priority if, say, the borrower grants a later fixed security. Whether this works in practice depends on the registration provisions: the better view in England is that registration of the floating charge with its negative pledge does not constitute notice to the later chargee.[45]

At the outset, however, it is useful to canvass the reasons for negative-pledge lending. Fundamentally it is because a bank is not always able to take security, given the bargaining power or nature of the borrower. Indeed, the borrower able to obtain funds simply on the basis of a negative pledge has an enhanced credit-standing in the market. Because a bank does not have the priority flowing from ordinary security, however, it needs some assurance that no third party will steal a march on it in the event of the borrower's insolvency. Hence the negative-pledge clause. Possibly the only two advantages to a bank—apart from the fact that otherwise the borrower may well take its business elsewhere—are that negative-pledge lending avoids the time and expense of taking security, and that a negative pledge acts as a curb on excessive lending by the borrower, since third parties may refrain from advancing funds if they cannot take security. Yet the disadvantages of negative-pledge lending are not all one way. In particular, there are a number of cases of borrowers finding the presence of negative-pledge clauses in existing loans a significant hurdle to their obtaining new credit, which was only available if the new lenders were able to obtain some sort of

---

[45] *AIB Finance Ltd.* v. *Bank of Scotland* [1994] BCC 184.

security interest in relation to the new assets they were to fund. Without a waiver by the old creditors of any breach of the existing negative-pledge clauses, new credit was blocked.[46]

B. AMBIT OF THE NEGATIVE PLEDGE

This leads conveniently to the first legal issue to be addressed, the ambit of a negative-pledge clause. It is not uncommon for negative-pledge clauses to make extensive claims. Even in relation to security strictly defined, the clause may be very wide. Existing security may have to be discharged, and purchase-money security may be blocked—the borrower undertakes not to create any security or 'permit any security to subsist'. In the event of the former the bank should probably ask itself whether it should be lending on an unsecured basis if other banks have not done so. To include purchase-money security could impede the future financing of new assets, although if it is not included the bank's position may be adversely affected as the unencumbered assets of the borrower depreciate in relation to the newly acquired, encumbered assets. Usually there will be a sensible exemption for security interests arising by operation of law, e.g. banker's liens.

Quasi-security devices, such as sale and leaseback and sale and repurchase of the borrower's own assets, while functionally equivalent to security, are not regarded as security in English law. Thus the negative-pledge clause may be drafted so as to extend to them expressly. But need hire purchase or leasing arrangements be included, when these enable a borrower to obtain new income-producing assets on credit? Moreover, since these are very common transactions, many borrowers would have to change their mode of business radically from the norm if the clause is not to be constantly breached in practice. For the same reason, including set-off in the negative-pledge clause would cause havoc to a borrower's business.

The negative-pledge clause needs to extend to security given by the borrower's subsidiaries, both as an anti-avoidance device and because they may take on excessive debt by encumbering themselves, thus reducing indirectly the capacity of their parent to repay. This is slightly tricky, since subsidiaries may not be parties to the agreement, and hence not bound by the clause. It is a matter of obliging the parent to use its control over its subsidiaries—'to procure them' in the standard terminology—not to breach the clause. What if a borrower sells a subsidiary to a bank for immediate payment, the bank takes security over its assets, and then sells the subsidiary back to the borrower, the price being deferred (in effect, a loan)? The security in this case is given by the subsidiary when it is owned by the bank, not when it is owned by the borrower, so no breach of the clause occurs. Recall, however, that the standard negative-pledge clause includes an undertaking that the borrower will ensure that none of its subsidiaries permits any security to *subsist*—this would effectively block

[46] D. Asiedu-Akrofi, 'Negative Pledge Clauses in International Loan Agreements' (1995) 26 *Law & Policy in Int'l Bus.*, 407, 430–4.

the transaction described. Indeed devices such as this, which involve the movement of assets into and from subsidiaries, may also be caught by the anti-disposal clause.[47]

C. BANK V. BORROWER FOR BREACH OF NEGATIVE PLEDGE

The second issue concerns the bank's legal remedies against the borrower for breach of the clause. Like the other covenants in a loan agreement, breach of the negative-pledge clause will trigger the default clause. It will also give rise to an action for damages if there is any loss caused by the breach. However, the default remedy is in many cases impractical, while an action for damages is obviously unattractive because of the delays and cost, doubly so if the borrower is now insolvent. The bank has three hopes. The first is that it can obtain an injunction to prevent breach of the basic negative-pledge clause, not to give security; the second is that it can obtain specific performance of an 'equivalent security' negative pledge; and the third is that, if an 'automatic security' negative pledge is in place, this will give it security which trumps any security taken by the third party.

(i) Injunction

A bank which is in the unusual position of getting wind that a borrower is about to breach a negative-pledge clause can seek an injunction to prevent that happening. The normal rule is that to obtain an injunction a party needs to show that damages are not an adequate remedy. However in England, but not in all US jurisdictions, the authorities say that an injunction will readily be granted for breach of a negative stipulation, regardless of the adequacy of damages. They assume, however (which is doubtful), that there is a bright line between positive and negative stipulations. Were it necessary to show that damages were an inadequate remedy, it would probably require the borrower's solvency to be in question. If solvent, the borrower could argue that the bank would be fully protected by acceleration and cancellation under the default clause, or by terminating for breach and claiming damages. The bank's only riposte may be that if it accelerated or terminated, it would be deprived of its right to a long term investment.

In exceptional cases, it may be possible to argue that even an injunction would be inadequate—primarily an urgent necessity to preserve the assets of the borrower pending final judgment or liquidation. There is some authority that in such circumstances the court may appoint a receiver, on application of the bank to take control of the assets from the borrower.[48]

---

[47] 314 above.

[48] Cf. *National Australia Bank Ltd.* v. *Bond Brewing Holdings Ltd.* [1991] 1 VR 386, (1990) 169 CLR 271. D. Allan, 'Negative Pledge Lending—Dead or Alive?' in R. Cranston and R. Goode (eds.), *Commercial and Consumer Law* (Oxford, Clarendon, 1993); P. Devonshire, 'Freezing Orders, Disappearing Assets and the Problem of Enjoining Non-Parties' (2002) 188 *LQR* 124, 142–4.

(ii) Specific Performance

The equivalent-security negative pledge is an undertaking by the borrower to give equal and rateable security in the assets over which the third party has taken security, or to give matching security in other assets. Can a bank obtain specific performance of this type of promise? Specific performance is discretionary, and as a matter of principle courts should ask whether damages are an adequate remedy. There are cases where specific performance has been granted on a promise to execute security, when money has actually been advanced. It has not mattered, for these purposes, whether the security was over real or personal property. This would seem justified in terms of principle in the event of a borrower's insolvency, since it is then more valuable to have a security interest than a claim for damages. But there is at least one major problem with the 'equal and rateable' clause: since specific performance cannot operate retro-spectively, the bank may well lose priority to the third party's security interest, if this has already been taken.

(iii) Automatic Security

An equivalent security clause does not purport to give security on breach—the bank has simply a contractual undertaking that the borrower will give equivalent security. The automatic security clause goes further. The assumption is that, although the bank remains unsecured until breach, the happening of that contingency automatically triggers security in favour of the bank, that security having a priority over what the third party has taken. However, banks should place little hope in 'automatic security' negative pledges.

Some commentators see no objection to automatic security clauses. The prop-erty over which security is to arise is identifiable, since it is the property over which the third party is taking its security. This is not in contention. These com-mentators then ask: if an agreement can provide for security to attach to future property, why should an agreement not provide for security to come into existence on the occurrence of a contingency, i.e. breach of the negative pledge?[49] But there is a difference. An agreement for security over future property is unconditional in nature, although whether it attaches depends on whether the property comes into the hands of the borrower. By contrast, an agreement for automatic security is conditional—the bank will never get security if the negative-pledge clause is observed.

For this reason other commentators invoke the principle that equity will not regard as done that which ought to be done, unless there is fresh consideration when the contingency occurs (e.g. new money advanced). Only then will what was a conditional agreement to give security be transformed into an unconditional,

---

[49] e.g. P. Gabriel, *Legal Aspects of Syndicated Loans* (London, Butterworths, 1986), 85–9; J. Stone, 'The "Affirmative" Negative Pledge' [1991] NZLJ 364, [1991] 9 JIBL 364; M. Young, 'Floating Charge Restrictive Clauses and Unsecured Negative Pledge Covenants' (1999) 10 *JBFLP* 205, 225.

enforceable undertaking.[50] Yet cannot the forbearance of the bank in calling default constitute the new value required?

Whichever view ultimately prevails—and we require an authoritative determination of the issue—automatic security clauses suffer from a very real practical defect, the lack of registration. Registration of security interests is demanded in many jurisdictions within a limited period after their creation, if they are to be perfected. The negative pledge in the original, unsecured loan agreement will not be registered. If a breach of it occurs, security is said to arise automatically. But if that security is not to be ineffective, it must be registered. In practice, the bank will often not learn about the breach quickly enough to be able to register within the requisite period.

D. BANK V. THIRD PARTY ON BREACH OF NEGATIVE PLEDGE

The final aspect to be considered is the right of the bank against a third party which takes security in breach of a negative-pledge clause. As a practical matter, the claim against the third party may be all the bank has if the borrower has become insolvent. There are at least three possibilities.

(i) The Rule in *De Mattos* v. *Gibson*

The first possibility is that the bank may obtain an injunction on the basis of the principle stated by Knight Bruce LJ in *De Mattos* v. *Gibson.*

Reason and justice seem to prescribe that at least as a general rule, where a man, by gift or purchase, acquires property from another, with knowledge of a previous contract, lawfully and for valuable consideration made by him with a third person, to use and employ the property for a particular purpose in a specified manner, the acquirer shall not, to the material damage of the third person, in opposition to the contract and inconsistently with it, use and employ the property in a manner not allowable to the giver or seller.[51]

Applying the *De Mattos* principle to a negative-pledge clause, it is arguable that the third party could be restrained by an injunction from exercising rights under the security. In the result, the third party would be treated as an unsecured creditor, along with the bank. The bank would then be in the same position as it would have been if the negative-pledge clause had not been breached. The third party would need to have actual knowledge of the negative pledge clause to be bound by the principle.

Whether the *De Mattos* principle would be applied in this way is open, however, to doubt. Courts in both England and the United States have been inclined to limit its application. It is said that the principle applies to situations where the bank has a

---

[50] e.g. R. Goode, *Legal Problems of Credit and Security* (London, Sweet & Maxwell, 1988), 19–22; J. Maxton, 'Negative Pledges and Equitable Principles' [1993] *JBL* 458.

[51] (1858) 4 De G & 276, 282, 45 ER 108, 110. See T. Mitchell, 'The Negative Pledge Clause and the Classification of Financing Devices' (1986) 60 *Am. Bankr. LJ* 153, 263; M. Ogilvie, 'Privity of Contract and the Third Party Purchaser' (1987–88) 42 *Can.Bus. LJ* 402; S. Worthington, *Proprietary Interests in Commercial Transactions* (Oxford, Clarendon, 1996), 101–6.

proprietary interest, although the plaintiff in *De Mattos* itself did not have such an interest. It is also said that the rule applies only in relation to ships, or a very limited range of property, although there is nothing in the *De Mattos* decision to suggest that it should be limited in this way. The only principled limitation would seem to be that the contractual right has to relate to specific assets. Arguably in the case of a negative pledge, these are the assets over which security has been taken. However, it is difficult to be definite about the ambit of the principle. In a few words its boundaries are uncertain, and its application to negative-pledge clauses not to be counted on.

(ii) Interference with Contractual Relations

In some cases the rule in *De Mattos* v. *Gibson* is aligned with the tort of interfering with contractual relations. In fact in *De Mattos* itself there was no tort. In any event, this tort provides the second possible claim which a bank may have against a third party taking security in breach of a negative-pledge clause.[52] The tort takes various guises, but in this context would involve the unjustified procurement or inducement by the third party of the breach of the clause.

Knowledge, intention, and causation are required. Some have argued that something less than actual knowledge may be all that is needed, at least at the interlocutory stage of legal proceedings, for example common knowledge about the way unsecured lending is conducted. But English courts abhor constructive knowledge in commercial transactions, and it would be going a considerable way to ascribe knowledge to third parties just because unsecured lending is usually on negative pledge terms. As for intention, if the third party knows about the negative-pledge clause, and yet goes ahead and takes security, this element would seem to be satisfied. The problem with causation is that the third party will argue that the borrower breached the clause because of its desire to obtain new funding. But since new funding inevitably involves breaching the clause, if the third party demands security, it is very difficult for it to argue that it has not induced the breach. Moreover, the law will not recognize as a justification for inducing the breach the willingness of the third party to provide finance, just because the borrower needs it.

The damages obtainable if the tort is established will be the loss suffered because the third party has a secure interest, and so now obtains a priority in payment, as opposed to an unsecured interest. In many cases this will be equivalent to what would be recovered from the borrower itself for its breach.

(iii) A Security Interest?

A final possibility in relation to the third party is to argue that the bank has a security interest from the outset, which has priority over any security subsequently given to a third party. Clearly under English law and similar common law systems this

---

[52] See *Law Debenture Trust Corporation* v. *Ural Caspian Oil Corporation* [1995] Ch. 152 (CA); J. Stone, 'Negative Pledges and the Tort of Interference with Contractual Relations' [1991] 8 *JIBL* 310. Another possibility, not discussed here, is the tort of conspiracy.

possibility must be given short shrift.[53] A negative pledge does not purport to create an immediate security interest: negative pledges are not registered as such under section 395 of the Companies Act 1985. If the bank does not get security against the borrower itself, it is difficult to see how it gets it against third parties.

Yet there are a few US decisions which support the idea that the bank gets an equitable mortgage (or equitable lien in American terms).[54] A closely-reasoned opinion in the Federal District Court of Southern New York, rejecting the idea, and consistent with the English approach, was reversed and remanded on appeal without reasons.[55] Nevertheless, it tends to have influenced most jurisdictions in the United States where the negative pledge has been considered: a negative pledge does not give rise to a security interest at the outset, whatever the position subsequently.

E. THE *PARI PASSU* CLAUSE

The negative-pledge clause is concerned with threats that the borrower might encumber its assets. The *pari passu* clause is an undertaking that the borrower will ensure that its obligations under the loan will rank at least equally with all its other present and future unsecured obligations. In practice the clause has little purchase. Even without it the borrower cannot subsequently subordinate the bank's loan, since this requires the consent of the bank (unless a sovereign borrower procures a change of the law in its jurisdiction). The *pari passu* obligation does not mean that the maturity of all indebtedness must coincide. Thus the borrower could incur further, unsecured payment obligations to a third party, whereby the latter is paid before the bank. Nor does it prevent payment of other indebtedness when the bank's loan is in default. That, however, may be a preference under the insolvency legislation, and thus reversable.

V. DEFAULT

A. THE DEFAULT CLAUSE

Under the general law default enables a bank to sue for its losses. A serious default means it can terminate the facility. It may also have the court appoint a receiver. But a written facility will invariably contain a default clause. This will contain a range of events which the lender is entitled to treat as a default. Significantly, an event of default will give remedies additional to those conferred by the general law. With

---

[53] T. Han, 'The Negative Pledge as a "Security" Device' [1996] *Singapore JLS* 415; J. Arkins, 'The Negative Pledge Clause and the "Security" it Provides' [2000] *JIBL* 198.

[54] e.g. *Connecticut Co. v. New York NH & HRR*, 107 A 646 (1919); *Coast Bank v. W. J. Minderhout*, 392 P 2d. 265 (SC Calif., 1964).

[55] *Kelly v. Central Hanover Bank & Trust Co.*, 11 F Supp. 497 (1935), 85 F 2d 61 (1936).

unsecured lending default will give the bank a discretion to accelerate payment and to cancel any of its outstanding obligations. With secured lending the agreement will generally also give a bank the power to appoint an administrator, who will have the power to run the business, or dispose of the assets, in order to meet the bank's claim.

(i) Events of Default

The events of default range from non-payment of interest and principal, through breach of the representations, covenants, and other obligations in the agreement, to acts which anticipate default, for example events indicating insolvency. The occurrence of the events set out in a default clause may not automatically constitute default, for there may be requirements that notice be given to the borrower, grace periods, materiality tests, and other limitations built into the clause. For example, a borrower with bargaining power may be able to have the clause drafted so that, to constitute default, payment must be overdue for, say, thirty days. Again, default might be defined so as not to occur unless a breach of the agreement is material or has an adverse effect on the ability of the borrower to repay.[56] Banks will resist such a provision as being uncertain. Indeed they will argue for a separate event of default if, in their opinion, something occurs which has a material and adverse effect on the financial condition or operations of the borrower, or its ability to repay. The only change a borrower may be able to negotiate is that the opinion be reasonable, rather than completely subjective. Otherwise the only limitation English law would impose on the bank is that its opinion be honest. There is no obligation on the bank to act in good faith. Events of default may have to be continuing if the bank wants to exercise its remedies under the default clause.

(ii) Cross Default

A crucial aspect of the default clause is how cross-default is defined.[57] This can be extraordinarily wide. Any default under *another* agreement with, say, Bank B, may be an event of default under this agreement with Bank A, even though Bank B has chosen not to call default. Indeed, any event which, with the giving of notice, lapse of a grace period, determination of materiality, or fulfilment of any other condition, would constitute an event of default under the other agreement with Bank B, may constitute an event of default here. The policy behind the cross-default clause is that default under the other agreement with Bank B may be symptomatic of a general malaise in the borrower. There is also the fear that Bank B may obtain a priority. If Bank A insists on a wide default clause, the hope the borrower may have is that Bank B observe its duty of confidentiality so that Bank A never learns about a potential event of default, or an event of default which is remedied. Otherwise, the cross-default clauses in the range of facilities which a borrower may have are potentially catastrophic.

---

[56] *Pan Foods* v. *ANZ Banking Group* (2000) 74 *ALJR* 791 (HCA).

[57] L. Buchheit, *How to Negotiate Eurocurrency Loan Agreements* (2nd edn., London, Euromoney, 2000), 96–100.

B. GENERAL LAW LIMITS ON ACCELERATION/CANCELLATION?

Whereas many other legal systems hedge in a bank's exercise of discretion by notions such as good faith, English law takes the view that a bank can invoke its default remedies without limitation. Technical breach of the default clause is no excuse for the borrower, nor is an inability to meet its obligations owing to circumstances beyond its control, for example the exchange-control authorities blocking payment. English law works on the principle of strict performance of contractual obligations, unmitigated by the absence of fault on the borrower's part. Thus a borrower cannot expect protection from equity exercising its jurisdiction to relieve against forfeiture. Decisions on forfeiture make it quite clear that it is not available in contracts which do not involve the transfer of possessory or proprietary rights, or in arm's-length transactions where time is of the essence.[58]

The only possible limitation on a bank exercising its default remedies is the rule against penalties. Generally speaking, a provision making the *total* sum payable on any default is not to be considered a penalty.[59] However, acceleration must be confined to the capital sum: a clause providing that in the event of any breach the capital sum is immediately payable, together with all anticipated interest, i.e. without discount for the fact that the interest is not earned, would constitute a penalty.[60] The clause is not a genuine pre-estimate of the loss incurred on default, since presumably the bank can immediately lay out the capital again and earn interest from another borrower. However, a default clause providing that the lenders shall forthwith be put in funds to cover all existing or future liability under outstanding bills of exchange drawn in connection with a loan is not a penalty, even if it be construed as covering potential liability for interest on the bills. The justification is that it is protecting the lenders against liability if the bills have been negotiated. In England, it is not the general practice to issue bills in association with loan agreements, although this is done elsewhere.

C. THE COMMERCIAL REALITIES

A bank with a wide default clause has a more powerful weapon than is provided by the legal remedies under the general law. But herein lies the rub: a default clause acts best *in terrorem*: if it has to be invoked the situation is probably lost. Some of the practical obstacles to invoking the default clause are obvious on the face of the clause itself. The cross-default clause is a notable example, because it is likely to be replicated in other loan agreements. It is a reminder that if default occurs under this loan, default may be triggered under other loans as well. As a result, the borrower may face a number of demands but be unable to meet any of them. In a rescheduling, even small lenders will have to be accommodated by the others. Consequently, banks may be

---

[58] e.g., *On Demand Information plc* v. *Michael Gerson (Finance) plc* [2002] UKHL 13, [2002] 2 WLR 919.
[59] *Wallingford* v. *Mutual Society* (1880) 5 App.Cas. 685.
[60] *The Angelic Star* [1988] 1 Lloyd's Rep. 122, [1988] 1 FTLR 94 (CA).

reluctant to call a default unless the borrower is in a near hopeless position. Even then, if it has security it may choose to exercise that instead.[61] Some of the practical obstacles to using the default clause derive from the very nature of lending. As one of the standard books on term-lending puts it, the lending bank will demand immediate repayment of the loan only in extreme circumstances:

because banks are in the business to lend money; if the borrower is able to repay, then it is probably still worth lending to . . . [A] demand for repayment which was met would almost certainly mean the end of any relationship with the company.[62]

Thus despite an event of default occurring—and for that matter breach of the agreement—a bank may well decide not to exercise its remedies, for example, by not giving notice of default to the borrower. The bank may simply waive the breach, in other words elect to have the contract continue on foot. In serious cases it may use the threat of invoking its remedies to negotiate a more favourable rescheduling. Note that the bank cannot be said to have waived its remedies unless it has full knowledge of the circumstances which would give rise to its right to call default. Moreover, to have waived an event of default it must have acted unequivocally. Acceptance of late payment *this* month most probably does not constitute waiver of late payment *next* month, although to protect its position the bank should state this in writing. Although there is generally a clause in the agreement that no failure to exercise a right shall constitute waiver, a bank as a matter of fact might well be held to have waived its rights under that clause.

---

[61] *The Maule* [1997] 1 WLR 528 (PC).

[62] J. A. Donaldson and T. H. Donaldson, *The Medium Term Loan Market* (London, Macmillan, 1982), 154–5.

12

BANKS AND THE CAPITAL MARKETS

As banks have become multifunctional institutions, core banking has become associated with securities activities. That has always been the situation with the universal banks of jurisdictions like Germany, but in England the clearing banks and merchant banks were for over a century institutionally separate.[1] That no longer being the case, banking law must acknowledge the reality and find some place in its overall framework for a discussion of securities law. This is doubly important because of the long-term decline in the share of bank lending in the financial system. As a source of finance it has been losing ground to securities markets. The intermediation of core banking—taking money on deposit and lending it—has been overtaken by dis-intermediation, as larger companies raise money directly on the securities markets through the issue of equities and debt securities.

Many banks have compensated for this decline in traditional finance by emphasizing their securities activities. These range from a traditional task of investment banks in advising, underwriting, and distributing new issues of securities, through to dealing on their own account on securities and derivatives markets.[2] Often such activities have an international dimension to them, with the overlap and integration of domestic and international markets. Securities issues, especially debt securities issues, are becoming international in character. The typical purchasers of securities will be large institutions like insurance companies, pension funds, and fund managers, whose portfolios will invariably range beyond the domestic.

---

[1] 20, 98 above.

[2] e.g. U. Cherubini *et al.*, 'The Role of Banks as Investors in Securities', in V. Conti and R. Hamaui (eds.), *Financial Markets' Liberalisation and the Role of Banks* (Cambridge, CUP, 1993).

I. TYPES OF SECURITIES, SUBORDINATION, AND CUSTODY

Capital can be classified in a variety of ways. One division is between secured and unsecured capital. Secured capital is a subject for a later chapter (Chapter 15). Unsecured capital can be divided into senior and subordinated capital. There is also the fundamental distinction between equity and debt capital. After exploring these different features in a little more detail, this section of the Chapter addresses an institutional matter fundamental to securities dealings, custody. At base this involves the safe-keeping of any instruments representing the capital. These days custody involves record-keeping and spills over into providing other services such as settlement.

A. TYPES OF SECURITIES

(i) Equity and Debt Securities

The basic legal distinction is between equity and debt capital. Equity capital represents, in commercial terms, the risk capital, since it is last in the queue to be paid, but if things go right there will be a considerable benefit. Those providing the debt capital—lenders and investors—will want the margin of safety which adequate equity capital provides. An appropriate debt:equity ratio (gearing) will provide a sufficient cushion so that debt servicing is not too great a burden on the cash flow of the enterprise. The availability of security, in particular guarantees, may make a lower debt:equity ratio acceptable. Legally the holders of equity capital—the shareholders of a company—have rights and obligations as the company's members. This is the subject of company, not banking, law.

Debt capital takes a variety of forms, in addition to the bank loans examined in the preceding chapter. A company may issue debt securities—bonds, notes, certificates of deposit, commercial paper, debentures, and so on. These terms have no fixed legal meaning, although commercially they often indicate features such as the maturity of the securities. Bonds are usually long-term securities, for instance, but commercial paper is short term. Certificate of deposit is typically the term used to describe debt securities issued by banks themselves. The fundamental legal character of the different types of debt security remains constant, a point frequently lost in the detailed accounts describing the documentation which at a particular time typically governs their issue and distribution. It is important to appreciate that debt securities called, for instance, 'commercial paper', have no fixed quality. Markets vary and change. So, too, does the terminology and the ways of doing things.

At base a debt security represents the simplest form of obligation in English law, i.e. debt. If there is a definitive instrument, it evidences the debt. The terms on which the debt is to be repaid will need to be specified, e.g. is the interest rate fixed or floating? Indeed, a range of contractual provisions will overlay the basic obligation to pay.

There may be anti-disposal and negative-pledge undertakings by the issuer. There may be events of default. The undertakings and events of default will be less onerous than discussed in relation to bank loans, where those providing the finance are in a stronger bargaining position.[3]

(ii) Registered, Bearer, and Paperless Securities

Both equity and debt securities may be issued in either registered or bearer form. Ownership of the former (even if only nominal) appears on a register kept by the issuer. In English law the transfer of a registered equity security results in a novation: the transferee is substituted for the transferor as a member of the company, with the same rights and obligations. Section 22(2) of the Companies Act 1985 provides that the transferee becomes a member of the company only when entered in the register of members.

By contrast, registered debt securities are transferred in English law by way of assignment. Until notice is given to the issuer, the assignment will remain equitable. If there is a trustee and the promise to pay is in favour of it rather than the investors, the assignment will be treated as of an equitable, rather than of a legal, interest. As with the assignment of any chose in action, the assignment of a registered debt security will be subject to equities.[4] Express provision will need to mitigate this right of an issuer to raise claims against transferees. Although the Companies Act 1985 contemplates that there may be a register of debt securities, there is nothing in the Act, as there is for shares, about the effect of registration.

Bearer securities are transferable by delivery. This is because English law treats both share certificates to bearer and bearer debt securities as negotiable instruments. There has been a considerable debate in North America about whether certain types of debt securities can be negotiable instruments. For example, it is said that a debt security with a floating interest rate is not, since it does not contain a promise to pay 'a sum certain'.[5] In English law this is beside the point. Certainly the statutory law requires of a promissory note that it contain an unconditional promise to pay a sum certain.[6] But negotiability can also arise at common law, as a matter of market practice (trade usage). Bearer debt securities have been held to be negotiable in this way, even those having a relatively short life.[7] In any event, a floating interest rate is arguably a sum certain, since at any particular point the rate is ascertainable. Whether the typical debt security, with its clauses qualifying the obligation to pay, contains the requisite 'unconditional' promise to pay, is more doubtful. But common law negotiability comes to the rescue. Negotiability is no longer a practical concern, since securities these days are immobilized in depositories.

Both registered and non-registered securities may not be evidenced by any

---

[3] 321 above.   [4] 358 below.
[5] e.g. J. Hiller and S. Ferris, 'Variable Interest Rates and Negotiability' (1989) 94 *Commercial LJ* 48.
[6] Bills of Exchange Act 1882, s. 83(1).
[7] W. Blair, 'Negotiability and Estoppel' [1988] 1 *JIBL* 8 reviews the case law.

definitive instruments representing individual securities. A global note may represent the whole of the issue, with individual ownership of the debt securities being evidenced by book entries. Individual investors may be contractually entitled to call, however, for definitive instruments to be issued. Dematerialization takes the process one step further—there is nothing to represent the securities, not even one composite (global) instrument. Dealing is done on a paperless basis, and ownership and transactions recorded electronically. Again, however, individual investors may be able to opt out of a dematerialized system and obtain definitive instruments. To protect those dealing in securities through an approved paperless system in the UK, where an uncertificated security ceases to be held in that form so that it must be registered, regulations confer on transferees an equitable interest on the transfer taking place.[8]

(iii) Convertible Securities

While there is a legal chasm between equity and debt capital, there is a commercial blurring.[9] One example is convertible debt. This may be evidenced by a debt security, which gives the holder the right to convert the debt into shares of the particular company. Legally, a convertible security of this nature gives the investor an option—a right which it may, but need not, exercise. The right passes with the security. There is some controversy in English law whether the right is a contractual right or simply an irrevocable offer which the investor may accept.

There are several problems associated with this type of debt security. First, the company could dilute the conversion value by making larger dividend payments to existing holders of equity capital, subdividing existing equity, issuing new equity, and so on.[10] Holders of debt securities have no standing to object to such measures, as they are not members of the company. Their protection must come from contractual undertakings set out in the debt securities, the so-called anti-dilution clauses. These bind the company, and any holder of the securities can enforce them.

Secondly, there are the problems thrown up by legislation. For example, there are limitations on the amount of equity any one person can hold, set out in the laws of various jurisdictions. For example, banks in the European Community cannot have more than a specified stake in industrial and commercial companies.[11] Some countries employ limits on foreign shareholdings in domestic enterprises. Several countries oblige a mandatory takeover bid once a certain level of shareholding has been reached

---

[8] Uncertificated Securities Regulations 2001, SI 2001 No 3755, r.31. See J. Benjamin, *Interests in Securities* (Oxford, OUP, 2000), 33–6.

[9] R. McCormick and H. Creamer, *Hybrid Corporate Securities: International Legal Aspects* (London, Sweet & Maxwell, 1987).

[10] W. Klein, 'The Convertible Bond' (1975) 123 *Univ. Penn. LR* 547, 565–7; P. Wood, 'International Convertible Bond Issues' [1986] 2 *JIBL* 69; M. Dunton and C. Parker, 'Exchangeable and Convertible Bonds' [2001] *JIBL* 287, 289–90.

[11] 35 above.

in a listed company.[12] (In the United Kingdom this is effected not through legislation but through the Takeovers Code.) In all such cases a holder of convertible debt securities must be aware of the consequences of exercising the right to convert, if this contravenes these limits.

(iv) Debt Securities and Deposit-taking

One quirk to issuing debt securities in the United Kingdom relates to the impact of FSMA 2000. It will be recalled that deposit and deposit-taking are widely defined there. So widely defined, in fact, that an ordinary commercial issuer, having nothing to do with banking, could infringe the provision penalizing the accepting of deposits without authorization in the course of business. The problem is especially acute with shorter term debt securities—commercial paper and medium-term notes—where issuers regularly return to the market and thus satisfy the test for carrying on business in English law. An exemption has been necessary to avoid this result.[13]

B. SUBORDINATED CAPITAL

The subordinated capital of an enterprise is capital which will only be repaid once other (senior) capital is repaid. In terms of payment priorities, the subordinated (or junior) capital falls between equity and straightforward (or senior) debt. Its fundamental legal character is, however, debt capital. Subordinated capital may be advanced by an insider to an enterprise, or by a sponsor of a project, to provide the capital which will support borrowings from third parties such as banks. It may also feature in work-outs, where existing suppliers, insiders, and creditors agree to subordinate their debt claims so as to attract further support from the banks. Banks themselves have issued subordinated securities, which count as Tier 2 capital for capital-adequacy purposes.[14] In takeovers and management buy-outs, institutional investors or a departing shareholder may agree to take subordinated debt.

It is easy enough for junior creditors to agree with a company (say) that their claims will be subordinated. The legal issue is how to structure a transaction so that the subordination stands up.[15] When the company is solvent, everyone will be paid. It is only on the insolvency of the company that the problem arises. In other words, how can the specified senior creditors be assured that the junior creditors will not be able to upset the arrangements on insolvency and have their claims treated as *pari passu* with those of the senior creditors?

---

[12] P. Lambrecht, 'The 13th Directive on Takeover Bids—Formation and Principles', in G. Ferranini, K. Hopt, and E. Wymeersch (eds.), *Capital Markets in the Age of the Euro* (Hague, Kluwer, 2002), 461–4; E. Wymeersch, 'The Mandatory Bid', in K. Hopt and E. Wymeersch (eds.), *European Takeovers. Law and Practice* (London, Butterworths, 1992).

[13] Financial Services and Markets Act 2000 (Regulated Activities) Order 2001, SI 2001 No 544, as amended, paras. 9, 77–8. See G. Fuller, *Corporate Borrowing: Law and Practice* (Bristol, Jordans, 1995), ch. 9.

[14] 90 above.

[15] See P. Wood, *Project Finance, Subordinated Debt and State Loans* (London, Sweet & Maxwell, 1995), chs. 6–11; P. Wood, *The Law of Subordinated Debt* (London, Sweet & Maxwell, 1990).

There are various ways of doing this. One possibility is for the junior creditors to agree that, on an insolvency, they will turn over everything paid to them to the senior creditors, until such time as the latter are paid in full. One problem with this type of turnover arrangement is set-off. In English law a creditor of an insolvent company has a right to set off claims which the company has against it. If there are such claims against the junior creditors which are set off, there may be nothing subject to the turnover agreement. Alternatively, if a junior creditor is itself insolvent—it may be a related company of the debtor and the whole group has collapsed—there will be nothing in the pot for the senior creditor. The senior creditor in this situation bears a double credit risk.[16]

A second type of contractual-debt subordination is a contingency debt arrangement. This is a means of overcoming the problems of set-off and a junior creditor's insolvency. Here junior creditors agree that, on the insolvency of the company, their claims are contingent on the senior creditors being fully paid. Since until that point the junior creditors do not have a claim, there cannot be any set-off. Nor is anything paid to them which is caught up in their own insolvency. A disadvantage of the contingent debt arrangement, over the turnover agreement, is that the senior creditors must share *pari passu* with ordinary creditors. With a turnover arrangement they obtain a double dividend compared with ordinary creditors—the payment due to them and that due to junior creditors.

Despite earlier doubts, contractual-debt subordination of whatever type does not fall foul of the *pari passu* principle. This principle supposedly underlies insolvency law, although with all the exceptions the law recognizes—secured debt, set-off, reservation of title clauses, and trust devices—it looks decidedly shaky. In several decisions the courts have upheld subordination arrangements, with the reasoning that the *pari passu* principle is not mandatory, but confers a private right on creditors which they may contractually relinquish.[17] Moreover, it has been held that contractual-debt subordination does not necessarily constitute a charge over a company's assets which, if unregistered, is void in the insolvency. An agreement may simply determine how the company should distribute its assets—it need not give senior creditors the property interest which is a prerequisite to security.[18]

So far we have simply assumed that senior creditors can enforce contractual subordination. If they are a party to the contract, they certainly can. It will not be possible for the company and junior creditors to agree to amend the subordination agreement without their consent. An inter-creditor (or priorities) agreement will be a feature of many of the more complex financings with a single borrower to which banks are

---

[16] B. Johnston, 'Contractual Debt Subordination and Legislative Reform' [1991] *JBL* 225, 240.

[17] e.g. *Re Maxwell Communications Corp. (No 2)* [1993] 1 WLR 1402, [1994] 1 All ER 737. See J. Lopes, 'Contractual Subordinations and Bankruptcy' (1980) 97 *Banking LJ* 204; G. Bourke, 'The Effectiveness in Australia of Contractual Debt Subordination where the Debtor becomes Insolvent' (1996) 7 *JBFLP* 107; S. Rajani, 'Enforceability of Subordination of Debt in a Liquidation' (2000) 16 *Insolvency L&P* 58.

[18] *United States Trust Co. of New York v. Australia and New Zealand Banking Group Ltd.* (1995) 37 NSW LR 131 (CA). See R. Goode, *Commercial Law* (2nd edn., London, Penguin, 1995), 664–6.

parties. The inter-creditor agreement will cover the rights of the various creditors and provide procedures for them to agree on matters such as calling default. Importantly, it will provide for any subordination.

In some situations, however, the senior creditors of the company will be unknown, future creditors. In the case of a securities issue, there may be many of them. In the absence of contract, one way they can have enforceable rights in English law is under a trust. The junior creditors could declare themselves as trustees of the amounts they agree to turn over to the senior creditors under the subordination agreements.[19] As well, this may destroy the mutuality necessary for set-off, because the senior creditor's proprietary interest in the recoveries as beneficiary under the turnover trust would be destroyed by a set-off between junior creditor and the company. Most turnover subordinations are by the trust route, and only rarely do parties agree that the junior creditor will pay *amounts equal* to recoveries to the senior creditor, rather than transferring the benefit of those recoveries.

C. CUSTODY

Banks play the dominant role in providing custody services. And custody is now central to the issue of and trading in capital markets instruments. Writing about the topic is, however, fraught with difficulties.[20] Custody services differ between jurisdictions, as do the relevant institutional arrangements and law. There is a big difference between the situations, say, in London and Russia, although through sub-custodian arrangements a 'global custodian' will provide customers with custody services in respect of numerous other countries, in addition to where it is actually located.

Certainly it can be said that modern custody is more than safekeeping. The basic custody services include settlement, cash management (e.g. dividends, interest payments, redemptions, and reinvestment), and communicating and acting on corporate events (e.g. voting rights, proxies). Additional custody services include securities lending, derivatives, and performance measurement. In practice, custody services are provided mainly by large banks. In any event providing custody services is a regulated activity, and must be authorized under the FSMA 2000.[21] Custodians are subject to conduct-of-business rules, e.g. about segregating their own assets and those held as custodian.[22] One catalyst for similar changes in Europe has been the Investment Services Directive.[23] This obliges Member States to ensure that investment firms make adequate arrangements for safeguarding investors' ownership rights in

---

[19] J. Powell, 'Rethinking Subordination' [1993] *LMCLQ* 357, 371.

[20] See R. Goode, 'The Nature and Transfer of Rights in Dematerialised and Immobilised Securities', in F. Oditah (ed.), *The Future for the Global Securities Market* (Oxford, Clarendon, 1996); J. Benjamin, *The Law of Global Custody* (London, Butterworths, 1996); A. Austen-Peters, *Custody of Investments: Law and Practice* (Oxford, OUP, 2000).

[21] FSMA 2000, Sched. 2, para 5.

[22] FSA Handbook, *Conduct of Business*, ch. 9.1.

[23] Dir. 93/22/EEC [1993] OJ L141/27, Art. 10.

investment instruments (especially in insolvency), and do not use instruments for their own account, except with express consent.

Customers of custodians come in a variety of shapes and sizes. They may be individual investors, fund managers, or institutions like insurance companies. They may be other banks or another part of the same bank (e.g. the fund-management arm). They will often be acting on behalf of their own customers in holding and depositing the securities.

The legal position of customers *vis-à-vis* the custodian will be spelt out in a written agreement. Custodians will be entrusted with discretion about how the securities are held, although for record purposes customers will each have an account, which will be credited and debited in accordance with instructions. The agreement should also answer some obvious questions. What liability is the custodian prepared to assume (if any), in the event of a depository or clearing system collapsing? Is the custodian entitled, for example, to use the securities for securities lending. (The term is a misnomer, since the securities are transferred outright to the third party—often securities dealers which need to settle trades—who undertake to return equivalent securities. The custodian takes security from the third party as collateral and shares any fees it earns with its customers.[24]) What duties does the custodian have in choosing and monitoring sub-custodians, which will be employed in the various jurisdictions where the issuers of the securities making up a portfolio are located? To what extent does it assume liability for their lapses? In the absence of agreement English law is generous to custodians, so long as they exercise reasonable care in choosing sub-custodians and keeping the sub-custodian arrangements under review.[25]

Apart from the rights and liabilities generated by the agreement, there are various other legal issues which arise in a customer's relations with a custodian. One concerns the consequences of the custodian's insolvency, negligence, or fraud. In established financial centres this is largely a theoretical possibility, but in emerging markets it is a risk which must be taken into account. Another is the conflict of interests which can arise between a bank's role, say, as fund manager and as custodian.[26] How security is created over a customer's securities is a third issue, discussed later in the book.[27] Partly the resolution of these issues depends on the nature of the relevant property; partly it depends on how the relevant law characterizes the relationship between customer and custodian.

Take a situation where customer B has securities deposited with Bank A, a custodian. As far as any moneys are concerned (e.g. moneys credited to the customer as dividends or interest) the customer is simply a creditor. The customer does not acquire any interest in, or charge over, any asset of the bank, and if the bank becomes insolvent, all the customer can do is to prove in the liquidation as an unsecured creditor for the amount which was, or ought to have been, credited to it.[28]

---

[24] 411 below.   [25] Cf. Trustee Act 2000, s. 23(1).   [26] 21 above.   [27] 407 below.
[28] *Space Investments Ltd.* v. *Canadian Imperial Bank of Commerce Trust Co. (Bahamas) Ltd.* [1986] 1 WLR 1072, [1986] 3 All ER 75 (PC).

As for the securities, take the simplest case: say definitive, bearer securities have been issued but are deposited with Bank A.

One way of characterizing this relationship in English law is as bailment. B is bailor, and the bank is bailee. Moreover, B does not lose its rights as bailor just because Bank A holds the securities, along with the same securities belonging to itself or others, and it is not possible to identify any one person's securities in the pool (e.g. by number). Bank A must still redeliver securities of the same type, denomination, and amount, even though not the identical securities. Title remains in all parties in the fungible pool in proportion to their respective deposits.[29]

Bailment as a way of characterizing the relationship would be of great advantage to B. On Bank A's insolvency, B would have a proprietary right, which could not be defeated by Bank A's creditors. B could also trace where the securities had been wrongfully converted into other forms. Importantly, bailment can continue to operate where B sells its securities to C, if Bank A attorns to C as the new owner. This is obviously important, because after their issue securities are typically traded, often frequently so, and in back-to-back trades. Arguably, attornment can work even if the securities sold are an undifferentiated portion of a larger quantity of identical securities, the custodian being estopped from arguing that severance and appropriation have not occurred.

In practice, however, there are often real obstacles to characterizing the relationship as bailment. Bailment is possible even if the exact property is not returned, but English (although not North American) law does not go as far as accepting that the bailee can convert the bailment into a loan, substitute other goods, and convert the loan back into a bailment. Yet this is what a custodian will claim to be able to do, not least in the case of securities lending. The problems for bailment are compounded when a sub-custodian is involved, as will often be the case in practice. Certainly English law recognizes sub-bailment and quasi-bailment (where the bailee never has possession). But can there be any sort of bailment if the securities go directly from issuer to sub-custodian, in other words if neither Bank A nor B ever has possession? Regardless of the agreement between Bank A and B, what if that between Bank A and the sub-custodian denies that other than contractual rights are involved? In the case of a transfer from B to C, how can the sub-custodian ever be regarded as attorning to C, when neither it nor C is ever likely to know of each other's existence? And when the sub-custodian is in a foreign jurisdiction, even if Bank A and customer B are in London, is a court, especially a court in the foreign jurisdiction, likely to apply the English law of bailment? If securities are represented by a global note or are dematerialized, then bailment is not an appropriate characterization, even in the simplest of cases governed by English law.[30] Possession is central to bailment, yet there is nothing that can be physically possessed.

---

[29] *Mercer v. Craven Grain Storage Ltd.* [1994] CLC 328 (PC).
[30] Cf. A. Beaves, 'Global Custody', in N. Palmer and E. McKendrick (eds.), *Interests in Goods* (2nd edn., London, LLP, 1998).

What, then, of trust as a means of characterizing the position of custodians. Can an intention be spelt out to constitute the custodian as trustee? If so, is there the requisite certainty in the subject matter of the trust? In the simplest case the records of a third party (the issuer; a securities clearing and settlement system) identify the custodian Bank A as holding the securities, but on behalf of B. English law would regard this as a clear indication of an intention to create a trust. The position is trickier if the securities are recorded in the name of Bank A alone, or its nominee. Here the custody agreement, and Bank A's own records, would be crucial to show the requisite intention, for in its absence the arrangement would be purely contractual and B would not have any beneficial interest in the event of Bank A's insolvency.

As far as the subject matter of a trust is concerned, the typical situation these days is that Bank A as custodian will hold A's securities in an undifferentiated mass along with securities of the same type held by others. The securities may be held by sub-custodians. There may not be any definite instruments, not even a global note, and the securities are completely dematerialized. The pool of securities of all types held by Bank A as custodian, including the type held by B, will be constantly shifting as Bank A's customers buy and sell, as Bank A buys and sells securities it owns, and as Bank A engages in securities lending. Despite all this English law has no difficulty with the subject matter of the trust. It has long recognized a trust over a fungible mass, so long as there is an intention to create a trust. The so-called problem of allocation, which has bewitched some commentators, does not arise as it does with tangibles such as goods. The subject matter of any trust is intangibles, which can never be differentiated (or allocated). In English law, the nature of B's beneficial interest is a functional interest in the shifting pool of securities of a particular issuer, held by Bank A as custodian.

In summary, the characterization of the relationship between customer and custodian will turn on the agreement. Superimposing bailment over this agreement will be defeated in practice, given the nature of modern custodial arrangements (e.g. stock lending by custodians, the use of sub-custodians) and modern securities (represented by a global note or dematerialized). Trust is a clear possibility, and is readily demonstrated where the customer is identified on third party records. ('Bank A—account client B'). There are difficulties of proof if the register simply identifies Bank A's nominee company as holder or the only records are those of the custodian or its sub-custodian. But there is no obstacle in principle to finding a trust, despite the fungibility of its subject matter, so long as the intention to create a trust is clear.

II. DISTRIBUTING SECURITIES ISSUES

Advising, arranging, and then distributing an issue of government or corporate securities is an investment banking activity which goes back centuries. On this ground alone it justifies attention. But it is also a matter which can demand a considerable legal input. The documentation can be voluminous, even if it is fairly standard. One reason for its standardization is the activities of trade associations of banks, such as the International Primary Market Association (IPMA), which consists of the leading banks involved in Eurobond issues. Moreover, there are a host of legal issues, which periodically bubble to the surface as issuers fail. Banks can then enter the frame as a convenient deep pocket for investors experiencing a loss.

A. MECHANICS OF DISTRIBUTION

(i) Brokerage, Placement, Underwriting, and Purchase

Analytically, without relating the discussion to the practices of any particular market, a bank's involvement with an issue of securities can involve, in broad terms, a hierarchy of four types of agreement with an issuer. The first can be described as a *brokerage agreement* with the issuer. With this there is no commitment on the bank's part, but it will agree to provide services such as disseminating the prospectus or offering circular, handling applications for securities, and maybe liaising with a stock exchange if the securities are to be listed. The bank will not be under a contractual obligation to solicit subscriptions.

At the next level the bank could conclude what might be termed a *placement agreement* with the issuer. Again there will be no obligation on it to take any securities, but it will be obliged to secure subscriptions for the securities. This could be with professional investors or the public generally. One legal issue is the standard to be expected of the bank in executing its task of placing the securities. In the absence of an express provision, it will need to exercise reasonable care and skill. What about a higher standard, such as best endeavours? English law could only reach this result by implying a term in the contract on the basis of market practice (trade usage). Notice that a bank may have an action against brokers, which it employs to assist it in placing the securities, if they breach their undertakings, thereby causing the bank loss.[31]

Thirdly, if a bank agrees to *underwrite* an issue of securities, it commits itself to take them up in the event that the issue is undersubscribed. It is clearly distinguished from a brokerage agreement and a placement agreement. Under section 195 of the Companies Act 1985, an underwriting agreement for debt securities is enforceable by specific performance. For an unfathomable reason equity issues are not covered, so to prevent the bank getting off the hook, and simply paying damages, other devices are

---

[31] e.g. *County Ltd. v. Girozentrale Securities* [1996] 3 All ER 834 (CA).

necessary (e.g. a director of the issuer being empowered on the underwriter's behalf to be allotted the number of securities underwritten).

The advantage of underwriting to the issuer is obvious: it knows that it will be paid for the securities. Underwriting by the bank may even enhance the marketability of the securities. Where more than one bank is acting as underwriter, there needs to be an agreement on whether their liability is several, or joint and several. An underwriting bank can enter sub-underwriting agreements with others, under which the latter agree to underwrite a certain amount of the securities. Other than by contract, an underwriting bank has no duty to the issuer in sub-underwriting its commitment.[32]

Finally, the bank could agree to purchase the whole of the securities and then sell them to investors (a *purchase agreement*). If it does so there is a clear risk in relation to its capital. Moreover, various consequences flow because in this situation it is acting as principal, rather than as agent of the issuer. First, if it is in direct contractual relations with those to whom it on-sells, investors can thus make contractual claims directly against it. (If it is simply an agent, contractual claims will generally only be against the issuer.) Secondly, a bank may become responsible for any faults in the prospectus, offering circular, or the like published by the issuer. To both consequences we return.

(ii) Obtaining the Mandate

How a bank becomes contractually involved in a distribution of an issuer's securities clearly depends on the circumstances. The issuer may have been a long-established customer of the bank, or have used it for a previous issue. At the underwriting/ purchase end of the spectrum the issuer may conduct an auction, or call for tenders by those wishing to be involved in a distribution. There may be a number of banks involved, which are organized as a syndicate.[33]

With short-term debt securities, which are to be regularly issued, the issuer might even establish a tender panel of those it is prepared to have tender to purchase and distribute any particular issue. The agreement establishing a tender panel may commit the issuer on how the securities will be allocated, depending on the level of bids. There is no duty of good faith in English law, so, although a bank which is a member of a tender panel may be contractually obliged to bid, it need not do so *bona fide* or reasonably. In practice tender panels are constituted when the issuer has the whip hand, and members of the panel are actively competing to take the securities.

In whatever way tendering is used in the distribution of securities, its legal character must be taken into account. In English law a tender is an offer. Since a bank in tendering is making an offer, it can withdraw it before acceptance if it decides it has pitched its bid incorrectly, or if the market changes. Conversely, the issuer is not obliged to accept the best bid in terms of price. Both rules are, of course, subject to contract. A bank could make an irrevocable tender: an issuer could commit itself to

---

[32] *Eagle Trust plc* v. *SBC Securities Ltd.* [1995] BCC 231. See E. Ferran, *Company Law and Corporate Finance* (Oxford, OUP, 1999), 630–3.

[33] 54ff. above.

accepting bids from the lowest upwards. Depending on the market, it may be that the practice is to deal with tenders in a certain way. If the practice meets the standards for a trade usage—it is certain, notorious and reasonable—the parties would be bound by the implied term. As a matter of fairness, English law does not permit referential tenders, in other words tenders expressed to be so many base points better than what another party bids.[34]

B. PROTECTION FOR THE BANK *VIS-À-VIS* THE ISSUER

A bank will want protection in distributing an issue, especially where it commits itself to purchase securities under an underwriting agreement or outright purchase. A basic concern is whether the prospects for the issue are sound. Clearly the issuer can be required to give representations and warranties as conditions precedent to the bank's obligation—about the truth and completeness of the prospectus or offering circular, that the issuer is not involved in any material litigation or arbitration, that it has obtained all necessary regulatory approvals, and so on. There is no legal objection to the representations and warranties having to remain accurate, until closing, or beyond.

The bank's commitment under the agreement could be made conditional on no event occurring which makes the representations and warranties incorrect. Additional conditions precedent to the bank's obligation could be that the issuer obtains a stock exchange listing, and that there be favourable certificates and reports from the issuer's directors and auditors. It is simpler and clearer if the bank can obtain a condition precedent in relation to the latter heads, rather than having to prove a breach of a warranty and representation. The bank can always waive non-compliance with a condition precedent if it is happy to continue its commitment.

Importantly, the bank can take an indemnity from the issuer for losses it occurs as a result of the distribution. These could be direct losses of the bank, or losses it incurs as a result of investors claiming against it. An indemnity clause in relation to the latter avoids the argument at common law that such damages are too remote—not being within the reasonable contemplation of the parties.[35] It can also usefully cover the costs to the bank of defending any action by investors. English law makes illegal a contract to indemnify a person in respect of liability for fraud. If a bank is unaware that a prospectus, say, is fraudulent, it could rely on the indemnity. But if it continues to promote the issue once it knows of the true state of affairs, or is reckless about them, it cannot invoke the indemnity against the issuer.[36]

Any delay between the bank undertaking a commitment and closing raises the possibility of events occurring which are adverse to the issue. A bank could be saddled with some very unattractive paper. Consequently, it will try to insist on a *force*

---

[34] *Harvela Industries Ltd.* v. *Royal Trust Co. of Canada* [1986] AC 207 (HL).

[35] E. Ferran, 'The Benefit of Warranties in Bond Issues' (1990) 11 *Co. Lawyer* 163, 164n.

[36] T. Prime, *International Bonds and Certificates of Deposit* (London, Butterworths, 1990), 77–9.

majeure, or market disruption clause, whereby it can avoid its commitment to take the securities in the light of specified events. These could include a material alteration in the financial condition or business of the issuer, or a change in national or international political, economic, legal, tax, or regulatory conditions. In English law such *force majeure* clauses are best regarded as limiting the bank's obligation, rather than as shielding it from liability for breach of contract.[37] Naturally the bank will wish to make the decision itself whether the events set out in the clause have occurred. One limit on its discretion, which the issuer may be able to negotiate, is that the bank's opinion be reasonably held. Another would be that the bank also hold the opinion that the happening of the event materially prejudices the prospects of success of the issue. The test of materiality would probably be whether the event would reasonably affect the mind of a reasonable investor. In the Euromarkets, the International Primary Market Association has agreed standard-form *force majeure* clauses.

C. BANK'S LIABILITY TO INVESTORS

(i) The Bank's Own Wrongdoing

In distributing an issuer's securities, a bank can obviously incur legal liability through its own conduct. Its sales people may make representations or negligent statements, or may even act fraudulently. Although in English law a representation can be innocent and still give investors a remedy, it must be a positive representation of fact. Moreover, omissions do not, in general, give rise to liability, unless they result in a half-truth.[38] Negligent misstatement is broader, covering both opinions and omissions, but at its heart there must be an assumption of responsibility by the bank.[39] As for a fraudulent statement, there will be a heavy burden on an investor to demonstrate the requisite knowledge or recklessness in relation to a falsity. Statute also requires that the statement be in writing.[40] In the case of each—misrepresentation, negligent statement, and fraudulent statement—the investor must have relied on what the bank said in purchasing the securities. In addition to the common law, the bank may be liable for breaches of the securities laws, a topic deserving separate treatment.[41]

   An investor's remedies will turn, in part, on the way a distribution is structured. On the one hand if the bank is acting as broker, or is placing the securities with investors on behalf of the issuer, any contract is with the issuer: the bank is simply the agent. Misrepresentations by the bank, within the scope of its actual or apparent authority, are attributable to the issuer, even though the brokerage or placement agreement forbids such behaviour.[42] Rescission will probably be the favoured contractual remedy

[37] W. Swadling, 'The Judicial Construction of Force Majeure Clauses', in E. McKendrick (ed.), *Force Majeure and Frustration of Contract* (2nd edn., London, LLP, 1995); G. Treitel, *Frustration and Force Majeure* (London, Sweet & Maxwell, 1994), 434–55.
[38] 209 above.   [39] 185 above.
[40] *UBAF Ltd.* v. *European American Banking Corporation* [1984] QB 713 (CA).   [41] 349 below.
[42] *Bowstead and Reynolds on Agency* (17th edn., London, Sweet & Maxwell, 2001), 422–3.

of investors. However, the right to rescind can be lost—investors may be taken to have affirmed the contract, e.g. by accepting dividends or interest payments; they may have disabled themselves from restoring the securities, e.g. by selling them in the secondary market; or they may be defeated by a simple lapse of time in taking action. Recission being barred, an investor will sue for damages. Contractual damages are *prima facie* the difference between the actual value of the securities and the value if the representation had been true. In practice the latter will often be higher than what they paid. With negligent misstatement and non-contractual fraud (deceit), investors are confined to their actual losses, and cannot obtain damages for the gains they might have expected. Thus what they pay for the securities is the benchmark for their losses. If the issuer is liable to investors, in practice the bank will often be liable in turn to the issuer under an indemnity given to it for any loss suffered.

On the other hand, if the investor buys from the bank, which sells securities which it has in turn bought from the issuer (as underwriter or under a purchase agreement), contractual remedies lie in the first instance against the bank. However, once allotted, the security will also give rise to a contract directly with the issuer. If investors rescind, recission will be of both the contract of sale with the bank, and the contract which an investor has directly with the issuer on the security. It almost goes with out saying that negligent statement or fraud by the bank, when acting as principal, makes it directly liable to investors.[43]

(ii) The Issuer's Wrongdoing: The Bank's Duty of Due Diligence

So far the discussion has revolved around the bank's own representations, negligent statements, and fraud in distributing an issuer's securities. If the issuer is responsible for such wrongs, then its liability to investors will be along lines parallel to those discussed. A detailed discussion of the issuer's liability is beyond the scope of this book, which is concerned with the position of banks as distributors of another's securities. But there is one matter which deserves attention—the liability of the *bank* for the issuer's wrongdoings.

Perhaps the best illustration is if the offering circular or prospectus is false. The bank distributes it to prospective investors, who consequently suffer loss. The issuer fails. As a practical matter, investors' remedies against the issuer are worthless. (So, too, are the bank's remedies against the issuer, previously discussed.) Investors therefore look to the bank as a deep pocket from which to recover their losses. This is not a theoretical possibility. In 1994 the Supreme Court of the Netherlands held that, in principle, the lead bank of a syndicated bond issue could be liable in such circumstances. The decision was based on a provision in the Dutch civil code, that persons commit a tort by publishing or making available misleading information in relation to services offered by them as principal, or on another's behalf, in the course of a business or profession. Liability was not confined to those parts of the prospectus which the bank had prepared. Indeed, the bank was not necessarily entitled to excuse

---

[43] *Smith New Court Securities Ltd.* v. *Scrimgeour Vickers (Asset Management) Ltd.* [1997] AC 254 (HL).

itself if the faulty contents had been approved by independent auditors. The court
noted, however, that if a person distributing a text has included a clear and
unambiguous statement that it is not responsible for particular parts, and that it does
not accept responsibility for them, it can effectively disclaim liability.[44]

The upshot is that banks distributing an issuer's offering circular or prospectus
may be liable unless they have undertaken a due diligence exercise. In other words,
they must make reasonable inquiries about the statements in it, and must reasonably
believe that these are true and that there are not material omissions. That the securities are listed on an exchange is not conclusive about the truth or completeness of
the prospectus: the bank must conduct its own investigations. This it can do by
discussions with the borrower and external checks.

To what extent does this represent the position in English law? Certainly it is
sometimes said that it is market practice to do due diligence—to check the issue as
well as the suitability of the issuer by discussions with it and by external checks. Even
if this is market practice, translating it into a legal duty is not a one-to-one process.
Under a brokerage or placement agreement, a bank is acting as agent and so is not
directly liable to an investor in contract. But it could be liable in negligence or fraud.
Handing on the issuer's prospectus, for instance, does not necessarily exculpate the
bank from negligence.[45] Here any market practice could be used to set the standard of
care which the law demands. Were the bank to know about a false statement or
material omission in the prospectus, or were the bank to be reckless about any faults
in it, fraud is a possibility. In very special circumstances banks may owe fiduciary
duties to investors.[46]

If the bank sells as underwriter, or has purchased an issue for on-selling, it acts as
principal. The potential liability to investors in contract is two-fold. First, in relation to
a misrepresentation in, say, the prospectus, it may be that investors can demonstrate
that they contracted on this basis. Secondly, if the market practice is to conduct a due
diligence exercise, then it may be possible to imply a term in the contract that due
diligence has been observed in this instance. Failure to do so constitutes a breach.
However, English law puts significant road blocks in the way of establishing a trade
usage.

Even if liability could be founded on these various bases, however, English common
law gives a free rein to banks to negate it by denials, disclaimers, and exclusion clauses.
(The one exception is fraud, where as a matter of public policy the courts treat
attempts at exclusion as void.) Thus offering circulars and prospectuses contain
prominent statements that the issuer is responsible for information in it, that it takes
responsibility, and that no person has been authorized to give any information or to
make any representations other than those in the document. For reasons already
given, exclusions and disclaimers will pass muster under the statutory law on unfair
contract terms.[47] However, in English law statutory liability cannot be excluded by

[44] *Association of Bondholders Coopag Finance BV v. ABN Amro Bank NV* [1994] RvdW 263.
[45] 211 above.   [46] 187 above.   [47] 149 above.

disclaimer or exclusion clauses. Thus a key issue, to which we return below, is whether a bank may be liable for an issuer's faulty prospectus under the securities laws.[48]

D. TRUSTEES TO DEBT ISSUES

As members of a company, shareholders are in theory able to protect their own interests. Not so holders of debt securities. Thus, Anglo-American practice has long been to appoint a corporate trustee for the holders of debt securities. Some civil law countries have emulated this practice. The corporate trustee will act as the independent representative of the investors, and have wide discretion whether to call default. For a century the Law Debenture Trust Corporation plc—a widely held public company—has been appointed as a trustee of many debt issues in the United Kingdom and abroad. However, a number of international banks have arms which can, and do, act as the trustees to issues of debt securities. Both for this reason, and since it is an important element in many such distributions, some discussion of the role of the corporate trustee is necessary.

(i) Appointment of a Trustee

Generally speaking, listed debt securities in the UK must have a corporate trustee, who has no interest in or relation to the issuer which can conflict with its position as a trustee. The listing rules set out the provisions which the trust instrument must contain.[49] In other jurisdictions the mandatory appointment of a corporate trustee, or its equivalent, is set out in the law. These even include civil law countries, where the concept of trust is unknown to the law. For example, in 1993 the Japanese Commercial Code was amended to make compulsory the appointment of a bank or trust bank as a 'commissioned company' for holders of debt securities, except for offerings to institutional investors or private placements. Commissioned companies have duties under the Commercial Code somewhat comparable to the corporate trustee in common law countries.[50]

However, some jurisdictions do not require a corporate trustee or anything equivalent. Moreover, some Euromarket issuers eschew a corporate trustee. There is a cost, including the increased documentation. Sovereign borrowers resent the suggestion that they will not act in the interests of investors. Instead a fiscal agent may be appointed—an agent of the issuer—with administrative tasks such as running any register, publishing notices, acting as a conduit for information, drawing bonds for redemption, and so on. In a common law jurisdiction a fiscal agent may be regarded as holding any moneys to be paid to investors on trust. In special circumstances investors may also have a claim in negligence against the fiscal agent. As for the claims against the issuer, the rights of securities owners will usually be set out in a deed poll. In English law rights under a deed poll are enforceable despite the absence of privity

---

[48] 349 below.
[49] FSA, The Listing Rules, Apr. 2002 edn., rr.13.10, 13.12, App. 2.   [50] S. 297ff.

of contract. Coupled with the possibility of an action under the Contracts (Rights of Third Parties) Act 1999, purchasers of securities in the secondary markets can therefore proceed against the issuer.

The notion of a trustee for investors is, in theory, protective. An independent body, with access to expert advice, can monitor the issuer and take remedial action if necessary. Instead of investors individually having to take action, the trustee can act in a representative capacity for their benefit. In reality the trustee of debt issues is somewhat removed from this picture. Moreover, often underplayed is the enormous advantage to issuers of having a trustee. They are saved from multiple suits, or from suit by the renegade investor who will not accede to a rescheduling. Moreover, a trustee can waive breaches on an issuer's part and agree to some modifications of the issuers responsibilities to investors.[51]

Trustees also facilitate certain financial arrangements such as subordinated debt and securitizations. There are advantages in having a security trustee, where a number of banks are involved and the collateral takes a variety of forms.[52]

(ii) The Position of Investors

The appointment of a trustee transforms the position of the investor. In the terms governing the debt security—the bond, note, or debenture—the issuer may undertake to pay the investor, but only the trustee will be entitled to enforce the terms and call default. This is the so-called 'no action' provision. The investor expressly relinquishes its right to proceed directly against the issuer, except in the situation where a specified number of investors direct the trustee to enforce the security, and it fails to do so within a reasonable period. Indeed, the terms may even strip the investor of the right to payment. The undertaking to pay is given to the trustee alone, which then distributes payments to investors. In this second situation the investor ceases to be a creditor of the issuer.

In English law an investor will probably take subject to such limitation, even if he or she does not see a debt instrument (which remains with a custodian or is dematerialized). The limitation will be set out in the prospectus or offering circular, and the trust instrument. Investors are bound by market practice if notorious and reasonable, even though they are unaware of it. It becomes a term of their contract with the issuer. For this reason an investor buying on the secondary market will also be bound. American law is more protective of investors in relation to no action clauses.[53]

Typically the terms will give a majority (as defined) of investors the right to direct the trustee to enforce them. Meetings for this, and other purposes such as rescheduling, must be called and conducted in accordance with the terms of the debt instrument

---

[51] See P. Wood, *International Loans, Bonds and Securities Regulation* (London, Sweet & Maxwell, 1995), 164–8.

[52] C. Duffett, 'Using Trusts in International Finance and Commercial Transactions' (1992) 1 *J. Int'l. Trust and Corporate Planning* 23.

[53] R. McClelland and F. Fisher, *The Law of Corporate Mortgage Bond Issues* (1937) (Buffalo, William S. Hein, 1983 reprint), 684ff.

and trust instrument. Investors have the power to decide the matters expressly conferred and none other. Since a majority can bind a minority, there are some common law limits on the conduct by the majority in having a resolution passed— but only if it is oppressive, discriminatory, or fraudulent.

(iii) Rights and Duties of a Trustee

The trustee of an issue is constituted by a trust instrument. Under this the issuer will give a series of undertakings to the trustee. Of prime importance is the undertaking to pay the interest and ultimately the principal. This will be underpinned by undertakings to conduct its business in a proper manner, to prepare proper accounts and have them audited, to provide the trustee with information and documents (e.g. accounts, notifications of default, certificates of compliance), to use reasonable endeavours to maintain any exchange listing, and so on. The trustee will also be entitled to enforce the undertakings of the issuer governing the securities themselves—such as the negative pledge clause—as if they were in the trust instrument. The trustee is the trustee of these various undertakings for the benefit of the investors.[54] Any failure on its part can be visited by an action by the investors as beneficiaries under a trust.

The trustee has conferred on it the discretion whether or not to call default, indeed, in some cases, whether or not default has occurred. (The events of default will be breaches of the undertakings governing the securities and the trust instrument.) Individual investors relinquish that right, although the documentation will confer on them the power to direct the trustee to call default if they constitute the requisite majority. The trustee will also be entrusted with a power to waive or authorize breaches by the issuer of its various undertakings, and to determine that they are not to be treated as events of default. A prerequisite to this may be that the trustee is of the opinion that none of this will materially prejudice the investors. Coupled with the discretion to call default will be a power to agree minor or technical modifications, although any substantial restructuring (e.g. reducing or cancelling any amount payable, or extending the period of payment) will demand the agreement of investors.

In general terms a corporate trustee is in no different position from any other trustee, and its conduct is controlled by the same rules. It must act with reasonable care and skill, and in the interests of the beneficiaries/investors. Care and skill in this context have been said to require the trustee to act as if it were the investor. Indeed a corporate trustee will be held to a higher standard than an ordinary trustee, since it carries on the specialist business of trust management.[55] As for acting in the interests of beneficiaries, the general law demands that the trustee take appropriate action not only when facts come to its knowledge, but also if it is put on inquiry that something is wrong. It is also in breach if it does not ensure an adequate flow of information from the issuer.[56]

---

[54] Cf. R. Goode, *Commercial Law* (2nd edn., London, Penguin, 1995), 630.
[55] *Bartlett* v. *Barclays Bank Trust Co. Ltd.* [1980] Ch. 515. See also Trustee Act 2000, s. 1(1).
[56] *Ibid.* 532, 534.

In practice, however, the documentation will subtract from the standards usually expected of trustees. Unless a trustee has actual knowledge or express notice of default, it will be entitled to assume that none has occurred (the so-called Ostrich clause). Although it is there to monitor the behaviour of the issuer, it will be able to rely on the certificates of the issuer's directors that all is well. Its absolute and uncontrolled discretion as to the exercise of its trust will enable it to release the issuer, and its directors, if the certificates are prepared negligently.[57] It will have no duty to disclose to investors any information it obtains about the issuer, except as specifically provided for in the trust deed. Provided it exercises reasonable care in the selection and review of agents, nominees, and custodians (which it will be empowered to appoint), it will not be responsible for their default.[58] Despite the general strictures about conflicts of interest, the trust instrument will enable the trustee to enter into contracts and financial arrangements with the issuer, including banking contracts and financial facilities. It will also be permitted to underwrite, distribute, or deal with the securities of the issuer or its affiliates, and to act as the trustee of other debt issues.

In some common law jurisdictions, legislation places a floor under the duties of trustees. Too great a substraction from the ordinary duties of trustees would constitute a breach of statute. The Trust Indenture Act of 1939 in the United States is one example, although its floor may be none too high.[59] English law offers statutory protection to investors with one hand—the duty to act with reasonable care and skill—but then subtracts from it with the other: 'The duty of care does not apply if or in so far as it appears from the trust instrument that the duty is not meant to apply'.[60] In one case there was judicial disapproval of a clause in a trust deed which enabled the trustee (which was a bank) to act as bankers to the company, to make advances, and to do other things in that capacity.[61] Judicial displeasure never manifested itself in a rule of law against such conflicts of interest (although in practice English banks withdrew from being trustees of debt issues).

At some point a trustee exempted from the duties laid down in the general law or statute must cease to be a trustee, although there seems to be very considerable leeway. Since 1948, the companies legislation has invalidated clauses in trust instruments for securities where these exempt or indemnify the trustee in advance 'for breach of trust where [it] fails to show the degree of care and diligence required of [it] as trustee, having regard to the provisions of the trust deed conferring on [it] any powers, authorities or discretions'.[62] What the provision promises in its opening words is denied by the qualifying phrase: trust deeds can set the standards at a low level from the outset. Under the Trustee Act 1925, a trustee is not liable for loss unless it happens through its own wilful default.[63] Yet there is authority that 'wilful default' here does not

---

[57] *New Zealand Guardian Trust Co. Ltd.* v. *Brooks* [1995] 1 WLR 96 (PC).
[58] Trustee Act 2000, s. 23(1).
[59] 15 USC §77 aaa-bbb; *Central Bank of Denver* v. *First Interstate Bank of Denver*, 511 US 164 (1994).
[60] Trustee Act 2000, Sched. 1, para. 7.
[61] *In re Dorman, Long & Company, Ltd.* [1934] 1 Ch. 635, 671.
[62] See now Companies Act 1985, s. 192(1).   [63] S. 30(1).

include gross negligence, and that a trustee is liable under this section only for reckless indifference.[64] Under the Act the court can also excuse a trustee from any breach of trust if it acted honestly and reasonably, and ought fairly to be excused, although there is a judicial reluctance to use this with professional trustees.[65] Even if the Unfair Contract Terms Act 1977 is applicable to trust instruments, it is very difficult to see how a lowering of the trustee's standard does not meet the test of reasonableness when the relevant contract involves a corporate trustee and a commercial issuer.

In the result it seems that the English trust instrument can remove the usual duties of a corporate trustee, although they can never be permitted to act fraudulently or recklessly.[66] Controlling the move away from core duties for corporate trustees therefore turns largely on self-regulation and legal practice. As mentioned, the listing rules of the FSA proscribe conflicts of interest for corporate trustees. Consequently, the bank with a corporate trustee arm would have at the least to establish effective Chinese walls.

III. SECURITIES REGULATION

Banks falling under the securities laws are obviously subject to both banking and securities regulation. For the bank it means superimposing a layer of additional regulation on basic banking regulation. In jurisdictions where banking and securities regulation are institutionally separate, there is also the problem of regulatory co-ordination. Clearly there are good reasons for the different regulators to co-operate. Chief among these are efficiency, and to avoid regulatory gaps and overlaps. The concept of 'lead regulator' is a means of achieving co-ordination. One of the regulators takes the lead, depending on the particular activity of the regulated institution.

Banking law as conceived in this book is imperialistic, but even it must draw the line at securities regulation. Until relatively recently, securities law outside the United States was relatively under-developed. Now in many jurisdictions it is a subject in its own right with a myriad of rules, of which only the expert securities lawyer can be master.[67] This part of the Chapter can only touch the surface of securities law, mainly as it relates to the activities of banks in the issue and distribution of securities. The discussion is limited to authorization (licensing), the responsibility of banks for information disclosed by issuers of securities, and the impact on banks of relevant marketing and other restrictions. To make the subject manageable, the discussion focuses on the securities law of the United Kingdom. In recent times this has received a dose of European Community law.

---

[64] The much criticized *Re Vickery* [1931] 1 Ch. 572.   [65] S. 61.

[66] Cf. P. Matthews, 'The Efficacy of Trustee Exemption Clauses in English Law' (1989) 53 *Conv.* 42.

[67] W. Blair, A. Allison, G. Morton, P. Richards-Carpenter, M. Walmsley, and G. Walker, *Banking and Financial Services Regulation* (3rd edn., London, Butterworths, 2002).

A. AUTHORIZATION

As with banking regulation, authorization (or licensing) in the field of securities regulation is preventive in design. As we have seen, a bank needs authorization to carry on a regulated activity in the United Kingdom.[68] Regulated activities include, in broad terms, engaging in one or more of the following: investments dealing, investments brokering, investments management, advising on investments, and running collective investment schemes.[69] Investments are defined widely to cover a whole range of securities, derivatives, interests in collective investment schemes, and so on.[70] The details of all this are beyond our horizon, although it is as well to remark that the securities regimes of other jurisdictions use different statutory hooks from the concept and definition of 'investments' used in the UK legislation. In the mainstream what is caught is the same, but this is not necessarily so at the edges.

Authorization is effected by the FSA. The details of the authorization regime are of no concern, although we should note that licensing as a tool of regulation cannot stand alone. It can prevent the unsavoury engaging in securities activities, but once someone has obtained a licence the threat to withdraw it can simply act *in terrorem*, rather than as a realistic means of influencing daily behaviour. That, as a matter of law, needs detailed rules. Contravention of the rules made under the FSMA 2000 can be enjoined or a restitution order sought to recover the profits accruing, or investors' losses, from a contravention.[71] Private, but not professional, investors can sue directly for their losses when the rules are broken.[72]

Given that securities activities frequently have a cross-border element, the issue arises of the jurisdictional reach of the licensing regime. The relevant sanction, which the foreign bank must have its eye on in this regard, is the unenforceability of its agreements if it is not licensed but ought to be. The Act draws a wide circle. It is clear on its face that one can carry on investment business in the United Kingdom without having a permanent place of business: engaging in the United Kingdom in one of the investment activities mentioned is sufficient.[73] There would, of course, need to be the continuity, or anticipation of continuity, which is a prerequisite in English law to the notion of carrying on business.

Nonetheless, the foreign bank may still be able to avoid the UK licensing regime, while engaged in some UK investment activity. The Act itself provides several gateways. One is if the foreign bank deals or acts as broker, through an authorized person.[74] Perhaps this is not a popular route, since banks generally prefer to avoid working through others in this area (not least because of the fees forgone). But another gateway is if the foreign bank in investment dealing—buying, selling, subscribing for or underwriting securities or contractually based investments—enters into a transaction as a result of an unsolicited approach by the person in the UK, or an

---

[68] 7, 85 above.   [69] Sched. 2, pt. I.   [70] Sched. 2, pt. II.
[71] Ss. 380, 382.   [72] S. 151.   [73] S. 1(3).
[74] Financial Services and Markets Act 2000 (Regulated Activities) Order 2001, SI 2001 No 544, as amended by SI 2001 No 3544, art. 72(1), (2).

approach which does not contravene the financial promotion regime. Approaching investment professionals, rather than private investors, is an easily achievable way of doing this.[75]

The other major avenue through which a foreign bank may avoid the UK licensing regime is if it can take advantage of the single passport created by the European Community Investment Services Directive (the ISD).[76] This is comparable to the way that banks authorized in one part of the European Community can provide services and open branches elsewhere, without being licensed in the host state.[77] Unlike the FSMA 2000, the ISD divides investment services into core and non-core services. An investment firm must be licensed in its home state to provide one or more of the core services before it can offer its services elsewhere unhindered.

The core services in the ISD are brokerage, dealing, managing, and underwriting. Brokerage is narrower, however, than under the FSMA 2000, where the concept is of 'arranging deals': under the ISD, brokerage consists of receiving and transmitting orders on behalf of others (although under the thirteenth recital to the ISD this seems to extend to bringing together investors, thereby effecting a transaction). Investment advice is a non-core service, along with custody services (broadly defined), and lending and foreign exchange in connection with investment services.[78] Consequently, if EC banks simply provide investment advice they need licensing under the Act, and will not benefit from the passport provided by the ISD. Moreover, the FSMA 2000 covers activities in a wider range of securities and derivatives than does the ISD. Commodity futures provide one example. A foreign bank's passport would not extend to dealing in, brokering, managing, or advising on these in the United Kingdom.

As with the passport created by the Credit Institutions Directive, prudential supervision under the ISD is carried out by the home-state regulator. This includes initial capital requirements, and being satisfied that controllers are fit and proper.[79] It also means taking such steps as ensuring adequate requirements for the safe custody of the securities and funds of investors.[80] Importantly for present purposes, host states remain responsible under the ISD for the conduct of investment business. The only limitation on the host state is that its controls be in the interest of the general good.[81] Thus the promotion and stabilization provisions of UK law, to be discussed shortly, apply to anyone in the United Kingdom, even to those entering under an ISD passport.

---

[75] 352 below.   [76] Dir. 93/22/EEC [1993] OJ L141/27.

[77] 433 below.   [78] ISD, Annex, Secs, A, C.

[79] ISD, Arts. 3(3), 4, 8, 9(5). See Capital Adequacy Dir., 101 above.

[80] ISD, Art. 10.

[81] See G. Ferrarini, 'Towards a European Law of Investment Services and Institutions' (1994) 31 *CML Rev.* 1283, 1297–1300; M. Tison, 'Conduct of Business Rules and their Implementation in the EU Member States', in G. Ferrarini, K. Hopt, and E. Wymeersch (eds.), *Capital Markets in the Age of the Euro* (Hague, Kluwer, 2002); J. Welsh, 'The Sophisticated Investor and the ISD', in *ibid.*, 112–14.

B. PROSPECTUS PROVISIONS

For a century, statute has demanded the disclosure of specified information in prospectuses issued by companies desirous of raising money by direct appeal to the public. The policy has been to arm potential investors with information sufficient for them to assess the risks of a particular investment. In practice the statutory aim can be achieved only indirectly—private investors cannot generally digest the information provided—by filtering out investors promoters who cannot reach the statutory standards, and by providing information to professional analysts, who in turn inform the public. Coupled with the compelled disclosure of information has been a liability imposed on those responsible for false prospectuses. The English approach in this regard has been adopted elsewhere, notably in the US securities laws.

In the United Kingdom there are two legal regimes for prospectuses. Both have been influenced by the European Community Prospectus Directive.[82] In brief, the first applies where there is to be a listing of the securities. The relevant law is contained in Part VI of the FSMA 2000, although the details are set out in the Listing Rules of the Financial Services Authority.[83] (The discussion below concentrates on the regulation of prospectuses, but the FSMA 2000 treats prospectus regulation as a sub-set of listing regulation. What is said below about prospectuses generally also applies to listing.) The second regime applies to public offers in the United Kingdom of securities which are not listed anywhere. This regime is provided for in the Public Offers of Securities Regulations 1995 (the POS Regulations).[84] Under both regimes a prospectus must contain not only the information specifically required in the Listing Regulations or the POS Regulations, but any other information which investors would reasonably require and reasonably expect in order to be able to make an informed assessment.[85] Where there is a material change in circumstances before the start of dealings in securities, there is an obligation to publish a supplementary prospectus.[86]

Both regimes apply only to offers of securities made to the public in the United Kingdom. Private placements of securities to sophisticated investors—fund managers, insurance companies, pension funds, etc.—are not subject to either prospectus regime. 'Offer to the public' is defined largely through the exemptions which apply in relation to certain issues and placings, for example, with 'professional' investors, covering in practice banks, fund managers, corporate treasurers, and so on. Other exemptions apply to securities offered to no more than fifty persons, and to a 'restricted circle' of those reasonably believed to be sufficiently knowledgeable to understand the risks. Securities offered in the Euromarket will likely fall within the professionals exemption, but there is also a specific exemption for 'Euro-securities'

---

[82] Dir. 89/298/EEC [1989] OJ L 124/8 as amended.

[83] See W. Chalk, 'The Official Listing of Securities', in Ashurst Morris Crisp, *The Financial Services and Markets Act* (London, Sweet & Maxwell, 2001), 180–91.

[84] SI 1995 No 1537.

[85] FSMA 2000, ss. 80(1), 86, Sched. 9, para. 2; POS Regs., r.9.

[86] FSMA 2000, ss. 81(1), 86, Sched. 9, para. 2; POS Regs., r.11.

provided advertising is to professional or sophisticated investors.[87] This may be a difficult condition to fulfil in practice.

(i) Bank Liability for the Issuer's Prospectus

The prospectus provisions are complex, and their full detail is not part of our agenda. However, there is one issue which demands further attention—the extent to which a bank distributing an issuer's prospectus can be liable if it is faulty. It will be recalled that there is a potential liability at common law, although in practice this can generally be negated.[88] This is not the case with the statutory law.

Under both regimes for prospectuses—the FSMA 2000 regime for listed prospectuses, and the POS regime for other public issues—it is primarily the issuer and its directors which have a statutory liability to pay compensation to investors who suffer loss. Both regimes also impose liability on those who accept (and are stated as accepting) responsibility, and those who have authorized the contents.[89] In theory, banks involved in the issue could be caught by these provisions, although in practice we have seen that they disclaim any responsibility. In any event, if somebody like a bank accepts responsibility or authorizes part only of the contents of a prospectus or supplementary prospectus, they are responsible only for that part, and only if included in substantially the form and content agreed. Moreover, there is no responsibility by reason only of giving advice in a professional capacity about the contents. A generous interpretation is that banks can advise in a 'professional capacity', along with solicitors and auditors. There seems no basis to a suggested distinction between advice about contents on the one hand, and actually proffering a form of words on the other.

There is also a potential liability imposed on others who are not issuers.[90] In the case of the Listing Regulations this arises because they contemplate in a roundabout way that a bank, say, making an offer in association with an issuer can be responsible for the prospectus unless it was drawn up primarily by the issuer or those acting on its behalf. In the case of the POS regime, this responsibility extends to directors of an 'offeror', unless the offer is made in association with the issuer. Depending on the circumstances, banks could be offerors.

Recall the distinction between brokerage, placement, underwriting, and purchase drawn earlier.[91] If a bank resells the securities it has taken as an underwriter, or has bought the issuer's securities to sell as a principal, then it could be said (within the Listing Regulations) to be acting in association with the issuer or (within the POS Regulations) to be an offerer. To avoid potential liability it will need to bring itself within one of the exemptions.

---

[87] Sched. 11, para. 20; Financial Services and Markets Act 2000 (Official Listing of Securities) Regulations 2001, SI 2001 No 2956 ('Listing Regs.'), r.12; POS Regs., r.7.

[88] 340–1 above.

[89] Listing Regs., r.6(1)(d),(e); POS Regs., r.13(d),(g).

[90] Listing Regs., r.10(2); POS Regs., r.13(1)(e).

[91] 335 above.

Those responsible for a faulty prospectus as an issuer, offeror, etc. are liable to pay compensation to investors who have suffered loss as a result.[92] (Failure to publish a prospectus at all may be visited by disciplinary action or, possibly, criminal penalty.) Liability extends beyond untrue or false statements giving rise to common law liability. Omissions are covered as well—omissions of specified information, as well as of the information demanded by the general duty to disclose what would be reasonably required and expected by investors. Recall also the duty to publish a supplementary prospectus: failure in this respect may also give rise to a liability to compensate. Also, by contrast with the common law, investors need not demonstrate reliance. The justification is that a faulty prospectus can affect the market value of securities. Investors can therefore claim compensation, even if they have never seen the prospectus. Claims are not excluded just because investors have acquired the securities in the secondary market (i.e. outside the initial offer). If an investor acquires securities with a knowledge that a statement is false or misleading, or of the omitted matter, or of a change in circumstances, then, as would be expected, there is no liability to compensate.

There are a range of statutory defences to prospectus liability.[93] For example, the bank which conducts itself with due diligence and reasonably believes that a statement was true and not misleading, or that a matter whose omission caused the loss was properly omitted, does not incur any liability if (1) it continued in that belief until the time when the securities were acquired; (2) they were acquired before it was reasonably practicable to bring a correction to the attention of potential investors; (3) if before they were acquired it had taken all reasonable steps to bring a correction to investors' attention; or (4) if the securities were acquired after such a lapse of time, the bank ought reasonably to be excused (provided it continued in the belief until after the commencement of dealings on any exchange). Another defence is if, before the investor acquired the securities, a correction had been effectively published, or the person responsible for the prospectus had taken all reasonable steps to secure its publication, and reasonably believed it had taken place.

C. PROMOTING SECURITIES ISSUES

The prospectus provisions of the securities laws apply to offers. Invitations and inducement are not offers in English law, and so do not fall within their scope. However, banks must navigate the financial promotion restrictions of the securities laws when they become involved in the issue and distribution of securities.

Historically controls on share hawking date back to section 92 of the Companies Act 1928. The target was those who personally hawked shares from house to house, which were totally unsuitable as investments for those being canvassed. Fraud was also thought to be rampant. Nothing in this respect is new. In 1994 the European Court of Justice upheld a 1991 Dutch prohibition on cold-calling investors about off-market

---

[92] S. 90; POS Regs., r.14.   [93] Sched. 10, para. 1; POS Regs., r.15.

commodities futures. The law was provoked by the infamous Dutch 'boiler houses', which peddled dubious securities around Europe. The prohibition extended to cold-calling those in other Member States from the Netherlands, but was justified as preserving the reputation of the Dutch financial sector.[94] The Financial Services Act 1986 regulated both investment advertisements and unsolicited calls, but under FSMA 2000 there is a uniform regime for all financial promotions.

Under FSMA 2000 it is an offence in section 21 for a person to communicate an invitation or inducement to engage in investment activity unless authorized or unless the contents of the investment communication have been approved by an authorized person. Since banks will generally be authorized under FSMA 2000 they will not fall into the net. Instead a bank may be called upon to approve an issuer's communications. If it does so, it must act in accordance with the relevant conduct of business rules applying to it as an authorized person.[95] Approving an unauthorized person's investment communications also means that a bank is accepting responsibility for its contents. Similarly, if a bank issues a communication itself, it must comply with the relevant rules. Failure on either count to comply with these rules can give rise under the Act to civil liability to private investors.[96] In very broad terms, the various rules oblige a bank to undertake due diligence. In addition, they mandate certain contents and risk warnings, in particular for communications directed at private investors.

Section 21 has a significant reach. 'Communication' has a wide meaning—advertisements, telephone calls, visits, e-mails, internet websites—and includes causing a communication to be made. The person acting as a mere conduit is excluded, but it is difficult to conceive of a bank engaged in securities actually falling into that category. 'Invitation' and 'inducement' are also words of wide import, although the test seems to be whether objectively the material has a promotional intent. The third aspect of section 21—engaging in investment activity—is confined to controlled activities or investments, whose meaning track that of regulated activities.[97] We pass by the detailed regime for financial promotion, except to note that there is a tighter control over the more immediate ('real-time' as opposed to 'non-real-time' communications), on the basis that the investor needs more protection if there is less time to reflect, although within the former the solicited communication is generally exempt (solicited real-time communications).[98]

Financial promotions from outside the UK are caught in the net if they are capable of having an effect, and directed at persons, in the UK.[99] (With unsolicited real-time communication the control is tighter: to escape it must be from outside the UK

---

[94] Case C–384/93 *Alpine Investments BV* v. *Minister van Financien* [1995] ECR I–1141.

[95] FSA Handbook, Conduct of Business, ch. 3.

[96] FSMA 2000, s. 150.

[97] Financial Services and Markets Act 2000 (Financial Promotion) Order 2001, SI 2001 No 1335 ('Financial Promotion Order'), art. 4.

[98] e.g. G. McMeel and J. Virgo, *Financial Advice and Financial Products* (Oxford, OUP, 2001), 328–30.

[99] FSMA 2000, s. 21(3); Financial Promotion Order, art. 12(1)(b), (3)–(6).

for the purposes of a business not carried on in the UK.)[100] When the Electronic Commerce Directive is implemented, however, the UK will relinquish control of financial promotion emanating through the internet from other European Community countries to the home-state regulator[101]—a break from the general approach of the single market for banking where marketing is for the host state, not the country of origin. It is with a considerable sense of relief that we note that the financial promotion regime has no application at all to communications made to investment professionals.[102]

D. SELLING RESTRICTIONS

In the light of the securities laws, those engaged in distributing an issuer's securities, such as banks, often undertake to the issuer that they will observe certain selling restrictions. For example, they may represent and agree that they will not offer or sell securities in circumstances which would result in an offer to the public. Clearly this is aimed at the prospectus provisions. Connected with the financial promotion provisions, the bank will also represent and agree that it will issue or pass on any document received in connection with the issue only to a professional investor. Finally, it will represent and agree generally to comply with the FSMA 2000. Similarly, the US and Japanese securities laws have spawned standard selling restrictions for issues in the Euromarkets.

Such selling restrictions operate in contract only. The bank contracts directly with the issuer or, if the bank is down the distribution chain, with those on a higher rung. In a complex distribution each member of the chain will also undertake to have anybody a rung down the chain agree to the selling restrictions. Contract cannot negate a contravention of the securities laws. Nor can it prevent it, but then neither can the various penalties attached to the securities laws themselves. The expectation is that institutions like banks, engaged professionally in the distribution of securities, will have in place procedures and practices to ensure compliance with the law. Whether that law is statutory in origin, or simply contract, ought to be irrelevant to those engaged in selling on a daily basis. All they need to know through instructions, procedures, and training is that they cannot sell to certain categories of person, or in certain parts of the world. Their marketing repertoire is limited. If they stray, the selling restrictions—contract—will not save a breach of the securities laws.

Not unnaturally the issuer will wish to avoid liability should any breach of the selling restrictions or the securities laws occur. Contract can seek to deny that anyone in the distribution chain has the issuer's authority to make representations, give information, and so on in breach of the securities laws. It may also seek to absolve the

---

[100] Art. 12(2).

[101] Directive 2000/31/EC [2000] OJ L178/1. See HM Treasury, *Implementation of the E-Commerce Directive in Financial Services*, Consultation Document, Dec. 2001; A Second Consultation Document, Mar. 2002.

[102] Financial Promotion Order, art. 19.

issuer from any responsibility if someone in the chain steps out of line. At the end of
the day, however, the issuer's liability depends on the terms of the securities laws. For
example, if its securities are offered to the public in the United Kingdom for the first
time, there must be a prospectus, whatever its intentions to have the offer confined to
professionals. If the issuer is the offeror of the securities—in other words, if those in
the distribution chain are simply broking or placing the securities—it is responsible if
there is no prospectus.[103] Since the issuer may be liable in this way for the acts of those
such as banks in the distribution chain, it will seek an indemnity from them for any
losses, costs, claims, or damages which it incurs as a result of their failure to observe
the selling restrictions.

E. STABILIZATION

Stabilization is nothing new. The common law took a dim view, although the leading
case[104] was largely negated by a subsequent, if poorly reported, decision that stabilization is unobjectionable if honestly done, within limits, in accordance with market
practice, and the fact disclosed.[105] Nonetheless, taken to extremes, it not only constitutes a breach of the civil law, but is also capable of founding criminal liability.[106] In
particular, it can constitute the offence which can be broadly characterized as market
manipulation, set out in section 397(2) of the Financial Services and Markets Act
2000. The section has an extraterritorial reach, in that stabilization committed abroad
can create the requisite false or misleading impression in the United Kingdom.

What, then, is stabilization? It is the practice of supporting the price of securities
during the issuing period. The idea is to mitigate the impact of the temporary over-
supply of securities on how the long-term price is viewed. It has been argued that it is
easily justifiable when there is already an existing market price for securities, in order
to protect existing holders. With a new issue, it is said to ease a situation of volatility.
Less clear is the rationale when the issue is mispriced.[107] Stabilization is effected
through those involved in the distribution purchasing on the secondary market, and
under- or over-allocating.

A breach of section 397(2) can be avoided if stabilization is conducted in accordance with the rules promulgated under the Act. The rules restrict the type of securities
and issues which can be stabilized; impose administrative requirements such as the
appointment of a stabilizing manager, the keeping of records, and the publication
of warnings that stabilising might occur; and restrict the permissible period and
methods of stabilization.[108]

---

[103] FSMA 2000, s. 84(1); POS Reg., r.16(2).
[104] *Scott* v. *Brown, Doering, McNab & Co.* [1892] 2 QB 724 (CA).
[105] *Sanderson and Levi* v. *British Westralian Mines and Share Corp. Ltd., The Times*, 19 July 1899.
[106] Cf. *R.* v. *Saunders* [1996] 1 Cr. App. R. 463.
[107] J. Dalhuisen, *The New UK Securities Legislation and the EC 1992 Program* (Amsterdam, North Holland,
1989), 108–9.
[108] Ss. 144, 397(4); FSA Handbook, Market Conduct, ch. 2.

13

LOAN SALES AND SECURITIZATION

The transfer of intangible property, whether absolute or by way of security, recurs in banking practice. We saw how depositors with insolvent banks have attempted to enhance claims against the deposit-protection scheme by purportedly transferring deposit claims to others.[1] Later we see that the hallmark of negotiable instruments—documentary intangibles—is their ready transferability. The payment obligation locked up in the instrument is transferred by its delivery, coupled with any endorsement.[2] A third example is that businesses sometimes transfer their debts and contracts—pure intangibles—to their banks. This happens for various reasons. In some cases it is by way of security for finance to be advanced. Security over debts and contract (e.g. in project finance) is taken up in Chapter 15. In times of trouble the transfer of debts and contracts occurs as a business responds to bank pressure to reduce or repay a financial facility already advanced. If this type of assignment becomes known, it can be very damaging for a business' credit.

Block discounts provide a fourth example of businesses transferring their debts and contracts to a bank, or at least that part of the bank group undertaking this type of financing. Often a business providing goods under rental agreements, or by means of hire purchase or conditional sale, will simply sell them to a financial institution, which as a matter of law will itself lease, hire, or sell them to the third parties. Depending on the circumstances, however, sometimes the business will instead block-discount the relevant contracts to the financial institution. There will be a master agreement, under which the business offers for sale batches of agreements it has entered into with customers.[3] Banks will be reluctant to discount contracts where the business is providing a service rather than supplying goods, because there is more scope for the business failing to live up to its obligations and thus for the third party refusing to pay.

Similarly with factoring. Although it has a fairly long history in other jurisdictions, it was only in 1960 that the first factoring company was established in Britain. Now all the major banks have subsidiaries involved in factoring business debts. This form of

---

[1] 80 above
[2] 378 below. Payment, of course, does not involve assignment (233 above).
[3] R. Goode, *Hire-Purchase Law and Practice* (2nd edn., London, Butterworths, 1970), ch. 28(c).

receivables financing affords mainly smaller businesses the opportunity to sell their trade debts at a discount to factoring companies, and thus to improve cash-flow. Recourse factoring enables the factor to recover from its business customer's account moneys advanced against what turn out to be bad debts. With non-recourse financing, the factor absorbs the losses on bad debts, or at least on some of them. There is also a distinction between full factoring, where a factor provides sales accounting functions, and a business' customers are informed that their invoices have been assigned, and confidential invoice discounting, where neither occurs, and the business continues to collect payments from its customers, but on the factor's behalf. While as a matter of law these different forms of factoring—recourse/non-recourse, full-service/confidential invoice discounting—turn on the particular contractual arrangements between the factor and its customer, they will build on the basic legal principles for transferring debts. Factoring is expertly dealt with in other books.[4]

This Chapter examines a further context in which contracts and debts are transferred—as banks and bank subsidiaries 'sell' their own assets, i.e. their loans, mortgages, credit card receivables, and so on. Commercially speaking this divides into loan sales and securitization. The motivations for these transactions are various—for example to reduce risk, to meet capital requirements, to allow for new lending, and to take advantage of financial and commercial opportunities. Before examining loan sales and securitization, however, let us first lay out the different legal techniques for transferring debts and contractual rights.

I. LEGAL TECHNIQUES FOR TRANSFERRING DEBTS/CONTRACTUAL RIGHTS

The legal techniques for transferring debts and contractual rights are various. As indicated, they are used in a variety of contexts. Understanding them is thus basic for appreciating how some important banking transactions are undertaken, not just the sale of loan assets and securitization.

A. NOVATION

Novation involves the substitution of a new contract for an existing one, with the approval of all the parties concerned. If O and P are in contractual relations, O obtains P's agreement for the discharge of their contract and its replacement with one between P and Q. Strictly this is not the transfer of the original contract, but its extinction and replacement by a new contract.

---

[4] See R. Goode, *Commercial Law* (2nd edn., London, Penguin, 1995), 800–19; F. Oditah, *Legal Aspects of Receivables Financing* (London, Sweet & Maxwell, 1991); F. Salinger, *Factoring Law and Practice* (3rd edn., London, Sweet & Maxwell, 1999).

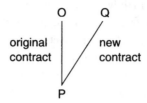

Since a new contract is involved, English law demands that some consideration move from the third party, Q.

One important difference between novation and assignment is that novation can effect a transfer of an obligation, for example an obligation of O to provide further finance to P. As we see shortly, assignment cannot transfer obligations. Novation is also distinguished from assignment in that, with novation, P must be involved. With assignment, P need not consent, nor need it even be notified. In either event—novation or assignment—P may continue to pay O, with O being formally appointed as agent to receive payment on P's behalf. In this event, O may hold those payments as trustee for Q.

B. ASSIGNMENT AND ITS LIMITATIONS

Assignment results in the transfer from the assignor to the third-party assignee of the right to proceed directly against the debtor or obligor. O assigns a debt or contractual right against P to Q, and Q can sue P. In a sense assignment is an exception to privity of contract. It matters not that the debt or right is disputed at the time it is assigned, and that litigation may be necessary to enforce or collect it.[5]

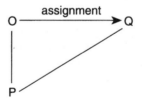

One limitation on assignment is that the agreement between the original parties (O and P) may prohibit it. In English law, a general prohibition on assignment is effective.[6] In our example O would be in breach of contract with P. Moreover, Q could not sue P. If P by its words or conduct waives a breach of the prohibition, the assignment is valid and Q can sue P. However, an assignment in breach of a prohibition is not

---

[5] *Camdex International Ltd.* v. *Bank of Zambia* [1998] QB 22 (CA).

[6] *Linden Gardens Trust Ltd.* v. *Lenesta Sludge Disposals Ltd.* [1994] 1 AC 85. G. McCormack, 'Debts and Non-Assignment Clauses' [2000] *JBL* 422. This is also New York common law: *Allhusen* v. *Caristo Construction Corp.*, 303 NY 446, 103 NE 2d 891 (1952).

invalid as between assignor and assignee. A prohibition on assignment would not preclude O agreeing with Q to account to Q for what P pays it.

A provision featuring in some contracts is that assignment is prohibited without the prior consent of the debtor or obligor (P), such consent not to be unreasonably withheld or delayed. The onus would be on the assignor (O) to prove that consent is being unreasonably withheld or delayed.[7] If consent were to be unreasonably withheld or delayed, the assignor could assign without consent, although it might play safe and seek a court declaration that it has the right to do so. The test whether consent is being unreasonably withheld or delayed is objective. A reasonable debtor or obligor might well object to assignment because of the characteristics of the intended assignee, for example its harsh attitude to default. The reasonable debtor or obligor need usually look to its interest only, although there may be cases where there is such a disproportion between the benefit to the assignor and the detriment to the debtor/obligor from the assignment, that it is not reasonable for the latter to withold consent.

A second limitation is that the debt or contract to be assigned must not be personal to the assignor and the debtor/obligor. It has been said that this limitation does not apply where the assignor has an accrued right to a debt, but the authorities do not support this. There is a real difficulty in formulating a basis for this rule. One authority states that the rule is whether it is clear that the debtor/obligor is willing to perform only in favour of the assignor, and if it would be unjust to force it to perform in favour of another.[8] It seems preferable, however, to invoke a more objective test: a debt or contract is personal for the purposes of this rule if the assignment would materially change the duty of the debtor/obligor, or materially increase the burden or risk imposed on it?[9] That an assignee may be more pressing and less indulgent than the assignor should not of itself prevent assignment, unless the result would be a considerably harsher regime for the debtor/obligor. If the original contract makes clear that assignment is contemplated (e.g. a contract between O and P and their respective assigns) then it is permissible, despite a personal element.[10]

A third limitation on assignment is summed up in the phrase that one can assign the benefit, but not the burden, of a contract. So clearly a debtor cannot assign a debt; nor can a lender assign continuing obligations. But there are various glosses on this rule. English law recognizes that a benefit and a burden of a contract may be inextricably linked—the burden acts as a limitation on the benefit—so that if the assignee wants the benefit it must accept the correlative burden. There is also a suggestion that English law recognizes a pure principle of benefit and burden: even if a benefit and burden are independent, an assignee may in some circumstances become liable, along with the assignor, for breach of the latter's duties. However, there has been a distinct lack of enthusiasm for a pure principle of benefit and burden.

---

7 *Hendry* v. *Chartsearch Ltd.* [1998] EWCA Civ. 1276 [1998] CLC 1382 (CA).
8 G. Treitel, *The Law of Contract* (10th edn., London, Sweet & Maxwell, 1999), 639.
9 *US Restatement on Contract, Second,* §317(2)(a).
10 *Tolhurst* v. *Associated Portland Cement Manufacturers* [1903] AC 414 (HL).

Another aspect of the third limitation is whether a person with duties to perform under a contract can delegate those duties (while still remaining liable). With some contracts it cannot matter to the debtor/obligor who performs continuing duties, so long as they are performed and satisfy the contractual standard. Only when these duties demand a level of personal skill or judgement can it be said that delegation is prohibited. In that event, English law should render nugatory an attempt to delegate duties.

C. LEGAL AND EQUITABLE ASSIGNMENT

English law has long recognized the equitable assignment of debts and contractual rights, but it was not until the Judicature Act 1873 that assignments were also upheld at law. The prerequisites for a legal assignment are now set out in section 136 of the Law of Property Act 1925: (i) it must be in writing; (ii) it must be absolute and not by way of charge (a mortgage of a debt or contractual right is not by way of charge); (iii) it must be of the whole of the debt; and (iv) written notice of the assignment must be given to the debtor or obligor. Often these prerequisites are not satisfied. However, even though the assignment is of part only of the debt, or no notice is given, there can still be a good assignment in equity. In any event, future debts and contractual rights are generally incapable of assignment at law and so must be assigned in equity. As a matter of practice, then, most assignments will be equitable, rather than legal.

One difference between legal and equitable assignment is that with equitable assignment, the assignor must generally be joined as either a claimant or defendant in a suit by the assignee against the debtor/obligor. This is to protect the debtor/obligor—the assignor might dispute the equitable assignment or disclose a prior interest of some third party—and to avoid a multiplicity of suits. But this is procedural, and if the assignor objects to being joined as claimant, it can be joined as defendant. Another difference is that with equitable assignment the assignor retains a right to sue the debtor/obligor, but as trustee for the assignee. If an assignor sues for a part of a debt which was not assigned, as a protection for the assignee it must be joined.[11] Equitable interests, such as a second mortgage, can be assigned only in equity and must be in writing.[12]

Although with equitable assignments notice does not need to be given to the debtor/obligor, it is generally advisable. First, the debtor/obligor can obtain a good discharge by paying the assignor if not notified of the assignment. Secondly, although the general rule is that interests have priority in order of the time of their creation, where a debt or contractual right is dealt with twice over, notice determines priorities under the rule in *Dearle* v. *Hall*.[13] Thus a subsequent assignee giving notice first obtains priority, provided that it did not know about the first dealing at the time of the assignment to it, or when it furnished consideration. It has been held that the rule

---

[11] There is some Antipodean authority that joinder is substantive with the equitable assignment of a legal right: G. Tolhurst, 'Equitable Assignment of Legal Rights' (2002) 118 *LQR* 98.

[12] Law of Property Act 1925, s. 53(1)(c).   [13] (1828) 3 Russ. 1, 38 ER 475.

applies not only to successive equitable assignments but also, more doubtfully, to an equitable assignment followed by a legal assignment to a *bona fide* purchaser without notice.[14] The rule cannot generally apply if the first assignment is legal since a legal assignment demands notice.

The third advantage of notice for the assignee is that it cuts off further 'equities' (cross-claims and defences), which the debtor/obligor may have against it. By contrast with a negotiable instrument, where the holder in due course takes free of equities,[15] an assignment does not transfer to the assignee any more rights than the assignor had. In other words, it subjects the assignee to the cross-claims and defences which the debtor/obligor had against the assignor. But notice prevents any further such equities arising. It has this effect in both legal and equitable assignment, the difference being that cross-claims and defences can continue to accrue against the equitable assignee, for as long as notice is not given to the debtor/obligor.

The equities subject to which an assignee takes are most notably set-offs, which the debtor/obligor acquires against the assignor before notice. Yet the law in this area is confused as to its theoretical base, and in practice its boundaries are blurred. This much seems clear. Say the debtor/obligor has a liquidated cross-claim against the assignor, which originated before notice of the assignment. That can be set off against the assignee, despite being unrelated to the debt or contract being assigned. This is the case, even though it was not due and payable until after the assignment. But an unliquidated claim for damages against the assignor, arising before notice, can be invoked against the assignee only if it is inseparably connected with the debt or contract being assigned. There is authority that if a debtor/obligor was induced to enter a contract by fraud or misrepresentation of the assignor, the debtor/obligor cannot set off the claim arising on it when the assignee claims against it. This seems wrong in principle and a travesty of the policy considerations underlying this area of the law.[16] Notice that the debtor/obligor can agree in the underlying contract that the debt or contract can be assigned free from equities.

D. TRUST; ATTORNMENT

For sake of completeness it should be mentioned that a creditor can always declare itself as trustee of a debt in favour of a third party. It is sufficient that the creditor is clear about its intention immediately and irrevocably to make itself trustee. Unless there is consideration, however, the property subject to the trust must exist at the time of the declaration of trust. In ordinary commercial contracts of loan that condition will be satisfied—the debt will not be a mere expectancy.[17]

---

[14] F. Oditah, 'Priorities: Equitable versus Legal Assignments of Book Debts' (1989) 9 *OJLS* 513.

[15] 378 below.

[16] See P. Wood, *English and International Set-Off* (London, Sweet & Maxwell, 1989), 882–3; F. Oditah, *Legal Aspects of Receivables Financing* (London, Sweet & Maxwell, 1991) 234–5.

[17] R. Meagher, W. Gummow, and J. Lehane, *Equity. Doctrines and Remedies* (3rd edn., Sydney, Butterworths, 1992), 179, 182.

There is also authority that if a person such as P in our example holds a fund for another (O), and O directs that P pay it to a third party (Q), if P accepts ('attorns'), then Q acquires a right to the fund. But this notion of attornment in relation to money rests on uncertain foundations and probably does not extend beyond funds, to include debts.[18]

II. SELLING LOAN ASSETS

'Selling loan assets' is banking jargon. It involves a bank (the seller) transferring part or all of its interest in a loan to another party (the buyer). 'Sale', 'seller', and 'buyer' are not accurate legal descriptions but are a convenient short-hand. Loans are, of course, a bank's assets, and hence the use of the term asset sale.

Loan sales arise in various contexts. The first is what was earlier described as a participation syndicate, where a bank enters a bilateral loan but then immediately sells off parts of the loan to other banks.[19] Secondly, many loan sales have been motivated by a need for banks to remove items from their balance sheet. Portfolio management, meeting capital-adequacy requirements, enhancing equity return, and reducing exposure to certain borrowers have been different aspects of this. Related to this second point is the third—there is now an active market in 'distressed debt'. Borrowers are in default, or dire financial straits, and the debt is sold at a discount to those who might be willing to assume the risk because, for instance, there is a favourable prospect for them in any ultimate rescheduling of the debt. There has been controversy as so-called vulture funds have bought up third world debt and then refused to participate in rescheduling, insisting on payment.[20] To an extent, the developing market in bank loans is dissolving the boundaries between credit and capital markets. Since loans are now more readily saleable, there are parallels with securities.

A. TECHNIQUES FOR LOAN SALES

The 'sale' of loan assets is effected in practice by novation, assignment, and what in market parlance is termed a sub-participation. A sub-participation is simply a contractual agreement between the 'selling' and 'buying' bank and has no effect whatsoever on the underlying loan. At law none of these techniques involves sale.

---

[18] R. Goff and G. Jones, *The Law of Restitution* (5th edn., London, Sweet & Maxwell, 1998), 689–93.

[19] 54 above.

[20] e.g. *Camdex International Ltd.* v. *Bank of Zambia* [1998] QB 22; *Elliott Associates LP* v. *Banco de la Nacion* 194 F 3d 363 (2d Cir. 1999). See R. Buckley, *Emerging Markets Debt* (London, Kluwer, 1999); R. Barratt, 'Distressed Debt. The Sale of Loan Assets' [1998] *JIBL* 50; R. Buckley, 'The Law of Emerging Markets Loan Sales' [1999] *JIBL* 100; R. Buckley, 'Lessons from the Globalisation of the Emerging Debt Markets' [2000] *JIBL* 103.

(i) Novation

Novation is the extinguishment of a contract between the borrower, B, and the seller, Bank X, and its substitution by a contract of the same nature between B and the buyer Y. All parties must agree to a novation.

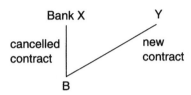

In a true syndicate the loan agreement may provide for the agent bank to agree to novation on behalf of syndicate members. Novation can be in relation to part only of a promised performance, for example part of the borrower's payment obligation. Novation can also subject the buyer to duties, as well as pass to it the benefit of the borrower's duty to pay. Thus it is especially appropriate where the original loan facility is revolving in nature, or where under it the borrower can still draw down fresh advances. Since novation extinguishes the borrower's original payment obligation, it threatens any security which the selling bank has taken. That must also be novated, or the security held by a security trustee in favour of any buyer of the loan.

An important practice has developed whereby some loan agreements incorporate at the outset the borrower's agreement to novate in favour of anyone introduced by the original bank. A form of novation certificate can be included in the loan agreement, which also provides that novation takes effect when a certificate is signed by the seller and buyer and by the party designated as the borrower's agent for this purpose. The result is that the borrower need not know at the time that the loan agreement has been novated. Most likely, however, it will have access to the register of novation certificates—knowledge *post hoc*. At first glance the technique seems contrary to the concept of novation set out in the authorities, where a contracting party must give consent at the time of novation, albeit that in some cases this is implied by conduct. The practice has been justified on the grounds that English law recognizes an offer made to the whole world.[21] Although generally speaking acceptance has no effect unless communicated to an offeror, this is overcome by the submission of the certificate to the party designated as the borrower's agent.

(ii) Assignment

In English law assignment as a technique of selling loan assets will be an assignment in equity. First, loan sales may relate to part only of a loan. In any event, banks are sometimes reluctant to notify a borrower of an assignment for commercial reasons, since it may be taken as a sign of the bank's weakness, a slight on the borrower or a

---

[21] *Carlill* v. *Carbolic Smoke Ball Co.* [1893] 1 QB 256. See M Hughes, 'Transferability of Loans and Loan Participations' [1987] 1 *JIBL* 5.

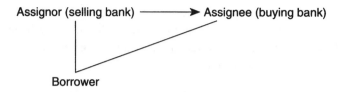

vote of no confidence in it. (Of course the latter are not problems with distressed debt.) Notice has distinct legal advantages, in particular preserving priorities and cutting off further cross-claims and defences. There may also be practical advantages, such as reducing the risk of the selling bank being pressured to provide new money on a rescheduling. However, with syndicated loans, where an agent bank is appointed, there is no risk that the borrower, if not notified, will get a good discharge by paying the wrong party—all payments must go to the agent bank.[22]

Some borrowers are sufficiently powerful to have assignments limited. They want to know who their banking partners are and wish to be in a position to track their exposure to particular parties. Thus they may insist on a clause in the loan agreement which requires their consent, or requires their consent although this is not to be unreasonably refused. Generally under these clauses consent will not be necessary with assignments to affiliates, or if the borrower is in default. An assignment without consent is not binding on the borrower. Where loans are being actively traded, loan sale agreements will generally contain unwind clauses, where a sale is made for which consent is not obtained within a specified period. As between seller and buyer, however, the agreement to assign is not a nullity. Invariably the borrower itself will be expressly prohibited from assigning its rights, notably its right to make further draw-downs.

With smaller, domestic loans there seems little scope for the rule invalidating assignments which materially increase the duties of the borrower. Borrowers have to repay, and it matters not to whom. Large, international loans contain clauses, however, which are ineffective because of this rule. The obligation of a borrower to gross up payments if the lender is subject to a withholding tax may operate only in relation to some lenders, e.g. those in jurisdictions not having a tax treaty with the borrower's jurisdiction. If the assignee is one of these, but not the assignor, then clearly the borrower can be materially disadvantaged. So, too, with the increased costs clause, which obliges the borrower to pay a lender facing an 'increased cost' as a result of participating in the loan (e.g. a reduction in the effective return to it or on its capital); and the illegality clause, which enables a lender to be prepaid by the borrower if it becomes unlawful in the bank's jurisdiction to maintain its participation in the loan.[23] If the borrower need not give its consent to an assignment, then the problem raised by such clauses needs to be addressed directly, by providing that the borrower's duties are not to be increased as a result of assignment.

---

[22] P. Wood, *International Loans, Bonds and Securities Regulation* (London, Sweet & Maxwell, 1995), 108.
[23] 307, 309 above.

There is no problem with assigning the benefit of a fully drawn-down loan. Distressed debt is clearly in this category. But the rules against assigning burdens and delegating duties have obvious application in the case of a revolving facility, or where the borrower is otherwise entitled to make further draw-downs under a loan agreement. If new moneys are provided by a third party in this situation, it should not be a cause of concern to the borrower. Money is money. But if this happens the borrower may not become liable to the third party. Rather, the legal characterization of this arrangement may be a loan from the third party to the selling bank, which on-lends to the borrower.

(iii) Sub-participation

A fundamental distinction is between a sub-participation and a risk participation. In a sub-participation the buyer pays an amount to the selling bank, and in return the selling bank agrees to pay an amount to the buyer, usually geared to payments by the borrower on the underlying loan. Because the sub-participant provides funds to the selling bank, this is sometimes called a funded sub-participation. In a risk participation, the third party involved, in return for a fee, simply gives the lending bank a guarantee in relation to the failure of the borrower to pay on the underlying loan. Nothing more will be said of risk participations here, although it is well to note that they are akin to credit derivatives in the securities markets.[24]

As a matter of law sub-participations can be characterized in various ways. Their characterization turns on the nature of the agreement between the selling bank and the buyer. The basic sub-participation involves the buyer paying an amount to the selling bank, which in return agrees to pay it amounts equal to a proportionate share of the payments of interest and principal received from the borrower. The loan agreement between the seller and borrower remains untouched by the sub-participation agreement. That agreement simply involves the selling bank and the buyer. The buyer has no claim whatsoever against the borrower. Thus if it defaults, the buyer cannot sue it. The buyer is thus exposed to double credit risk—of default by both the borrower and the selling bank. No notice of the agreement need be given to the borrower.

As described, the basic participation is simply a contractual arrangement between the selling bank and buyer. Payments to the third party are contingent on payment of principal and interest by the borrower. Of course the particular sub-participation

---

[24] M. Hughes, 'Creating a Secondary Market for Loans' [1998] *BJIBFL* 352, 354.

agreement between the seller and buyer could go further, while still leaving the under-lying loan contract intact. What characterization is adopted should turn on the documentation, rather than *a priori* reasoning.[25] First, the sub-participation agreement could constitute a separate loan, distinct from the underlying loan. Payments to the buyer would then be of what it originally paid the selling bank, but geared to what the selling bank receives from the borrower. Secondly, payments under the sub-participation agreement could be secured on the underlying loan or its proceeds. Yet this is impractical. A mortgage of the contract itself involves assignment, which is precisely what sub-participation is designed to avoid. Moreover, security is generally objectionable because it is in breach of negative-pledge clauses and/or registrable. Thirdly, the selling bank could expressly agree to be trustee for the buyer of amounts received from the borrower.[26]

In the case of a sub-participation, the buyer has a double credit risk. The first risk is that the borrower will default: payments to it are typically geared to the borrower's payments to the selling bank. As with novation and assignment, the documentation will provide that the selling bank does not accept any responsibility in this event. Not only is there this risk, but if the selling bank fails the buyer faces loss, even if the borrower itself is healthy. The essence of a sub-participation is that the buyer does not have a direct claim against the seller. Unless the buyer can establish that it has a security interest over the loan, or that the seller holds the proceeds on trust, its only claim is in the seller's insolvency.

B. THE SALE AGREEMENT AND ITS IMPLICATIONS

Loan sales are typically governed by written terms. These may be in the original loan agreement, which anticipates that parts of it will be sold. Mention has been made of novation certificates. Otherwise there will be a separate agreement. Standard terms are used in some parts of the market, e.g. those of the London-based Loan Market Association or New York-based Emerging Markets Traders Association.[27] Independently of the sale agreement, a seller may be liable for a misrepresentation or negligent statement.

Any sale certificate or agreement will contain basic information about what exactly is being sold. It also helps to make clear in the case of novation and assignment whether interest accrued, but unpaid at the settlement date, is for the account of the buyer or to be split between buyer and seller. Other than such basics, the context of the particular loan sale determines its terms. It will generally be made clear that the seller is making no representation and has no responsibility regarding the loan agreement (validity, enforceability, etc.). It may also be made explicit that buyers must

---

[25] See J. Ziegel, 'Characterization of Loan Participation Agreements' *(1988) 14 Can. Bus. LJ* 336; I. Davidson, 'Trading Loan Assets', in G. Burton (ed.), *Directions in Finance Law* (Sydney, Butterworths, 1990), 155–9.

[26] e.g. *Hibernia National Bank* v. *FDIC,* 733 F 2d 1403 (10th Cir. 1984).

[27] M. Chamberlin and A. Werner, 'EMTA's Standard Terms Speed up Loan Settlements', *IFLR,* v. 15, Apr. 1996, 48; Loan Market Association, *Loan Transferability. A Paper* (London, LMA, 2001).

undertake their own independent investigation of the financial condition of the borrower and cannot rely on the selling bank.[28] In some cases, however, the market is such that sellers must give some representations and warranties assuring buyers what is being sold. Thus with an assignment, the seller may represent that the buyer will obtain good title, free of any security interests or claims; that the seller is in compliance with its obligations under the loan agreement; and that the loan is not subject to any set-off, defence, or counterclaim due to an act or omission of the seller.

(i) Confidentiality

One reason that a potential buyer of a loan asset must do its own credit appraisal is that in English (but not New York[29]) law the seller will be under a duty of confidentiality in relation to the borrower. That duty encompasses the very existence of the facility, unless it is a matter of public record. Disclosing a copy of the agreement and the state of the account, if this could be done without revealing the name of the borrower, might not constitute breach of the duty. But if the buyer goes ahead, it will need to know the borrower's identity. That requires the latter's consent. The borrower's express consent may be given at the time of sale. What if the loan agreement contemplates loan sales? That of itself does not imply consent to the disclosure of information. Typically, however, a clause will permit the seller to disclose a copy of the agreement and information which the seller has acquired under or in connection with the agreement. This will not cover information acquired by the seller otherwise, notably as banker to the borrower.

(ii) Rescheduling

Since loan sales are often of distressed debt, the role of the seller and buyer in any restructuring of the borrower is crucial. Ultimate buyers of distressed debt often do so with an eye to making their profit at that point. With novation the buyer is in direct contractual relations with the borrower, and thus entitled to participate in its restructuring. With assignment the same result follows, although here because either in law or equity the buyer has ownership and control of the debt. In the case of equitable assignment notice will need to be given to the borrower, if this has not already been done, so that the buyer can be actively involved in the rescheduling. With both novation and assignment the seller may continue to have a role in any rescheduling, if it has not sold off all of the loan.

A sub-participation is quite different. The buyer has no entitlement as against the borrower. At most the sale agreement may confer certain rights on the buyer, for example to be consulted about aspects of any rescheduling. Breach of these gives the buyer an action, but only against the selling bank. The selling bank, as the party to the loan agreement, retains its full discretion to exercise or refrain from exercising rights, to agree to amendments, and to waive breaches. It is not agent or trustee of the buyer

---

[28] e.g. *National Westminster Bank* v. *Utrecht America Finance Company* [2001] 3 All ER 733, 738–9.
[29] 172 above.

in this regard, although arguably it has fiduciary duties towards it.[30] It is easy to see why in the distressed debt market sub-participation is far from being the favoured technique for buyers who are seeking a profit on a restructuring.

(iii) Set-off

Say a borrower has a deposit with its lender. In theory it can set this off against payments due under the loan, although in practice this will generally be prohibited by a term in the loan agreement. But what if the loan is sold: can the borrower set off that deposit against the buyer? What if the borrower has a deposit with the buyer: can it set off against that?

Set-off turns on mutuality. Whether set-off is possible therefore depends initially on how the technique used to effect the loan sale affects mutuality. With novation the answers are fairly elementary. The borrower can no longer set off any deposit it has with the seller if the whole loan agreement has been novated. Its loan contract is now with the buyer. There is no mutuality between its claim on the deposit (against the seller) and its payment obligation (to the buyer). But because it is now in direct contractual relations with the buyer, it can now set off any deposit it has with the buyer, subject, of course, to contract.

Sub-participation also produces clear results. The borrower's payment obligation remains with the seller throughout. If not prohibited by the loan agreement, the borrower can continue to set off in relation to any deposit it has with the seller, whether before or after the loan sale. The sale document needs to ensure that the buyer gets paid its full amount, even if the seller has not received the full amount directly because of any set-off. Any deposit with the buyer is of no avail to the borrower. There is no mutuality between the borrower and the buyer. That the borrower knew also of the sale is immaterial.[31]

Assignment is slightly tricky. As far as deposits with the buyer are concerned, the borrower can set these off as soon as assignment occurs. From that point there is mutuality between the two. If the borrower has a deposit with the seller it can set off—subject to contract—until it receives notice of the assignment.[32] Thus it continues to get a good discharge by paying the seller what it owes on the loan agreement, less the deposit. Since an assignment is always subject to equities, the borrower can also set off against the buyer after notice. It may not be notified of the assignment until sometime later. Equities continue to accrue. Consequently, the buyer could find a borrower setting off deposits placed with the seller (1) before assignment; and (2) after assignment, but before the borrower receives notification of the assignment. Consequently, loan-sale documentation by means of assignment typically contains a representation and warranty on the part of the seller that the buyer will receive the asset free of any set-offs. Typically it also excludes the borrower's right of set-off against the buyer.

---

[30] 58 above.

[31] *In the matter of Yale Express System, Inc.*, 245 F Supp. 790 (SDNY 1965).

[32] *In re Pinto Leite* [1929] 1 Ch. 221; *FDIC* v. *Mademoiselle of California*, 379 F 2d 660 (9th Cir. 1967).

C. REGULATION

The market in loan assets is not directly controlled. For a time it looked as if policy favoured a moratorium on trading in distressed debt, on the basis that the operation of the secondary market could disrupt company workouts under the so-called 'London Approach'. This is the rescue policy, pursued by the Bank of England, although without a statutory backing, which seeks to avoid the unnecessary collapse of potentially viable businesses as a result of disagreements between creditors. Under the London approach the Bank of England may become involved in a workout to overcome these by seeking compromises. The fear was that, with an active secondary market, banks might sell distressed debt to those unsympathetic to the London approach. In the result, the Bank gave a cautious welcome to the secondary market in distressed debt, recognizing that in some instances it might even assist corporate rescues by providing a solution to disagreements among existing lenders.[33]

In the interests of sound banking, there is some regulation of the sale by banks of loan assets. Bank regulators are especially concerned about how sales affect risks. This in turn determines whether a bank will be treated as having removed a loan from its balance sheet, relevant of course in calculating if it has adequate capital. The policy of the Financial Services Authority (FSA) is one of clean break—a bank should not have any further involvement with the assets sold, either explicitly and implicitly, so that reputational linkages with the seller should be broken as far as possible.[34] The FSA's minimum requirement to regard a sale by means of assignment as a clean transfer is a warrant from the seller that there is no right of set-off. If the assignment is not notified to the borrower, there are additional risks to the parties. For example, the seller may be subject to pressure to reschedule or renegotiate, or to advance further moneys. Consequently, the FSA requires banks to have controls on the volume of loans sold.[35]

With sub-participation the FSA says that the seller may take a charge over the underlying loan, although in practice this would be commercially objectionable, and in any event often in breach of negative-pledge clauses. Overall, the FSA's policy is that the following conditions be met:

(i) the transfer does not contravene the terms and conditions of the underlying loan agreement and all the necessary consents have been obtained;

(ii) the seller has no residual economic interest in the part of the loan which has been transferred, and the buyer has no formal recourse to the seller for losses;

(iii) the seller has no obligation to repurchase the loan;

(iv) the seller has given satisfactory notice (and the buyer has acknowledged this)

---

[33] P. Kent, 'The London Approach: Distressed Debts Trading' (1994) 34 *BEQB* 172.
[34] FSA Handbook, Prudential Sourcebook. Banks, para 2.12.3.
[35] *Ibid.*, paras. 5.2–5.5.

that it is under no obligation to repurchase or support any losses suffered by
the buyer;

(v) the documented terms of the transfer are such that, if the loan is rescheduled
or renegotiated, the buyer and not the seller would be subject to the
rescheduled or renegotiated terms;

(vi) where payments are routed through the seller, it is under no obligation to
remit funds to the buyer unless and until they are received from the borrower.[36]

It is not especially clear whether the securities laws apply to trading in loan assets.[37]
Were they to apply, then trading in loan assets would be subject to the criminalization
of practices such as misrepresentation, manipulation, and insider dealing.[38] Moreover,
there also opens the Pandora's box of authorization, marketing controls, and so on.[39] In
as much as the securities laws demand sellers to disclose information, banks selling
loan assets are confined by their duty of confidentiality to borrowers. Setting up a
Chinese wall to separate off traders in loan assets from other parts of the bank is only
a partial solution. Perhaps in practice the issue of the securities laws is not a live one,
since banks will be authorized under them in any event. In addition, if the sale of loan
assets is confined to professionals, the exemptions for this apply.[40]

Under the Financial Services and Markets Act 2000 the legal issue revolves, in the
main, around whether a loan asset is an 'investment', and whether its sale constitutes
the carrying on of a regulated activity. In the typical loan facility the borrower is given
a right to draw-down, but until it does so there is no indebtedness. Consequently, the
facility agreement does not 'create' or 'acknowledge' indebtedness, and so is not a
debenture—one of the definitions of investment in Schedule 2 to the Act. Moreover,
there is a specific exemption from the definition of regulated activity for one simply
accepting an instrument creating or acknowledging indebtedness in respect of a loan
which 'he or his principal has made, granted or provided'.[41] The picture may change,
however, on sale of a loan asset. First, the latter exemption will not normally apply
since the buyer will not provide new moneys, i.e. will not itself make, grant, or provide
a loan. Secondly, any new instrument in relation to the sale might well be such as to
'create' or 'acknowledge' an indebtedness, whether the sale be by way of novation,
assignment, or sub-participation.[42]

[36] *Ibid.*, para. 6.2.
[37] For the US: *Banco Espanol de Credito* v. *Security Pacific National Bank*, 973 F 2d. 51 (2nd Cir. 1992);
R. Roberts and R. Quinn, 'Levelling the Playing Field: the Need for Investor Protection for Bank Sales of Loan
Participations' (1995) 63 *Fordham LR* 2115.
[38] 24 above.   [39] 345 above.   [40] 349–50, 353 above.
[41] Financial Services and Markets Act 2000 (Regulated Activities) Order 2001, SI 2001 No 544, as amended,
r.17(1).
[42] Cf. R. Tennekoon, *The Law and Regulation of Investment Finance* (London, Butterworths, 1991), 134–9.

III. ASSET SECURITIZATION

Asset securitization is the process of pooling and repackaging loans into securities, which are then sold to investors.[43] Throughout the discussion it is assumed that bank loans are being securitized, although there is no reason that other financial intermediaries should not securitize their loans. In effect what a bank is doing in securitizing its loans is raising money on the security of some of its assets, i.e. its loans. The securities issued to investors, giving them an interest in the pool, are said to be 'asset-backed', because payment on them is based on the flow of payments by borrowers on the underlying loans. It is easier to securitize where the loans are standard. They are more easily valued, and it is probably also easier to estimate default rates. The higher the gross spreads on loans, the more easily securitized, because even with wide fluctuations in default levels the income stream is strong enough to pay the investors holding the securities. Asset securitization involves home mortgages, credit card receivables, personal loans, and so on. The amounts involved are enormous.[44]

What has been the driving force behind securitization? For banks an important motivation has been balance-sheet management. For example, the bank removes loans from its balance sheet, thus improving the return on capital, while still profiting from having entered them in the first place. Securitization also helps the bank in raising funds. There might be a tidy profit, notwithstanding bad debts, given the disparity between interest rates on the securities and on the underlying loans. Moreover, as bank regulators have tightened capital-adequacy requirements, banks have had to get loans off their books. Once this is done it also means they have greater freedom to engage in new lending. By selling loans, banks are also increasing their liquidity. Selling loans is thus a means of reconciling the conflicting demands of continuing to make loans, satisfying return on assets requirements, and generating profits. Of course there are also profits from the fees involved in running a scheme and selling the securities. Another motivation has been to diversify sources of funding; for example, some governments have promoted mortgage-backed securities in the hope of generating more long-term funding for residential mortgages. As with other innovations in financial markets, sometimes securitization is driven by tax advantages.

---

[43] Project backed securization—not discussed here—securitizes the cash flow from the whole business of one project or group of projects: D. Petkovic, 'Whole Business' Securitisations of Project Cash Flows' [2000] *JIBL* 187; Zhang Xin, 'The Emergence of Project-Backed Securitiztion', *IFLR*, Jan. 2000, 24; 'Trends and Developments in Cross-Border Securitisation' [2000] *BJIBFL* 269, 318, 363.

[44] J. Shenker and A. Colletta, 'Asset Securitization: the Evolution, Current Issues and New Frontiers' (1991) 69 *Tex. LR* 1369, 1371–2.

A. FORMS OF SECURITIZATION

There are various theoretical possibilities in English law as regards the legal structure of a securitization issue.[45] In broad outline, the first is that the investors' certificates represent the bank's undertaking to pay a proportionate share of the principal and interest. A declaration of this nature would be legally enforceable by investors if (a) it were done by way of deed poll; or (b) it were done by way of trust. In the first case the investors would have a contractual right to payment; in the second, they would have a right as beneficiaries under a trust. As far as a bank is concerned this first possibility is a non-starter, since it does not remove the loans from its books.

The second possibility is that the investor holds a 'pass-through' security, which represents the beneficial ownership of part of a portfolio of loans. The bank establishes a special trust, settles a portfolio of loans on the trust, and beneficial interests in the trust are sold to investors. The bank continues to service the loans, i.e. collects the principal and interest, and passes this on to the trust, less a servicing fee. The beneficial interests in the trust, represented by the securities, entitle investors to receive a proportionate share of that principal and interest as property of the trust. In other words, the amounts repaid by borrowers on their loans are 'passed through' to investors as beneficial owners.[46] Whilst the trust structure has been widely used in securitizations in the United States, tax problems have been an impediment to its common adoption in Britain.

The third possibility is that the loans are transferred to a special-purpose company, and the investor holds a security instrument issued by it. Typically, the security will be a bond, note, or other debt instrument. (Shares could also be issued, for example cumulative preference shares with a dividend calculated to reflect the amount of interest and principal received.) The assets of the issuer are loans. The securities entitle the investor to certain payments during their lifetime. The securities may be of varying types (e.g. maturity, ranking). Unlike the first possibilities, therefore, the cash flows are not 'passed through' to investors as a matter of law, although in effect this is the result. The term 'pay-through' securities has sometimes been used for this arrangement. Since it is the method most used in Britain, it is the focus of the following discussion.[47]

The actual issuer of the securities which investors hold will be a specially established vehicle, sometimes incorporated in a tax haven, with no creditworthiness in itself. Consequently, the securities as issued by the special-purpose vehicle will need credit enhancement. Credit enhancement involves providing a cushion to investors to reflect potential losses and uncertainty. Credit enhancement can be provided for externally, such as through a demand guarantee, or insurance, issued by an

[45] Cf. T. Baums and E. Wymeersch, *Asset Backed Securitization in Europe* (The Hague, Kluwer, 1996).
[46] A. Finch, 'Securitisation' (1995) 6 *JBFLP* 247, 251.
[47] D. Bonsall, *Securitisation* (London, Butterworths, 1990).

independent third party for a fee.[48] Internal credit enhancement is typically by a subordinated loan to the issuer, or by the issuer issuing a class of subordinated securities. The flow of funds from the borrowers is used first to pay the investors, and only if they are fully paid is payment made on the subordinated loan or subordinated securities. Credit enhancement is thus provided through capitalizing the issuer. Either way, credit enhancement can result in the issuer having a credit rating higher than that of the bank.

Diagrammatically, this type of securitization can be shown as follows.

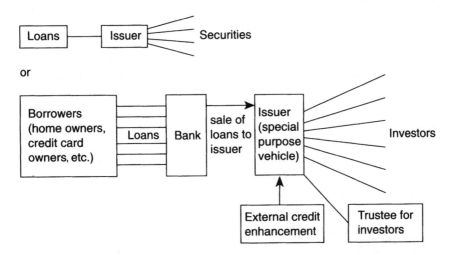

The rating of the securities will be entrusted to one of the rating agencies. It will concentrate on the underlying assets and any credit enhancement. The underlying assets must be capable of generating cash flows for the investors. The rating agency will focus on potential risks to these flows, including legal risks. Indeed, the issuer's lawyer will need to give the rating agency a lengthy legal opinion about risks. One dimension to the legal risks concerns the transfer of the loans, receivables, or mortgages to the issuer.

B. TRANSFER OF LOAN ASSETS

Earlier in the Chapter, we saw that in English law there is generally no obstacle to transferring a loan from one lender to another. Novation and assignment are the methods of doing this. Because the borrower must consent to novation, it is not a practical method of transferring numerous assets like home loans, credit-card receivables, and personal loans. The same applies with assignment if, in the original loan agreement, the borrower's specific consent must be obtained to any transfer. Even giving notice of an assignment is problematic. A bank would not want to contact all the relevant borrowers, both for reasons of cost and also because it might adversely affect their reputation if it were known that they were selling their customers' loans.

---

[48] 390 below.

Typically, therefore, in a securitization the loans are assigned to the issuer by the technique recognized in English law as equitable assignment. Because no notice is given, a borrower's claims against the bank are not cut off and may be raised against the issuer if it exercises its remedies on default.

In English law it is possible to assign only the benefits of a contract, not the burdens. Thus a bank can assign the benefit of receiving the principal and interest payable under a loan, but it cannot assign the burden of making further advances. This is obviously relevant with credit-card loans, which are revolving in nature. Thus it is the receivables, rather than the loans, which are assigned. So, too, with leasing contracts: if the bank obtains certain tax advantages as owner (leasor) it will want to transfer the receivables, not the contracts as a whole.

In theory any security or insurance, coupled with a loan, can also be transferred on the same principles as the assignment of the loan itself. In practice there are a number of problems. For example, a security interest might be registered, as with a home mortgage. The transaction costs of making any changes in the register for a pool of mortgages are so great that what typically happens is that there is an agreement to transfer, with the issuer (or trustee for the investors, if any) being given a power of attorney to effect a complete transfer if necessary. Since there is only an agreement to transfer, the issuer (or trustee) may need the help of the court. Specific performance will generally be granted for the transfer of a mortgage, but an element of uncertainty is introduced since specific performance is a discretionary remedy. Moreover, the issuer faces the risk, however remote, of a subsequent dealing with the same mortgage, especially if the third party can get priority through registration.[49]

C. RISK

The extent and location of risk is crucial in a securitization. On the one hand a bank will seek to minimize its risks once the loans have been transferred. On the other hand, unless the risks for investors are minimized, the securities are unlikely to be widely marketable. There is a tension between these goals.

As far as the bank is concerned, novation means that the bank has no further obligations or liabilities under the loans. On the other hand assignment cannot absolve the bank from its obligations, for example to make further advances. More-over, as explained earlier, the bank remains subject to claims which accrued before borrowers were notified of the assignment. Consequently, the transfer of loans, receivables, and mortgages by means of assignment means that the bank remains subject to some risk. Moreover, the bank will often continue to service the loans, i.e. collect the principal and interest and pass this on to the issuer, and is thus exposed to 'operational' risk. Legally, it might be in breach of its duties as agent of the issuer, or it might be liable for misrepresentations made to the borrowers. These various risks for the banks have influenced bank regulation, as we shall see.

---

[49] E. Ferran, *Mortgage Securitisation: Legal Aspects* (London, Butterworths, 1992), 39–57.

What risks face the issuer? Once the loans are transferred to the issuer, then it must bear the credit risks attached to the underlying transactions. The most basic credit risk is non-payment. Another is the possibility that borrowers will bring cross-claims or raise defences when payment is sought from them. For example, if the loans fall under the Consumer Credit Act 1974, the borrowers may have claims for faulty goods against the credit provider, as well as against the supplier.[50] Yet another risk, if interest rates have fallen, is that borrowers may seek to repay loans early, but any new loans transferred will be at less profitable rates. Apart from credit enhancement, these risks can be minimized in a number of ways. For example, the transfer of the loans may be at a discount, taking potential risks into the calculation of price. Another possibility is to over-collateralize the issuer, in other words to transfer more loans to the issuer than required to fund payment on the securities, but taking into account that a certain proportion will cause problems. But these are mainly commercial solutions: what of more legal approaches? For example, the bank may give certain representations and warranties to the issuer in the documentation concerning the quality of loans being transferred, for example on the inquiries it conducted prior to granting them and the satisfaction by the borrowers of its lending criteria. In the event of a breach of these representations and warranties, the issuer will have recourse against the bank.

If the bank fails (e.g. becomes insolvent), there is little credit risk to the issuer if the loans have been transferred to it, either by novation or assignment. The only credit risk would seem to be if the transfer of assets to the issuer is a voidable disposition under the insolvency law, e.g. a preference within the specified period of the insolvency.[51] Even if the bank collects the principal and interest as agent for the issuer, this will go directly into a bank account in the name of the issuer, and not to the bank itself. If held on trust, it is not subject to claims by the bank's creditors. To isolate the issuer as much as possible from the risk of the bank failing and claims by bank creditors, it is made 'insolvency remote'. As well as the other steps mentioned, its shares will be held not by the bank, but by a neutral entity, distinct from the bank, or on trust for charitable purposes. Then there is no chance of its being treated as a subsidiary within the definition of the Companies Act 1985.[52] However, it has been suggested that if the bank fails, borrowers may be more inclined to delay or default on their obligations because they no longer have a continuing relationship with the bank. Borrowers may also be more likely to raise any possible defences to their payment obligations. Law can do little in this regard.

If the issuer fails—the ultimate risk for investors—their position depends on the structure of the securitization. If the securities they hold are debt instruments, they rank equally with other creditors. In fact the issuer will be prevented from incurring debts, other than strictly in association with the securitization. It will have no employees who could have preference claims in its insolvency. Just as in a bank's insolvency, transactions can be attacked in the issuer's as well. For example, the

---

[50] Ss. 56, 75   [51] Insolvency Act 1986, s. 239.   [52] Companies Act 1985, s. 736.

liquidator might argue that the transfer of the assets was at an undervalue—not a fanciful threat if the bank has set the price on the high side, as a method of extracting yet more profit from the securitization. Credit enhancement obviously becomes relevant on the issuer's failure.

So far the focus has been on credit risks faced by the issuer and the investors. But there are other risks as well. For example, there is liquidity (or income) risk.[53] There might be a mismatching of the flow of funds from borrowers to bank to issuer, and what is required to be paid to investors. One method of addressing this is to oblige the bank in administering the loans to increase the interest rate to borrowers, to cover any shortfall. It goes without saying that this technique is a serious matter for borrowers. Other methods are preferable, such as building in a cushion by committed facilities, reserves, or subordinated capital.

D. REGULATION

There is a tension in securitization between accommodating the risk to banks and the risk to investors. Bank regulators are concerned with the former; they have not been primarily interested in the latter. Moreover, there is another group affected if consumer loans are securitized—the borrowers. Their concerns have not always been to the forefront of the debate. It is appropriate to begin with them.

(i) Consumer Borrowers

Borrowers must be protected in a securitization of consumer loans—home mortgages, credit card receivables, personal loans, and so on. One aspect is interest-rate policy. What if the issuer sets interest rates at a higher level than the bank would have fixed? What if the issuer adopts a less indulgent attitude to default than the bank? What if the issuer discourages early repayment—which can disrupt the matching of income flows from borrowers to bank to issuer, and from issuer to investors—by imposing stiff penalties?

To make the securities marketable, the issuer must retain a certain control over these matters, even if the bank will normally continue to administer the loans as its agent. Thus in the documentation the bank may undertake to reset interest rates to cover any shortfalls in the funds available to the issuer, which cannot be met elsewhere. In this event the issuer or any trustee for investors will usually be given a power of attorney to reset the rate if the bank fails to do so. Although the documentation may confine the issuer (or trustee) in the extent to which either can require the bank to enforce default, the bank will in turn be obliged to comply with any reasonable directions. Any protection for borrowers in the documentation, however, depends on the degree to which a bank thinks its reputation may be affected if they suffer. This is not good enough when the commercial pressures for securitization may be pulling in the opposite direction.

---

[53] R. Beaumont, 'Securitisation in the United Kingdom', in J. Norton, P. Spellman, and M. Dupler (eds.), *International Asset Securitisation* (London, Lloyd's of London Press, 1995), 47–51.

In Britain limited steps have been taken, and these primarily through soft law. A statement of practice has been drawn up on government initiative. The Council of Mortgage Lenders expects its members to comply with it. Under it home mortgages can be assigned without the specific consent of the borrowers at the time of transfer if arrears policy is left in the hands of the lender, as agent of the issuer, and if the issuer has undertaken that its approach on interest rates and arrears will be identical to that of the original lender. Just what constitutes an identical approach is a debatable matter. Specific consent involves providing borrowers with certain information so that they can make an informed decision.[54] In 1991 the Law Commission took the view that a voluntary statement of practice may be insufficient protection for residential mortgages, and that legislation may be necessary.[55] Neither the Statement of Practice nor the Law Commission addresses the position of borrowers outside the context of home mortgages.

(ii) Bank Supervision

If bank regulators are to be persuaded that securitized assets have been completely removed from the balance sheet of a bank, they will want to know what has been done to isolate the risks attached to them. One concern will be whether the loans have been transferred to the vehicle in accordance with the general standards set for the sale of loan assets.[56] Another will be with the operational and moral risks which a bank may have in relation to securitized assets if it continues to administer them, even though investors do not have any legal recourse to it. The continued identification of a bank with a securitized pool means that its commercial reputation is committed and a completely clean break is not achieved. Banks may come under pressure to support losses incurred by investors (or to smooth cash flows) and maybe inclined to do so in order to protect their name. Consequently, the FSA requires that the association of a bank with an issuer must be severely limited: *inter alia* (i) any offering circular must contain a highly visible, unequivocal statement that the bank does not stand behind the issue or the issuer and will not make good any losses in the portfolio; (ii) the bank should not have any share capital in the issuer or otherwise have a proprietary interest in or control over the issuer; (iii) the issuer's name should not include the name of the bank or any reference to it; and (iv) the bank should not provide any general continuing support.[57] There are separate, and additional conditions, to be met with certain securitizations such as revolving credits.

Another dimension to the impact which bank regulators have had on securitization is the risk weighting they have attached to a bank's holding of the securities of an issuer. A bank after all will want to hold a diversified portfolio of the debt instruments on the market, for its own account and in the funds it manages. After considerable

---

[54] CML, Statement of Practice, Transfer of Mortgages, 1989 (2002).
[55] Law Commission, *Transfer of Land—Land Mortgages*, Report No 204, 1991, 40–3.
[56] 374 above.
[57] FSA Handbook, Prudential Sourcebook. Banks, ch. SE, paras. 6.3, 7.

debate on whether the risk weighting for mortgage-backed securities was 100 per cent—a distinct disincentive to banks holding the securities as part of their portfolio, and thus to the development of the market in securitized assets—the Bank of England now takes the view that they fall within the 50 per cent risk weighting applied under the EC Credit Institutions Directive.[58]

(iii) Securities Regulation

The securities issued will be subject to the ordinary securities laws. Depending on the structure of the issue, they will be treated in different ways under these laws. For example, in the United Kingdom, debt instruments will be regarded as 'investments' and subject to the ordinary issue and marketing controls.[59]

---

[58] Dir. 2000/12/EC [2000] OJ L126/1, Art. 43(1)(c). See Basle Commitee on Banking Supervision, *Working Paper on the Treatment of Asset Securitisations* (Basle, BIS, 2001).

[59] 345 above.

14

TRADE FINANCE

Finance for the trade in goods and services may simply involve techniques already considered. Buyers and suppliers may be lent moneys by their bank in the ordinary way (see Chapter 11). The bank's repayment may be guaranteed by an export-credit agency. The bank may take security over its customer's business (Chapter 15). If a supplier is confident that there is little risk of not being paid, it may agree to open-account trading: the buyer orders goods or services, the supplier provides them, and the buyer then pays by one of the various methods considered in Part III of the book. Open-account trading is widely used for trade between European countries. One advance on open-account trading is the documentary collection: the supplier retains control of the goods by not handing over the transport documents (e.g. the bill of lading) until the buyer pays (documents against payment) (D/P) or obliges itself to pay by accepting a bill of exchange (documents against acceptance) (D/A). The bank here acts as an intermediary. The ICC Uniform Rules for Collections are relevant to documentary collections.[1]

This Chapter touches on some forms of financing the trade in goods and services, notably bills of exchange, letters of credit, and demand guarantees. It should be emphasized that this is not an exhaustive catalogue.[2] International factoring, in which banks are involved, is used by sellers to handle a stream of smaller-value transactions. In broad terms it is the sale of debts to the factor (bank).[3] Export-credit agencies have already been mentioned. Countertrade covers a not insignificant part of the world's trade. Banks have an essential role: for example, they operate the trust or escrow accounts in which the proceeds from (say) the sale of oil are held to satisfy the claims of (say) the exporter of machinery.[4]

There is a wealth of case law, and a glittering array of commentaries, on bills of exchange, letters of credit, and demand guarantees. Not only does space preclude a lengthy analysis, but it is difficult for anyone to add to the sum total of human knowledge on these topics. Thus this Chapter aims to do nothing more than highlight a few aspects of the use of these devices in international trade, from the point of view of practical banking.

---

[1] ICC No 522, 1995. See 273 above.
[2] See, e.g., H. Palmer, *International Trade and Pre-Export Finance* (London, Euromoney, 1999).
[3] See UNIDROIT Convention on International Factoring, 1988.
[4] M. Rowe, *Countertrade* (2nd edn., London, Euromoney, 1990).

I. BILLS OF EXCHANGE

Bills of exchange feature in a variety of ways in trade-related credit. Mention has been made of the documentary collection: one type of documentary collection, D/A, is for the buyer to have to accept a bill of exchange, or to arrange acceptance of a bill of exchange, before the transport and other documents relating to the shipment are handed over to it. In effect the buyer is getting credit from the seller. For convenience we refer to this type of bill of exchange as a trade bill. Secondly, under an acceptance credit facility a seller or a buyer may raise trade-related finance, independently of the other, by drawing a bill on his or her bank, which is then discounted. A seller drawing bills under an acceptance credit will be looking to payment by the buyer, possibly under a trade bill, to pay its bank. Thirdly, there is the special form of trade finance known as forfaiting, where the forfaiter agrees to discount bills of exchange which are backed, usually by a leading bank in the buyer's country. In section II of this Chapter we see, fourthly, how payment under a letter of credit may be effected by the seller drawing a bill of exchange on the issuing or confirming bank.

Bills of exchange, because they are negotiable instruments, have a number of advantages over other methods of providing trade credit. First, the claim on the bill is generally dissociated from any claim in relation to the underlying transaction. By contrast, a supplier of goods on open account may be faced with disputes about the quality of the goods and services: if it draws a bill of exchange on the buyer, the latter will generally speaking have to raise those matters separately, after paying the bill. Secondly, a person buying a bill of exchange—such as a bank buying a bill in the bills market—generally obtains a good title to it, even though the transferor had a defective title or no title at all. As would be expected, there is a condition that the buyer of the bill acts in good faith, and without notice of the defect. Clearly this feature is facilitative of market transactions in bills. By contrast, those buying debts or contractual obligations can never be in a better position than their sellers. Indeed, as we saw in Chapter 13, they may be in a worse position because they take subject to equities (claims) and are subject to new equities.

Thirdly, the claim embodied in a bill is transferred by delivery, or indorsement and delivery, and a holder of a bill can sue in its own name. Under the general law contractual claims can be transferred by assignment and novation, but, as we saw in Chapter 13, there are difficulties associated with these techniques. Moreover, transferees under an equitable assignment need to join the transferor when suing the debtor/obligor. These factors have sometimes inhibited the development of a market in certain types of claims. By contrast, negotiability has been conducive to the development of a market in bills, as they can be freely bought and sold.[5] Central banks use the bills market as one technique to effect monetary policy.

---

[5] See U. Jahn, *Bills of Exchange* (3rd edn., Paris, ICC, 1999).

A. TRADE BILLS

Trade bills may be payable on demand, or, more likely, at some fixed time after sight or date, to give a period of credit.[6] The advantage to the buyer is thus obvious: it is being supplied with goods or services on deferred-credit terms. Indeed, if the buyer has the bargaining power, the collection order may specify that its acceptance of the bill be deferred until arrival of the goods. Bills of exchange in international trade tend on the whole to favour buyers, by contrast with letters of credit, where the seller can claim payment as soon as it ships the goods. The disadvantage of bills of exchange to buyers, as we shall see, is that they are liable to any holder in due course of the bill, irrespective of the underlying contract. Trade bills may contain a clause which makes it clear that the buyer must pay any bank charges, in addition to the face value.

Say a supplier draws a bill to its own order, i.e. with itself as payee, and with the buyer as drawee. If the buyer accepts, it has primary liability on the bills.[7] In the terminology of the Act, it becomes the acceptor. In other words, it must pay the payee (the supplier in our case), and anyone to whom the supplier negotiates the bill. Bills payable to order are negotiated by indorsement and delivery: an indorsement in blank, specifying no indorsee, is payable to the bearer and negotiated by delivery.[8] Once the bill is negotiated, however, the supplier, as drawer, becomes liable on the bill if the buyer dishonours it.[9] In other words, the supplier's (drawer's) liability is secondary to that of the buyer (acceptor).

The bill may be further negotiated. Again the buyer has primary liability on the bill. However, the scheme of the Act is to establish a chain of liability. If the buyer dishonours the bill, each party on the bill is liable to parties below it. Conversely, each party can claim against a party above it on the bill. Ultimately, the supplier (drawer) may have to bear the loss of the buyer's default. Under section 48 of the Act, if the buyer dishonours the bill, the holder must give notice of the dishonour to the drawer and each indorser if they are not to be discharged. The Act lays down detailed rules on how this is to be done. Trade bills, because they will generally be 'foreign bills' within the terms of the Act, must also be protested. This is a formal procedure, provided for in section 51, and provides evidence that the bill was dishonoured by the buyer: it is necessary if the holder in due course is to retain its right of recourse against prior indorsers and the drawer.

Now assume the bill is first negotiated to the supplier's bank. The bank discounts the bill, i.e. it buys the bill at less than its face value, to reflect the fact that it is out of its money until the bill matures. The supplier is, of course, paid immediately, which is the very object of the exercise. The bank claims against the buyer on maturity of the bill. It collects the bill on its own account. In the event of non-payment, the bank will have

---

[6] Bills of Exchange Act 1882, s. 11(1). See *Hong Kong & Shanghai Banking Corp. Ltd.* v. *G D Trade Co. Ltd.* [1998] CLC 238 (CA). Cf. *Korea Exchange Bank* v. *Debenhams (Central Buying) Ltd.* [1979] 1 Lloyd's Rep. 548 (CA).

[7] Ss. 17, 54(1).   [8] Ss. 31, 34.   [9] S. 55(1)(a).

recourse against the supplier, its customer.[10] The bank, having discounted the bill, has clearly given value. It is a holder for value in terms of the Act.[11] So, too, are other banks, which subsequently buy the bill in the market. The strongest position to be in, however, is as a holder in due course, for a holder in due course takes a bill free from any defect of title of prior parties, as well as from personal defences available among them.

To be a holder in due course, a holder for value must have taken the bill, complete and regular on the face of it, before it was overdue, without notice that it had previously been dishonoured (if that was the case), in good faith, and with no notice of any defect in the title of the party negotiating it.[12] Good faith demands honesty.[13] Whether a holder has notice of a defect in the transferor's title depends on its actual knowledge or whether it wilfully shut its eyes to the obvious.[14] Trade-related bills will frequently refer to the underlying transaction: that certainly does not make them irregular, although care is needed to ensure that the order to pay remains unconditional.[15] Just because the indorsements are out of order does not necessarily mean that the bill is irregular on its face.[16] But the supplier's indorsement might be irregular because of a discrepancy with its signature as drawer.[17] A material alteration certainly makes the bill irregular; indeed, under the Act, it avoids the bill.[18]

Bills of exchange are negotiated in the market every day without problems occurring. Since they are handled by professionals, there is less scope for fraud than with cheques. This point should not be lost sight of in the welter of case law involving fraudulent bills: these cases are atypical in practice. The Act even contains a presumption that a holder of a bill is *prima facie* deemed to be a holder in due course.[19] Occasionally a bank is the victim of fraud and loses its right to claim as a holder in due course. Implication of a bank employee in fraud may mean that the bank takes bills without good faith, or in other circumstances such that it does not become a holder in due course.[20] Moreover, if a signature on a bill is forged, the scheme of the Act is that no rights can be acquired through that signature.[21] The victim of the fraud must suffer the loss. Thus, if the discounting bank has taken a bill with a forged indorsement of its customer, the supplier, it cannot claim against the buyer/acceptor. If that bank has subsequently sold the bill in the market, however, it will be liable on its indorsement to others which take it.[22]

---

[10] S. 55(2)(a). Instead of negotiating the bill, the seller's bank may collect it on the seller's behalf. It may make an advance—a proportion of the bill's face value—to the seller against the collection. Under the general law it has a lien on the bill, and consequently under s. 27(3) of the Act it is a holder to the extent of the advance.

[11] S. 38.   [12] S. 29(1).   [13] S. 90.   [14] 186 above.   [15] S. 3(3)(b).

[16] *Yeoman Credit* v. *Gregory* [1963] 1 WLR 343, [1963] 1 All ER 245; *Lombard Banking Ltd.* v. *Central Garage and Engineering Co. Ltd.* [1963] QB 220.

[17] e.g., *Arab Bank Ltd.* v. *Ross* [1952] 2 QB 216 (CA).   [18] S. 64; 264 above.

[19] S. 30(2).   [20] See also s. 29(2).   [21] S. 24.   [22] Ss. 55(2), 58.

B. THE UNDERLYING TRANSACTION

If the bank, having bought a trade bill and still holding it, seeks payment from the buyer/acceptor on its maturity, can it be defeated by any claim which the buyer has in relation to the underlying contract—failure of consideration, late or defective performance, and so on? In general, the bank, as holder in due course of the bill, 'holds the bill free from any defect of title of prior parties, as well as from mere personal defences available to prior parties among themselves'.[23] So whatever claims the immediate parties to the bill—the buyer and supplier—might be able to raise in proceedings between themselves,[24] the bank should not be troubled by them.

In one decision,[25] the Court of Appeal gave a bank judgment for the whole amount of the bills it had discounted for suppliers, but stayed judgment against the buyers in respect of that proportion of the amount which the bank was said to hold as trustees for the suppliers. The buyers were acceptors of the bills, but they claimed liquidated damages against the suppliers for breach of contract. Under the facility letter with the suppliers, the bank had credited part of what it had paid for the bills, undertaking to credit the remaining proportion as and when the bills were met on maturity. It was said that when a holder of a bill holds it as a trustee for someone else, a defendant can raise against it any defence or set-off which it would have against the person who is really behind the transaction. The decision was subsequently disapproved in a later decision of the Court of Appeal, where the rule of practice was emphatically restated: 'pay upon the bill of exchange and pursue claims later'.[26]

C. ACCEPTANCE CREDITS

Instead of a straightforward loan, a bank facility may involve the borrower in drawing bills of exchange on the bank. These are then discounted in the market. Because the bank will have accepted the bills, these facilities are sometimes called acceptance credits.[27] In some jurisdictions, acceptance credits may be available for a range of financing purposes; in others, they tend to be trade-related, providing credit for both buyers and sellers. An important reason for the latter in the United Kingdom is the attitude of the Bank of England. For monetary control reasons the bank will only discount bills which are short-term and not for capital purposes.[28] The Bank expects banks whose paper it discounts to generate only bills having the characteristics it will discount.

Acceptance credits will be issued under a facility agreement. Typically this will

---

[23] S. 38(2).

[24] In an action by a supplier/payee on a bill, the buyer/acceptor may raise an absence or total failure of consideration, or have a liquidated cross-claim: e.g. *Nova (Jersey) Knit Ltd.* v. *Kammgarn Spinnerei GmbH* [1977] 1 WLR 713, [1977] 2 All ER 463 (HL). Generally speaking, defective goods do not give rise to a liquidated claim: to do so they must be worthless.

[25] *Barclays Bank Ltd.* v. *Aschaffeburger Zellstoffwerke AG* [1967] Lloyd's Rep. 387.

[26] *Cebora SNC* v. *SIP (Industrial Products) Ltd.* [1976] 1 Lloyd's Rep. 271, 279.

[27] E. P. Ellinger, E. Lomnicka, and R. Hooley, *Modern Banking Law* (3rd edn., Oxford, OUP, 2002), ch. 17.

[28] *Bank of England, Open Market Operations: Eligible Banks and Eligible Bills*, Notice, 1 Mar. 2000.

contain provisions broadly along the lines of those in the loan agreements discussed in Chapter 11. Thus there will be clauses regarding availability and charges, conditions precedent, representations and warranties, limited undertakings, and a default clause giving the bank a wide (or unlimited) discretion to demand repayment of any outstanding drawings (with interest) and to declare the aggregate face value of any outstanding bills immediately repayable. As regards availability, the agreement may oblige the customer to request utilization of the facility. If approved, the customer will then draw bills payable to its order, on its bank, with an agreed maturity date after acceptance (e.g. one, two, three, six, or twelve months). The bills may then be returned to the customer, or delivered to its order, or the bank may discount them on the customer's behalf disbursing the proceeds (less charges) to the customer. On the date of maturity the customer will be obliged by the facility agreement to provide the bank with funds equal to the face value of the bills.

One issue never authoritatively decided is whether a bill drawn under an acceptance credit facility is an accommodation bill under the Bills of Exchange Act 1882. Section 28(1) provides that an accommodation party to a bill is one who signs a bill as a drawer, acceptor, or indorser, without receiving value, and for the purpose of lending its name to some other person. Under section 59(3) of the Act an accommodation bill is discharged if the party accommodated—the customer—pays the bill. If a bank under an acceptance credit is not an accommodation party, and the customer pays any holder directly, the bill is not discharged under this subsection. Thus it is said that the customer could unjustly sue the bank on the bill. In fact it is difficult to see how a bank can be an accommodation party under section 28(1) when, under the typical acceptance credit facility, it charges an acceptance fee, i.e. it receives value. However, in the unlikely event that the customer pays an acceptance credit bill directly and claims against the bank because the bill is still extant, the bank would be protected under the typical acceptance credit facility by the default clause and the obligation on the customer to put the bank in funds at the date of maturity.

D. FORFAITING

Forfaiting is generally used for large transactions. It is the discounting of bills of exchange or promissory notes on a non-recourse basis. The supplier draws a bill of exchange, which the forfaiter agrees to discount at a previously agreed fixed price.[29] The supplier thus receives immediate payment, although the discount reflects the risk the forfaiter is taking. Central to forfaiting is that the supplier will have drawn the bill 'without recourse'. Crucial for the forfaiter is thus the *aval* or guarantee which the forfaiter will require on the bill. This will usually be provided by a leading bank in the buyer's country. Forfaiting is a specialist activity. Forfaiters in turn sell the bills and notes they have discounted.

---

[29] Promissory notes of the buyer, as well as other instruments, may be involved in forfaiting: the discussion concentrates on bills.

Assume the supplier has drawn a bill of exchange on the buyer covering the price of goods, and payable in the future. If it is an order bill it will be indorsed, and the forfaiter will take the instrument. Were the forfaiter's customer to refuse to release the instrument, on grounds of commercial confidentiality,[30] it might be difficult for the forfaiter to sue on the instrument. Under the Bills of Exchange Act 1882, delivery is essential to complete the contracts of the drawer and acceptor, and to the bill's negotiation.[31] Delivery can be effected by a constructive transfer of possession, but this would involve the forfaiter's customer somehow constituting itself as agent of the forfaiter, and holding the instrument on the latter's behalf, rather than on its own account.

If the buyer has accepted the bill, it is obviously primarily liable. Having drawn the instrument, the supplier ordinarily has a secondary liability if the buyer does not pay. If the forfaiter then supplies the bill in the secondary market, it too will be liable on the bill if it has indorsed it. There is, however, a special feature of bills which are forfaited: the supplier will typically avoid liability on the bill by signing as drawer and indorsing 'without recourse' or *sans recours*.

By contrast with the Geneva Uniform Law on Bills of Exchange and Promissory Notes, under which a drawer cannot release itself from its guarantee of payment,[32] the Bills of Exchange Act 1882 permits drawers and indorsers to negate liability to a holder.[33] 'Without recourse' or *sans recours* must be on the bill itself, for if it is in a separate contract between the supplier and forfaiter it will only be effective between those parties. The negation of liability does not affect the negotiability of the bill.

Although not liable on the bill, can a supplier still be liable, for example, to the same extent as a transferor by delivery?[34] Under section 58 a transferor by delivery (in our case, the supplier) warrants to its immediate transferee (in our case, the forfaiter) that the bill is genuine, that the transferor has a right to transfer it, and that at the time of transfer the transferor is not aware of any fact which renders it valueless.[35] These warranties may include, for example, that the signatures on the bill are genuine and that the bill relates to a genuine transaction. However, it is difficult to see how a party signing 'without recourse' can be held to these warranties. In an ordinary sale of an instrument there are no implied terms that the instrument is genuine or relates to a genuine transaction.[36] In theory such terms could be implied by trade usage. There is a

---

[30] See I. Guild and R. Harris, *Forfaiting* (Cambridge, Woodhead Faulkner, 1985), 6. See also H. Waterman, 'Forfaiting', in J. Norton and R. Auerback (eds.), *International Finance in the 1990s* (Oxford, Blackwell, 1993).

[31] Ss. 21, 31.

[32] Art. 9. However, this problem does not apply to makers of promissory notes (Art. 77). Forfaiting in Geneva countries may thus involve notes, rather than bills, since suppliers may not be happy with a separate contractual undertaking of the forfaiter not to sue on a bill. See H.-U. Jäger, 'Export Factoring and Forfaiting', in N. Horn (ed.), *The Law of International Trade Finance* (Deventer, Kluwer, 1989).

[33] S. 16(1). See for promissory notes, s. 89.

[34] *Chalmers and Guest on Bills of Exchange* (15th edn., London, Sweet & Maxwell, 1998), 472ff.

[35] S. 58(3).

[36] A point recognized in an old American case used to support the suggestion that the warranties in s. 58(3) apply: *Dumont* v. *Williamson* (1867) 17 LT 71, 72.

suggestion that in the forfait market sellers have an obligation to sell bills constituting a valid claim, and that as well the words 'without recourse' do not exclude liability if there is some fundamental defect in the transaction. In the forfait market 'without recourse' is said to mean 'that any purchaser takes on the credit risk that the acceptor and guarantor may not pay and also the risk that force majeure may prevent payment'.[37] It is a matter of inquiry whether all this meets the stringent tests for trade usage in English law.[38]

The forfaiter will rely primarily on the guarantee or *aval* of the bank in the buyer's country in the event of non-payment by the buyer. The guarantee or *aval* is also necessary for the marketability of the paper, since without the name of a leading bank on it the forfaiter will be unlikely to sell it in the secondary market. *Avals* are recognized in the Geneva Uniform Law: *avals* are given either on the bill itself or an *allonge*, are expressed by the words *bon pour aval* or their equivalent, and signed.[39] The giver of an *aval* is bound in the same manner as the person for whom it has become guarantor.[40] Thus in our case, if the buyer has accepted the bill, the bank *avalizing* the bill for account of the buyer assumes the liability of an acceptor.

It is hornbook law that '[a]n *aval* for the honour of the acceptor, even if on the bill, is not effectual in English law'.[41] However, this problem is generally academic because the Bills of Exchange Act 1882 does recognize the undertaking of the 'quasi' or 'anomalous' indorser: if someone like a bank, not the holder of a bill, backs it with its signature, it is liable as an indorser to a holder in due course.[42] Unlike the *aval*, the undertaking of the quasi- or anomalous indorser is limited to those who became parties to the bill after its signature was placed on it. This can be the position with forfaiting, since the forfaiter will sign as an indorser of the bill. To be liable to the payee, however, the parties need to practice alchemy: the bank will *avalize* the bill, which will then be endorsed by the payee back to the bank, then endorsed by the bank back to the payee. However, an *aval* may well be enforceable as an ordinary guarantee. In any event, forfaited bills will often be *avalized* in countries which recognize the *aval*. English law will then give effect to an *aval*, since the Bills of Exchange Act 1882 provides that the obligations created by it are determined by the law of place where the contract of *aval* is made.[43]

II. LETTERS OF CREDIT

If a supplier is doubtful about the credit of a prospective foreign buyer, it may still be willing to trade if a bank can be brought into the picture. The supplier accepts an undertaking by the bank to pay in substitution for the payment obligation of

---

[37] I. Guild and R. Harris, note 30 above, 40.   [38] 143 above.   [39] Art. 31.
[40] Art. 32.   [41] *Steele* v. *M'Kinlay* (1880) 5 App. Cas. 754, 772.   [42] S. 56.
[43] S. 72(2). *G. & H. Montage GmbH* v. *Irvani* [1990] 1 Lloyd's Rep. 14 (CA).

the buyer. This is essentially the function performed by the letter of credit: it is an arrangement whereby a bank (the issuing bank), acting at the behest of its customer (the buyer in our case), undertakes to pay a beneficiary (the supplier). The requirement for a letter of credit will be contained in the underlying contract between supplier and buyer. Payment to the beneficiary may be direct (but often on deferred terms); by the bank accepting and paying bills of exchange drawn by the beneficiary; or by the bank authorizing another bank to pay or to negotiate the credit. Payment is against stipulated documents and in compliance with the terms and conditions of the credit.[44]

There is an obvious advantage to the supplier being paid under a letter of credit, compared with a bill of exchange.[45] With a bill of exchange, by the time the buyer accepts, the goods may have reached, or be about to reach, their destination. If the buyer then fails to accept the bill, the supplier may incur considerable expense in retrieving the situation. Even if the buyer accepts the bill, there is a risk that it will dishonour it on maturity. By contrast, with a letter of credit the supplier obtains payment from a bank as soon as it presents complying documents. This can be at the time of shipment—once it has obtained the transport documents evidencing shipment. The transport documents are the key documents to be presented, along with the invoice, an insurance policy, and certificates on matters such as quality, inspection, and origin.

Much international trade does not involve letters of credit. For example, only a small proportion of trade within Europe is covered by letters of credit. Suppliers are prepared to take the risk, they have a longstanding relationship with their buyers, or their buyers have sufficient bargaining power to demand other means of payment— incidentally also avoiding bank charges for opening a letter of credit. But in other parts of the world letters of credit are typical: partly this reflects the respective bargaining position of the parties, partly tradition, and partly also the law. Where exchange control is in place, a government may insist on payment by letters of credit to underpin it.

A. BASIC FEATURES

Letters of credit are typically governed by the Uniform Customs and Practices for Documentary Credits (UCP), published by the International Chamber of Commerce.[46] These will be incorporated into the letter of credit by reference. There is a good argument that an English court will imply them in any event, as representing

---

[44] ICC Uniform Customs and Practices for Documentary Credits, UCP 500, 1993, Art. 2. For the history of letters of credit: E. P. Ellinger, *Documentary Letters of Credit* (Singapore, Uni. of Singapore Press, 1970), 5–7.

[45] A. Watson *et al.*, *Finance of International Trade* (7th edn., London, IFS, 2001), 106–7.

[46] On the development of the UCP: E. P. Ellinger, 'The Uniform Customs—their Nature and the 1983 Revision' [1984] *LMCLQ* 578. Art. 5 of the Uniform Commercial Code of the United States, revised in 1995, deals with letters of credit. See J. Dolan, *The Law of Letters of Credit* (3rd edn., Arlington, A. S. Pratt & Sons, 1996).

modern banking practice in relation to the principles underlying letters of credit.[47] If
the UCP is incorporated in a letter of credit, it clearly overrides any common law rule
to the contrary. However, if the credit itself adopts a different approach, that must be
given preference over the UCP. Since the UCP ostensibly represents the customs and
practices of the banking community, it should be given a purposive interpretation. In
fact, with time, the UCP has become increasingly legalistic in character.

Letters of credit are typically, and presumptively,[48] irrevocable. They can be neither
amended nor cancelled without the agreement of the beneficiary: once issued, a buyer
cannot have its bank revoke.[49] A revocable credit may be used to satisfy a formality, e.g.
exchange-control regulations. Letters of credit become binding on a bank when they
are issued to a beneficiary. There has been considerable discussion about how this can
be reconciled with the conventional demands of English contract law, notably that
consideration must flow from the promissee (the beneficiary).[50] Attempts to invoke
agency (the bank as the buyer's agent) and reliance (on the part of the beneficiary) do
not bear close examination. Justification through the Contracts (Rights of Third
Parties) Act 1999 is unnecessary. The fact is that English law takes a pragmatic view
and upholds the letter of credit, and other abstract payment obligations, despite
conceptual difficulties.[51]

The credit may be transmitted to the supplier through an intermediary bank in its
own country. The intermediary bank may simply advise the credit and assume no
liability on it. Its only liability is to take reasonable care to check the apparent authen-
ticity of the credit it advises.[52] However, the intermediary bank may be requested to
confirm the credit, in other words, to undertake independently to pay, provided the
stipulated documents are presented and that the terms of credit are complied with.[53] A
confirming bank is in the same position as the issuing bank, in terms of its rights and
obligations. Where an issuing bank is not willing to request the confirmation of a
letter of credit (e.g. it may not have suitable credit lines with other banks, or there may
be political or other restrictions), the beneficiary may request a bank in its jurisdiction, maybe its own bank, to undertake to pay, according to the terms of the credit,
should the issuing bank fail to do so. The issuing bank is not told. Despite the way this
practice is described—a silent confirmation of a letter of credit—it is an independent
undertaking by a bank, outside the terms of letter of credit law, and enforceable
simply on its own terms.[54]

A letter of credit may involve banks other than those mentioned—the issuing,
advising, and confirming bank. The letter of credit may stipulate that it may be paid at
another bank, a nominated bank. In a freely negotiated credit any bank is a nominated

---

[47] R. Jack, A. Malek, and D. Quest, *Documentary Credits* (3rd edn., London, Butterworths, 2001), 15.
[48] UCP, Art. 6(c).   [49] UCP, Art. 9(d)(ii).
[50] See B. Kozolchyk, 'Letters of Credit', *International Encyclopedia for Comparative Law*, ix, ch. 5, 135–43.
[51] See R. Goode, 'Abstract Payment Undertakings', in P. Cane and J. Stapleton (eds.), *Essays for Patrick Atiyah* (Oxford, Clarendon, 1991).
[52] UCP, Art. 7(a).   [53] Art. 9(b); 10(d).
[54] Cf. *Dibrell Bros. International SA v. Banca Nazionale de Lavoro*, 38 F 3d 1571 (11th Cir. 1995).

bank.[55] Negotiation credits, and the separate topics of transferable credits and assignment, are beyond our remit.[56]

B. FUNDAMENTAL PRINCIPLES

A fundamental principle of letters-of-credit law is that a bank's undertaking on a letter of credit is separate from any underlying contract. Banks are in no way concerned with, or bound by, such contracts. Consequently, a bank undertaking to pay on a letter of credit is not subject to any claims or defences which the applicant for the credit—the buyer in our example—might have against the supplier, or indeed against the bank itself.[57] Similarly, the beneficiary (supplier) can in no way avail itself of a contractual relationship between the applicant and the issuing bank, or between the issuing bank and other banks.[58] The three (or more[59]) contracts—buyer–beneficiary/supplier; buyer–issuing bank; issuing bank–beneficiary/supplier—are independent of each other.

Fraud is the one exception to the principle of autonomy. Fraud will justify a bank in not paying a beneficiary under a credit. In well used terminology 'fraud unravels all'. In the leading English case on fraud in letters of credit, the House of Lords said:

The exception for fraud on the part of the beneficiary seeking to avail himself of the credit is a clear application of the maxim *ex turpi causa non oritur actio* or, if plain English is to be preferred, 'fraud unravels all'. The courts will not allow their process to be used by a dishonest person to carry out a fraud.[60]

Common law fraud involves dishonesty: it is a false act or a false statement done knowingly or without belief in its truth, or recklessly (not caring whether it is true or false).[61] Common law fraud requires no corrupt motive: it is infinite in variety. In the context of letters of credit, common law fraud would involve dishonestly making a demand or asserting other than a *bona fide* demand. Proof of fraud, by a buyer seeking to restrain its bank from paying, will rarely be possible.[62]

A second fundamental principle with letters of credit is that banks deal in documents and not with the goods, services, or performances to which the documents

---

[55] Art. 10.

[56] See Art. 48; *Bank Negara Indonesia* v. *Lariza (Singapore) Pte. Ltd.* [1988] 1 AC 583 (PC); A. Ward and G. McCormick, 'Assignment and Documentary Credits' [2001] *JIBL* 138.

[57] Art. 3(a).

[58] Art. 3(b).

[59] If there is a confirming bank there are at least two more contracts: confirming bank–beneficiary/supplier; issuing bank–confirming bank: cf. *United City Merchants (Investments) Ltd.* v. *Royal Bank of Canada* [1983] 1 AC 168.

[60] *Ibid.* at 184. See also *Szetejn* v. *J. Henry Schroder Banking Corp.*, 31 NYS 2d 631 (1941); X. Gao, 'Presenters Immune from the Fraud Rule in the Law of Letters of Credit' [2002] *LMCLQ* 10.

[61] *Derry* v. *Peek* (1889) 14 App. Cas. 337.

[62] e.g., *United Trading Corporation SA* v. *Allied Arab Bank Ltd.* [1985] 2 Lloyd's Rep. 554 (CA); *Czarnikow–Rionda Sugar Trading Inc.* v. *Standard Bank London Ltd.* [1999] 2 Lloyd's Rep. 187.

relate.[63] All a bank has to do is to determine, on the basis of the documents alone, whether they appear on their face to be in compliance with the terms and conditions of the letter of credit.[64] If they do, the bank must pay; if they do not, the bank may refuse to take up the documents.[65] Documents not stipulated in the credit will not be examined by the bank, and if a letter of credit contains conditions without stating the documents to be presented, a bank will disregard them.[66] The description of the goods in the commercial invoice must correspond with the description in the credit, although in all other documents they may be described in general, although not inconsistent, terms.[67]

The duty of a bank is to make payment only against documents which comply strictly with the terms of a letter of credit.[68] Thus it may reject documents where the goods are described differently from the credit, even if it is universally understood in a trade that the descriptions are interchangeable—a bank is not to be bound to know each trade of its many customers.[69] The bank must give notice of rejection without delay, although it has a reasonable time to examine for discrepancies.[70] Banks are thus protected in refusing to pay under a letter of credit if there is a discrepancy in the documents. In practice, discrepancies are rampant: one survey in the 1980s found that there were discrepancies, initially, in over 60 per cent of presentations of documents.[71] A more recent survey of United States and Japanese banks found that banks paid despite discrepancies in over 70 per cent of documents presented.[72] Many of these discrepencies are easily remedied, and many will be waived by the bank's customer, the buyer.

To what standard are banks to be held in examining the documents? This issue arises where a bank has paid, but subsequently discrepancies in the documents are discovered. As a general rule, banks must act for their customers with reasonable care and skill.[73] So, too, in the context of letters of credit. As Article 13(a) of the UCP puts it: 'Banks must examine all documents stipulated in the credit with reasonable care, to ascertain whether or not they appear, on their face, to be in compliance with the terms and conditions of the credit.' In other words, banks are not strictly liable if they fail to uncover discrepancies in the documents. They can refuse to pay beneficiaries in the absence of strict compliance, but their own customers cannot hold them to a higher standard than reasonable care. In determining what is reasonable care, the UCP refers to international standard banking practice, as reflected in the

---

[63] UCP, Art. 4.   [64] Art. 14(b).   [65] Art. 14(b).

[66] Art. 13(a)(c). See *Banque de l'Indochine* v. *J. H. Rayner (Mincing Lane) Ltd.* [1983] QB 711 (CA).

[67] Art. 37(c).

[68] Certain tolerances in the amount, quantity, or unit price are permissible: UCP, Art. 39.

[69] *J. H. Rayner & Co. Ltd.* v. *Hambro's Bank Ltd.* [1943] 1 KB 37.

[70] Art. 16; *Seaconsar Far East Ltd.* v. *Bank Markazi Jumhouri Islamic Iran* [1999] 1 Lloyd's Rep. 36 (CA).

[71] SITPRO, 'Letter of Credit Management and Control: A Midland Bank Survey on Errors on Letter of Credit Documentation' (London, unpublished, 1985).

[72] R. Mann, 'The Role of Letters of Credit in Payment Transactions' (2000) 98 *Michigan LR* 2494.

[73] 186 above.

UCP itself.[74] Banking practice requires prompt decision-making by banks when documents are presented for payment.[75] If the credit is ambiguous or unclear, the bank may need to clarify the matter with its customer,[76] but if not it commits no breach by adopting a reasonable interpretation.[77] Visual inspection is all that is called for.

C. TRUST RECEIPTS

Except for the most creditworthy of customers, banks are generally happier lending money if they can take some sort of security. This applies in international trade as much as to anywhere else. An obvious avenue for banks financing buyers is to take security over the goods themselves. This can be done relatively easily by a bank taking the bill of lading, representing the goods, which may still be on the high seas. At common law the bill of lading is a document of title, so a pledge of it is equivalent to a pledge of the goods themselves.[78] But the buyer will need access to the bill of lading to deal with the goods when they arrive at the port or in relation to third parties. The trust receipt is a document, signed by the importer, which facilitates this, without destroying the bank's security interest. The buyer undertakes that, in consideration of the bank releasing the bill of lading to it, it will hold it on trust for the bank, together with the goods and the proceeds of their sale.

Legally the term 'trust' is a misnomer, although no doubt some lawyer thought it might offer some protection in insolvency (since property held on trust is excluded from the insolvent's estate) and in relation to the proceeds of sale. And it might also have been used to bring home to lay merchants their obligations to their bank in relation to the goods. But legally no trust is involved and at most one could say that the buyer has certain obligations to its bankers as a result of signing the trust receipt.

In the typical case of a merchant buying goods, the bill of lading is made out to the order of the banker (but the buyer to be notified). Insurance is effected in the name of the bank. In consideration of the banker giving the buyer credit (e.g. by issuing a letter of credit in the seller's favour) the buyer signs an agreement with the bank to the effect that the bank remains the owner of the goods, the bill of lading, the policy of insurance, and the proceeds of these until repayment of the amount of the credit. The agreement probably refers to the buyer giving a trust receipt and security, if required, once the goods have arrived and are released to the buyer for resale or use. Once

---

[74] Art. 13(a). See B. Kozolchyk, 'Strict Compliance and the Reasonable Document Checker' (1990) 56 *Brooklyn LR* 45.

[75] The UCP specifies a reasonable time to take up or refuse the documents, not to exceed 7 days: Art. 13(b). But this goes more to the rights of the beneficiary than those of the buyer/applicant.

[76] 140 above.

[77] *Commercial Banking Co. of Sydney* v. *Jalsard Pty. Ltd.* [1973] AC 279 (PC); *Gian Singh & Co.* v. *Banque de L'Indochine* [1974] 1 WLR 123, [1974] 2 All ER 754 (PC); *Credit Agricole Indosuez* v. *Muslim Commercial Bank Ltd.* [2001] 1 Lloyds Rep. 1 (CA).

[78] 400 below.

notified of the arrival of the goods, the buyer obtains the bill of lading and other documents upon signing a trust receipt.

The trust receipt was first upheld by US courts and then by the House of Lords in 1894.[79] It had no difficulty in concluding that the bank was entitled to the proceeds of sale over the sellers, who were claiming the remainder of the unpaid purchase price. Under English law, it said, there could be no doubt that a pledgee like the bank might hand back to the pledgor as his agent goods it had pledged for the purposes of sale, without diminishing the power of the security. So long, then, as there is a valid pledge of documents or goods to the bank, the trust receipt is effective.[80]

The commercial efficacy of the trust receipt led subsequent courts in England to deflect attacks on it. When in one case it was argued that trust receipts created a security which was void because they were not registered under the bills-of-sale legislation, the court held that security (pledge) rights of the bank were complete on the deposit of the bills of lading and other documents of title, before the trust receipts came into existence. Their object was to enable the bank to realize the goods over which it had a charge 'in the way in which goods in similar cases have for years and years been realised in the City [of London] and elsewhere'.[81] The exception where a bank would be defeated was if the buyer were fraudulent and sold or otherwise disposed of the goods obtained under a trust receipt to innocent third parties.[82]

III. DEMAND GUARANTEES

Demand guarantees are the undertaking of a bank to pay a beneficiary, independent of the principal contract, possibly on written demand, possibly on presentation of a certificate by some independent third party, or possibly on submission of a court judgment or an arbitral award. They are typically used in construction contracts and contracts for the international sale of goods and are designed to safeguard the employer of the construction company, or the buyer under the sales contract, against non-performance by the construction company or seller (the customer requesting the demand guarantee).[83] Among the range of demand guarantees are the performance guarantee, given for a specified percentage of the contract sum, and the advance-payment guarantee, to ensure the beneficiary's right to repayment of the advance if performance is not furnished. In practice, the demand guarantee may be issued by a bank in the beneficiary's country, at the request of the customer's (principal's) bank.

---

[79] *North Western Bank Ltd. v. John Poynter, Son & Macdonalds* [1895] AC 56. See K. Frederick, 'The Trust Receipt as Security' (1922) 22 *Columbia LR* 395, 546.
[80] [1895] AC 56.
[81] *In re David Allester Ltd* [1922] 2 Ch. 211, 218.
[82] *Lloyds Bank Ltd. v. Bank of America National Trust and Savings Association* [1938] 2 KB 147, 166 (CA).
[83] R. Goode, *Guide to the ICC Uniform Rules for Demand Guarantees* (Paris, ICC, 1992), 9.

A. LEGAL CHARACTER

A fundamental principle of demand guarantees is that they are by their nature separate transactions from the contract or tender conditions on which they may be based. In other words, their legal basis is 'pay first, argue later'.[84] As the ICC's Uniform Rules for Demand Guarantees put it: 'The duty of a Guarantor [bank] under a Guarantee is to pay the sum or sums therein stated on the presentation of a written demand for payment and other documents specified by the Guarantee which appear on their face to be in accordance with the terms of the Guarantee.'[85] The principal might sue the beneficiary on the underlying contract, if of the opinion that although called there has not been default. However, any disadvantage because the bank cannot invoke defences from the underlying contract pertains to the principal, not the bank, in view of the principal's invariable obligation to reimburse the bank irrespective of those defences.

In English law the nature of a demand guarantee and of the obligations undertaken under it is determined by construing the guarantee as a whole.[86] The primary nature of the obligation undertaken by a bank under a demand guarantee may be evident from a clause such as follows: 'We hereby waive the necessity of your demanding the said debt from the Main Contractor before presenting us with the demand'. That the bank undertakes a primary obligation means that the obligation is independent of the principal contract. Reference in the principal contract to the demand guarantee in no way detracts from the independence principle: it serves to identify the purpose behind the issue of the demand guarantee and the risk against which it provides protection.

Although the purpose of a demand guarantee will be to indemnify the beneficiary for any losses resulting from the principal's default on the underlying contract, its right to claim payment under it is to be determined solely by reference to the terms and conditions set out in the demand guarantee itself. The bank does not become involved in any dispute between the principal and the beneficiary, and any such dispute is irrelevant to the rights and obligations on the guarantee.

[T]he obligation of the bank is to perform that which it is required to perform by that particular contract, and that obligation does not in the ordinary way depend on the correct resolution of a dispute as to the sufficiency of performance ... under the ... contract; the bank ... is simply concerned to see whether the event has happened upon which its obligation to pay has arisen.[87]

The position in English law is therefore clear. Whether the beneficiary or the principal is in breach of the underlying contract, and as a result the other party is entitled to a remedy, is not a relevant issue between the beneficiary and the bank. If the principal believes that it is not in breach of the principal contract, it can institute

---

[84] R. Bertrams, *Bank Guarantees in International Trade* (2nd edn., The Hague, Kluwer, 1996), 60.

[85] ICC No 458, 1992, Art. 2(b). Cf. UN Convention on Independent Guarantees and Stand-By Letters of Credit, 1995, Art. 2.

[86] *Trafalgar House Construction (Regions) Ltd.* v. *General Surety & Guarantee Co. Ltd.* [1996] AC 199 (HL).

[87] *Howe Richardson Scale Co.* v. *Polimex-Cekop* [1978] 1 Lloyd's Rep. 161, 165 (CA).

proceedings against the beneficiary under that contract and the court or arbitrator may order it to pay an amount equivalent to that paid under the guarantee to the principal. The fact that the court or arbitrator may later find that the beneficiary is liable does not mean that payment by the bank under the guarantee should not have been made, nor that the demand for payment was fraudulent.[88]

For the sake of completeness, three additional points may be made. First, unless required by the demand guarantee, there is no need for notices of demand to be given to a principal before a beneficiary makes demand. Secondly, once a demand guarantee is issued, the principal cannot act to have it revoked. This follows because English law regards the principal as having instructed the bank to assume an irrevocable undertaking. The analogy is with irrevocable letters of credit. Thirdly, if the bank's customer is unable to reimburse it in full, after the bank has paid out, the bank may be subrogated to any claims which the beneficiary has.[89]

B. FRAUD AND ENJOINING BANKS FROM PAYING

There has been long discussion about abusive calling of demand guarantees, and it has given rise to a substantial body of litigation in many jurisdictions. Beneficiaries, it is said, have fraudulently made demand when there is no breach of the underlying contract, or when breach is easily remedied or in the process of being remedied. Abusive calling has on occasions been said to be politically motivated. The courts in civil law jurisdictions have invoked doctrines of the abuse of rights and fraud to enjoin the beneficiary's drawing on the bank's payment. The English courts have taken a quite different approach.[90]

In the seminal English case on demand guarantees, *Edward Owen*, Lord Denning MR cross-referred to the fraud exception in letter of credit cases—'established or obvious fraud to the knowledge of the bank': 'the bank ought not to pay under the credit if it knows that the documents are forged or that the request for payment is fraudulently made in circumstances when there is no right to payment'.[91] These principles apply as well to demand guarantees. It is thus clear that in English law the fraud exception is very narrow—clear fraud of which the bank has notice. It does not apply

---

[88] *Edward Owen Engineering Ltd.* v. *Barclays Bank International Ltd.* [1978] QB 159 (CA); *Cargill International SA Ltd.* v. *Bangladesh Sugar & Food Industries Corp.* [1998] 1 WLR 461, [1998] 2 All ER 406 (CA).

[89] A. Ward and G. McCormack, 'Subrogation and Bankers' Autonomous Undertakings' (2000) 116 *LQR* 121.

[90] e.g. Note, 'Fraud in the Transaction: Enjoining Letters of Credit During the Iranian Revolution' (1980) 93 *Harv. LR* 992; N. Horn and E. Wymeersch, 'Bank-guarantees, Standby Letters of Credit, and Performance Bonds in International Trade', in N. Horn (ed.), *The Law of International Trade Finance* (Deventer, Kluwer, 1989), 482–528; B. Kozolchyk, 'Bank Guarantees and Letters of Credit: Time for a Return to the Fold' (1989) 11 *U Penn. J Int'l. Bus. L* 7, 38ff; R. Bertrams, *Bank Guarantees in International Trade* (2nd edn., The Hague, Kluwer, 1996), chs. 14–16.

[91] *Edward Owen Engineering Ltd.* v. *Barclays Bank International Ltd.* [1978] QB 159, at 169. See H. Bennett, 'Performance Bonds and the Principle of Autonomy' [1994] *JBL* 574; C. Debattista, 'Performance Bonds and Letters of Credit: A Cracked Mirror Image' [1997] *JBL* 289.

simply because the principal says that there has not been any default. Failure by the beneficiary to reply, or to produce any evidence of the principal's default or breach of contract, does not establish fraud. The view of the English courts is that if a bank has undertaken to pay on demand without proof or conditions, it should do so. So long as the beneficiary makes an honest demand, the banks are bound to pay: of course banks will rarely, if ever, be in a position to know whether the demand is honest or not. So the general rule is pay.

In summary, therefore, the fraud exception with respect to demand guarantees in English law requires common law fraud, and the fraud must be clearly particularized and established. A court will require strong corroborative evidence of the allegation, usually in the form of contemporary documents, particularly those emanating from the beneficiary.[92] It is therefore very difficult for a principal to establish the fraud exception in relation to demand guarantees before an English court. There is no doubt that in this regard English law is more stringent than that of other jurisdictions as regards the test for, and evidence necessary to establish, fraud. It follows because, as a matter of policy, English courts assume that, were they to find fraud too readily, international commercial practice would be adversely affected.

Alongside fraud are challenges to the instrument itself, for example that it was obtained by a conspiracy between, or financial misrepresentation by, the customer and beneficiary so as to undermine the genuineness of the underlying transaction. The English Court of Appeal has said that the mere appearance of a valid instrument does not commit the bank: if it can establish that there is a real prospect of success that there was such a conspiracy or misrepresentation, and that it has avoided the instrument on this basis, it is unjust for the court to give summary judgment to the beneficiary in an action against the bank for payment.[93] If this decision is not to undermine years of learning, it must be given a narrow ambit, involving wrongdoing by the customer and beneficiary combined. The general rule must be that banks pay on letters of credit, except for the narrow fraud exception involving a beneficiary.

Under what circumstances will an English court, on application of a principal, grant an injunction against a beneficiary or bank, preventing payment under a demand guarantee? In general terms, it can be said that fraud justifies a court granting such an injunction. However, there is a stringent approach:

Judges who are asked, often at short notice and ex parte, to issue an injunction restraining payment by a bank under an irrevocable letter of credit or performance bond or guarantee should ask whether there is any challenge to the validity of the letter, bond or guarantee itself. If there is not or if the challenge is not substantial, prima facie no injunction should be granted and the bank should be left free to honour its contractual obligation, although restrictions may well be imposed on the freedom of the beneficiary to deal with the money after he has received it.[94]

---

[92] *United Trading Corporation SA v. Allied Arab Bank Ltd.* [1985] 2 Lloyd's Rep. 554, 561 (CA).
[93] *Solo Industries UK Ltd. v. Canara Bank* [2001] Lloyd's Rep. Banking 346 (CA).
[94] *Bolivinter Oil SA v. Chase Manhattan Bank* [1984] 1 WLR 392, 393, [1984] 1 All ER 351, 352 (CA).

The justification is that demand guarantees are given to avoid suing abroad or to avoid lengthy litigation. They are intended to give immediate payment and issues between the parties are to be resolved at a later date. As a result of one Court of Appeal decision it seemed as if a principal could circumvent this approach by obtaining an injunction not against the bank, but against the beneficiary, preventing it from making a demand under a demand guarantee.[95] The decision is inconsistent with principle and has been subsequently disapproved.[96]

A further major obstacle faces a principal in obtaining an injunction. This is because of the general principle of English law that an injunction is discretionary and equitable in nature, and will not issue if damages are an adequate remedy. In the context of demand guarantees, the high standard is weighed against claimants. If the threatened payment is in breach of contract then the principal will have a good claim for damages against the bank. An interim injunction would be inappropriate, because it would interfere with the bank's obligations to the beneficiary, and because it might cause greater damage to the bank (e.g. reputation) than the principal could pay on its undertaking in damages.[97]

An English court will not take cognizance of any injunction issued by a foreign court in an action by a beneficiary against a bank on a demand guarantee. In the leading case on this point, involving letters of credit,[98] the Court of Appeal acknowledged that, wherever possible, it would seek to recognize and uphold the order of the court of a friendly state in the interests of comity. However, it also emphasized the countervailing importance of letters of credit in international trade. To recognize the injunction would strike at the very heart of the other country's international trade, since no foreign supplier would deal with that country on letters of credit because it could no longer be confident of being paid.

C. INDEMNITIES

Banks will often take an express indemnity from a customer, under which they will have recourse to debit its account. The indemnity will authorize a bank to pay (e.g. to pay and/or accept bills of exchange drawn under a letter of credit; to pay under a demand guarantee) and will give it an indemnity against all losses, expenses, and liabilities by reason of having taken a particular course (e.g. paid the letter of credit; a demand guarantee). With demand guarantees the indemnity will be especially significant, since, unlike other areas of international trade, there will be no goods over which security can be taken. In practice, there will often be a chain of indemnities (counter-indemnities)—from the customer to its bank, and then from the customer's bank, through intermediate banks, to the bank in the beneficiary's country which actually issues the demand guarantee.

---

[95] *Themehelp Ltd.* v. *West* [1996] QB 84 (CA).
[96] *Group Josi Re* v. *Walbrook Insurance Co. Ltd.* [1996] 1 WLR 1152, [1996] 1 All ER 791 (CA).
[97] *Harbottle (Mercantile) Ltd.* v. *The National Westminster Bank Ltd. & Ors* [1978] QB 146, 155 (CA).
[98] *Power Curber International Ltd.* v. *National Bank of Kuwait* [1981] 1 WLR 233, [1981] 3 All ER 607 (CA).

The nature of the indemnity in English law is clear: it is a primary undertaking, in no way dependent for its content or enforceability on the terms or validity of any other contract.[99] The customer's obligations under an indemnity clearly turn on the words used. The bank will want reimbursement whether or not there is an argument that it need not have paid: thus an indemnity, under which the customer undertakes to reimburse the bank what it was obliged to pay under a demand guarantee, will be unacceptable to a bank. Indeed, if the indemnity is drafted broadly enough, it will enable the bank to claim against the customer even if the demand guarantee is legally unenforceable.[100] With counter-indemnities it is essential that their wordings mirror each other, so there is no possibility of the chain of liability being broken.[101] Moreover, in the absence of express choice-of law-clauses to the contrary, an English court will infer that the parties intended the same law to govern the demand guarantee and any counter-guarantees.[102]

---

[99] R. Goode, *Commercial Law* (2nd edn., London, Penguin, 1995), 822–3.
[100] *Gulf Bank KSC v. Mitsubishi Heavy Industries (No 2)* [1994] 2 Lloyd's Rep. 145 (CA).
[101] *Turkiye Is Bankas SA v. Bank of China* [1998] 1 Lloyd's Rep. 250 (CA).
[102] *Wahda Bank v. Arab Bank plc* [1996] 1 Lloyd's Rep. 470 (CA).

15

SECURITY

Lending is in some cases unsecured, where the standing of the borrower is such that the banks cannot demand it or, because of the creditworthiness of the borrower, do not regard it as necessary. At one time international lending was of this character, although much international lending is now oriented to particular projects, and security is taken. At the other end of the scale, the local shop or the village money-lender may also grant credit without security, since informal sanctions ensure repayment. In terms of the number of commercial borrowings banks enter, however, cases of unsecured lending are in the minority. Security, even if only limited security or personal security in the form of a guarantee, will usually be required, so that in the event of default the bank can recoup itself out of the collateral. Indeed, in relation to project financings, the security required by the banks will often be of a comprehensive nature, e.g. a fixed and floating charge, a charge over shares, a charge over bank accounts, a legal assignment of material contracts, and so on. With large lendings the security might be granted in favour of a security trustee, to hold to the benefit of the lending syndicate. Within a corporate group, each member may contribute to the security, and there will be cross-guarantees. There might be other forms of security enhancement, such as on-demand guarantees.[1]

I. SECURITY—ITS NATURE AND RATIONALE

Security, strictly defined, is an interest in property which secures the performance of an obligation, in our case payment. Thus in addition to being able to proceed on the personal undertaking to repay, the bank as lender has rights against the property. This has an obvious advantage if the borrower becomes insolvent. In addition to security strictly defined, there is what is sometimes called 'personal security', where a third party agrees to guarantee another's debts. Third parties sometimes give security in the strict sense to support a borrower's undertaking to repay. For reasons of space, guarantees are not discussed in this book.[2]

---

[1] 390 above.

[2] See *Halsbury's Laws of England* (4th edn. (reissue), London, Butterworths, 1993), v. 20 (R. Salter); J. Phillips and J. O'Donovan, *The Modern Contract of Guarantee* (2nd edn., Sydney, Law Book Co., 1992); G. Andrews and R. Millett, *Law of Guarantees* (3rd edn., London, Sweet & Maxwell, 2000).

In examining security in the strict sense, this Chapter concentrates on security over personal property. This is not meant to suggest that mortgages over realty are unimportant, or do not give rise to legal problems. Although in some states (e.g. those of the Pacific Ocean) land held communally cannot be mortgaged, mortgages over real property are almost universal. Indeed, in many societies, land is treated as the most valuable, or main form of, property to be proffered as security. This has significant equity implications, since those without land are effectively denied credit. But the rules governing mortgages over land are fairly well established. It is because the legal challenge has come with attempts to extend security to forms of personal property that it deserves our attention.

Security law raises important issues of public policy. One is the implication for financial stability, in enabling those engaged in wholesale financial markets to manage counterparty credit and liquidity risks.[3] Another, more mundane, is the role of security in inducing banks to lend in situations when they might chose to utilize their funds in other ways, e.g. investing in government bonds or, at the other end of the spectrum, on derivatives markets. In the absence of security, a commercial entity in financial difficulty may be tempted to pay those other than the bank first, e.g. to ensure a continued supply of goods and services. It is argued that security lowers the cost of credit. The exact degree to which security produces these results is, however, a matter of contention.[4] In the event of a business' solvency coming into question, security is also said to foster rescue efforts because the lender, feeling secure, is willing to allow time, and because with one lender or group of lenders in the driving seat there is a greater likelihood of the business being carried on or sold as a going concern, when compared with the situation of many creditors fighting over the carcass. In fact critics argue that strong security has exactly the opposite effect, since the banks are tempted to act too hastily and to recoup themselves too readily by selling assets.

A favourable security law can greatly advantage lenders to the detriment of other interests in society. Often this is overlooked, because security law is treated in isolation from areas such as insolvency and consumer-protection law. For example, English law is very favourable to those, such as banks, which take security. The result is that in the event of insolvency the whole of the assets can fall to be realized outside the winding-up, in violation of any *pari passu* principle, and to the detriment of unsecured creditors.[5] To argue that the unsecured creditors voluntarily accept the risk and can demand a premium in the form of a higher price ignores the realities. Many unsecured creditors do not have accurate information about the risks involved and, even if they did, would have little choice but to do business or take employment where they can. Many attempts to give greater protection to unsecured creditors have fallen

---

[3] Working Group of the Committee on the Global Financial System, *Collateral in Wholesale Financial Markets* (Basle, BIS, 2001).

[4] e.g. R. Scott, 'A Relational Theory of Secured Financing' (1986) 86 *Colum. LR* 901.

[5] See *Insolvency Law and Practice. Report of the Review Committee*, Cmnd. 8558 (London, HMSO, 1982), 32 (the Cork Committee).

by the wayside, although legislation in most jurisdictions gives some a preference in an insolvency.

Perhaps greater success has been achieved in redressing the inequality of bargaining power when consumers give banks security. As we saw in Chapter 7, the courts have used doctrines such as undue influence to upset some third party security.[6] But more could be done: why have courts not read down the 'all-moneys clause' in bank security agreements, when many ordinary customers do not understand that the property secured is at stake for *any* debts which are incurred in the future, and that it is not confined to the indebtedness presently being incurred.[7] Statute has gone some of the way to protecting ordinary customers. Thus the Consumer Credit Act 1974 imposes some curbs: for example, security given in relation to a regulated agreement, whether by the debtor or a third party, must be in writing. Moreover, a mortgage or charge by a debtor over personal property must be embodied in a regulated agreement, and a copy supplied to the debtor in accordance with the Act. Similarly, a guarantee or indemnity from a third party must be in the prescribed form and have the prescribed contents, and the third party is entitled to copies of the guarantee or indemnity and the regulated agreement.[8]

The weight of academic writing on security has long criticized the law's untidiness, formalism, and impenetrability to non-lawyers. These defects have provided the impetus for moves to simplify personal-property security law, which culminated in the United States in the famous Article 9 of the Uniform Commercial Code (UCC). Aspects of the Article 9 system which have attracted particular praise are the more rational approach to defining security interests, a concern with substance, not form, a common set of rules for all security and the comprehensive system of registration of security interests which determines priorities. Article 9 has proved a beacon for law reformers elsewhere, although so far only Canadian jurisdictions and New Zealand have adopted it. Recommendations in England for an Article 9 system—in particular, the official inquiries conducted by the Crowther Committee and by Professor Diamond—were rejected by the government, the banks, and City of London lawyers on the grounds that they were unnecessary and costly.[9] The European Bank for Reconstruction and Development published a Model Law on Secured Transactions in 1994, which is less elaborate than Article 9.[10]

If the substantive law of security could be more rational, so too could the

---

[6] 213 above.

[7] *Smith* v. *ANZ Bank* (1996) NSW Con R 55–774(CA). See generally *AIB Group (UK) Ltd.* v. *Martin* [2001] UKHL 63, [2002] 1 WLR 94 (HL); 220 above.

[8] See R. Goode, *Consumer Credit Legislation* (London, Butterworths, looseleaf), paras. 105–8.

[9] *Report of the Committee on Consumer Credit*, Cmnd. 4596 (London, HMSO, 1971); A. L. Diamond, *A Review of Security Interests in Property* (London, HMSO, 1989) respectively.

[10] J. Simpson and J.-H. Röver, 'An Introduction to the European Bank's Model Law in Secured Transactions', in J. Norton and M. Andenas (eds.), *Emerging Financial Markets and the Role of International Financial Organisations* (London, Kluwer, 1996); J. Simpson and J. Menze, 'Ten Years of Secured Transactions Reform' [2001] *JIBLF* 54; F. Dahan, 'Secured Transactions Law in Western Advanced Economies' [2001] *JIBFL* 60.

terminology. The notion of personal security has been mentioned. It is not security at all in its strict sense. English terminology does not clearly distinguish between the security agreement which creates the security, and the property securing the obligation. Article 9 of the UCC calls the latter the collateral, which is the term used here. Unfortunately the term collateral is not used widely by English lawyers (or those with a similar common law heritage). Then there is the infelicity, possibly even confusion to the novice, when we deal with securities over securities—securities in the latter, quite different, sense being the compendious description for stocks, shares, bonds, debentures, notes, and so on.

II. TYPES OF SECURITY: PLEDGE, MORTGAGE, AND CHARGE

Article 9 of the Uniform Commercial Code is unusual in adopting a uniform framework for security over personal property. By contrast, almost all other systems of law, both common law and civil law, have a diversity of security types, each governed by its own rules as to creation, enforceability, and priorities. However, jurisdictions divide on how extensive security interests may be; whether security can cover non-specified and future property of the debtor, or indeed the debtor's future indebtedness; and whether intangible, as well as tangible property, can serve as collateral. As a broad generalization, common law systems have been remarkably flexible in what security can be created, what it can cover, and how it can be enforced. Some civil law systems, such as Germany and Japan, have been reasonably sympathetic to new forms of security, but others, such as France, Italy, Spain, and many Latin-American countries, have been hostile.[11]

Among the objections those jurisdictions have had to extensive security is that a debtor can give the impression of wealth, even if its assets are subject to security. A registration system for security can obviate this objection. Taking security over future property has been deprecated in these jurisdictions, because it is seen as preferring the creditor with an existing security which automatically extends to the debtor's future property. Again techniques such as purchase-money security—which is over new property specifically purchased with an advance—can reduce the force of this objection. But there are other social policies antipathetical to extensive security, like the *pari passu* principle alluded to previously, which are less easily refuted.

---

[11] P. Wood, *Comparative Law of Security and Guarantees* (London, Sweet & Maxwell), 1995.

A. OVERVIEW

Pledge is a fundamental and time-honoured method of taking security in all, or almost all, jurisdictions. It is a possessory security[12] and in English law enables the pledgee to sell the collateral on default. Apart from pledge, English law divides security over personal property into mortgages and charges. A legal mortgage is constituted by an absolute assignment of ownership to the mortgagee bank, coupled with the right—the equity of redemption—to have the property reassigned on repayment. If the power of sale does not arise at law, the agreement will invariably confer it on the mortgagee. Although legal mortgages can cover future property, there generally needs to be some *novus actus* on the part of the mortgagor on obtaining the property contemplated by the contract, and designed to implement the promise to secure it. No such requirement is needed for an equitable mortgage, which can be constituted by an agreement for value to secure both present and future property. On acquisition of the asset, the mortgage takes effect as from the date of the agreement. Equitable mortgages can also arise from an agreement for value to give a legal mortgage and on the mortgage of an equitable interest. Whereas equitable mortgage involves a transfer of the collateral (at least in equity), the conventional view is that a charge is simply an agreement to appropriate it, in the event of default, to the satisfaction of the chargee's claim. This may not be justified, and a charge may involve a proprietary interest.

Banks use all these techniques—pledge, mortgage, and charge—to take security over personal property. Because a prerequisite to pledge is a transfer of possession, however, it has a limited, but nonetheless important, scope. Mortgage also features, but chattel mortgages never took hold in England because of the obstacles thrown up to registering them under the bills-of-sale legislation. Hire purchase and other forms of title finance such as leasing have been used instead. Nonetheless, banks use the mortgage when they take security over intangibles, in particular over account receivables and contracts. Finally, the charge: charges are taken over specific property, but in England this type of security came into its own in the form of the floating charge. Let us examine pledge, mortgage, and charge in particular banking contexts.

B. PLEDGING GOODS AND DOCUMENTS

Banks sometimes use pledge in financing dealers' stock-in-trade and international trade. To obtain the requisite possession of the collateral, the bank is not confined to taking actual delivery. Constructive delivery will suffice, for example the borrower

---

[12] Lien is a possessory security, which arises by operation of law or agreement. A lien can only arise on property which has been the subject of a transaction between the parties. It enables one party to retain the collateral until the other pays a charge connected with the thing, or the general account which has arisen in respect of similar dealings. Banks sometimes take a 'letter of lien' over goods, but in English law this is not a true lien and must take effect as a pledge, mortgage, charge, or declaration of trust. (So, too, a 'letter of hypothecation'.) An important lien for banks is that over negotiable instruments deposited for collection, or for retention until maturity (379 above), but this has nothing to do with the present topic of security taken in the context of financing.

could contract with the bank to hold goods as the bank's bailee—not on its own account as owner—and give the bank the keys to its warehouse, silo, or other premises. So called field warehousing—an American idea—builds on this. The goods are set aside in a separate part of the borrower's premises, and movement in and out of it controlled by the borrower's staff, who are temporarily employed by an independent field-warehouse company acting for the bank. In general, where goods are in the custody of a third party which holds them for a borrower, a pledge can be effected by the borrower ordering the third party to hold them for the bank, the change being perfected by the third party attorning to the bank, that is, acknowledging that it holds for the bank. Unless there is a trust, it seems that there cannot be an attornment when the third party holds the borrower's property in bulk with those of others, such that it is not identifiable, e.g. grain in a silo.[13]

In addition to recognizing constructive possession, English law also gives a certain flexibility by permitting the pledge of documents which by delivery, or endorsement and delivery, can pass control of goods or an interest in contractual obligations. Thus bills of exchange, promissory notes, and certificates of deposit can be, and frequently are, pledged to banks. So too are documents of title, notably bills of lading. The fiction is that their delivery is constructive delivery of the goods they represent. Thus banks finance importers by taking security over bills of lading, but then releasing them under a so-called trust letter or trust receipt so that the goods can be disposed of. This is one of those many situations where English law places mercantile advantage above doctrinal purity: it is rationalized with the argument that, although the bank is relinquishing possession (on which pledge depends), it is doing so for only a restricted purpose, and the pledge is thus preserved.[14] English law also upholds a pledge of bearer securities, but it does not as yet recognize a pledge of other securities, or of other documents such as hire purchase and credit sale agreements.[15]

C. RECEIVABLES FINANCING BY WAY OF SECURITY

Receivables, or accounts receivable, are the debts earned in conducting business—the proceeds from sales and from providing services (including rental payments and freight). Banks, or at least their factoring subsidiaries, are major participants in receivables financing. One method of receivables financing is through the outright sale of a company's receivables. The sale will be at a discount on the face value of the receivables. The company obtains immediate payment, although the sale may be with recourse, obliging it to indemnify the bank against any losses (primarily bad debts). Another method of receivables financing is against the security of the receivables.

---

[13] Cf. *Maynegrain Pty. Ltd.* v. *Compafina Bank* [1982] 2 NSW LR 141, 146–7. On appeal to the Privy Council this issue was not discussed: [1984] 1 NSW LR 258.

[14] 389 above.

[15] Cf. N. Palmer, 'Pledge', in M. Gillooly (ed.), *Securities over Personalty* (Sydney, Federation, 1994), 138; N. Curwen, 'General and Special Property in Goods' [2000] *Leg.S* 181.

While it has some merits, this has distinct disadvantages.[16] Notably, the security must be registered under section 395 of the Companies Act as a charge over the company's book debts ('charge' in this section includes mortgage).

There is a clear legal distinction between an outright sale of receivables, and a bank providing finance on the security of receivables. With the latter the bank has a right to payment, and the company a right to redeem. In practice, however, the line between the two is blurred. A good example is non-recourse lending on the security of receivables when the bank's right to payment is exclusively from the receivables themselves. While presented as a loan on security, this is functionally equivalent to an outright sale, since the bank must look exclusively to the receivables to be paid. While English courts will determine the true character of a transaction when this is not apparent on its face, they are reluctant to go behind the legal form chosen in the documentation and recharacterize the transaction.[17]

In theory receivables financing by way of security can involve a pledge, charge, or mortgage.[18] Pledge is impractical, except for certain businesses, since it can only be used over a limited range of documentary intangibles. A charge over receivables is, as indicated, a mere right to be paid out of the proceeds. There is no transfer of the receivables, and the bank cannot take action against the debtors. To enforce the charge the bank's remedy is against the chargor for an assignment of the receivables. Thus in practice if a charge is used in receivables financing it will be coupled with a power of attorney, enabling the bank to convert it into a mortgage at any time, and to appoint a receiver.[19]

Mortgage in the context of receivables financing involves assignment. In general this is by way of legal assignment or equitable assignment.[20] Either the receivables or their proceeds can be assigned. There is no objection to assigning receivables to be generated in the future, although this should be a present assignment of future receivables, rather than a contract to assign receivables in the future. The assignment will give the bank the power to enforce any of the receivables (although in the case of equitable assignment it must join the company in any proceedings). However, it will not be bound to do so, and the agreement will provide that it is not responsible if it does not. Any moneys received by the company on payment of the receivables may be held on trust for the bank. In the agreement the company will make certain representations and warranties as to the nature of the debts being assigned, e.g. that they are valid. Assignment of debts represented by documents will turn on the instrument:

---

[16] F. Salinger, *Factoring Law and Practice* (3rd edn., London, Sweet & Maxwell, 1999), 3–4.

[17] *Lloyds and Scottish Finance Ltd.* v. *Cyril Lord Carpets Sales Ltd.* (1979) [1992] BCLC 609 (HL); *Welsh Development Agency* v. *Export Finance Co. Ltd.* [1992] BCLC 148, [1992] BCC 270 (CA); *Orion Finance* v. *Crown Financial Management* [1996] BCC 622 (CA). Cf. *On Demand Information plc* v. *Michael Gerson (Finance) plc* [2002] UKHL 13, [2002] 2 WLR 919 (HL).

[18] It must be doubtful that there can be an attornment of a receivable. R. Goff and G. Jones, *The Law of Restitution* (5th edn., London, Sweet & Maxwell, 1998), 689–93.

[19] R. Goode, *Legal Problems of Credit and Security* (2nd edn., London, Sweet & Maxwell, 1988), 117; F. Oditah, *Legal Aspects of Receivables Financing* (London, Sweet & Maxwell, 1991), 96.

[20] 355–60 above.

for example, a negotiable instrument is assigned by delivery if to bearer, and by endorsement and delivery if to order.

D. SECURITY OVER CONTRACTS—PROJECT FINANCE

In particular circumstances banks take security over the contracts a company has entered. The leading example is in project finance. It is often said in this context that security is defensive, especially when the project is in an emerging economy: the bank may be unable to realize much of the collateral, so that the best it can obtain is a priority over third-party claims. Certainly the government in the jurisdiction of the project may not consent to the enforcement of any security taken over the licence or concession it has granted. Seizing the operating assets may be of little use (e.g. rigs, pipelines), although not if they can be readily moved and sold (e.g. diggers, platforms).[21] However, the contracts the project company has entered—the project contracts—can offer valuable collateral. For example, taking security over a right to receive tariff payments under a throughput contract is an obvious course if the project being funded is something like an oil or gas pipeline. Similarly, a long-term supply contract is especially valuable collateral, especially if the buyer is obliged to pay the project company even if it is unable to take the product (a take or pay contract).[22]

There are few problems in English law in assigning rights under a contract by way of security. With project contracts, the rights assigned will not be confined to payments under the contract but will extend to all benefits and interests, present and future, even if the contract is varied. One obstacle is if there is a restriction on assignment in the project contract, for this means that the consent of the other party—the construction company, the user in a throughput project, or the buyer in a production project—must be obtained. Moreover, even if consent to assignment by way of security is obtained, this does not necessarily extend to assignment by way of sale on execution of the security. In practice, all parties involved will have understood that bank finance is not available without security over the project contracts, so that generally consent will have been built in at the outset.[23]

It has been said that a further obstacle to taking security over project contracts is that the identity of the project company is a matter of fundamental importance to the other parties. Therefore contractual rights, other than to payment, are too 'personal' to be assigned.[24] In practice, as indicated, other parties to project contracts would have understood from the outset that there was to be assignment to the bank, and a contractual provision to this effect removes any objection on this score. Consent to assignment will invariably be a condition precedent to draw-down and covered by elaborate direct agreements.

---

[21] See P. Wood, *Project Finance, Subordinated Debt and State Loans* (London, Sweet & Maxwell, 1995), App., pt. 1, §4, 227.

[22] P. Nevitt, *Project Financing* (5th edn., London, Euromoney, 1989), 278–83.

[23] e.g. G. Vinter, *Project Finance* (2nd edn., London, Sweet & Maxwell, 1998), 94, 103, 149.

[24] J. Lehane, 'Project Securities' [1983] *AMPLA Yearbook* 183, 186.

In the assignment agreement the project company will make various representations and warranties to the bank as to the enforceability of a project contract, and that
it has not otherwise been assigned or encumbered. It might also represent that there
are no equities between it and the other contracting party which are to the detriment
of the bank. Despite the assignment, the project company will remain liable to
perform any obligations arising under the project contract. Conversely, the other
party to the contract will remain liable to perform, and cannot argue because of the
assignment that its liability for damages disappears into a 'black hole'.[25]

Typically the project company will covenant to give notice of the assignment to the
other party and to use its best endeavours to procure an acknowledgment and consent
from it. It will also consent not to agree to any material variation or release, nor to
terminate a project contract. The bank will not be obliged to take any action under a
project contract. Of course the bank will be able to enforce its security. Often in
project finance security is as much to enable the bank to carry on the project contract
as to sell it. The power of attorney in favour of the bank underpinning this possibility
has been mentioned.

E. THE FLOATING (UNIVERSAL BUSINESS) CHARGE

Many legal systems eschew the notion of a universal security over all a company's
assets, whether specified or not, and whether present or future. In many civil law
countries like France security over a business's assets is effective only if the assets can
be identified, which tends to exclude raw materials and stock in trade. These, and
intangibles such as receivables and intellectual property rights, may serve as collateral
in other ways. Countries such as Germany are less onerous in requiring the collateral
to be specified. But no civil law jurisdiction has an instrument as favourable to the
banks as the English floating charge.

Central to bank financing in England and a considerable number of Commonwealth jurisdictions is the floating charge. The typical floating charge covers all assets
in a company's possession from time to time, even if unspecified. It includes both
present and future assets of the company. The collateral under a floating charge will
extend beyond goods to include securities, receivables, and other intangibles such as
intellectual property rights. A company can deal with all of these in the ordinary
course of business until the charge crystallizes (which can be automatic or on the
occurrence of specified events).[26] Thus it can create a second floating charge (although
it will rank after the first), and a company's other creditors can set off debts they owe
the company against what it owes them. In this light the floating charge is best
conceived of as a present security in a shifting fund of assets, which the company is

---

[25] *Bovis International Inc. v. Circle Limited Partnership* [1995] NPC 128. See D. Petkovic, 'Security over
Contracts in Project Financings' (1996) 14 *IBFL* 81.

[26] The classic descriptions are in *Illingworth v. Houldsworth* [1904] AC 355, 357, 358; *Re Yorkshire Wool-
combers Accociation Ltd.* [1903] 2 Ch. 284, 295 (CA). See also *Smith (Administrator of Cosslett (Contractors)
Ltd.) v. Bridgend CC* [2001] UKHL 58, [2001] 3 WLR 1347, [2002] 1 All ER 202 (HL).

free to manage in the ordinary course of its business. The agreement constituting a floating charge will invariably include a power in the event of default (widely defined) to appoint an administrative receiver without resort to the court. Discretion can be conferred on the administrative receiver to recoup the lender by carrying on business, or by selling assets without any application to the court.[27]

There are some legal limits to the creation of a floating charge. Under section 245 of the Insolvency Act 1986 a floating charge is invalid within the suspect period—in the case of most bank lending, twelve months—except to the extent of new value provided by way of consideration for the creation of the charge. Under the Companies Act 1985, section 395(1), a registrable, but unregistered, charge is void as against the liquidator, administrator, and any creditor of the company. The reference to other creditors must be read restrictively: only creditors who subsequently take security in the property the subject of the unregistered charge can claim it is void and deferred to their claims. Section 395(2) specifically provides that the avoidance of a charge under subsection (1) is without prejudice to the repayment obligation, and indeed the money secured becomes immediately repayable. Presumably acceleration is justified on the basis that the lender should not have to leave his now unsecured moneys out for the full period contemplated by the security. On the other hand, if lenders had to do this it would provide a powerful incentive to secure registration. Clearly other forces are at work here, notably a sentiment not to make life too hard for banks and other financiers.

A bank with a floating charge can block the appointment of an administrator. Thus even though a bank is sufficiently protected by specific security, it will take a 'featherweight' floating charge to be in the position to do this. A bank with a fixed charge does not have this power, although a fixed charge confers other advantages, such as tighter control over the collateral, and a priority in relation to the claims of preferential creditors and to the expenses of any administration or liquidation.

Whether a bank's charge over book debts is a fixed or floating charge has led to a raft of litigation. One line of authority, now disapproved, favoured freedom of the parties, or at least the banks, to create a fixed charge by the company undertaking not to dispose of the book debts and paying their proceeds on collection into an account with the bank, without restriction on the use of the account.[28] Clearly this method could only be used by banks with which the company had a current account. The justification was that a debt and its proceeds can be separated and a fixed charge created over the former but not the latter. While this separation is still possible in theory, it is said by the second line of authority to make no commercial sense since ownership of a debt is worthless if it carries no right to proceeds.[29] This second line of

---

[27] At the time of writing the Enterprise Bill 2002 is proposing to prevent holders of a floating charge appointing an administrative receiver, except for certain capital market financings.

[28] *Siebe Gorman & Co. Ltd.* v. *Barclay's Bank Ltd.* [1979] 2 Lloyd's Rep. 142. Cf. *Re New Bullas Trading Ltd.* [1994] BCC 36, [1994] BCLC 485 (CA).

[29] *Agnew* v. *Commissioner of Inland Revenue* [2001] UKPC 28, [2001] 3 WLR 446. See C. Hanson and G. Yeowart, 'Book Debt Charges after *Brumark*: Where are We Now?' [2001] *JIBFL* 456.

authority, which is now dominant, is that it is not sufficient, if there is to be a fixed charge, for the company simply to undertake not to dispose of debts to third parties. A right of the company to destroy the debts by collecting them in its accounts for its own ends is said to be inconsistent with a fixed charge. This approach seems inconsistent with the way English law generally attempts to facilitate commercially beneficial transactions, and with older authority which accepts mortgages and charges over stock in trade and book debts although the company still has a general license to deal.[30] In any event, under this second line of authority an effective fixed charge over book debts is subject to two conditions—that they cannot be disposed of without the bank's consent, and that they are paid into a separate bank account with withdrawals actually being controlled by the bank.[31] Since the latter is likely to impede a company's main source of cash flow, banks are not generally likely to be able to take a fixed charge over book debts. If any charge is to be taken, it will need to be a floating charge.

III. SOME CURRENT ISSUES

Although the general principles of security law are well established, there is considerable ferment regarding their application in particular contexts. A hardy perennial in English law is whether a bank can take a charge over a customer's deposit with itself. There is an argument that this is conceptually impossible: how can a bank have a proprietary interest in its own obligation to pay its customer? However, there is now clear authority that banks can take security over debts they owe customers (e.g. deposits, accounts).[32] To the same effect banks can take a contractual set-off, which enables them to withhold payment of the cash deposit pending ascertainment of the customer's liability on any loan account, and to combine the deposit with the loan account deficit.[33]

Considerable attention is being given at present to the efficiency and proper functioning of securities clearing and settlement arrangements. These are largely domestic systems (such as CREST in the UK), together with the well-established systems for international bonds—which have been extending their remit in recent times—Euroclear in Belgium and Clearstream in Luxembourg. Both domestic and international systems are underpinned by law.[34] For example, both Belgium and Luxembourg amended their legislation in the 1990s after doubts were raised, *inter alia*, about the rights in an insolvency of customers of Euroclear and Clearstream. The

---

[30] R. Gregory and P. Walton, 'Fixed and Floating Charges—A Revelation' [2001] *LMCLQ* 123.

[31] *Re Holidair Ltd.* [1994] 1 IR 416.

[32] *In Re Bank of Credit and Commerce International SA (No 8)* [1998] AC 214, [1997] 4 All ER 568 (HL). See generally G. McCormack, 'Security Interests in Deposit Accounts' [2002] *Insol.L* 7.

[33] See Financial Law Panel, *Security Over Cash Deposits* (London, FLP, 1994) and *Security Over Cash Deposits. A Supplemental Practice Recommendation* (London, FLP, 1996).

[34] For the UK: E. Micheler, 'Modernising Securities Settlement in the UK' (2002) 23 *Company L.* 9.

solution was to provide legislatively for rights equivalent to co-ownership by customers of fungible securities held by the settlement systems.[35] In late 2001 the European Central Bank and the Committee of European Securities Regulators established a project on clearing and settlement of securities in Europe. The central bank interest arises from the relevance of these arrangements for the smooth operation of monetary policy and payment systems, and for financial stability; the interest of securities regulators is in maintaining market efficiency and ensuring investor protection. Coupled with this the European Commission is examining how to create more efficient systems and to establish a level playing field for securities settlement systems, and the need for an overall EU legal framework.[36]

This section examines three broad areas of security law of great practical importance which in recent times have experienced considerable change. Taking security over securities—the first to be examined—must face the problems thrown up by changing technology, in particular the immobilization and dematerialization of securities. Quasi-security—the second area examined—has a long history but has rather suddenly become central to the efficient operation of securities markets in the form of 'repos' (sales and repurchases). Thirdly, there is some discussion of the problems arising with cross-border security, a regular feature of international financing.

A. SECURITY OVER SECURITIES

A bank may take security over a customer's securities, i.e. over stocks and shares (so-called equity) or over debt securities such as bonds, debentures, certificates of deposit, or the like. The securities may be bearer securities, so that title passes by delivery of the instrument. Otherwise the securities are registered securities, and generally speaking title does not pass until the transfer is registered with the issuer. However, this will turn on the rules of the issuer, and the law of the jurisdiction where it is located. A bank may be reluctant to take securities which are not listed on an exchange, because of the problems of valuation and of disposing of them if the security is realized. Often as part of a wider security package, however, a bank may take security over the shares a parent has in its subsidiaries. If the bank needs to execute the security, it may be able to sell off the whole group.

In England it is possible to pledge bearer securities by handing over the certificates themselves. Registered securities cannot be pledged. Security over them is a matter of creating a mortgage or charge. Constituting a legal mortgage, by transferring the shares into the name of the bank or its nominee, has the disadvantage that the bank must account for dividends etc. and otherwise be involved in the administrative work of holding securities. Customers can agree to create a legal mortgage, and although

---

[35] See Belgium: L. De Ghenghi and B. Servaes, 'Collateral Held in the Euroclear System' [1999] *JIBFL* 83; Luxembourg: A. Schmitt and J. Dif, 'Circulation of Securities and other Fungible Instruments' [2002] *JIBL* 44.

[36] Both the ECB/CESR and EC work builds on e.g. Committee on Payment and Settlement Systems and Technical Committee of the International Organization of Securities Commissions, *Recommendations for Securities Settlement Systems* (Basle, BIS, 2001).

this constitutes an equitable mortgage it leaves the door open to fraud, since without more the bank does not have control over their disposition. The risk is that in the event of the mortgagor's fraud (e.g. it is able to persuade the issuer to effect another mortgage or a sale) a third party can get priority over the bank if, acting *bona fide* and without notice, it becomes the legal mortgagee or transferee.[37]

More casual arrangements are fraught with danger. Take a situation where A simply agrees that its securities portfolio is to be security in favour of the bank. At most this constitutes a charge. Assume the securities are specified, but that the agreement gives A the right to substitute other securities, albeit that A must furnish the bank with a description of the substituted securities. A may be a broker or financial institution with a portfolio of securities which is constantly shifting. Giving A the liberty to deal with the securities in this way is the badge of a floating charge, so that under section 395 of the Companies Act 1985 it is void unless registered. The only way this result may be avoided is to state that a fixed charge is intended—generally a fixed charge need not be registered—and to fetter A's discretion to substitute, with the bank actually vetting the process.[38] Note that there is an argument that even a fixed charge over short-term money-market securities may be registrable because they are book debts. Charges over book debts of a company are, of course, separately registrable under section 395.

All this is relatively straightforward. Complications are introduced, however, by current market practice. To reduce transaction costs and risk, securities are increasingly in central custodial and settlement systems. The securities are fungible: a party (A) with securities in the system will not be entitled to the return of exactly the same, but only of equivalent, securities. Transfer of A's securities to B will be effected by a movement on their accounts with the system. The securities will remain immobilized and unidentified unless taken out of the system. If dematerialized, so there are no definitive instruments, the securities will never be identified other than through their presence and movement on the accounts. In any event, A may have a fractional beneficial interest in the securities held by the system.[39]

There are various ways of creating security in these circumstances. Say A wishes to give security to a bank, and both A and the bank are members of the system. First, A can comply with any rules of the system which lay down a means of giving security ('the rules method'). Secondly, there may be nothing in the rules to prevent A creating a mortgage by an outright transfer of its interest in the securities to the bank ('the mortgage method'). The mortgage would be recorded in an agreement. The bank would be obliged to retransfer A's interest in the securities on repayment. Thirdly, and similarly, A may be able to transfer the securities into a separate account in its own name, but designate it as being held for the bank (the 'designated account method'). The bank's security interest here is equitable. A's interests are unconditionally

[37] See *MCC Proceeds Inc. v. Lehman Brothers International (Europe)* [1998] EWCA Civ. 3068, [1998] 4 All ER 675 (CA).

[38] *Dresdner Bank v. Ho Mun-Tuke Don* [1993] 1 Singapore LR 114 (CA).   [39] 331–4 above.

appropriated to the bank's security interest. Clearly there are dangers with the designated account method, since A may deal with the securities to the detriment of the bank, which has no control over the account.

The important point is that with all these methods of creating security over securities in a central custodial and settlement system—the rules method, the mortgage method, and the designated-account method—the bank has not perfected any security interest in the underlying securities. It could be said that this should not matter, at least with the first two methods. If A complies with the rules for giving security to the bank (the rules method), it will be to the bank and it alone that the system is prepared to account. The system will allow it to sell on default. The system, its members, and issuers are after all bound by the rules. With the mortgage method, the bank will be recorded as owner in the accounts kept by the system, and so again the system will recognize a sale by it if it sells to enforce its security interest. The designated-account method is a greater problem, because ultimately it may involve applying for a court order for A to transfer the securities to the bank.

A further complication is that often these days securities are held by a custodian and managed on behalf of their owner by a fund manager. It may be the custodian or fund manager who has the relationship with any custodial and settlement system. The system may hold the securities to the order of them, rather than to that of the owner. Even though they may hold the securities on behalf of them, since the owner does not have any direct relationship with the system, it will not be able to use it to create a security interest.

The complexity and uncertainty in taking security (collateral) over securities in Europe has led the European Commission to propose a directive to create a uniform legal framework.[40] In policy terms it is designed to limit credit risk in cross-border financial transactions involving the provision of securities and cash as collateral. The proposal is a priority measure under the European Community's Financial Services Action Plan. First, it seeks to ensure relatively simple and effective regimes for the creation of security under either a title transfer or pledge structure. Thus it restricts the imposition of the onerous formalities which operate in some of the civil law jurisdictions on both the creation and enforcement of security. Secondly, it provides a limited protection of security arrangements in insolvency, in particular the realization of collateral. There is specific protection of close-out netting and of arrangements for topping up security (e.g. when the securities are marked to market) or substituted.

---

[40] Proposal for a Directive of the European Parliament and of the Council on Financial Collateral Arrangements, COM (2001) 168 final. See also International Swaps and Derivatives Association, Collateral Law Reform Group, *Collateral Arrangements in the European Financial Markets. The Need for National Law Reform* (London, ISDA, 2000.)

B. QUASI-SECURITY—REPOS AND STOCK LENDING

There are a range of devices which, while functionally equivalent to security, are intended as a matter of law to amount to something different. Contractual set-off, negative-pledge clauses, and subordination agreements are examples encountered earlier in this book. These do not constitute a security interest, since they do not involve rights in an asset which bind third parties generally.[41] English courts generally respect the legal form the parties impose on a transaction and do not recharacterize it in another way. A number of important consequences flow from characterizing such devices as other than security. Importantly, quasi-security does not have to be perfected to preserve its validity and priority in an insolvency. It may not be caught by contractual restrictions, such as negative-pledge clauses.[42] As far as banks are concerned, whether a transaction falls into one category rather than another can have implications for their capital adequacy. There are also tax and accounting implications.[43]

Repos are another quasi-security device. They consist of a spot sale and a forward purchase of property—typically securities—by a seller. Sellers can raise money from buyers, who have 'security' in the form of the securities they have purchased for the duration of the agreement. Thus the market-maker in securities can finance its inventory, and the fund manager can also raise short-term moneys, without disturbing its underlying, portfolio. The repurchase price which the seller must pay will reflect the use which it has had of the buyer's money, i.e. an 'interest' component. Repurchase may be at a certain time or on demand by either party. Central banks use repos as an instrument of monetary policy.

When banks undertake repo transactions, the securities will be transferred between the parties by use of the various electronic securities settlements systems for government and commercial securities. Others without ready access to these systems may be confined to hold-in-custody or non-deliverable repos, where the securities remain with the seller. Clearly this involves risks, e.g. the seller entering into more than one repo in relation to the same securities. To overcome the risks, a third-party bank may take custody of the securities on behalf of the buyer.

The standard repo is functionally equivalent to a loan of money on security, since the lender (buyer) owns the securities for the duration of the agreement. There is some Anglo-American authority that repos constitute a loan on security, with consequences such as invalidity through a failure to register as such.[44] The standard master agreements now in use for repos in the London, New York, and other markets seek to avoid such adverse consequences by carefully characterizing the transactions

[41] R. Goode, *Commercial Law* (2nd edn., London, Penguin, 1995), 652ff.
[42] 315 above.
[43] P. Wood, *Title Finance, Derivatives, Securitisations, Set-Off and Netting* (London, Sweet & Maxwell, 1995), 18–24.
[44] e.g. *Chase Manhattan Asia Ltd. v. Official Receiver and Liquidator of First Bangkok City Finance Ltd.* [1990] 1 WLR 1181, [1990] BCC 514 (PC); *RTC v. Aetna Cas & Sur. Co. of Illinois*, 25 F 3d 570 (7th Cir. 1994).

concluded under them. For example, the Global Master Repurchase Agreement[45] is worded as applying to transactions in which one party ('seller') agrees to sell to the other ('buyer') securities and financial instruments (other than equities, and net-paying securities) ('securities'), against the payment of the purchase price by buyer to seller, with a simultaneous agreement by the buyer to sell to the seller securities equivalent to such securities at a date certain, or on demand, against the payment of the purchase price. Consistently with their usual approach to matters of form and substance in commercial transactions, English courts should not penetrate behind this characterization as a sham. There is no equity of redemption or specifically enforceable right for the seller to have the securities returned: the agreement simply provides a right to have equivalent securities.

The standard documentation for repos also covers matters such as the ability to call margins, or to reprice if the value of the securities falls; substitution; events of default; and a close-out/netting provision in the case of insolvency. The latter is important, since without security the non-defaulting party is simply an unsecured creditor. Annexes to the documentation can take into account the characteristics of particular securities. For example, the Bank of England has published an annex to the Global Master Repurchase Agreement for London to cater for government securities (gilts), enabling a netting of obligations under gilt repos with non-gilt repos.[46]

Stock lending is a variation of the repo. It is an integral feature of efficient securities markets, enabling timely settlement and liquidity. A fund manager or securities dealer 'borrows' securities when it has gone short or there are delays in settlement. It undertakes to return securities of the same type, value, and denomination. On the other side of the equation are those such as custodians, who obtain their customers' permission to lend the securities. There is a fee paid to the 'lender' for use of its securities which, in the case of a custodian, is shared with its customers.

The seller of the securities in a stock-lending transaction will take other securities with similar risk characteristics. This is provided for in the standard stock-lending agreements, along with an obligation to mark to market so that adjustments to the 'collateral' can be made if there has been a decline in its value. The agreements are also drafted to ensure that, in the event of default by one party, the non-defaulting party has an unencumbered right to close out and set-off. The 'borrower' is obliged to pay the 'lender' all cash benefits, such as dividends, arising in respect of what is borrowed.

At one time the standard agreements provided that, although absolute title was to

---

[45] Published by the Bond Market Association (formerly the Public Securities Association) and the International Securities Market Association (ISMA). A 2000 version of the Global Master Repurchase Agreement (GMRA) replaces the original 1992 version, revised in 1995. See K. Tyson-Quah (ed.), *Cross-Border Securities Repo, Lending and Collaterisation* (London, Sweet & Maxwell, 1998), pt. II (G. Morton, P. Brigantic, D. StC Nelson, and E. Bettelheim); B. Hur, 'Some Legal Aspects in Cross-Border Repurchase Transactions Involving Immobilised Securities' [2000] *JIBFL* 366 (pt. 1).

[46] See e.g., Stock Lending and Repo Committee, *Gilt Repo Code of Best Practice* (London, Bank of England, 1997), 7.

pass in relation to the stock lent, the collateral was transferred by way of security.[47] Fears that this constituted a floating charge led to a change in the standard agreements from the early 1990s. Absolute title to the 'collateral' now passes under the standard documentation and, as with repos, the only right of the lender is to have equivalent securities. For this reason the right of set-off on a borrower's default is crucial, since the lender does not have a secured interest.

C. CONFLICT OF LAWS

It is not unusual for a commercial financing, and the security associated with it, to have a cross-border element. Borrowers may have assets in more than one jurisdiction, or the credit itself may be directed to an entity abroad. Yet the English rules of private international law governing security are not always clear. There is relatively little authority, and often it is quite old. The commentators are sometimes in conflict. Even recent authority lacks a unanimity of approach.

Many countries adopt the *lex situs* as the paramount influence in relation to the proprietary effects of a transfer of property, including a transfer of property by way of security. The proper law of a security transaction is not favoured, for then the parties themselves could determine its effects on third parties. Following this line it would seem to follow that, whether security over securities has been perfected should also be determined by the *lex situs*. The same rule should also apply to negotiable instruments. But what is the *lex situs*? One approach is to say that the *lex situs* of securities is the place of incorporation of the issuer.[48] Another approach is to say that the *lex situs* is the place where the securities are situated.[49] In the case of registered securities, this is normally where the register is kept. In the case of negotiable securities, this is where the pieces of paper representing the securities are at the time of transfer. Presumably with immobilized securities, which are not registered, where the securities are situated is where the relevent depository/settlement system is located.[50] So too, with dematerialized securities, although there is an argument that the concept of *lex situs* is artificial when applied to an intangible, so that it would be preferable for English conflict of laws to embody a direct rule applying the law of the place of the depository/settlement system.[51] However, where legislation in jurisdiction such as the United States and Belgium provides that the applicable law is the law of the place of the relevant depository/settlement system maintaining the securities account, it is by means of creating a security entitlement or a co-ownership right, i.e. what would

[47] T. Herrington, 'The Legal Structure of Stock Lending in the UK', 10 *IFLR*, No 8, Aug. 1991, 22.
[48] *Macmillan Inc. v. Bishopsgate Investment Trust plc (No 3)* [1996] 1 WLR 387, 405, 424 (CA).
[49] *Ibid.* 411.
[50] *Dicey and Morris on the Conflict of Laws* (13th edn., London, Stevens, 1999), 977–8.
[51] R. Goode, 'Security Entitlements as Collateral and the Conflict of Laws', *JIBFL* Sept. 1998, Special Supplement, 22. Cf. C. Bernasconi, R. Potok, and G. Morton, 'General Introduction', in R. Potok (ed.), *Cross-Border Collateral: Legal Risk and Conflict of Laws* (London, Butterworths, 2002), 27ff; cf. J. Benjamin, *Interests in Securities* (Oxford, OUP, 2000), 153–4.

ordinarily attract the *lex situs* rule.[52] The place of the relevant depository/settlement system maintaining the securities account is also the solution to the conflict of laws problem adopted in the proposed European Community Directive on financial collateral arrangements,[53] and it is at the heart of proposals by the Hague Conference on Private International Law.[54]

It seems that a foreign company can validly contract under English law to give a floating charge over its English assets. So long as the company has the power to grant a mortgage under the law of its place of incorporation, it is immaterial that the latter does not recognize the floating charge.[55] However, a floating charge given by an English company may not be recognized by the law of a foreign jurisdiction where certain assets of the company are situated. Prudence requires that security over them should be taken in accordance with that law. Even if the foreign jurisdiction does recognize floating charges, local registration is obviously the sensible course. But the question of who can act for a company is typically regarded by legal systems as a matter of the *lex domicilii*. If English law recognizes an administrative receiver appointed under a floating charge with power to sell, a foreign jurisdiction may as well.

As for assignment—a legal basis for security over contracts and other choses in action—the result of the Rome Convention is that matters concerning it are now determined according to the proper law of the contract or chose, as also is the relationship between the assignee and the debtor/obligor, and whether the debtor/obligor's obligations are discharged.[56] Thus the law governing the contract, debt, or other chose determines how notice of the assignment is to be given to the other party/debtor, the effect of that notice, what force prohibitions on assignment have, and who has priority in the event of successive assignments whether fraudulent or by mistake of the same contract, debt, or other chose.[57] The mutual rights and obligations of assignor and assignee are determined by the proper law of the assignment.[58]

---

[52] UCC §§8–110; 9–103 (b)(d). See J. Rogers, 'Policy Perspectives on Revised UCC Article 8' (1996) 43 *UCLA LR* 1431, 1449–57. For Belgian law: L. De Ghenghi and B. Servaes, 'Collateral Held in the Euroclear System' [1999] *JIBFL* 83, 84–7.

[53] Proposal for a Directive of the European Parliament and the Council on Financial Collateral Arrangements, COM (2001) 168 final, 10 (Art. 10). Art. 9(2) of the Settlement Finality Directive (283 above), which in broad outline adopted the same approach, has not been implemented in the UK.

[54] Hague Conference on Private International Law, Preliminary Draft Convention on the Law Applicable to Certain Rights in Respect of Securities Held with an Intermediary, 17 Jan. 2002; C. Bernasconi, *The Law Applicable to Dispositions of Securities Held Through Indirect Holding Systems* (Hague, Hague Conference on Private International Law, 2000).

[55] L. Collins, *Essays in International Litigation and Conflict of Laws* (Oxford, Clarendon, 1994), 443.

[56] Rome Convention on the Law Applicable to Contractual Obligations, Art. 12(2).

[57] See *Raiffeisen Zentralbank Österreich AG v. Five Star General Trading LLC* [2001] EWCA Civ. 68, [2001] QB 825, [2001] 3 All ER 257 (CA). See R. Stevens, 'The English Conflict of Law Rules', in M. Bridge and R. Stevens, *Cross-Border Security and Insolvency* (Oxford, OUP, 2001).

[58] Art. 12(1).

IV. INEFFECTIVE SECURITY

If something goes wrong with the security or part of a security package, what are the consequences for the bank? At one level the security might simply lose priority: a bank remains secured, but it is postponed to others. Beyond that the security might be ineffective, but only for some purposes. The solution of partial voidness for non-registration under section 395 of the Companies Act 1985 is an example. If the security is ineffective, a number of questions arise. Will a court in setting aside the security impose any terms on the party seeking this outcome? Does ineffectiveness annul the obligation to repay any credit the bank has advanced as part of the transaction? As to the latter, the legislation may provide a definite answer, as with the Companies Act which states explicitly that this is not to be the consequence of non-registration of a charge. In other cases the courts have struggled against the draconian result of nullity. Conceptually this might be justified, in that the ineffective security can be severed from the payment obligation. Even if severance is not possible, a restitutionary action may survive, at least for the principal sum advanced.[59]

A. VITIATING FACTORS IN FORMATION

An issue which regularly exercises the minds of those in commercial practice is whether security is vitiated because the company officers have not addressed adequately the issue of its commercial benefit to the company. Clearly the issue does not arise when the company is giving security to support its own financing, but it can raise its head when the company gives a guarantee or security to support borrowings by others, e.g. other members of a corporate group. The requirement of commercial benefit derives from the obligation of company officers to act *bona fide* in the interests of the company. Their natural tendency is to look to the interests of a corporate group as a whole, and while this does not automatically vitiate the security their company has given to a member of the group to support a loan to another member of the group, it potentially exposes it to attack.[60]

The company granting security must be able to show direct benefit (e.g. part of the loan ultimately has flowed through to it) or indirect benefit (a financial strengthening of the group, of which it is an integral part). Downstream security by a parent company in favour of its subsidiaries is more likely to survive scrutiny than upstream security, especially if a subsidiary could have survived insolvency had it not given the security. A bank, knowing that security is not in the interests of a corporate borrower,

---

[59] *Goss* v. *Chilcott* [1996] AC 788 (PC).

[60] *Rolled Steel Products (Holdings) Ltd.* v. *British Steel Corporation* [1986] Ch. 246 (CA). See R. Pennington, 'Personal and Real Security for Group Lending', in R. Goode (ed.), *Group Trading and the Lending Banker* (London, CCLS, 1988); D. Prentice, 'Group Indebtedness', in C. Schmitthoff and F. Wooldridge (eds.), *Groups of Companies* (London, Sweet & Maxwell, 1991); J. Stumbles, 'Corporate Benefit and the Guarantee' in G. Burton (ed.), *Directions in Finance Law* (Sydney, Butterworths, 1990).

cannot enforce it. In practice doubts can be overcome by having the company in a general meeting ratify the grant of security, although this raises another set of issues, e.g. ratification is ineffective if the company giving security is not fully solvent.

Fraud and duress obviously render a security contract voidable in law and equity; if the innocent party so elects the contract is avoided *ab initio*. Similarly, contracts of security may be set aside in equity as a result of innocent misrepresentation, equitable fraud, undue influence, and unconscionability.[61] In these categories of cases as well, rescision dissolves the security completely, rather than merely discharging the parties from future performance. Statute, however, now enables a court to declare a security subsisting in the event of an innocent or negligent misrepresentation of, say, a minor nature: the victim is denied rescision and receives damages instead.[62] All this is trite law, but it should not be overlooked that normal equitable principles apply when security is set aside in equity. The normal equitable defences of laches, acquiescence, and confirmation may be invoked.

As regards remedies, equity will order the delivery up of a security instrument for cancellation. An account may be ordered to be taken, and terms imposed. If the parties cannot be restored to their precise original positions by the setting aside of the security, the court will look at all the circumstances and do what is fair and just in practical terms. Where there is no deceit or intention to defraud (e.g. innocent misrepresentation), a court will be less ready to pull a transaction to pieces, but in cases of conscious fraud it will exercise its jurisdiction to the full.[63] Equity couches its relief in such cases, guided by broader considerations such as the equitable maxims, e.g. those who seek equity must do equity. This maxim has been used in cases of illegal money-lending where, for example, borrowers sought to have security declared void. It would be wrong to think that equity confines these broader considerations to cases involving *restitutio in integrum*. *Restitutio in integrum* will often be irrelevant in this sort of case, for example a surety receives no benefit that can be required to be restored. The mere fact that on the basis of a guarantee the bank has advanced moneys, which it will be unable to recover save from the security, may not in itself (on *restitutio in integrum* principles) preclude rescission.[64]

Somewhat surprisingly, the courts have turned their back on this learning where security is rescinded because the bank taking it is implicated in the misrepresentation, undue influence, or legal wrong of others.[65] The typical situation, as in *O'Brien* itself, is the husband inducing his wife, by misrepresentation or undue influence, to give security over her share in the matrimonial home to support his business debts with the bank. A matter which the House of Lords in *O'Brien* left open was whether a wife, who establishes that the bank had constructive notice of the husband's wrongdoing, can have the security set aside *in toto*, or whether in particular circumstances she can

---

[61] 212 above.   [62] Misrepresentation Act 1967, s. 2(2).

[63] *Spence* v. *Crawford* [1939] 3 All ER 271, 283–5, *per* Lord Wright.

[64] See *Mackenzie* v. *Royal Bank of Canada* [1934] AC 468 at 476 (HL).

[65] 216ff above.

do so only on terms. (In fact in that case the O'Briens did make a payment of £60,000 to Barclays at an interlocutory stage of the proceedings, after the trial judge had ordered possession, suspended on terms that that amount be paid. This seemed to do justice, in a general sense, since Mrs O'Brien's case on appeal was that, although it was an all-moneys charge, her husband's misrepresentation, and her understanding, was that the charge was limited to £60,000.) Subsequently the Court of Appeal held that, in an *O'Brien* situation, it is not open for a court to set aside a security on terms that a wife acknowledges it is valid for the amount which was actually represented to her.[66] It is noticeable that the court recognized the morality, perhaps even the justice, of requiring the wife to acknowledge the security in the amount she intended to grant. It seems unfortunate that it held that terms could never be imposed to achieve practical justice for both parties. Notice, however, that where on *O'Brien* or *Etridge* grounds security is not effective in relation to the indebtedness on the husband's business account, it can still bind the wife in relation to other indebtedness covered by it such as in relation to the home mortgage.[67]

B. NON-COMPLIANCE WITH FORMALITIES

There are various kinds of formalities in the case of a contract of security. The simplest is that the security be in writing. It is still possible for some security to be created orally, as in the case of a commercial pledge of goods. Even here there will usually be writing in practice, because the bank will not take physical possession of the goods. Both directly and indirectly statute now obliges writing for many forms of security. For example, the enactment of section 2 of the Law of Property (Miscellaneous Provisions) Act 1989 means that, even if it were possible previously, a deposit of title deeds will not of itself operate as an effective equitable mortgage or charges.[68] Statutory registration requirements for security mean that, as a practical matter, it must often be in written form, even if writing is not required as a matter of law.

What of the consequences of non-compliance with the formality of registration itself? The idea of registration is to perfect a security interest, i.e. to make the security effective against third parties (other than the borrower). Banks, others contemplating taking security, and purchasers can check the register to see whether there is security already. As a matter of legislative policy non-registration could be made to affect priority; secondly, it could render a secured lender unsecured; or, thirdly, it could invalidate the security completely, and possibly also other rights a lender might have.

Perhaps the best-known registration requirement in England is for company charges under section 395 of the Companies Act 1985. As presently drafted, the Act does not lay down a system of priorities, although in practice registration may affect

---

[66] *TSB Bank plc* v. *Camfield* [1995] 1 WLR 430, [1995] 1 All ER 951. Cf. *Commercial Bank of Australia Ltd.* v. *Amadio* (1983) 151 CLR 447, 481.

[67] *Barclays Bank plc* v. *Burgess* [2002] EWCA Civ. 291 (CA). See also *Dunbar Bank plc* v. *Nadeem* [1998] 3 All ER 876 (CA).

[68] e.g. *United Bank of Kuwait plc* v. *Sahib* [1997] Ch. 107 (CA).

priorities if a third party thereby obtains actual notice of a previous charge. Instead, the Act provides that failure to register makes the charge void as against the liquidator, administrator, and any creditor of the company. Under the legislation the security is not void against the company itself, perhaps because this would prejudice purchasers from a security-holder which exercised its power of sale. Only the security is affected by non-registration, and the avoidance of a charge is without prejudice to the repayment obligation.

Contrast the result of failing to register a charge under the Companies Act with that obtaining for bills of sale. (As indicated earlier, bills of sale have never been of great practical significance in effecting commercial security over goods.) Under the legislation, a bill of sale by way of security is void if not in statutory form or registered.[69] Non-compliance with the statutory form means that, not only is the security aspect void, but also the personal covenant to pay interest. Seeking to avoid the draconian consequences of this, the courts in such cases have granted a restitutionary remedy for money had and received, and coupled it with an obligation to pay interest at a reasonable rate—unhappily for the money-lenders in some of the cases, the courts have held the reasonable rate to be 5 per cent, rather than the some 60 per cent set out in the agreements.[70] Analytically, the courts are simply recognizing that a borrower has a personal obligation to repay the principal, apart from any security. If legislation avoids the security, that cannot affect this obligation, although it may strike at any provision in the security about interest. Only in requiring payment of 5 per cent interest are these cases legally unorthodox—at common law there is no obligation to pay interest in the absence of a stipulation to that effect—and then it could be argued that they are doing rough justice.

Does this approach apply to the much more common situation where the security given is governed by the Consumer Credit Act 1974, but the Act's various formalities for the security, and in other respects, are not met? Although in some cases non-compliance under the Act simply causes the security to be enforceable only by order of the court, in other circumstances the security 'shall be treated as never having effect'.[71] If the security is to be treated as never having effect, and if it contains payment obligations, then on first impression, these too must be nullified. A debtor's personal obligation to repay the credit advanced will remain unaffected, although whether a court should couple an action for money had and received with an obligation to pay reasonable interest (as in the bill of sale cases) is open to doubt.

C. STATUTORY VULNERABILITY

Security is vulnerable to a range of statutory provisions. The money-lenders legislation has already been alluded to; it can render security unenforceable.[72] In commercial

---

[69] Bills of Sale Act 1878 (Amendment) Act 1882, ss. 8, 9.

[70] e.g., *Davies* v. *Rees* (1886) 17 QBD 408 (CA).

[71] e.g. s. 106(a).   [72] e.g. *Orakpo* v. *Manson Investments Ltd.* [1978] AC 95 (HL).

practice security must always be tested for vulnerability were an insolvency to occur within the suspect periods after its grant set by the Insolvency Act 1986, notably section 239 (preferences), section 245 (floating charges). Breach of the former provision means the court must make such order as it thinks fit for restoring the position to what it would have been if the company had not entered into the preferential transaction. Specific orders contemplated include wholly or partly releasing or discharging any security. Breach of section 245 means that the floating charge is invalid except to the extent of 'new money' provided by way of consideration for the creation of the charge. Section 238 (transactions at an undervalue) cannot be used to invalidate a mortgage or charge to secure existing indebtedness because no assets of the company have ceased to be its property and its total assets have not been reduced. *Quaere* whether the same reasoning applies to a guarantee of a third person's indebtedness given for no or nominal consideration.

An instance of statutory illegality frequently encountered in commercial practice is the financial assistance provision of the Companies Act 1985 (section 151). That provision and its predecessors make it unlawful for a company or its subsidiaries to give financial assistance directly or indirectly for the purpose of enabling a person to acquire its shares. Financial assistance is now defined widely to mean financial assistance given by way of guarantee or security. The prohibition had its origins in the common law objections to a company reducing its capital and legislative fears of asset-stripping takeovers. It was subsequently considered as much directed at making sure a company uses its funds for proper purposes. Concern about the prohibition's over-inclusiveness led in 1981 to the introduction of certain 'gateway' provisions—now Companies Act 1985, sections 155 to 158—which were intended to permit assistance (subject to strict safeguards) so long as the interests of minority shareholders and of the company's creditors were protected. Because of European Community law only private companies can pass through these gateways.

The English legislation has never spelt out the civil consequences of a breach of this prohibition; it simply has attached to it a criminal penalty. The courts have filled the gap and held that security given is caught by section 151 as an illegal contract. The classic situation is where a bank is asked to advance money to someone to enable it to effect a takeover of a company. The bank wants security as backing. But security given by the company itself runs up against the prohibition; in practice the bank may not be prepared to provide the finance without that security. As a matter of policy, the unenforceability of security 'is likely to deter potential lenders from lending money on security which might be held to contravene the statute and is likely to be more efficacious in achieving the policy of the sections than the very small maximum penalty on the company.'[73]

The consequence of the security being unenforceable in the classic situation described seems to be that the bank becomes an unsecured creditor. The loan itself seems not to be tainted by the illegality and the unenforceable security can be severed

---

[73] *Heald* v. *O'Connor* [1971] 1 WLR 497, 502.

from it. There seem to be no public-policy objections to this outcome. Of course this will be very cold comfort when the purchaser is in financial difficulties. In practice the gateway provisions are often invoked to validate the security. But for banks the matter is not wholly satisfactory. Uncertainty as to the possible voidness of transactions may inhibit them from becoming involved in financing transactions. Canadian legislation provides that the rights of third parties are affected only if it can be shown that they knew, or ought reasonably to have known, that the company was acting or proposing to act in breach of the prohibition.[74] But banks advancing money will know the purpose for which it is to be used and if they know the purpose, they will not come within the saving provision. At the time of writing the government is proposing to repeal the restrictions on financial assistance completely for private companies.[75]

[74] See *Financial Assistance by a Corporation: Section 42 The Business Corporations Act (Alberta)* Discussion Report 5, 1987, 111. But see *Petro-Canada v. Cojef Ltd.* [1993] 3 WWR 76.

[75] See D. Cabrelli, 'In Dire Need of Assistance? Sections 151–158 Companies Act 1985 Revisited' [2002] *JBL* 272.

PART V

THE INTERNATIONAL DIMENSION

16

INTERNATIONAL BANKING

Running through this book is the theme that modern banking and finance are importantly international in character. Right from the outset the multinational, as well as multifunctional, nature of banking enterprises and operations was underlined. Chapter 3 identified this multinational character of banking activity as a bugbear for bank regulators.[1] Even if a bank's customers are from the local jurisdiction, the various transactions they want effected (and examined in Part II) often have a cross-border dimension. We saw that the payment systems discussed in Part III of the book are, in terms of their use, international systems.[2] The financing techniques outlined in Part IV need have no national boundaries in terms of the lenders or borrowers.

This final part of the book draws together, and makes explicit, some of these threads. After some introductory material on the growth of international banking, and the role of the law in this, this Chapter turns to the form in which foreign banking is conducted. The legal restrictions on banks entering certain jurisdictions are then examined. Finally considered are the measures designed to facilitate international banking. One type of measure is regional in scope: the Credit Institutions Directive of the European Community is perhaps the best example. The second type is more ambitious and is worldwide in its reach. The General Agreement on Trade in Services, negotiated in 1993 as part of the Uruguay Round of Multilateral Trade Negotiations, is considered in this context.

I. NATURE OF INTERNATIONAL BANKING

Retail banking is still largely oriented to particular jurisdictions: customers have feelings of loyalty to domestic banks, as well as being governed by inertia. Thus banks pursuing an international strategy at the retail level have often expanded by acquisition, retaining the local character of their new subsidiary. At the wholesale level, however, international banking has a long history. Bankers met at the medieval fairs to settle payments for cross-border trade.[3] In the eighteenth century Hope & Co. floated loans for states such as Russia and Sweden on the Amsterdam stock market

---

[1] 104 above.   [2] Especially 236–7 above.
[3] F. Braudel, *The Wheels of Commerce* (London, Collins, 1982), 90–2.

and elsewhere.[4] In its wake the Anglo-American merchant banks of the nineteenth century went cross-border with their involvement in trade finance and foreign-securities issues.[5] The period of western colonialism provided a further catalyst, its legacy still evident in the presence of western-dominated banks in some Asian and African countries.[6] Most importantly, since the 1960s there has been a spread of banks internationally.

A. RECENT GROWTH IN INTERNATIONAL BANKING

The 1960s to the mid-1980s saw an explosion in international banking by banks physically establishing in other jurisdictions. Several factors contributed. One was the enormous growth in world trade and foreign direct investment. US and European banks in particular followed their multinationals around the world.[7] Secondly, there was financial innovation, so that banks with experience in matters such as securities, mergers and acquisition, fund management, and derivatives established themselves in international financial centres where this could be exploited. Thirdly, international banking was facilitated by the innovations in technology and communications.

Since the mid-1980s there has been a deceleration in the growth of international banking, but not a contraction. Some banks have taken advantage of the single market of the European Community and of the economic liberalization in emerging and developing economies. There is a globalization, to use the buzz-word, of financial markets. The largest banks have offices across the globe, and many banks are in international financial centres such as London, New York, Frankfurt, Paris, Tokyo, Switzerland, and Singapore.

What has been the effect of legal regulation on the growth of international banking? The evidence suggests that legal factors are much less important than those already mentioned in the overall level of international banking activity, although the comparative burden of regulation influences its pattern of distribution.[8] An oft-cited example of the latter is the concentration of Euromarket activities in London from the 1960s, as a reaction to various measures of the US government which made New York a less attractive site.[9] As indicated, many countries have liberalized their economies in recent years by removing exchange controls and limits on the movement of capital. Lowering the barriers in this way has encouraged many foreign banks to locate in

[4] M. Buist, *At Spes non Fracta: Hope & Co. 1770–1815. Merchant Bankers and Diplomats at Work* (The Hague, Martinus Nijhoff, 1974).

[5] S. Chapman, *The Rise of Merchant Banking* (London, Allen & Unwin, 1984).

[6] e.g. F. King, *The Hong Kong Bank in the Period of Development and Nationalism, 1914–1984* (Cambridge, Cambridge UP, 1988).

[7] e.g. E. Roussakis (ed.), *International Banking: Principles and Practices* (New York, Praeger, 1983); R. Pecchioli, *The Internationalisation of Banking: The Policy Issues* (Paris, OECD, 1983).

[8] R. Brealey and E. Kaplanis, *The Growth and Structure of International Banking* (City Research Project, London, Subject Report XI, 1994).

[9] See R. Cranston, 'Doctrine and Practice in Commercial Law', in K. Hawkins (ed.), *The Human Face of Law* (Oxford, Clarendon, 1997).

these countries. However, if history is any guide, a sharp growth in international banking activity will come more from an increase in world trade than from removing legal barriers. In other words, it turns more on the overall success of the World Trade Organisation (WTO), rather than on any impact made by that specific part dealing with banking and financial services, i.e. the GATS.

B. FORMS OF INTERNATIONAL BANKING

At one level banks can provide services internationally by employing other banks elsewhere in the world. Correspondent banking is crucial if banks are to give effect to the payment instructions of their customers and for aspects of trade finance. Except for need, or where it is more efficient economically, however, banks prefer not to act in a major way through correspondents. The system of correspondent banking was discussed earlier.[10]

Secondly, with modern communications and technology banks can offer services across borders, without having a physical presence in other jurisdictions. Many financial services can be provided across borders in this way—fund management, acting on behalf of clients in securities and derivatives markets, financial advice, and so on. Even banking in the strict sense does not demand a bank's presence in a jurisdiction, as long as capital can flow freely. Given modern payment systems, it is possible to deposit money in banks elsewhere in the world, in currencies different from one's own. Arranging loan finance to elsewhere in the world is, of course, an historic feature of banking activity in international financial centres. The Credit Institutions Directive of the European Community is designed, in part, to foster European banks providing services across borders within the European Union. Licensing in the home jurisdiction is sufficient and there is no need for a bank to be authorized if it offers services *into* other Member States.[11] The General Agreement on Trade in Services (GATS) also recognizes cross-border provision into other jurisdictions as a means of trading in services, which it seeks to encourage.[12]

However, banking really demands a presence in a jurisdiction, rather than acting through others, or simply providing services into that jurisdiction. Only thus can a bank participate fully in the interbank markets and exchange markets located there, and only thus can it establish close and direct relations with customers there. The focus of the rest of the discussion is therefore on international banking through a structural presence—in particular, the right to establish, and the right to operate once established, unimpeded by discriminatory measures. The different structural forms which a physical presence can take in other jurisdictions have already been considered—the representative office, the branch, or the full-blown subsidiary or incorporated affiliate.[13]

It is possible to subdivide international banking activities, depending on the nationality of the parties and the currency of the transaction. Transactions with

---

[10] 39 above.   [11] 100 above.   [12] 435 below.   [13] 9 above.

non-residents, but in the local currency, are traditional foreign banking activities. Offshore banking is that sub-set of international banking which is confined to transactions with non-residents, and in foreign currencies. Eurocurrency activity is more extensive than the latter, covering transactions with both residents and non-residents, but in foreign currencies only.[14] There is judicial support for this definition of Eurocurrency activity.[15] Diagrammatically,

	Local currency	Foreign currency
Residents	Domestic banking	— *+
Non-residents	Foreign banking+	Offshore banking*+

* Eurocurrency banking
+ International banking

Whether the definitions offered here have operative effect depends on the precise terms of the applicable law. For example, the categorization by the host-country regulatory law of a bank may determine which transactions it can lawfully enter there.[16] The categorization of its activities by the home country may determine what reserve requirements its central bank will impose and the coverage of deposit insurance.[17]

II. THE HOST-COUNTRY RESPONSE

A. FACILITATING FOREIGN BANKS

Most countries positively encourage foreign banks. Thus London has long been a home to foreign banking. The legislative and judicial climates have been conducive. At one time there was a statutory prohibition on associations of a certain size being formed for the purposes of banking, unless specially registered. This seemed to point to the exclusion of foreign banks from carrying on business in Britain.[18] Whatever may have been the origin of the practice, it became clearly established that foreign banks could carry on business in England, without any general authority to that effect.[19]

---

[14] See R. Johnson, *The Economics of the Euro-Market* (London, Macmillan, 1983), 2; H. Scott and P. Wellons, *International Finance* (7th edn., NY, Foundation Press, 2000), 3.

[15] *Libyan Arab Foreign Bank* v. *Bankers Trust* [1989] QB 728, 735; *Citibank NA* v. *Wells Fargo*, 495 US 660, 684 (1990).

[16] 426 below.   [17] 120, 79 above.

[18] *Lindley on Partnership and Companies* (3rd edn., London, Maxwell, 1873), i, 193; ii, 1516–7.

[19] *Grant on the Law Relating to Bankers and Banking Companies* (7th edn., London, Butterworth, 1924), 505.

Once licensing was introduced for banks under the Banking Act 1979 foreign banks had, too, to go through the process. If they simply established a representative office, without taking deposits, it was sufficient to give notice and certain basic information to the Bank of England.[20] Even that is unnecessary since the Financial Services and Markets Act 2000, so long as representative offices do not engage in regulated activity or financial promotion of investment activity.[21]

Likewise other international financial centres are hospitable to the establishment of foreign banks. That does not mean that the path for foreign banks need be legally straightforward. The complex regime for foreign banks in the United States is well-known.[22] Moreover, foreign banks may be encouraged to pursue wholesale or foreign currency, rather than general, banking. That may occur through a special legal regime for offshore banking.

B. LIMITING FOREIGN BANKS

Many countries still refuse to open up their economies wholesale to foreign banks. Other countries, while preaching access, practise *de facto* discrimination. Neither *de jure* nor *de facto* obstacles to foreign banks are inherently objectionable. Countries may have quite legitimate concerns about the spread of foreign banks. One concern may be of foreign economic domination. Another objection to particular foreign banks establishing in a jurisdiction may be that the banks of that jurisdiction are denied access to the home country of those foreign banks. The concept of reciprocity—designed to deal with this—is examined below. However, the resistance to change is not always motivated by praiseworthy concerns. A cosy cartel of local banks is sometimes a factor against change. A fear of foreign competition can, of course, be a legitimate objection to wholesale access, at least in the short term, if foreign banks are so better capitalized and resourced with skills and technology that within a short time they would wipe the floor.[23]

(i) Formal Limits on Access

Putting *de facto* discrimination to one side, the law may limit expressly the establishment of foreign banks. First, foreign banks may be banned completely. This is unfashionable these days. Secondly, the law may permit some foreign banks but confine them to certain spheres, such as wholesale banking. A third approach is to put a ceiling on the number of licences granted to foreign banks. It may be done directly by writing criteria into the licensing provisions, such as whether a foreign bank will make a contribution to training and competitive conditions in the jurisdiction. There may also be a cap on foreign banks, in terms of absolute numbers, or in terms of a

[20] Banking Act 1979, s. 40.   [21] 12 above.

[22] C. Lichtenstein, 'Standards and Administrative Practices Regarding Treatment of Foreign Banks in the United States', in J. Norton, Chia-Jui Cheng, and I. Fletcher (eds.), *International Banking Operations* (London, Kluwer, 1994); M. Gruson and R. Reisner, *Regulation of Foreign Banks* (Albany, Matthew Bender, 2000), v. 1.

[23] OECD, *Banks Under Stress* (Paris, OECD, 1992), 64.

maximum percentage of assets held by all licensed banks in the jurisdiction. A further approach is to license foreign banks but to require that a certain percentage of shares be held locally. Coupled with this may be an obligation to have local managers and directors. Neither of these requirements—local shareholders and officers—need be especially onerous.

Such restrictions on foreign banks are not uncommon. The free movement of banks may now be a fact of life in Western Europe, an approach enshrined in the Treaty of Rome and the EC Credit Institutions Directive. But many countries, quite legitimately, have wanted to limit the entry of foreign banks. Even developed countries—members of OECD such as Canada and Australia—have restricted foreign banks.[24] Banking is treated as special: it has to do with control of the economy. Foreign control of the banking system would be, at the very least, a symbolic surrender of economic sovereignty. The GATS has had to recognize this.

Yet in the last decade restrictions on foreign banks have been eroded. For example until 2002 foreign banks operating in China were confined to foreign currency business. The few foreign banks licensed to conduct renimbi business needed to be located in Shanghai and Shenzhen and were permitted only limited dealings with Chinese companies. As a result of China's accession to the WTO in 2002, foreign banks will be permitted to engage in renimbi business with foreign customers. After two years foreign banks will be permitted to conduct renimbi business with Chinese companies in cities such as Shanghai and Shenzhen; three years on foreign banks will be able to take up to a third interest in joint venture securities firms, and after 2007, foreign banks should be conducting renimbi business with Chinese entities and individuals.[25]

(ii) *De Facto* Discrimination

While our brief is the law, the *de facto* barriers to market access should never be forgotten. In the GATS this is taken into account by defining a government 'measure' as any measure 'whether in the form of a law, regulation, rule, procedure, decision, administrative action or any other form'.[26] Non-governmental measures, if taken by a delegation of powers, are covered, but private practices are not measures covered by the general obligations of the GATS.

The position in Japan is illustrative. *De jure* discrimination either dissolves on close examination or has been removed. For example, Chapter VII of the Japanese Banking Law 1981 provides for the licensing of each branch or agency of a foreign bank established in Japan. But limiting banks to one branch per application operates for Japanese banks as well. Moreover, the previous restrictions on foreign banks dealing

---

[24] M. Ogilvie, 'The Foreign Bank Entry Regime and the Search for a 21st Century Banking Policy for Canada' [1998] *JBL* 397; R. McDowell and R. Elliott, 'Canada Opens the Door to New Ownership of Financial Institutions', *IFLR*, Aug. 2000, 22; K. Chalmers, 'Regulatory Issues Affecting Foreign Bank Entry into Australia' (1995) 6 *JBFLP* 285, 287, 290.

[25] S. Cornelius and K. Axup, 'The Financial Services Sector in China after the WTO' (2001) 12 *JBFLP* 326, 327.

[26] Art. 28(a).

in government bonds, establishing trust banking subsidiaries, and so on have been abandoned.

However, if *de jure* discrimination is no longer a problem, the concern of foreign banks is about *de facto* measures, cutting them off from full access to the Japanese market.[27] One example is said to be the absence of full information about applicable rules, because of the government's penchant for informal 'administrative guidance' over published law. This would be covered by the GATS definition. In fact features of the Japanese economic and social system, such as the *keiretsu* relationships previously mentioned,[28] are much more important than legal style in creating hurdles for foreign banks in Japan. These would obviously be 'private practices' in GATS terms.

C. THE CONCEPT OF RECIPROCITY

Reciprocity is a concept with a potential for limiting the number of foreign banks in a jurisdiction. The reciprocity provision in the Credit Institutions Directive of the European Community is an example.[29] It was inserted because of the concerns which Member States had about access for their banks to the United States and Japan. There were, and are, domestic reciprocity provisions,[30] but it was thought that a uniform European response was desirable.

In Article 23(5) of the Credit Institutions Directive there is a minimum standard of national treatment of EC banks by third countries, i.e. they must treat EC banks the same as domestic banks. Breach of this may lead the European Commission to open negotiations with the third country so that EC banks receive national treatment, but it may also lead to Member States being required to prevent entry to third-country banks. Entry bans cannot, however, be retrospective, so that third-country banks which gained access before 1 January 1993 are not subject to this sanction. (The grandfather clause also enables authorized subsidiaries of third-country banks to acquire holdings in EC banks without sanction.) In Article 23(4) there is the higher standard, that third countries grant EC banks 'effective market access comparable to that granted by the Community' to third-country banks. Here there is no direct sanction, and all that may occur is that the EC Council of Ministers authorizes the Commission to negotiate with a third country to obtain 'comparable competitive opportunities' for EC banks.

Things are not as simple as this broad outline suggests. The first difficulty is the ambiguity in the text. Article 23(5) certainly refers to 'national treatment', but the full context is 'Community [banks] in a third country do not receive national treatment offering the same competitive opportunities as are available to domestic [banks], and the conditions of effective market access are not fulfilled'. There has been some

---

[27] H. Scott and P. Wellons, *International Finance* (7th edn., New York, Foundation Press, 2000), ch. 8(1).

[28] 31 above.

[29] Directive 2000/12/EC [2000] OJ L126, Title IV. Similarly, the Investment Services Dir. 93/22/EEC [1993] OJ L141/27, Art. 7.

[30] e.g. Financial Services Act 1986, s. 183; Banking Act 1987, s. 91; FSMA 2000, ss. 405–7.

discussion about whether the 'and' is conjunctive or disjunctive, in other words, whether the Commission can take action only if the third country fails to provide both reciprocal national treatment and effective market access, or whether it can act on lack of market access alone.[31] If the former, quotas on banking entrants to a third country would not breach Article 23(5). Certainly the phrase 'effective market access' is an empirical matter, directed to both the *de jure* and *de facto* situations.[32] It is not completely clear that this is the case with the qualification to 'national treatment' (i.e. 'offering the same competitive opportunities').

National treatment is largely concerned with discriminatory treatment, not offering the same competitive opportunities. Barriers can also result from non-discriminatory differences in national rules. Hence Article 23(4), which uses as a benchmark effective market access granted by the Community to third-country banks. Again, however, the parameters of the principle are ill-defined. One interpretation is that third countries have to enable EC banks to engage in the activities, and to provide the services, which are open to third-country banks in the EC. Under the Directive subsidiaries of third-country banks may, if authorized in one EC jurisdiction, establish themselves in other EC jurisdictions, or provide services cross-border, without further authorization. Included in the activities which a bank can thus engage in are securities activities.[33] The obvious question which arises is whether EC banks are being accorded 'effective market access comparable to that granted by the Community' if, in a third country with a federal system (e.g. the United States), they must obtain authorization in each state or province, or if in the third country (again the United States) there are restrictions on a bank's non-core activities. A second, more expansive, interpretation of 'effective market access' would examine end-results, for example market shares: do EC banks have a market share in a third country, comparable to that of that third country's banks in the EC?[34]

Neither interpretation commends itself. The first interpretation seems to be untenable because it would mean the Commission entering into negotiations with the United States for removal of state limitations on bank branching, or federal restrictions on the non-core activities of banks. As for the second interpretation, it places too strained an interpretation on when market access can be regarded as 'effective'. Market shares are influenced by a range of economic and social factors, such as the size of the market, the history of banking in that market, and customer preferences there. At most, market shares might form part of the evidence used in negotiating effective market access.

The Commission has said that it is concerned with restrictions which it considers inhibit freedom to establish a full commercial presence in another country. This

---

[31] e.g. P. Vigneron and A. Smith, 'The Concept of Reciprocity in Community Legislation: the Example of the Second Banking Directive' [1990] 5 *JIBL* 181, 183.

[32] EC Commission, *Treatment Accorded in Third Countries to Community Credit Institutions, Insurance Companies and Investment Firms*, COM (95) 303 final, 29 June 1995, 13.

[33] Art. 18(1), Annex 1.

[34] See S. Key, 'Is National Treatment still Viable? US Policy in Theory and Practice' [1990] 9 *JIBL* 365, 366.

suggests that the Commission believes that the liberalization of banking through multifunctional, or universal, banking is a goal of negotiations. Recall that this higher standard of market access (compared with the minimum standard of national treatment) is not coupled with sanctions, so that the ambiguity in the Directive is not fatal for individual third-country banks.

Apart from ambiguity, a second difficulty in the reciprocity provisions is their coverage. The wording of Article 23(1) suggests that their ambit is the subsidiaries of third-country banks, and does not extend to branches. In other words, a third-country bank establishing a branch in the EC will not be subject to the reciprocity provisions, even if the third country does not afford national treatment to EC banks. The justification probably is that branches will not have a right to establish their presence in the Community through the single licence. For this reason third countries' banks will have an incentive to establish subsidiaries, not branches, in the EC.

Another aspect of coverage is whether 'leapfrogging' is possible. In other words, could a third-country bank, whose country does not afford national treatment to EC banks, establish a subsidiary in a country which does, and then enter the EC through that other country, thereby avoiding the reciprocity provisions? Article 23(5) speaks of blocking entry in relation to 'direct or indirect parent undertakings governed by the laws of the third country in question'. Article 23(1) and (6) uses the language of 'a direct or indirect subsidiary of one or more parent undertakings which are governed by the laws of the third country in question', and of such undertaking proposing to acquire a holding in an EC bank. Of course an undertaking is 'governed by the laws of a third country' if it has a presence in that country, even though this may not be the centre of gravity of the bank's operations, which is probably what the phraseology is aimed at. 'Subsidiary' is defined in the Directive by cross-referencing to the Seventh Council Directive of 13 June 1983 on consolidated accounts, but there is no mention there of 'indirect' parents or subsidiaries. It seems likely that the concept of 'indirect' parents and subsidiaries, however imprecise, was introduced by the Commission after the problem of 'leapfrogging' was drawn to its attention. Certainly it did not appear in the earlier draft of the Directive. Much will depend on how these provisions have been translated into the laws of the Member States.

Finally, there is the issue of policy. It is understandable that the EC should want to ensure that, once its banks are established in third countries, they are not discriminated against. But there are good reasons for countries not to provide completely open entry to foreign banks, notably their desire to continue national control of key economic institutions. The IMF and the World Bank accept this. And EC Member States have sometimes said that there must be limits on the foreign control of their own national banks.[35] In interpreting Article 23(5) it would be unacceptable if the Commission, or the European Court of Justice, took a different view. As mentioned earlier, third countries' quotas on entry could escape the reach of Article 23(5) if it is read conjunctively.

---

[35] See 17 above.

Non-discrimination cannot mean completely equal treatment. This can be justified by the text of Article 23(5), in that it qualifies national treatment by the phrase 'offering the same competitive opportunities as are available to domestic [banks]'. As Scott correctly observes on the broader policy issue:[36]

Some countries, like Japan and South Korea, have been criticised by the US for giving domestic institutions preferable access to the discount windows of their central banks. Since discount window loans are usually at rates below those charged in the private inter-bank market, it is claimed that this results in a competitive disadvantage for foreign banks. However, these same foreign banks would be less susceptible to 'window guidance' than their domestic counterparts. Such guidance may dictate making relative unprofitable loans. The US is myopic in looking only at the funding side of discount window access.

The Directive, in Article 23(4), goes further than national treatment by requiring that EC banks have freedom to establish an effective market access in non-member countries, albeit that this is not backed by the threat of retaliatory action. The possibility of the Commission opening negotiations with a non-member country may, however, give EC banks access, especially if the non-member is dependent on the EC for its markets for other goods and services. Yet will this type of access always be desirable? More generally, is the liberalization inherent in EC policy the right one?

From the standpoint of EC banks, the answer to these questions may be in the affirmative, but from a broader perspective one cannot be as definite. Despite the success of the universal bank in many parts of Europe can it be said that, in other social and economic contexts, the combination of activities such as banking and securities is the most conducive to a safe and efficient financial sector? Moreover, in developing countries should the EC seek an effective market access for its banks at the inevitable expense of local institutions, just because developing-country banks seek to establish in Europe—an important location to finance trade and to raise capital for development, and an avenue to financial information and expertise. In other words, 'free trade' for EC banks is not just a matter of banking, but of the foreign relations of the Community with the world.[37] It is a notion pregnant with ideological and political ramifications.

III. REGIONAL AND INTERNATIONAL MEASURES

Never before has the world seen an era of financial liberalization comparable to the present. Restrictions on foreign banks are some of its many victims. The battle for liberalization has been waged, as a matter of law, through foreign-investment and

---

[36] H. Scott, 'Reciprocity and the Second Banking Directive', in R. Cranston (ed.), *The Single Market and the Law of Banking* (2nd edn., London, LLP, 1995), 101–2.

[37] See P. Eeckhort, *The Internal Market and International Trade. A Legal Analysis* (Oxford, Clarendon, 1994).

free-trade treaties. In the past, foreign-investment treaties generally excluded core banking from their ambit.[38] Financial services were not part of the General Agreement on Tariffs and Trade (the GATT). Now, however, bilateral, regional, and multilateral treaties promote, in varying degrees, access by foreign banks.

Of limited geographical scope is NAFTA, the North American Free Trade Agreement, between Canada, Mexico, and the United States, which came into effect in 1994. Chapter 14 of the NAFTA obliges the parties to provide (a) access to the financial-service providers of the other parties, and (b) the better of national treatment, or most-favoured-nation treatment, to the other parties' financial institutions, cross-border financial-service providers, and eligible investors. However, cross-border branching is subject to national discretion, and Mexico has detailed reservations in Annex VII relating to the terms and conditions on which it will open its financial markets.[39]

This section examines, albeit briefly, two examples of multinational financial liberalization—the Single Market programme of the European Community and the General Agreement on Trade in Services (the GATS). The first provides very free access within the European Community to banks from other Member States. The GATS is ambitious in geographical coverage, although for quite understandable reasons many developing countries were not prepared to have incorporated in it the financial liberalization for banking advocated by developed countries such as those in the OECD.

A. THE SINGLE LICENCE AND THE SINGLE EUROPEAN MARKET

Throughout this book we have encountered the Credit Institutions Directive of the European Community. It and its predecessors (notably the Second Banking Directive) and the Investment Services Directive have been part of the agenda for a single European market. The aim has been to create one market in banking services, with no internal barriers to EC banks establishing branches in other parts of the EC, or in providing services cross-border. The aim is achieved through 'mutual recognition': a bank based in one EC Member State has a 'passport' to establish branches, or to provide services, in other EC Member States. A 'single licence' is required, rather than licensing in each Member State. The passport does not apply to a branch of a bank established outside the European Community: the third-country bank must incorporate a subsidiary in the Community and be licensed in at least one jurisdiction there. Mutual recognition is coupled with the harmonization of certain basic prudential standards.

It can be argued that the Directives have added little, if anything, to the rights of

---

[38] e.g. Treaty of Friendship, Commerce and Navigation Between the United States of America and Japan, 4 UST 2063, Art. 7(2).

[39] See K. Schefer, *International Trade in Financial Services. The NAFTA Provisions* (Hague, Kluwer, 1999), 157, 198, 229.

establishment and to provide services which were already enjoyed under the Treaty of Rome.[40] Even if this were the case as a matter of strict law, the Directives have given certainty to these rights of banks to move across borders, without the need to wring them out of the decisions of the European Court of Justice. If a bank is to take advantage of the passport to establish branches or provide services on the territory of another European Community state, it must notify its intention to its own (home) regulator, which will in turn inform the regulator in the host state.[41] In 1997 the European Commission adopted a non-restrictive interpretation of this provision in relation to providing banking services cross-border. Its Banking Communication treats a banking service as being provided within the territory of another Member State only if the bank is located there. This so-called characteristic performance test means, as the Banking Communication noted, that banking services provided via the internet are not 'within the territory' of the Member State which is the residence of the customer, but rather within that where the bank is located.[42] The upshot is that the occasions on which a bank must notify under the Directive are much reduced.

One important practical issue is what difference the single licence has made. At the time the Directive was being finalized, its proponents detected a positive stimulus from the nearness of 1992. Whatever the flurry of activity at that time, there has been only a gradual effect on banking markets generally, and thus the increase in competition which the Directive is supposed to achieve. This is partly because banks have been uncertain about domestic legal rules elsewhere. The absence of harmonization within the European Community on tax matters has given rise to instances where banks have been hindered in providing cross-border services.[43]

As already remarked, retail banking services do not in general travel well across cultures and nationalities. In theoretical terms banking, especially retail banking, does not fit the model of 'contestable' markets. Branch networks of existing dominant banks, their reputation for soundness, and switching costs for consumers—all create non-legal barriers to entry. Consequently, while European competition in wholesale banking will continue to be strong, and competition for medium-sized firms and wealthy individuals will grow, the likelihood is of only gradual changes in European retail banking.[44] What has occurred are certain defensive measures by banks to the potential increase in competition. This has taken the form of some cross-border

---

[40] J. Usher, 'The Implications of the Single Market for Banking and Finance: an Overview', in R. Cranston (ed.), *The Single Market and the Law of Banking* (2nd edn., London, LLP, 1995). See also J. Usher, *The Law of Money and Financial Services in the European Community* (2nd edn., Oxford, Clarendon, 2000).

[41] Credit Institutions Directive 2000/12/EC [2000] OJ L126, Art. 20–1.

[42] See M. Dassesse, 'Localisation of Financial Services: Regulatory and Tax Implications', in M. Andenas and W. Roth (eds.), *Services and Free Movement in EU Law* (Oxford, OUP, 2001); R. Cranston and C. Hadjiemmanuil, 'Banking Integration in the European Community' in J. Norton, M. Andenas, and M. Footer (eds.), *The Changing World of International Law in the Twenty-First Century* (Hague, Kluwer, 1998), 380–2.

[43] M. Dassesse, 'Retail Banking Services in the Single Market', in R. Cranston (ed.), *The Single Market and the Law of Banking* (2nd edn., London, LLP, 1995), 69ff.

[44] See F. Heinemann and M. Jopp, *The Benefits of a Working European Retail Market for Financial Services* (Bonn, Europe Union Verlag, 2002), 45–53.

acquisitions, and the establishment of some cross-border networks of banks. That the promise of increased competition, which the Directive holds out, is likely to be long in gestation, is not of itself objectionable.

B. THE GATS

The General Agreement on Trade in Services (the GATS) is binding on those who enter the agreement establishing the World Trade Organization. It came into effect in 1995. It comprises two main parts, the general framework with annexes, and the individual schedules of commitments of member countries. Important obligations of the general framework apply only when a party makes a specific commitment. The GATS has implications for banking: in 1997 financial services became a permanent feature of the GATS as a result of the Financial Services Agreement.[45]

The definition of trade in services in Article 1 includes the cross-border provision of services, and their delivery through a commercial presence in the host jurisdiction. Determining the origin of a foreign service or supplier is provided for elsewhere.[46] As we have seen, the GATS includes *de jure* steps along with laws, regulations, administrative actions, and so on, as the 'measures' of members against which the GATS is directed.[47] Notwithstanding the provisions of the Agreement, the Annex on Financial Services enables members to take prudential measures for investor protection and the integrity of the financial system. This exemption must not be used, however, as a means of avoiding a member's commitments. Nonetheless, this carve out means that priority is being given to the goods of bank regulation over the demands of competition and financial liberalization.

There are three key concepts in the GATS—most-favoured nation treatment, market access, and national treatment. Most-favoured nation treatment is central to the GATS, as it was also to the GATT (the General Agreement on Tariffs and Trade). In the context of banking it obliges a country to accord no less favourable treatment to the banks of one foreign country than that accorded to the banks of any other foreign country.[48] In the case of banking most-favoured nation treatment is not a major problem. If countries exclude, or limit, foreign banks, they generally do so indiscriminately. Exceptions to the general obligation include regional economic arrangements, such as the European Community, and reciprocity provisions.

Secondly, market access. This is concerned with the different types of limitations on foreign banks identified above—the numbers, assets, types of legal entity through which banking services may be offered, and so on.[49] Many countries do not agree with the view that a very liberal regime of market access is desirable. Consequently, the market-access provision of the GATS is a fudge: each member simply agrees to

---

[45] M. Footer, 'GATT and the Multilateral Regulation of Banking Services' (1993) 27 *Int'l. Lawyer* 343; R. Lastra, 'Cross-Border Trade in Financial Services', in I. Fletcher, L. Mistelis, and M. Cremona (eds.), *Foundation and Perspectives of International Trade Law* (London, Sweet & Maxwell, 2001), 434. See also P. Sauvé and R. Stern (eds.), *GATS 2000: New Directions in Services Trade Liberalisation* (Washington DC, Brookings, 1999).

[46] Art. XXVIII.   [47] 429 above.   [48] Art. II.   [49] Art. XVI.

accord access under the terms, limitations, and conditions it agreed. These can include limitations on the number of banks, the volume of their transactions, the number of persons employed, and conditions as to their form and the distribution of any branches. If, however, a Member State does agree to market access for foreign banks, then it is committed to allow any necessary transfers of capital.

Thirdly, there is national treatment. This operates once a bank obtains market access. It commits members to treat foreign banks in the same way as domestic banks, although, as with market access, it is a fudge and, under the GATS, members can make treatment subject to conditions and qualifications.[50] The approach to national treatment which the OECD countries would on the whole want is embodied in an 'Understanding', attached to GATS, but with no legal force. It is designed to obtain more ambitious liberalization commitments from those who schedule in accordance with it, although it seems that almost the same degree of liberalization could be obtained under the general approach.

The process of liberalization to which the GATS has given an impetus will not be fast. Many emerging and developing countries have legitimate concerns about the spread of foreign banks. Article XIX recognizes that the GATS is a halfway house: it commits members to enter successive rounds of negotiation, beginning not later than five years from the date of the Agreement, with a view to achieving progressively higher levels of liberalization.

[50] Art. XVII.

17

CROSS-BORDER BANKING

I. INTRODUCTION

Consider these situations:

Case 1
Banking regulation in country X requires banks to have a certain amount of capital if they are to continue in business, while banking regulation in country Y requires banks to have a greater amount of capital. A bank is incorporated in country X, but has a branch in country Y.

Case 2
A, a resident of country X, sends money to country Y. The transfer is denominated in the currency of country Z and involves correspondent banks in country Z. Country Z takes proceedings against A for money-laundering and seizes amounts in clearing accounts there.

Case 3
A bank in country X transfers to another bank there assets with a company in country Y. A bank in country Z claims that this was for the purposes of putting those assets beyond the reach of creditors like itself, in breach of the legislation in country Y.

Case 4
A bank in country X lends money to an entity, A, in country Y. Country Y declares a moratorium on its debts and those owed by entities within its borders.

Case 5
There is a breach in the foreign relations between countries Y and Z. (This may be a unilateral breach or because country Y is acting in accordance with a United Nations Security Council Resolution or with a regional decision, e.g. of the European Community). As a result country Y freezes the assets of country Z, its entities and leaders, held by country Y's nationals anywhere in the world. A bank with its head office in country Y refuses to repay deposits which an entity of country Z has in one of the bank's branches in country X. The entity sues the bank in country X.

Case 6
Banks A and B are parties to a syndicated loan agreement. Bank A agrees to purchase

Bank B's share in the agreement by way of a 'take-out agreement', but Bank A now claims that Bank B concealed from it certain adverse information about the borrower. Bank A issues recission proceedings in jurisdiction X pursuant to the law there of fraudulent concealment. Bank B applies in jurisdiction Y for an anti-suit injunction preventing Bank A from pursuing the claim in jurisdiction X. The take-out agreement is governed by the law of jurisdiction Y, there is a non-exclusive jurisdiction clause for Y's courts, and under the agreement each party is unambiguously protected from actions for non-disclosure by the other.

Case 7
A bank is incorporated in country Z with branches in many other countries, including countries X and Y. A regulatory body in country X orders the bank to produce records maintained at its branch in country Y, relating to the bank account of a customer. The bank declines to produce the documents, asserting that compliance with the order without the customer's consent, or an order of the courts of country Y, will violate the bank secrecy laws of that country.

These examples illustrate some of the legal problems arising because banking is carried out internationally. Clearly many are not new, nor are most confined to banking. What follows is an outline of how these problems have been handled. Then an examination is made of the broader principles underlying the resolution of the harder cases. Comity, balancing, co-operation, and harmonization are considered. The breadth of the subject matter precludes an exhaustive treatment. Reference is made to principles of both domestic and international law.

II. THE PROBLEMS EXAMINED

A. REGULATING THE MULTINATIONAL BANK

In case 1, the bank operates in various jurisdictions and is subject to parallel, but not conflicting, regulatory regimes. There is no question but that, in international law, both jurisdictions have competence to prescribe and enforce their capital-adequacy and other rules. The bank must comply with both regulatory regimes. Where the branch in country Y is separately incorporated, it will generally have to meet the requirements of a fully independent bank there. Where it is not separately incorporated, regulation of its capital there will usually be tailored to take into account its capital base in country X. As we saw in Chapter 3, regulatory authorities will usually supervise a bank group on a consolidated, as well as an individual, basis.[1] Across many jurisdictions the regulatory regimes are now very similar: there has been a remarkable degree of international harmonization in banking regulation since the 1980s.[2]

---

[1] 109 above.   [2] 63ff above.

However, in other respects such as financial promotion there is still significant divergence and banks must comply with the requirements of each jurisdiction in which they operate.

B. EXTRATERRITORIAL JURISDICTION

Cases 2 and 3 raise the issue of the reach of the law of one country beyond its borders.

(i) International Law

As a matter of international law, a country has clear competence to prescribe as regards resources and persons within its own territory (the territorial principle). Moreover, nationality provides a basis for a country to prescribe, although it may not enforce its law over nationals in another country's jurisdiction (the nationality principle). A problem with nationality as a basis of jurisdiction is identity: which are a country's nationals? In case 5, country Y claims that its nationals include any branches of its banks around the world. That might be acceptable to other countries in the case of branches and representative offices, but once there is a subsidiary or incorporated affiliate it becomes a different story.

The third possible basis of extraterritorial jurisdiction is the effects doctrine. One interpretation is that this is not a claim to extraterritorial jurisdiction, but to territorial jurisdiction: if an offence committed outside a country is concluded or consummated in the jurisdiction, the courts have jurisdiction. Another interpretation is that a country has the jurisdiction to prescribe rules of law governing conduct which has effects within its jurisdiction. The US view, set out for example in the third edition of the *Restatement on Foreign Relations Laws*, is that international law enables the exercise of jurisdiction over conduct having significant effects in a state. The European Court of Justice gives some support to the effects principle.[3] It has been given legislative force in some jurisdictions: for example, in the United Kingdom the restrictions on financial promotion apply to communications outside if they are capable of having an effect within the jurisdiction and are directed there.[4]

International law has recognized universal jurisdiction in a limited number of situations, notably gross breaches of human rights. National courts can try defendants, whether or not they are nationals and whether the offences occurred within the jurisdiction. Terrorism and terrorist financing have been added to the list of offences giving rise to universal jurisdiction. The General Assembly of the United Nations adopted the International Convention for the Suppression of the Financing of Terrorism in 1999, which is now in force (April 2002). It obliges parties to establish crimes in this regard and to take steps for the confiscation of such funds.[5] In the United

---

[3] R. Higgins, *Problems and Process. International Law and How We Use It* (Oxford, Clarendon, 1994), 75.

[4] FSMA 2000, s. 21(3); Financial Services and Markets Act 2000 (Financial Promotions) Order 2001, SI 2001 No 1335, art. 12.

[5] 73 above.

Kingdom the Terrorism Act 2000 criminalizes terrorist fund-raising funding, using or possessing money or other property for terrorism, and terrorist money-laundering. We have seen how banks can get caught up in this.[6] It establishes universal jurisdiction for these offences, so they can be prosecuted even if the criminal act was committed outside the United Kingdom, so long as this would have been an offence if done there.[7] It also enables the United Kingdom to meet its obligation under the 'extradite or prosecute' provision of the Convention: it must extradite for prosecution elsewhere if it decides not to prosecute itself.[8]

(ii) Domestic Law: The Principles

These differing views of international law are reflected in the domestic laws of states. Thus civil law countries may use a nationality principle and proceed against a national no matter where in the world an offence is committed. Some common law countries adopt what has been described as 'subjective territoriality' and assume jurisdiction if any element of an offence is committed there. English law, however, has been bedeviled by an analytical distinction between conduct offences and result offences. With a conduct offence, an English court will only assume jurisdiction if the last element comprising it is carried out in England. Jurisdiction over a result offence depends on whether the offence has an effect in England.[9]

Take an example. English customers of an English bank, who obtain foreign currency at a German bank through the use of some sort of payment card, when they know that their account is overdrawn and they have no overdraft arrangement, are guilty of obtaining money by deception from the German bank (to use the English terminology for such behaviour). Because all elements of that offence are committed abroad, however, an English court does not regard itself as having jurisdiction. But because a customer in such circumstances can also be guilty of another offence, obtaining a pecuniary advantage by deception in the form of borrowing by way of overdraft, a prosecution can be brought in England where the overdraft arises. The policy behind the decision of the court which established the latter proposition is explicit in the judgment: 'If an English court had no jurisdiction when a person resident here with a bank account here uses his cheque card abroad dishonestly, a great deal of dishonesty may go unpunished'.[10]

In another example, the chairman and managing director of a small London merchant bank, WSTC, was convicted *inter alia* of obtaining property by deception. A repurchase agreement contract was entered into in relation to securities allegedly held in Canada, and payment was made by one New York bank into an account with WSTC's New York bank. It was argued on appeal that the moneys were obtained in New York, not England. The Court of Appeal was unimpressed: the appellant and

---

[6] 73–5 above.   [7] S. 63.   [8] S. 64.

[9] G. Gilbert, 'Crimes sans Frontières' (1992) 63 *Brit. Y'book Int'l L* 415; L. Leigh, 'Territorial Jurisdiction and Fraud' [1988] *Crim. LR* 280.

[10] *R. v. Bevan* (1987) 84 Cr. App. R., 143, 148. See also *R. v. Ngan* [1998] CAR 331 (CA).

those to whom he made the representation were in London, it was in London the telephone call was made, all relevant documentation save for the crediting of the New York account came into existence in London, and it was in and from London that the appellant and WSTC conducted their business. Again the policy aspect of the court's reasoning was explicit:

The reliance of international banking on advancing communications technology had added new weapons to the armoury of fraudsters, especially those whose purpose it was to perpetrate fraud across national boundaries. . . . The court had to recognise the need to adapt its approach to the question of jurisdiction in the light of such changes.[11]

As in so many areas of English law, an arid conceptualization gives way in most cases to pragmatism in practice.

Legislation now gives effect to this pragmatic approach for certain offences in the Theft Acts of 1968 and 1978 and the Forgery and Counterfeiting Act 1981. Part I of the Criminal Justice Act 1993, finally brought into effect in 1998 except for certain conspiracies, requires only that one element of those offences be committed in England. It need not be the last element of the offence. Moreover, a conspiracy, or attempt to commit these offences abroad, can be proceeded against in England. An important factor behind these changes is the national interest in London remaining a major banking and financial centre. 'Should it be thought that large scale frauds could be carried out here with impunity, confidence in London as a major international centre would rapidly be undermined'.[12] To this extent, English law is more in line with the approach in other common law jurisdictions.

(ii) Domestic Law: The Practice

As a matter of the domestic law of a country, the reach of its legislation will depend partly on its terms, and partly on how it is interpreted. For example, the US Money Laundering Control Act of 1986 contains a specific declaration of extraterritorial jurisdiction over prohibited conduct if 'the conduct is by a United States citizen or, in the case of a non-United States citizen, the conduct occurs in part in the United States'.[13] In one sense this is a clear claim to extraterritorial jurisdiction. In another sense, much depends on what conduct is regarded as occurring in part in the United States. The United States takes the view that the Act applies to transactions involving foreign banks and foreign nationals situated abroad if, for example, one foreign national transfers funds from one foreign location to another foreign location via the United States. An example would be a payment in US dollars between foreign banks routed through the CHIPS system in New York.[14] Under US law, laundered money never becomes clean, and New York prosecutors now seize the balance in New York

---

[11] *R. v. Smith (Wallace Duncan)* [1996] 2 CAR 1. Cf. *R. v. Manning* [1999] QB 980 (CA).

[12] Law Commission, *Jurisdiction Over Offences of Fraud and Dishonesty with a Foreign Element*, Law Com. Rep. No 180, 1989, para. 2.24.

[13] 18 USC §1956(f)   [14] 237 above.

correspondent accounts on the basis that they facilitated the money-laundering transactions.[15]

If legislation is unclear, administrative practices and judicial decisions will shape its interpretation. Presumptions of statutory interpretation may enter the process, for example, that legislation is intended to extend to the territory of a country, but not outside; and to persons and matters within that territory, but not to others (not even to nationals outside the territory). At the end of the day, however, such presumptions are only one aspect of how a court will construe legislation.

Experience in the banking area suggests that courts will not be slow to give legislation an extraterritorial effect. Illustrative is the decision from which the facts of Case 3 are taken, where an English court recognized the extraterritorial impact of section 423 of the Insolvency Act 1986, which even outside of insolvency proceedings permits a court to set aside a transfer of assets which it finds has been for the dominant purpose of putting them beyond the reach of creditors.[16] The court held that the location of the assets in England gave it jurisdiction, but in the circumstances of the case it exercised its discretion to decline jurisdiction. The allegations were speculative and lacking evidential support that the bank had the requisite purpose in entering the transaction, and there was no impelling reason why the court should assume jurisdiction just because the assets were in England.

Policy loomed large in an earlier decision of the English Divisional Court on the reach of the drug-trafficking legislation. That empowers the authorities to apply to a judge for a production order for the purpose of an investigation into drug trafficking. On ordinary principles, such an order overrides bank confidentiality.[17] An officer of the bank and an account holder were indicted in the United States for money-laundering and drug offences. While searching the bank official's premises in England, customs officers saw files in a locked cabinet relating to the bank accounts of General Noriega, who had been named in another indictment in the United States relating to drug trafficking. The Divisional Court held that the legislation extended to investigations being conducted by authorities of other countries, and that the UK authorities could make the information available to the foreign enforcement authorities. The court reasoned that the relevant legislation contained express reference to offences against corresponding provisions in the corresponding laws in other signatory countries to the Single Convention on Narcotic Drugs 1961, and that the drafters had the international obligations of the United Kingdom under the convention in mind.[18]

This discussion of jurisdiction has concentrated on criminal and regulatory offences. It will be recalled, however, that the civil law in England now plays its part in pursuing the fraudulent and their ill-gotten proceeds. Thus a bank may be held accountable on the ground that it dishonestly assisted a fiduciary in a breach of duty, or received money knowing that it had been paid in breach of fiduciary duty.[19]

---

[15] e.g. *Marine Midland Bank* v. *United States*, 11 F 3d 1119 (2nd Cir. 1993).
[16] *Re Banco Nacional de Cuba* [2001] 1 WLR 2039, [2001] 3 All ER 923.   [17] 176 above.
[18] *R. v. Southwark Crown Court, ex p. Customs and Excise* [1990] 1 QB 650 (CA).
[19] 196 above.

In an English Court of Appeal decision,[20] a manager of the claimant at its Tokyo office, and his accomplice, siphoned off moneys, which then passed through bank accounts in the United States and London. The moneys were then invested with a company controlled by an individual with Spanish domicile, and after deposit in the company's London account were transferred to the Isle of Man and further afield. The claim against the Spaniard, properly analysed, was for dishonest assistance of a breach of trust or fiduciary duty. The court held that for the purposes of the Brussels Convention, now the Brussels Regulation,[21] this was a claim in tort, delict, or quasi-delict. It followed that instead of suing in Spain, the place of domicile, it was possible to sue in England as the jurisdiction where the harmful event (the investment) occurred. However, there are a number of crucial issues not addressed by the judgment. What of claims in knowing receipt, arguably restitutionary in nature, as opposed to dishonest assistance? And given the large number of jurisdictions likely to be associated with many large frauds, when in fact does the harmful event occur for the purposes of the Brussels Regulation?

C. MORATORIA AND FREEZES

Cases 4 and 5 involve whether country X will recognize the laws of country Y, either the moratorium of country Y declared with respect to debts owed to a bank (Case 4), or the freeze imposed by country Y on deposits of country Z with country Y's nationals, such as the bank, including the bank's branch in country X (Case 5). In such cases Y's competence to prescribe is only partly, if at all, in issue, especially if in the case of a freeze it is acting pursuant to a UN Security Council Resolution. As a matter of construction, even when the freeze is lifted it may impose a permanent prohibition on any claim against a bank which by virtue of the freeze was prevented from performing its payment obligations.[22] What is at issue concerns the secondary competence of country X and its courts to apply Y's law.

From the point of view of international law, country Y is entitled to impose a moratorium or freeze. A moratorium applied to entities in country Y falls directly within the territorial principle. There is a separate issue of whether a moratorium is in breach of Article VIII(2)(a) of the IMF, which obliges members not to restrict the making of payments and transfers for current international transactions without approval of the IMF.[23] However, the issue is never a live one in practice because the IMF does not generally disclose whether or not it has given approval.

What of a freeze, in particular one applying to country Y's nationals, such as the branch of one of its banks situated in country X? When the UK government

---

[20] Casio Computer Co. Ltd. v. Kaiser [2001] EWCA Civ. 661.

[21] EC Regulation 44/2001 [2001] OJ L12/1, Art. 5(3).

[22] *Shanning International Ltd.* v. *Lloyds TSB Bank plc* [2001] 1 WLR 1462 (HL).

[23] S. Zamora, 'Exchange Control in Mexico: A Case Study in the Application of IMF Rules (1984) 7 *Hous. J.Int'l. L* 103, 108–28; R. Edwards, 'Extraterritorial Application of the US Iranian Assets Control Regulations' (1981) 75 *AJIL* 870, 873–6.

imposes sanctions against payments to undesirable governments, rebel groups, or organizations (e.g. terrorists), the statutory instrument extends these to foreign branches of UK banks. Its actions can be justified on the nationality principle.[24] Whether a freeze is legitimate if extended to UK foreign subsidiaries, as under some US sanctions,[25] in addition to UK foreign branches, is more doubtful. As a matter of corporations law, a foreign subsidiary is separate from its parent, whereas a branch is part of the same entity. From the point of view of control, however, the subsidiary may be as much subject to direction by the parent as a branch is by its head office. It would seem wrong to determine the issue simply on the basis of corporate form. In practice, if the freeze is being imposed by other countries as well (pursuant, say, to a Security Council Resolution), the foreign subsidiary will be caught by the freeze as implemented by the law of those other countries.[26]

No doubt the courts of country Y will impose its moratorium or freeze, as the mandatory law of the forum, even though the proper law of the transaction is that of another jurisdiction. Of course it may be that on its true interpretation the law does not apply: in criminal proceedings, for example, the courts of country Y may construe it narrowly.[27] If money is lent in breach of this type of law, the English approach is that it is irrecoverable as an illegal contract—it is not unjust enrichment for the borrower not to be made to repay.[28]

The real question is whether, as a matter of domestic law, the courts of country X will apply the moratorium or freeze imposed by country Y. In Britain and the United States, the court decides this independently of international law. Indeed, in certain circumstances in England, foreign law in breach of international law will be given effect, unless it constitutes a grave infringement of human rights.[29] England invokes principles of conflict of laws, the United States, the act-of-state doctrine. Article VIII, section (2)(b), of the IMF is interpreted so as not to apply.

(i) Conflict of Laws—The English Approach

In England, the courts invoke the principles of conflict of laws set out in the Rome Convention on the Law Applicable to Contractual Obligations.[30] Under Article 8, the ordinary rules in the Convention apply to issues of illegality. Thus, if the proper law of the payment obligation is country Y, its moratorium will be given effect. The only caveat is whether the United Kingdom recognizes the legitimacy of the body purporting to act as the government of country Y. Similarly with country Y's freeze order.

---

[24] e.g. The Afghanistan (United Nations Sanctions) Order 2001, SI 2001 No 396, art. 1(4)(b).

[25] K. Alexander, 'Extra-territorial UK Economic Sanctions and Third Party Liability for Non-US Banks and Companies' [2001] *BJIBFL* 272, 281.

[26] W. Blair, 'Interference of Public Law in the Performance of International Monetary Obligations', in M. Giovanoli (ed.), *International Monetary Law* (Oxford, OUP, 2000), 411.

[27] Cf. *Swiss Bank Corporation* v. *Lloyds Bank Ltd.* [1982] AC 584 (HL).

[28] *Boissevain* v. *Weil* [1950] AC 327 (HL); Contracts (Applicable Law) Act 1990, s. 2(2).

[29] *Re Helbert Wagg* [1956] Ch. 323, 346; *Oppenheimer* v. *Cattermole* [1976] AC 249, 278 (HL).

[30] [1980] OJ L266/1.

What, however, if the proper law of the obligation is country X? Article 7(1) of the Convention confers a discretion to apply the mandatory rules of a foreign country with which there is a close connection, and consequently some European courts might give effect to the moratorium or freeze. As it was entitled to, the United Kingdom has excluded the application of Article 7(1). An English court must therefore resolve the issue in terms of the common law or of other provisions of the Convention. Invoking Article 8, one would apply the proper law, the law of country X. If country X were England, English law would disregard the effect of the moratorium or freeze on the payment obligation.

One objection which the obligor might raise is that, although not illegal in England, payment would be illegal by the place of performance. That could be said to be country Y in case 4, if that is where entity A, the obligor, has the bulk of its assets. With case 5 it might be said to be country Y, if payment is to be in the currency of country Y, and therefore would typically go through a clearing system there. In English common law there is authority that illegality in a foreign place of performance would be given effect to, although the proper law is England.[31] The principle, however, is a narrow one in that it applies only if at the time of conclusion of the contract the real object was for it to be performed in a way unlawful by the place of performance.[32] In any event, country Y might not have been treated as the place of performance in case 4, even in the absence of express provision, since fulfilling the payment obligation would not necessarily have involved an act there. Nor would country Y have been treated as the necessary place of performance in case 5. Although payment in a country's currency is normally routed through a clearing system there, this need not always be the case. Payment may be effected through correspondent accounts elsewhere.[33]

As far as the Rome Convention is concerned illegality by the place of performance is not expressly mentioned. Some European countries might apply the law of the place of performance under Article 7(1), as the mandatory law of a foreign country with which the situation has a close connection. Its exclusion from UK law means resort may be had to other provisions of the Convention. One possible basis for giving the law of the place of performance effect is Article 10(2): 'In relation to the manner of performance . . . regard shall be had to the law of the country in which performance takes place'. Two points should, however, be made: first, the phrase 'manner of performance' has a narrow remit, covering relatively minor matters, rather than the substance of the obligation (which, in cases 4 and 5, is payment itself). Secondly, the Article confers a discretion—regard shall be had to the law of the place of performance, but it is not necessarily determinative.

Another possible basis for giving the law of the place of performance effect is

---

[31] e.g. *Libyan Arab Foreign Bank* v. *Bankers Trust Co.* [1989] QB 728; *Ispahani* v. *Bank Melli Iran* [1998] Lloyd's Rep. Banking 133.

[32] *Royal Boskalis Westminster NV* v. *Mountain* [1999] QB 674 (CA). See e.g. F. Reynolds, 'Illegality by *Lex Loci Solutionis*' (1992) 108 *LQR* 553.

[33] 237 above.

Article 16, which provides that any law specified by the Convention may be refused application if that would be manifestly incompatible with the public policy of the forum. Could a court regard illegality according to the place of performance as raising significant public policy considerations such as comity? It would seem not. The parties have chosen another law to govern the transaction. Why should their expectations be undercut by the fact that other countries (country Y in our cases 4 and 5) subsequently introduced a moratorium or freeze? In any event, with both Articles 10(2) and 16, the common law reasoning as to where performance takes place would probably still be applicable. In other words, in both cases 4 and 5 performance need not be treated as occurring in the countries where it is illegal (country Y).

(ii) Act of State—The US Approach

US courts invoke the act-of-state doctrine, whereby their courts will not inquire into the validity of public acts, such as moratoria or freeze orders, of a recognized foreign power having effect within its own territory. The situs of the obligation affected by the moratorium or freeze is thus crucial, since the doctrine does not apply if this is outside the territory of the foreign state. Thus the US courts have enforced payment obligations under cross-border loans, despite a moratorium in the borrower's country, where repayment of the loan had to be made in New York or the jurisdiction clause required settlement of disputes there. Choice of New York law as the governing law generally leads to a finding that the situs of the obligation is there.[34] There are close similarities between the factual inquiries necessary in English and US courts for determining respectively the proper law (in the absence of an express choice) and the situs of the obligation. Not surprisingly, the results produced are similar, despite the different doctrines.

(iii) Article VIII(2)(b) of the IMF

Article VIII, section 2(b) of the IMF provides:

Exchange contracts which involve the currency of any member and which are contrary to the exchange control regulations of that member maintained or imposed consistently with this Agreement shall be unenforceable in the territories of any member.[35]

In an interpretation of the Article, the Executive Directors of the IMF have said that, as a result, a court or tribunal in a member country cannot refuse recognition of the exchange-control regulations of the other members which are maintained or imposed consistently with the IMF Agreement.[36] Consequently, such contracts must be treated

---

[34] *Libra Bank Ltd.* v. *Banco Nacional de Costa Rica SA*, 570 F Supp. 870 (SDNY 1983); *Allied Bank International* v. *Banco Credito Agricola de Cartago*, 757 F 2d 516 (2d Cir. 1985). See M. Gruson, 'Scope of *Lex Monetae* in International Transactions', in M. Giovanoli (ed.), *International Monetary Law* (Oxford, OUP, 2001), 446–9.

[35] F. Mann, *The Legal Aspect of Money* (5th edn., Oxford, Clarendon, 1992), ch. XIII cites some of the vast literature on this topic.

[36] 'Unenforceability of Exchange Contracts', Decision No 446–4, 10 June 1949.

as unenforceable, notwithstanding that under the private international law of the forum the law under which the foreign-exchange control regulations are maintained or imposed is not the law which governs the exchange contract or its performance.

The argument for a wide interpretation of this Article is that the paramount purpose of the Fund is to promote international monetary co-operation.[37] If exchange control or a moratorium has been imposed by country Y, consistently with the IMF Treaty, courts in other Member States such as country X should, in a co-operative spirit, give effect to it. In favour of a narrow interpretation is commercial convenience: it would place an intolerable burden on banks and others if they had to be conversant with the foreign-exchange law of each country involved in any particular transaction, before they could be sure that it would not be unenforceable as being in breach of exchange-control law. Not surprisingly the narrow interpretation has won the day in international financial centres such as London, New York, and Singapore, even now after modern information systems should automatically flag up transactions affected by particular foreign exchange laws. This may also reflect a rather unrefined sensibility to international treaty obligations in these jurisdictions.

Thus English, New York, and Singapore courts confine the expression 'exchange contracts' to contracts to exchange the currency of one country for the currency of another.[38] Foreign-exchange dealings would be covered, as would currency swaps if involving the currency in question, but not loans or securities purchases, even if in that foreign currency. A more generous interpretation would be that an exchange contract is a contract which has an impact on the foreign-exchange resources of the country. This accords with the policy behind exchange control and moratorium laws, which is to protect a state's reserves of foreign exchange. Thus countries like France give effect to another country's exchange restrictions affecting loans or securities deals, and Germany will also, so long as they affect current (but not capital) payments.[39]

Moreover, when Article VIII 2(b) renders exchange contracts 'unenforceable', the common law interpretation is that it means precisely that, rather than void or illegal. Thus acts undertaken in performance of a contract caught by the section are not unlawful (e.g. set-off). Clearly an action in tort independently of the contract would be permissible. Civil law countries such as Germany have difficulty with the common law term 'unenforceable'. In Germany it has been taken to mean a precondition to suit: the claimant has to prove that the exchange controls invoked by the defendant are inconsistent with the IMF Articles, or that Article VIII 2(b) does not apply for other reasons.

---

[37] J. Gold, *The Fund Agreement in the Courts* (Washington DC, IMF, 1989), iv, 16, 21, 31–2.

[38] *United City Merchants (Investment) Ltd.* v. *Royal Bank of Canada* [1983] 1 AC 168 (HL); *Libra Bank Ltd.* v. *Banco Nacional de Costa Rica SA*, 570 F Supp. 870 (SDNY 1983); *Singapore Finance Ltd.* v. *Soetanto* [1992] 2 SLR 407.

[39] J. Gold, 'The IMF's Article VIII, Section 2(b) and Scrupulosity', in J. Norton, M. Andenas, and M. Footer (eds.), *The Changing World of International Law in the Twenty-First Century* (Hague, Kluwer, 1998).

D. ANTI-SUIT INJUNCTIONS

Anti-suit injunctions require a party not to commence, or to discontinue, proceedings in a foreign court. They have been sought in a variety of situations. When the Iranian central bank instituted action in an English court for repayment of a deposit with the London branch of an American bank, the latter attempted to have a US court enjoin the litigation. The ground was that repayment was in breach of the US regulations freezing Iranian assets. The US court refused and referred to the close connection of the matter with England.[40] While the different US federal circuits are divided as to which standards to apply, there are suggestions that anti-suit injunctions will be granted only if the foreign proceedings threaten the jurisdiction of a US court (primarily if the foreign court is not merely proceeding in parallel but is attempting to carve out exclusive jurisdiction over an action), or undermine strong public policies of the United States.[41]

Case 6 is based on an English decision, where the Court of Appeal granted an injunction against US litigation. English courts grant injunctions in such cases, it held, because it is vexatious and oppressive for a party to maintain an action in breach of an agreement not to do so. In such circumstances English courts do not feel any diffidence from restraining foreign court proceedings in the interests of comity.[42]

A court's competence to grant an anti-suit injunction seems to derive from its jurisdiction to adjudicate. Since all that is required for this is a presence within the jurisdiction, there is a wide potential for anti-suit injunctions. If there is competence to grant an anti-suit injunction, on what grounds will this be done? As indicated there need to be strong reasons not to grant an anti-suit injunction if the foreign proceedings are in breach of contract (e.g. an exclusive jurisdiction clause; an agreement not to sue for non-disclosure as in the case above). Otherwise, greater regard will be paid to comity.[43] However, where the action can be brought both in England and elsewhere, the approach of an English court will most likely be to grant an anti-suit injunction where England is the forum with which the action has its most real and substantial connection; by proceeding in the foreign court the party is acting vexatiously or oppressively; and the injunction will not deprive the party unjustly of an advantage in the foreign forum.[44] In a leading case, a US Court of Appeals indicated that it would issue an anti-suit injunction more sparingly than would an English court, although there is a difference between US jurisdictions with some being laxer.[45] Where the

---

[40] *Chase Manhattan Bank NA* v. *State of Iran*, 484 F Supp. 832 (SDNY 1980).

[41] *Gau Shan Co. Ltd.* v. *Bankers Trust Co.*, 956 F 2d 1349 (6th Cir. 1992).

[42] *National Westminster Bank* v. *Utrecht-America Finance Company* [2001] EWCA Civ. 658, [2001] 3 All ER 733 (CA).

[43] *Donohue* v. *Armco Inc.* [2001] UKHL 64, [2002] 1 All ER 749 (HL).

[44] *Société Nationale Industrielle Aérospatiale* v. *Lee Kui Jak* [1987] AC 871 (PC); *Airbus Industrie GIE* v. *Patel* [1999] 1 AC 119 (HL). See K. Anderson, 'What Can the United States Learn from English Anti-Suit Injunctions?' (2000) 25 *Yale J. Int'l L* 195.

[45] *Laker Airways* v. *Sabena, Belgian World Airlines*, 731 F 2d 909 (DC Cir., 1984). See T. Hartley, 'Comity and the Use of Antisuit Injunctions in International Litigation' (1987) 35 *Amer J Comp. L* 487.

substantive issue can be decided only by a foreign forum, an English court will still contemplate an anti-suit injunction, if the grounds mentioned above are established. A US court will not grant an anti-suit injunction if the foreign forum is the only one available.

E. SECRECY LAWS

A real problem is case 7, which has generated a great deal of controversy. An official body in country X, such as the securities regulators, orders a bank, with a presence in the jurisdiction, to produce information about a customer from a branch in another jurisdiction, in breach of the law there. The rules about jurisdiction to prescribe and enforce do not assist. Both jurisdictions have a competence to prescribe—country X can prescribe the behaviour of the customer (e.g. on its securities markets) and the bank (to produce the information), while country Y can prescribe confidentiality for accounts with banks there. Country X's competence to enforce the law is territorial, but this is satisfied because its orders are directed to the bank, which is in the jurisdiction.

(i) US Regulatory Efforts

In terms of case law, the problem seems to have arisen in the context of US regulatory efforts (rather than those of other jurisdictions) seeking disclosure elsewhere and then running up against bank secrecy laws in those other jurisdictions.[46] Notable US orders of this nature have involved grand jury subpoenas issued in relation to investigations by enforcement bodies.[47] The orders initially were made against US banks with foreign branches, because the US head office supposedly had control over its foreign branches. Later the orders were extended to foreign banks with branches in the United States. In a notable development, officers of foreign banks visiting the United States have been subpoenaed to produce information.

In deciding whether to give weight to foreign secrecy laws, the US courts examine the good faith of the bank and the nature of the relevant foreign law. Good faith will not necessarily guarantee the withdrawal or modification of an order, although bad faith will result in the imposition of sanctions for failure to comply. Good faith requires the bank to supply documents in the United States, and information not caught by the secrecy provisions, and to endeavour to comply with the production order if possible under the terms of the foreign law (for example, by applying for permission to the foreign court).[48] Foreign law is examined to ensure that the material falls within the secrecy protection and to determine whether there are comparable investigatory provisions to those in the United States. US courts have also found it

---

[46] Cf. *Brannigan* v. *Davidson* [1997] AC 238 (PC) criticized in C. McLachlan, 'The Jurisdictional Limits of Disclosure Orders in Transnational Fraud Litigation' (1998) 47 *ICLQ* 3, 39–46.

[47] Cf. *Spencer* v. *R.* [1985] SCR 278, involving the Canadian tax authorities.

[48] e.g. *In re Grand Jury Proceedings Bank of Nova Scotia*, 740 F 2d 817 (11th Cir. 1984), cert. denied 469 US 1106 (1985).

significant that a foreign secrecy law is civil, rather than criminal, and that there may be a defence to a criminal prosecution under the foreign law if production is pursuant to the order of a US court.

An extension of case 7 is the extraterritorial asset transfer ordered in the *Standard Chartered* case.[49] In this case the Securities and Exchange Commission brought an insider-trading action against Lee, a non-United States national, resident in Hong Kong. Standard Chartered was not a party to the case, and it was not claimed to be involved in the scheme or in any wrongdoing. No relief was sought against it. Its connection was that, at the time of the insider trading, Lee had bank accounts with one of its Hong Kong branches. Nevertheless, a US District Court made orders against Standard Chartered in New York, requiring it to pay a sum into court equal to the balances in the Hong Kong accounts, which was to be paid over to the victims of Lee's insider trading and as a penalty. The court accepted that the amounts in the account were impressed with a constructive trust, but apparently there was virtually no evidence that they represented insider trading profits. Standard Chartered was still exposed in Hong Kong to liability for claims for repayment by the account-holders. The upshot is that a bank having a presence in the United States can be ordered to pay over an amount representing balances held by any one of its branches elsewhere, irrespective of the law of that jurisdiction and of the liability of the bank there.

(ii) The Approach Elsewhere

What has been the reaction of other courts to such orders? Even if it is a US bank which is ordered by a US subpoena, other common law courts have applied traditional conflict-of-laws analysis. If the proper law of the bank account is England, English courts have generally upheld bank confidentiality, despite the US order.[50] Moreover, it seems to follow that the 'compulsion of law' qualification to the duty of confidentiality does not include an order directed at the bank from a foreign court.[51] It is doubtful if this line can be maintained. Chapter 6 argued that bank confidentiality, properly analysed, always involves a weighing of the public interest, and that these days there is a strong public interest against using the banking system as a channel for wrongdoing or unlawful action. Bank confidentiality should have little weight in this balance; assisting foreign regulators must often outweigh it.

Where the US courts have used established international procedures for obtaining evidence, such as letters rogatory, English courts have been more responsive. In one case it was said that, although an English court might not accede to a request when this was against the public interest—and there was a public interest in maintaining bank confidentiality:

[t]here is, in my view, also clearly a public interest, and a very strong one, in not permitting the confidential relationship between banker and client to be used as a cloak to conceal

---

[49] *United States Securities and Exchange Commission v. Wang*, 699 F Supp. 44 (SDNY 1988).
[50] *X AG v. A bank* [1983] 2 All ER 464.
[51] *FDC Co. Ltd. v. Chase Manhattan Bank NA* [1990] 1 HKLR 277, 283 (CA).

improper or fraudulent activities evidence of which would otherwise be available to be used in legal proceedings, whether here or abroad.[52]

Such sentiments are likely to weigh heavily in the future.

The approach of the English courts to requests to them to breach foreign bank secrecy has already been touched on. In the leading decision Hoffmann J held that only very exceptionally would the court order a third party within the jurisdiction to disclose documents abroad in breach of secrecy duties there. Alternative avenues such as letters of request and applications to the foreign court were to be preferred.[53] The English Court of Appeal has endorsed this approach when holding that garnishee orders can be directed at a multinational bank owing money abroad, which has a branch in London, so long as the bank is not at a real risk of having to pay twice. The justification is that a garnishee order does not require a multinational bank to do anything abroad, but simply to pay the judgment debt in England (although this may discharge the foreign debt by reason of private law principles and contractual terms).[54] However, if the bank cannot confirm that it holds money in the foreign jurisdiction because of bank secrecy laws there, the appropriate course is for the claimant to register its judgment there and apply for production of the debtor's account with the bank.[55]

III. RESOLVING A CLASH OF JURISDICTIONS

The case studies illustrate the potential for clashes between the laws of different jurisdictions applying to a bank. Regulatory requirements may differ for the one bank operating in two jurisdictions (case 1); the law in one jurisdiction makes unlawful behaviour which is at least partly conducted abroad (case 2); in one jurisdiction there is a claim for repayment by or against a bank, but another jurisdiction forbids repayment (cases 4 and 5); one jurisdiction requires a bank to disclose information, but that is in breach of the law in another (cases 3, 7); and one jurisdiction says a bank may be sued, another that the proceedings in that jurisdiction ought not to proceed (case 6). Case 2 also raises a different issue, making fraudsters liable in the jurisdiction most appropriate to prosecuting them. How are such clashes resolved?

In some cases clashes are not resolved and there is a stand-off. Thus the Helms-Burton Act purportedly extends to non-US entities, such as banks financing transactions which affect any property nationalized by the Cuban government.[56] There are

---

[52] *The Santa Fe Case* (1984) 23 ILM 511, 516.

[53] *Mackinnon v. Donaldson, Lufkin & Jenrette Securities Corp.* [1986] Ch. 482.

[54] *Société Eram Shipping Co. Ltd.* v. *Cie Internationale de Navigation* [2001] 1 All ER (Comm) 843, [2001] 2 Lloyd's Rep. 394.

[55] *Kuwait Oil Tanker Co. SAK* v. *Qabazard* [2002] EWCA Civ. 34, para. 32 (CA).

[56] 22 USC §6082.

other such US provisions. An EU Regulation provides that no US judgment giving effect to the Act is enforceable and, in general, that European banks should not comply with it.[57]

A. AVOIDING PROBLEMS

While a clash of jurisdictions may exist, it may not manifest itself, or it may be avoided. The bank may simply comply with the differing regulatory requirements of the jurisdictions where it operates. If there is regulatory liability in more than one jurisdiction, the authorities in one may not take further action following proceedings in the other. Foreign law may be recognized under ordinary rules about conflict of laws. While one jurisdiction may maintain that there is liability there, it respects an order of a foreign court to the contrary, and takes appropriate executive or judicial action. Bank regulation may avoid jurisdictional clashes by requiring information to be made available to the regulators, who can then pass it on to regulators in other jurisdictions.[58]

In England there is no directly relevant common law doctrine which enables the courts to avoid extraterritorial claims, although there is authority that an English court will take into account that a foreign law or court order purports to operate extraterritorially. One line of cases where the fact of extraterritoriality of an English court order has influenced a decision involve an exercise of discretion, such as the grant of an injunction.[59] A narrow view of the English authorities, then, is that the fact that a court order has extraterritorial effect is a factor which the court will take into account in exercising a discretion. If that exercise of jurisdiction should be given effect to on ordinary principles of conflict of laws, however, its extraterritoriality will not, as a matter of some independent principle, be refused effect by an English court.

B. JUDICIAL DECISION-MAKING: COMITY AND BALANCING

As a matter of judicial decision-making, how might jurisdictional clashes be avoided, or at least mitigated, while still achieving the policy objectives of the two jurisdictions? One approach has been to refine the concept of jurisdiction.[60] Jurisdiction to prescribe and jurisdiction to enforce have been further divided into the primary and secondary competence to prescribe and enforce. Economic sovereignty has been introduced as a notion for refining discussions of jurisdiction. While the concept of jurisdiction can narrow the issues, it is not definite enough to provide complete answers. Moreover, it

---

[57] Council Regulation 2271/96 [1996] OJ L309/1.

[58] 104, 105 above, 455 below.

[59] *British Nylon Spinners Ltd.* v. *Imperial Chemical Industries Ltd.* [1953] Ch. 19; *X AG* v. *A bank* [1983] 2 All ER 464; *Midland Bank* v. *Laker Airways* [1986] 1 QE 689. Cf. *Williams and Humbert Ltd.* v. *W. & H. Trademarks (Jersey) Ltd.* [1986] AC 368, 379.

[60] e.g. A. Lowe, 'The Problems of Extraterritorial Jurisdiction' (1985) 34 *ICLQ* 724.

does not assist to resolve the situation where more than one state has jurisdiction to prescribe or to enforce.

The two concepts which common law courts have invoked to mitigate a clash of jurisdictions are comity (the English approach) and balancing interests (the US approach). Comity means that, in decision-making, courts ought to have due regard to the position of persons affected by foreign law. English courts have had regard to comity, both in defining the reach of foreign legislation and in judicial decision-making. In the leading banking cases,[61] orders against, respectively, the head office of a UK bank, and the London branch of a US bank, were set aside. In the first, the Court of Appeal held that, although it could make the order under the Bankers' Books Evidence Act 1879, it should not in its discretion do so because of the danger of a conflict of jurisdictions between the High Court in England and the foreign court (which previously had refused to make such an order). In the second, the judge set aside an order under that Act, and a subpoena, because there was an alternative remedy available to the plaintiff in a foreign jurisdiction (actually New York), and it was not a case of 'hot pursuit'.

Comity, however, is an ill-defined concept, and for that reason can be arbitrary in its application. Moreover, comity requires abnegation: in its absence, the doctrine is still-born in practice. Comity has appealed to US academic writers, but in recent times only occasionally to its courts. In the main the US courts have accorded overwhelming weight to US interests in cases involving foreign banking laws.

Balancing interests is another approach to minimizing jurisdictional clashes. The law of one jurisdiction may require a bank to act, but in breach of the law of another, so that the courts of the first will balance the different interests carefully before deciding to apply it. Developed by the US courts in the context of anti-trust activities, the notion of balancing interests is now incorporated in general terms in the *Restatement on Foreign Relations Law*.[62] This provides that, when it is not unreasonable for each of two states to exercise jurisdiction to prescribe in relation to a person or activity, but the prescriptions of the two are in conflict, each state has an obligation to evaluate its own, as well as the other state's, interest in the light of all the relevant factors, and to defer to the other if that state's interest is clearly greater.[63]

While balancing might once have provided a method of reconciling jurisdictional conflicts, it no longer provides much hope. As a general technique, it fails unless some weight is assigned to the various interests, in particular those of the foreign state. The *Restatement* provides only that the foreign state's interests must clearly be greater before the United States exercises its jurisdiction to prescribe. No weights are attached to the interests identified for the making of production orders. In any case, is the weight to be attached, say, to bank secrecy laws for one jurisdiction to be greater than that which attaches to those of another? Collins has suggested:

---

[61] *R. v. Grossman* (1981) 73 Cr. App. R. 302; *MacKinnon v. Donaldson, Lufkin and Jenrette Securities Corpn.* [1986] 1 Ch. 482.

[62] *Restatement of the Law. The Foreign Relations of the United States* (3rd edn., 1987), §403.

[63] P. Muchlinski, *Multinational Enterprises and the Law* (Oxford, Blackwell, 1995), 131ff, 149ff.

It is one thing to pay respect to Swiss secrecy laws; they have their origin in the protection of basic human rights and not in the facilitation of fraud and crime, and Switzerland is a country with a strong international currency and an indigenous banking business. Can the same respect be due the Cayman Islands? The banking business there consists of branches of foreign banks which act largely as accommodation addresses for the transfer of funds.[64]

In practice, balancing when invoked by US courts has almost invariably resulted in a finding that jurisdiction lies. While referring to the laws of other jurisdictions, US courts have given them short shrift.[65] One can also question whether, as a matter of institutional competence, the judiciary is in the best position to evaluate what is essentially a foreign-policy issue, the weight to be given to the interests of a foreign state.

C. INTERNATIONAL CO-OPERATION

Of major importance is the attempt to resolve jurisdictional clashes by means of international co-operation. There are various ways of slicing this topic, but the one adopted here is classifying the co-operation on the basis of whether as a matter of legal form it is unilateral, bilateral, or multilateral.

(i) Unilateral Co-operation

With multinational banking, information required by one bank regulator will generally be required by bank regulators in any other jurisdiction where a bank has a presence. The attitude of the local judiciary is often crucial, as we have seen, to regulatory efforts by foreign agencies. The trail may be blocked by an injunction, as the local courts effectively elevate a local public policy, such as bank secrecy, into a universal human right. The reality of modern banking and bank regulation was recognized in an important decision directing a bank to comply with a Bank of England notice, even though the bank was co-operating with the US Federal Reserve Board. Hirst J said that the bank's counsel

seeks to draw a line down the centre of the Atlantic, and to suggest that in some way the supervisory operations of the Federal Reserve Board and those of the Bank of England are separate and unconnected. In fact, in the world of international banking today, supervisory authorities in various countries can, should, and no doubt do regularly cooperate on matters of mutual supervisory concern.[66]

Local legislation may provide an avenue to foreign regulators to side step the courts. It may have no basis in treaty or other international agreement. Thus the Financial

---

[64] L. Collins, 'Problems of Enforcement in the Multinational Securities Market: a United Kingdom Perspective' (1987) 9 *U Pa. J International Bus. Law* 487, 515.

[65] *In re Grand Jury Proceedings*, 691 F 2d 1384 (11th Cir. 1982), cert. denied 462 US 1119 (1983); *In re Grand Jury Proceedings, the Bank of Nova Scotia*, 740 F 2d 817 (11th Cir. 1984), cert. denied 469 US 1106 (1985).

[66] *A v. B Bank* [1992] 1 All ER 778, 792. See also *Bank of Crete SA v. Koskotas (No 2)* [1992] 1 WLR 919, 925, [1993] 1 All ER 748, 754.

Services Authority is under a general duty not to disclose confidential information it obtains in the course of its regulation of banks.[67] However, one of the gateways is if disclosure to regulators elsewhere will facilitate the carrying out of their regulatory functions.[68] There is another gateway for the disclosure of confidential information if it is for the purposes of a criminal investigation or criminal proceedings whether in the United Kingdom or elsewhere.[69]

(ii) Bilateral Co-operation

There has been considerable progress with mutual legal-assistance treaties, especially between the United States and foreign countries.[70] These provide for the law-enforcement machinery of one country to be made available to assist investigations in other countries. Assistance can include locating persons, obtaining testimony, and providing records (even confidential records). Modern mutual legal-assistance treaties cover conspiracy, if only implicitly, and are in terms wide enough to cover most other criminal offences (save, in some cases, fiscal offences). US mutual-assistance treaties cover grand jury proceedings, but not always proceedings which are quasi-criminal, such as forfeiture. The procedures under the treaties are not exclusive. Mutual legal-assistance treaties may permit disclosure otherwise in breach of local bank secrecy laws.

Mutual legal-assistance treaties have been heavily criminal, however, so that they do not necessarily cover regulatory offences. Nor are they always sufficient to cover the preliminary inquiries before an offence can be prosecuted. Here, however, a memorandum of understanding (MOU) may be available. These fall short of being legally binding international instruments. MOUs have been popular in areas such as securities regulation.[71] An inquiry pursuant to a MOU may lead to the penetration of local bank secrecy.

(iii) Multilateral Co-operation

The Hague Convention on the Taking of Evidence Abroad in Civil and Commercial Matters 1970 is a well-known example.[72] Chapter I of the Convention applies to letters of request, issued by the judicial authorities of a Contracting State in civil or commercial matters, to obtain evidence intended for use in judicial proceedings. A request can include oral testimony and the inspection of documents. Civil or commercial proceedings include tax proceedings, and probably also a claim for the restitution of

---

[67] FSMA 2000, s. 348.

[68] S. 349(5); Financial Services and Markets Act 2000 (Disclosure of Confidential Information) Regulations 2001, SI 2001 No 2188, r.12(1)(a).

[69] R.4.

[70] e.g. Treaty between the UK and USA concerning the Cayman Islands relating to mutual assistance in criminal matters, Cm. 1316 (London, HMSO, 1990).

[71] See D. McClean, *International Judicial Assistance* (Oxford, Clarendon, 1992); W. Gilmore (ed.), *Mutual Assistance in Criminal and Business Regulatory Matters* (Cambridge, Cambridge UP, 1995).

[72] Cmnd. 6727 (London, HMSO, 1976).

profits in relation to insider-dealing.[73] Clearly, however, the Convention does not cover the collection of evidence for regulatory proceedings having a criminal element. Nor, since it is confined to requests from courts, does it apply to the seeking of evidence by US grand juries.

Under the Convention, countries like the United Kingdom have declared that they will not execute letters of request for obtaining the pre-trial discovery of documents.[74] The Convention has thus not resolved some of the contentious extraterritorial claims by some states. The United States view is that the Convention does not provide an exclusive and mandatory procedure for obtaining evidence abroad, and thus courts are not deprived of the jurisdiction they otherwise possess to order a foreign party to produce evidence located within a signatory nation.[75] Where the Convention applies, however, proceedings otherwise to obtain evidence may cause objection on the part of other countries.

Outside the civil law, multilateral co-operation is patchy, at least as a matter of law on the books. For Europe there is the Convention on Mutual Assistance in Criminal Matters of 1959, supplemented by the Convention on Mutual Assistance in Criminal Matters between the Member States of the European Union of 2000.[76] Of particular importance is the Protocol to the latter, which in general terms obliges Member States of the EU to take measures to ensure that requests from each other can be answered as to whether someone subject to a criminal investigation for a serious offence holds or controls one or more accounts and, if so, the details.[77] The particulars of specified bank accounts and of operations through them must also be provided, clarifying the 2000 Convention. There are limitations to thwart fishing expeditions, requests to monitor specific accounts must be carried out, and banks must be prevented from tipping off customers about a request. However, the Protocol does not abolish dual criminality as a basis for refusing a request, although the European Council has undertaken to address this issue. In the United Kingdom Part I of the Criminal Justice (International Co-operation) Act 1990 gives compulsory powers to obtain evidence for foreign investigations and criminal proceedings.[78] The evidence can be obtained despite a bank's duty of confidentiality. Thus a request by the Nigerian government and the Swiss government to assist in tracing moneys looted by a former military ruler of Nigeria was given effect, in part, by referring the matters to the director of the Serious Fraud Office, who used her own statutory powers to obtain information about deposits in London bank accounts.[79] No doubt in practice a great deal of multilateral

---

[73] *Re State of Norway's Application (Nos 1 & 2)* [1990] 1 AC 723 (HL).

[74] Evidence (Proceedings in Other Jurisdictions) Act 1975, s. 2(4) See *Genira Trade & Finance Inc.* v. *CS First Boston and Standard Bank (London) Ltd.* [2001] EWCA Civ. 1733 (CA).

[75] *Société Nationale Industrielle Aérospatiale* v. *US Dist. Court*, 482 US 522 (1987).

[76] Cm. 1928 (1992); Cm. 5229 (2001) respectively.

[77] Council Act of 16 Oct. 2001 [2001] OJ C326/1.

[78] S. 4 (as amended). See also Proceeds of Crime Act 2002, ss. 432(1)(a), 439; *Seeking Mutual Legal Assistance in Criminal Matters from the United Kingdom* (London, Home Office, 1999).

[79] *R (Abacha)* v. *Secretary of State for the Home Department* [2001] EWHC Admin. 787.

co-operation between bank regulators occurs on an informal basis. This is fostered through the Basle Committee on Bank Supervision, meetings of non-G10 regulators, and the work within the European Community.

D. INTERNATIONAL HARMONIZATION

As we saw in Chapter 3 the activities of the Basle Committee on Banking Supervision, the Financial Action Task Force and others have resulted in important principles of banking regulation being harmonized across jurisdictions. In Europe this has been underpinned by the work of the European Community. Especially relevant to the discussion in this Chapter is harmonization with respect to money-laundering and terrorist financing.[80] Associated with harmonization within the European Community, of course, has been mutual recognition. Moreover, the Basle and European initiatives have also meant that co-operation between bank regulators in different jurisdictions has been facilitated on individual matters.

IV. CONCLUSION

Jurisdictional clashes over banking matters continue to occur. Some are resolvable in accordance with established legal doctrine, some in accordance with bilateral and multilateral agreements between states. Little seems achievable in reducing the conflict by pursuing notions of jurisdiction, comity, and the balancing of interests. Rather, shared concerns on substantive issues—as in recent times with money-laundering and terrorist financing—are more likely to lead to deference by, and co-operation between, jurisdictions. Banks sometimes find themselves involved indirectly in these jurisdictional clashes. Legally, there is little they can do to avoid this. In practice they could avoid being caught in the jurisdictional clashes, which occur when enforcement agencies pursue the unmeritorious and criminal across borders, by scrutinizing their customers and ceasing to do business in offshore centres of dubious reputation.

[80] 71 above.

INDEX